THE PORTRAICTUER OF CAPTAYNE IOHN SMITH ADMIRALL OF NEW ENGLAND.
Æta 37
A° 1616

Dictionary of Literary Biography • Volume Twenty-four

American Colonial Writers, 1606-1734

Dictionary of Literary Biography

1: *The American Renaissance in New England*, edited by Joel Myerson (1978)

2: *American Novelists Since World War II*, edited by Jeffrey Helterman and Richard Layman (1978)

3: *Antebellum Writers in New York and the South*, edited by Joel Myerson (1979)

4: *American Writers in Paris, 1920-1939*, edited by Karen Lane Rood (1980)

5: *American Poets Since World War II*, 2 volumes, edited by Donald J. Greiner (1980)

6: *American Novelists Since World War II*, Second Series, edited by James E. Kibler, Jr. (1980)

7: *Twentieth-Century American Dramatists*, 2 volumes, edited by John MacNicholas (1981)

8: *Twentieth-Century American Science-Fiction Writers*, 2 volumes, edited by David Cowart and Thomas L. Wymer (1981)

9: *American Novelists, 1910-1945*, 3 volumes, edited by James J. Martine (1981)

10: *Modern British Dramatists, 1900-1945*, 2 volumes, edited by Stanley Weintraub (1982)

11: *American Humorists, 1800-1950*, 2 volumes, edited by Stanley Trachtenberg (1982)

12: *American Realists and Naturalists*, edited by Donald Pizer and Earl N. Harbert (1982)

13: *British Dramatists Since World War II*, 2 volumes, edited by Stanley Weintraub (1982)

14: *British Novelists Since 1960*, 2 volumes, edited by Jay L. Halio (1983)

15: *British Novelists, 1930-1959*, 2 volumes, edited by Bernard Oldsey (1983)

16: *The Beats: Literary Bohemians in Postwar America*, 2 volumes, edited by Ann Charters (1983)

17: *Twentieth-Century American Historians*, edited by Clyde N. Wilson (1983)

18: *Victorian Novelists After 1885*, edited by Ira B. Nadel and William E. Fredeman (1983)

19: *British Poets, 1880-1914*, edited by Donald E. Stanford (1983)

20: *British Poets, 1914-1945*, edited by Donald E. Stanford (1983)

21: *Victorian Novelists Before 1885*, edited by Ira B. Nadel and William E. Fredeman (1983)

22: *American Writers for Children, 1900-1960,* edited by John Cech (1983)

23: *American Newspaper Journalists, 1873-1900,* edited by Perry J. Ashley (1983)

24: *American Colonial Writers, 1606-1734,* edited by Emory Elliott (1984)

Yearbook: 1980, edited by Karen L. Rood, Jean W. Ross, and Richard Ziegfeld (1981)

Yearbook: 1981, edited by Karen L. Rood, Jean W. Ross, and Richard Ziegfeld (1982)

Yearbook: 1982, edited by Richard Ziegfeld; associate editors: Jean W. Ross and Lynne C. Zeigler (1983)

Documentary Series, volume 1, edited by Margaret A. Van Antwerp (1982)

Documentary Series, volume 2, edited by Margaret A. Van Antwerp (1982)

Documentary Series, volume 3, edited by Mary Bruccoli (1983)

Documentary Series, volume 4: *Tennessee Williams,* edited by Margaret A. Van Antwerp and Sally Johns (1984)

Dictionary of Literary Biography • Volume Twenty-four

American Colonial Writers, 1606-1734

Edited by
Emory Elliott
Princeton University

A Bruccoli Clark Book
Gale Research Company • Book Tower • Detroit, Michigan 48226
1984

Matthew J. Bruccoli and Richard Layman, *Editorial Directors*
C. E. Frazer Clark, Jr., *Managing Editor*

Manufactured by Edwards Brothers, Inc.
Ann Arbor, Michigan
Printed in the United States of America

Library of Congress Cataloging in Publication Data
Main entry under title:

American colonial writers, 1606-1734.

(Dictionary of literary biography; v. 24)
"A Bruccoli Clark book."
Includes index.
1. American literature—Colonial period, ca. 1600-1775—History and criticism. 2. American literature—Colonial period, ca. 1600-1775—Bio-bibliography. 3. Authors, American—Colonial period, ca. 1600-1775—Biography—Dictionaries. I. Elliott, Emory, 1942- II. Series.
PS185.A39 1983 810'.9'001 83-20577
ISBN 0-8103-1703-6

This volume is for a few of the scholars
who have made
American seventeenth-century literature
a vital field of study:
Sacvan Bercovitch
Everett Emerson
David Levin
Ann Stanford
Larzer Ziff
and
in memory of
Richard Beale Davis

Contents

Plan of the Series

... Almost the most prodigious asset of a country, and perhaps its most precious possession, is its native literary product–when that product is fine and noble and enduring.

Mark Twain*

The advisory board, the editors, and the publisher of the *Dictionary of Literary Biography* are joined in endorsing Mark Twain's declaration. The literature of a nation provides an inexhaustible resource of permanent worth. It is our expectation that this endeavor will make literature and its creators better understood and more accessible to students and the literate public, while satisfying the standards of teachers and scholars.

To meet these requirements, *literary biography* has been construed in terms of the author's achievement. The most important thing about a writer is his writing. Accordingly, the entries in *DLB* are career biographies, tracing the development of the author's canon and the evolution of his reputation.

The publication plan for *DLB* resulted from two years of preparation. The project was proposed to Bruccoli Clark by Frederick G. Ruffner, president of the Gale Research Company, in November 1975. After specimen entries were prepared and typeset, an advisory board was formed to refine the entry format and develop the series rationale. In meetings held during 1976, the publisher, series editors, and advisory board approved the scheme for a comprehensive biographical dictionary of persons who contributed to North American literature. Editorial work on the first volume began in January 1977, and it was published in 1978.

In order to make *DLB* more than a reference tool and to compile volumes that individually have claim to status as literary history, it was decided to organize volumes by topic or period or genre. Each of these freestanding volumes provides a biographical-bibliographical guide and overview for a particular area of literature. We are convinced that this organization—as opposed to a single alphabet method—constitutes a valuable innovation in the presentation of reference material. The volume plan necessarily requires many decisions for the placement and treatment of authors who might properly be included in two or three volumes. In some instances a major figure will be included in separate volumes, but with different entries emphasizing the aspect of his career appropriate to each volume. Ernest Hemingway, for example, is represented in *American Writers in Paris, 1920-1939* by an entry focusing on his expatriate apprenticeship; he is also in *American Novelists, 1910-1945* with an entry surveying his entire career. Each volume includes a cumulative index of subject authors. The final *DLB* volume will be a comprehensive index to the entire series.

With volume ten in 1982 it was decided to enlarge the scope of *DLB* beyond the literature of the United States. By the end of 1983 twelve volumes treating British literature had been published, and volumes for Commonwealth and Modern European literature were in progress. The series has been further augmented by the *DLB Yearbooks* (since 1981) which update published entries and add new entries to keep the *DLB* current with contemporary activity. There have also been occasional *DLB Documentary Series* volumes which provide biographical and critical background source materials for figures whose work is judged to have particular interest for students. One of these companion volumes is entirely devoted to Tennessee Williams.

The purpose of *DLB* is not only to provide reliable information in a convenient format but also to place the figures in the larger perspective of literary history and to offer appraisals of their accomplishments by qualified scholars.

We define literature as the *intellectual commerce of a nation*: not merely as belles lettres, but as that ample and complex process by which ideas are generated, shaped, and transmitted. *DLB* entries are not limited to "creative writers" but extend to other figures who in this time and in this way influenced the mind of a people. Thus there will be volumes for historians, journalists, publishers, and screenwriters. By this means readers of *DLB* may be aided to perceive literature not as cult scripture in the keeping of cultural high priests, but as at the center of a nation's life.

DLB includes the major writers appropriate to each volume and those standing in the ranks immediately behind them. Scholarly and critical coun-

*From an unpublished section of Mark Twain's autobiography, copyright © by the Mark Twain Company.

sel has been sought in deciding which minor figures to include and how full their entries should be. Wherever possible, useful references will be made to figures who do not warrant separate entries.

Each *DLB* volume has a volume editor responsible for planning the volume, selecting the figures for inclusion, and assigning the entries. Volume editors are also responsible for preparing, where appropriate, appendices surveying the major periodicals and literary and intellectual movements for their volumes, as well as lists of further readings. Work on the series as a whole is coordinated at the Bruccoli Clark editorial center in Columbia, South Carolina, where the editorial staff is responsible for the accuracy of the published volumes.

One feature that distinguishes *DLB* is the illustration policy—its concern with the iconography of literature. Just as an author is influenced by his surroundings, so is the reader's understanding of the author enhanced by a knowledge of his environment. Therefore *DLB* volumes include not only drawings, paintings, and photographs of authors, often depicting them at various stages in their careers, but also illustrations of their families and places where they lived. Title pages are regularly reproduced in facsimile along with dust jackets for modern authors. The dust jackets are a special feature of *DLB* because they often document better than anything else the way in which an author's work was launched in its own time. Specimens of the writers' manuscripts are included when feasible.

A supplement to *DLB*—tentatively titled *A Guide, Chronology, and Glossary for American Literature*—will outline the history of literature in North America and trace the influences that shaped it. This volume will provide a framework for the study of American literature by means of chronological tables, literary affiliation charts, glossarial entries, and concise surveys of the major movements. It has been planned to stand on its own as a vade mecum, providing a ready-reference guide to the study of American literature as well as a companion to the *DLB* volumes for American literature.

Samuel Johnson rightly decreed that "The chief glory of every people arises from its authors." The purpose of the *Dictionary of Literary Biography* is to compile literary history in the surest way available to us—by accurate and comprehensive treatment of the lives and work of those who contributed to it.

The *DLB* Advisory Board

Foreword

Since the early nineteenth century, when the first literary histories of the American colonies and the early United States began to be produced, critics and historians have bemoaned the thinness of the early American literary heritage. With some embarrassment over the crudeness of American writings compared to the grace of the contemporary works of the English and Scottish poets, commentators provided a set of excuses to explain why Americans had failed as literary artists. One argument was that the colonists had been too busy clearing a wilderness and establishing laws, governments, schools, and commerce to devote time and energies to belles lettres. Another was that Puritanism was such a powerful force in the culture that its dictates against the indulgence of the imagination and toward utilitarianism suppressed aesthetic achievement and encouraged only literature of the most pedestrian and didactic form. The reasoning followed that since the clergy often controlled the presses in New England and were the masters of the written word, the sermon was the only literary form to reach the public in the Northern colonies. To account for the paucity of literary production in the middle colonies and the South, there was the ready explanation that the climate and geography did not favor the creation of cultural centers or energetic literary output. And when these excuses were not enough, there was always the plea that the vast majority of the colonists were illiterate, poor people who were outcasts of Europe. So convincing was this set of descriptions that many generations of Americans were taught that American literature really began with the essays of Ralph Waldo Emerson and the tales of Hawthorne and Melville.

Not until the second and third decades of this century was this interpretation of the American literary past seriously called into question. In the 1930s four great teacher-scholars—Thomas Johnson, Perry Miller, Samuel Eliot Morison, and Kenneth Murdock—began to reassess the writings of seventeenth-century New England by examining them in their aesthetic and religious contexts. The literary merits of both the early sermons and other forms of writing, such as autobiographies, histories, diaries, and elegies, became more apparent in light of this more sophisticated historical understanding. At the same time the discovery of the poetry of Edward Taylor led to a revision of the image of the Puritan minister and a greater appreciation of the imaginative range of the Puritan mind. Under the direction of these and a growing number of scholars of colonial American literature, there began a reassessment of the literature of colonial New England that continues today. Almost concurrent with these discoveries has been a significant effort to unearth, catalogue, and evaluate the literary production of the Southern and middle colonies. Through the painstaking and persistent work of such prominent scholars as Richard Beale Davis, Lewis Leary, J. A. Leo Lemay, and Harrison Messerole, a host of early American poets and men of letters have been recovered from historical obscurity. Even after completing his monumental three-volume history of Southern literature, Davis was still at work in the last weeks of his life in the archives of small local libraries in the Carolinas discovering early Southern poetry and published sermons. The result of all this remarkable scholarly achievement is that we now have a wealth of materials and a much more complete understanding of the complex nature of the literary achievement of the colonial writers.

Through the three volumes of *DLB* devoted to early American writing, of which this is the first, we hope to accomplish at least two important goals. First, to provide treatments of the lives and works of the major figures of the period, such as the Mathers, Bradstreet, Taylor, and Edwards, which are informed by the most recent critical interpretations of the works. Second, we wish to preserve in these volumes the sometimes fragmentary knowledge we currently have of some of the more elusive figures of our literary past. This volume necessarily contains a number of quite brief entries because, at present, we may know only that a certain writer produced one fine poem or a handful of sermons. More information about these writers and evidence of other works may emerge in the years to come, particularly if this reference work stimulates others to follow up the available evidence recorded here. With the exception of the bibliographies for Increase and Cotton Mather, whose published works number in the hundreds, the lists of books at the beginnings of entries include all the authors' separate publications, excluding broadsides, the most ephemeral pamphlets, and works of doubtful attribution. While original spellings have been preserved, idiosyncrasies of colonial typography, such as the swash *s*, have not.

The enthusiasm with which the contributors

to this volume welcomed the opportunity to investigate and present the lives and writings of the authors who appear in these pages has been typical of the liveliness, even zeal, that has characterized the work in the field of early American literature in the last three or four decades. After the groundbreaking work of the scholars of the 1930s and 1940s, there followed two generations of scholars who have taken up the challenge of rewriting the literary history of early America and putting to rest the myths and rationalizations that served for over a century to explain the alleged lack of a heritage where, in fact, a rich and complex imaginative life remained to be discovered and explored. Though the list of those who have labored in this effort is a long and distinguished one, I have chosen to dedicate this volume to a few of the leading scholars who seem to me to have played, in the last twenty years, most significant roles in stimulating and furthering our study and appreciation of seventeenth-century American literature.

–Emory Elliott

Acknowledgments

This book was produced by BC Research. Karen L. Rood, senior editor for the *Dictionary of Literary Biography* series, was the in-house editor.

The production manager is Lynne C. Zeigler. Art supervisor is Alice A. Parsons. The production staff included Angela D. Bardin, Mary Betts, Josie A. Bruccoli, Patricia Coate, Claudia Ericson, Lynn Felder, Joyce Fowler, Laura Ingram, Sharon K. Kirkland, Nancy H. Lindsay, Cynthia D. Lybrand, Walter W. Ross, Patricia C. Sharpe, and Joycelyn R. Smith. Joseph Caldwell is photography editor. Jean W. Ross is permissions editor. Joseph Caldwell, Claudia Ericson, and Charles L. Wentworth did the photographic copy work.

A project of this magnitude is necessarily the work of many hands, and for such a book to be also of consistent high quality requires the commitment of hearts and minds as well. Credit should go to the contributors who patiently and cheerfully endured too many impersonal form letters from me during our two years of work together. To each of you, a hearty thanks for your goodwill and fine work.

While we would not have this volume without the collective commitment of the contributors, the book certainly would never have seen print without the splendid individual performance of our editor at BC Research, Ms. Karen Rood. Ms. Rood's superb editing skills, her unwavering professionalism, and her genuine scholarly interest in the material were exemplary throughout; she is indeed a person of exceptional talents, and I have been most fortunate to be able to work with her.

Closer to home, I have been able again to count upon the assistance of the mainstay of the Princeton American Studies Program, Mrs. Helen Wright. Aiding me as she has American studies faculty since 1946, Helen helped to organize the complicated assignments for this and two forthcoming volumes of the *DLB*, and she typed and helped to mail those form letters. During the copyediting stage I received considerable assistance from my research assistant, Ms. Susan Mizruchi, who proved to be a remarkably capable editor as well as the most promising scholar I already knew her to be. Also assisting with final details and in searching for materials for reproduction in the volume has been another graduate student in the Princeton English department, Ms. Elizabeth Dant.

The skillful aid of the reference staff at the John Carter Brown Library at Brown University was essential in providing illustrations for this book. Norman Fiering, director, and Everett Wilkie, reference librarian, have earned my gratitude.

Valuable assistance was also given by the staff at the Thomas Cooper Library of the University of South Carolina: Lynn Barron, Sue Collins, Michael Freeman, Gary Geer, Alexander M. Gilchrist, Jens Holley, David Lincove, Marcia Martin, Roger Mortimer, Harriet B. Oglesbee, Jean Rhyne, Karen Rissling, Paula Swope, and Ellen Tillett.

Finally, I acknowledge the contribution of those closest to me whose understanding and support are essential to the completion of any project I assume: my children Scott, Mark, Matthew, Constance, and Laura, and as ever, my wife, Georgia.

Dictionary of Literary Biography • Volume Twenty-four

American Colonial Writers, 1606-1734

Dictionary of Literary Biography

James Alexander
(1691-2 April 1756)

John R. Holmes
Kent State University

BOOKS: *The Arguments of the Council for the Defendent, In Support of A Plea to the Jurisdiction, Pleaded to a Bill filed in a Course of equity, At the suit of The Attorney General, Complainant, Against Rip Van Dam, Defendant, In the Supream Court of New-York,* by Alexander and William Smith (New York: Printed by John Peter Zenger, 1733);

The Proceedings of Rip Van Dam, Esq; In order for obtaining Equal Justice of His Excellency William Cosby, Esq., by Alexander and Smith (New York: Printed by John Peter Zenger, 1733);

The Vindication of James Alexander, One of His Majesty's Council for the Province of New-York, and of William Smith, Attorney at Law, From the Matters charged and suggested against them in two Pamphlets lately published . . . , by Alexander and Smith (New York: Printed by John Peter Zenger, 1734);

The Complaint of James Alexander and William Smith to the Committee of the General Assembly of the Colony of New-York, &c., by Alexander and Smith (New York: Printed by John Peter Zenger, 1735);

A Brief Narrative of the Case and Tryal of John Peter Zenger, Printer of the New-York Weekly Journal . . . (New York: Printed by John Peter Zenger, 1736);

A bill in the Chancery of New-Jersey. At the suit of John, Earl of Stair, and others, Proprieters of the Eastern Division of New Jersey . . . , by Alexander and Joseph Murray (New York: Printed & sold by James Parker, 1747).

James Alexander

James Alexander, a colonial New York attorney and statesman, was a contributor to and editor of the *New York Weekly Journal.* He is of literary interest primarily for his lifelong advocacy of freedom of the press, particularly in the celebrated libel trial of New York printer John Peter Zenger. His political prose anticipates that of Paine, Jefferson, and Hamilton, and his *A Brief Narrative of the Case and Tryal of John Peter Zenger . . .* (1736), which went through fifteen editions in both New York and London by

1800, has been called by Charles R. Hildeburn "the most famous publication in America before the *Farmer's Letters*."

Born in the village of Muthill in Pertshire, Scotland, son of David Alexander, James Alexander was to become the seventh Earl of Stirling, though he never claimed the title. Alexander studied science and mathematics at Edinburgh and joined the Scottish army as engineering officer in the unsuccessful Jacobite uprising of 1715. When the Scots forces were routed by the British, Alexander fled to Devon, where his cousin Henry, fifth Earl of Stirling, arranged his passage to America. He arrived at New York on 17 August 1715, and by November he had obtained a position as surveyor-general of New Jersey. He began studying law in 1718, serving as court recorder in Perth Amboy, New Jersey, as well as becoming deputy secretary of New York. Such double duty was fairly common: New York and New Jersey were not totally separate political entities at that time, sharing a governor and several administrative offices between them. In March of 1719 he moved to New York to oversee the surveying of its border with New Jersey; later that year he was admitted to the Council of New York as deputy clerk.

In 1721 he married Polly Spratt, widow of the Dutch merchant David Provoost, with whom she had two children. With Alexander she had five children in the next five years; the last, born in 1726, was their first and only son, William. Named after the first Earl of Stirling, court poet to James I and Charles I, William was to become the eighth Earl of Stirling and a general of the American Revolutionary Army.

James Alexander was admitted to the bar in 1723 and named attorney general for the province of New Jersey and member of the Council of New Jersey. In October he was named naval officer to the New York Council, where he defended the rights of colonists to trade with the Indians and the French, rights which had been suspended by Governor William Burnet (who served from 1720 to 1728) to protect the trade of London merchants. This defense was the first of Alexander's attempts to limit the powers of the colonial governor, and his first victory: the Privy Council in London accepted Alexander's recommendations and issued a Royal Instruction prohibiting governors from "assenting to *private* bills." In the ensuing years, however, Alexander came to realize that further victories could not be gained without comprehensive legal reform. In 1725 he made a formal motion in council for such a reform in order to place more control of the courts in the Provincial Assembly and less in the hands of the governor. The motion made little progress in the council but was picked up by the assembly, which moved to abolish the Court of Chancery. On 25 November 1727, when the resolution was presented to Governor Burnet, he dissolved the assembly. Such a furor resulted that the colonial authorities were obliged to remove Burnet in March 1728. The new governor, John Montgomerie, avoided Burnet's excesses, but such discretion was the result of a change of administration, not of law: the potential for gubernatorial abuses of court remained, and in Governor William Cosby that potential was realized. It was during Cosby's administration (1732-1736) that Alexander's most heated opposition appeared—as well as his most powerful prose.

The first issue to reunite the opposition against Cosby was that of "Van Dam's salary." When Montgomerie died on 1 July 1731, Rip Van Dam, as senior councilman of New York, assumed the office until Cosby's arrival. When he reached New York in August 1732, Cosby demanded half of Van Dam's interim salary and used his own appointees in the New York Supreme Court to sue for it. Alexander, along with William Smith, took up Van Dam's legal defense, filing a 1 February 1733 rule declaring the supreme court invalid. When it came before the grand jury on 9 April, Chief Justice Lewis Morris agreed, affirming that the court had no jurisdiction in equity; Cosby had Morris removed from office. This action gave the opposition party their leader, Morris, and another complaint against Cosby. Alexander became the party spokesman in court and in the press. He had been having articles published in the *New York Gazette*, but he found its editor, Francis Harison, to be a de facto censor for Cosby. Finding printer John Peter Zenger sympathetic to the opposition, Alexander published the proceedings of Van Dam's trial at Zenger's press. On 5 November, following an overwhelming Morrisite victory in the assembly elections, Alexander launched the party's newspaper, the *New York Weekly Journal*, from Zenger's press. It was the first politically and editorially independent paper in America. The best pieces in it were Alexander's editorials on freedom of the press, offering the legal and philosophical basis for opposing the governor. Arguing that the paper defamed his administration and, therefore, threatened public order, Cosby tried on 15 January 1734 to gain indictments for seditious libel against the publishers through James De Lancey, who had replaced Morris as chief justice: the grand jury refused to grant them.

A threatening letter placed on Alexander's doorstep on Friday evening, 1 February, gave the journal editor a chance to respond more openly than

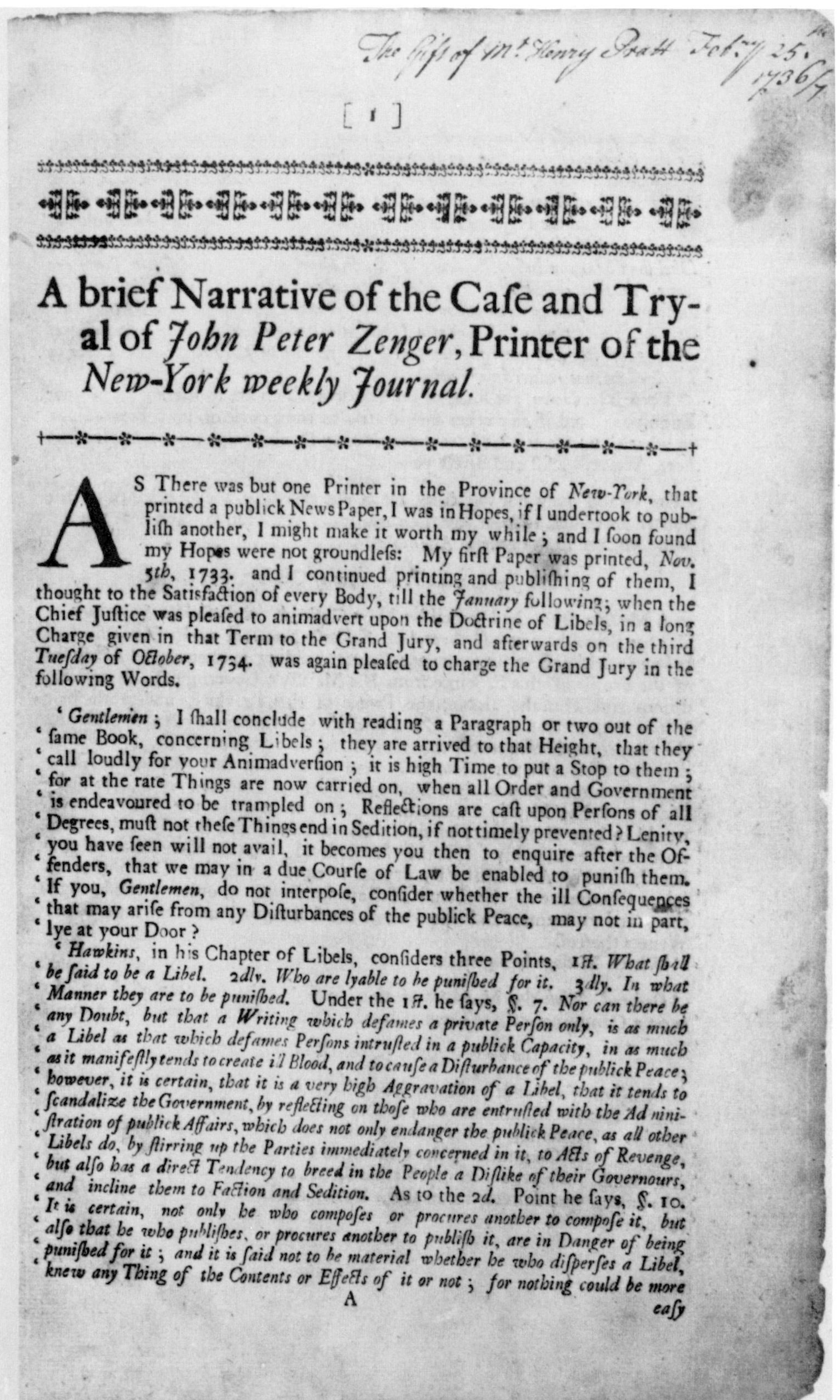

[1]

A brief Narrative of the Caſe and Tryal of *John Peter Zenger*, Printer of the *New-York weekly Journal.*

AS There was but one Printer in the Province of *New-York*, that printed a publick News Paper, I was in Hopes, if I undertook to publiſh another, I might make it worth my while; and I ſoon found my Hopes were not groundleſs: My firſt Paper was printed, *Nov.* 5*th*, 1733. and I continued printing and publiſhing of them, I thought to the Satisfaction of every Body, till the *January* following; when the Chief Juſtice was pleaſed to animadvert upon the Doctrine of Libels, in a long Charge given in that Term to the Grand Jury, and afterwards on the third *Tueſday* of *October*, 1734. was again pleaſed to charge the Grand Jury in the following Words.

‘*Gentlemen*; I ſhall conclude with reading a Paragraph or two out of the ſame Book, concerning Libels; they are arrived to that Height, that they call loudly for your Animadverſion; it is high Time to put a Stop to them; for at the rate Things are now carried on, when all Order and Government is endeavoured to be trampled on; Reflections are caſt upon Perſons of all Degrees, muſt not theſe Things end in Sedition, if not timely prevented? Lenity, you have ſeen will not avail, it becomes you then to enquire after the Offenders, that we may in a due Courſe of Law be enabled to puniſh them. If you, *Gentlemen*, do not interpoſe, conſider whether the ill Conſequences that may ariſe from any Diſturbances of the publick Peace, may not in part, lye at your Door?

‘*Hawkins*, in his Chapter of Libels, conſiders three Points, 1ſt. *What ſhall be ſaid to be a Libel.* 2dly. *Who are lyable to be puniſhed for it.* 3dly. *In what Manner they are to be puniſhed.* Under the 1ſt. he ſays, §. 7. *Nor can there be any Doubt, but that a Writing which defames a private Perſon only, is as much a Libel as that which defames Perſons intruſted in a publick Capacity, in as much as it manifeſtly tends to create ill Blood, and to cauſe a Diſturbance of the publick Peace; however, it is certain, that it is a very high Aggravation of a Libel, that it tends to ſcandalize the Government, by reflecting on thoſe who are entruſted with the Adminiſtration of publick Affairs, which does not only endanger the publick Peace, as all other Libels do, by ſtirring up the Parties immediately concerned in it, to Acts of Revenge, but alſo has a direct Tendency to breed in the People a Diſlike of their Governours, and incline them to Faction and Sedition.* As to the 2*d.* Point he ſays, §. 10. *It is certain, not only he who compoſes or procures another to compoſe it, but alſo that he who publiſhes, or procures another to publiſh it, are in Danger of being puniſhed for it; and it is ſaid not to be material whether he who diſperſes a Libel, knew any Thing of the Contents or Effects of it or not; for nothing could be more*

A

eaſy

First page for Alexander's defense of John Peter Zenger

in his unsigned editorials. Identifying the handwriting as that of rival editor and Cosbyite Francis Harison, Alexander ordered a council investigation, and printed the proceedings and his own account as a pamphlet, *The Vindication of James Alexander*... (1734).

Failing in a second attempt to gain a grand jury indictment, De Lancey went to the council and succeeded in having Zenger arrested as the *Journal*'s printer on 17 November 1734. Alexander continued to publish the paper while he and Smith defended Zenger in the celebrated case. As in the Van Dam case, Alexander's bold strategy was to challenge the legality of the court. When Smith and Alexander refused to retract the protest, De Lancey cited them for contempt and had them disbarred on 16 April 1735. *The Complaint of James Alexander and William Smith* . . . (1735) is a record of their final address to the court. Zenger was acquitted on 4 August 1735 through the efforts of Philadelphia lawyer Andrew Hamilton, though the defense had been prepared by Alexander, who recorded it in *A Brief Narrative of the Case and Tryal of John Peter Zenger, Printer of the New-York Weekly Journal* . . . (1736).

Cosby died the following March, and Alexander was returned to the bar, though he continued to meet opposition from subsequent governors for the rest of his career. Reelected to the council in 1737, he led an opposition party majority in the General Assembly. Attacks on *A Brief Narrative of the Case and Tryal of John Peter Zenger*... appearing in July of that year occasioned one of Alexander's finest defenses of a free press, which appeared in Benjamin Franklin's *Pennsylvania Gazette* (17 November-8 December 1737). This association with Franklin led to Alexander's charter membership in the American Philosophical Society when it was founded in 1744. Alexander was also instrumental in legal action that led to the rejection of New Jersey's territorial claims against New York (1748), in raising funds (1751) to establish King's College (now Columbia University), in preventing his old enemy (now governor) James De Lancey from dissolving the Council of New York (1753), and in several unsuccessful attempts to secure religious freedom for disenfranchised Quakers, Jews, and Roman Catholics. He died in Albany while working on a tax bill to pay the colony's debts.

Recent historians have pointed out that the Zenger case set no legal precedent, and that virtually every practice that Alexander opposed continued after his death. No later political prose was demonstrably indebted to Alexander's, but he kept alive in print and in court the Lockean language of individual rights that was the foundation of the political writings of the American Revolution. James Alexander's contribution to American literature goes beyond his own writings, however: as editor of the *New York Weekly Journal* he offered a forum for local rhymesters and satirists. Much of the verse was doggerel-verse propaganda, but a few of the anonymous contributors were competent versifiers, and some mock advertisements, interviews, and letters to the editor were fine pieces of satire. Alexander also reprinted the best of the British periodical literature in the *Journal* when it supported his own views, particularly the *Spectator* essays of Addison and Steele and *Cato's Letters* of Gordon and Trenchard. Both of these were models for Alexander's own essays in the *Journal*. In these editorials, in his pamphlets, and in editing the works of other writers, James Alexander provided the first independent journalism in America.

References:

Vincent Buranelli, *The Trial of Peter Zenger* (New York: New York University Press, 1957);

Charles R. Hildeburn, *Sketches of Printers and Printing in Colonial New York* (New York: Dodd, Mead, 1895);

Stanley Nider Katz, Introduction to *A Brief Narrative of the Case and Trial of John Peter Zenger* (Cambridge: Harvard University Press, 1972);

Livingston Rutherford, *John Peter Zenger, His Press, His Trial, and a Bibliography of Zenger Imprints* (Gloucester, Mass.: Peter Smith, 1904);

William Smith, *A History of the Province of New-York*, edited by Michael Kammen (Cambridge: Harvard University Press, 1972).

George Alsop

(June 1636-post 1673)

Robert D. Arner
University of Cincinnati

BOOK: *A Character of the Province of Mary-Land . . .* (London: Printed by T. J. for Peter Dring, 1666); edited by John Gilmary Shea (New York: W. Gowans, 1869).

George Alsop is the author of one of the wittiest books to emerge from colonial America, *A Character of the Province of Mary-Land . . .* (1666), which grew directly out of his experiences as an indentured servant. The book combines prose and verse in promoting an image of Maryland as a land of unparalleled opportunity, a virgin womb awaiting fertilization, and in discussing a number of topics related directly or indirectly to Maryland's economic destiny, including the Susquehanna Indians, English politics, and the virtues of commerce.

Alsop was born in Westminster parish, a London suburb, sometime around mid-June 1636. The son of a tailor, Peter Alsop, and his wife Rose, Alsop appears to have been of modest economic means, which helps to explain his championing of the lot of indentured servants. A staunch Anglican and Royalist, Alsop fled England during Cromwell's reign, arriving in Maryland after a terrifying voyage of five months in late December 1658 or early January 1659. He served a four-year term of indenture to a Maryland planter and fur trader named Thomas Stockett, like Alsop a Royalist and Anglican, at whose house Alsop probably had the opportunity to observe the Indians at firsthand. Alsop remained in Maryland, probably because of a serious illness, for some time after his term of indenture expired in 1662. Late in 1663 or early in 1664, he returned to England, working through most of 1665 on his book. The same year *A Character of the Province of Mary-Land . . .* appeared, Alsop began a career as a minister; a last indirect reference to him occurs in his father's will of 1672.

As the title of his book makes clear, Alsop conceived of his work within a seventeenth-century literary tradition that featured short sketches, usually bawdy and satiric, of character types or countries; Owen Felltham, for instance, to whose *Resolves, Divine, Moral, and Political* (1628) Alsop refers, had previously had *A Brief Character of the Low Countries* (1652) published. In addition, Alsop

Frontispiece portrait of George Alsop from the first edition of A Character Of the Province of Mary-Land . . .

also annexed the aims and purposes of promotional literature to the character and added verses and letters to his father, brother, and a cousin, producing a type of literary hybrid not uncommon in colonial literature. Alsop's language is equally acrobatic, now seriously urging the extension of agriculture and trade, then deliberately descending into self-parody and collapsing from rhetorical overextension. Indeed, style seems a standing metaphor for the age of political turbulence in which Alsop was writing. Old coherencies were gone; not even the Restoration could reestablish the notion of divine right, as the Glorious Revolution of 1688 would shortly show, and beggary and other economic hardships abounded. But there existed also the exciting prospect of America, liberating language in a litany of absent things that, unlike Henry James's two centuries later, bespoke mainly American possibility, the call to discard as entirely outworn the social structures of Europe: "Here's no Newgates for pilfering Felons, nor Ludgates for Debters, nor any Bridewells to lash the soul of Concupiscence into a chaste Repentance."

Throughout the first part of Alsop's book, Maryland is portrayed as a "natural womb" of "superabounding plenty," a sort of Peaceable Kingdom *cum* Eden whose "Wolves, Bears, and Panthers" live only in remote wilderness areas and are so degenerated anyway as to be merely comical rather than threatening and whose "Trees, Plants, Fruits, Flowers, and Roots . . . are the only Emblems or Hieroglyphicks of our Adamitical or Primitive situation. . . ." Europe, by contrast, is represented by the allegorical figures of "Famine (the dreadful Ghost of penury and want)," by the "common and folding-handed Beggar," and by clamoring, competitive tradesmen who vie with beggars for the attention of passersby in London's crowded streets and alleys. Rustic, agricultural innocence is juxtaposed to urban corruption and nastiness. Maryland's Edenic innocence is qualified somewhat by the success of sexual adventurers, who find easy pickings in the province, but the most dangerous serpents in the American Garden seem to be the Indians, "great Warriors" to be sure but also cruel cannibals who appear to be forever in thrall to "Devillish powers, and Hellish commands" and who strike Alsop not as noble savages (though at some moments he tends toward that idea) but rather as parodies of human beings. Though conscious of the problems of European society throughout *A Character of the Province of Mary-Land . . .* , as his portraits indicate, Alsop reserves most of his explicitly anti-Cromwell, anti-Puritan commentary for the fourth and final section of his book, a gathering of letters to his friends and relatives in which he also announces his sickness and his conviction of sin and desire to dedicate his life to "the love of God."

The modern reader coming to Alsop's *A Character of the Province of Mary-Land . . .* will find it a book of many moods—serious and sober, self-parodic, satiric, outrageously humorous—and in Alsop's prose and verse one finds a delightful example of the bawdy, extravagant wit of the seventeenth century. Alsop can be seen as a

Alsop's map of Maryland from the first edition of his book

transitional figure between the madcap merriment of old England and—in his exploitation of the contrast between earthy, even scatological subject matter and high rhetorical modes as well as in his pastoral celebration of the land and its rural people—various comic traditions that have come to be known as Southern humor.

References:

Jay Broadus Hubbell, *The South in American Literature* (Durham: Duke University Press, 1954), pp. 61-62;

Harry H. Kunesch, Jr., ed., "George Alsop's *A Character of the Province of Maryland*, A Critical Edition," Ph.D. dissertation, Pennsylvania State University, 1970;

J. A. Leo Lemay, *Men of Letters in Colonial Maryland* (Knoxville: University of Tennessee Press, 1972), pp. 48-69;

Ted-Larry Pebworth, "The 'Character' of George Alsop's *Mary-land*," *Seventeenth-Century News*, 34 (Summer-Fall 1976): 64-66;

Moses Coit Tyler, *A History of American Literature, 1607-1765*, 2 volumes (New York: Scribners, 1878), I: 57-61.

A
CHARACTER
Of the PROVINCE of
MARY-LAND,
Wherein is Defcribed in four diftinct Parts, (*Viz.*)
I. *The Scituation, and plenty of the Province.*
II. *The Laws, Cuftoms, and natural Demeanor of the Inhabitant.*
III. *The worft and beft Ufage of a* Mary-Land *Servant, opened in view.*
IV. *The Traffique, and vendable Commodities of the Countrey.*
ALSO
A fmall *Treatife* on the wilde and naked *INDIANS* (or *Sufquehanokes*) of *Mary-Land*, their Cuftoms, Manners, Abfurdities, & Religion.
Together with a Collection of Hiftorical LETTERS.

By *GEORGE ALSOP.*

London, Printed by *T. J.* for *Peter Dring*, at the fign of the Sun in the *Poultrey*: 1666.

Title page for Alsop's description of Maryland, which portrays the colony as a land of Edenic innocence and plenty

John Barnard

(6 November 1681-24 January 1770)

Susan Mizruchi
Princeton University

BOOKS: *The Hazard and the Unprofitableness of Losing a Soul for the Sake of Gaining the World* (Boston: Printed by B. Green, 1712);

The Peaceful End of the Perfect and Upright Man . . . (Boston: Printed by B. Green & sold by Benjamin Eliot, 1714);

Two Sermons: The Christians Behaviour Under Severe and Repeated Bereavements, and The Fatal Consequence of a Peoples Persisting in Sin, Preached in the Time of Measles (Boston: Printed by B. Green, 1714);

The Nature and Manner of Man's Blessing God; with our Obligations Thereto . . . (Boston: Printed by T. Crump for Samuel Gerrish, 1717);

Elijah's Mantle . . . (Boston: Sold by S. Gerrish, 1724);

Ashton's Memorial. An history of the Strange Adventures and Signal Deliverances of Mr. Phillip Ashton . . . (Boston: Printed by T. Fleet for S. Gerrish, 1725; London: Printed for R. Ford & S. Chandler, 1726);

Sermons on Several Subjects; to Wit, A Confirmation of the Truth of the Christian Religion . . . (London: Printed for Samuel Gerrish, 1727);

Two Discourses Addressed to Young Persons . . . (Boston: Printed for S. Gerrish, 1727);

Sin Testify'd Against by Heaven and earth . . . (Boston: Printed for J. Phillips, 1728);

The Worship of God . . . (Boston: Printed for S. Gerrish, 1729);

The Certainty, Time and End, of the Birth of our Lord and Saviour Jesus Christ: with the Accomplishment of the Several Prophecys, Relating Thereto . . . (Boston: Printed for S. Gerrish, 1731);

The Throne Established by Righteousness . . . (Boston, 1734);

A Call To Parents, and Children; or The Great Concern of Parents: and The Important Duty of Children . . . (Boston: Printed by T. Fleet for Daniel Henchman, 1737);

The Lord Jesus Christ the Only, and the Supream Head of the Church . . . (Boston: Printed by S. Kneeland & T. Green for H. Foster, 1738);

A Zeal for Good Works, Excited and Directed . . . (Boston: Printed by G. Rogers for S. Eliot, 1742);

The Imperfection of the Creature and the Excellency of the Divine Commandment . . . (Boston: Printed & sold by Rogers & Fowle, and by D. Gookin, 1747);

Janua Coelestis . . . (Boston: Printed & sold by Rogers & Fowle, and by D. Gookin, 1750);

A New Version of the Psalms of David . . . (Boston: Printed by J. Draper for T. Leverett, 1752);

A Proof of Jesus Christ His Being the Ancient Promised Messiah . . . (Boston: Printed & sold by J. Draper, 1756);

The True Divinity of Jesus Christ . . . (Boston: Printed & sold by Edes & Gill, 1761);

The Religion of Antichrist or, Notes on the Book of the Revelation of John, and Other Prophecies . . . (London: J. Chater & Th. Vernor, 1770).

A friend and contemporary of the Mathers, regarded by some as their "mimic and tool," John Barnard is best remembered, in the words of Perry Miller, as "one of the finest examples of the eighteenth-century New England parson." As minister at Marblehead, Massachusetts, from 1716 to the year of his death, the enlightened and politically aware Barnard proved himself to be a master of the jeremiad, and, as Sacvan Bercovitch has noted, he played a role in "harnessing the Puritan vision to the conditions of eighteenth-century life." Barnard had a number of sermons published during his lifetime as well as a version of the psalms of David with hymns, an effort which one early reviewer noted did not lead him "to discover that he had music in his soul." Barnard's autobiography, which is more noteworthy for its clerical gossip than for its eloquence, was circulated among his friends and acquaintances and was finally published in 1836. He also progressively championed the benefits of inoculation and was well acquainted with the intricacies of linguistics, mathematics, and shipbuilding. In a 6 May 1768 letter to President Ezra Stiles of Yale College, Dr. Charles Chauncy wrote that Barnard, "Had he turned his studies that way, would perhaps have been as great a mathematician as any in this country, I had almost said in England itself. He is equalled by few in regard either of readiness of invention, liveliness of imagination, or strength and clearness in reasoning." Barnard's claim to literary distinction is based primarily on his published sermons, which combine energetic argument with theological erudition.

John Barnard, in his own words, "was born at Boston, 6th November, 1681, descended from reputable parents, John and Esther Barnard, remarkable for their piety and benevolence, who devoted me to the service of God, in the work of the ministry from my very conception and birth." A precocious child, Barnard, by the time he was six years old, had read the Bible through "thrice, and was appointed to tutor children both older and younger than himself at the local 'reading-school.'" When he was eight Barnard was sent to the Boston Latin School, then under the tutelage of the renowned Ezekiel Cheever. Barnard was, by his own accounts, a bright pupil whose sole intellectual shortcoming was a lack of "poetical fancy." "Nor had I anything of a poetical genius," he continues, "till after I had been at College some time, when upon reading some of Mr. Cowley's works, I was highly pleased, and a new scene opened before me."

Barnard entered Harvard College in 1696, during Increase Mather's presidency. At Harvard, known as "Johnny" to all, he was a popular though unremarkable student. After his graduation in 1700 Barnard applied himself more seriously to scholarly studies, particularly to the subjects of mathematics, divinity, and Hebrew. In his postcollege years Barnard was active in the ministry, preaching at various pulpits in and around Boston. But he experienced a round of professional disappointments, being passed over for permanent pulpits at Reading, Newton, and the North Church in Boston. Barnard attributed these failures to his temporary disfavor with the Mathers, who thought his sermons smacked of Arminianism, and to his candid friendship with the generally unpopular Governor Joseph Dudley. Finally in July of 1716, he was ordained minister for the church at Marblehead in a ceremony which featured a sermon by Barnard, with "the Charge" given by Cotton Mather and "the Right Hand of Fellowship" given by Benjamin Colman. Two years later, on 18 September 1718, Barnard was married to Anna Woodbury. They had no children.

In Marblehead Barnard served as more than his congregants' spiritual adviser. He showed a propensity for commercial affairs, which exemplifies the more liberal interests of the eighteenth-century minister. Observing the poverty of the town fishermen and the inefficient way in which they allowed their fish to be distributed and marketed by American and European merchants in the bigger ports, Barnard encouraged them to eliminate the middlemen and deal directly with foreign markets. Largely as a result of Barnard's efforts, by 1766 all the fish caught by Marblehead fishermen were locally cured and distributed, mostly to foreign markets. Town wealth increased accordingly.

In his autobiography Barnard interprets the affair in scriptural terms. Formerly, "The people contented themselves to be the slaves that digged in the mines, and left the merchants of Boston, Salem, and Europe, to carry away the gains; by which means the town was always in dismally poor circumstances . . ." But now, "we have between thirty and forty ships, brigs, snows, and topsail schooners, engaged in foreign trade. From so small a beginning the town has risen into its present flourishing circumstances, and we need no foreigner to transport our fish, but we are able ourselves to send it all to the market. Let God have the praise, who has redeemed the town from a state of bondage into a state of liberty and freedom." It is evident from Barnard's detailing of his own efforts to bring prosperity to Marblehead that rational human agency goes hand in hand with Providential favor.

Belief in the powers of human reason in both government and daily life is the trademark of Barnard's sermonizing. Barnard's election sermon of 29 May 1734, *The Throne Established by Righteousness* . . . , provides a good illustration of Barnard's thoughts on government and human nature. Barnard begins his address, significantly, with an appeal to human reason: "That the supreme Ruler of the world is to be acknowledged in all our ways and more especially in all the grand and important concerns, whether of public societies or of private persons, is a principle that stands in the strongest light to the natural reason and conscience of every man who is not sunk into the lowest stupidity and the vilest atheism." Barnard then moves to assert that while government is ordained by God, a ruler's authority derives from the commission of the people ruled. Barnard, like Jonathan Edwards in his 1748 eulogy for Col. John Stoddard, emphasizes the practical necessities of leadership. Government, he insists, is for the good of the governed, and there must be mutual respect between the governors and the governed. Governments must abide by constitutions of written laws, which act as checks on the powers of leaders. And good leaders will distribute the rewards of official positions in

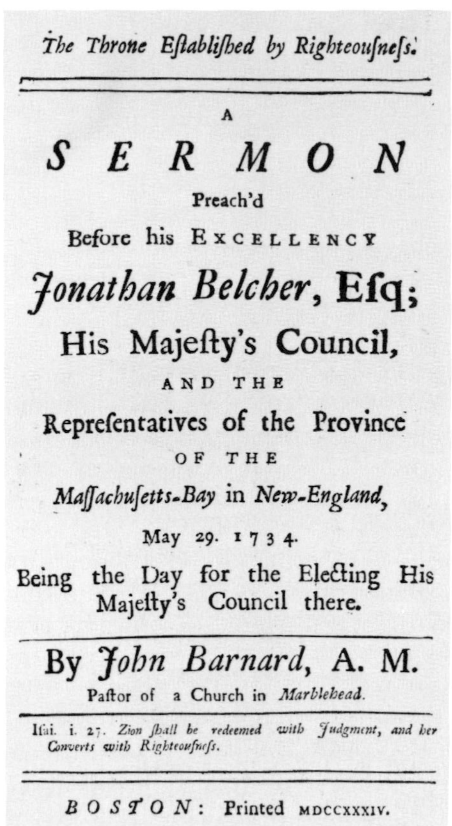

The Throne Eſtabliſhed by Righteouſneſs.

A

SERMON

Preach'd

Before his EXCELLENCY

Jonathan Belcher, Eſq;

His Majeſty's Council,

AND THE

Repreſentatives of the Province

OF THE

Maſſachuſetts-Bay in *New-England*,

May 29. 1734.

Being the Day for the Electing His Majeſty's Council there.

By *John Barnard*, A. M.

Paſtor of a Church in *Marblehead*.

Iſai. i. 27. *Zion ſhall be redeemed with Judgment, and her Converts with Righteouſneſs.*

BOSTON: Printed MDCCXXXIV.

Title page for Barnard's 1734 election sermon, which argues that government is ordained by God but derives its authority from the governed (John Carter Brown Library, Brown University)

accordance with ability and merit. Never shall governmental favors be given to those "who have the impudence to offer at the purchasing of them." Rather, "the distribution shall be made to able men, men suitably qualified, furnished with wisdom and knowledge, sagacity and penetration, fortitude and resolution, vigor and diligence." Barnard also relegates to the responsibilities of government the promotion of industry and manufactures. Governments should actively facilitate the prosperity of their constituents by "due encouragement of labor and industry, by proper premiums for serviceable manufactures, by suppressing all that tends to promote idleness and prodigal wasting and consuming of estates, by a due testimony against all fraud and deceit and unrighteousness in dealings, by cultivating frugality and good husbandry."

Barnard stresses the rational processes of government, the role human reason can play in bringing about an orderly and just society. The force and benevolence of God speaks through the rational designs of men. Appropriately, Barnard's election sermon focuses on human possibility, on the promised fulfillment of God's divine errand for the benefit of future generations of Americans. Though Barnard in his sermon expresses unshakable loyalty to English governors, it would not be long before similar testimonies to the reasonableness of man would be invoked for the purposes of more nativist forms of government.

A "sweet reasonableness" is the predominant tone of Barnard's sermons. It is not surprising that Barnard guided his congregation at Marblehead through the enthusiasms of the Great Awakening with a minimal amount of conflict. Barnard's persuasiveness was a model for other congregations as well. His sermon *A Zeal for Good Works, Excited and Directed . . .*, preached at Boston on 25 March 1742, was recognized as a contribution to the checking of religious disorders throughout New England. The spirit of Barnard's works can be summed up in his own words, "zeal guided by knowledge, tempered with prudence, and accomplished with charity."

Other:

"Autobiography of the Rev. John Barnard," Massachusetts Historical Society *Collections*, third series 5 (1836): 177-243;

The Throne Established by Righteousness . . ., in *The Wall and the Garden: Selected Massachusetts Election Sermons 1670-1775*, edited by A. W. Plumstead (Minneapolis: University of Minnesota Press, 1968), pp. 223-280.

References:

"Historical Account of Marblehead," Massachusetts Historical Society *Collections*, first series 8 (1802), p. 54;

"Letter from President Stiles to John Barnard" and "Letter from Dr. Charles Chauncy to President Stiles of Yale," Massachusetts Historical Society *Collections*, first series 10 (1809), pp. 157, 166;

Perry Miller and Thomas Johnson, *The Puritans* (New York: American Book Company, 1938), pp. 270-276, 556;

Clifford K. Shipton, *Sibley's Harvard Graduates: Biographical Sketches of Those Who Attended Harvard College*, volume 4 (Cambridge & Boston: Harvard University Press, 1933), pp. 501-512;

Moses Coit Tyler, *A History of American Literature* (Ithaca: Cornell University Press, 1949), pp. 412-414.

Robert Beverley

(circa 1673-1722)

Robert D. Arner
University of Cincinnati

BOOKS: *An Essay upon the Government of the English Plantations on the Continent of America . . .*, attributed to Beverley (London: Printed for Richard Parker, 1701);

The History and Present State of Virginia . . . (London: Printed for R. Parker, 1705; revised and enlarged edition, London: Printed for F. Fayram & J. Clarke & for T. Bickerton, 1722; Richmond: J. W. Randolph, 1855);

An Abridgement of the Public Laws of Virginia . . ., attributed to Beverley (London: Printed for F. Fayram & J. Clarke & T. Bickerton, 1722).

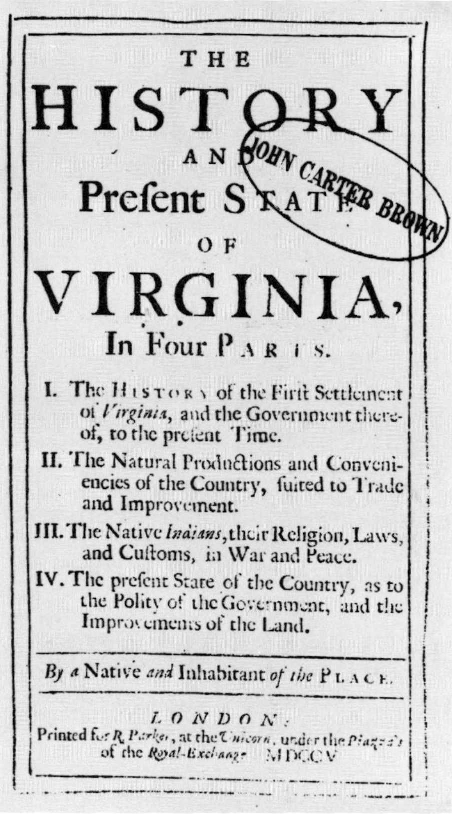

THE

HISTORY

AND

Prefent STATE

OF

VIRGINIA,

In Four PARTS.

I. The HISTORY of the Firft Settlement of *Virginia*, and the Government thereof, to the prefent Time.

II. The Natural Productions and Conveniencies of the Country, fuited to Trade and Improvement.

III. The Native *Indians*, their Religion, Laws, and Cuftoms, in War and Peace.

IV. The prefent State of the Country, as to the Polity of the Government, and the Improvements of the Land.

By a Native *and* Inhabitant *of the* PLACE.

LONDON:

Printed for *R. Parker*, at the *Unicorn*, under the *Piazza's* of the *Royal-Exchange*. MDCCV

Title page for Beverley's history, written to counter John Oldmixon's account of the colony (John Carter Brown Library, Brown University)

Robert Beverley's claim to literary fame rests entirely upon one book, *The History and Present State of Virginia* (1705), which betrays a deep-seated ambivalence toward the march of civilization. On the one hand, Beverley envisages a productive society based upon wise laws, honest governors, and hard work. On the other, he locates the symbolic center of his book in Indian civilization, condemning the "curse of Industry" and imagining a static, nearly perfect pastoral society without laws of any sort but those dictated by nature; English "improvements" only ruin things.

Beverley was born in Middlesex County, Virginia, sometime about 1673, the son of Major Robert Beverley, a man who stood steadfastly by Gov. Sir William Berkeley during Bacon's Rebellion. Upon his father's death, Beverley inherited a plantation in Gloucester County and some six thousand additional acres in King and Queen County, where he eventually built an estate and married Ursula Byrd, the sister of William Byrd II of Westover; she died shortly thereafter, and Beverley never remarried. In 1696, he was appointed to the important posts of clerk of the General Court, clerk of Council, and clerk of the General Assembly; he also served as a burgess from Jamestown in 1699, 1700-1702, and 1703-1706. While on a business trip to England in 1703, Beverley read a manuscript of John Oldmixon's account of the *British Empire in America* and determined to write his own history and set the record straight. He also wrote letters to friends in Virginia alleging that Gov. Francis Nicholson was plotting against the liberties of Virginians, and for his pains Nicholson removed him from the office of clerk of the court of King and Queen County. Retiring from public life, Beverley spent the remaining years of his life transforming the interior of Beverley Park into a Spartan abode—reminiscent, so he claimed, of Indian simplicity—and attempting to establish viniculture in Virginia. He died in 1722, having barely finished a revision of *The History and Present State of Virginia* in which he toned down his political commentary markedly and to some extent modified his appreciation of the Indians.

The History and Present State of Virginia is divided into four sections, the first of which, relying heavily upon Capt. John Smith's *Generall Historie*

of Virginia (1624), brings the readers up to the founding of the College of William and Mary and the present situation of the colony. This part is marked by open criticism of a number of royal governors—Lord Culpeper, Sir Edmund Andros, and, of course, Francis Nicholson among them—who in various ways attempted to infringe upon the liberties of Virginians. The criticism is written from a Whig perspective and seems to derive more than one idea from John Locke's *Two Treatises of Government* (1690). Like Locke, for example, Beverley does not believe that one generation ought to make laws binding upon succeeding generations, and he favors maintaining the constitutional liberties of all Englishmen. One may well see in this section the seeds of political ideas that were to flower in the prose of Thomas Jefferson (who read Beverley).

The second and third sections of Beverley's book extend the concept of history to include natural history, detailing the flora and fauna of Virginia and elaborating upon the life led by the local Indians, "happy, I think, in their simple State of Nature, and in their enjoyment of Plenty, without the Curse of Labour." For rhetorical purposes, indeed, Beverley identifies his own language and political pose as those of an Indian, and he hopes European readers will pardon any infelicities or barbarities of style or sentiment. Finally, in part four, Beverley addresses the present and future prospects of the colony, praising the "Liberties and Priviledges" extended to all immigrants—except, of course, the slaves. On that subject, Beverley betrays the same tragic myopia that would later afflict Thomas Jefferson, an inability to understand that the craving for liberty was not to be discovered in white breasts alone but in black men and women also. Despite this flawed vision, Beverley's history remains one of the most interesting literary documents produced in the pre-Revolutionary South, one that can still be read with pleasure and excitement.

References:

Robert D. Arner, "The Quest for Freedom: Style and Meaning in Robert Beverley's *History and Present State of Virginia*," *Southern Literary Journal*, 8, no. 2 (Spring 1976): 79-98;

David Freeman Hawke, Introduction to *The History and Present State of Virginia* (Indianapolis & New York: Bobbs-Merrill, 1971);

Jon Kukla, "Robert Beverley Assailed: Appellate Jurisdiction and the Problem of Bicameralism in Seventeenth-Century Virginia," *Virginia Magazine of History and Biography*, 88 (1980): 415-429;

Leo Marx, *The Machine in the Garden: Technology and the Pastoral Ideal in America* (New York: Oxford University Press, 1967), pp. 75-88;

Louis B. Wright, Introduction to *The History and Present State of Virginia* (Chapel Hill: University of North Carolina Press, 1947; republished, Charlottesville: University Press of Virginia, 1968).

Arthur Blackamore

(1679-death date unknown)

Carl Bredahl
University of Florida

BOOKS: *The Perfidious Brethern, or the Religious Triumvirate* . . . (London: Printed for T. Bickerton, 1720);

Ecclesiae Primitiva Notitia, or a Summary of Christian Antiquities . . . (London: Printed for E. Bell, 1722);

Luck at Last; or The Happy Unfortunate (London: Printed by H. Parker & sold by T. Werner, 1723).

Arthur Blackamore, master of the Grammar School of the College of William and Mary between 1707 and 1716, is known primarily for two books published in London in 1720 and 1723 and a poem written in America in 1716. Born in London, Blackamore matriculated at Christchurch College, Oxford, in May 1695. In 1707 he was sent as a schoolmaster to Virginia, where whatever benefits he gained from his contacts with William Byrd II and lieutenant-governor Alexander Spotswood were overshadowed by his increasingly troublesome alcoholism. To commemorate Spotswood's 1716 western expedition, designed to protect the colony from Iroquois raids by establishing compacts with friendly Indians, Blackamore composed "Expeditio Ultramontana," a poem later translated from the Latin by the Reverend George Seagood and printed in the *Maryland Gazette* for 17-24 June 1729.

Because of his problem with alcohol, Blackamore was removed from his position at the Grammar School, returning to London in 1717. There he maintained his contacts with Virginia and had three works published. His first, *The Perfidious Brethern, or The Religious Triumvirate* (1720), was dedicated to Spotswood and supported Spotswood's controversy with the local clergy over the right of appointment of ministers to Anglican parishes. Blackamore speaks of "*One*; who should he be set forth as he ought, would appear to be a false Priest: Like the worst of the following Triumvirate: of *equal Piety*, and as *black Example*." The book contains three short narratives which exemplify the perfidy of priests of various religions and situations. A minor work, *Ecclesiae Primitiva Notitia, or a Summary of Christian Antiquities*, was published in two volumes in London in 1722. Apparently with justification, this publication incurred the anger of Joseph Bingham (1668-1723), who felt that Blackamore had stolen from Bingham's own ten-volume work, *Antiquities of the Christian Church* (1708-1722).

In 1723 was published Blackamore's third work, *Luck at Last; or The Happy Unfortunate*. *Luck at Last* . . . draws on a plot from Mrs. Alphra Behn's *The Wandering Beauty* (1698) and is a forerunner of Samuel Richardson's *Pamela* (1740-1742) in its sentimental adventure and moral admonitions. Some realism is achieved through the use of a mildly bawdy beggars' idiom and references to Virginia. Richard Beale Davis sums up Blackamore's literary importance when he notes that if Blackamore "had remained in the colony he might have been our Swift or our Defoe. As it is, we must now assign him a place among those who wrote significantly and cogently about Virginia."

Other:

"Expeditio Ultramontana," translated by George Seagood, *Maryland Gazette*, 17-24 June 1729; republished in *William and Mary Quarterly*, first series 7 (1898-1899): 30-36;

Luck at Last, in *Four Before Richardson*, edited by William H. McBurney (Lincoln: University of Nebraska Press, 1963), pp. 1-81.

References:

Richard Beale Davis, "Arthur Blackamore: The Virginia Colony and the Early English Novel," *Virginia Magazine of History and Biography*, 75 (January 1967): 22-34;

Davis, *Intellectual Life in the Colonial South 1585-1763* (Knoxville: University of Tennessee Press, 1978), pp. 1458-1459, 1487;

William H. McBurney, Introduction and note in *Four Before Richardson*, edited by McBurney (Lincoln: University of Nebraska Press, 1963), pp. xvi-xix, 5.

James Blair

(circa 1655-18 April 1743)

Homer D. Kemp
Tennessee Technological University

BOOKS: *Our Saviour's Divine Sermon on the Mount* . . . (5 volumes, London: Printed for J. Brotherton, 1722; enlarged edition, 4 volumes, London: Printed for J. Brotherton & J. Oswald, 1740);

The Present State of Virginia, and the College, by Blair, Henry Hartwell, and Edward Chilton (London: J. Wyat, 1727).

For fifty-four years James Blair—parish rector, Anglican commissary, president of the College of William and Mary, and councillor—dominated church life and was a major force in political life in Virginia. One of the three ablest Anglican commissaries in the colonial South, Blair was politically powerful enough to effect the dismissal of three strong royal governors and has been called, for his period, "the most articulate spokesman in Virginia" against the exercise of royal authority. With friends in England such as John Locke, three successive Archbishops of Canterbury, and two Bishops of London, Blair ruthlessly destroyed those who opposed him. Tough-minded, impervious to criticism, iron-willed, ruthlessly ambitious, avaricious, solitary, imperious, articulate, idealistic, and pragmatic, Blair was a complex man of tireless abilities and a violent temper who also was a conscientious and effective pastor, a powerful speaker, and an able writer. As he left office in 1721, partially due to Blair's machinations, Governor Alexander Spotswood indignantly dubbed Blair "that old Combustion."

Portrait by J. Hargreaves, 1705 (College of William and Mary)

Blair was born sometime between May 1655 and May 1656, the son of Robert Blair, minister of Avah in Banffshire, Scotland. In 1667, at the age of twelve, young James entered the preparatory grammar school at Marischal College, Aberdeen, and matriculated at the University of Edinburgh in 1669. He took his M.A. in 1673 and was ordained into the Church of Scotland in 1679, serving as rector of Cranston in the diocese of Edinburgh until his refusal in 1682 to sign the test oath that was one of the Stuart efforts to disarm Scottish opposition to the accession of James II. Blair was far from alone among Protestant clergymen in Scotland who balked at the Roman Catholic James II's requirement that all Scottish administrators, soldiers, scholars, and churchmen sign an oath that would have placed James at the head of the Scottish church. After a period of working as a law clerk in the Rolls Office in London, during which time he cultivated several powerful friendships, Blair accepted an appointment to a rectorship in Virginia.

Arriving in Virginia in the autumn of 1685, Blair assumed his duties in Henrico parish on Virginia's westernmost frontier, where on 2 June

1687 he married Sarah Harrison, daughter of Colonel Benjamin Harrison, thus aligning himself with a politically and socially prominent family. Appointed Virginia's first Anglican commissary in late 1689, Blair began his campaign for the establishment of a college in Virginia. Through his tireless efforts and fierce resolve, including a trip to England to lobby for his cause (1691-1693), the College of William and Mary was chartered in 1693 with Blair as president.

In 1694 Blair's friends in England secured his appointment to the Royal Council of Virginia; he was the first clergyman on that body. Now part of the inner circle of Virginia's leaders, Blair was named in 1695 rector of James City parish, the oldest and most desirable in the colony, where he served until he went to Bruton parish in Williamsburg in 1710. The first of Blair's thirty years of squabbles with Virginia governors also began in 1695. In 1697 Blair carried this fight with Sir Edmund Andros to the Board of Trade in England, where Blair's great debating abilities and ruthlessness won the governor's dismissal.

Blair developed a friendship with one of the members of the board, John Locke, and coauthored with him "Some of the Cheif Greivances of the present Constitution of Virginia with an Essay towards the Remedies thereof," an essay which was the basis for a longer report written by Blair, Henry Hartwell, and Edward Chilton. On 20 October 1697, the three men submitted their report to the Board of Trade, entitling it "An Account of the Present State and Government of Virginia." It languished in government files, however, until it was published in 1727 as *The Present State of Virginia, and the College*. Although largely overlooked in Southern colonial historical surveys, this sociopolitical appraisal—combined with promotional literature for the College of William and Mary—is a significant view of developing political attitudes in Virginia. Blair's hand is seen throughout the work in its call for restricting the broad powers of the governor and council and for the correction of abuses of power.

Swiss diarist Francis Louis Michel's 1702 sketch of the first building at the College of William and Mary. Blair was the college's first president (Colonial Williamsburg).

Blair's battles with Andros's successor, Francis Nicholson, and Nicholson's successor, Alexander Spotswood, were fierce and ended the same way, with their removal. In these disputes Blair found himself aligned with Virginia's political establishment against the majority of the clergy. The clergy and the governor were pressing for the right of the governor to induct ministers into their parishes; Blair sided with the local vestries in their right to appoint and dismiss ministers. The Blair-Nicholson feud inspired a little body of literature, including a number of satiric poems largely by clergymen. Back in England, the novelist Arthur Blackamore, who had been dismissed from William and Mary for alcoholism, perhaps modeled the villain Whiskero of *The Perfidious Brethern* . . . (1720) on his old enemy James Blair.

Throughout his stormy public life, Blair remained a conscientious parish minister. His effectiveness as a pulpit orator can be seen in his *Our Saviour's Divine Sermon on the Mount* . . . (1722), a massive five-volume edition of 117 sermons preached at Jamestown and Williamsburg between 1707 and 1721. Although he was a brilliant and learned theologian, Blair's sermons are for the most part practical discourses aimed at an ordinary audience and deal with Christian behavior, morality, and ethics. This collection spread Blair's name throughout the English-speaking world; it remained in libraries in England and America for over a century. Regarded highly by church historians, the series exemplifies one Southern homiletic tradition which Richard Beale Davis describes as "the quiet unraveling of texts which

J. Hargreaves portrait of Sarah Harrison Blair, 1705 (College of William and Mary)

touched upon some aspect of everyday life, in as plain a style as was any ever found in New England."

From the late 1720s until his death on 18 April 1743 Blair's life was relatively quiet and largely solitary. He never adopted the robust life-style and camaraderie of Virginia society and never formed many close friendships; moreover, his policy positions and truculent nature alienated most of his clergy. In the final analysis, James Blair has been judged a powerful force both for good and bad in Virginia's history. He founded, against almost insurmountable odds, the South's only colonial college, and he doggedly opposed abuses of royal power. Moses Coit Tyler called him the actual founder of "intellectual culture" in Virginia, and Parke Rouse, Blair's biographer, credits him with being unequaled in contributing to Virginia's intellectual maturation.

Other:

"A Proposition for encouraging the Christian education of Indian, Negroe and Mulotto Children" (1699), *Archives of Maryland,* 19 (1899): 100, 484ff; 23 (1903): 83;

"Some of the Cheif Greivances of the present Constitution of Virginia . . . ," in "Virginia at the Close of the Seventeenth Century: An Appraisal by James Blair and John Locke," by Michael Kammen, *Virginia Magazine of History and Biography,* 74 (April 1966): 141-169.

References:

Robert A. Bain, "The Composition and Publication of *The Present State of Virginia, and the College,*" *Early American Literature,* 6 (Spring 1971): 31-54;

George M. Brydon, *Virginia's Mother Church* Richmond: Virginia Historical Society, 1947), I: 273-326;

Richard Beale Davis, *Intellectual Life in the Colonial South, 1585-1763,* 3 volumes (Knoxville: University of Tennessee Press, 1978);

Hunter Dickinson Farish, ed., Introduction to *The Present State of Virginia, and the College* (Williamsburg: Colonial Williamsburg, Inc., 1940), pp. xi-lxxii;

Samuel C. McCulloch, "James Blair's Plan of 1699 to Reform the Clergy of Virginia," *William and Mary Quarterly,* third series 4 (January 1947): 85-86;

William Meade, *Old Churches, Ministers and Families of Virginia* (1857; Baltimore: Genealogical Publishing, 1966), I: 154-156, 157-165;

Samuel R. Mohler, "Commissary James Blair, Churchman, Educator, and Politician of Colonial Virginia," Ph.D. dissertation, University of Illinois, 1944;

Edgar L. Pennington, *Commissary Blair* (Hartford, Conn.: Church Missions Publishing, 1936);

William Stevens Perry, *The History of the American Episcopal Church, 1587-1883,* 2 volumes (Boston: Osgood, 1885), I: 113-128;

Parke Rouse, Jr., *James Blair of Virginia* (Chapel Hill: University of North Carolina Press, 1971).

William Bradford

Frank Shuffelton
University of Rochester

BIRTH: Austerfield, England, March 1590, to William and Alice Hanson Bradford.

MARRIAGES: 10 December 1613 to Dorothy May; child: John. 14 August 1623 to Alice Carpenter Southworth; children: William, Mercy, Joseph.

DEATH: Plymouth, New England, 9 May 1657.

BOOKS: *History of Plymouth Plantation . . .*, edited by Charles Deane, *Collections of the Massachusetts Historical Society*, fourth series, no. 2 (1856); republished as *Of Plymouth Plantation, 1620-1647*, edited by Samuel Eliot Morison (New York: Knopf, 1922);

William Bradford: The Collected Verse, edited by Michael G. Runyan (St. Paul: John Colet Press, 1974).

When William Bradford's *Of Plimmoth Plantation* (the title he himself gave the work) was first published from his manuscript as *History of Plymouth Plantation* (1856), it was immediately recognized as a uniquely valuable historical record and almost as quickly seen as one of the finest examples of seventeenth-century American literature. The intervening years have not seen any lessening of its historical importance to scholars, although there have been different opinions about the ultimate validity of Bradford's view of his fellow Pilgrims. More interesting, its appreciation as a major literary work has continued to grow. Hailed by Kenneth Murdock as an "American classic" and by Peter Gay as an "authentic masterpiece," *Of Plimmoth Plantation* has, by virtue of the imaginative richness and vision with which it comprehends the facts of emigration and settlement, become one of the essential texts for anyone wishing to understand the American experience.

Bradford's literary reputation depends almost entirely on his history—the morally earnest but awkward verses he wrote toward the end of his life and the didactic, although sometimes effective, dialogues he offered to the young men of Plymouth show him more as a good Puritan than as a great artist—and in a curious way his history has almost become his best biography, curious because of its impersonal subjection of Bradford's private hopes and trials to the account of the vicissitudes of the covenanted community. Elected governor thirty-one times in the thirty-seven years he lived in Plymouth, Bradford characteristically refers to himself in his history, when events require such a reference, as "the governor" rather than by proper name or by a first-person pronoun, yet Moses Coit Tyler, for one, praised the "manliness" of character that shines through its pages, and that character is ultimately Bradford's own.

If the "hero" in *Of Plimmoth Plantation* is the church at the center of the civil polity, Bradford's devotion to and identification of himself with the covenanted community fuels his narrative with a personal energy and vigor. One might draw certain broad parallels between *Of Plimmoth Plantation* and the form of Puritan spiritual autobiography. After a brief overview of Satan's war on mankind, Bradford focuses on the gathering of the church into a covenanted group, downplaying genealogy and youthful tribulations in favor of a detailed account of the community's sometimes stumbling progress toward sanctity and self-clarification. Just as the spiritual autobiographer submerges the personal or eccentric into the universal pattern of grace, so Bradford sinks himself and the specific biographies of the Plymouth church members into a narrative of the fortunes of his church and community; specific facts about individual Saints are brought forward to illustrate truths about the community, whereas Bradford gives his villains extensive space in which to demonstrate their egoism and hypocrisy. Finally, if the autobiographer is of necessity uncertain of the specific nature of his coming end, he is confident of the heavenward direction of his life, and so Bradford ends his narrative amid the ambiguities of history yet sure that the experience he depicts reveals in its totality God's providential care.

Bradford was born at Austerfield, a small village near the southern border of Yorkshire, probably in early March of 1590 since his baptismal entry in the local parish register is dated on the nineteenth. His father, also William, belonged to a family of relatively well-to-do yeomen, and his mother, born Alice Hanson, came from a similar background. This comfortable beginning was, however, soon disrupted; his father died in July 1591, and, when his mother remarried, young William was sent to live with his grandfather Bradford. When his grandfather died two years later, he rejoined his mother, but following her death in the next year, he was taken in by his uncles, Thomas and Robert Bradford. His uncles intended him to become a farmer, but as a child Bradford was, according to Cotton Mather, afflicted with "a long sickness," which may have kept him indoors for long stretches, giving him a chance to read the Bible and perhaps books such as John Foxe's *Actes and Monuments* (1563), more familiarly known as the *Book of Martyrs*. The nature of Bradford's formal education is unknown; certainly a great deal of the learning that lies behind the pages of his history is the result of private reading rather than formal schooling. Probably he went to a local dame school, possibly for some time to a nearby grammar school, but the turning point of his life came in early adolescence when he went to hear Richard Clyfton, a noted nonconformist preacher, at Babworth, a village about eight miles from Austerfield. Bradford later described Clyfton as "a grave and reverend preacher, who by his pains and diligence had done much good, and under God had been a means of the conversion of many," and among that many was Bradford himself.

Despite the opposition of his family, he continued to attend upon Clyfton, and when the latter organized a covenanted Separatist church in neighboring Scrooby, Bradford became a member. Here he met the two men who most influenced the remainder of his life, William Brewster and John Robinson. Brewster, nearly twenty-five years his senior, had attended Cambridge for a time, where he was "first seasoned with the seeds of grace and virtue"; he entertained the Scrooby meetings in his house, and he eventually became the elder of the church of Plymouth. Bradford's elegiac description of Brewster in *Of Plimmoth Plantation* suggests the character he chose as a model for his own: "He was wise and discreet and well spoken, having a grave and deliberate utterance, of a very cheerful spirit, very sociable and pleasant amongst his friends, of a humble and modest mind, of a peaceable disposition, undervaluing himself and his own abilities and sometime overvaluing others. Inoffensive and innocent in his life and conversation, which gained him the love of those without as well as those within; . . . He was tenderhearted and compassionate of such as were in misery, but especially of such as had been of good estate and rank and were fallen unto want and poverty either for goodness and religion's sake or by the injury and oppression of others; he would say of all men these deserved to be pitied most." The "manliness" of character that Bradford projects in his history is another version of Brewster's cheerful spirit, modest mind, and compassion, and his lengthy, heartfelt character sketch of Brewster suggests that the older man was at once Bradford's best friend and a substitute for the father he never really knew. John Robinson, an alumnus of Christ's College, Cambridge, joined the Scrooby church, soon becoming its teacher and then, in Holland, Clyfton's successor as pastor. Robinson established a larger reputation as an important defender of the principles of Separatism, but he was distinguished from many other Separatist spokesmen by his moderation and tolerance. Although he never came to America, his ideas and advice, his emphasis on the importance of compassion, guided Bradford both in his conduct as governor and in his strategy as historian.

Bradford's covenanting with the Scrooby congregation marks the point at which his biography merges with the history he would come to write. He made the storm-tossed passage to Amsterdam in 1608, removed with the church to Leyden in the following year, and married Dorothy May, daughter of a member of the English Church in Amsterdam, in 1613. Their only child, John (circa 1615-1678), remained in Holland when the Pilgrims sailed for America and joined his father after nearly a seven-year separation; in the meantime Dorothy Bradford had drowned at Cape Cod on 7 December 1620, within days of the first landfall, a fact unrecorded in *Of Plimmoth Plantation*, and William had taken a second wife, Alice Carpenter Southworth, widow of Edward Southworth, a former member of the Leyden church. Bradford had three children by his second wife—William (1624-1704), Mercy (1627-?), and Joseph (1630-1715)—and his household after John's arrival in America also included Alice Southworth's two sons by her previous marriage, Constant and Thomas, as well as sons of Robert Cushman and George Morton, friends and associates who had died after the emigration. Against this pattern of removals, separations, deaths, and reunions, Bradford wrote his history of the Scrooby Separatists' passage to Holland and America, a history celebrating their unity in adversity and mourning their fragmentation in their moment of worldly success.

Bradford began to write *Of Plimmoth Planta-*

tion in 1630, a response, some scholars claim, to the arrival of the Massachusetts Bay Colony settlers in that year and to a fear of being overwhelmed by that more populous enterprise. The manuscript of the history as Bradford left it was divided into two books, the first covering the origins of the Plymouth church and their wanderings from Scrooby to America, the second covering in annalistic order the fortunes of the plantation from the landing in 1620 until the year 1646. Bradford apparently wrote the first book, nearly a quarter of the whole manuscript, in 1630, and came back in the years between 1646 and 1650 to compose the second book, using for source material his letter book and probably a diary of some sort which no longer exists.

Because *Of Plimmoth Plantation*'s first book is a coherent narrative that begins with references to "the first breaking out of the light of the gospel in our honourable nation of England" and to the "wars and oppositions . . . Satan hath raised, maintained, and continued against the Saints," critics such as Kenneth Murdock and Robert Daly have in their different fashions emphasized Bradford's narrative as a form of providential history. But while there is certainly a great deal of justice to this view, it is important to recognize, as David Levin and Alan Howard have explained, that Bradford's understanding of the working of providence in the world was sophisticated and complex and that he recognized the frequent ambiguities raised by a belief in providence. Correspondingly, because the second book is seemingly more fragmented, has less sense of "plot," and closes with an outbreak of sin in Plymouth, the dispersal of the church, and the death of Brewster, writers like Daly and Peter Gay see Bradford as ending in sadness, despair, and a sense of failure. But Levin, with whom Howard concurs, opposes this view with a contention that Bradford's "pattern of . . . historical organization is perennially dialectical, cyclical, alternating," moving between success and failure and ending with a perception of history that is perhaps more nearly ironic than it is despairing.

When Bradford in his first pages determines to explain "the very root and rise" of the Plymouth Plantation, he does seem more concerned with establishing as a frame the dialectical, oscillating movement of history than with asserting God's providential hand directing all. He opens with an evocation of the Reformation seen in its broadest terms which is immediately opposed by Satan's wars expressed first as overt persecution of the Saints by the Roman Church, but when the "main truths of the gospel" thrive on "the blood of the martyrs" and balk these stratagems, Satan in turn attempts to undermine the Saints from within by means of "errours, heresies, wonderful dissensions amongst the professors themselves, working upon their pride and ambition." Bradford then enlarges the scope of his frame by pointing to the contentions "in the ancient times" of Arians against orthodox and by suggesting that "the like method Satan hath seemed to hold in these later times," implicitly arguing that as Satan's maneuvers failed in the past, so would they now. Bradford then passes on to an account of the Reformation in England, repeating the familiar pattern of an outbreak of gospel truth, overt prosecution (Queen Mary's martyrs), triumph of the reformers, then contentions between the "zealous professors" and those who wished to preserve episcopal authority and "popish trash," which in turn leads to seeing "further into things by the light of the Word of God. How not only these base and beggarly ceremonies were unlawful, but also that the lordly and tyrannous power of the prelates ought not to be submitted unto." Thus for Bradford if "the light of the gospel" draws men forward in history, their progress in truth and virtue is marked by the attempts of pride and ambition to overthrow them.

At the same time as Bradford is setting up a reciprocal relationship between the bright and dark moments of human experience, he is continuously narrowing his focus from a briefly sketched general view of history to the specific case of the Plymouth immigrants. Beginning with the whole Continental Reformation seen in terms of the opposition of Satan and gospel truth, he moves to the English Reformation delineated in terms of the opposition of Mary and the martyrs for whom John Foxe spoke, then to reformation "in the North parts" of England and the struggle of the "many . . . enlightened by the Word of God" against "apparitors and pursuivants and the commissary courts." Similarly his attention shifts from spiritual forces at work on history from the outside to the actions of men caught up in the toils of history; he leads his reader finally to a consideration of the North-country Christians who "shook off this yoke of antichristian bondage, and as the Lord's free people joined themselves (by a covenant of the Lord) into a church estate, in the fellowship of the gospel, to walk in all His ways made known or to be made known unto them, according to their best endeavours, whatsoever it should cost them, the Lord assisting them. And that it cost them something this ensuing history will declare." If the light of the gospel is requisite to make these "the Lord's free people," Bradford nevertheless calls the reader's attention to their own activity in joining themselves together and to the costs they will pay in history for their action.

Having drawn the connection between the grace inherent in the Word of God and the activity of the Saints, Bradford in his second chapter finds historically appropriate terminology for this grace and uses the word *providence* for the first time; the members of the Scrooby church were not dismayed, he says, by the prospect of immigrating to Holland, "for their desires were set on the ways of God and to enjoy his ordinances; but they rested on His providence, and knew Whom they had believed." In the course of his narrative Bradford shows providence operating in two different modes. At times God seems to intervene almost directly with a special providence capable of transforming a situation with an instructive or happy turn of events which might seem merely accidental to a skeptic; thus on the voyage to America, when John Howland was washed overboard in a storm, "it pleased God that he caught hold of the topsail halyards which hung overboard" and was brought safely back onto the ship. But for the most part Bradford believes that God's providence works through second causes, orchestrating complex and varied human motives, some sacred, some profane, to bring about a benevolent result, albeit a result that can be understood by men only with some difficulty. When, for example, the group was boarding a ship to pass over to Holland, the authorities fell upon them, capturing some, mostly women and children. "Being thus apprehended," writes Bradford, "they were hurried from one place to another and from one justice to another, till in the end they knew not what to do with them." If it was unreasonable to jail women and children, the magistrates also found it impossible to send them home since they had sold all in order to emigrate, but finally "they were glad to be rid of them in the end upon any terms, for all were wearied and tired with them." Pointing the moral, Bradford adds, "Though in the meantime they (poor souls) endured misery enough . . . thus in the end necessity forced a way for them." Providence for Bradford is occasionally God's special pleasure, but more often it appears as necessity, in the long run supportive and protective but never simply so, often bringing misery before rejoicing. And the misery is central, for providence brings suffering as often as deliverance, since painful experiences test the peoples' faith, bring them closer together, and prevent overweening self-confidence.

Bradford ends his first book with the immigrants thus directed by God's special providence and by necessity, resolving to pitch their dwellings at the spot they have named Plymouth, and the last words here record that they on "the 25th day [of December, 1620] began to erect the first house for common use to receive them and their goods," affirming their preservation of community in the face of bitter adversity. The second book of his history records the vicissitudes which beset this communal spirit in the New World, but Bradford has not left his Pilgrims in their safe haven before asking, "What could now sustain them but the Spirit of God and His grace? may not and ought not the children of these fathers rightly say, 'Our fathers were Englishmen which came over this great ocean, and were ready to perish in this wilderness; but they cried unto the Lord and He heard their voice and looked on their adversity.' " His manuscript note at this point calls attention to the last phrase of the children's directed memory as a quotation from Deuteronomy, the book written by Moses, "on this side Jordan in the wilderness." Bradford's exaltation of the community in the closing pages of the first book is an act of typological piety, linking his spiritual Israelites with those of the Old Testament, and at the same time it places the Plymouth settlers in the course of their history; the time of wandering is over, spiritual principles are settled, and now the Pilgrims must face the spiritual uncertainties of history as they strive to build their own Canaan.

Walter P. Wenska has noted that Bradford's second book "is much denser and less schematic than the first book, primarily because Bradford is more concerned with ascertaining than asserting the meaning of history. As a result, his Pilgrims are less often depicted as players in a universal drama. Their roles reduced from mythic to prosaic proportions, they are seen more often and more clearly as men enmeshed in the circumstantiality of time." If there is in the opening pages an observable movement toward the local and the specific, here in the second book that movement finds its culmination through the detailed examination of circumstances and of human character and motive. Bradford's hero continues to be the covenanted community of the church, but henceforth its tribulations come not from Satan's oppositions but from the designs of proud and ambitious men to manipulate the Plymouth settlement for selfish ends. He opens the second book with an explicit recognition of the internal threat to the colony; the *Mayflower* carried in addition to the Pilgrims a group of settlers who were not originally associated with the Leyden church but who were sent on their "particular" by the London Adventurers who backed the colony. The famous Mayflower Compact was intended in part to quiet "the discontented and mutinous speeches that some of the strangers amongst them had let fall . . . in the ship," and Bradford's insertion of the compact and its circumstances in the first paragraph of the second book, out of its proper chronological order (a fact he especially calls attention to), reasserts the value of the covenant, extends its principles to civil life, and points to the origin within the community itself of many of its future difficulties.

Storms, starvation, and the trials of the wilderness ultimately served to bind the Saints more closely one to another, but the machinations and greed of a few of the strangers among them and of some self-serving, conniving Adventurers posed a divisive and thus more serious threat. Bradford draws upon all the resources of his literary art in order to conform the reader's judgment to his own, and most notably he both portrays these questionable actors by means of specifically described passages and skillfully inserts letters to reveal men's characters in their own words. He typically refrains from final and absolute judgments on his villains beyond recording the sentences that providence itself seems to impose, but he effectively portrays actions so as to lead the reader to judgment long before he himself and the Pilgrims appear to weary of giving a rogue one more chance to repent. Bradford's patience in dealing with those who would deceive the planters is both a condition of his art and an expression of a basic principle; perhaps the most important of all the letters he inserts in his text is John Robinson's farewell admonition, urging that "watchfulness must be had that we neither at all in ourselves do give, no, not easily take offense being given by others." Robinson goes on in detail to enjoin charity in their treatment of others, both on spiritual and expediential grounds. Charity is an essential sign of grace, "For how unperfect and lame is the work of grace in that person who wants charity to cover a multitude of offenses, . . . Neither have they ever proved sound and profitable members in societies which have nourished their touchy humor." Robinson's formulation of Christian charity became the ethical norm of Plymouth, and Bradford so explains events to demonstrate the Pilgrims' charitable behavior toward others and to indict their enemies less for any material harm they cause than for their lack of charity.

For example, Thomas Weston, one of the Adventurers who provided financial backing, approached the Leyden church when it was thinking about emigration and urged them "not to meddle with the Dutch or too much depend on the Virginia Company. For if that failed, . . . he and such merchants as were his friends, together with their own means, should set them forth." Bradford notes Weston's previous friendship to the Leyden group, but in this first mention of him maintains a neutral stance which does not hint at the difficulties that came later. Yet within a few pages Bradford begins to reveal Weston's unreliable character as he tries to change the conditions of the agreement arrived at in Leyden, and Bradford casts doubt on his motives by suggesting that Weston's justification for altering the earlier contract may have been pretended. He then modifies this doubt without allaying it by including a letter from Robinson to John Carver, warning, "You know right well we depended on Mr. Weston alone. . . . He did this in his love I know, but things appear not answerable from him hitherto." Robinson puts the best face on Weston's behavior, and Bradford's use of this letter offers the reader the possibility of understanding Weston not as a deceiver and covenant breaker but as a well-intentioned man inclined to overreach himself. When Weston reappears in the history, however, he arraigns himself in his own words as a self-serving schemer; in a letter sent in the summer of 1621 he confides that he "durst never acquaint the Adventurers with the alterations of the conditions first agreed on between us" and goes on to promise that he "will never quit the business though all the other Adventurers should." Promises following a stated willingness to deceive his own partners are hardly encouraging, and Bradford glosses this letter with an answer to Weston's complaints and an observation that "he was the first and only man that forsook them. . . . So vain is the confidence in man." Weston later tried to cut out his merchant partners by sending over a private group of traders and settlers while in the meantime warning the Pilgrims not to believe what they might hear about him from the other Adventurers. Further letters from Weston and the other Adventurers reveal the full scope of his double-dealing, but Bradford, now aware that Weston "pursued his own ends and was embittered in spirit," still refrains from an outright condemnation of his betrayal of his own partners and the Plymouth settlers. The Pilgrims in fact "give his men friendly entertainment, partly in regard of Mr. Weston himself, considering what he had been unto them and done for them, . . . and partly in compassion to the people, who were now come into a wilderness (as themselves were)." Weston's ill-planned schemes failed; he himself arrived to make more trouble in Plymouth but was treated considerately, and after further problems with

Captain Robert Gorges he disappeared from New England history. Bradford's careful revelation of Weston shows us no simple villain but a man with complex motives who slowly reveals his moral confusion through the gradual unfolding of the historical process. Bradford judges Weston but only after the reader's judgment has been shaped by the evidence to accord with his own. He sees Weston's flaws yet continues to deal with him in a spirit of Christian charity, reserving final judgment on his basic goodness or depravity for God, who alone knows the hearts of other men.

A more threatening presence but one who revealed himself much more quickly was the Reverend John Lyford, sent over by the Adventurers in 1624 as a possible minister. Bradford's portrayal of Lyford's arrival emphasizes his extravagant display of piety, thus hinting at some basic imbalance in his character: "When this man first came ashore, he saluted them with that reverence and humility as is seldom to be seen, and indeed made them ashamed, he so bowed and cringed unto them, and would have kissed their hands if they would have suffered him." Lyford soon desired to join the church, made a confession of faith, and frequently was invited to consult with Governor Bradford, Elder Brewster, and the assistants, yet not long after this he was seen to fall in with John Oldham, one of the more discontented of those in Plymouth on their "particular," and was found to be plotting against the civil and ecclesiastical government of the colony. Confronted with the letters he wrote to the Adventurers complaining of unjust treatment, Lyford groveled again, "and confessed he 'feared he was a reprobate, his sins were so great that he doubted God would not pardon them, he was unsavory salt,' etc." His repentance turned out to be more dissembling on his part, for he continued to write to the Adventurers in justification of his earlier actions. When he was again to be censured, "his wife was so affected with his doings as she could no longer conceal her grief and sorrow of mind," and she revealed Lyford's former tawdry and profligate career as a minister in Ireland from whence he had to flee an outraged congregation. Bradford's and the Plymouth court's judgment of Lyford was reinforced by the Adventurers' hearing of the case, in which they independently discovered the same unsavory background and decided he was "unmeet forever to bear ministry any more, what repentance soever he should pretend." Bradford's final notice of Lyford follows his wanderings in America and his death in Virginia, concluding "so I leave him to the Lord." Lyford, like Weston, is turned over to God for ultimate judgment, but in the meantime Bradford and the Plymouth settlers have dealt with him patiently and charitably, arriving at their merely historical judgment only after he has refused opportunities to repent and has threatened the community's harmony and stability.

History, then, for Bradford is complex and ambivalent; he so presents Lyford that we see him finally as an egregious self-deceiver even more than as a deceiver of others. The trials and threats to the community strengthen its bonds and motivate more strenuous efforts to succeed, and when historical events seem to affirm the Pilgrims' success (the arrival of the Massachusetts settlers in 1630), Bradford can claim, "Thus out of small beginnings greater things have been produced by His hand that made all things of nothing, and . . . as one small candle may light a thousand, so the light here kindled hath shone unto many, yea in some sort to our whole nation." But the providential design of history remains ambiguous; the unconverted wilderness that surrounds the covenanted community recedes before its labors but reappears as sin within its own heart. The native American population appears first in opposition when the Pilgrims explore Cape Cod, then in friendship when Samoset, Squanto, and Hobomok arrive to help plant their first crops. When John Robinson heard of the first Indian killings on Cape Cod in 1620, he cried, "Oh, how happy a thing had it been, if you had converted some before you had killed any!" But the wilderness is for Bradford unconvertible; the friendly alliance with Massasoit and the Wampanoags is followed by the nearly disastrous Pequot War. Victory over the Pequots leaves the English enmeshed in the rivalry between the Narragansetts and the Mohegans, and they acquiesce in the disgraceful murder of the Narragansett chief, Miantonomo, thus bringing about the possibility of further bloodshed. Success in the American wilderness is purchased by complicity in savage behavior.

As has been suggested, much of the recent criticism of the history has taken up the question of its ending and its significance for Bradford's fully developed view of the Pilgrims' experiment. *Of Plimmoth Plantation* has no real ending in the sense of a formal narrative conclusion but instead terminates rather abruptly after two entries for the year 1646, one on the arrival in Plymouth of a famous pirate and his crew, the other on the departure of Edward Winslow for London to answer complaints and scandals laid against them by Samuel Gorton, a notorious Rhode Island

Of plimoth plantation

And first of ye occasion, and Indusments ther vnto; the which that I may truly vnfould, I must begine at ye very roote & rise of ye same. The which I shall endeuor to manefest in a plaine stile; with singuler regard vnto ye simple trueth in all things, at least as ~~farr~~ near as my slender Judgmente can attaine the same.

1. Chapter

It is well knowne vnto ye godly, and judicious, how euer since ye first breaking out of ye lighte of ye gospell, in our Honourable Nation of England (which was ye first of nations, whom ye Lord adorned ther with, after ye grosse darknes of popery which had couered & ouerspred ye Christian worled) what warrs, & opposissions euer since Satan hath raised, maintained, and continued against the Saincts, from time, to time, in one sorte, or other. Some times by bloody death & cruell torments; other whiles Imprisonments, banishments, & other hard vsages; As being loath his kingdom should goe downe, the trueth preuaile; and ye Churches of God reuerte to their anciente puritie; and recouer, their primatiue order, libertie & bewtie. But when he could not preuaile by these means, against the maine trueths of ye gospell; but that they began to take rootting in many places; being watered with ye blooud of ye martires, and blessed from heauen with a gracious encrease. He then begane to take him to his anciente strategemes, vsed of old against the first Christians. That when by ye bloody, & barbarous persecutions of ye Heathen Emperours, he could not stoppe, & subuerte the course of ye gospell; but that it speedily ouerspred, with a wounderfull celeritie, the then best known parts of ye world. He then begane to sow errours, heresies, and wounderfull dissentions amongst ye professours them selues (working vpon their pride, & ambition, with other corrupte pasions, incidente to all mortall men; yea to ye saints them selues in some measure) By which wofull effects followed; as not only bitter contentions, & hartburnings, schismes, with other horrible confusions. But Satan tooke occasion & aduantage therby to foyst in a number of vile ceremoneys, with many vnprofitable cannons, & decrees which haue since been as snares, to many poore, & peaceable souls, euen to this day. So as in ye anciente times, the persecutio-

First page of the manuscript for Bradford's history, which he began in 1630 (Massachusetts Historical Society)

troublemaker. Bradford's last words are the headings, "Anno 1647" and "Anno 1648," but he has no entries under them. "And so," Peter Gay says, "Bradford ends his history in silence." Bradford's account of those years in the 1640s, just before he ceased his narrative, discusses an outbreak of flagrant sin (bestiality) in Plymouth, the murder of Miantonomo, the death of William Brewster, and the exodus of some of the church members to found a new town on Cape Cod, leaving "this poor church . . . like an ancient mother grown old and forsaken of her children, though not in their affections yet in regard of their bodily presence and personal helpfulness." Because of these disheartening accounts Gay, for one, argues Bradford was "obsessed" with declension. Jesper Rosenmeier in a typological analysis points to the failure of Bradford's millennial hopes in 1646 and after—the breaking forth of new gospel light happens in revolutionary England, the country they left, not in New England—as a source for his nostalgic melancholy. Alan Howard and David Levin have replied to Gay by arguing that the cyclical quality of Bradford's history leaves him not ultimately despairing but on the down side, so to speak, of one of history's cycles; Howard points to the balance of affirmation and loss in the famous trope just noted of the Plymouth church as an "ancient mother," still possessing her children's affection even if deprived of their physical presence. Certainly, if we consider Bradford's history as a variant of spiritual autobiography, his arrival at an advanced age calls for a farewell to the material world and an anticipation of the purely spiritual world to come. The logic of spiritual progress, after all, leads to a seeing of the world as increasingly an occasion of sin.

Yet it is clear that Bradford's final vision is melancholy, nostalgic, and deeply aware of the intractable ambiguities of history. When writing the second book in the late 1640s, he went back to the first book he had written in a more optimistic moment fifteen years before, and, on the blank page opposite a letter of 1617 to the Virginia Company which emphasized that "We are knit together as a body in a most strict and sacred bond and covenant of the Lord," he laments, "That subtle serpent hath slyly wound in himself under fair pretences of necessity and the like, to untwist these sacred bonds and ties, and as it were insensibly by degrees to dissolve, or in a great measure to weaken the same." He falls back upon the abstract principles of motivation he began with and poignantly recognizes that necessity can be diabolical pretenses as well as providential direction.

If the history simply stops, whether weighed down by a sense of declension, failure of millennial hopes, or simply the logic of old age, Bradford himself kept on writing in defense of the faith that had brought him this far. Beginning in 1648 he composed three historical and theological dialogues between "Yonge-men borne in New-England And some Ancient-men, which came out of Holand and Old England," of which only the first and third survive. In these the young men respectfully approach the ancients for enlightenment on the "true and simple meaning of those of the *Separation*"; the first dialogue discusses the origins of congregational independency in England, and the third, written in 1652, describes four forms of church government, Papist, Episcopal, Presbyterian, and Independent, in order to argue for the Independent form as the nearest approach to the primitive Christianity supposedly sanctioned by the New Testament. As Rosenmeier has pointed out, the forms Bradford turns to in preference to historical narrative convey their own message; the earlier "belief in the union of actor and act, form and essence, seems to disintegrate." Where the historian spoke of a unified "them," the dramatist-narrator of the dialogues speaks in terms of a distance between "we," "us," and "you." In *Of Plimmoth Plantation* the reader is implicated in the narrative process, but in the dialogues the young men are passive, disembodied listeners who are exhorted by the unrealized voices of the ancients.

In the 1650s Bradford turned to versification, speaking to the younger generation without benefit of a public mask in poems such as "On the Various Heresies in Old and New England," "A Word to New Plymouth," "A Word to New England," and "Some Observations of God's Merciful Dealing with Us in This Wilderness." His seven poems display more piety and talent for rhetorical organization than they do poetic genius, but they do attest to a widespread desire in early New England to realize experience and moral truth in poetic form. Unfortunately, these survive, except for one 351-line fragment, only in an unreliable copy of Bradford's original manuscript. In addition to his history, the dialogues, and the poems, Bradford's writing is preserved in a number of fragmentary exercises in Hebrew, his letter book, from which he drew selectively when writing *Of Plimmoth Plantation.* He also had an undetermined part in the authorship of *A Relation . . . of the beginning and proceedings of the English Plantation setled at Plimoth . . .* (1622)—commonly known as *Mourt's Relation,* which was mostly written by Edward Winslow. In his final poem, "Epitaphium Meum," Bradford characterized himself as "a man of

Though I am growne aged, yet I have had a longing desire, to see with my owne eyes, somthing of that most ancient language, and holy tongue, in which the Law and oracles of God were write; and in which God, and angels spake to the holy patriarks, of old time; and what names were given to things, from the creation. And though I canot attaine to much herein, yet I am refresh=ed, to have seen some glimpse hereof; (as Moyses saw the Land of Ca=nan afarr of) my aime and desire is, to see how the words, and phrases lye in the holy texte; and to discerne somewhat of the same, for my owne contente.

חֶסֶד יְהוָה מָלְאָה הָאָרֶץ The earth is full of ye mercie of Jehovah.	שָׁם פָּחֲדוּ פַחַד לֹא הָיָה פָחַד Ther they feared a fear, wher no fear was.
וַיַּרְא אֱלֹהִים כִּי טוֹב And God saw that it was good.	הוֹן יֹסִיף רֵעִים רַבִּים Riches gather many friends
לֹא טוֹב הֱיוֹת הָאָדָם לְבַדּוֹ It is not good that man should be alone.	רַע רַע יֹאמַר הַקּוֹנֶה It is naught, it is naught, saith the buyer.
כַּבֵּד אֶת־אָבִיךָ וְאֶת אִמֶּךָ honour thy father, and thy mother	מָצָא אִשָּׁה מָצָא טוֹב he that findeth a wife findeth good
וּשְׂמַח מֵאֵשֶׁת נְעוּרֶיךָ And rejoyce with the wife of thy youth	וַאֲנִי בְּרֹב חַסְדְּךָ אָבוֹא בֵיתֶךָ But I in multitude of thy mercies, will come into thy house.
זְנוּת וְיַיִן וְתִירוֹשׁ יִקַּח־לֵב whordome, and wine, & new wine take away the harte	וְהָיָה כְּעֵץ שָׁתוּל עַל־פַּלְגֵי מָיִם And he shall be as a tree planted by the brooks of waters.
קוֹל דְּמֵי אָחִיךָ צֹעֲקִים אֵלַי The voyce of thy brothers blood crieth unto me.	חַכְמוֹת נָשִׁים בָּנְתָה בֵיתָהּ A wise woman buildeth her house
דָּן דִּין עָנִי ing Judge the	נְקִי כַפַּיִם וּבַר לֵבָב Innocente in hands, & pure in hart

Page from Bradford's Hebrew exercises, bound at the front of the manuscript for Of Plimmoth Plantation *(Massachusetts Historical Society)* sorrows," waiting "Until my happy change shall come," but this self-image of the resigned Christian should be balanced by that of the pious inquirer into God's truth; at one point in the manuscript containing his Hebrew exercises, he stopped to explain why he was studying this language: "Though I am growne aged, yet I have had a longing desire to see, with my owne eyes, somthing of that most ancient language, and holy tongue, in which the Law and Oracles of God were write; and in which God and angels spake to the holy patriarks of old time; and what names were given to things from the creation. And though I canot attaine to much herein, yet I am refresh—to have seen some glimpse hereof; (as Moyses saw the land of Canan a farr off.) My aime and desire is, to see how the words and phrases lye in the holy texte; and to discerne somewhat of the same, for my owne contente."

Other:

Edward Winslow, *A Relation or Journal of the beginning and proceedings of the English Plantation setled at Plimoth in New England . . .* [*Mourt's Relation*], contains material by Bradford (London: Printed for John Bellamie, 1622);

"Governour Bradford's Letter Book," edited by Jeremy Belknap, *Collections of the Massachusetts Historical Society*, first series 3 (1794): 27-76;

"A Dialogue or 3d Conference betweene some Yonge-men borne in New-England, and some Ancient-men, which came out of Holand and Old England, concerning the Church, and the governmente thereof," *Proceedings of the Massachusetts Historical Society*, first series 11 (1870): 396-464;

"A Dialogue or the sume of a Conference between som younge men borne in New England and sundery Ancient men that came out of holland and Old England Anno dom 1648," *Collections of the Colonial Society of Massachusetts*, 22 (1920): 115-141.

References:

E. F. Bradford, "Conscious Art in Bradford's History of Plymouth Plantation," *New England Quarterly*, 1 (April 1928): 133-157;

Robert Daly, "William Bradford's Vision of History," *American Literature*, 44 (January 1973): 557-569;

Peter Gay, *A Loss of Mastery: Puritan Historians in Colonial America* (Berkeley: University of California Press, 1966);

Norman S. Grabo, "William Bradford: *Of Plymouth Plantation*," in *Landmarks of American Literature*, edited by Hennig Cohen (New York: Basic Books, 1969), pp. 3-19;

Alan B. Howard, "Art and History in Bradford's *Of Plymouth Plantation*," *William and Mary Quarterly*, third series 28 (April 1971): 237-266;

David Levin, "William Bradford: The Value of Puritan Historiography," in *Major Writers of Early American Literature*, edited by Everett Emerson (Madison: University of Wisconsin Press, 1972), pp. 11-31;

Isidore S. Meyer, *The Hebrew Exercises of Governor William Bradford* (Plymouth: Pilgrim Society, 1973);

Samuel Eliot Morison, Introduction to *Of Plymouth Plantation 1620-1647 by William Bradford, Sometime Governor Thereof* (New York: Knopf, 1952);

Kenneth B. Murdock, *Literature and Theology in Colonial New England* (Cambridge: Harvard University Press, 1949);

Floyd Ogburn, Jr., *Style as Structure and Meaning: William Bradford's Of Plymouth Plantation* (Washington, D.C.: University Press of America, 1981);

Jesper Rosenmeier, " 'With My Owne Eyes': William Bradford's *Of Plymouth Plantation*," *Typology and Early American Literature*, edited by Sacvan Bercovitch (Amherst: University of Massachusetts Press, 1972), pp. 67-105;

Michael G. Runyan, Introduction to *William Bradford: The Collected Verse* (St. Paul, Minn.: John Colet Press, 1974);

Bradford Smith, *Bradford of Plymouth* (Philadelphia: Lippincott, 1951);

Walter P. Wenska, "Bradford's Two Histories: Pattern and Paradigm in *Of Plymouth Plantation*," *Early American Literature*, 13 (Fall 1978): 151-164;

Perry D. Westbrook, *William Bradford* (Boston: Twayne, 1978).

Papers:

Bradford's papers are at the Massachusetts Historical Society.

Anne Bradstreet

Wendy Martin
Queens College

BIRTH: Northhampton, England, 1612 or 1613, to Thomas Dudley and Dorothy Yorke.

MARRIAGE: Circa 1628 to Simon Bradstreet; children: Samuel, Dorothy, Sarah, Simon, Hannah, Mercy, Dudley, and John.

DEATH: Andover, Massachusetts, 16 September 1672.

BOOKS: *The Tenth Muse Lately Sprung Up in America . . .*, as "a Gentlewoman in those parts" (London: Printed for Stephen Bowtell, 1650); revised and enlarged as *Several Poems Compiled with Great Variety of Wit and Learning, Full of Delight*, as "a Gentlewoman in New-England" (Boston: Printed by John Foster, 1678);

The Works of Anne Bradstreet in Prose and Verse, edited by John Harvard Ellis (Charlestown, Mass.: Abram E. Cutter, 1867);

The Tenth Muse (1650) and, From the Manuscripts, Meditations Divine and Morall Together with Letters and Occasional Pieces by Anne Bradstreet, edited by Josephine K. Piercy (Gainesville, Fla.: Scholars' Facsimiles and Reprints, 1965);

The Complete Works of Anne Bradstreet, edited by Joseph R. McElrath, Jr., and Allan P. Robb (Boston: Twayne, 1981).

Anne Bradstreet was the first woman to be recognized as an accomplished New World Poet. Her volume of poetry *The Tenth Muse Lately Sprung Up in America . . .* received considerable favorable attention when it was first published in London in 1650. Eight years after it appeared it was listed by William London in his *Catalogue of the Most Vendible Books in England*, and George III is reported to have had the volume in his library. Bradstreet's work has endured, and she is still considered to be one of the most important early American poets.

Although Anne Dudley Bradstreet did not attend school, she received an excellent education from her father, who was widely read—Cotton Mather described Thomas Dudley as a "devourer of books"—and from her extensive reading in the well-stocked library of the estate of the Earl of Lincoln, where she lived while her father was steward from 1619 to 1630. There the young Anne Dudley read Vergil, Plutarch, Livy, Pliny, Suetonius, Homer, Hesiod, Ovid, Seneca, and Thucydides as well as Spenser, Sidney, Milton, Raleigh, Hobbes, Joshua Sylvester's 1605 translation of Guillaume du Bartas's *Divine Weeks and Workes*, and the Geneva version of the Bible. In general, she benefited from the Elizabethan tradition that valued female education. In about 1628—the date is not certain—Anne Dudley married Simon Bradstreet, who assisted her father with the management of the Earl's estate in Sempringham. She remained married to him until her death on 16 September 1672. Bradstreet immigrated to the new world with her husband and parents in 1630; in 1633 the first of her children, Samuel, was born, and her seven other children were born between 1635 and 1652: Dorothy (1635), Sarah (1638), Simon (1640), Hannah (1642), Mercy (1645), Dudley (1648), and John (1652).

Although Bradstreet was not happy to exchange the comforts of the aristocratic life of the Earl's manor house for the privations of the New England wilderness, she dutifully joined her father and husband and their families on the Puritan errand into the wilderness. After a difficult three-month crossing, their ship, the *Arbella*, docked at Salem, Massachusetts, on 22 July 1630. Distressed by the sickness, scarcity of food, and primitive living conditions of the New England outpost, Bradstreet admitted that her "heart rose" in protest against the "new world and new manners." Although she ostensibly reconciled herself to the Puritan mission—she wrote that she "submitted to it and joined the Church at Boston"—Bradstreet remained ambivalent about the issues of salvation and redemption for most of her life.

Once in New England the passengers of the *Arbella* fleet were dismayed by the sickness and suffering of those colonists who had preceded them. Thomas Dudley observed in a letter to the Countess of Lincoln, who had remained in England: "We found the Colony in a sad and unexpected condition, above eighty of them being dead the winter before; and many of those alive weak and sick; all the corn and bread amongst them all hardly sufficient to feed them a fortnight." In addition to fevers, malnutrition, and inadequate food supplies, the colonists also had to contend with Indian attacks on the settlement. The Bradstreets and Dudleys shared a house in Salem for many months and lived in spartan style; Thomas Dudley complained that there was not even a table on which to eat or work. In the winter the two families were confined to the one room in which there was a fireplace. The situation was tense as well as uncomfortable, and Anne Bradstreet and her family moved several times in an effort to improve their worldly estates. From Salem they moved to Charlestown, then to Newtown (later called Cambridge), then to Ipswich, and finally to Andover in 1645.

Although Bradstreet had eight children between the years 1633 and 1652, which meant that her domestic responsibilities were extremely demanding, she wrote poetry which expressed her commitment to the craft of writing. In addition, her work reflects the religious and emotional conflicts she experienced as a woman writer and as a Puritan. Throughout her life Bradstreet was concerned with the issues of sin and redemption, physical and emotional frailty, death and immortality. Much of her work indicates that she had a difficult time resolving the conflict she experienced between the pleasures of sensory and familial experience and the promises of heaven. As a Puritan she struggled to subdue her attachment to the world, but as a woman she sometimes felt more strongly connected to her husband, children, and community than to God.

Bradstreet's earliest extant poem, "Upon a Fit of Sickness, Anno. 1632," written in Newtown when she was nineteen, outlines the traditional concerns of the Puritan—the brevity of life, the certainty of death, and the hope for salvation:

> O Bubble blast, how long can'st last?
>   That always art a breaking,
> No sooner blown, but dead and gone,
>   Ev'n as a word that's speaking.
> O whil'st I live, this grace me give,
>   I doing good may be,
> Then death's arrest I shall count best,
>   because it's thy decree.

Artfully composed in a ballad meter, this poem presents a formulaic account of the transience of earthly experience which underscores the divine imperative to carry out God's will. Although this poem is an exercise in piety, it is not without ambivalence or tension between the flesh and the spirit—tensions which grow more intense as Bradstreet matures.

The complexity of her struggle between love of the world and desire for eternal life is expressed in "Contemplations," a late poem which many critics consider her best:

> Then higher on the glistering Sun I gaz'd,
> Whose beams was shaded by the leavie Tree,
> The more I look'd, the more I grew amaz'd,
> And softly said, what glory's like to thee?
> Soul of this world, this Universes Eye,
> No wonder, some made thee a Deity:
> Had I not better known, (alas) the same had I

Although this lyrical, exquisitely crafted poem concludes with Bradstreet's statement of faith in an afterlife, her faith is paradoxically achieved by immersing herself in the pleasures of earthly life. This poem and others make it clear that Bradstreet committed herself to the religious concept of salvation because she loved life on earth. Her hope for heaven was an expression of her desire to live forever rather than a wish to transcend worldly concerns. For her, heaven promised the prolongation of earthly joys, rather than a renunciation of those pleasures she enjoyed in life.

Bradstreet wrote many of the poems that appeared in the first edition of *The Tenth Muse* . . . during the years 1635 to 1645 while she lived in the frontier town of Ipswich, approximately thirty miles from Boston. In her dedication to the volume written in 1642 to her father, Thomas Dudley, who educated her, encouraged her to read, and evidently appreciated his daughter's intelligence, Bradstreet pays "homage" to him. Many of the poems in this volume tend to be dutiful exercises intended to prove her artistic worth to him. However, much of her work, especially her later poems, demonstrates impressive intelligence and mastery of poetic form.

The first section of *The Tenth Muse* . . . includes four long poems, known as the quaternions, or "The Four Elements," "The Four Humors of Man," "The Four Ages of Man," and "The Four Seasons." Each poem consists of a series of orations; the first by earth, air, fire, and water; the second by choler, blood, melancholy, and flegme; the third by childhood, youth, middle age, and old age; the fourth by spring, summer, fall, and winter. In these quaternions Bradstreet demonstrates a mastery of physiology, anatomy, astronomy, Greek metaphysics, and the concepts of medieval and Renaissance cosmology. Although she draws

A Bradstreet

heavily on Sylvester's translation of du Bartas and Helkiah Crooke's anatomical treatise *Microcosmographia* (1615), Bradstreet's interpretation of their images is often strikingly dramatic. Sometimes she uses material from her own life in these historical and philosophical discourses. For example, in her description of the earliest age of man, infancy, she forcefully describes the illnesses that assailed her and her children:

> What gripes of wind my infancy did pain,
> What tortures I in breeding teeth sustain?
> What crudityes my stomach cold has bred,
> Whence vomits, flux, and worms have issued?

Like the quaternions, the poems in the next section of *The Tenth Muse . . .* , "The Four Monarchies" (Assyrian, Persian, Grecian, and Roman), are poems of commanding historical breadth. Bradstreet's poetic version of the rise and fall of these great empires draws largely from Sir Walter Raleigh's *History of the World* (1614). The dissolution of these civilizations is presented as evidence of God's divine plan for the world. Although Bradstreet demonstrates considerable erudition in both the quaternions and monarchies, the rhymed couplets of the poems tend to be plodding and dull; she even calls them "lanke" and "weary" herself. Perhaps she grew tired of the task she set for herself because she did not attempt to complete the fourth section on the "Roman Monarchy" after the incomplete portion was lost in a fire that destroyed the Bradstreet home in 1666.

"Dialogue between Old England and New," also in the 1650 edition of *The Tenth Muse . . .* expresses Bradstreet's concerns with the social and religious turmoil in England that impelled the Puritans to leave their country. The poem is a conversation between mother England and her daughter, New England. The sympathetic tone reveals how deeply attached Bradstreet was to her native land and how disturbed she was by the waste and loss of life caused by the political upheaval. As Old England's lament indicates, the destructive impact of the civil strife on human life was more disturbing to Bradstreet than the substance of the conflict:

> O pity me in this sad perturbation,
> My plundered Towers, my houses devastation,
> My weeping Virgins and my young men slain;
> My wealthy trading fall'n, my dearth of grain

In this poem, Bradstreet's own values begin to emerge. There is less imitation of traditional male models and more direct statement of the poet's feelings. As Bradstreet gained experience and confidence, she depended less on poetic mentors and relied more on her own perceptions.

Another poem in the first edition of *The Tenth Muse* . . . that reveals Bradstreet's personal feelings is "In Honor of that High and Mighty Princess Queen Elizabeth of Happy Memory," written in 1643, in which she praises the Queen as a paragon of female prowess. Chiding her male readers for trivializing women, Bradstreet refers to the Queen's outstanding leadership and historical prominence. In a personal caveat underscoring her own dislike of patriarchal arrogance, Bradstreet points out that women were not always devalued:

> Nay Masculines, you have thus taxt us long,
> But she, though dead, will vindicate our wrong,
> Let such as say our Sex is void of Reason,
> Know tis a Slander now, but once was Treason.

These assertive lines mark a dramatic shift from the self-effacing stanzas of "The Prologue" to the volume in which Bradstreet attempted to diminish her stature to prevent her writing from being attacked as an indecorous female activity. In an ironic and often-quoted passage of "The Prologue," she asks for the domestic herbs "Thyme or Parsley wreath," instead of the traditional laurel, thereby appearing to subordinate herself to male writers and critics:

> Let Greeks be Greeks, and women what they are
> Men have precedency and still excell,
> It is but vain unjustly to wage warre;
> Men can do best, and women know it well
> Preheminence in all and each is yours;
> Yet grant some small acknowledgement of ours.

In contrast, her portrait of Elizabeth does not attempt to conceal her confidence in the abilities of women:

> Who was so good, so just, so learned so wise,
> From all the Kings on earth she won the prize.
> Nor say I more then duly is her due,
> Millions will testifie that this is true.
> She has wip'd off th' aspersion of her Sex,
> That women wisdome lack to play the Rex

This praise for Queen Elizabeth expresses Bradstreet's conviction that women should not be subordinated to men—certainly it was less stressful to make this statement in a historic context than it would have been to confidently proclaim the worth of her own work.

The first edition of *The Tenth Muse*... also contains an elegy to Sir Philip Sidney and a poem honoring du Bartas. Acknowledging her debt to these poetic mentors, she depicts herself as insignificant in contrast to their greatness. They live on the peak of Parnassus while she grovels at the bottom of the mountain. Again, her modest pose represents an effort to ward off potential attackers, but its ironic undercurrents indicate that Bradstreet was angered by the cultural bias against women writers:

> Fain would I shew how he same paths did tread,
> But now into such Lab'rinths I am lead,
> With endless turnes, the way I find not out,
> How to persist my Muse is more in doubt;
> Which makes me now with *Silvester* confess,
> But *Sidney's* Muse can sing his worthiness.

Although the ostensible meaning of this passage is that Sidney's work is too complex and intricate for her to follow, it also indicates that Bradstreet felt his labyrinthine lines to represent excessive artifice and lack of connection to life.

The second edition of *The Tenth Muse* . . . , published in Boston in 1678 as *Several Poems* . . . , contains the author's corrections as well as previously unpublished poems: epitaphs to her father and mother, "Contemplations," "The Flesh and the Spirit," the address by "The Author to her Book," several poems about her various illnesses, love poems to her husband, and elegies of her deceased grandchildren and daughter-in-law. These poems added to the second edition were probably written after the move to Andover, where Anne Bradstreet lived with her family in a spacious three-story house until her death in 1672. Far superior to her early work, the poems in the 1678 edition demonstrate a command over subject matter and a mastery of poetic craft. These later poems are considerably more candid about her spiritual crises and her strong attachment to her family than her earlier work. For example, in a poem to her husband, "Before the Birth of one of her Children," Bradstreet confesses that she is afraid of dying in childbirth—a realistic fear in the seventeenth century—and begs him to continue to love her after her death. She also implores him to take good care of their children and to protect them from a potential stepmother's cruelty:

> And when thou feel'st no grief, as I no harms,
> Yet love thy dead, who long lay in thine arms:
> And when thy loss shall be repaid with gains
> Look to my little babes my dear remains.
> And if thou love thy self, or love'st me
> These O protect from step Dames injury.

Anne Bradstreet's husband, Simon, circa 1685 (Boston Athenaeum). There are no existing portraits of Anne Bradstreet.

Not only is this candid domestic portrait artistically superior to the strained lines of "The Four Monarchies," it gives a more accurate sense of Bradstreet's true concerns.

In her address to her book, Bradstreet repeats her apology for the defects of her poems, likening them to children dressed in "home-spun." But what she identifies as weakness is actually their strength. Because they are centered in the poet's actual experience as a Puritan and as a woman, the poems are less figurative and contain fewer analogies to well-known male poets than her earlier work. In place of self-conscious imagery is extraordinarily evocative and lyrical language. In some of these poems Bradstreet openly grieves over the loss of her loved ones—her parents, her grandchildren, her sister-in-law—and she barely conceals resentment that God has taken their innocent lives. Although she ultimately capitulates to a supreme being—"He knows it is the best for thee and me"—it is the tension between her desire for earthly happiness and her effort to accept God's will that makes these poems especially powerful.

Bradstreet's poems to her husband are often singled out for praise by critics. Simon Bradstreet's responsibilities as a magistrate of the colony frequently took him away from home, and he was very much missed by his wife. Modeled on Elizabethan sonnets, Bradstreet's love poems make it clear that she was deeply attached to her husband:

> If ever two were one, then surely we
> If ever man were lov'd by wife, then thee;
> If ever wife was happy in a man
> Compare with me ye women if you can

Marriage was important to the Puritans, who felt that the procreation and proper training of children were necessary for building God's commonwealth. However, the love between wife and husband was not supposed to distract from devotion to God. In Bradstreet's sonnets, her erotic attraction to her husband is central, and these poems are more secular than religious:

> My chilled limbs now nummed lye forlorn;
> Return, return sweet *Sol* from *Capricorn*;
> In this dead time, alas, what can I more
> Than view those fruits which through thy heat I bore?

Anne Bradstreet's brother-in-law, John Woodbridge, was responsible for the publication of the first edition of *The Tenth Muse* . . . . The title page reads "By a Gentlewoman in those parts"—and Woodbridge assures readers that the volume "is the work of a Woman, honored and esteemed where she lives." After praising the author's piety, courtesy, and diligence, he explains that she did not shirk her domestic responsibilities in order to write poetry: "these poems are the fruit but of some few hours, curtailed from sleep and other refreshments." Also prefacing the volume are statements of praise for Bradstreet by Nathaniel Ward, the author of *The Simple Cobler of Aggawam* (1647), and Reverend Benjamin Woodbridge, brother of John Woodbridge. In order to defend her from attacks from reviewers at home and abroad who might be shocked by the impropriety of a female author, these encomiums of the poet stress that she is a virtuous woman.

In 1867, John Harvard Ellis published Bradstreet's complete works, including materials from both editions of *The Tenth Muse* . . . as well as "Religious Experiences and Occasional Pieces" and "Meditations Divine and Morall" that had been in

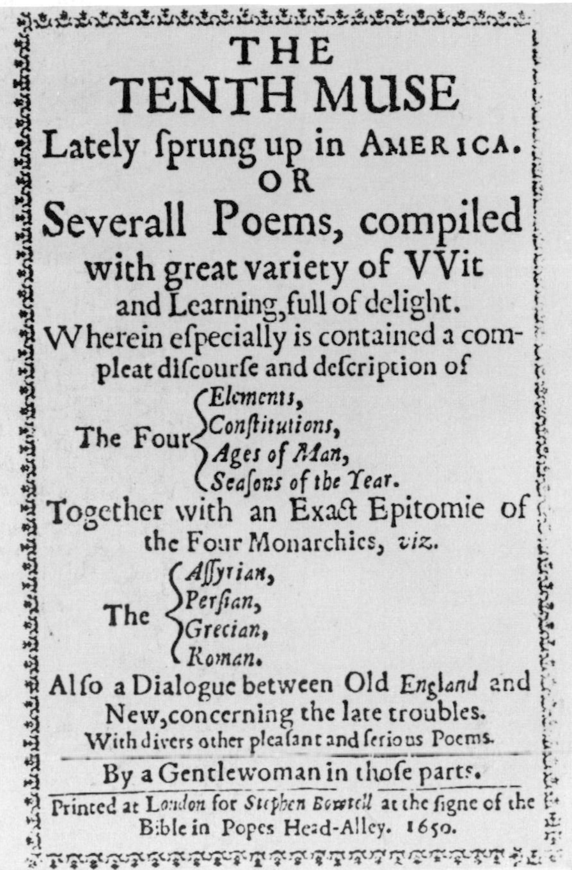
THE
TENTH MUSE
Lately ſprung up in AMERICA.
OR
Severall Poems, compiled
with great variety of VVit
and Learning, full of delight.
Wherein eſpecially is contained a compleat diſcourſe and deſcription of
The Four { *Elements*, *Conſtitutions*, *Ages of Man*, *Seaſons of the Year*. }
Together with an Exact Epitomie of
the Four Monarchies, *viz.*
The { *Aſſyrian*, *Perſian*, *Grecian*, *Roman*. }
Alſo a Dialogue between Old *England* and
New, concerning the late troubles.
With divers other pleaſant and ſerious Poems.
By a Gentlewoman in thoſe parts.
Printed at *London* for *Stephen Bowtell* at the ſigne of the
Bible in Popes Head-Alley. 1650.

Title page for Anne Bradstreet's collection of poems. The manuscript was carried to London by her brother-in-law John Woodbridge, who arranged for its publication.

the possession of her son Simon Bradstreet, to whom the meditations had been dedicated on 20 March 1664. Bradstreet's accounts of her religious experience provide insight into the Puritan views of salvation and redemption. Bradstreet describes herself as having been frequently chastened by God through her illnesses and her domestic travails: "Among all my experiences of God's gractious Dealings with me I have constantly observed this, that he has never suffered me long to sit loose from him, but by one affliction or other hath made me look home, and search what was amiss." Puritans perceived suffering as a means of preparing the heart to receive God's grace. Bradstreet writes that she made every effort to submit willingly to God's afflictions which were necessary to her "straying soul which in prosperity is too much in love with the world." These occasional pieces in the Ellis edition also include poems of gratitude to God for protecting her loved ones from illness ("Upon my Daughter Hannah Wiggin her recovering from a

Pages from the manuscript for "Meditations Divine and Morall" (Stevens Memorial Library, North Andover, Massachusetts)

dangerous fever") and for her husband's safe return from England. However, these poems do not have the force or power of those published in the second edition of *The Tenth Muse . . .* and seem to be exercises in piety and submission rather than a complex rendering of her experience.

The aphoristic prose paragraphs of "Meditations Divine and Morall" have remarkable vitality, primarily because they are based on her own observations and experiences. While the Bible and the *Bay Psalm Book* are the source of many of Bradstreet's metaphors, they are reworked to confirm her perceptions: "The spring is a lively emblem of the resurrection, after a long winter we see the leaveless trees and dry stocks (at the approach of the sun) to resume their former vigor and beauty in a more ample manner than when they lost in the Autumn; so shall it be at that great day after a long vacation, when the Sun of righteousness shall appear, those dry bones shall arise in far more glory then that which they lost at their creation, and in this transcends the spring, that their lease shall never fail, nor their sap decline" (40).

More often, her meditations consist of drawing moral lessons from her domestic activities—house cleaning, baking, preserving, caring for her children—or from her observations of nature:

> Diverse Children have their different natures; some are like flesh which nothing but salt will keep from putrefaction; some again like tender fruits that are best preserved with sugar: those parents are wise that can fit their nurture according to their Nature. (10)

> Yellow leaves argue want of sap, and gray haires want of moisture; so dry and sapless performances are symptoms of little spirituall vigour. (30)

> The finest bread hath the least bran; the purest hony, the least wax; the sincerest christian, the least self love. (6)

Perhaps the most important aspect of Anne Bradstreet's poetic evolution is her increasing confidence in the validity of her personal experience as a source and subject of poetry. Much of the work in the 1650 edition of *The Tenth Muse . . .* suffers from being too imitative, too strained. The often wooden lines with forced rhymes reveal Bradstreet's grim determination to prove that she could write in the lofty style of the established male poets. But her deeper emotions were obviously not engaged in the project. The publication of her first volume of poetry seems to have given her confidence and enabled her to express herself more freely. As she began to write of her ambivalence about the religious issues of faith, grace, and salvation, her poetry became more accomplished.

Bradstreet's recent biographers, Elizabeth Wade White and Ann Stanford, have both observed that Bradstreet was sometimes distressed by the conflicting demands of piety and poetry and was as daring as she could be and still retain respectability in a society that exiled Anne Hutchinson. Bradstreet's poetry reflects the tensions of a woman who wished to express her individuality in a culture that was hostile to personal autonomy and valued poetry only if it praised God. Although Bradstreet never renounced her religious belief, her poetry makes it clear that if it were not for the fact of dissolution and decay, she would not seek eternal life: "for were earthly comforts permanent, who would look for heavenly?"

In a statement of extravagant praise Cotton Mather compared Anne Bradstreet to such famous women as Hippatia, Sarocchia, the three *Corinnes*, and Empress Eudocia and concluded that her poems have "afforded a grateful Entertainment unto the Ingenious, and a Monument for her Memory beyond the stateliest *Marbles*." Certainly, Anne Bradstreet's poetry has continued to receive a positive response for more than three centuries, and she has earned her place as one of the most important American women poets.

SEVERAL
POEMS
Compiled with great variety of Wit and Learning, full of Delight;
Wherein especially is contained a compleat Discourse, and Description of
The Four { ELEMENTS. CONSTITUTIONS, AGES of Man, SEASONS of the Year.
Together with an exact Epitome of the three first *Monarchyes*
Viz. The { *ASSYRIAN, PERSIAN, GRECIAN.*
And beginning of the Romane Common-wealth *to the end of their last King:*
With diverse other pleasant & serious *Poems*,
By a Gentlewoman in *New-England.*
The second Edition, Corrected by the Author, and enlarged by an Addition of several other Poems found amongst her Papers after her Death.
Boston, Printed by *John Foster*, 1678.

Title page for the revised edition of The Tenth Muse Lately Sprung up in America, *thought to be the first book by a woman to be published in America (John Carter Brown Library, Brown University)*

References:

Helen Campbell, *Anne Bradstreet and Her Time* (Boston: Lothrop, 1891);

Jane Donahue Eberwein, "The 'Unrefined Ore' of Anne Bradstreet's Quaternions," *Early American Literature*, 9 (1974): 19-24;

Anne Hildebrand, "Anne Bradstreet's Quaternions and 'Contemplations,' " *Early American Literature*, 8 (1973): 117-125;

Rosemary M. Laughlin, "Anne Bradstreet: Poet in Search of Form," *American Literature*, 42 (1970): 1-17;

Wendy Martin, "Anne Bradstreet's Poetry: a Study in Subversive Piety," in *Shakespeare's Sisters*, edited by Sandra Gilbert and Susan Gubar (Bloomington: Indiana University Press, 1979), pp. 14-31;

Martin, *The Lives and Work of Anne Bradstreet, Emily Dickinson, and Adrienne Rich* (Chapel Hill: University of North Carolina Press, 1983);

Josephine K. Piercy, *Anne Bradstreet* (New York: Twayne, 1965);

Kenneth A. Requa, "Anne Bradstreet's Poetic Voices," *Early American Literature*, 9 (1974): 3-18;

Robert Richardson, "The Puritan Poetry of Anne Bradstreet," *Texas Studies in Literature and Language*, 9 (1967): 317-331;

Alvin H. Rosenfeld, "Anne Bradstreet's 'Contemplations': Patterns of Form and Meaning," *New England Quarterly*, 43 (1970): 79-96;

Ann Stanford, "Anne Bradstreet: Dogmatist and

Rebel," *New England Quarterly*, 39 (1966): 373-389;
Stanford, *Anne Bradstreet: The Worldly Puritan* (New York: Burt Franklin, 1974);
Elizabeth Wade White, *Anne Bradstreet* (New York: Oxford University Press, 1971).

Thomas Bray

(1656-15 February 1730)

Michael A. Lofaro
University of Tennessee

SELECTED BOOKS: *Proposals for the Incouragement and Promoting of Religion and Learning in the Foreign Plantations; And to Induce such of the Clergy of this Kingdom, as are Persons of Sobriety and Abilities, to accept of a Mission into those Parts* (London, 1695);

A Course of Lectures on Church Catechism (Oxford, 1696); republished as *Catechetical Discourses on the Whole Doctrine of the Covenant of Grace, Delivered in 32 Lectures, on the Preliminary Questions and Answers of the Church-Catechism . . .* (London: Printed by John Brudenell for W. Haws, 1701);

Bibliotheca Parochialis: Or, A Scheme Of Such Theological Heads Both General and Particular, As Are Most peculiarly Requisite to be well Studied by every Pastor of a Parish . . . (London: Printed by E. H. for Robert Clavel, 1697);

An Essay Towards Promoting all Necessary and Useful Knowledge, Both Divine and Human, In all the Parts of His Majesty's Dominions, Both at Home and Abroad (London: Printed by E. Holt for Robert Clavel, 1697);

A Short Discourse Upon the Doctrine of our Baptismal Covenant, Being An Exposition upon the Preliminary Questions and Answers Of Our Church-Catechism. Proper to be read by all Young Persons . . . (London: Printed by E. Holt for Rob. Clavel, 1697);

Apostolick Charity, its Nature and Excellence Consider'd. In a Discourse Upon Dan. 12.3 . . . (London: Printed by W. Downing for W. Hawes, 1698); expanded and republished with *Proposals for the Incouragement and Promoting of Religion . . .* and "A Circular Letter . . ." (London: Printed for W. Hawes, 1699);

Bibliotheca Catechetica: Or, the Country Curates Library . . . (London: Printed for W. Hawes, 1699);

Thomas Bray

The Necessity of an Early Religion Being a Sermon Preach'd the 5th of May Before the Honourable Assembly of Maryland (Annapolis: Printed by Tho. Reading for Evan Jones, 1700);

The Acts of Dr. Bray's Visitation Held at Annopolis [sic] *in Mary-Land, May 23, 24, 25. Anno 1700* (London: Printed for W. Downing, 1700);

A Memorial, Representing The Present State of Religion, On The Continent of North-America (London: Printed by William Downing, 1700);

Several Circular Letters to the Clergy of Mary-land, subsequent to their late Visitation, to enforce such resolutions as were taken therein (London: Printed by William Downing, 1701);

For God, or for Satan: being a Sermon preach'd at St. Mary le Bow, before the Society for Reformation of Manners, December 27. 1708 . . . (London: Printed & sold by J. Downing, 1709);

The Good Fight of Faith, in the Cause of God against the Kingdom of Satan. Exemplified in a sermon preach'd at the parish-church of St. Clements Danes, Westminster, on the 24th of March, 1708/9. At the funeral of Mr. John Dent . . . (London: Printed & sold by J. Downing, 1709);

Papal Usurpation and Persecution as it has been exercis'd in Ancient and Modern Times with respect to princes & people; a fair warning to all Protestants . . . (London: Printed by J. Downing, 1712).

COLLECTION: *Rev. Thomas Bray, His Life and Selected Works,* edited by Bernard C. Steiner, Maryland Historical Society Fund Publication, no. 37 (Baltimore: John Murphy for the Maryland Historical Society, 1901).

The importance of the Reverend Thomas Bray to the mission of the English church is hard to underestimate. He was the motivating force in the founding of missionary and philanthropic societies that were to have worldwide implications and a profound effect upon the American colonies: the Society for Promoting Christian Knowledge (founded 1699); the Society for the Propagation of the Gospel in Foreign Parts (founded 1701); and the Associates of Dr. Bray (founded 1723, enlarged 1729—a group which supported the founding of Georgia).

Thomas Bray was born in 1656 at Marton in Shropshire. Although he matriculated at Hart Hall, Oxford, on 12 March 1675, he soon left because of a lack of funds. Returning to Oxford, he graduated from All Souls College on 11 November 1678. He subsequently took an M.A. at Oxford in 1693 and both bachelor and doctor of divinity degrees at Magdalen Hall, Oxford, on 17 December 1696.

Bray's relationship to the American Plantations began in the autumn of 1695 (not in the spring of 1696 as was previously thought) when he was appointed Commissary to Maryland by Bishop Compton of London. The position did not carry with it the religious power of one in episcopal orders, but it did allow the assumption of certain civil and managerial functions granted him as the bishop's representative. Bray could call conventions, hold visitations, and superintend the conduct of the clergy, but he felt that his first and primary duty was to provide clergy for the colonial church from "New found land" to the "West Indies." He succeeded in doing so in part by securing the passage of the Maryland Establishment Act, which provided the legal basis for state support of the Anglican church, and by the initiation of a system of libraries. He knew that benefices and the availability of books, whose cost placed them beyond the reach of many ministers, would help to attract capable men to the American church.

Although the efforts behind his success were orchestrated mainly from England, Bray felt that his position as commissary also required his presence in the colonies. He set sail for America on 20 December 1699, arrived in Maryland on 12 March 1700, and stayed until the following year.

Of Bray's major works from this period that specifically involved America, two were preached or written in England for export to America. *Apostolick Charity* . . . (1698), preached at St. Paul's on 19 December 1697 at the ordination of missionaries bound for the plantations, was prefaced by Bray's "A General View of the English Colonies in America, with Respect to Religion." When republished in 1699 it was expanded with his *Proposals for the Incouragement and Promoting of Religion and Learning in the Foreign Plantations* and "A Circular Letter to the Clergy of Mary-Land." Another of Bray's English works which was redirected for use in America was his *Catechetical Discourses* . . . (1701). This retitled third edition of his *A Course of Lectures on Church Catechism* (1696) was merely given a preface that focused upon the conditions in the colonies. The lectures were essentially unchanged.

Two other major works were presented by Bray in Maryland. *The Acts of Dr. Bray's Visitation* . . . (1700), which documented Bray's exercising of his powers as commissary, revealed that he encouraged his ministers in their work, sought to provide them with clerks and with skilled workmen to build their churches, issued a formal censure of a profligate minister, dealt with a case of unintentional bigamy, and treated other matters as well. The major thrust of his comments in *The Acts of Dr. Bray's Visitation*... and in *The Necessity of an Early Religion*... (1700)—the only extant sermon of those Bray delivered in America—and, in fact, the major thrust in all of his works, whether English or American, was remarkably consistent. Theologically, he seldom wavered from the basics of the Baptismal Covenant: men must "know and believe of their Creation by, and dependence on God; Of the

Fall of Man, his Rebellion against his Maker, and of his siding with the Devil; Of our Redemption through the Mediation of Jesus Christ the Son of God, and his rescuing us from the Dominion of Satan; Of the terms of our Reconciliation with our Maker, and of that Covenant of Grace which he procur'd for us, has preach'd unto us, and we have entered into; And lastly of the necessity of regeneration, and Sanctification through the Holy Spirit." Practically, Bray regarded education and religious instruction as the primary and logical means with which to achieve salvation.

Thomas Bray was truly an aggressive force in the Church of England both at home and in the Plantations. Just as he selflessly invested his own money in his library and missionary schemes, he ardently opposed all those who stood in the way of his grand vision. When he said of himself "I am called a *Projector* (a very mean and contemptible Character with such as are accounted Men of Wisdom) upon the account of these Designs I am continually forming," his wit underlines the foresight that allowed him to rise above his critics. The American sermons and related literature were an integral part of his overall program for the colonies and exemplified the same pragmatic, organized, and efficient qualities evident in almost all of his activities and in the man himself. Bray died in London on 15 February 1730, but lived long enough to know that his work would indeed be carried on.

References:

Verner W. Crane, "Dr. Thomas Bray and the Charitable Colony Project, 1730," *William and Mary Quarterly*, third series 19 (January 1962): 49-63;

Charles T. Laugher, *Thomas Bray's Grand Design: Libraries of the Church of England in America, 1695-1785* (Chicago: American Library Association, 1973);

John W. Lydekker, "Thomas Bray (1658-1730), Founder of Missionary Enterprise," *Historical Magazine of the Protestant Episcopal Church*, 12 (September 1943): 187-214;

Samuel C. McCulloch, "Dr. Thomas Bray's Commissary Work in London, 1696-1699," *William and Mary Quarterly*, third series 2 (October 1945): 333-348;

Edgar L. Pennington, "The Beginnings of the Library in Charles Town, South Carolina," *Proceedings of the American Antiquarian Society*, new series 44 (April 1934): 159-187;

Pennington, *The Reverend Thomas Bray*, The Church Historical Society, publication no. 7 (Philadelphia: The Church Historical Society, 1934);

Nelson Waite Rightmyer, *Maryland's Established Church* (Baltimore: The Church Historical Society for the Diocese of Maryland, 1956);

Percy C. Skirven, *The First Parishes of the Province of Maryland* (Baltimore: Norman, Remington, 1923);

Bernard C. Steiner, "Rev. Thomas Bray and His American Libraries," *American Historical Review*, 2 (October 1896): 59-75;

James W. Thomas, *Chronicles of Colonial Maryland* (Baltimore: Cushing, 1900);

H. P. Thompson, *Thomas Bray* (London: S.P.C.K., 1954);

John C. Van Horne, " 'Pious Designs': The American Correspondence of the Associates of Dr. Bray, 1731-1775," Ph.D. dissertation, University of Virginia, 1979;

Joseph T. Wheeler, "Thomas Bray and the Maryland Parochial Libraries," *Maryland Historical Magazine*, 34 (September 1939): 246-265;

Lawrence C. Wroth, "Dr Bray's 'Proposals for the Incouragement of Religion and Learning in the Foreign Plantations'—A Bibliographical Note," *Massachusetts Historical Society Proceedings*, 65 (February 1936): 518-534.

Thomas Budd

(birth date unknown-1698)

Jeffrey M. Jeske
University of California, Los Angeles

SELECTED BOOKS: *Good Order Established in Pennsilvania & New Jersey in America, Being a true Account of the Country; with its Produce and Commodities there made* ... (Philadelphia: Printed by William Bradford, 1685);

A True Copy of Three Judgments given forth by a Party of Men, called Quakers at Philadelphia, against George Keith and his Friends. With two answers to the said Judgments, by Budd and others (Philadelphia: Printed by William Bradford, 1692);

A Brief answer to two papers procured from Friends in Maryland, the one concerning Thomas Budd's favouring John Lynam, &c. the other concerning his owning George Keith's Principles and Doctrines (Philadelphia, 1692);

A Just Rebuke to several Calumnies, Lyes and Slanders Reported against Thomas Budd (Philadelphia: Printed by William Bradford, circa 1692);

An Expostulation with Thomas Lloyd, Samuell Jennings, and the rest of the Twenty-eight unjust Judges and Signers of the Paper of Condemnation against George Keith and the rest of his Friends. And Complaint for Public Hearing and Tryal before all impartial People, by Budd and others (Philadelphia: Printed by William Bradford, 1692);

A Testimony and Caution to such as do make a profession of Truth who are in scorn called Quakers, and more especially such who profess to be Ministers of the Gospel of Peace, that they should not be concerned in Worldly Government, by Budd and John Hart (Philadelphia, 1692);

The Great Doctrines of the Gospel of Christ, Owned, Believed and asserted in several Declarations or Sermons Preached in London, by Sundry Servants of Christ of the Society of Christian Quakers, by Budd, George Keith, John Raunce, and Charles Harris (London: Printed for Nath. Crouch, 1694).

Good Order Eſtabliſhed
IN
Pennſilvania & New-Jerſey
IN
AMERICA,
Being a true Account of the Country;
With its Produce and Commodities there made.

And the great Improvements that may be made by means of **Publick Store-houſes** for **Hemp, Flax** and **Linnen-Cloth**; alſo, the Advantages of a **Publick-School**, the Profits of a **Publick-Bank**, and the Probability of its ariſing, if thoſe directions here laid down are followed. With the advantages of publick **Granaries**.

Likewiſe, ſeveral other things needful to be underſtood by thoſe that are or do intend to be concerned in planting in the ſaid Countries.

All which is laid down very plain, in this ſmall Treatiſe; it being eaſie to be underſtood by any ordinary Capacity. To which the *Reader* is referred for his further ſatisfaction.

By Thomas Budd.

Printed in the Year 1685.

Title page for Budd's first book, which recommends a comprehensive plan of public education (John Brown Library, Brown University)

Thomas Budd, a prominent seventeenth-century Quaker, was born in England but moved to New Jersey in 1668. He was active there as a proprietor for the Friends, particularly in Indian affairs, and in *Good Order Established in Pennsilvania & New Jersey in America* . . . (1685), written during a trip to England in 1685, he recommended a comprehensive plan of public education which was largely adopted. A New Jersey town—Buddtown—was named after him.

In 1692, Budd became a chief supporter of George Keith, whose attempt to purify the Society of Friends through stricter membership rules and a more uniform orthodoxy created a massive upheaval in both England and America. Budd led several prominent colonial Quakers to secede from the Society of Friends and join Keith's Christian Quakers; he also wrote several works dealing with the resulting controversies. In 1692, amid a conflict involving the relationship of church and state, Budd, Keith, and Peter Boss were charged with seditious libel, convicted, and fined. Budd's account of the affair was published in *A True Copy of Three Judgments* . . . (1692). Other polemical documents by Budd published in the same year are *A Brief answer to two papers procured from Friends in Maryland*. . . ; *A Just Rebuke to several Calumnies, Lyes and Slanders Reported against Thomas Budd*; *An Expostulation with Thomas Lloyd, Samuell Jennings, and the rest of the Twenty-eight unjust Judges*. . . , by Budd and others; and *A Testimony and Caution to such as do make a profession of Truth who are in scorn called Quakers*. . . , by Budd and John Hart. In 1693, Budd accompanied Keith to England, where their case was heard and rejected at the English Friends' Yearly Meeting; in the following year they and others reasserted their positions in *The Great Doctrines of the Gospel of Christ*. . . . Afterward, Budd remained a schismatic, reiterating his opinions in "A Test for Truth Against Error" (written circa 1697) and eventually becoming a member of the Anglican church.

References:

J. William Frost, *The Keithian Controversy in Early Pennsylvania* (Norwood, Pa.: Norwood Editions, 1980);

Rufus M. Jones, *The Quakers in the American Colonies* (New York: Russell & Russell, 1962).

Mather Byles

(15 March 1707-5 July 1788)

Kenneth A. Requa

BOOKS: *A Poem on the Death of His Late Majesty King George* . . . (Boston, 1727);

A Poem Presented to His Excellency William Burnet, Esq; on His Arrival at Boston, July 19, 1728 (Boston, 1728);

The Character of the Perfect and Upright Man . . . (Boston: Printed for S. Gerrish, 1729);

A Discourse on the Present Vileness of the Body . . . (Boston: Printed by S. Kneeland & T. Green for N. Proctor, 1732);

To His Excellency Governour Belcher, on the Death of His Lady. An Epistle (Boston, 1736);

On the Death of the Queen. A Poem . . . (Boston: Printed by J. Draper for D. Henchman, 1738);

The Glories of the Lord of Hosts, and the Fortitude of the Religious Hero . . . (Boston: Printed & sold by Thomas Fleet & Joseph Edwards, 1740);

The Flourish of the Annual Spring . . . (Boston: Printed & sold by Rogers & Fowle, 1741);

The Visit to Jesus by Night. An Evening Lecture (Boston: Printed & sold by Rogers & Fowle, 1741);

The Comet: A Poem (Boston: Printed & sold by B. Green & D. Gookin, 1744);

God Glorious in the Scenes of Winter . . . (Boston: Printed by B. Green for D. Gookin, 1744);

Poems on Several Occasions (Boston: Printed by S. Kneeland & T. Green, 1744);

The Glorious Rest of Heaven . . . (Boston: Printed by B. Green for D. Gookin, 1745);

The Prayer and Plea of David, to be Delivered from Blood-Guiltiness . . . (Boston: Printed & sold by S. Kneeland, 1751);

God the Strength and Portion of His People . . . (Boston: Printed by John Draper, 1752);

Divine Power and Anger Displayed in Earthquakes. A Sermon Occasioned by the Late Earthquake . . . (Boston: Printed by S. Kneeland, 1755);

The Man of God thoroughly Furnished to Every Good Work . . . (New London: Printed & sold by Nathaniel Green & Timothy Green, Jr., 1758);

The Vanity of Every Man at His Best Estate . . . (Boston: Printed by Green & Russell, 1761);

The Death of a Friend Lamented (Boston: Printed by Richard Draper, 1772).

COLLECTION: *Works*, edited by Benjamin Franklin V (Delmar, N.Y.: Scholars' Facsimiles & Reprints, 1978).

Mather Byles, the chief published poet of early eighteenth-century America, flourished during the

Mather Byles

Portrait by John Singleton Copley, 1774

high tide of provincial spirit in New England. He was a poet whose verse was influenced by English Augustan poetry and a moderate clergyman whose published sermons are notable more for polished prose than for theological thought. During the American Revolution, he was an unrepentant—but passive—Tory, and throughout his life, he maintained a well-deserved reputation as Boston's eccentric wit.

His father, Josias Byles, a Boston saddler, died when Mather Byles was little more than a year old. Since his mother, Elizabeth Mather Byles, the sister of Cotton Mather and daughter of Increase Mather, did not remarry, young Mather came strongly under the influence of those two great Boston ministers. He entered Harvard College in 1721 and managed to overcome serious illness in time to graduate in 1725.

Rather than going immediately into the ministry, as was expected, Byles turned to literary work. In 1727, he became an editor of and the most celebrated contributor to the *New England Weekly Journal*, a new and, for that era, a strongly literary journal. Byles contributed polite and instructive essays, but most notably he published in that journal most of his important poems, including "Eternity" (1727), "Written in Milton's *Paradise Lost*" (1727), "A Poem on the Death of King George I" (1727), and "The Conflagration" (1729).

Like his American Puritan poet predecessors, Byles selected subjects that would "improve" his readers. His presentation, however, indicates the truer purpose of his verse was to construct tasteful imitations of the new Augustan poetic fashions from England. For instance, "The Conflagration" is less the versified sermon on the day of doom a reader would expect than it is an occasion for the poet to take "high flights." Byles strains for an epic voice to capture the grand scenes, including his curious turn of having the earth, purified by escatalogical fires, blossom into spring. Similarly, his "Written in Milton's *Paradise Lost*" scarcely pauses over the subject of Milton's epic as Byles attempts his own mighty lines to recreate the sounds and scenes of Milton.

The influence of Alexander Pope is evident throughout these early poems. Subject, treatment, diction, and versification all show the debt of provincial Byles to his English master. More than once tributes to Pope, such as this one from "To an Ingenious Young Gentleman, on his Dedicating a Poem to the Author," show up: "O Pope! thy fame is spread around the sky, / Far as waves can flow, far as winds can fly!" Among the other English masters Byles copied, the most notable influence on him was Isaac Watts, who provided the models for several hymnlike poems Byles wrote. In 1729, Byles began to send letters to Pope, Watts, and other English poets. The message to each was similar: they were the glorious lights of English verse, Byles a humble provincial. Pope responded once in a letter Byles proudly displayed for years after. Watts continued an occasional correspondence until 1742, encouraging Byles in each letter to carry on his poetic efforts and to improve in piety.

Although his early poetic efforts won him high praise in New England and some notice from abroad, Byles by 1730 began to seek a ministerial post. In 1732, he was chosen the first pastor of the Hollis Street Church in Boston. In 1734, he married Anna Gale, niece of Governor Jonathan Belcher, who had been the major founder of the church and instrumental in securing the pastorate for Byles. In his first years as pastor, Byles continued to write some poems, but his new duties and connections apparently crowded out his interests in verse. By 1744 he virtually had given up poetry.

In that year, the same year in which his wife died, most of his poems were collected in *Poems on Several*

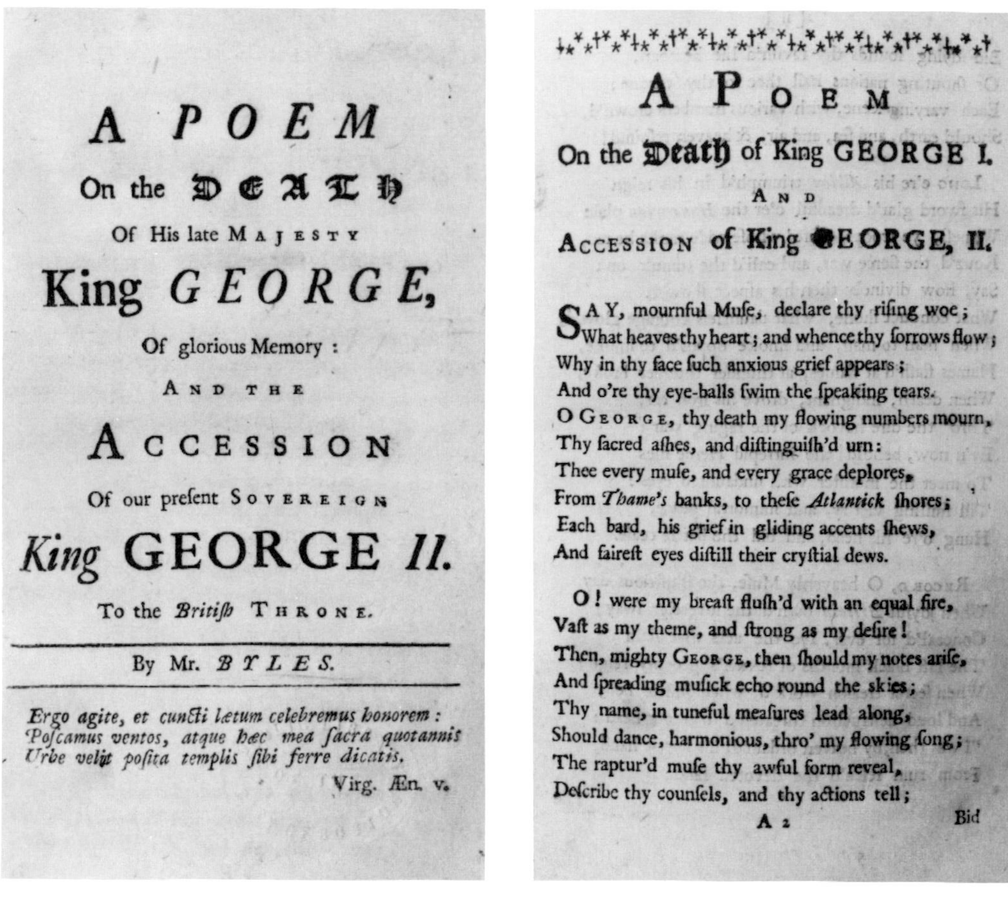

A POEM

On the DEATH

Of His late MAJESTY

King GEORGE,

Of glorious Memory :

AND THE

ACCESSION

Of our preſent SOVEREIGN

King GEORGE II.

To the Britiſh THRONE.

By Mr. BYLES.

Ergo agite, et cunčti lætum celebremus honorem :
Poſcamus ventos, atque hæc mea ſacra quotannis
Urbe velit poſita templis ſibi ferre dicatis.
Virg. Æn. v.

A POEM

On the Death of King GEORGE I.

AND

ACCESSION of King GEORGE, II.

SAY, mournful Muſe, declare thy riſing woe;
What heaves thy heart; and whence thy ſorrows flow;
Why in thy face ſuch anxious grief appears;
And o're thy eye-balls ſwim the ſpeaking tears.
O GEORGE, thy death my flowing numbers mourn,
Thy ſacred aſhes, and diſtinguiſh'd urn:
Thee every muſe, and every grace deplores,
From *Thame's* banks, to theſe *Atlantick* ſhores;
Each bard, his grief in gliding accents ſhews,
And faireſt eyes diſtill their cryſtial dews.

O! were my breaſt fluſh'd with an equal fire,
Vaſt as my theme, and ſtrong as my deſire!
Then, mighty GEORGE, then ſhould my notes ariſe,
And ſpreading muſick echo round the skies;
Thy name, in tuneful meaſures lead along,
Should dance, harmonious, thro' my flowing ſong;
The raptur'd muſe thy awful form reveal,
Deſcribe thy counſels, and thy actions tell;

A 2 Bid

Title page and first page of text for the separate publication of Byles's elegy for George I (Thomas Cooper Library, University of South Carolina)

Occasions. Byles announced in the preface that the poems were "for the most part written as the amusements of looser hours" and that "he gives up at once these lighter productions, and bids adieu to the airy muse." Also in 1744, other earlier poems by Byles were collected, along with poetic tributes to him, in *A Collection of Poems By Several Hands.* Taken together, the collected poems are but a modest achievement, their contribution to American poetry being equally modest.

Byles's other publications were his sermons, the first of which was printed in 1729. As late as the 1750s, he continued occasionally to have sermons published. Lacking the doctrinal fire of the earlier Mather sermons, Byles's sermons are most notable for carefully fashioned polite prose. Since he was a moderate in his theological positions, Byles stayed free of disputations and emphasized, instead, such comparatively pleasant topics as lessons to be drawn from the seasons, virtuous living, and eternal rest. He aimed, he once said, to present "old thoughts in a newer, or stronger, or more agreeable, or at least *different* light."

Until the first stirring of the American Revolution, Byles maintained his ministerial prestige in Boston, serving faithfully and with little controversy in his church. In 1747, he married Rebecca Tailer, daughter of William Tailer, who had been twice lieutenant-governor of Massachusetts and once acting governor. And in 1765, he received an honorary Doctor of Divinity degree from Aberdeen University. As revolutionary furor grew, however, Byles began to fall into disfavor because of his Tory leanings. As the crisis polarized colonists, Byles became clearly—and willingly—marked. Never an active political advocate of the crown, he maintained social connections among the Tory aristocracy and sharply criticized what he saw as mindless loyalism. His position was well summed up in the remark he made at the funeral of Crispus Attucks: "They call me a brainless Tory; but tell me, my young friend, which is better, to be ruled by one tyrant 3,000 miles away, or by 3,000 tyrants not a mile away?"

During the British occupation of Boston, troops were garrisoned in the Hollis Street Church. When the colonial troops returned in 1776, Byles was ejected from the pastorate, since he was believed to have allowed, if not encouraged, the use of and subsequent damage to the church. On 2 June 1777 he was called before a special session on peace, declared an enemy of the United States, and sentenced to exile. The sentence was altered, however, so that Byles was instead placed under house arrest for two years.

Byles's reputation as a wit had been growing. "Punning Byles invokes our smiles," said Thomas Morton Jones in "The Boston Ministers, A Ballad" (1774). "He visits folks to crack his jokes, / Which never mend their hearts. . . . / And throws out wit, or what's like it, / To everyone he meets." His troubles during the Revolution, however, seem to have brought out the best in his wit. On the British occupation of Boston he remarked, "Our greviences" are "reddressed"; he referred to his house guard as "my observe-a-Tory"; and he said about the various removals and replacements of his guard, "I have been guarded, re-guarded, and disregarded."

1776. August 9th. This Church having been for Some Time. driven. (by the Cruel hand of Brittain) from their habitations, and their house of Worship. been Turned into a Barrack. by Their Enemies.-- have now by the great Goodness of God. an opportunity to Visit their habitations .. — This day assem= =bled in the Meetinghouse. to. Consider the Conduct of the Revd. Doct. Byles our pastor who. remaind in the Town. during. the time of its. being in Possesion of the Enemy. and to our great greif. appears to have Joined them. against the Liberties of our Country — This being a matter of Great Importance and we being few in Number. It. was Moved. that. the Church Should Unite with the Congregation. In the Consideration & determination of this Matter. which. being put. Pass'd in the affirmative unanimously. and the Congregation unanimously Agreed. to the Proposal —

A page from the records of the Hollis Street Church, which states the congregation's intention to call Byles to account for allegedly allowing the British troops garrisoned in the church to damage the interior of the building. Byles angrily denied their charges, but he was dismissed from his pastorate a week later.

With the end of the war and the calming of revolutionary passions, Byles was left to settle into a quiet retirement. He never attempted to regain a pulpit, and he never returned to the production of verse. Others collected and recorded his humorous sayings, but Byles himself made no effort to publish or preserve those curious verbal productions. He died on 5 July 1788.

Like several other colonial poets, Byles has virtually sunk to obscurity since the discovery of the poems of Edward Taylor. Considered by his literate contemporaries a bright light in American letters, he seems to modern readers and critics a minor poet who at best can be said to be better than most others in a dark age of American poetry—between Taylor and the Connecticut Wits. Given his minor contributions as a poet, it is likely that he will continue to be noted more for his role as a moderate clergyman during the waning days of the old theology, as a Tory, and as an eccentric wit.

Other:

"Bombastic and Grubstreet Style: A Satire," *New England Weekly Journal*, no. 5 (24 April 1727);

A Collection of Poems by Several Hands, includes poems by Byles (Boston: B. Green/Cornhill: D. Gookin, 1744).

References:

C. Lennart Carlson, "John Adams, Matthew Adams, Mather Byles, and the *New England Weekly Journal*," *American Literature*, 12 (November 1940): 347-348;

Arthur W. H. Eaton, *The Famous Mather Byles* (Boston: Butterfield, 1914);

Clifford K. Shipton, "Mather Byles," *Sibley's Harvard Graduates*, volume 7 (Boston: Massachusetts Historical Society, 1945), pp. 464-493;

Austin Warren, "To Mr. Pope: Epistles from America," *PMLA*, 48 (March 1933): 61-73.

Papers:

The Hollis Street church records (1732-August 1739), mostly in Byles's hand, are at the Boston Public Library. The Massachusetts Historical Society has the Byles Family Papers, 1728-1835, a two-volume collection of material by and about Byles and his children. The New England Historic Genealogical Society has Byles's letterbook, transcripts of letters by Byles and his daughters, 1727-1784. The American Antiquarian Society has Byles's own copies of the *New England Weekly Journal* (1727-1737) with his annotations and revisions.

William Byrd II

Richard M. Preston
Princeton University

BIRTH: Virginia, 28 March 1674, to William and Mary Byrd.

EDUCATION: Middle Temple, Inns of Court, London, 1692-1695.

MARRIAGES: 1706 to Lucy Parke; children: Evelyn, Wilhelmina. 1724 to Maria Taylor; children: Anne, Maria, William, Jane.

DEATH: Westover Plantation, Virginia, 26 August 1744.

SELECTED BOOKS: *A Discourse Concerning the Plague, With Some Preservatives Against It. By a Lover of Mankind*, attributed to Byrd (London: Printed for J. Roberts, 1721);

The Westover Manuscripts: Containing The History of the Dividing Line Betwixt Virginia and North Carolina; A Journey to the Land of Eden, A.D. 1733; and A Progress to the Mines. Written from 1728 to 1736 . . ., edited by Edmund Ruffin (Petersburg, Va.: Printed by Edmund & Julian C. Ruffin, 1841);

History of the Dividing Line and Other Tracts . . ., 2 volumes (Richmond, 1866); revised as *The Writings of "Colonel William Byrd of Westover in Virginia, Esqr.,"* edited by John S. Bassett (New York: Doubleday, Page, 1901);

Description of the Dismal Swamp and A Proposal to

William Byrd II, circa 1692-1695. This portrait by an unknown artist hangs in the capitol building at Williamsburg (Colonial Williamsburg).

Drain the Swamp, edited by Earl G. Swem (Metuchen, N.J.: Printed for C. F. Heartman, 1922);

A Journey to the Land of Eden and Other Papers, edited by Mark Van Doren (New York: Macy-Masius, 1928);

The Secret History of the Line, in *William Byrd's Histories of the Dividing Line betwixt Virginia and North Carolina*, edited by William K. Boyd (Raleigh: North Carolina Historical Commission, 1929);

The Secret Diary of William Byrd of Westover, 1709-1712, edited by Louis B. Wright and Marion Tinling (Richmond: Dietz Press, 1941);

Another Secret Diary of William Byrd of Westover, 1739-1741, With Letters & Literary Exercises, 1696-1726, edited by Maude H. Woodfin, translated and collated by Tinling (Richmond: Dietz, 1942);

The London Diary (1717-1721) and Other Writings, edited by Wright and Tinling (New York: Oxford University Press, 1958).

COLLECTION: *The Prose Works of William Byrd of Westover: Narratives of a Colonial Gentleman*, edited by Wright in a collated edition with a modernized text (Cambridge: Harvard University Press, 1966).

William Byrd II, the proprietor of Westover plantation in Virginia, left an entertaining and varied body of factual reportage about colonial America during the age of Pope and Swift. Byrd's four travel narratives, as well as his diaries, letters, and miscellaneous writings, give a revealing picture of the Virginia planter's world. He was an urbane, inquisitive, eccentric man, who, with sly humor, surveyed life from beneath an upcurved eyebrow and a cumulonimbus wig. Byrd's eye moved over flora and fauna, landscapes and people. He wrote about Indians, gentry, women, slaves, medicine, natural history, folklore, diet, religion, and sex. He sailed back and forth between London coffeehouses and the New World and seemed equally at ease surveying the Dismal Swamp of Virginia or picking up a prostitute in St. James's Park in London. He chewed ginseng root to prolong his life. He ate almost nothing but milk and boiled or fried meat. He could chat in Latin. He managed vast estates, regularly practiced calisthenics, lechery, and prayer, and read seven languages. True to the aristocratic tradition, he wrote mainly to amuse his friends in England and America. Although Byrd's major works circulated in manuscript for many years, none of them was printed during his lifetime.

His father, William Byrd I, was a London goldsmith who immigrated to Virginia at age eighteen and inherited an estate there from an uncle. He became a wealthy planter and Indian trader and, when his son reached age seven, sent him to England under the care of relatives, to be given a gentleman's education.

William Byrd II stayed in England until he was twenty-six. He learned Greek and Latin at Felsted Grammar School in Essex under the famous tutor Christopher Glasscock, witnessed the Glorious Revolution of 1688, and eventually, in 1692, entered the Middle Temple in London to study law. The Middle Temple, which formed one of the Inns of Court, was a haven for wits and writers during the seventeenth century. It was here that Byrd cultivated lifelong friendships with Sir Robert Southwell, president of the Royal Society, and with Charles Boyle (later the Earl of Orrerey). Byrd also formed acquaintances with the dramatists William Congreve, William Wycherley, and Nicholas Rowe. Through the influence of Southwell, Byrd was elected to the Royal Society and kept up an interest in natural science all his life. He also developed a lifelong relish for (discreet) debauchery.

In 1696, his father asked him to come home. Once back in Virginia, the son immediately entered the House of Burgesses, beginning his lifetime of political activity in the colony. As a member of the oligarchy of planters, Byrd served in a number of high offices and frequently opposed the interests of the English crown in favor of Virginia.

Virginia was a provincial country of tobacco plantations dropped in green rectangles among river estuaries. The nearest market town was London, a two months' sail away. Byrd soon found a need to return to England, but he was back in Virginia again in 1705, to take over his inheritance at the death of his father. (All told, Byrd lived in England five separate times, a total of thirty years of his life.)

A year after his father's death he married Lucy Parke, daughter of Daniel Parke, governor of the Leeward Islands. When Daniel Parke died in 1710, Byrd voluntarily assumed some of the Parke family debts in order to acquire a huge Parke landholding in Virginia. The Parke debts turned out to be more than Byrd expected, and for the rest of his life he was often harassed by the need for money. Yet he kept buying more and more land; for in land rested his hope for wealth. Two of his travel narratives were inspired by journeys into the backcountry to inspect his holdings there and try to make them pay.

During the early years of his marriage, Byrd settled into the daily routine of an ambitious planter. He kept a diary in cryptic shorthand, published in 1941 as *The Secret Diary of William Byrd of Westover, 1709-1712*. The first of three known Byrd diaries, it was discovered in 1939 at the Huntington Library in California. This find spurred the discovery of two other Byrd diaries at other libraries. When deciphered, the diaries revealed an amazingly detailed record of the minutiae of Tidewater life. They are the fullest set of diaries we have from the Southern colonies during that period. A typical entry (of 30 July 1710) reads: "I rose at 5 o'clock and wrote a letter to Major Burwell about his boat which Captain Broadwater's people had brought round and sent Tom with it. I read two chapters in Hebrew and some Greek in Thucydides. I said my prayers and ate boiled milk for breakfast. I danced my dance. I read a sermon in Dr. Tillotson and then took a little [nap]. I ate fish for dinner. In the afternoon my wife and I had a little quarrel which I reconciled with a flourish. Then she read a sermon in Dr. Tillotson to me. It is to be observed that the flourish was performed on the billiard table. I read a little Latin. In the evening we took a walk about the plantation. I neglected to say my prayers but had good health, good thoughts, and good humor, thanks be to God." He customarily read ancient languages at sunrise. Then he "danced his dance"—meaning that he did some form of calisthenics. We learn in these pages that Byrd was fascinated with medical lore. And we learn that Byrd was already dabbling at composition, perhaps light verse or satiric sketches.

During part of the period covered in the second diary, published in 1958 as *The London Diary (1717-1721)*, Byrd was in London. His wife had died in 1716 of smallpox, and Byrd immediately set out to capture an heiress with a fortune by day, tastier game by night. As he wrote in the entry for 9 July 1718, "I rose about 8 o'clock and read a chapter in Hebrew and some Greek in Lucian. I said my prayers and had milk for breakfast. The weather was cloudy and cold, the wind west. I danced my dance. About 11 o'clock came Daniel Horsemanden and stayed half an hour and then I went to Mrs. Southwell's and sat about an hour with her and then went to Ozinda's [a popular chocolate-house] and won a guinea. About two I went to Colonel Blakiston's for dinner and ate some fried lamb. . . . Then I went to Will's Coffeehouse and drank a dish of chocolate, and about ten went to the bagnio and bathed and then lay all night with Annie Wilkinson and rogered her twice. I neglected to say my prayers."

He lived in private quarters off the Strand, placing his two daughters with friends. Now in his early forties, he wooed in succession three heiresses, failing with each of them. Meanwhile, he conducted business for the colony of Virginia and spent much time gossiping and making contacts at the Virginia Coffeehouse, where the colony's gentry gathered. In the evenings he roamed the city, sometimes settling for an encounter in the bushes of St. James's Park. He finally married Maria Taylor in 1724, respectable but without money, who gave him an heir named William.

In 1721, when Byrd was spending time in Virginia, there appeared in London *A Discourse Concerning the Plague, With Some Preservatives Against It. By a Lover of Mankind*. The tract advised heavy use of the "great antipoison" tobacco. If Byrd was this "Lover of Mankind," as many scholars think, then it is the only complete book he had published during his lifetime.

After one last trip to England, Byrd returned to Virginia in 1726 to stay. Here, during the last two decades of his life, he wrote out the works for which he is best known, four factual narratives of travel through the backcountry. Byrd took up the pen to

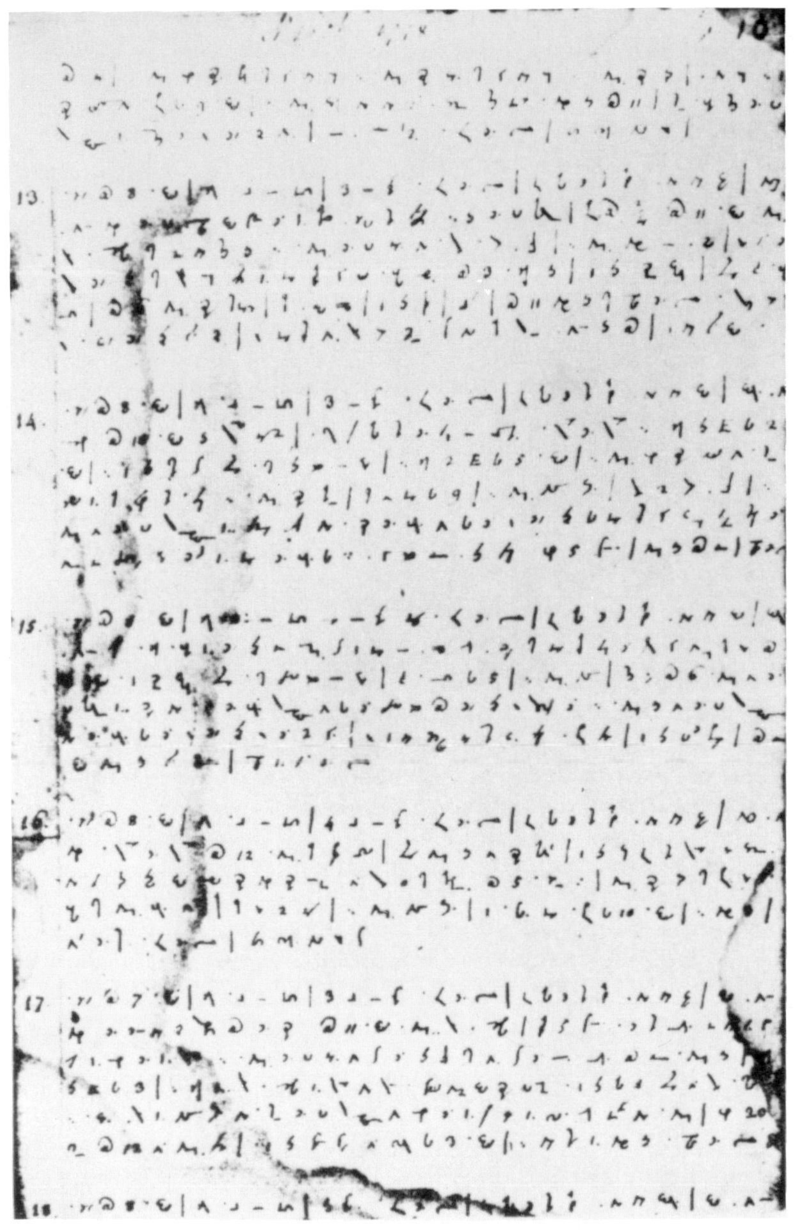

Entries for 13-17 March 1718 in Byrd's London diary, written in his invented shorthand (Virginia Historical Society)

fill the intellectual vacancies in the routine of a planter's life, a life—busy as it was with overseers, slaves, politics, tobacco, ship movements, and visitors—that could be tedious. The practice of letters was for Byrd an amusement and a refuge. He read and wrote in his library, which at his death contained some 3,600 volumes, making it one of the largest in the Colonies, equaled only by Cotton Mather's.

In 1728, Byrd accepted the leadership of a Virginia commission to settle a boundary dispute between Virginia and North Carolina. His party of surveyors and workmen met up with a similar commission from North Carolina, and they pushed the dividing line between the two states westward from the Atlantic shore, through the Dismal Swamp, and on to the upper Roanoke River. Chewing ginseng root to keep up his strength, Byrd jotted notes. It took him nearly ten years to finish the narrative based on this journey, his best known work, *The History of the Dividing Line Betwixt Virginia and North Carolina*. . . . The narrative was

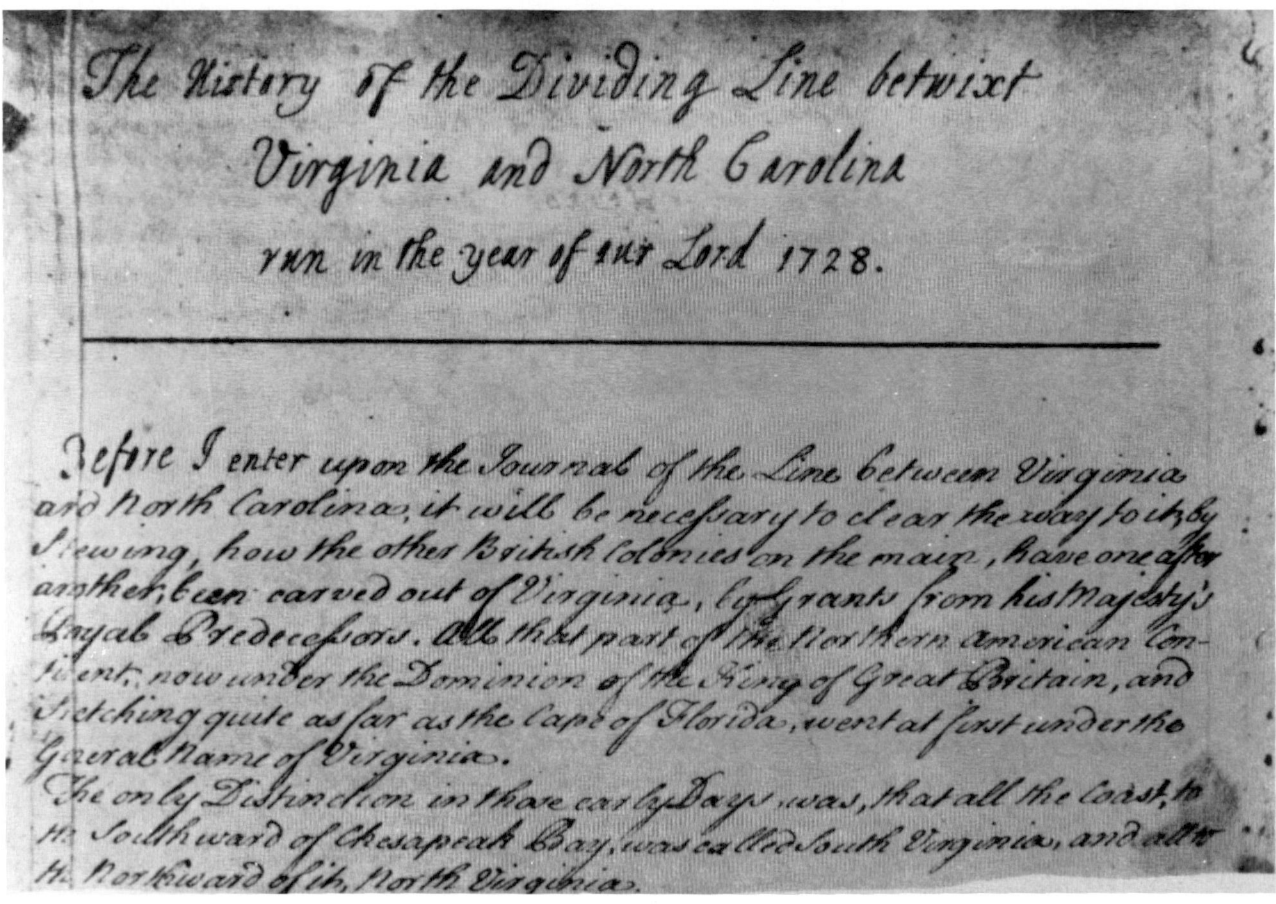
The History of the Dividing Line betwixt Virginia and North Carolina run in the year of our Lord 1728.

Before I enter upon the Journal of the Line between Virginia and North Carolina, it will be necessary to clear the way to it, by shewing, how the other British Colonies on the main, have one after another, been carved out of Virginia, by Grants from his Majesty's Royal Predecessors. All that part of the Northern American Continent, now under the Dominion of the King of Great Britain, and stretching quite as far as the Cape of Florida, went at first under the General Name of Virginia.

The only Distinction in those early Days was, that all the Coast, to the Southward of Chesapeak Bay, was called South Virginia, and all to the Northward of it, North Virginia.

First page of the manuscript for one of Byrd's accounts of the 1728 survey of the boundary between Virginia and North Carolina. This longer version, intended for a sophisticated London audience, is propagandistic on behalf of Virginia (Virginia Historical Society).

not published until 1841, but since then it has become known as a classic portrait of backwoods life in the mid-eighteenth century. Byrd had a reporter's eye and a magisterial sense of ridicule. He enjoyed mocking North Carolinians: they were lazy, he said, vicious, "full of gross humors." Their noses frequently fell in from eating too much pork. "Nay, 'tis said that once, after three good pork years, a motion had like to have been made in the House of Burgesses [of North Carolina] that a man with a nose should be incapable of holding any place of profit in the province; which extraordinary motion could never have been intended without some hopes of a majority." It is clear that Byrd had a sophisticated London audience in mind.

Richmond Croom Beatty, in his biography of Byrd, asserted that Byrd is "primarily a humorist." Byrd's comic spirit was based on firmly aristocratic standards of behavior and taste; those who tried to assume dignity and failed became the butts of his ridicule.

After passing through the "filthy quagmire" of the Dismal Swamp, they moved into the country of the Nottoway Indians. Here, Byrd picked up ethnological information. His chief informant was one Ned Bearskin, a guide and hunter, who told him about Indian beliefs and customs. Byrd examined the problem of Indian-white relations, and he proposed an interesting solution: intermarriage. In this way, he argued, Indians might be brought painlessly to civilization over a span of generations; for "all nations of men have the same natural dignity, and we all know that very bright talents may be lodged under a very dark skin. The principal difference between one people and another proceeds only from the different opportunities of improvement." (Byrd kept slaves. He felt, however, that the slave system would prove disastrous.)

In 1851 a manuscript by Byrd, titled *The Secret History of the Line,* turned up in Philadelphia. It was finally published in 1929. A shorter, alternate version of the *History of the Dividing Line, The*

Secret History of the Line was probably written first, for a small circle of Virginia friends. In *The Secret History of the Line,* Byrd disguised the names of the party. The other commissioners were given names such as "Meanwell" and "Firebrand." Introducing himself as a character named "Steddy," Byrd told the narrative in the third person, much as Xenophon in the *Anabasis* and Julius Caesar in the *Commentaries* told the histories of their campaigns in the third person. For his private audience, Byrd included sexual escapades, including six occasions when members of the Virginia party (but not Byrd himself) assaulted women. Finally, in *The Secret History of the Line,* Byrd made no attempt to disguise the personal hatreds that had existed between various members of the group. The *History of the Dividing Line,* the longer and more public work, was frankly propagandistic on behalf of the colony of Virginia.

Two other trips resulted in narratives: *A Progress to the Mines,* the story of his investigation into iron smelting at Fredericksburg; and *A Journey to the Land of Eden, A.D. 1733,* a narrative of an inspection tour of his landholdings (which he had named "Eden") on the Dan River. Although both are shorter than the *History of the Dividing Line,* these works, first published in 1841, are full of

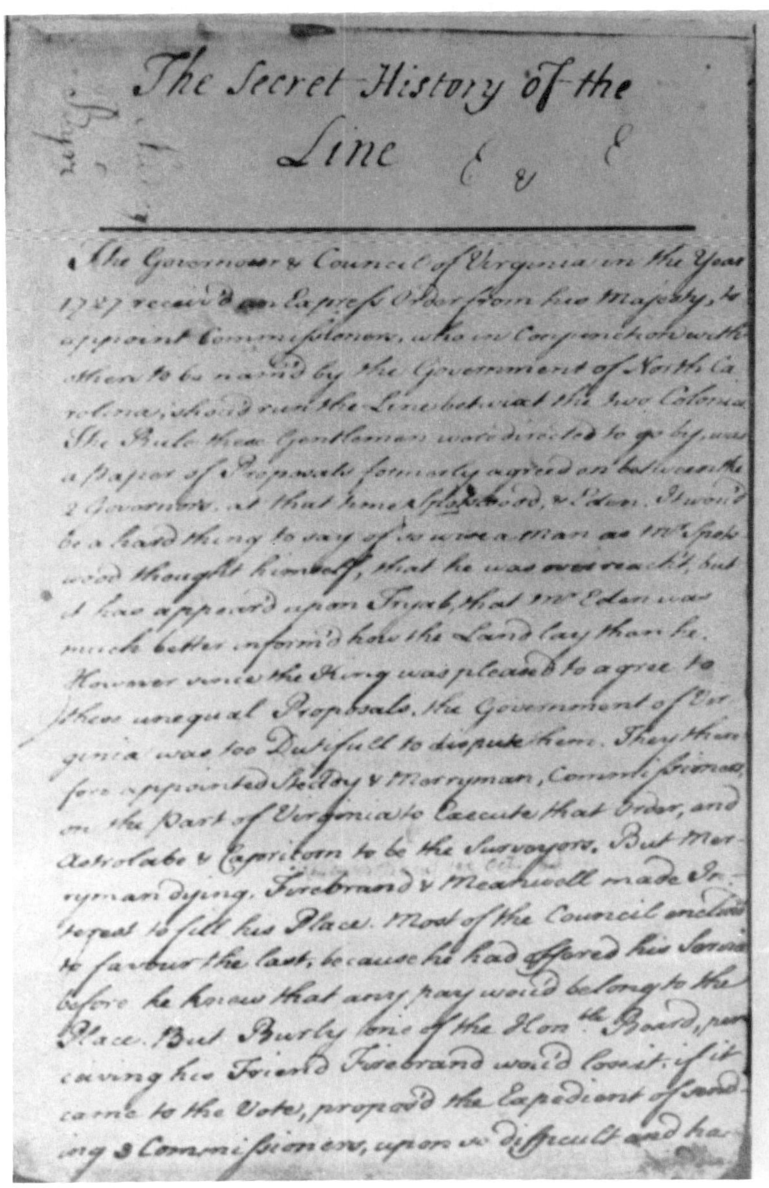

The Secret History of the Line

The Governour & Council of Virginia in the Year 1727 receiv'd an Express Order from his Majesty, to appoint Commissioners, who in Conjunction with others to be nam'd by the Government of North Carolina, shou'd run the Line between the two Colonies. The Rule these Gentlemen were directed to go by, was a Paper of Proposals formerly agreed on between the 2 Governors, at that time Spotswood, & Eden. It wou'd be a hard thing to say of so wise a Man as Mr. Spotswood thought himself, that he was over-reacht, but it has appear'd upon Tryal, that Mr. Eden was much better inform'd how the Land lay than he. However since the King was pleas'd to agree to those unequal Proposals, the Government of Virginia was too Dutifull to dispute them. They therefore appointed Steddy & Merryman, Commissioners on the Part of Virginia to Execute that Order, and Astrolabe & Capricorn to be the Surveyors. But Merryman dying, Firebrand & Meanwell made Interest to fill his Place. Most of the Council enclin'd to favour the last, because he had offer'd his Service before he knew that any pay wou'd belong to the Place. But Burly one of the Hon.ble Board, perceiving his Friend Firebrand wou'd loose it if it came to the Vote, propos'd the Expedient of sending 3 Commissioners, upon so difficult and hav-

First page of the manuscript for Byrd's more private account of his 1728 surveying trip. Intended for his friends, this version describes the party's sexual escapades and the animosities that existed among various members of the group (American Philosophical Society).

entertaining lore and facts about frontier life. In *A Journey to the Land of Eden*, Byrd told how "we laid the foundation of two large cities: one . . . to be called Richmond, and the other at the point of Appomattox River, to be named Petersburg."

Why did William Byrd not arrange to have his books printed? "I have one infirmity," he wrote to his friend Peter Collinson in England, "never to venture anything unfinished out of my hands. The bashful bears hide their cubs 'till they have licked them into shape, nor am I too proud to follow the example of those modest animals." And he was content (as an aristocrat should be) to let his manuscripts circulate among his friends.

Byrd's third and last secret shorthand diary known to exist covers his later years, from 1739 to 1741. A steady intake of ginseng and meat had not weakened his humors. At age sixty-seven he noted, "I rose about 6 and played the fool with Sarah, God forgive me. However, I prayed and had coffee."

Byrd was a practicing member of the Anglican church and clearly a devout man. Yet he took his transgressions with an easier heart than, say, Cotton Mather. Byrd's library held 300 volumes of works on theology—many of the same titles, curiously, that Cotton Mather was reading.

Probably neither England nor Virginia wholly satisfied William Byrd; he was a traveler between worlds. He hungrily read the *Tatler* and other news pamphlets as they came off ships from England. Byrd filled the eighteen-foot-wide hallway of Westover with portraits of Southwell, the Earl of Orrerey, the Marquis of Halifax, and other noted Englishmen—windows with a view back over the Atlantic. "Thus my Lord," he wrote to Orrerey, "we are very happy in our Canaans if we could but forget the onions and fleshpots of Egypt." At the same time, Byrd showed a constant fascination for the factual mystery of America—its botany and folklore, its range of peoples. One of his favorite authors was Petronius Arbiter, who penned a ribald natural history of the human maggotry that infested Nero's Rome. Byrd's factual reporting is not "imagined" in the sense that Petronius's fiction is, but imaginative in a different way: Byrd captured the density of color, the microscopic detail, and the absurd contradictions of colonial life in a coherent body of writing. Faced with a continent too strange to be imagined, he had to report. This necessity connects him with a long tradition of factual narrative in American literature that extends from William Bradford's *History of Plimoth Plantation*, through Henry David Thoreau's *Walden*, and into the present day with Tom Wolfe, another Virginian (born in Richmond, the city Byrd founded) with aristocratic dress and an incinerating wit.

William Byrd II died in 1744 at three-score and ten years, leaving an estate of 179,440 acres. The family buried him in his garden of boxwood and honeysuckle. The imposing brick house he built at Westover still stands today, not far from Colonial Williamsburg.

References:

Richmond Croom Beatty, *William Byrd of Westover* (Boston: Houghton Mifflin, 1932); republished, with an introduction and an annotated bibliography by M. Thomas Inge (Hamden, Conn.: Archon, 1970);

Alden Hatch, *The Byrds of Virginia* (New York: Holt, Rinehart & Winston, 1969);

Louis B. Wright, *The First Gentlemen of Virginia* (San Marino, Cal.: The Huntington Library, 1940).

Papers:

The manuscript for *The Secret History of the Line* is in the library of the American Philosophical Society in Philadelphia. The Virginia Historical Society owns the famous "Westover Folio" containing Byrd's other travel narratives; the Virginia Historical Society also owns his diary of 1717-1721 and an unpublished commonplace book. The Huntington Library in San Marino, California, owns his diary of 1709-1712. The University of North Carolina Library owns the diary of 1739-1741.

Joseph Capen

(20 December 1658-30 June 1725)

Georgia Elliott
Princeton University

BOOK: *A Funeral Sermon Occasioned by the Death of Mr. Joseph Green, Late Pastor of the Church in Salem Village* (Boston: Printed by B. Green for Samuel Gerrish, 1717).

Joseph Capen was born in Dorchester, Massachusetts, the son of John Capen. Little is known of his childhood. He graduated from Harvard College in the class of 1677 with an M.A. degree and served as minister in Dorchester for a short time. In 1684 he became the pastor of the church in Topsfield, Massachusetts, where he remained until his death in 1725. His broadside, a funeral elegy on the death of John Foster, who established the first printing press in Boston, was published in 1681. This elegy, *A Funeral Elegy Upon the much to be Lamented Death and most Deplorable Expiration of the Pious, Learned, Ingenious, and Eminently Usefull Servant of God Mr. John Foster,* is believed to be one source of the famous epitaph that Benjamin Franklin composed when he was twenty-three:

The Body
Of
Benjamin Franklin
Printer
(Like the cover of an old book,
Its contents torn out,
And stript of its lettering and guilding,)
Lies here, food for worms.
Yet the work itself shall not be lost,
For it will, as he believed, appear once more,
In a new
And more beautiful edition,
Corrected and amended
By
The Author.

Capen's elegy uses strikingly similar imagery and the same conceit:

Thy body, which no activeness did lack,
Now's laid aside like an old almanac;
But for the present only's out of date,
'Twill have at length a far more active state.
Yea, though with dust thy body soiled be,
Yet at the resurrection we shall see
A fair edition, and of matchless worth.
Free from *Errata,* new in Heaven set forth;
'Tis but a word from God, the great Creator,
It shall be done when he saith *Imprimatur.*

All copies of the original broadside of Capen's elegy have been lost, but Thomas C. Simonds reprinted the poem from a copy of the manuscript in his *History of South Boston* (1857).

Capen's only other publication was a funeral sermon on the death of Joseph Green, *A Funeral Sermon Occasioned by the Death of Mr. Joseph Green, Late Pastor of the Church in Salem Village* (1717). Included with the sermon was a prefatory epistle by Increase Mather and an elegy by Capen. All indications are that Capen lived his life free from controversy in the faithful performance of his pastoral duties.

Other:

A Funeral Elegy Upon the much to be Lamented Death and most Deplorable Expiration of the Pious, Learned, Ingenious, and Eminently Usefull Servant of God Mr. John Foster, in *History of South Boston,* by Thomas C. Simonds (Boston: Clapp, 1857);

Harold Jantz, *The First Century of New England Verse,* includes Capen's elegy (Worcester, Mass.: American Antiquarian Society, 1944).

References:

James Savage, *Genealogical Dictionary of the First Settlers of New England,* volume 1 (Baltimore: Genealogical Publishing, 1977), p. 334;

John Langdon Sibley, *Biographical Sketches of Graduates of Harvard University,* volume 2 (Cambridge: Sever, 1881), pp. 519-522.

Charles Chauncy

Peter White
University of New Mexico

BIRTH: Boston, Massachusetts, 1 January 1705, to Charles and Sarah Walley Chauncy.

EDUCATION: B.A., Harvard College, 1721; M.A., Harvard College, 1724.

MARRIAGES: 14 February 1727 to Elizabeth Hirst; children: Charles, Elizabeth, Sarah. 8 January 1738 to Elizabeth Townsend. 15 January 1760 to Mary Stoddard.

DEATH: Boston, Massachusetts, 10 February 1787.

This painting, attributed to Nathaniel Smibert, is believed to be a portrait of Charles Chauncy (Harvard University Portrait Collection).

SELECTED BOOKS: *Man's Life considered under the Similitude of a Vapour, that appeareth for a little Time, and then vanisheth away . . .* (Boston: Printed by B. Green, 1731);

Early Piety recommended and exemplify'd . . . (Boston: Printed by S. Kneeland & T. Green for B. Gray, 1732);

Nathanael's Character display'd. A Sermon, Preach'd The Lord's Day after the Funeral of the Honourable Nathanael Byfield, Esq. . . . (Boston, 1733);

The Character and Overthrow of Laish considered and applied . . . (Boston: Printed by S. Kneeland & T. Green for D. Henchman, 1734);

Prayer for help a seasonable duty upon the ceasing of Godly and Faithful Men . . . (Boston: Printed by T. Fleet, 1737);

The only Compulsion proper to be made Use of, in the Affairs of Conscience and Religion . . . (Boston: Printed by J. Draper for J. Edwards, 1739);

Joy, the Duty of Survivors, on the Death of Pious Friends and Relatives . . . (Boston: Printed by S. Kneeland & T. Green, 1741);

An Unbridled Tongue a sure Evidence, that our Religion is Hypocritical and Vain . . . (Boston: Printed by Rogers & Fowle, 1741);

The New Creature Describ'd, and Consider'd as the sure Characteristick of a Man's being in Christ . . . (Boston: Printed by G. Rogers for J. Edwards & S. Eliot, 1741; Edinburgh: Printed for S. Clark, 1742);

Enthusiasm described and caution'd against . . . (Boston: Printed by J. Draper for S. Eliot & J. Blanchard, 1742);

The Gifts of the Spirit to Ministers consider'd in their diversity . . . (Boston: Printed & sold by Rogers & Fowle . . . also by S. Eliot, 1742);

The out-pouring of the Holy Ghost . . . (Boston: Printed by T. Fleet for D. Henchman & S. Eliot, 1742);

A Letter from a Gentleman in Boston, to Mr. George Wishart, one of the Ministers of Edinburgh, concerning the State of Religion in New-England, anonymous (Edinburgh, 1742);

Seasonable Thoughts on the State of Religion in New-England . . . (Boston: Printed by Rogers & Fowle for Samuel Eliot, 1743);

Ministers cautioned against the Occasions of

Contempt . . . (Boston: Printed by Rogers & Fowle for Samuel Eliot, 1744);

Ministers exhorted and encouraged to take heed to themselves . . . (Boston: Printed by Rogers & Fowle for S. Eliot, 1744);

Cornelius's Character. A Sermon Preach'd the Lord's-Day after the Funeral of Mr. Cornelius Thayer . . . (Boston: Printed for D. Gookin, 1745);

A Letter to the Reverend Mr. George Whitefield, Vindicating certain Passages he has excepted against, in a late Book entitled, Seasonable Thoughts on the State of Religion in New-England . . . (Boston: Printed by Rogers & Fowle for S. Eliot, 1745);

Marvelous Things done by the right Hand and holy Arm of God in getting him the Victory . . . (Boston: Printed & sold by T. Fleet, 1745; London: Printed for M. Cooper, 1745);

The Counsel of two Confederate Kings to set the Son of Tabeal on the Throne, represented as evil, in it's natural Tendency and moral Aspect . . . (Boston: Printed for D. Gookin, 1746);

Civil Magistrates must be just, ruling in the fear of God . . . (Boston: Printed by order of the House of Representatives, 1747);

The Blessedness of the Dead who die in the Lord . . . (Boston: Printed by Rogers & Fowle, 1749);

The Idle-Poor secluded from the Bread of Charity by the Christian Law . . . (Boston: Printed by Thomas Fleet, 1752);

The horrid Nature and enormous Guilt of Murder . . . (Boston: Printed by Thomas Fleet, 1754);

Earthquakes a Token of the righteous Anger of God . . . (Boston: Printed & sold by Edes & Gill, 1755);

The Earth delivered from the Curse to which it is, at present, subjected . . . (Boston: Printed & sold by Edes & Gill, 1756);

Charity to the distressed Members of Christ accepted as done to himself . . . (Boston: Printed by Green & Russell, 1757);

The Opinion of one that has perused the Summer Morning's Conversation, concerning Original Sin, wrote by the Rev. Mr. Peter Clark . . . , as A. B. (Boston: Printed & sold by Green & Russell, 1758);

All Nations of the Earth blessed in Christ, the Seed of Abraham . . . (Boston: Printed & sold by John Draper, 1762);

The Validity of Presbyterian Ordination asserted and maintained . . . (Boston: Printed & sold by Richard Draper & by Thomas Leverett, 1762);

Twelve Sermons . . . (Boston: Printed by D. & J. Kneeland for Thomas Leverett, 1765);

A Discourse occasioned by the Death of the Reverend Jonathan Mayhew . . . (Boston: Printed by R. & S. Draper, Edes & Gill, and T. & J. Fleet, 1766);

A Discourse On "the Good News from a Far Country" . . . (Boston: Printed by Kneeland & Adams, 1766);

The Duty of Ministers to "make known the Mystery of the Gospel;" And the Duty of People to "pray for them" that they may do it "with Boldness," or Fortitude . . . (Boston: Printed & sold by Edes & Gill, 1766);

A Letter To a Friend, Containing Remarks on certain Passages in a Sermon Preached by the Right Reverend Father in God, John, Lord Bishop of Landaff . . . (Boston: Printed by Kneeland & Adams for Thomas Leverett, 1767; enlarged edition, London: Printed for S. Bladon, 1768);

A Sermon Preached May 6, 1767. At the Ordination of the Reverend Simeon Howard . . . (Boston: Printed by R. Draper, Edes & Gill, and T. & J. Fleet, 1767);

The Appeal to the Public answered, In Behalf of the Non-Episcopal Churches in America . . . (Boston: Printed by Kneeland & Adams for Thomas Leverett, 1768);

A Discourse Occasioned by the Death of the Reverend Dr. Joseph Sewall . . . (Boston: Printed & sold by Kneeland & Adams, 1769);

A Discourse occasioned by the Death of the Reverend Thomas Foxcroft . . . (Boston: Printed by Daniel Kneeland for Thomas Leverett, 1769);

A Reply to Dr. Chandler's 'Appeal Defended:' Wherein His Mistakes are rectified, his False Arguing refuted, and the Objections against the planned American Episcopate shewn to remain en full force . . . (Boston: Printed by Daniel Kneeland for Thomas Leverett, 1770);

Trust In God, the Duty of the People in a Day of Trouble . . . (Boston: Printed by Daniel Kneeland for Thomas Leverett, 1770);

A Compleat View of Episcopacy . . . (Boston: Printed by Daniel Kneeland for Thomas Leverett, 1771);

"Breaking of Bread," in remembrance of the dying Love of Christ . . . (Boston: Printed for Thomas Leverett, 1772);

Christian Love as exemplified by the first christian church . . . (Boston: Printed by Thomas Leverett, 1773);

A Letter to a Friend. Giving a concise, but just, representation of the hardships and sufferings the town of Boston is exposed to, and must undergo in consequence of the late Act of the British Parliament . . . (Boston: Printed & sold at Greenleaf's, 1774);

The accursed Thing must be taken away from among a People, if they would reasonably hope to stand before their Enemies . . . (Boston: Printed by Thomas & John Fleet, 1778);

Divine Glory Brought to View in the Final Salvation of All Men . . . (Boston: Printed & sold by T. & J. Fleet, 1783);

The Mystery hid from Ages and Generations . . . (London: Printed for Charles Dilly, 1784);

The Benevolence of the Deity . . . (Boston: Printed by Powars & Willis, 1784);

Five Dissertations on the Scripture Account of the Fall . . . (London: Printed for C. Dilly, 1785);

A Sermon, Delivered at the First Church in Boston, March 13th, 1785 . . . (Boston: Printed by Greenleaf & Freeman, 1785).

Charles Chauncy, who was minister of Boston's First Church for sixty years, has, until recently, stood in the shadow of his greatest antagonist, Jonathan Edwards, the revivalist, philosopher, and president of Princeton. It was Chauncy's unfortunate fate to have been pitted against such a man as Edwards, for otherwise he might have been known solely as a man of learning and influence, a defender of the New England Congregational way, and as a creditable proponent of the enlightened world of the American Revolution and the beginnings of Unitarianism. Instead, because he was Edwards's rival during the Great Awakening (circa 1740-1744) and because he was perhaps incapable of understanding and unwilling to accept Edwards's position, he has been chiefly portrayed by historians as an intellectual inferior, a stubborn, conservative, overcautious opponent of anything that resembled a "passionate" or "affectionate" response to religious matters.

Although he could count among his friends and supporters some of Boston's finest families and therefore enjoyed a position of great prestige in the community, Chauncy appealed to the growing upper and middle classes of New England, who were safe, sound, and secure in their belief that God would save the sober. The solid Yankee merchants and mariners of New England needed a voice to ratify their compact with rationality. Chauncy drew up the contract and signed the papers for them.

There are several anecdotes in the biographical literature on the Chauncys that perhaps best illustrate this minister's prosaic and literalistic temperament. In book 2 of John Milton's *Paradise Lost* some of the fallen angels are condemned to participate in a variety of hellish pastimes. The most torturous punishments are inflicted upon those poor devils who

> sat on a hill retired,
> In thoughts more elevate, and reason'd high
> Of Providence, foreknowledge, will and fate,
> Fix'd fate, free will, foreknowledge absolute
> And found no end, in wand'ring mazes lost.

One hundred years after Milton expressed his exasperation with the legalistic intricacies of Calvinism, Charles Chauncy found himself wandering in the same theological maze. For Chauncy, however, the first obstacle he faced in following the finer threads of an argument resided in the manner of presentation, so he sent out a call for someone to translate Milton's great Christian epic into prose. Throughout his life, Chauncy was a persistent advocate of the "commonsensical" approach to religion, philosophy, and literature. "Trust in Christ as mediator and Redeemer," he urged his congregation, and pay "less regard to metaphysical niceties." Chauncy characterized the proper literary style as one which "avoids all pomp of words, all show of learned subtlety by the artful use of scholastic, systematical, and metaphysical terms," and he admitted that "If I have wrote in a mystical, perplexed, unintelligible way, I own it is a fault not to be overlooked." He so despised rhetoric that he prayed he might never become an orator. The prayer, as one of his friends remarked, was unequivocally answered. Chauncy's request for an expository *Paradise Lost* and his prayers against oration hint at why he was unable to understand Edwards and why he advocated the eighteenth-century theology that might be called supernatural rationalism, or Arminianism.

Everything in Charles Chauncy's ancestral background seemed to point the way his life would eventually go. He was the great-grandson of Charles Chauncy (1592-1671), the second president of Harvard College; he was the grandson of Isaac Chauncy (died 1712), a controversial minister in London; and he was the son of Charles Chauncy (died 1711), one of Boston's leading merchants. His mother, Sarah Walley, was the daughter of Judge Walley of the supreme court of Massachusetts. Although orphaned at the age of six, young Charles Chauncy received his primary education at Boston's fine Latin School and entered Harvard in 1717, at the age of twelve. (Jonathan Edwards had entered Yale College the year before.) Chauncy graduated from Harvard in 1721 and studied theology at Cambridge until 1727, when he was elected associate to Thomas Foxcroft, with whom he ministered to the congregation at the "Old Brick" First Church in Boston for the next sixty years.

Thus, Charles Chauncy came from a family which had from the early seventeenth century achieved recognition in the ministry, business, and law. He drew from his great-grandfather and father his resistance to Episcopacy and his support of Congregationalism. He followed the wishes of his educated, wealthy, cosmopolitan parishioners in denouncing revivalism and in trumpeting the arrival of Deism, Universal Salvationism, and the benevolence of God. Nothing would stand in Chauncy's way of guaranteeing that the social, political, and ecclesiastical structures of Boston's First Church would remain intact, thereby reassuring his congregation of his fidelity to their principles. His insistence upon sobriety in religion and regulation of the emotions was evident in his personal habits, as observed and recorded by Bezaleel Howard: "The Dr. was remarkably temperate in his diet and exercise. At Twelve o'clock he took one pinch of snuff, and only one in twenty-four hours. At one o'clock, he dined on one dish of plain, wholesome food, and after dinner took one glass of wine, and one pipe of tobacco, and only one in twenty-four hours. And he was equally methodical in his exercise, which consisted chiefly or wholly in walking. I said, 'Doctor, you live by the rule.' 'If I did not, I should not live at all.' "

Charles Chauncy began his ministry in a crucial time in the evolution of American Protestantism. At the end of the first quarter of the eighteenth century, the old, Puritanical world had begun visibly to crumble, and a more liberal brand of Calvinism gained a foothold in Boston. Arminianism, named after the sixteenth-century Dutch Remonstrant Jacobus Arminius, emphasized the rational aspects of religious thought and worship, and it advocated the belief that man had free will. Various scholars have taken pains to point out that Arminianism never really existed in the churches of New England, that it was something of a New England bogeyman, or that the established clergy actually feared the rise of Episcopalianism. Other cultural historians have argued persuasively that Arminianism, particularly the type that Edwards denounced, had in fact infected the churches of the standing order. Many religious historians have attempted to prove that federal theology and the preparation scheme for conversion of the Puritans "contained a built in equivocacy whereby the Arminian camel could get its nose under the Puritan tent so unobtrusively that few of the insiders noticed when the stakes of orthodoxy began to loosen."

Whatever the case, certain historical facts do seem to indicate that orthodox Calvinism had begun a slow process of change as early as 1662, when New Englanders adopted the Half-Way Convenant (a practice which liberalized the requirements for church membership), and continued through the demoralizing Reforming Synod of 1679, through Solomon Stoddard's use of the Lord's Supper as a converting ordinance in his "harvests," and finally through the widespread influence of English theists and Common Sense Scottish Philosophers, whose works confirmed and deepened American liberalizations of strict Reforming theology. The enlightenment had begun in New England.

Thus, Charles Chauncy inherited a congregation from a society that was becoming increasingly worldly and disinclined to accept the rigidity of pure Calvinistic doctrine. Edwards's *Personal Narrative* reveals that even he struggled with the difficult notion of predestination. With the Great Awakening in 1740, many established clergymen such as Chauncy felt that revivalism would lead to a catastrophic collapse of all that they had managed to build. The entire social order was threatened by these "out-pourings" of the spirit sweeping over the New England countryside. Among the great revivalist preachers—George Whitefield, John Davenport, Gilbert Tennent, and Jonathan Edwards—Chauncy identified Edwards as his chief antagonist, the leader of the movement to spread envy, strife, and schism throughout the colonies.

It is true that Chauncy did see some good in the growing interest in religious matters at the start of the Great Awakening. In the first two years of the Awakening (1740-1741), Chauncy was notably restrained: his *The New Creature Describ'd . . .* (1741) and *An Unbridled Tongue . . .* (1741) deal only indirectly with the commotion of the revival. He urged his readers to consider that the convert has a change in his inward frame of mind and in his outward course and manner of life. Matters of religion are serious spiritual matters, not to be discussed lightly but with the solemnity that reason should bestow upon language. By 1742, however, Chauncy probably agreed to have his *A Letter from a Gentleman in Boston, to Mr. George Wishart . . .* published anonymously in Edinburgh. This document reveals his increasing discomfort with revivalism and displays for the first time his insistence upon personal restraint: he warns that the new converts "place their Religion so much in the Heart and Fervour of their Passions, that they too much neglect their Reason and Judgement."

Chauncy gradually came to believe that the whole movement had gotten out of control by 1742, when he had his first major denunciation of the Awakening's "New Lights" published in Boston. His chief objections always emanated from his perception that the exhorters, whether lay or ordained, appealed merely to the passions of the individual auditors. Because he based his understanding of the nature of the religious experience upon the rationalism of the day, he deeply distrusted the role of the emotions, or affections, as they were called in contemporary literature.

Various prorevivalists, in turn, attempted to provoke the laity against the antirevivalists, who then responded by publicly condemning "evangelical preaching" and by publishing accounts of the dangerous explosion of the emotions in New England. In essence, the antirevivalists like Chauncy were spurred into action partially by their fear that they were losing support among the congregation. They saw their power and authority dwindling, just

ENTHUSIASM
deſcribed and caution'd againſt.

A
SERMON

Preach'd at the *Old Brick Meeting-Houſe* in *Boston*,
the LORD's DAY after the COMMENCEMENT,
1742.
With a *Letter* to the Reverend Mr. JAMES DAVENPORT.

By *Charles Chauncy*, D.D
One of the Paſtors of the *first Church* in ſaid *Town*.

——Non ſum idoneus ad habenda, aut interpretanda ſomnia, neque eam facultatem aut ſcientiam mihi expeto; et pactum feci cum Domino Deo meo, ne vel viſiones, vel ſomnia, vel etiam angelos mihi mittat. Contentus enim ſum hoc dono, quòd habeo ſcripturam ſanctam, quæ abunde docet, et ſuppeditat omnia, quæ ſunt neceſſaria cum ad hanc, tum ad futuram vitam. Huic credo, et acquieſco, ac certus ſum, me non poſſe falli.——Moveor infinita illa multitudine illuſionum, præſtigiarum, impoſturarum, quibus mundus horribiliter ſub papatu, longo tempore, deceptus eſt per ſathanam: Deinde ſufficientia ſcripturæ ſanctæ, cui ſi non adhibuero fidem, profectò nec angelo, nec viſioni, nec ſomnio facile credam. *Lutherus*, in Comment. in Gen. 37. fol. 6 Edit. An. 1554.

——Multi enim fanatici ſpiritus me adorti ſunt, quorum alius ſomnia, alius viſiones, alius revelationes jactabat, quibus nitebantur me erudire. Sed reſpondi, me non expetere ejuſmodi revelationes; et ſi quæ offerentur, me iis non habiturum fidem. Idque ardentibus votis precatus ſum, ut daret mihi Deus certum ſenſum et intellectum ſcripturæ ſanctæ. Si enim verbum habeo, ſcio me recta via ingredi, nec facile falli aut errare poſſe. Hæc mea ſententia eſt, quam non muto. *Ibid* ad Cap. 40 fol. 61.

BOSTON:
Printed by J. DRAPER, for S. ELIOT in Cornhill, and J. BLANCHARD at the Bible and Crown on Dock Square. MDCCXLII.

Title page for Chauncy's first full-scale attack on the excesses of the Great Awakening (John Carter Brown Library, Brown University)

as John Cotton and John Wilson saw their influence wane in 1637 when Anne Hutchinson, the Antinomian, drew the people of Boston to her home for instruction and biblical commentary. The historical analogy here is confirmed by the fact that Chauncy and other antirevivalists occasionally made published comparisons between Hutchinson's anarchical movement and the widespread disruptions of the normal order in 1740.

Chauncy's first full-scale attack upon the Awakening, *Enthusiasm described and caution'd against* . . . (1742), thrust him into a position of leadership among the clergy who feared the unsettling aspects of emotional "extravagance." In the first part of this work, Chauncy shows how the Awakening has caused dissension in the local churches. He says, "This is the nature of Enthusiasm . . . 'Tis a kind of religious Phrenzy" under which people practice a "sort of extatic violence," and are thrown "into convulsions and distortions, into quakings and tremblings." The proud egotistical converts declare themselves prophets moved by the spirit, but they are merely "under the influence of a deluded imagination." The most troubling aspect of revivalistic practice is that the convert's pride causes him to become "infinitely stiff and tenacious, but impatient of contradiction, censorious and uncharitable." Furthermore, they question the authority of their own ministers, even to the point of questioning their religious commitment. Chauncy summarized his opinion of the enthusiast as one who has extraordinary fervor, uncommon bodily motion, excessive confidence, a weak understanding, and an argumentative nature.

There are several ways to account for Chauncy's rather reactionary remarks about the Great Awakening. For centuries, even before the Great Migration of the Puritans to New England in the 1630s, elements within the Protestant faith had warred with one another over the question of the balance between the head and the heart in religious worship. Because Reformation theologians placed so much emphasis upon the workings of grace and the efficacy of faith, many believers incorrectly deduced that human behavior and Christian conduct in this world had become irrelevant matters, or at least matters thrown open to wide-ranging and varied interpretation. Consequently, the Reformation inadvertently spawned splinter groups of zealots, absurdists, revolutionaries, eccentrics, and absolute anarchists. The Puritans, led by graduates of Oxford and Cambridge, established a tradition of carefully—some might say painfully—grounding every doctrine or practice on a rational, intellectual, and biblical foundation. The patriarchs among the first generation of New England's settlers feared "extremism" in any form, whether Antinomian, Baptist, Quaker, Fifth Monarchy, Leveller, or Familist. Chauncy sincerely believed that the Great Awakening might give birth to another of the "monstrous" forms of anarchical and absurdist practice. He understandably convinced himself and others that he was rejecting the "out-pouring" of the spirit as his ancestors had rejected all things convulsive, threatening, and repugnant to the dignified Christian. And typically, as Cotton Mather scientifically scrutinized the hysterical "witches" of Salem in 1692, Chauncy used his own Lockean empirical tools to gather data and test hypotheses about the more recently "possessed." Like a figure out of Spenser or Bunyan, Chauncy was Reason fighting against allegorical Rabble.

But the problems were more complicated in 1740 than they had been for the Medieval and Renaissance thinkers. As Perry Miller brilliantly concluded in his biography of Edwards, Chauncy, the supposed modernist from urbane and enlightened Boston, unfortunately relied upon the outmoded theories of the compartmentalizing Lockeans, while Edwards, the Connecticut Valley mystic and the last of the Puritanical conservatives, developed truly advanced theories of man as a dynamic, whole, and spiritual being. Edwards's man had the freedom to choose, the ability to perceive and love, and the obligation to practice Christian duty. Chauncy could never look past the behavioral abuses, what Edwards called the "no signs" of the *Religious Affections*, to the general principles of the operations of the human psyche.

In *Some Thoughts Concerning the Revival of Religion* . . . (1742), which Perry Miller and Alan Heimert have called the major document of the Great Awakening, Edwards used church doctrine, psychological insight, and historical vision to demonstrate that "the Very life and soul of all true religion" consists "in the religious affections . . . which are not properly distinguished from the will, as though they were two faculties in the soul." Therefore, he concluded, since there is this holistic connection between the understanding, the will, and the affections, "our people . . . need to have their hearts touched."

In 1743 Charles Chauncy set out to collect firsthand, eyewitness accounts of the horrors of the "New Birth" conversion experience in New England. However, his original plan had to be modified so that he might answer Edwards's *Some Thoughts Concerning the Revival of Religion*. Confident now that Edwards was his worthiest opponent, Chauncy composed *Seasonable Thoughts on the State of Religion in New-England* . . . (1743), while he simultaneously prepared for the press "two volumes in octavo" essentially containing an amalgam of the antirevivalists' criticisms. He was also engaged in answering "hundreds of letters . . . from all parts of the country." Chauncy was a compiler and editor for many of those critics who shared his opinions. He used his office at the First Church as a kind of political clearinghouse.

In *Seasonable Thoughts* . . . Chauncy made the best summary of his own primary beliefs: "The plain Truth is that an *enlightened Mind*, and not *raised Affections*, ought always to be the Guide of those who call themselves Men; and this, in the Affairs of Religion, as well as other Things. *Reasonable* Beings are not to be guided by *Passion* or *Affection*. . . ." *Seasonable Thoughts* . . . reads like a handbook or compendium of the most salient features of Rationalism. One is under the obligation to use restraint, common sense, and a well-instructed judgment, thereby preserving order and regularity in society. Additionally, however, there is evidence in Chauncy's treatise of a deep-seated fear that he, as well as other avowed antirevivalists, will lose power and influence, that the arrogant and headstrong will lash out at their superiors. Chauncy sees the Great Awakening as a cynical and desperate attempt to overthrow God's ordained. Time and again, he characterizes emotional spiritual exercise as delusion, vain imagination, extraordinary, and furious behavior. Converts are likely to become conceited, impressionistic, and bent upon "bringing forward a State of Tumult and Disorder." Such individuals, Chauncy proposes, "ought to be taken in Hand by Authority." The minister of Boston's First Church clearly saw his own stable and predictable world crumbling.

If asked to isolate the major causes of New England's degeneration, Chauncy would probably have mentioned first lay-exhorting, itinerant preaching, and internal ecclesiastical bickering. At the annual convention of ministers in Boston on 31 May 1744, Chauncy preached a sermon which was subsequently published under the title of *Ministers cautioned against the Occasions of Contempt* . . . (1744). This sermon, with *Ministers exhorted and encouraged to take heed to themselves* . . . (1744) and his *A Letter to the Reverend Mr. George Whitefield* . . . (1745), reveals Chauncy's extreme discomfort with the current state of ministerial competition for the congregation's attention. On the one hand, it is clear that Chauncy is justifiably concerned about preserving the traditional structure of the congregation as a clearly defined geographical and political entity. On the other hand, however, Chauncy is irate about the tactics employed by the more theatrical "New Light" clergy. For example, he accuses George Whitefield of gross egotism when Whitefield writes of his successes in bringing the people to a state of "sore weeping . . . drowned in Tears . . . or with Hearts leaping for Joy." He sees the revivalists such as Whitefield and Tennent, and even Edwards, as mere showmen who encourage the most outrageous breaches of decorum, such as laughing and smiling during services, making extraordinary bodily movements, publicly criticizing dissenting ministers, and, finally, engaging in shady business practices. The "New Lights," argued Chauncy, were more intent upon hearing themselves than listening to others preach and were using the people to pressure ministers to join their movement. Interestingly, Chauncy makes a special point of attacking English itinerant preachers as foreigners and newcomers in an established, American land. From this point of view, one might discover in Chauncy's works on the Great Awakening some hint of his, and the general, growing opposition to British interference in colonial affairs. But whatever his motives, Chauncy tried his best in these three final works on the Great Awakening to ease the envy and strife in New England, to temper the behavior of the more radical evangelicals, and to serve as a spokesman for the "Old Light" party headquartered in Boston.

In the fifteen years following the collapse of the Great Awakening, Chauncy busied himself with devising plans to combat his physical ailments, which involved traveling to such remote places as North Carolina, and with recommending more complicated military strategies to British and American generals. His advice included the stern, and as we know now, the wise admonition to use native officers and troops familiar with the manner of fighting in the wilderness. It was during this period that "Old Brick" Chauncy aligned himself with Jonathan Mayhew in the traditional cause of resisting Anglican attempts to establish bishops in America. When Mayhew died of a stroke at forty-five, Chauncy became the chief spokesman for American, Congregational independence from English interference on these shores. For over a hundred years, the descendants of John Cotton and others renowned for their Congregational polity had rejected any suggestion that the Anglican church be allowed to gain an official foothold in America. Chauncy, never one to be outwritten, had published *A Compleat View of Episcopacy* . . . (1771), a 474-page denunciation of Thomas Chandler's appeal on behalf of the Anglicans. Chauncy's attack, which had the effect of finally ending the controversy, included dozens of objections to the English "plot": bishops were just the first step in a complete church hierarchy, and practices here would resemble those in England, with the results that the colonies would be restricted and the civil liberties of the people would be curtailed. The insidious intentions of the Anglicans in this case were, according to Chauncy, no less dangerous and insulting than the infringements upon colonial rights occasioned by the Stamp Act of 1765, which Chauncy had also vehemently opposed. Such political foresight and fervor is all the more admirable when one considers that Chauncy had to cope at the same time with a succession of disasters, including the death of his second wife, financial insecurity, loneliness because his children had all married and moved, and general depression because his poor health inhibited extended study.

By the end of the 1760s, however, Chauncy had somehow regained enough strength to undertake a massive campaign to make Congregationalism more appealing and more suited to the times. For the next twenty years Chauncy studied what he considered to be the quintessential elements of Christian doctrine: the nature of man and God, the fall of man and original sin, and the hope of an everlasting life. Thus in the mid-1780s Chauncy had published the three works that formed the cornerstone of his theology: *The Benevolence of the Deity* . . . (1784); *The Mystery hid from Ages and Generations* . . . (1784); and *Five Dissertations on the Scripture Account of the Fall* . . . (1785). Throughout these treatises, Chauncy shows a heavy reliance upon John Locke and the Common Sense Scottish Philosophers. His indebtedness is most clearly seen when one summarizes his major convictions: man is a naturally intelligent, free moral agent; the light of Reason, supplemented by the light of Revelation, enables man to grasp the eternal truths of existence; God is a benevolent governor and father who works to promote human happiness and who permits, but does not determine, the existence of evil; religion is primarily the intellectual assent to self-evident principles of ethics; and salvation is dependent upon the faith within the reach of all men.

In order to understand Chauncy's idea of a Benevolent God it is first necessary to understand his concept of the nature of man: "There are two grand principles in human nature, self-love and benevolence, the former determining us to private, and the

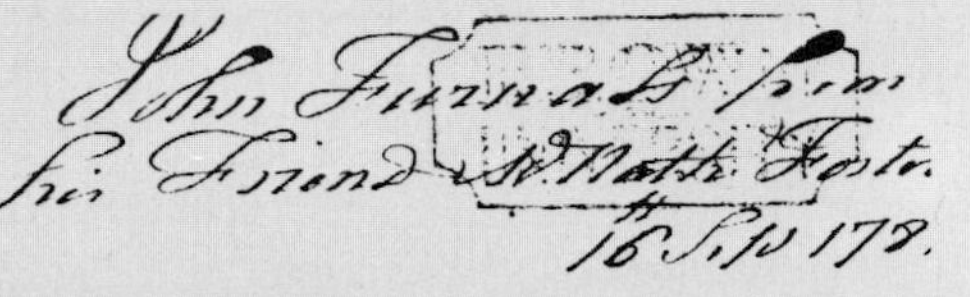

THE BENEVOLENCE
OF THE DEITY,
FAIRLY AND IMPARTIALLY
CONSIDERED.
IN THREE PARTS.

The firſt explains the ſenſe, in which we are to underſtand Benevolence, as applicable to GOD.

The ſecond aſſerts, and proves, that this perfection, in the ſenſe explained, is one of his eſſential attributes.

The third endeavours to anſwer objections.

Under one or other of theſe heads, occaſion will be taken to view man as an *intelligent moral agent*; having within himſelf an *ability* and *freedom* to WILL, as well as to *do*, in oppoſition to NECESSITY from any extraneous cauſe whatever:—To point out the ORIGIN OF EVIL, both *natural* and *moral*:—And to offer what may be thought ſufficient to ſhew, that there is no *inconſiſtency* between *infinite benevolence* in the Deity, which is always guided by *infinite wiſdom*, and any *appearances of* evil in the creation.

BY CHARLES CHAUNCY, D. D.
SENIOR PASTOR OF THE FIRST CHURCH OF
CHRIST IN BOSTON.

AMERICA: MASSACHUSETTS;
BOSTON: PRINTED BY POWARS & WILLIS.
MDCCLXXXIV.

The Myſtery hid from Ages and Generations, made manifeſt by the Goſpel-Revelation:

OR,

THE SALVATION
OF
ALL MEN
THE GRAND THING AIMED AT IN THE SCHEME OF GOD,

As opened in the New-Teſtament Writings, and entruſted with JESUS CHRIST to bring into Effect.

IN THREE CHAPTERS.

The Firſt, exhibiting a GENERAL EXPLANATION of this glorioſly benevolent Plan of GOD.——*The Second*, proving it to be the TRUTH OF SCRIPTURE, that MANKIND UNIVERSALLY, in the FINAL ISSUE of this Scheme, ſhall REIGN IN HAPPY LIFE FOR EVER.——*The Third*, largely anſwering OBJECTIONS.

By *One who wiſhes well to the whole Human Race.*

Charles Chauncy, D.D.

Ωσπερ εβασιλευσεν η αμαρτια εν τω θανατω ουτω και η χαρις βασιλευση δια δικαιοσυνης εις ζωην αιωνιον, δια Ιησου Χριστου του Κυριου ημων. Apoſtle *Paul*.

LONDON:
PRINTED FOR CHARLES DILLY, IN THE POULTRY.
M.DCC.LXXXIV.

FIVE
DISSERTATIONS
ON THE
SCRIPTURE ACCOUNT
OF THE
FALL; AND ITS CONSEQUENCES.

BY

CHARLES CHAUNCY, D. D.
Miniſter of the Firſt Church in BOSTON, NEW ENGLAND.

LONDON:
PRINTED FOR C. DILLY, IN THE POULTRY.
MDCCLXXXV.

Title pages for the works that form the cornerstone of Chauncy's theology, a system that is heavily indebted to John Locke and the Scottish Common Sense Philosophers (John Carter Brown Library, Brown University) latter to public good." Self-love is a calm and dispassionate principle employed by man for his self-preservation. Benevolence is "that quality of the human mind, without which we could not be the objects of one another's esteem. . . ." This quality of benevolence is exercised within the bounds of Right Reason and directed by wisdom for the "disposing and promoting to the communication of human happiness." Where Edwards defined benevolence as "consent, propensity, and union of heart to Being in General," Chauncy preferred to see it as "a certain state of mind inclining man to pursue pleasure, both for his own private good, and the good of others." Our powers of intelligence and volition qualify us to "discern what will conduce to these ends." Chauncy never entertains the idea of moral ambiguity; as a matter of fact, he states, "There is such a thing as eternal and immutable truth." Objective truth is discovered through "the first power in our nature (call it common sense, moral discernment, moral sense, or give it any other name that may be thought better)." This power enables us "at once, without the labor of a long train of reasoning, to distinguish between moral good and moral evil. . . ." Only idiots and madmen are exempt. Given this definition of man, one need only "remove from his ideas, even of a good man, all frailties and defects, and add to it boundless perfection in mode and degree," and he shall "entertain just thoughts of the Divine Benevolence."

Chauncy did not hesitate to compare God to man; in fact, he believed this analogy the only proper method of instruction: "When I speak of goodness as a natural disposition in the Deity," Chauncy said, "I would be understood to mean a certain state of mind, call it inclination, propension, disposition, or whatever else may be thought proper, analogous to what is signified by a benevolent disposition in men. . . . 'Tis natural to us, one of the principles implanted in our original frame." The only difference between God and man is that God is benevolent to the greatest degree, manner, and proportion. God dispenses this goodness through "the established course of nature." Increase Mather saw God as a prime mover and first cause, actively involved in the daily events as well as "Illustrious Providences" of life, but Chauncy's God was a Divine Administrator who worked through the "general plan, constitution, or system" of a Newtonian universe.

Chauncy accused his opponents of constructing a system which encourages fatalism, which views God as a malevolent and arbitrary despot, which releases man from moral obligation and makes him an irrational victim of emotional impulses. Determinism, Chauncy felt, is a system of mechanized gloom in which "virtue and vice are idle names," praise and blame are "vulgar notions," God is reduced to "a vain imagination," and religion only serves the purposes of "politicians and priests."

Given Chauncy's view of the nature of God and man, his next logical step was the elimination of the doctrine of election. In *Five Dissertations on the Scripture Account of the Fall. . .* , Chauncy sees election as that horrendous scheme whereby wailing infants are dashed into the pit: "What! make them first open their eyes in torments; and all this for a sin which they certainly had no hand in. . . ." Strict Calvinists endeavored to visualize election from God's point of view. To them God was benevolent because he freely saved some undeserving few even though they could not, on their own, live up to the demands of the law. For Chauncy, "our being free moral agents is that which not only makes us living images of the Deity . . . but capable participants . . . of that happiness which is the highest." Chauncy looked upon predestination from a single point of view and concluded that "A more shocking idea can scarce be given to the Deity than that which represents him as arbitrarily dooming the greater part of the race of men to eternal misery."

Chauncy preferred to believe that God, as a more rational and systematic Being, would devise a plan in which the righteous, temperate, and disciplined would, through the redemptive acts of Christ, eventually be rewarded with everlasting happiness. Although Chauncy's system, completely outlined in his 406-page treatise called *The Mystery hid from Ages and Generations. . .* , represents a radical break from the Calvinism of his ancestors, it does not eliminate the prospects of hell, nor does it hold out the possibility of salvation without faith and good works. Repentant sinners, argued Chauncy, must first undergo excruciating pains in the bottomless pit for an indeterminate period in order to be purged of their sins and qualified to receive the fruits of heavenly reward. Chauncy's theory of Universal Salvation, simply called Universalism, rested upon the belief that because Christ had atoned for the sins of the world, the divine will is such that all men be saved. Arbitrary predestination thwarts Christ's mediatorial sacrifice and illogically contradicts God's will. In works which appeared earlier than *The Mystery hid from Ages and Generations . . .* Chauncy had skillfully laid the foundation for these radical ideas. In several of his *Twelve Sermons . . .* (1765), for example, he had ingeniously devised a scheme whereby observation of the law (works) became the tool to obtain faith, the absolutely essential qualification for justification, or salvation. Couched in the familiar Puritan language of type (works) and antitype (faith), this answer anticipated the objections of those who would later see Universalism as salvation by merit or works, in other words, as Catholicism.

Had Charles Chauncy's active life ceased with his involvement in the debates about the Great Awakening, historians could fairly portray him as Edwards's foil. However, Edward M. Griffin reminds us in the only full-length biography of "Old Brick" Chauncy, that this physically frail minister played an important role in almost all of the major events of his time, including the French and Indian Wars, the controversy over the proposed establishment of an Anglican Episcopacy in America, the rise of the enlightenment, the opposition to the Stamp Act, the strategies of the Revolution, and the beginnings of Unitarianism. It seems not unreasonable to assert that Charles Chauncy was, after Franklin and Edwards, one of the most representative men of the eighteenth century in America. The fact that cultural historians have not given him adequate credit is perhaps due to a general distaste for the neoclassical writers and thinkers. The period between the death of Edwards and the emergence of Ralph Waldo Emerson, with several notable exceptions, of course, has been slighted if not ignored in this century. When considered at all, Chauncy has been usually pictured as either the villain or the bore, but he deserves the more sensible treatment accorded to him by Griffin: Chauncy was, says Griffin, "a man whose importance transcended that of spokesman for the opposition in the Great Awakening or antagonist to Jonathan Edwards. He was a significant figure in his own right. His story was in many ways the story of eighteenth-century America. It deserves to be told."

Charles Chauncy, circa 1786 (Massachusetts Historical Society)

Biography:

Edward M. Griffin, *Old Brick: Charles Chauncy of Boston, 1705-1787* (Minneapolis: University of Minnesota Press, 1980).

References:

Francis A. Christi, "The Beginnings of Arminianism in America," *Papers of the American Society of Church History*, second series 3 (1912);

William Chauncey Fowler, *Memorials of the Chaunceys* (Boston: Henry Dutton, 1858);

Edwin Scott Gaustad, "Charles Chauncy and the Great Awakening: A Survey and Bibliography," *Papers of the Bibliographical Society of America*, 45 (Second Quarter): 125-135;

Gaustad, *The Great Awakening in New England* (New York: Harper, 1957);

C. C. Goen, ed., *Jonathan Edwards: The Great Awakening*, volume 4 of *The Works of Jonathan Edwards*, edited by John E. Smith (New Haven & London: Yale University Press, 1972);

Alan Heimert and Perry Miller, eds., *The Great Awakening* (New York: Bobbs-Merrill, 1967);

Clifford K. Shipton, *Sibley's Harvard Graduates: Biographical Sketches of Those Who Attended Harvard College*, volume 6 (Boston: Massachusetts Historical Society, 1942), pp. 569-571;

William B. Sprague, *Annals of the American Unitarian Pulpit* (New York: Carter, 1865).

Papers:

The American Antiquarian Society, the Boston Public Library, the Massachusetts Historical Society, the New York Public Library, and the Yale University library have collections of Chauncy's papers.

Ezekiel Cheever

(25 January 1615-21 August 1708)

Wesley T. Mott
University of Wisconsin

BOOKS: *A Short Introduction to the Latin Tongue, For the Use of the Lower Forms in the Latin School. Being the Accidence Abbridg'd and Compiled* ... (Boston: Printed by B. Green for Benj. Eliot, 1709);

Scripture Prophecies Explained ... (Boston: Printed by Green & Russell, 1757).

Ezekiel Cheever, the most influential schoolmaster in early New England, was born in London and educated at Christ's Hospital and Emmanuel College, Cambridge. He came to Boston in 1637 but soon moved on as one of the founders of the New Haven colony. There in 1639 he opened a school in his home, where his pupils included the future Puritan poet Michael Wigglesworth. Cheever also served as deputy to the General Court and preached occasionally. But when he charged the elders of his church with usurping the congregation's authority, he was tried and censured by the church (1649). Cheever responded with staunch conviction: "I had rather suffer any thing from men, than make shipwreck of a good conscience, or go against my present light though erroneous, when it is not discovered."

While at New Haven, it is believed, Cheever wrote his extraordinarily popular *A Short Introduction to the Latin Tongue* . . . (1709). Commonly known as the *Accidence*, it was a standard text in American schools into the eighteenth century; an edition of the *Accidence* was published as late as 1806. Cheever also wrote *Scripture Prophecies Explained* . . . (1757), three concise essays stressing his millennial beliefs. The world, he declared, will not be "annihilated" but "perfected," as the saints enjoy "bodily resurrection." And Christ will "personally" return a thousand years "before the general judgment" to establish an "outward glorious visible kingdom."

About 1650 Cheever moved back to the Massachusetts Bay Colony, serving as schoolmaster at Ipswich (1650-1661), Charlestown (1661-1670), and the Boston Latin School (1671-1708). Each town where he taught sent a disproportionately large number of students to Harvard College. His friend Judge Samuel Sewall wrote on the day Cheever died that he had "Labour'd . . . Skillfully, diligently, constantly, Religiously, Seventy years. A rare Instance of Piety, Health, Strength, Serviceableness." And Cotton Mather, a former pupil of Cheever's, preached the funeral sermon for this "*Master in our Israel*," emphasizing that Cheever yoked learning to piety: "The *Bible* is the Sacred *Grammar*, where / The *Rules of speaking well*, contained are. / He taught us *Lilly*, and he *Gospel* taught; / And us poor Children to our *Saviour* brought." Cheever "us from *Virgil* did to *David* train," for "Who Serv'd the *School*, the *Church* did not forget." As teacher of countless New England leaders and through his *Accidence*, Cheever exerted a profound impact on early American verse and rhetoric.

Other:

"The Trial of Ezekiel Cheever before the Church at New Haven [1649]," attributed to Cheever, Connecticut Historical Society *Collections*, 1 (1860): 22-51.

References:

Elizabeth Porter Gould, *Ezekiel Cheever: Schoolmaster* (Boston: Palmer, 1904);

John T. Hassam, "Ezekiel Cheever," *New-England Historical and Genealogical Register*, 57 (January 1903): 40-50;

Hassam, "Ezekiel Cheever and Some of His Descendants," *New-England Historical and Genealogical Register*, 33 (April 1879): 164-202.

Cadwallader Colden

(7 February 1688-28 September 1776)

Frank Shuffelton
University of Rochester

BOOKS: *The Interest of the Country in Laying Duties . . .*, attributed to Colden (New York: Sold by J. Peter Zenger, 1726);

The History of the Five Indian Nations Depending on the Province of New York (New York: Printed & sold by William Bradford, 1727; expanded edition, London: Printed for Thomas Osborne, 1747);

An Explication of the First Causes of Action in Matter; and of the Cause of Gravitation (New York: Printed by J. Parker, 1745; London: Printed for J. Brindley, 1746); revised as *The Principles of Action in Matter* (London: Printed for R. Dodsley, 1751);

The Conduct of Cadwallader Colden, Esquire, Lieutenant Governor of New-York; Relating to the Judges' Commissions,—Appeals to the King,—And the Stamp-Duty, attributed to Colden (London, 1767; New York: Printed by James Parker?, 1767).

Portrait by John Wollaston, Jr., circa 1749-1752 (Metropolitan Museum of Art)

Cadwallader Colden was one of the many young Scottish doctors, merchants, lawyers, and ministers who sought their fortunes in eighteenth-century America; by the time of his death at the age of eighty-eight he had played a prominent role in the government of colonial New York, had accumulated a comfortable estate, and had become a member of the international scientific community as well as one of early America's leading scientists. An industrious writer, he left behind papers that eventually would fill nine volumes of the collections of the New York Historical Society, but his chief claim to literary remembrance rests on his authorship of the first full-length history in English of the Iroquois or Five Nations.

The son of a Berwickshire clergyman, he was himself sent to the University of Edinburgh to be educated for the ministry, but he decided to become a physician instead and after his graduation in 1705 studied medicine in London. In 1710 he followed the suggestion of an aunt and moved to Philadelphia, where he practiced medicine but also branched out as a merchant of sorts, sending cargoes to the Southern colonies and the West Indies. He made a brief return to Scotland in 1715 where he married Alice Christie on 11 November 1715, but from soon after the time of his return to Philadelphia his life and reputation were linked to the New World. He had already begun the prolific occasional writing which he would continue to pursue, and he had begun to have articles on his scientific interests published in journals. During Colden's visit home he had met the astronomer Edmund Halley and had had a paper on "Animal Secretions" read at a meeting of the Royal Society. But the turning point of his life came on a visit to New York in 1718 when he met Governor Robert Hunter, a Scotsman like himself and author of a satiric play on New York politics. Impressed with Colden's talents, Hunter persuaded him to move to New York after promising him the offices of master in chancery and surveyor-general of the colony. Thus began a fifty-eight-year career which included membership on the Governor's Council and service as lieutenant-governor during some of the colony's most difficult years.

Colden's scientific interests were encouraged by Hunter's successor, William Burnet, and his office as surveyor-general took him among the native American tribes, particularly the Mohawks, whom he came especially to admire. After the funds promised to support his compilation of a catalogue of New York plants and animals dried up in the 1720s, Colden decided to write his *The History of the Five Indian Nations Depending on the Province of New York* (1727), returning to complete a botanical catalogue over a decade later. His history of the Iroquois relies on the earlier narratives of Baron de Lahontan (*Nouveaux Voyages . . . dans l Amérique Septentrionale,* 1703) and Claude Charles Bacquevillê de la Potherie (*Histoire de l'Amérique Septentrionale,* 1722), undertaking to correct the biases of the French writers who until then had been the Europeans' main source of knowledge concerning the remarkable confederacy of the Five Nations. In the first edition of 1727, Colden begins his account with the first European contacts and carries it down to 1688, adding in the 1747 edition a second part which describes events up to the Treaty of Ryswyck, which ended King William's War (1689-1697). Inspired in part by his wide-ranging curiosity, Colden's *The History of the Five Indian Nations* is more specifically motivated by the political, economic, and military problems of New York in the 1720s; a staple of the colonial economy was the fur trade in which the most powerful New York families had a heavy stake. When the traders discovered it was more profitable to deal with the French and their Indian allies than with the Iroquois, even during wartime, relations with the Five Nations were seriously jeopardized; Colden wished to demonstrate the crucial role the Iroquois played and could play in defending New York against the expansion of the French empire in North America. Accordingly, he stresses the Iroquois' courage and loyalty, their essential nobility, and their military and diplomatic genius.

Colden never learned much of the native language, and his inability to find and keep a skilled interpreter prevented him from learning as much about the Five Nations' culture as he would have liked; this ethnographic element is conspicuously missing from the history beyond a brief comment or two, but Colden's duties as one of the frequent envoys to the Iroquois enabled him to give copious examples of their treaty-making procedures and to analyze their political behavior. His inclusion of numerous speeches by Iroquois chiefs makes the history important, among other reasons, as an exemplary collection of Indian oratory, but Colden's ulterior motive in preserving Indian public speaking is to strengthen his favorite comparison of the Iroquois to the classical, republican Romans.

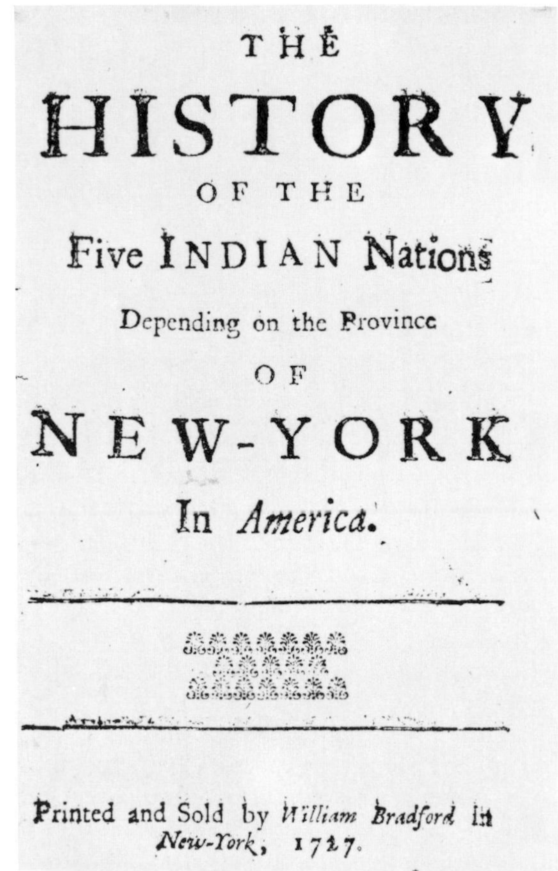
THE HISTORY OF THE Five INDIAN Nations Depending on the Province OF NEW-YORK In America.

Printed and Sold by William Bradford in New-York, 1727.

Title page for Colden's history of the Iroquois nations, in which he compares them favorably to the classical Roman republic (John Carter Brown Library, Brown University)

As Richard Slotkin has pointed out, Colden's book "offered an image of the Indian shaped by the new scientific thought of both Europe and America," a body of thought that included Lockean political and social theory and Shaftesburian ethics. Colden echoes Locke's claim that in the beginning all was America, saying that if we wish "to know the Manners of our Earliest Progenitors: if I be not mistaken, the Indians are living Images of them."

Furthermore, he contends, "here we may with more certainty see the Original Form of all Government, . . . and that the Patriarchal, and other Schemes in Politicks are no better than hypotheses in Philosophy," for "Each Nation is an absolute Republick." Thus Colden's Five Nations are cast in the mold of republican behavior exemplified for Europeans by republican Rome. If they are admittedly "a poor Barbarous People," a "bright and Noble Genius shines thro' " their barbarity; "None of the greatest Roman Hero's have discovered a greater love to their Country, or a greater Contempt of death." Decanesora, their greatest speaker, "was tall and well made, and his Features, to my thinking," says Colden, "resembled much the Bustos of Cicero." These "faithful Friends" to the British nation have, however, sullied their stoic and republican virtue "by that cruel Passion Revenge," but if the English could but "plant in them, and cultivate that general Benevolence to Mankind, which is the true Principle of Vertue," the Five Nations might become the equals of the Greeks and Romans.

If Colden presents the Iroquois as a justification of the Lockean thesis on the origins of political order, he also uses them as a norm to criticize New York's Anglo-Dutch culture and its short-sighted pursuit of mere pecuniary gain. Both the governors and the people of New York have been too often ruled by "their Passion for Money," and as a public official and private citizen Colden seldom missed a chance to criticize their selfishness and lack of public spirit. A "general Benevolence to Mankind" he felt to be at times as remote from the political life of New York as it was from the foreign policy of the Five Nations, and he advised governors, chided his neighbors, and complained to his friends in a stream of letters and reports, mostly unpublished at the time of his death. If he was a political force, his political writings had little effect, partly because of the antagonism his personality generated in others, partly because he was not a terribly effective polemical writer. Colden's interests reflected the wide-ranging amateurishness of the virtuoso, his vanity made him constantly sensitive to perceived insults and rebuffs, and his self-righteous pomposity never attracted a wide circle of admirers. His writings on political and social issues are accordingly diffuse, defensive, and slightly patronizing, products of a Scots carpetbagger who is often right but seemingly never appreciated. The letters that fill the New York Historical Society's collections of his papers offer modern readers valuable comments and records of New York's colonial political life, but in their own times they were of little value in giving it definition or direction.

In addition to his political activity and his historical writing, Colden made an impression on the scientific world of his day and is still remembered as an important scientific figure in the colonies. He maintained his interest in medicine, publishing essays on Bishop Berkeley's tar water, the "Iliac Passion," yellow fever, and pokeweed as a cancer cure, but he was most respected as a botanist. A correspondent with Linnaeus, Gronovius, Peter Collinson, and American botanists such as John Bartram and Alexander Garden, Colden saw his "*Plantae Coldenghamiae in provincia Novaboracensi Americes sponte crescentes*," published in 1749 and 1751 by Linnaeus in the *Acta Regiae Societatis Scientiarum Upsaliensis*, and his training of his daughter Jane gained her respect in her own right as a botanist from the likes of Garden and Collinson. But it is typical of Colden's misdirection of his talents that he abandoned botany, turned to physics, and set out to correct Newton, claiming "to have discover'd the Cause of Generation." His *An Explication of the First Causes of Action in Matter* (1745; revised in 1751 as *The Principles of Action in Matter*) betrayed his ignorance of advanced mathematics and of the work of Huygens, Leibniz, the Bernouillis, and Euler. As Brook Hindle has observed, "The initial reaction to Colden's theory was one of bewilderment," and either bewilderment or flat rejection continued to be the response. Colden never gave up trying to promote his theory and deposited his last manuscript revision in the University of Edinburgh Library, hoping for some future vindication. The vindication never came, and when Colden died in 1776, the meaning of his long and loyal career as a servant of the Crown in New York was in the process of being rejected by a newly independent state. But it was not until the mid-nineteenth century that the work of Henry R. Schoolcraft and, most notably, Lewis Henry Morgan superseded his *The History of the Five Indian Nations . . .* with more authoritative accounts of the Iroquois, and Colden's history remains a valuable piece of colonial writing on the native Americans.

Other:

"A Memorial Concerning the Furr-Trade of New-York," in *Papers Relating to An Act of the Assembly of the Province of New York, for Encourage-ment of the Indian Trade, &c., And for Prohibiting the Selling of Indian Goods to the French. . . ,* probably compiled by Colden

(New York: Printed & sold by William Bradford, 1724);

"Plantae Coldenghamiae in provincia Noveboracensi Americes sponte crescentes," in *Acta Regiae Societatis Scientiarum Upsaliensis,* 4 (1749): 81-136; 5 (1751): 47-82.

Letters:

"Letters on Smith's History of New York," *Collections of the Historical Society of New York,* 1 (1868): 177-235; 2 (1869): 203-212;

The Colden Letter Books, Collections of the New York Historical Society, 9-10 (1876-1877);

The Letters and Papers of Cadwallader Colden, Collections of the New York Historical Society, 50-56 (1917-1923); 67-68 (1934-1935).

References:

Louis Leonard Gitin, "Cadwallader Colden as Scientist and Philosopher," *New York History,* 16 (1935): 166-177;

Brooke Hindle, "Cadwallader Colden's Extension of Newtonian Principles," *William and Mary Quarterly,* third series 13 (October 1956): 459-475;

Hindle, "A Colonial Governor's Family: The Coldens of Coldengham," *New York Historical Society Quarterly,* 45 (July 1961): 233-250;

Alfred R. Hoermann, "Cadwallader Colden and the Mind-Body Problem," *Bulletin of the History of Medicine,* 50 (1976): 392-404;

Hoermann, "A Savant in the Wilderness: Cadwallader Colden," *New York Historical Society Quarterly,* 62 (October 1978): 270-288;

Alice Maplesden Keys, *Cadwallader Colden; A Representative Eighteenth-Century Official* (New York: Columbia University Press, 1906);

Roy N. Lokken, "Cadwallader Colden's Attempt to Advance Natural Philosophy Beyond the Eighteenth-Century Mechanistic Paradigm," *Proceedings of the American Philosophical Society,* 122 (December 1978): 365-376;

Richard Slotkin, *Regeneration Through Violence: The Mythology of the American Frontier* (Middletown, Conn.: Wesleyan University Press, 1973), pp. 199-202;

Raymond Phineas Stearns, *Science in the British Colonies of America* (Urbana: University of Illinois Press, 1970), pp. 559-575;

A. J. Wall, "Cadwallader Colden and His Homestead at Spring Hill, Flushing, Long Island," *New York Historical Society Quarterly,* 8 (April 1924): 11-20.

Papers:

The New York Historical Society Library has the largest collection of Colden's papers.

Benjamin Colman

(19 October 1673-28 August 1747)

Wyn Kelley
Stanford University

SELECTED BOOKS: *Faith Victorious. As It Was Represented in a Sermon Preached to the Honorable Artillery Company in Boston . . .* (Boston: Printed by B. Green & J. Allen for Samuel Sewall, Jr., 1702);

The Government and Improvement of Mirth, According to the Laws of Christianity . . . (Boston: Printed by B. Green for Samuel Phillips, 1707);

Imprecation Against the Enemies of God . . . (Boston: Printed by B. Green for Nicholas Boone, 1707);

Practical Discourses upon the Parable of the Ten Virgins (London: Printed for Thomas Parkhurst 1707; Boston: Printed & sold by Rogers & Fowle & by J. Edwards, 1747);

A Poem on Elijah's Translation, Occasion'd by the Death of the Reverend and Learned Mr. Samuel Willard . . . (Boston: Printed by B. Green for Benj. Eliot, 1707);

The Piety and Duty of Rulers to Comfort and Encourage the Ministry of Christ . . . (Boston: Printed by B. Green, sold by Benj. Eliot, 1708);

A Sermon Preached Before the Governor and

Council on July 22d, 1708: Being the Day of the Proclamation of the Happy Union of the Two Kingdoms of England and Scotland (Boston: Printed by B. Green, sold by Benj. Eliot, 1708);

The Duty and Honour of Aged Women, A Sermon on the Death of Madam Abigail Foster (Boston: Printed by B. Green for Joanna Perry, 1711);

The Hainous Nature of the Sin of Murder . . . (Boston: Printed by John Allen, 1713);

A Devout Contemplation on the Meaning of Divine Providence in the Early Death of Pious and Lovely Children . . . (Boston: Printed by John Allen for Joanna Perry, 1714);

A Devout and Humble Enquiry Into the Reasons of the Divine Council in the Death of Good Men . . . (Boston: Printed by T. Fleet & T. Crump for Samuel Gerrish, Daniel Henchman & Benjamin Gray, 1715);

A Gospel Ministry the Rich Gift of the Ascended Savior Unto His Church . . . (Boston: Printed by T. Fleet & T. Crump for Samuel Gerrish, 1715);

A Holy & Useful Life Recommended from the Happy End of It. A Sermon Preach'd upon the Death of the Honourable and Truly Vertuous Isaac Addington . . . (Boston: Printed by B. Green for Benj. Eliot, 1715);

A Humble Discourse of the Incomprehensibleness of God . . . (Boston: Printed by B. Green for Samuel Gerrish, 1715);

Some of the Honours that Religion Does Unto the Fruitful Mothers in Israel . . . (Boston: Printed by B. Green for Samuel Gerrish, 1715);

A Brief Enquiry into the Reasons Why the People of God Have Been Wont to Bring into Their Penitential Confessions, The Sins of Their Fathers and Ancestors (Boston: Printed by T. Fleet & T. Crump for Samuel Gerrish, 1716);

The Honour and Happiness of the Vertuous Woman . . . (Boston: Printed by B. Green, 1716);

A Sermon for the Reformation of Manners . . . (Boston: Printed by T. Fleet & T. Crump for Samuel Gerrish, 1716);

A Sermon Preach'd at Boston in New-England: On Thursday the 23d of August 1716. Being the Day of Publick Thanksgiving for the Suppression of the Late Vile and Traitorous Rebellion in Great Britain (Boston: Printed by T. Fleet & T. Crump, sold by Samuel Gerrish, 1716);

A Sermon Preach'd at the Ordination of Mr. William Cooper . . . (Boston: Printed by B. Green for Samuel Gerrish & Daniel Henchman, 1716);

Four Sermons Preached at the Lecture in Boston . . . (Boston: Printed by B. Green for S. Gerrish & D. Henchman, 1717);

A Holy Walk with God. Funeral Sermon Preached Upon the Death of the Truly Vertuous and Religious Grove Hirst . . . (Boston: Printed by B. Green, 1717);

Industry and Diligence in the Work of Religion: A Sermon Preached in Boston, after the Funerals of . . . The Reverend Mr. William Brattle, . . . and the Reverend Mr. Ebenezer Pemberton (Boston: Printed by B. Green for Samuel Gerrish & Daniel Henchman, 1717);

The Rending of the Vail of the Temple at the Crucifixion . . . (Boston: Printed & sold by B. Green, 1717);

The Religious Regards We Owe to Our Country . . . (Boston: Printed by B. Green, 1718);

The Blessing of Zebulun & Issachar . . . (Boston: Printed by B. Green for Samuel Gerrish, 1719);

Some Reasons and Arguments Offered to the Good People of Boston, and Adjacent Places, for the Setting Up of Markets in Boston (Boston: Printed by J. Franklin for S. Gerrish & J. Edwards, 1719);

Early Piety again Inculcated . . . (Boston: Printed by S. Kneeland for D. Henchman & J. Edwards, 1720);

Ossa Josephi, Or, The Bones of Joseph. Consider'd

in a Sermon Preached at the Lecture in Boston, After the Funeral of the very Honourable and Excellent Joseph Dudley (Boston: Printed by B. Green for Benj. Eliot, 1720);

The Hope of the Righteous in their Death. A Sermon Preached on the Lord's-Day after the Funeral of William Harris . . . (Boston: Printed by S. Kneeland, 1721);

Some Observations on the New Method of Receiving the Small-Pox by Ingrafting or Inoculation . . . (Boston: Printed by B. Green for Samuel Gerrish, 1721);

A Discourse Had in the College-Hall at Cambridge, March 27, 1722. Before the Baptism of Rabbi Judah Monis . . . (Boston: Printed by S. Kneeland for Daniel Henchman, 1722);

Jacob's Vow Upon His Leaving His Father's House (Boston: Printed by James Franklin, 1722);

A Blameless & Inoffensive Life. A Sermon after the Funeral of David Stoddard . . . (Boston: Printed by B. Green, 1723);

David's Dying Charge to the Rulers and People of Israel . . . (Boston: Printed by B. Green, 1723);

The Death of God's Saints Precious in His Sight. A Sermon on the Death of Mrs. Jane Steel (Boston: Printed by B. Green, 1723);

God Deals With Us as Rational Creatures . . . (Boston: Printed by B. Green for D. Henchman, 1723);

The Prophet's Death; Lamented and Improved in a Sermon Preached September 1, 1723, to the North Church in Boston, on the Lord's Day, after the Funeral of Their Venerable and Aged Pastor Increase Mather . . . (Boston: Printed by T. Fleet for Nath. Belknap, 1723);

God's Concern for a Godly Seed. Two Sermons Preached in Boston, March 5, 1723 . . ., by Colman and William Cooper (Boston: Printed by S. Kneeland for J. Edwards, 1723);

The Master Taken Up from the Sons of the Prophets. A Sermon Preached at Cambridge Upon the Sudden Death of the Reverend & Learned John Leverett, President of Harvard College (Boston: Printed for Samuel Gerrish, 1724);

The Doctrine and the Law of the Holy Sabbath . . . (Boston: Printed by T. Fleet for Thomas Hancock, 1725);

It is a Fearful Thing to Fall into the Hands of the Living God. A Sermon Preached to Some Miserable Pirates July 10, 1726. On the Lord's Day Before Their Execution (Boston: Printed for John Phillips & Thomas Hancock, 1726);

Fidelity to Christ and to the Protestant Succession in the Illustrious House of Hanover . . . (Boston: Printed by T. Fleet for T. Hancock, 1727);

The Judgment of Providence in the Hand of Christ: His Voice to Us in the Terrible Earthquake . . . (Boston: Printed for J. Phillips & T. Hancock, 1727);

Parents and Grown Children Should Be Together at the Lord's Table . . . (Boston: Printed for S. Gerrish, 1727);

Prayer to the Lord of the Harvest for the Mission of Labourers into His Harvest. A Sermon Preached in the Old South Meeting-house in Boston, August 9. 1927. At the Ordination of the Reverend Ebenezer Pemberton . . . (Boston: Printed by Gamaliel Rogers for Daniel Henchman, 1727);

An Argument for, and Persuasive Unto the Great and Important Duty of Family Worship (Boston: Printed by Gemaliel Rogers for Thomas Hancock, 1728);

Death and the Grave Without Any Order. A Sermon Preached July 7. 1728. Being the Lord's Day after a Tragical Duel and Most Lamented Death (Boston: Printed for John Phillips & Thomas Hancock, 1728);

The Duty of Young People to Give Their Hearts Unto God . . . (Boston: Printed for D. Henchman & T. Hancock, 1728);

The Holy Walk and Glorious Translation of Blessed Enoch. A Sermon Preached at the Lecture in Boston, Two Days After the Death of the Reverend and Learned Cotton Mather . . . (Boston: Printed for J. Phillips & T. Hancock, 1728);

Some of the Glories of our Lord and Saviour Jesus Christ (London: Printed by S. Palmer for Thomas Hancock in Boston & for F. Osborne, T. Longman, R. Ford & T. Cox in London, 1728);

The Credibility of the Christian Doctrine of the Resurrection . . . (Boston: Printed for Thomas Hancock, 1729);

The Faithful Ministers of Christ Mindful of Their Own Death. A Sermon Preached at the Lecture in Boston; Upon the Death of the Learned and Venerable Solomon Stoddard . . . (Boston: Printed for D. Henchman, John Phillips & T. Hancock, 1729);

Dying in Peace in a Good Old Age. A Sermon Preach'd the Lord's-Day after the Funeral of the Honorable and Aged Simeon Stoddard . . . (Boston: Printed by S. Kneeland & T. Green for J. Phillips, 1730);

Government the Pillar of the Earth . . . (Boston: Printed for T. Hancock, 1730);

Narrative of the Success and Method of Inoculating the Small Pox in New-England . . . (Boston: Printed for S. Gerrish & D. Henchman, 1730);

The Friend of Christ, and of His People. A Sermon Preached at the Lecture in Boston, April 1, 1731. Before His Excellency the Governour and the General Court: Upon the News of the Death of the Much Honoured Thomas Hollis (Boston: Printed by B. Green for T. Hancock, 1731);

Ministers and People Under Special Obligations to Sanctity, Humility & Gratitude . . . (Boston: Printed by S. Kneeland & T. Green for S. Gerrish, 1732);

God is a Great King . . . (Boston: Printed by S. Kneeland & T. Green for T. Hancock, 1733);

The Fast Which God Hath Chosen . . . (Boston: Printed & sold by S. Kneeland & T. Green, 1734);

A Brief Dissertation on the Three First Chapters of Genesis . . . (Boston: Printed by S. Kneeland & T. Green for J. Edwards & H. Foster, 1735);

Reliquiae Turellae et Lachrymae Paternae . . . The Father's Tears over his Daughter's Remains (Boston: Printed by S. Kneeland & T. Green for J. Edwards & H. Foster, 1735);

A Dissertation on the Image of God Wherein Man Was Created . . . (Boston: Printed & sold by S. Kneeland & T. Green, 1736);

The Merchandise of a People Holiness to the Lord . . . (Boston: Printed by J. Draper, 1736);

The Peaceful End of a Perfect and Upright Life Remark'd and Contemplated in a Sermon after the Death of the Universally Esteemed Thomas Steel . . . (Boston: Printed by S. Kneeland & T. Green, 1736);

Righteousness and Compassion the Duty and Character of Pious Rulers . . . (Boston: Printed by J. Draper for D. Henchman, 1736);

The Great Duty of Waiting on God in Our Straits & Difficulties . . . (Boston: Printed by J. Draper for J. Edwards & H. Foster, 1737);

It is of the Lord's Mercies that We Are Not Consumed . . . (Boston: Printed by J. Draper for J. Edwards & H. Foster, 1737);

Christ Standing for an Ensign of the People . . . (Boston: Printed by J. Draper for J. Edwards & S. Eliot, 1738);

Faithful Pastors Angels of the Churches. A Sermon Preached to the Bereaved Flock, March 4, 1739. On the Lord's-Day after the Funeral of the Rev. Mr. Peter Thacher . . . (Boston: Printed by J. Draper for D. Henchman & S. Eliot, 1739);

The Unspeakable Gift of God . . . (Boston: Printed by J. Draper for H. Foster, 1739);

The Wither'd Hand Stretched Forth at the Command of Christ, and Restored . . . (Boston: Printed by J. Draper for J. Edwards, 1739);

The Faithful Servant in the Joy of His Lord. A Funeral Sermon on the Death of the Honorable Samuel Holden . . . (Boston: Printed by J. Draper for D. Henchman, 1740);

Souls Flying to Christ Pleasant and Admirable to Behold . . . (Boston: Printed by G. Rogers & D. Fowle for J. Edwards & S. Eliot, 1740);

The Lord Shall Rejoice in His Works . . . (Boston: Printed by J. Draper, 1741);

The Great God Has Magnified His Word to the Children of Men . . . (Boston: Printed by T. Fleet for D. Henchman, 1742);

The Declaration of a Number of Associated Pastors of Boston and Charles-Town Relating to the Rev. Mr. Davenport, and His Conduct (Boston: Printed & sold by S. Kneeland & T. Green, 1742);

The Glory of God in the Firmament of His Power . . . (Boston: Printed & sold by S. Kneeland & T. Green, 1743);

The Case of Satan's Fiery Darts in Blasphemous Suggestions and Hellish Annoyances . . . (Boston: Printed by Rogers & Fowle for J. Edwards, 1744);

Jesus Weeping Over his Dead Friend, and With His Friends in Their Mourning. A Sermon Preached the Lord's Day after the Funeral of the Reverend Mr. William Cooper . . . (Boston: Printed by Rogers & Fowle for J. Edwards, 1744);

One Chosen of God and Called to the Work of the Ministry, Willingly Offering Himself. A Sermon Preached at the Ordination of the Reverend Mr. Samuel Cooper . . . (Boston: Printed by Rogers & Fowle for J. Edwards, 1746);

The Vanity of Man as Mortal . . . (Boston: Printed by Rogers & Fowle for D. Henchman, 1746).

The man who preached the funeral sermons for Solomon Stoddard, Increase Mather, Cotton Mather, Joseph Dudley, John Leverett, William Brattle, and Ebenezer Pemberton and who corresponded with Jonathan Edwards and obtained the English publication of Edwards's *A Faithful Narrative* occupies a modest place in American literary history. Seen primarily as a transitional figure, who in his nearly fifty-year career steered Boston from the Puritan isolationism of the late-seventeenth century into the more rationalistic spirit of the eighteenth, he has been recognized for his influence on sermonic style. In his own day, as pastor of the Brattle Street Church, fellow and overseer of Harvard College, missionary to the Indians, active participant in efforts to secure the charter to protect New England churches, and correspondent of Isaac Watts and numerous other English divines, Colman played a significant role in colonial history.

Born in Boston on 19 October 1673, the second son of Elizabeth and William Colman, he began his education at five with Ezekiel Cheever. Under the care of this inspiring tutor and his pious mother, Colman progressed rapidly, entering Harvard College in 1688. There, in the catholic atmosphere engendered by John Leverett and William Brattle, he absorbed both orthodox theology and new science. The death of his mother and the "Decline of his Father's worldly Estate" inclined him to accept the offer to preach at Medford when he graduated in 1692. But feeling himself too young to make his vocation, he returned to Harvard after six months to complete his M.A. in 1695. Finding no further opportunities to preach in Boston, he immediately set sail for England.

The voyage provided numerous adventures. French pirates engaged Colman's ship, and although he "fought like a Philosopher" the brigands caught, stripped, and incarcerated passengers and crew. Luckily one of Colman's fellow passengers hid some of his gold for him so that he lived comfortably as a prisoner for some months in France. He arrived in London destitute and sick but boarded with Thomas Parkhurst, a Dissenting bookseller, and quickly managed to meet the leading Dissenters in London. Through their efforts he received invitations to preach at Ipswich, Cambridge, and finally Bath, where he continued two years. There he flourished in the esteem of Elizabeth Singer, a beautiful and accomplished poet, who, as much as the civilizing influences of London, contributed to Colman's genteel education.

In 1699 a liberal group of Cambridge, Massachusetts, men of substance completed the Brattle Street Church, an alternative to the Mathers' Second Church, and invited Colman to preach and to inaugurate certain changes in church practice: the abolition of public professions, the reading of scripture without exegesis, and a more liberal policy for church admission. Anticipating opposition from the Mathers, the group urged him to be ordained in England. Colman answered the call, arrived in Boston in November 1699, and with the founders drew up *A Manifesto of Declaration* for the new church. The Mathers overcame their resentment enough to preside at the Fast Day to inaugurate the church in January 1700 and after a short, fierce exchange of pamphlets eventually accepted Colman as a ministerial brother.

In fact, although Colman appeared as a force for change, he remained throughout his life a theological conservative who sought earnestly for peace and unity among the churches, who supported the idea of synods, and who welcomed Stoddard and the Mathers in his early years, Whitefield and Edwards in his later career. His real innovations appear not in doctrine but in style. He figures prominently as a model of lucid, elegant prose, as a reader of modern philosophy and science, and as a warmly persuasive preacher of the beauty and grace of God.

His first published sermon, *Faith Victorious . . .* (1702), an address to the Artillery Company of Boston, showed his flexibility in adapting the Gospel to a military occasion. He found a more congenial subject, however, in his *The Government and Improvement of Mirth . . .* (1707), a sprightly discourse on the benefits of religious joy which in its paeans to God imitates the Psalms. In the same year he produced his most renowned work, *Practical Discourses upon the Parable of the Ten Virgins* (1707). Colman used the story of the virgins to review

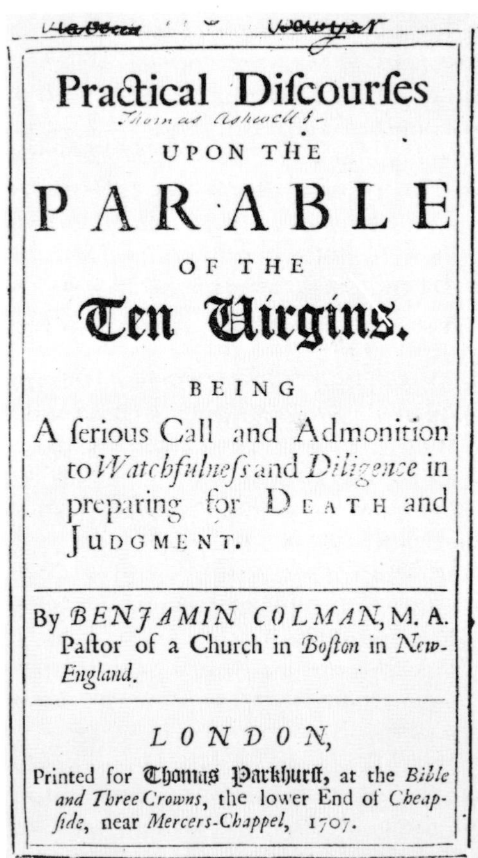

Practical Diſcourſes
UPON THE
PARABLE
OF THE
Ten Virgins.
BEING
A ſerious Call and Admonition to *Watchfulneſs* and *Diligence* in preparing for DEATH and JUDGMENT.

By *BENJAMIN COLMAN*, M. A. Paſtor of a Church in *Boſton* in *New-England.*

LONDON,
Printed for Thomas Parkhurſt, at the *Bible and Three Crowns*, the lower End of *Cheapſide*, near *Mercers-Chappel*, 1707.

Title page for Colman's best-known work, a series of sermons in which he employs the parable of the virgins to illustrate the main doctrines of Calvinism (John Carter Brown Library, Brown University)

the main doctrines of Calvinism: preparation, repentance, conversion, election, judgment, and redemption. At the same time he found the image of the virgins' intimate relation with the bridegroom Christ an attractive vehicle with which to work on his congregation's emotions: "The Heart of Christ is laid open to the Believer, as his is naked to him; every Disciple is there a *John*, and laid in his Bosom, having his ear with his Heart." Throughout his career Colman aimed always to assist his hearers in imagining the joys of God's presence, without neglecting but in a real measure balancing its terrors. The year ended with *A Poem on Elijah's Translation* (1707), Colman's longest poetic effort, in praise of Samuel Willard and the Harvard tradition. Throughout his life he read, admired, and imitated the poetry of Horace, Milton, Waller, Watts, Blackamore, and Pope.

Decades of preaching and publishing sermons for funerals, ordinations, elections, and fast days followed this momentous year. Colman had nearly ninety works published in his lifetime, demonstrating a wide range of concerns, patriotic, medical, and charitable, besides theological. He employed the Puritan plain style, limiting his metaphors to simple and natural images, using the language of ordinary men. Yet his sermons abound in rich varieties of diction, in poetic rhythms, and in joyous exclamations of pious faith. As Perry Miller has noted, "His ideal of style meant shedding the archaisms of the Mathers, but it also designed a prose in which ordinary emotions were given greater play." These ordinary emotions, couched in the most refined language, gave his sermons their urbane eloquence. Many of them, for clarity of argument and force of logic, remain convincing today. Among the most interesting are: *A Humble Discourse of the Incomprehensibleness of God* (1715), one of the best examples of Colman's hymnal praises of God; *The Religious Regards We Owe to Our Country* (1718), a patriotic call to duty; *Ossa Josephi* (1720), a curiously successful elegy for the problematic Governor Dudley; *Some Observations on the New Method of Receiving the Small-Pox by Ingrafting or Inoculation* (1721), a spirited defense of Dr. Zabdiel Boylston's part in the smallpox controversy; *God Deals With Us as Rational Creatures* (1723), a characteristic blend of Puritan and Enlightenment thought; *Some of the Glories of our Lord and Saviour Jesus Christ* (1728), a summary theological statement much admired by Dissenters in England; and *Souls Flying to Christ Pleasant and Admirable to Behold* (1740), a positive response to the preaching of George Whitefield and Gilbert Tennant. Shy of controversy, classically moderate, Addisonian in style, Colman infused his sermons with Puritan passion and Awakening sensibility.

Soon after his installation at Brattle Street, on 8 June 1700, Colman married Jane Clark with whom he enjoyed a happy marriage until her death on 27 October 1730. A son, Benjamin, born 1 September 1704, died a few weeks later. On 25 February 1708 was born Jane, on whom Colman lavished much paternal tenderness and ministerial solicitude. She married Ebenezer Turrell in 1726, but suffering from weak health, an overwhelming anxiety about religion, and the deaths of three infants, she died on 26 March 1735. Colman responded to her death with a wrenchingly personal funeral sermon, *Reliquiae Turellae et Lachrymae Paternae* (1735). Colman's second daughter, Abigail, born on 14 January 1715, eloped with a ne'er-do-well and died repentant on 17 May 1745. After the death of his first wife, Colman married a widow, Sarah Clark (no relation to Jane), on 6 May 1732. When she died on 24 April 1744, he soon married another widow, Mary Frost, on 12 August 1745. He died painlessly on 28 August 1747.

Colman's services as fellow (1717-1724) and

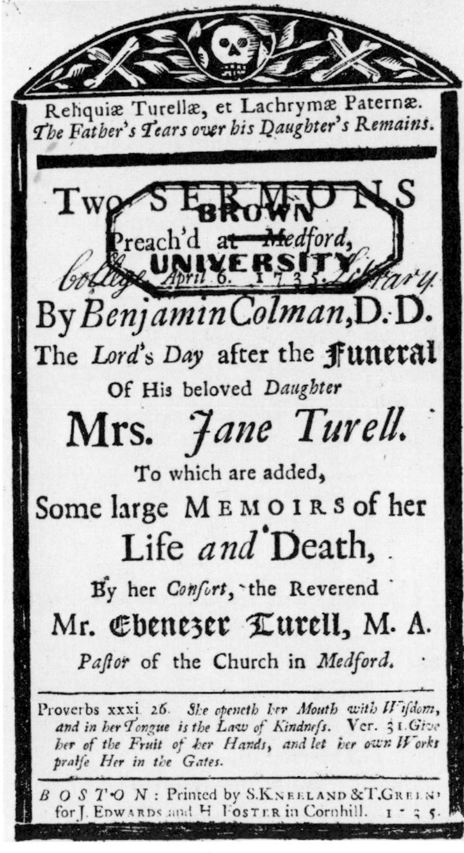

Reliquiæ Turellæ, et Lachrymæ Paternæ.
The Father's Tears over his Daughter's Remains.

Two SERMONS
Preach'd at Medford,
April 6. 1735.

By *Benjamin Colman*, D.D.
The *Lord's Day* after the **Funeral**
Of His beloved *Daughter*
Mrs. *Jane Turell.*
To which are added,
Some large MEMOIRS of her
Life *and* Death,
By her *Consort*, the Reverend
Mr. **Ebenezer Turell**, M. A.
Pastor of the Church in *Medford.*

Proverbs xxxi. 26. *She openeth her Mouth with Wisdom, and in her Tongue is the Law of Kindness.* Ver. 31. *Give her of the Fruit of her Hands, and let her own Works praise Her in the Gates.*

BOSTON: Printed by S.Kneeland & T.Green, for J. Edwards and H. Foster in Cornhill. 1735.

Title page for Colman's deeply personal funeral sermon for his favorite daughter, Jane overseer of Harvard College (particularly in attracting wealthy donors), as agent for the Society for the Propagation of the Gospel in New England, and as correspondent to kings and ministers in support of the colony's charter and churches won him widespread respect. He received an honorary doctorate in divinity from the University of Glasgow in 1731. Eclipsed at his death in part by the developments of the Great Awakening, he nevertheless retained a distinguished reputation on both sides of the Atlantic. Although no recent published biography of Colman exists, he has received some attention from historians. Beyond the critical appraisals of Perry Miller, however, little has appeared in print on his significance as a literary figure.

References:

Howard C. Adams, "Benjamin Colman: A Critical Biography," Ph.D. dissertation, Pennsylvania State University, 1976;

Clayton H. Chapman, "Benjamin Colman and Philomela," *New England Quarterly*, 42 (June 1969): 214-231;

Chapman, "Benjamin Colman's Daughters," *New England Quarterly*, 26 (June 1953): 169-192;

Chapman, "The Life and Influence of Benjamin Colman," Th.D. dissertation, Boston University School of Theology, 1947;

Theodore Hornberger, "Benjamin Colman and the Enlightenment," *New England Quarterly*, 12 (June 1939): 227-240;

"Memoir of the Rev. Benjamin Colman, D.D.," *New England Historical and Genealogical Register*, 3 (1849): 105-122, 220-232;

Perry Miller, *Jonathan Edwards* (New York: Sloane, 1949), pp. 17-21;

Miller, *The New England Mind, From Colony to Province* (Cambridge: Harvard University Press, 1953);

Chester P. Sadowy, "Benjamin Colman (1673-1747) as Literary Artist," Ph.D. dissertation, University of Pennsylvania, 1974;

Clifford K. Shipton, *Sibley's Harvard Graduates: Biographical Sketches of Those Who Attended Harvard College*, volume 4 (Cambridge: Harvard University Press, 1933), pp. 120-137;

Ebenezer Turrell, *The Life and Character of the Reverend Benjamin Colman, D.D.* (Boston: Rogers & Fowle, 1749; reprinted, Delmar, N.Y.: Scholars' Facsimiles and Reprints, 1972).

Papers:

The Massachusetts Historical Society has the largest collection of Colman manuscripts and letters as well as volumes from Colman's library. The Houghton Library of Harvard University has the only manuscripts of sermons by Colman, including the Bath sermons.

Ebenezer Cook

(circa 1667-circa 1732)

Robert D. Arner
University of Cincinnati

BOOKS: *The Sot-Weed Factor, Or, a Voyage to Maryland* . . . (London: Printed & sold by B. Bragg, 1708);

Sotweed Redivivus: Or the Planters Looking-Glass . . . , as E. C. Gent (Annapolis: Printed by William Parks, 1730);

The Maryland Muse. Containing I. The History of Colonel Nathaniel Bacon's Rebellion in Virginia. Done in Hudabrastick Verse, from an Old Ms. II. The Sotweed Factor, or Voiage to Maryland. The Third Edition, Corrected and Amended (Annapolis: Printed by William Parks, 1731).

Ebenezer Cook (or Cooke) is the best American writer of satire before Benjamin Franklin, and even Franklin, it is arguable, did not produce any single piece better than *The Sot-Weed Factor* . . . (1708). In this poem and in "The History of Colonel Nathaniel Bacon's Rebellion in Virginia," both composed in the hudibrastic verse form popularized by Samuel Butler, Cook initiated a tradition of Southern

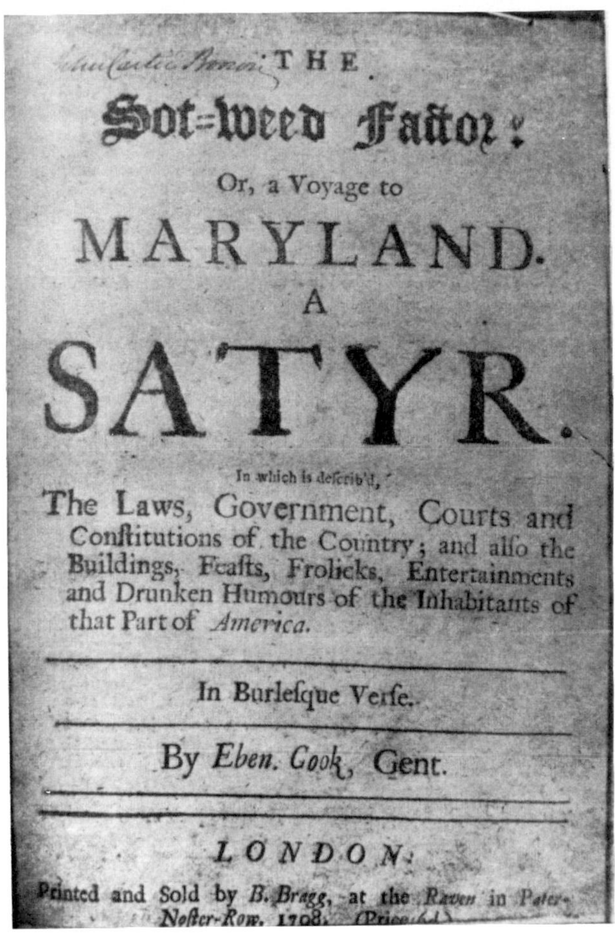

THE
Sot-Weed Factor:
Or, a Voyage to
MARYLAND.
A
SATYR.
In which is deſcrib'd,
The Laws, Government, Courts and Conſtitutions of the Country; and alſo the Buildings, Feaſts, Frolicks, Entertainments and Drunken Humours of the Inhabitants of that Part of *America.*

In Burleſque Verſe.

By *Eben. Cook*, Gent.

LONDON:
Printed and Sold by *B. Bragg*, at the *Raven* in *Pater-Noſter-Row.* 1708. (Price 6d.)

Title page for Cook's first book, a poem satirizing foolish Englishmen who come to America expecting a new Eden

humor that eventually spawned Mark Twain and William Faulkner and that remains vitally alive today. His portraits of what he called the "planting rabble" of Maryland, his deflation of the contradictory American dreams of pastoral innocence and unlimited economic advancement, and his irreverent handling and comic mythologizing of history are also very much in the mainstream of American literary traditions and entitle him to more careful critical attention than he has hitherto received.

Little is known of Cook's life. The son of Andrew and Anne Bowyer Cooke, he was born in London sometime around 1667 and first came to Maryland around 1694, when his signature appears on a remonstrance against the removal of the capital from St. Mary's City to Annapolis. He appears to have returned to London around 1700 and again sometime before 1708, the year *The Sot-Weed Factor* . . . was published, perhaps remaining long enough to probate his father's will on 2 January 1712. He is next mentioned in public records on 30 October 1717, when he sold to his cousin Edward Cook a tract of land called Malden that he had inherited from his father. Whether he was in London or Maryland at the time of the sale is impossible to establish, but he turns up again in Maryland records as the deputy of Henry Lowe 2nd, a receiver-general of the province, in 1720, and for the next several years he seems to have supported himself as a land agent for Lowe, Lowe's brother Bennett Lowe, and John Gresham; he was also admitted to the bar of Prince George's County and seems to have been practicing law intermittently since at least September 1700, when he was appointed the "true and Lawfull Attorney" of one "Edwd Ebbitt Citizen." After 1722, Cook's name virtually disappears from public records, and his existence can be traced only through his poems, which also provide clues that he had fallen on hard times and was sorely in need of money. His last poem, an elegy commemorating Benedict Leonard Calvert, was written in 1732, when the poet would have been in his mid-sixties, and it is probable that he died shortly thereafter.

Cook's best poem is *The Sot-Weed Factor* . . . , a complexly ironic work that burlesques the foolish expectations of Englishmen who come to America anticipating a new Eden and a land of unbounded economic opportunity. Penniless and friendless in England, the sot-weed factor (tobacco merchant) sails for Maryland, intending to get rich quickly; after a tempestuous sea journey, he arrives in the province and encounters a gallery of rogues and scoundrels who eventually cheat him of the goods he has brought and send him raging back to England, leaving behind a "dreadful Curse" upon a land "where no Man's Faithful, nor a Woman Chast." This indictment is, of course, intentionally hyperbolic, a measure both of the sot-weed factor's infantile egocentrism and of Cook's skill at manipulating a comic character type, the disgruntled merchant adventurer, who figures prominently in all sorts of literature about the New World, from Thomas Hariot's *A Briefe and True Report of the New Found Land of Virginia* . . . (1588) onward. John Hammond's *Leah and Rachel, or, The Two Fruitful Sisters Virginia and Mary-land* (1656) provides perhaps the best gloss on the sot-weed factor's enraged frustration when Hammond complains about Englishmen who "vilifie, scandalize, and cry down such parts of the unknown world" as have been settled by their own countrymen "as if because removed from us, we either account them people of another world or enemies."

Though episodic in nature, *The Sot-Weed Factor . . .* is held together by a number of recurrent images and motifs which help to characterize the speaker of the poem and project his fears of cultural transformation. One of these, the motif of misogyny, is introduced early in the poem through the speaker's apparently casual reference to "Pandora's Box" (Pandora is the classical counterpart of Eve, mother of all the ills of mankind) and carries through to the final allegation that all women in Maryland are whores or concubines, transforming Mary's or the Virgin's land into a nightmare of sexual license. A series of animal metaphors reveals not only the predatory nature of Maryland's inhabitants but also the speaker's fascination with ingestion and appetite, an infantile fixation that eventually extends into cannibalism in the concluding verse. Most important of these thematic and unifying devices is the curse itself, with which the poem both opens and closes, for it establishes Maryland as a fallen world, the "Land of *Nod*" or some other cursed realm, and allows the reader to chart the speaker's regression from civilization to primitive savagery, from satire to imprecation. The substitution of a "wish" for this "dreadful Curse" in the so-called third edition (no copy of any second edition is known to have been printed) of *The Sot-Weed Factor . . .* , published with "The History of Colonel Nathaniel Bacon's Rebellion in Virginia" in *The Maryland Muse* (1731), is a major mistake, for it deprives the poem of internal consistency and a psychologically as well as stylistically valid conclusion.

Between *The Sot-Weed Factor . . .* and *An ELOGY on the Death of Thomas Bordley, Esq . . .* , a broadside printed in Annapolis by William Parks in 1726, there is a long silence broken only by a few scattered references to Cook's career as lawyer and land agent. The "ELOGY" has the distinction of being the first belletristic writing published in the Colonial South. It is also the first work Cook signed as "Poet Laureate of Maryland." The poem was occasioned by the death of a prominent member of the Lower House of the Maryland Assembly, who, along with Daniel Dulany, championed the extension of English Statute Law to the province. Bordley arranged with Andrew Bradford of Pennsylvania for the publication of the *Votes and Proceedings of the Lower House* in 1725, authoring the preface himself and lamenting that the "Character of a great Commoner" so revered in England was unknown in Maryland because the laws were not printed; the next year, he was instrumental in bringing the printer William Parks to Annapolis, thereby insuring that the *Votes and Proceedings . . .* would continue to be published and, incidentally, providing local writers such as Cook with ready access to a printer. A lawyer himself, Cook sympathized with Bordley in this controversy, once ironically remarking that he could not be charged with plagiarism in *The Sot-Weed Factor . . .* because "the Laws of Great Britain are not allow'd to extend to the wilds of America," and he may have intended some of the legalistic imagery of his elegy to speak obliquely to the issue.

Cook's next work, "An Elegy on the Death of the Honorable Nicholas Lowe," was published in the *Maryland Gazette* on 24 December 1728. It is puzzling in that Cook seems to mock his subject, the brother of Henry and Bennett Lowe, who "[liv]'d and dy'd a Batchelor at last" rather than marry his servant, Mary Young, who Cook may have felt deserved better treatment. No hard biographical evidence directly linking Cook and Lowe has turned up, however, so this explanation must remain conjectural.

Two years after the elegy on Lowe, William Parks printed Cook's *Sotweed Redivivus: Or the Planters Looking-Glass . . .* (1730), another hudibrastic poem dominated, however, by classical allusions—Horace and Aesop seem the most immediate sources—and by the Augustan metaphor so frequently employed in English poetry of the eighteenth century. The speaker, identified with the sot-weed factor of the first satire but more like the one who revises his curse in the "third edition" of the same poem, discusses with the "Cockerouse" of the earlier work a variety of the evils besetting Maryland: the scarcity of currency and coin, the single-crop system, the absolute powers of English merchants to establish taxes and prices for tobacco, the lack of established commercial centers and a provincial merchant fleet, absentee landholders, and the unchecked importation of African slaves. Like *The Sot-Weed Factor . . .* , the poem features unfavorable portraits of poor whites but is nonetheless not a satire so much as it is a poem of counsel and advice.

In his last satire, "The History of Colonel Nathaniel Bacon's Rebellion in Virginia," published in *The Maryland Muse . . .* along with the first American edition of *The Sot-Weed Factor*, Cook employs mock-epic techniques as a way of elevating himself above the masses, suggesting cultural continuity between England and the colonies, diminishing Bacon's martial exploits, and containing Bacon's radicalism within a literary framework that bespeaks aristocratic traditions of order. The poem versifies the causes, initial military

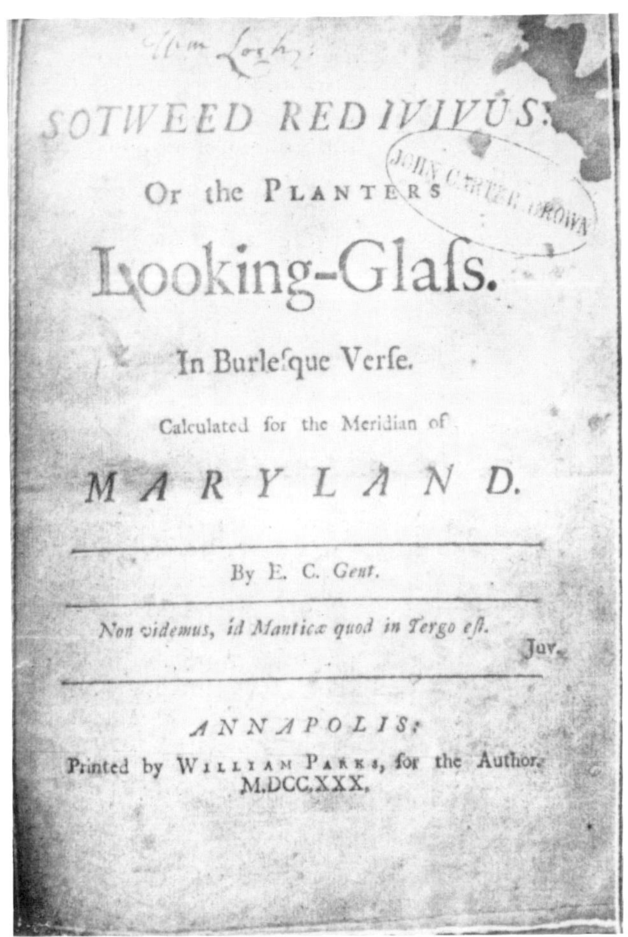
SOTWEED REDIVIVUS:

Or the PLANTERS

Looking-Glaſs.

In Burleſque Verſe.

Calculated for the Meridian of

MARYLAND.

By E. C. Gent.

Non videmus, id Manticæ quod in Tergo eſt.

Juv.

ANNAPOLIS:

Printed by WILLIAM PARKS, for the Author.

M.DCC.XXX.

Title page for Cook's second poem about the sot-weed factor (John Carter Brown Library Brown University)

successes, and eventual defeat of Nathaniel Bacon, who in 1676 led a frontier militia against the British governor Sir William Berkeley in a series of skirmishes that later American historians often looked upon as a foreshadowing of the American Revolution. Not as successful as *The Sot-Weed Factor* . . . , "The History of Colonel Nathaniel Bacon's Rebellion" is still well worth reading for its treatment of one of the legendary episodes of colonial history and its gallery of rogues, scoundrels, and cowards who seem inescapably to populate Cook's imaginative vision of the brave new world of America.

Cook's final poems, "An Elegy on the Death of the Honourable William Lock, Esqr. . ." and "In Memory of the Honble Benedict Leonard Calvert Esqr. Lieutenant Governor in the Province of Maryland . . . ," which both date from 1732, exist in manuscript copies only, though the elegy on Lock appears once to have been published. As elegies, they are competent but undistinguished verses, noteworthy perhaps only for their continuing dislike of "Mechanic Souls" who made Calvert's brief term as lieutenant governor of Maryland an unpleasant experience. Lock's and Calvert's virtues are rehearsed, and their ascent into the regions of the blessed is assured, as the formula demands.

Although his work has been known to scholars of American literature for a long time, Cook has been entirely omitted by the authors of all but a few of the many studies of American humor. The recent appearance of his work in several of the most popular anthologies of American literature makes it unlikely that such oversights will happen again. *The Sot-weed Factor* . . . stands alone among his poems as a major literary work, but his total output, though small, is sufficient to establish him as an important minor figure in American literary history, one whose work must be taken into account when the colonial legacy to American literature is calculated.

Other:

"An Elegy on the Death of the Honorable Nicholas Lowe," *Maryland Gazette,* 24 December 1728.

References:

Robert D. Arner, "The Blackness of Darkness: Satire, Romance, and Ebenezer Cooke's *The Sot-Weed Factor,*" *Tennessee Studies in Literature,* 21 (1976): 1-10;

Arner, "Clio's *Rhimes*: History and Satire in Ebenezer Cooke's 'History of Bacon's Rebellion,' " *Southern Literary Journal,* 6 (Spring 1974): 91-106;

Arner, "Ebenezer Cooke: Satire in the Colonial South," *Southern Literary Journal,* 8 (Fall 1975): 153-164;

Arner, "Ebenezer Cooke's *Sotweed Redivivus*: Satire in the Horatian Mode," *Mississippi Quarterly,* 28 (Fall 1975): 489-496;

Arner, "Ebenezer Cooke's *The Sot-weed Factor*: The Structure of Satire," *Southern Literary Journal,* 4 (Fall 1971): 33-47;

Donald V. Coers, "New Light on the Composition of Ebenezer Cooke's *Sot-Weed Factor,*" *American Literature,* 49 (1978): 604-605;

Edward H. Cohen, *Ebenezer Cooke: The Sot-weed Canon* (Athens: University of Georgia Press, 1975);

Jay B. Hubbell, *The South in American Literature* (Durham: Duke University Press, 1954), pp. 63-65;

J. A. Leo Lemay, *Men of Letters in Colonial*

Maryland (Knoxville: University of Tennessee Press, 1972), pp. 77-110;

James Talbot Poole, "Ebenezer Cooke and the Maryland Muse," *American Literature*, 3 (December 1931): 296-302;

Bernard C. Steiner, *Early Maryland Poetry* (Baltimore: John Murphy, 1900);

Lawrence C. Wroth, "The Maryland Muse," *American Antiquarian Society Proceedings*, new series 44 (October 1934): 267-335.

Papers:

The manuscript for Cook's elegy on Benedict Leonard Calvert is at the U.S. Naval Academy; the manuscript for Cook's elegy for Nicholas Lowe is at the Maryland Historical Society.

John Cotton

Everett Emerson
University of North Carolina at Chapel Hill

BIRTH: Derby, England, 4 December 1584, to Roland Cotton (mother's name unknown).

EDUCATION: A.B., Trinity College, Cambridge, 1602; A.M., 1606; B.D., 1613; Emmanuel College, Cambridge.

MARRIAGES: 3 July 1613 to Elizabeth Horrocks. 6 April 1632 to Sarah Hawkridge Story; children: Seaborn, Sarah, Elizabeth, John, Mariah, Rowland.

DEATH: Boston, Massachusetts, 23 December 1652.

BOOKS: *Gods Promise to his Plantation* . . . (London: Printed by William Jones for John Bellamy, 1630; Boston: Printed by Samuel Green, sold by John Usher, 1686);

An Abstract or the Lawes of New England, As they are now established (London: Printed for F. Coules & W. Ley, 1641); republished, with scriptural quotations, as *An Abstract of Laws and Government*... (London: Printed by M. S. for Livewel Chapman, 1655);

The Way of Life. Or God's Way and Course . . . (London: Printed by M. F. for Luke Fawne & S. Gellibrand, 1641);

Gods Mercie Mixed with his Justice . . . (London: Printed by G. M. for Edward Brewster & Henry Hood, 1641); republished as *The Saints Support & Comfort, in the Time of Distress and Danger* . . . (London: Printed & sold by Thomas Basset, 1658);

A Coppy of A Letter of Mr. Cotton of Boston . . . (London, 1641);

A Briefe Exposition Of the Whole Book of Canticles, or, Song of Solomon... (London: Printed for Philip Nevel, 1642); republished as *A Brief Exposition With Practical Observations Upon the whole Book of Canticles* (London: Printed by T. R. & E. M. for Ralph Smith, 1655);

The Powring out of the Seven Vials . . . (London: Printed & sold by Henry Overton, 1642);

The Churches Resurrection... (London: Printed by R. O. & G. D. for Henry Overton, 1642);

The True Constitution of A particular visible Church, proved by Scripture . . . (London: Printed for Samuel Satterthwaite, 1642); corrected as *The Doctrine of the Church* . . . (London: Printed for Samuel Satterthwaite, 1643);

A Modest and Cleare Answer to Mr. Balls Discourse of set formes of Prayer... (London: Printed by R. O. & G. D. for Henry Overton, 1642);

A Letter of Mr. John Cottons Teacher of the Church in Boston, New-England, to Mr. Williams a Preacher There . . . (London: Printed for Benjamin Allen, 1643);

Sixteene Questions of Serious and Necessary Consequence... (London: Printed by E. P. for Edward Blackmore, 1644); republished as *Severall Questions of Serious and Necessary Consequence*... (London: Printed for Thomas Banks, 1647);

The Keyes of the Kingdom of Heaven... (London: Printed by M. Simmons for Henry Overton, 1644);

The Way of the Churches of Christ in New-England... (London: Printed by Matthew Simmons, 1645);

The Covenant of Gods Free Grace . . . (London:

J Cotton

This 1649 portrait of John Cotton was later repainted as a portrait of Increase or Cotton Mather (Connecticut Historical Society).

Printed by Matthew Simmons for John Hancock, 1645);

A Treatise of Mr. Cottons, Clearing certaine Doubts concerning Predestination (London: Printed by J. D. for Andrew Crook, 1646);

The Controversie Concerning Liberty of Conscience in Matters of Religion . . . (London: Printed for Thomas Banks, 1646);

A Conference Mr. Cotton held at Boston . . ., parts 1 and 3 by Cotton, part 2 by Francis Cornwell (London: Printed by J. Dawson, sold by Fr. Eglesfield, 1646); republished as *Gospel Conversion . . .* (London: Printed by J. Dawson, 1646);

Milk for Babes. Drawn Out of the Breasts of Both Testaments . . . (London: Printed by J. Coe for Henry Overton, 1646); republished as *Spiritual Milk for Boston Babes in Either England. Drawn Out of the Breasts of Both Testaments for Their Souls Nourishment . . .* (Cambridge: Printed by Samuel Green for Hezekiah Usher, 1656);

The Grounds and Ends of the Baptisme of the Children of the Faithfull (London: Printed by R. C. for Andrew Crooke, 1647);

The Bloudy Tenent, Washed, and Made White in the Bloud of the Lambe . . . (London: Printed by Matthew Symmons for Hannah Allen, 1647);

Singing of Psalmes a Gospel-Ordinance . . ., by Cotton and Thomas Shepard (London: Printed by Matthew Simmons for Hannah Allen & John Rothwell, 1647);

The Way of Congregational Churches Cleared . . . (London: Printed by Matthew Simmons for John Bellamie, 1648);

Of the Holinesse of Church-Members (London: Printed by F. N. for Hanna Allen, 1650);

Christ The Fountaine of Life . . . (London: Printed by Robert Ibbitson, 1651);

The New Covenant . . . (London: Printed by M. S. for Francis Eglesfield & John Allen, 1654); republished in *The Covenant of Grace . . .* (1655);

A Briefe Exposition With Practicall Observations Upon The Whole Book of Ecclesiastes (London: Printed by T. C. for Ralph Smith, 1654);

Certain Queries Tending to Accommodation and Communion of Presbyterian & Congregationall Churches (London: Printed by M. S. for John Allen & Frances Egglesfield, 1654);

The Covenant of Grace . . . (London: Printed by Matthew Simmons for Francis Eglesfield & John Allen, 1655); revised and enlarged as *A Treatise of the Covenant of Grace . . .* (London: Printed by Ja. Cottrel for John Allen, 1659);

An Exposition upon The Thirteenth Chapter of the Revelation (London: Printed by Matthew Simmons for Livewel Chapman, 1655);

A Brief Exposition With Practical Observations Upon the Whole Book of Canticles. Never before Printed (London: Printed by T. R. & E. M. for Ralph Smith, 1655);

A Practicall Commentary, Or an Exposition With Observations, Reasons, and Uses upon The First Epistle Generall of John (London: Printed by R. I. & E. C. for Thomas Parkhurst, 1656);

A Defence of Mr. John Cotton From the imputation of Selfe Contradiction . . . (Oxford: Printed by H. Hall for T. Robinson, 1658);

Some Treasure Fetched out of Rubbish . . ., part 1 and probably part 2 by Cotton, part 3 by Robert Nichols (London, 1660);

A Discourse about Civil Government in a New Plantation Whose Design is Religion (Cambridge: Printed by Samuel Green & Marmaduke Johnson, 1663);

A Sermon Preached by the Reverend, Mr. John

Cotton, Teacher of the First Church in Boston in New-England. Deliver'd at Salem, 1636. To which is Prefixed, A Retraction of His Former Opinion Concerning Baptism, Utter'd by Him Immediately Preceeding The Sermon Here Emitted (Boston, 1713);

A Treatise I. Of Faith. II. Twelve Fundamental Articles of Christian Religion. III. A Doctrinal Conclusion. IV. Questions and Answers upon Church-Government . . . (Boston, 1713).

COLLECTION: *John Cotton on the Churches of New England,* edited by Larzer Ziff (Cambridge: Harvard University Press, 1968).

After a career of more than twenty years in England, John Cotton joined the Massachusetts Bay Colony and became a minister of the Boston church, where he was a powerful voice, though his involvement in several crucial controversies for a time limited his authority. Though recognized as a spokesman for the congregational system of church government and a defender of the New England Way, he regarded himself as chiefly a preacher, and of his thirty-seven publications, many merely pamphlets, nineteen are sermons or sermon collections.

The son of a lawyer, John Cotton attended grammar school in his natal place, Derby, in the English midlands. In 1597 he matriculated at Trinity College, Cambridge University, and, after completing undergraduate studies, he became a fellow of Emmanuel College, a Puritan institution that was to supply the Massachusetts Bay Colony with several of its leaders. He remained at Cambridge for some fifteen years, during which time he was influenced by three great Puritan preachers, William Perkins, Laurence Chaderton, master of Emmanuel College, and Richard Sibbes. A popular preacher who attracted crowds because of his elegant, heavily ornamented style, he continued to be uncertain about his relationship to God until he heard a plain-style sermon preached by Sibbes. Then, judging that God had effectually called him to salvation, he took up this simpler evangelical style, and, though he lost some of his popularity, he soon decided that the change was distinctly for the better. In 1612 he was appointed vicar of the handsome St. Botoph's Church in Boston, Lincolnshire, and within a few years he had established within his church an inner circle of the elect who entered into a covenant to "follow after the Lord in the purity of his worship," as he was later to report in *The Way of Congregational Churches Cleared* . . . (1648).

During his years in the English Boston John Cotton preached many sermons, some of which were published as long as twenty-five years after they were first delivered. Typically these sermons were not prepared for publication by the author but were published from notes made by those who heard the sermon. Of the five volumes of sermons that survive from Cotton's English years, a characteristic one is *Gods Mercie Mixed with his Justice* . . . (1641), in which he uses the customary Puritan sermon form. It begins with a biblical text, which is carefully elucidated. One or more doctrines are drawn from this text, and each is explained, often by citation of analogous passages from other portions of the Bible. Next, the reasons for the doctrine are set forth in the most theological (and sometimes philosophical) part of the sermon. Finally the preacher applies the doctrines to the condition of his listeners. The uses, as they were called, was usually the most colorful part of the sermon and frequently showed the preacher's knowledge of psychology. The longest of Cotton's sermon volumes is on the quintessential Puritan topic, the conversion process. This collection, *The Way of Life* . . . (1641), does not describe how a Christian is to live; rather it describes the way to life, the means of salvation. That way is the sermon, for like other Puritans Cotton taught the Pauline doctrine that "faith cometh by hearing." The most interesting single sermon of those that Cotton delivered in England is doubtless *Gods Promise to his Plantation* . . . (1630), preached in 1630 to John Winthrop and his followers, soon to depart for Massachusetts from Southampton. Taking as his text II Samuel 7.10 ("Moreover I will appoint a place for my people Israel, and I will plant them that they may dwell in a place of their own and move no more"), Cotton defended the colonists' enterprise and in particular stressed that their move would permit them to obtain "the liberty of the ordinances," that is, the proper administration of baptism and holy communion, and the establishment of preaching and church discipline, all vital concerns of the congregational wing of the Puritan party.

At the age of forty-nine John Cotton made his way to America, arriving in September 1633 at the town that had been named for his home parish. He reported that his people of St. Botolph's wanted him "to minister in this country to such of their town as they had sent before hither, and such as were willing to go along with me, or to follow me." He soon joined the Boston church and became its second minister; the other minister was John Wilson, who had been with the church since its founding in 1630. Soon after Cotton's arrival, Anne Hutchinson

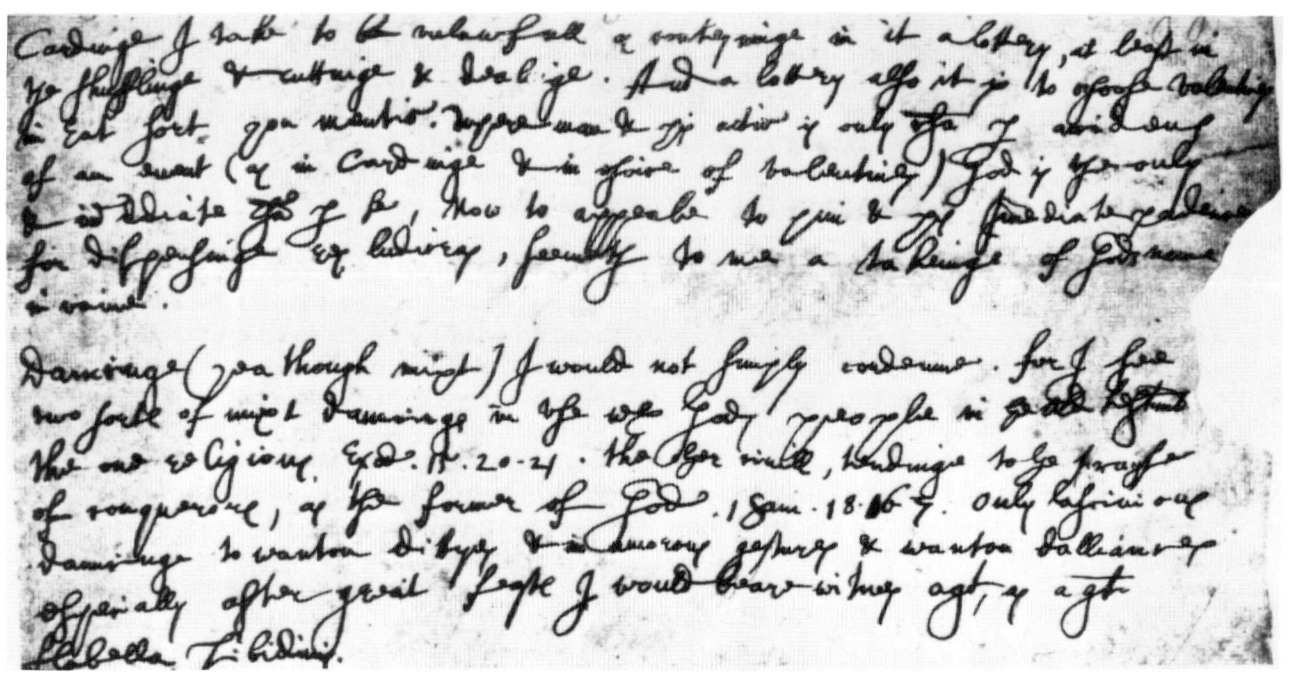

One of the oldest manuscripts in the Massachusetts Archives, this tracing of part of a rough draft of a 3 March 1626 letter from Cotton to the Reverend R. Levett presents Cotton's views on card playing and dancing (Archives of the Commonwealth, Boston, Massachusetts).

arrived, and within a year or two theological disputes began to occur. Ostensibly these centered around Hutchinson, who gathered at her Boston house those whom she sought to teach about the doctrine of justification; in fact, her gatherings soon amounted to a running criticism of local ministers. Anne Hutchinson, who had been Cotton's admirer in Lincolnshire, stressed the distinction between Cotton's emphasis on faith and the other ministers' emphasis on good works as a means of recognizing saving grace. By stressing and in time exaggerating the distinction, Hutchinson encouraged a spirit of individualism that the leaders of the new colony found threatening and dangerous. Badly tarred by Hutchinson's brush, Cotton barely survived the dispute, the "Antinomian controversy," which led to the exile of Hutchinson and many of her followers. Cotton was saved, it appears, by his theological sophistication, most fully demonstrated by the careful distinctions in *A Conference Mr. Cotton held at Boston* . . . (not intended for publication but published in 1646) and by his willingness to make a significant concession to the opposition. Another reason, no doubt, for his survival is that he had already begun the important work of preparing descriptions and defenses of the New England Way, Congregational church government. The first of these, *The True Constitution of A particular visible Church, proved by Scripture* . . . , was published in 1642, but Cotton had earlier expressed himself significantly in a sermon delivered at Salem in 1636, published in 1713, many years after his death.

Cotton's full-scale descriptions and justifications became probably his most important works. Among them are *The Way of the Churches of Christ in New-England* . . . , which apparently circulated in manuscript in England for some time before it was published in 1645; the more authoritative but less interesting *The Keyes of the Kingdom of Heaven* . . . (1644); and a reply to an attack on Cotton by English and Scottish Presbyterians, Cotton's *The Way of Congregational Churches Cleared* . . . (1648). Though the last of these is interesting for the personal comments it contains, the most important is doubtless *The Way of the Churches of Christ in New-England* . . . , since it describes in detail how New England Congregational worked in its earliest days. At that time those coming to the Massachusetts Bay Colony were expected to join a church, in part by declaring "that it was the principal end of their coming, to enjoy the presence of the Lord in the liberty and purity of his ordinances." Much of the book is a description of the officers of a church, how they are selected, their qualifications and responsibilities.

Another task that Cotton undertook in his role as spokesman for the standing order in Massachusetts was to reply to attacks from Roger Williams, who had been an important minister in the colony before he was exiled. Cotton replied to Williams's *The Bloudy Tenent of Persecution* (1644) with *The Bloudy Tenent, Washed, and Made White in the Bloud of the Lambe* . . . (1647). The issues were many, and the argument was complicated by differences in their reading of scripture, but it was especially significant that Williams rejected Cotton's advocacy of the New England Way, in which church and state were two cooperating powers, with the state justified in punishing those who attack religious truth. Cotton argued that Massachusetts was the modern equivalent of ancient Israel and that magistrates were analogous to the ancient kings. Another work that sets forth Cotton's notions on the proper relation of church and state, *A Discourse about Civil Government in a New Plantation Whose Design is Religion* (published posthumously in 1663), was not prompted by the controversy with Williams. Here Cotton defends the early practice of the government of Massachusetts, which restricted the franchise to church members.

Of Cotton's many published American sermons, perhaps the most interesting are two works of the 1640s, *The Powring out of the Seven Vials* . . . (1642), which suggests that the destruction of iniquity and the bringing in of the millenium are about to occur, and *The Churches Resurrection* . . . (1642), in which he urges New Englanders not to return to the Old Country but to recommit themselves to their covenant with God, whom Cotton saw to be at work in the English Puritan revolution then just beginning. Cotton was one of three Americans invited to participate in the Westminster Assembly (1642), designed to reform the Church of England, but he chose to remain in America. He soon saw that what was happening in England resulted in the dissemination of heresies, such as anabaptism (rejection of infant baptism), which was one of the issues taken up in the Synod of 1646. The synod resulted in the Cambridge Platform, a definition of New England Congregationalism largely drawn from Cotton's writings and to which he provided a preface.

Highly successful as a minister in Boston, even though he devoted much energy to his writings (especially those on church policy), Cotton even had time to think of those who had remained behind, his former parishioners back in Lincolnshire, to whom he addressed himself in *Of the Holinesse of Church-Members* (1650). While they had remembered him with annual financial gifts and now sought his return, he reminded them not only of his age (sixty-six) but of their failure to limit church membership to "professed saints," and he urged that his old church adopt the New England practice. The years in America had indeed resulted in Cotton's intimate identification with the Massachusetts Bay Colony and its peculiarities. His death in 1652 did not see an end to his influence, for nearly a dozen of his writings appeared after his death. Cotton's works lack the attractive vigor of Thomas Hooker's or Thomas Shepard's; they are most important because they are the writings of the semiofficial spokesman of that remarkable experiment in communal living, the Massachusetts Bay Colony. He has been the subject of two book-length studies, and he has figured prominently in the recent interest in religious typology. Students of literature have not, however, found him especially appealing.

Bibliography:

Julius H. Tuttle, "Writings of Rev. John Cotton," in *Bibliographical Essays: A Tribute to Wilberforce Eames* (Cambridge, Mass.: Privately printed, 1924);

Edward Gallagher and Thomas Werge, *Early Puritan Writers: A Reference Guide* (Boston: Hall, 1976), pp. 59-97.

Biography:

Larzer Ziff, *The Career of John Cotton: Puritanism and the American Experience* (Princeton: Princeton University Press, 1962).

References:

Sacvan Bercovitch, "Typology in Puritan New England: The Williams-Cotton Controversy Reassessed," *American Quarterly*, 19 (Summer 1967): 166-191;

Everett Emerson, *John Cotton* (New York: Twayne, 1965);

Norman S. Grabo, "John Cotton's Aesthetics: A Sketch," *Early American Literature Newsletter*, 3 (Spring 1968): 4-10;

David D. Hall, *The Antinomian Controversy, 1636-1638: A Documentary History* (Middletown, Conn.: Wesleyan University Press, 1968);

Edmund Morgan, *Visible Saints: The History of a Puritan Idea* (New York: New York University Press, 1963);

Jesper Rosenmeier, " 'Clearing the Medium': A Reevaluation of the Puritan Plain Style in Light of John Cotton's *A Practicall Commentary Upon the First Epistle Generall of John*,"

William and Mary Quarterly, 37 (October 1980): 577-591;

Rosenmeier, "New England's Perfection: The Image of Adam and the Image of Christ in the Antinomian Crisis, 1634 through 1638," *William and Mary Quarterly*, 27 (July 1970): 435-459;

Rosenmeier, "The Teacher and the Witness: John Cotton and Roger Williams," *William and Mary Quarterly*, 25 (July 1968): 408-431;

Darrett B. Rutman, *Winthrop's Boston: A Portrait of a Puritan Town, 1630-1649* (Chapel Hill: University of North Carolina Press, 1965);

William K. B. Stoever, "Nature, Grace and John Cotton: The Theological Dimension in the New England Antinomian Controversy," *Church History*, 44 (March 1975): 22-33;

Larzer Ziff, ed., *John Cotton on the Churches of New England* (Cambridge: Harvard University Press, 1968).

Papers:

There is a collection of Cotton's papers at the Boston Public Library.

John Danforth

(8 November 1660-26 May 1730)

Robert Daly
State University of New York at Buffalo

BOOKS: *An Almanack or Register of Coelestial Configurations &c: For the Year of Our Lord God 1679* . . . (Cambridge: Printed by Samuel Green, 1679);

Kneeling to God, at Parting With Friends: Or the Fraternal Intercessory Cry of Faith & Love . . . (Boston: Printed by B. Green & J. Allen & sold by S. Phillips, 1697);

The Right Christian Temper in Every Condition . . . (Boston: Printed by B. Green & J. Allen for Samuel Sewall, Jr., 1702);

The Vile Prophanations of Prosperity by the Degenerate among the People of God . . . (Boston: Printed by Samuel Phillips, 1704);

The Blackness of Sins Against Light . . . (Boston: Printed & sold by Timothy Green, 1710);

King Hezekiah's Bitterness and Relief . . . (Boston: Printed by T. Green?, 1710);

Judgment Begun at the House of God: And The Righteous Scarcely Saved . . . (Boston: J. Allen for N. Boone, 1716);

Cases of Conscience about Singing Psalms, Briefly Considered and Resolved. An Essay, by Several Ministers of the Gospel . . . , by John Danforth, Samuel Danforth II, Peter Thatcher, and others (Boston: Printed by S. Kneeland for S. Gerrish, 1723);

A Sermon Occasioned by the Late Great Earthquake, and the Terrors That Attended It. Prepared for, and (in Part) Delivered at a Fast in Dorchester, November 7, 1727 . . . (Boston: Printed by Gamiel Rogers for John Rogers for John Eliot, 1728).

The most prolific of the poets in the Danforth family, John Danforth was the son of Samuel and Mary Danforth and the elder brother of Samuel Danforth II. He was born in Roxbury, Massachusetts, graduated from Harvard in 1627, served as a fellow of the college, and was, on 28 June 1682, ordained as pastor of the Congregational society in Dorchester, where he remained for the rest of his long life. On 21 November 1682, he married Elizabeth Minot. They had three sons, Elijah, John, and Samuel. Extremely studious and learned, he excelled in mathematics and literature, and he traveled to Assonet Neck near Dighton, Massachusetts, to make a careful transcription of the curious carvings on Dighton Rock in the Taunton River, to see if he might be able to decipher those mysterious marks, some made by Indians and others possibly made by the lost Portuguese explorer Miguel Cortereale in 1511.

Danforth experimented with poetry in many genres, exchanged manuscripts of verses with Edward Taylor and Samuel Sewall, and managed to have nearly every poem he wrote published, often appending them to appropriate sermons. His notion of the poet as one who performs a public service for his community is evident not only in his many

THE

MERCIES

Of the YEAR,

COMMEMORATED:

A SONG for

Little *CHILDREN*

IN

NEW-ENGLAND.

December 13*th* 1720.

[1]

HEaven's MERCY ſhines, *Wonders* & *Glorys* meet;
Angels are left in ſweet *ſurprize* to ſee't.
The *Circle* of the *Year* is well near Run:
Earth's-*Conflagration* is not yet begun.

[2]

Heaven ſpares the *Bulwark* of our *Peace*, King GEORGE;
Our CHARTER holds; and *Priviledges* large.
Our GOVERNOUR and SENATORS can meet;
And Greet, and *Join* in Conſultations ſweet.

[3]

Though *Great* our *Loſs* in GREENWOOD's bleſs'd Tranſlation;
Yet well fill'd *Pulpits* bleſs the *Little Nation*.
New Churches Gather'd; Th' *Eaſtern Peace* not loſt;
And *Satan's* overthrown with all his Hoſt.

[4]

Sickneſs from Diſtant Lands Arrives, and Fears;
JEHOVAH in the *Mount* as oft *Appears*.
Contagion ſtops with Precious *Captain* GORE;
How *Great* our *Loſs*? But *Heav'n* will draw no more.

[5]

Tho' ripening HEAT came *late*, yet *Froſt* held off,
We Reap the *Harveſt*, and have *Bread* enough.
Proviſion's dear, Goods high, Bills low, Caſh none;
And yet the *Suffering Tribe* is not *Undone*.

[6]

A *Miracle*! That Ocean-Seas of Sin,
Have not prevail'd to let a Deluge in!
That Earth's upheld to bear the heavy Load!
Adore the *Grace* of a Long-ſuffering GOD!

[7]

Some Vices in the Church not yet ſubdu'd;
Old Barren Vines and Trees, not yet down hew'd.
Sinners, not ſent to their Deſerved Place;
A YEAR is added to their DAY of Grace.

[8]

The Fugitive may be returned home;
The Foe to GOD, a Favourite become:
Who have no ſhelter from Thy Jealous Eye,
JESUS! for ſhelter to thy Wounds may Fly.

[9]

The *whole Years ſpace* for Faith, Repentance, Prayer;
The *Moſt* have not improved well, I Fear:
Look then, *with broken Hearts*, upon your ways;
And ſee, your *Future Lives*, JEHOVAH *Praiſe*.

PSALM CVII. *laſt Part.*

TRANSLATED

by the Reverend

Mr. *Iſaac Watts*

And by him Intitled,

A *Pſalm* for

New-England.

[1]

WHen GOD provok'd with daring Crimes,
Scourges the madneſs of the Times,
He turns their Fields to barren Sand,
And Drys the Rivers from the Land.

[2]

His Word can Raiſe the Springs again,
And make the wither'd Mountains Green.
Send ſhowry Bleſſings from the Skies;
And Harveſts in the Deſart riſe.

[3]

Where nothing dwelt but Beaſts of Prey,
Or Men as Fierce and Wild as they,
He bids th' Oppreſs'd and Poor Repair,
And builds them Towns, and Cities there.

[4]

They Sow the Fields, and Trees they Plant,
Whoſe Yearly Fruit, ſupplies their Want.
Their Race Grows up from fruitful Stocks;
Their Wealth Increaſes with their Flocks.

[5]

Thus they are Bleſs'd. But if they Sin,
He lets the Heathen Nations in;
A Savage Crew invades their Lands;
Their Princes Dye by Barbarous Hands.

[6]

Their Captive Sons, expoſs'd to ſcorn,
Wander unpityed and Forlorn,
The Country lies unfenc'd, untill'd;
And Deſolation ſpreads the Field.

[7]

Yet, if the humbled Nation mourns,
Again His Dreadful hand, He Turns;
Again He makes their Citys Thrive;
And bids the Dying Churches Live.

[8]

The Righteous, with a Joyful Senſe,
Admire the Works of Providence:
And Tongues of Atheiſts ſhall no more,
Blaſpheme the GOD that Saints Adore.

[9]

How Few with Pious Care, Record,
Theſe wondrous dealings of the LORD?
But Wiſe Obſervers ſtill ſhall find,
The LORD is Holy, Juſt and Kind.

FINIS.

Apparently the broadside printing of Danforth's New Year's poem (accompanied by "A Psalm for New-England" by Isaac Watts) that Danforth sent Edward Taylor in 1721 (John Carter Brown Library, Brown University) elegies but also in his frequent allusions to Vergil, George Herbert, and others who had served as public poets and supporters of their communities. In many of the elegies, moreover, the source of comfort is that the subject of the poem, though apparently isolated from the grieving community, has gone to another community (salvation was a communal affair for Danforth, as for many Puritans), there to await a joyous reunion with friends only temporarily left behind. In all his lyrics, almanac verse, epigrams, anagrams, epitaphs, and verse epistles, Danforth worked, as he did in his elegies, to serve the community of poets, the community of the elect, and the community of Dorchester, where he died in 1730.

Other:

Harrison T. Meserole, ed., *Seventeenth-Century American Poetry,* includes poems by Danforth (New York: New York University Press, 1968);

Thomas A. Ryan, ed., "The Poetry of John Danforth," *Proceedings of the American Antiquarian Society,* 78 (April 1968): 129-193.

References:

Harold S. Jantz, *The First Century of New England Verse* (New York: Russell & Russell, 1962);

John Joseph May, *Danforth Genealogy* (Boston: C. H. Pope, 1902);

Marjorie Wolfe McCune, "The Danforths: Puritan Poets," Ph.D. dissertation, Pennsylvania State University, 1968;

John Langdon Sibley, *Biographical Sketches of the Graduates of Harvard University,* volume 2 (Cambridge: Charles William Sever, 1881): 507-514.

Samuel Danforth I

(September 1626-19 November 1674)

Robert Daly

State University of New York at Buffalo

BOOKS: *MDCXLVII. An Almanack for the Year of Our Lord 1647 . . .* (Cambridge, Mass.: Printed by Matthew Daye & sold by Hez. Usher, 1647);

MDCXLVIII. An Almanack for the Year of Our Lord 1648 . . . (Cambridge: Printed by Matthew Daye, 1648);

MDCXLIX. An Almanack for the Year of Our Lord 1649 . . . (Cambridge: Printed by Samuel Green, 1649);

A Catechism (Cambridge: Printed by Samuel Green, 1651);

An Astronomical Description of the late Comet, or Blazing Star, as it appeared in New-England in the 9th, 10th, 11th, and in the Beginning of the 12th Moneth, 1664. Together With a Brief Theological Explanation Thereof. (Cambridge: Printed by Samuel Green, 1665; London: Printed for P. Parker, 1666);

A Brief Recognition of New-Englands Errand into the Wilderness; Made in the Audience of the General Assembly of the Massachusetts Colony, at Boston in N.E. on the 11th of the third Moneth, 1670. being the day of Election there. (Cambridge: Printed by Samuel Green & M. Johnson, 1671);

The Cry of Sodom Enquired Into: Upon the Occasion of the Arraignment and Condemnation of Benjamin Goad, for His Prodigious Villany . . . (Cambridge: Printed by Marmaduke Johnson, 1674).

Tutor and fellow of Harvard College, poet, astronomer, and for twenty-four years pastor of the church at Roxbury, Massachusetts, Samuel Danforth was born in Framlingham, Suffolk, England, the second son of Nicholas and Elizabeth Danforth. His mother died when he was three years old. He and his father immigrated to New England when he was eight. Though his expressions of shock when reciting from pagan poets to his Harvard tutor caused him to be thought unhealthily pious, he went on to graduate in 1643 and seems to have recovered well enough to fill his almanac for 1647 with poems modeled on Vergil and full of classical deities busily celebrating the circle of the seasons and the growth and beauty of New England.

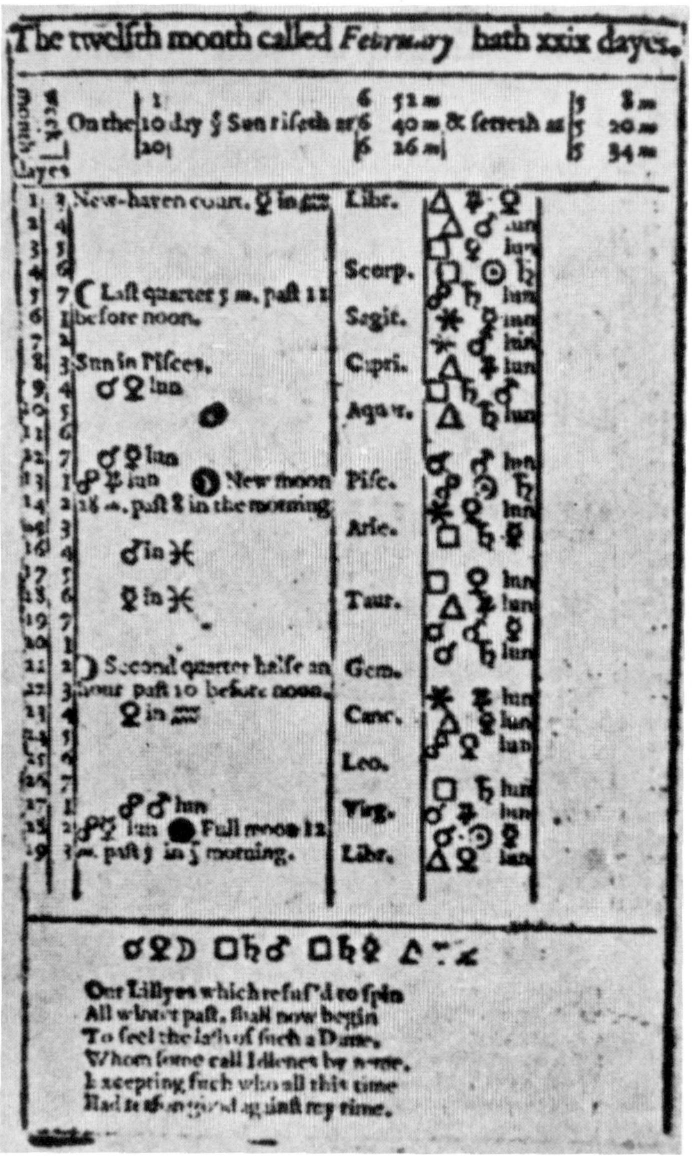

The twelfth moneth called February hath xxix dayes.

Our Lillyes which refus'd to spin
All winter past, shall now begin
To feel the lash of such a Dame,
Whom some call Idleness by name,
Excepting such who all this time
Had [illegible] against my time.

A page from Danforth's almanac for 1647 with his poetic warning against idleness

In 1641 he was invited by the Reverend Mr. Thomas Welde to become colleague pastor of the church at Roxbury, there to serve with the Reverend Mr. John Eliot, whose missionary work among the Indians often took him away from his domestic ministry. Danforth accepted the call, was ordained on 24 September 1650, and served the Roxbury congregation for the rest of his life. On 5 November 1651 he married Mary Wilson of Boston. They had twelve children, many of whom died young. Two sons, John and Samuel II, became ministers and poets.

Something of his erudition and the quality of his mind can be gathered from his description and explanation of the comet that appeared at the turn of the years 1664-1665. Danforth argued that comets have natural causes, obey mathematical laws, and should therefore be studied scientifically by astronomers; they are also signs sent to man by God, carriers of divine portents, and therefore to be studied by theologians as well. Like his brother Thomas, a colonial governor, and his sons John and Samuel II, also well-known as poets and scientists as well as for their ministry, he took an active part in all affairs of New England, sacred and secular.

Other:

Harrison T. Meserole, ed., *Seventeenth-Century*

American Poetry, includes poems by Danforth (New York: New York University Press, 1968).

References:

Harold S. Jantz, *The First Century of New England Verse* (Worcester, Mass.: American Antiquarian Society, 1944);

John Joseph May, *Danforth Genealogy* (Boston: C. H. Pope, 1902);

Marjorie Wolfe McCune, "The Danforths: Puritan Poets," Ph.D. dissertation, Pennsylvania State University, 1968;

Samuel Eliot Morison, *The Puritan Pronaos* (New York: New York University Press, 1936);

Kenneth B. Murdock, *Handkerchiefs from Paul* (Cambridge: Harvard University Press, 1927);

John Langdon Sibley, *Biographical Sketches of the Graduates of Harvard University*, volume 1 (Cambridge: Charles William Sever, 1873), pp. 88-92.

Samuel Danforth II

(18 December 1666-14 November 1727)

Robert Daly
State University of New York at Buffalo

BOOKS: *The New-England Almanack for the Year of Our Lord 1686* . . . (Cambridge: Printed by Samuel Green, 1686);

Piety Encouraged . . . (Boston: Printed by B. Green, 1705);

The Duty of Believers to Oppose the Growth of the Kingdom of Sin . . . (Boston: Printed by John Allen, 1708);

The Woful Effects of Drunkenness . . . (Boston: Printed by B. Green & sold by Samuel Gerrish, 1710);

An Exhortation to All: To Use Utmost Endeavours to Obtain a Visit of the God of Hosts, for the Preservation of Religion, and the Church, upon Earth. In a Sermon Preached Before His Excellency the Governour, the Honorable Council and Representatives of the Province of Massachusetts-Bay, in N.E. on May 26, 1714, Being the Anniversary Day of the Election of Councellors of Said Province. (Boston: Printed by B. Green & sold by Samuel Gerrish, 1714);

Cases of Conscience about Singing Psalms, Briefly Considered and Resolved. An Essay, by Several Ministers of the Gospel . . . , by Samuel Danforth II, John Danforth, Peter Thatcher, and others (Boston: Printed by S. Kneeland for S. Gerrish, 1723).

The son of Samuel and Mary Danforth and the younger brother of John Danforth, Samuel Danforth II was born in Roxbury, Massachusetts. Like his father and elder brother, he began writing poetry at Harvard, graduating in 1683, and entered the ministry, becoming pastor of the Congregational church at Taunton, Massachusetts, in 1688. In addition to serving as minister at Taunton, he ran a gristmill, taught Indian children, wrote an unpublished Indian dictionary (a portion of which is in the library of the Massachusetts Historical Society), and served as a lawyer and physician as well. On 4 October 1688, he married Hannah Allen of Boston. They had fourteen children, ten of whom outlived their father.

In "Ad Librum," the poem with which he introduced the almanac for 1686, Danforth attempted to read the signs placed by God throughout the universe and brought his own considerable knowledge of astronomy to bear on his reading. In his broadside *An Elegy on the Memory of the Worshipful Major Thomas Leonard* (1713), Danforth considered in detail Leonard's work as a doctor and lawyer in attempting to understand and articulate the religious significance of Leonard's life. Both poems are enlivened by his precise observations of a world that he saw as a book to be read carefully for the messages put there by its Maker. All contemporary accounts of his forty-one-year ministry in Taunton portray him as a man of great learning and considerable influence, especially with young people.

Other:

Harrison T. Messerole, ed., *Seventeenth-Century American Poetry*, includes poems by Danforth

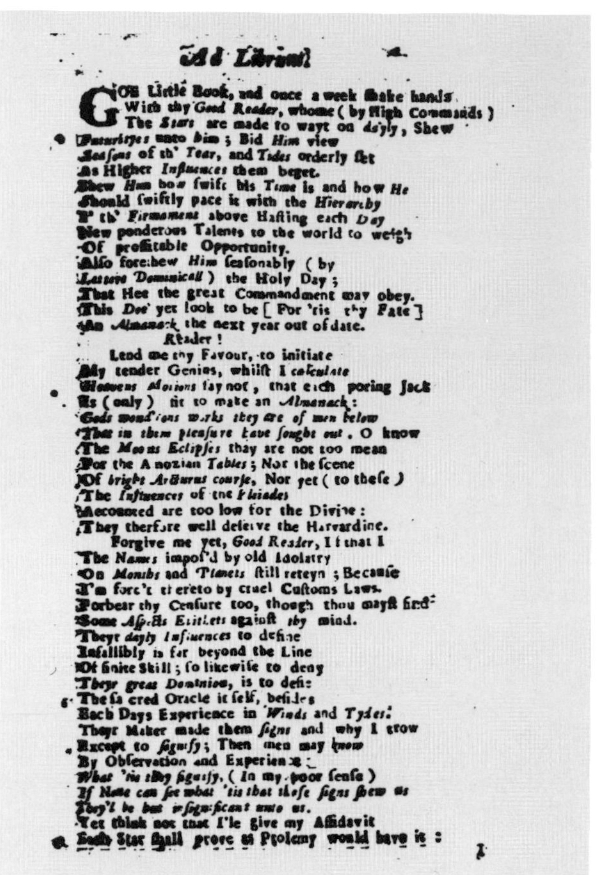

Ad Librum

GOE Little Book, and once a week ſhake hands
With thy *Good Reader*, whome (by High Commands)
The *Stars* are made to wayt on da'yly, Shew
Futuritys unto him; Bid *Him* view
Seaſons of th' *Year*, and *Tides* orderly ſet
As Higher *Influences* them beget.
Shew *Him* how ſwift his *Time* is and how *He*
Should ſwiftly pace it with the *Hierarchy*
I' th' *Firmament* above Haſting each *Day*
New ponderous Talents to the world to weigh
Of profitable Opportunity.
Alſo foreſhew *Him* ſeaſonably (by
Lettere Dominicall) the Holy Day;
That Hee the great Commandment may obey.
This *Doe* yet look to be [For 'tis thy *Fate*]
An *Almanack* the next year out of date.
Reader!
Lend me thy Favour, to initiate
My tender Genius, whilſt I *calculate*
Heavens Motions ſay not, that each poring Jack
Is (only) fit to make an *Almanack*:
Gods wond'rous works they are of men below
That in them pleaſure have ſought out. O know
The *Moons Eclipſes* thay are not too mean
For the A nozian *Tables*; Nor the ſcene
Of *bright Arcturus courſe*, Nor yet (to theſe)
The *Influences* of the *Pleiades*
Accounted are too low for the Divine:
They therfore well deſerve the Harvardine.
Forgive me yet, *Good Reader*, If that I
The *Names* impos'd by old Idolatry
On *Months* and *Planets* ſtill reteyn; Becauſe
I'm forc't thereto by cruel Cuſtoms Laws.
Forbear thy Cenſure too, though thou mayſt find
Some *Aſpects* Epithets againſt *thy* mind.
Theyr *dayly Influences* to define
Infallibly is far beyond the Line
Of finite Skill; ſo likewiſe to deny
Theyr great Dominion, is to defie
The ſacred Oracle it ſelf, beſides
Each Days Experience in *Winds* and *Tydes*.
Theyr Maker made them *ſigns* and why I trow
Except to *ſignifiy*; Then men may *know*
By Obſervation and Experience:
What 'tis they ſignify, (In my poor ſenſe)
If None can ſee what 'tis that theſe ſigns ſhew us
They'l be but inſignificant unto us.
Yet think not that I'le give my Affidavit
Each Star ſhall prove as Ptolemy would have it:

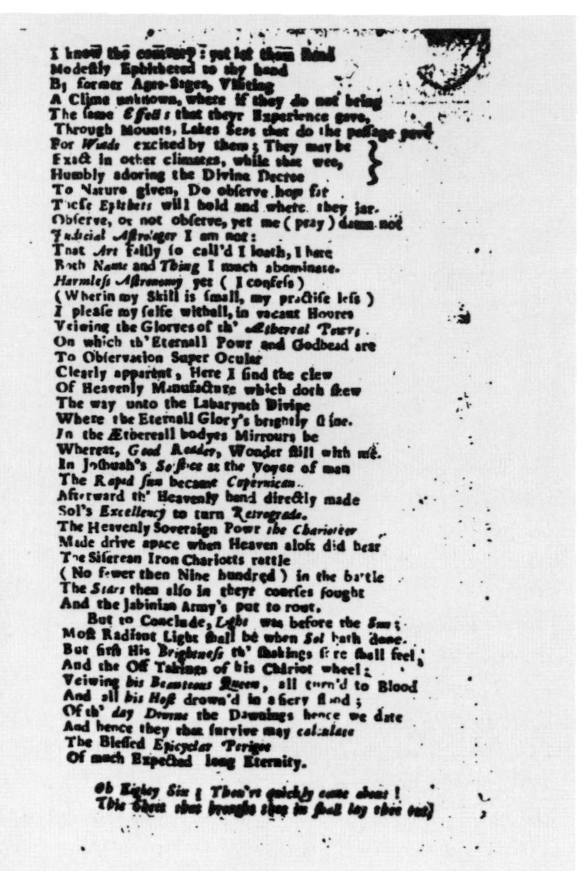

I know the contrary: yet let them ſtand
Modeſtly Epithete'd to thy hand
By former Ages-Sages, Viſiting
A Clime unknown, where if they do not bring
The ſame *Effects* that theyr Experience gave,
Through Mounts, Lakes Seas that do the paſſage pave
For *Winds* excited by them; They may be
Exact in other climates, while that wee,
Humbly adoring the Divine Decree
To Nature given, Do obſerve how far
Theſe *Epithets* will hold and where they jar.
Obſerve, or not obſerve, yet me (pray) damn not
Judicial Aſtrologer I am not:
That *Art* falſly ſo call'd I loath, I here
Both *Name* and *Thing* I much abominate.
Harmleſs Aſtronomy yet (I confeſs)
(Wherin my Skill is ſmall, my practiſe leſs)
I pleaſe my ſelfe withall, in vacant Houres
Veiwing the Gloryes of th' *Æthereal Towrs*,
On which th' Eternall Powr and Godhead are
To Obſervation Super Ocular
Clearly apparent, Here I find the clew
Of Heavenly Manufacture which doth ſhew
The way unto the Labarynth Divine
Where the Eternall Glory's brightly ſhine.
In the Æthereall bodyes Mirrours be
Whereat, *Good Reader*, Wonder ſtill with me.
In Joſhuah's *Soſtice* at the Voyce of man
The *Rapid ſun* became *Copernican*.
Afterward th' Heavenly hand directly made
Sol's *Excellency* to turn *Retrograde*.
The Heavenly Sovereign Powr *the Charioteer*
Made drive apace when Heaven aloft did hear
The Siſerean Iron Chariotts rattle
(No fewer then Nine hundred) in the battle
The *Stars* then alſo in theyr courſes fought
And the Jabinian Army's put to rout.
But to Conclude, *Light* was before the *Sun*;
Moſt Radiant Light ſhall be when *Sol* hath done.
But firſt His *Brightneſs* th' ſhakings fire ſhall feel,
And the Off Takings of his Chariot wheel;
Veiwing *his Beauteous Queen*, all turn'd to Blood
And all *his Hoſt* drown'd in a fiery flood;
Of th' *day Divine* the Dawnings hence we date
And hence they that ſurvive may *calculate*
The Bleſſed *Epicyclar Perigee*
Of much Expected long Eternity.

Oh Eighty Six! Thou'rt quickly come about!
This Sheet that brought thee in ſhall lay thee out.

Pages from Danforth's almanac for 1686 with his introductory poem (from a facsimile at John Carter Brown Library, Brown University; location of original unknown)

(New York: New York University Press, 1968).

References:

Harold S. Jantz, *The First Century of New England Verse* (Worcester, Mass.: American Antiquarian Society, 1944);

John Joseph May, *Danforth Genealogy* (Boston: C. H. Pope, 1902);

Marjorie Wolfe McCune, "The Danforths: Puritan Poets," Ph.D. dissertation, Pennsylvania State University, 1968;

John Langdon Sibley, *Biographical Sketches of Graduates of Harvard University*, volume 3 (Cambridge: Charles William Sever, 1885), pp. 243-249.

Daniel Denton
(circa 1626-1703)

Paul Royster

BOOK: *A Brief Description of New-York: Formerly Called New-Netherlands . . .* (London: Printed for John Hancock & William Bradley, 1670; New York: Gowans, 1845).

Daniel Denton, son of the first Presbyterian minister in America, wrote a promotional tract in 1670 to encourage English settlement of territories lately seized from the Dutch. Denton's *A Brief Description of New-York . . .* gives an account of the geographical features and general economy of the country surrounding New York, relates some customs of the native inhabitants, and offers incentives and advice to prospective settlers.

Denton was born around 1626 in Yorkshire, England, son of Helen Windlblank and the Reverend Richard Denton. In the 1640s he accompanied his father to Massachusetts, Connecticut, and eventually Long Island. In 1650 he was made town clerk of Hempstead, where his father was pastor, and in 1656 he held the same position in the town of Jamaica. When his father removed to Halifax, Nova Scotia, Denton remained on Long Island, and in 1664 he became one of the grantees of a patent at Elizabethtown, New Jersey. In 1665 and 1666 he served as justice of the peace in New York. Around 1659, Denton married Abigail Stevenson, who bore three children and from whom he was divorced in 1672. The two elder children, Daniel and Abigail, remained with their father, while the infant daughter, Mercy, accompanied her mother, who subsequently remarried. Denton left New York for England in 1670 (which may have occasioned his divorce), and there he evidently participated in settlement enterprises and possibly in the newly acquired (by the English) fur trade.

A Brief Description of New-York: Formerly Called New-Netherlands . . . is a twenty-five-page pamphlet describing the topography, climate, soil, fauna and flora, settlements, crops, products, trades and occupations of the area between the Hudson and Delaware rivers, including Manhattan Island, Staten Island, and Long Island. Denton also included in his pamphlet some anecdotal relations of Indian customs and society. Quite understandably, he did not describe the Indians as a threatening presence, noting that "it hath been generally observed, that where the *English* come to settle, a Divine Hand makes way for them; by removing or cutting off the *Indians*, either by Wars one with the other, or by some raging mortal Disease." Likewise, Denton gave little attention to the Dutch inhabitants of New York, other than to remark how much more effective British force would be in controlling the Indians.

A

Brief Deſcription

OF

NEW-YORK:

Formerly Called

New-Netherlands,

With the Places thereunto Adjoyning.

Together with the

Manner of its Scituation, Fertility of the Soyle, Healthfulneſs of the Climate, and the Commodities thence produced.

ALSO

Some Directions and Advice to ſuch as ſhall go thither: An Account of what Commodities they ſhall take with them; The Profit and Pleaſure that may accrew to them thereby.

LIKEWISE

A Brief RELATION of the Cuſtoms of the *Indians* there.

By *DANIEL DENTON*.

LONDON,

Printed for John Hancock, *at the first shop in* Popes Head Alley, *in* Cornhil, *at the Three Bibles, and* William Bradley, *at the Bible in the* Minories, 1670.

Title page for Denton's promotional tract, written to encourage Englishmen to settle in territory the British had recently seized from the Dutch (John Carter Brown Library, Brown University)

The recurrent theme of Denton's tract is the New World's availability of land, and it lays its greatest stress on the material advantages and opportunities of colonial life: "here any one may furnish himself with land, and live rent-free, yea, with such a quantity of land, that he may weary himself with walking over his fields of Corn, and all sorts of Grain." The pamphlet's strongest appeal is to "those which Fortune hath frowned upon in *England*, to deny them an inheritance amongst their Brethren, . . . [who] may procure here inheritances of land and possessions, stock themselves with all sorts of Cattel, enjoy the benefit of them whilst they live, and leave them to the benefit of their children when they die." Denton identified America (specifically New York) with this particular trajectory of success, and his tract represents an early prototype of the myth of American soil as the "land of opportunity": "How many poor people in the world would think themselves happy, had they an Acre or two of Land, whilst here is hundreds, nay thousands of Acres, that would invite inhabitants."

Denton's pamphlet reflects other characteristic colonial attitudes as well—most notably a sense of the self-reliant egalitarian flavor of American society, "where a Waggon or Cart gives as good content as a Coach, and a piece of their home-made Cloth, better than the finest Lawns or richest Silks," and a typically Puritan reference to America as the new Promised Land: "I must needs say, that if there be any terrestrial *Canaan*, 'tis surely here, where the Land floweth with milk and honey." Denton was anxious in this last passage to be understood in a literal as well as typological sense, and indeed the secular note dominates throughout the tract. Denton's early vision of the westward expansion of English culture and his mode of representing the American wilderness as an agrarian frontier were well on their way to becoming conventional tropes in a formalized rhetoric of the New World. Denton's book exemplifies the migration of ideas from New England southward and westward across the continent, and also the capacity of those ideas to adapt and develop in response to local circumstances.

After *A Brief Description of New-York . . .* , Denton published nothing more. He returned to America in 1673, settling in Piscataway in East Jersey, where he was appointed magistrate. The next year, however, he removed to Springfield, Massachusetts, where he taught school and served as the town recorder. In 1676 he married Hannah Leonard by whom he had six children—Hannah, Samuel, Sarah, Elizabeth, Thomas, and Alice. He returned to Jamaica, New York, in 1684, became county clerk of Queens County in 1689, and died intestate in 1703.

References:

George D. A. Combes, *Genealogy of the Descendents of Reverend Richard Denton* (Ann Arbor: University Microfilms, 1980);

William Hubbard, *A General History of New England from the Discovery to MDCLXXX*, revised edition (Boston: Little & Brown, 1848);

Frank Melville Kerr, "The Reverend Richard Denton and the Coming of the Presbyterians," *New York History* (April 1940);

Benjamin F. Thompson, *History of Long Island . . .* , revised and enlarged edition, 2 volumes (New York: Gould Banks, 1843).

Jonathan Dickinson

(22 April 1688-7 October 1747)

Paul W. Harris
University of Michigan

(Princeton University Archives)

SELECTED BOOKS: *Remarks upon Mr. Gales Reflections on Mr. Walls History of Infant-Baptism* . . . (New York: Printed by William Bradford for T. Wood, 1721);

A Sermon Preached at the Opening of the Synod at Philadelphia, September 19, 1722 . . . (Boston: Printed by T. Fleet for S. Gerrish, 1723);

A Defence of Presbyterian Ordination. In Answer to a Pamphlet, Entituled, A Modest Proof, of the Order and Government Settled by Christ, in the Church . . . (Boston: Printed for Daniel Henchman, 1724);

Remarks upon the Postscript to the Defence of a Book Lately Reprinted at Boston, entituled, A Modest Proof of the Order, &c. . . . (Boston: Printed for D. Henchman, 1724);

Remarks upon a Discourse Intituled an Overture. Presented to the Reverend Synod of Dissenting Ministers sitting in Philadelphia, in the Month of September, 1728 . . . (New York: Printed by J. Peter Zenger, 1729);

The Reasonableness of Christianity. In Four Sermons . . . (Boston: Printed by S. Kneeland & T. Green for Samuel Gerrish, 1732);

The Scripture-Bishop. Or, The Divine Right of Presbyterian Ordination and Government, Consider'd in a Dialogue Between Praelaticus and Eleutherius (Boston: Printed for D. Henchman, 1732);

The Scripture-Bishop Vindicated. A Defense of the Dialogue Between Praelaticus and Eleutherius, upon the Scripture-Bishop, or the Divine Right of Presbyterian Ordination and Government . . . (Boston: Printed by S. Kneeland & T. Green for D. Henchman, 1733);

A Sermon Preached at the Funeral of Mrs. Ruth Pierson, Wife of the Reverend Mr. John Pierson . . . (New York: Printed by William Bradford, 1733);

Remarks Upon a Pamphlet, Entitled, A Letter to a Friend in the Country . . . (Philadelphia: Printed & sold by Andrew Bradford, 1735);

The Vanity of Human Institutions in the Worship of God . . . (New York: Printed by John Peter Zenger, 1736);

A Defence of a Sermon Preached at Newark, June 2, 1736, Entituled, The Vanity of Human Institutions in the Worship of God, Against the Exceptions of Mr. John Beach . . . (New York: Printed by J. Peter Zenger, 1737);

The Reasonableness of Nonconformity to the Church of England, in Point of Worship . . . (Boston: Printed & sold by Kneeland & Green, 1738);

The Danger of Schisms and Contentions, With Respect to the Ministry and Ordinances of the

Gospel... (New York: Printed & sold by J. Peter Zenger, 1739);

A Call to the Weary & Heavy Laden to Come Unto Christ for Rest... (New York: Printed & sold by William Bradford, 1740);

Observations on that Terrible Disease Vulgarly Called the Throat-Distemper. With Advices as to the Method of Cure (Boston: Printed & sold by S. Kneeland & T. Green, 1740);

The Witness of the Spirit... (Boston: Printed & sold by S. Kneeland & T. Green, 1740);

The True Scripture-Doctrine Concerning Some Important Points of Christian Faith . . . (Boston: Printed by D. Fowle, 1741);

A Display of God's Special Grace . . . (Boston: Printed by Rogers & Fowle for S. Eliot, 1742);

A Protestation Presented to the Synod of Philadelphia, May 29, 1742, by Dickinson and others (Philadelphia, 1742);

A Defence of the Dialogue Intitled A Display of God's Special Grace . . . (Boston: Printed by J. Draper for S. Eliot, 1743);

The Nature and Necessity of Regeneration... (New York: Printed & sold by James Parker, 1743);

Reflections upon Mr. Wetmore's Letter in Defence of Dr. Waterland's Discourse of Regeneration . . . (Boston: Printed by J. Draper for S. Eliot & J. Blanchard, 1744);

Familiar Letters to a Gentleman, Upon a Variety of Seasonable and Important Subjects in Religion . . . (Boston: Printed & sold by Rogers & Fowle & by J. Blanchard, 1745);

A Brief Illustration and Confirmation of the Divine Right of Infant Baptism... (Boston: Printed & sold by S. Kneeland & T. Green, 1746);

A Vindication of God's Sovereign Free Grace . . . (Boston: Printed & sold by Rogers & Fowle & by J. Blanchard, 1746);

A Second Vindication of God's Sovereign Free Grace . . . (Boston: Printed & sold by Rogers & Fowle, 1748);

Sermons and Tracts . . . (Edinburgh: Printed for M. Gray, 1793).

Jonathan Dickinson was the foremost intellectual leader of American Presbyterianism during its formative decades and the key figure in the founding of the College of New Jersey (later Princeton University). His prolific output of books, pamphlets, and published sermons earned him a reputation as a formidable controversialist.

Dickinson was born on 22 April 1688 in Hatfield, Massachusetts, to Hezekiah and Abigail Dickinson. He graduated from Yale in 1706 and in 1709 was ordained pastor at Elizabethtown, New Jersey, where he remained for the rest of his life. He also served as the community's physician. In 1717 his congregation entered the Presbyterianism church, which in its early years in America had a loose organization virtually indistinguishable from the ministerial associations being formed by Connecticut Valley Congregationalists.

Dickinson soon emerged as the spokesman for those ministers whose conception of Presbyterian polity derived, like his, from New England backgrounds. The model for their principal opponents was the Presbyterianism of Scotland, and they sought to impose the formal creed of that church. In contrast, Dickinson advocated the Bible as the church's sole creed, arguing that man-made interpretations were more likely to sow divisions than to check heresy. Concerned with maintaining denominational unity, he played a major role in fashioning the compromise Adopting Act of 1729, which required creedal subscription but allowed a loophole for conscientious scruples over any article in the creed deemed nonessential to a true Christian faith. Thereafter Dickinson avoided intradenominational controversy until the Great Awakening renewed discord. Seeking to restrain the censorious behavior of both enthusiasts and antirevivalists, he articulated a moderate evangelicalism similar to the views of Jonathan Edwards. He expressed his views in several works, including his most systematic theological discourse, *The True Scripture-Doctrine* . . . (1741). When his moderate strategy failed to prevent a Presbyterian schism, Dickinson reluctantly joined in forming the prorevival Synod of New York in 1745.

Dickinson's interest in promoting piety and preserving union also informed his many controversial writings against the Anglicans, as well as a smaller group against the Baptists over the issue of infant baptism. The Anglican controversy began after the "Yale apostasy" of 1722, when Samuel Johnson, Timothy Cutler, and three others converted to the Church of England. Dickinson answered the Anglican attack on the validity of Presbyterian ordination by defending ministerial equality against the hierarchical structure of Anglicanism, and in a series of increasingly weighty tomes he sought to bury his opponents under a mass of scriptural and historical evidence. The controversy broadened in 1736 with the publication of Dickinson's sermon on *The Vanity of Human Institutions in the Worship of God*..., in which he returned to his earlier theme that substituting human inventions for the Bible undermined piety

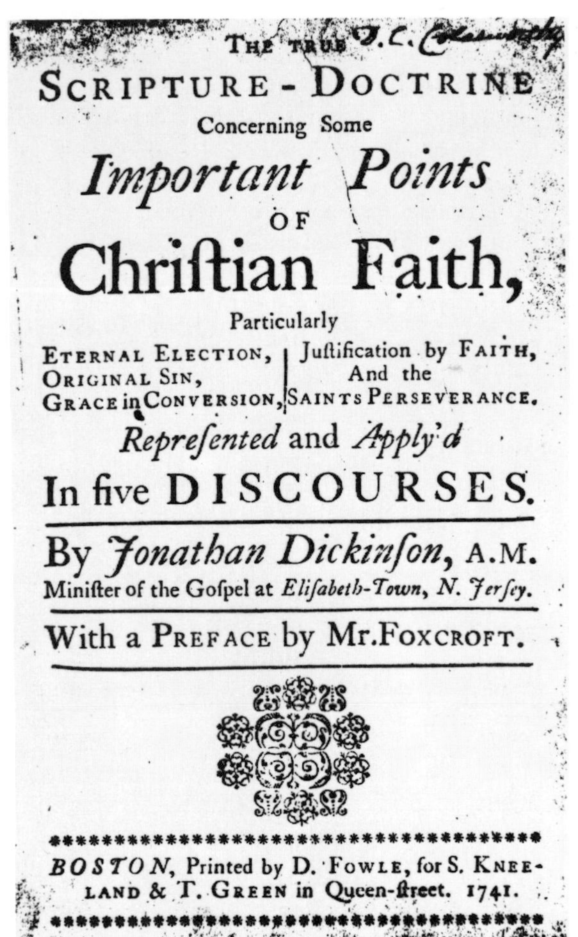

THE TRUE
SCRIPTURE-DOCTRINE
Concerning Some
Important Points
OF
Chriſtian Faith,
Particularly

ETERNAL ELECTION,	Juſtification by FAITH,
ORIGINAL SIN,	And the
GRACE in CONVERSION,	SAINTS PERSEVERANCE.

Repreſented and *Apply'd*
In five DISCOURSES.

By *Jonathan Dickinſon*, A.M.
Miniſter of the Goſpel at *Eliſabeth-Town, N. Jerſey.*

With a PREFACE by Mr. FOXCROFT.

BOSTON, Printed by D. FOWLE, for S. KNEELAND & T. GREEN in Queen-ſtreet. 1741.

Title page for Dickinson's most systematic theological discourse, in which he expresses moderate evangelical views similar to those of Jonathan Edwards (John Carter Brown Library, Brown University)

and was the root source of persecution and schisms. That sermon and its two defenses, *A Defence of a Sermon Preached at Newark . . .* (1737) and *The Reasonableness of Nonconformity to the Church of England, in Point of Worship . . .* (1738), are the clearest statements of the political basis of Dickinson's lifelong advocacy of the Bible as the exclusive and complete constitution of the church. In these works, he employs a strict-constructionist approach to scripture and argues against the coercive imposition of artificial forms in Christian worship. Dickinson's reliance on scriptural precedent for determining forms of organization and worship should not, however, be confused with biblical literalism, since he was willing to admit an allegorical interpretation of Adam's fall. Rather, his strict-constructionist approach was used to combat the corrosive effects of formalism on piety and to defend both local autonomy and individual freedom of conscience.

To Dickinson, creeds, forms, and hierarchies were a weak substitute for close attention to ministerial qualifications, comprising education, character, and Christian experience. In line with this long-standing commitment, he was among a group of clerical and lay Presbyterians who in 1746 succeeded in gaining a charter for the College of New Jersey, and he was promptly elected its first president. Until his death on 7 October 1747, he conducted classes in his home. Dickinson was largely responsible for the distinctive combination of catholicity and piety that characterized the early years of the college.

References:

Keith J. Hardman, "Jonathan Dickinson and the Course of American Presbyterianism, 1717-1747," Ph.D. dissertation, University of Pennsylvania, 1971;

Leonard J. Trinterud, *The Forming of an American Tradition* (Philadelphia: Westminster Press, 1949).

William Douglass

(circa 1691-21 October 1752)

Davis D. Joyce
University of Tulsa

SELECTED BOOKS: *The Abuses and Scandals of Some Late Pamphlets in Favour of Inoculation of the Small-Pox* . . . (Boston: Printed by J. Franklin, 1722);

Inoculation of the Small-Pox as Practised in Boston . . . (Boston: Printed by J. Franklin, 1722);

Postscript. Being a Short Answer to Matters of Fact, &c. Misrepresented in a Late Doggerel Dialogue (Boston: Printed by J. Franklin, 1722);

A Dissertation Concerning Inoculation of the Small-Pox . . . (Boston: Printed for D. Henchman & T. Hancock, 1730);

A Practical Essay Concerning the Small-Pox . . . (Boston: Printed for D. Henchman & T. Hancock, 1730; London: Printed for W. Innys, 1730);

The Practical History of a New Epidemical Eruptive Military Fever, With an Angina Ulcusculosa which Prevailed in Boston New England, in the years 1735 and 1736 . . . (Boston: Printed & sold by Thomas Fleet, 1736);

An Essay, Concerning Silver and Paper Currencies; More Especially with Regard to the British Colonies in New England (Boston: Printed by S. Kneeland & T. Green, 1738);

A Discourse Concerning the Currencies of the British Plantations in America. Especially with Regard to their Paper Money . . . (London: Printed for T. Cooper, R. Amey & Mrs. Nutt, 1739; Boston: Printed & sold by S. Kneeland & T. Green, 1740);

1743 Mercurius Nov-Anglicanus, or An Almanack . . . , as William Nadir (Boston: Printed & sold by Rogers & Fowle, 1742);

1744. Mercurius Nov-Anglicanus, or An Almanack . . . , as Nadir (Boston: Printed & sold by Rogers & Fowle, 1743);

1745. Mercurius Nov-Anglicanus, or An Almanack . . . , as Nadir (Boston: Printed & sold by Rogers & Fowle, 1744);

1746. Mercurius Nov-Anglicanus, or An Almanack . . . , as Nadir (Boston: Printed & sold by Rogers & Fowle, 1745);

1747. Mercurius Nov-Anglicanus, or An Almanack . . . , as Nadir (Boston: Printed by Rogers & Fowle, 1746);

1748. Mercurius Nov-Anglicanus, or An Almanack . . . , as Nadir (Boston: Printed & sold by Rogers & Fowle, 1747);

A Summary, Historical and Political, of the First Planting, Progressive Improvements, and Present State of the British Settlements in North-America, volume 1, nos. 1-16 (Boston: Printed & sold by Rogers & Fowle, 1747); volume 1, nos. 17-28 (Boston: Printed & sold by Rogers & Fowle, 1748); volume 1, nos. 29-36 (Boston: Printed & sold by Rogers & Fowle, 1749); volume 1, complete (Boston: Printed & sold by Rogers & Fowle, 1749); volume 2, nos. 1-14 (Boston: Printed & sold by Daniel Fowle, 1750); volume 2, nos. 15-23 (Boston: Printed & sold by Daniel Fowle, 1751); volume 2, part 1 (Boston: Printed & sold by Daniel Fowle, 1752); two volumes (London: Printed for R. Baldwin, 1755).

William Douglass was better known as a doctor than as a man of letters; indeed, from 1721—when he rose to prominence as a result of his pamphlets opposing Cotton Mather and others on their plan to inoculate the populace of Boston for smallpox—to his death in 1752, Douglass was the generally accepted head of the medical profession in that city and one of the most distinguished American physicians of the day. Douglass's primary literary contribution was *A Summary, Historical and Political, of the First Planting, Progressive Improvements, and Present State of the British Settlements in North-America* (1747-1752). Max Savelle may have exaggerated a bit when he credited this work with being "the first important literary and documentary expression to an American continental self-consciousness" and Douglass with being the first author "to present the American colonies as a unity," but his statement does illustrate the importance some have attached to Douglass's historical/literary endeavors.

Not much is known about Douglass before his arrival in New England in 1716. He was born in Gifford, Haddington County, Scotland, sometime in 1691. His father, George Douglass, was wealthy enough to provide him with a good education, for he attended the University of Edinburgh, then went to Leyden to complete his medical studies under the renowned Hermann Boerhaave. Boerhaave, however, was not the major influence on the young Douglass; that was the notable maverick Archibald Pitcairne of Edinburgh, who favored a clinical approach to medicine similar to that of the great English physician Thomas Sydenham. After practical experience at a city hospital in Paris, Douglass moved to Bristol, in England, and began a promising medical practice. When presented with an opportunity, however, he departed for New England, which he found profitable and much to his liking. He was to spend the rest of his life in Boston.

Douglass's writings before *A Summary, Historical and Political, . . . of the British Settlements in North-America* focused on two subjects: medicine and currency. His major contribution in the field of medical writing was a 1736 pamphlet entitled *The Practical History of a New Epidemical Eruptive Military Fever, With an Angina Ulcusculosa which Prevailed in Boston New England, in the years 1735 and 1736. . . .* Though he did not call it that, Douglass was clearly describing scarlet fever; indeed, his essay is generally credited as the first adequate clinical description of the disease, antedating the better-known essay by John Fothergill in London by twelve years.

Currency may seem a strange subject for a physician such as Douglass, but it became almost an obsession with him, and his work in this area, especially the 1739 pamphlet entitled *A Discourse Concerning the Currencies of the British Plantations in America . . . ,* earned him favorable mention in Adam Smith's *The Wealth of Nations* (1776). Thomas Hutchinson called him "the oracle of the anti-paper party," and though Douglass's language was, as usual, somewhat vituperative, his views were really more moderate. As David Freeman Hawke has pointed out, "To a degree it resembled his reaction to inoculation: he did not adamantly oppose the experiment but only the rash way legislatures performed it."

If the remarks on paper money were excerpted from Douglass's *A Summary, Historical and Political, . . . of the British Settlements in North-America* they would make a fair-sized volume. This work is the one for which Douglass is best known in the field of literature and historiography. Yet, as a historian, Douglass fell far short of the best standards of his day. He was extremely contentious. He especially delighted in attacking the works of

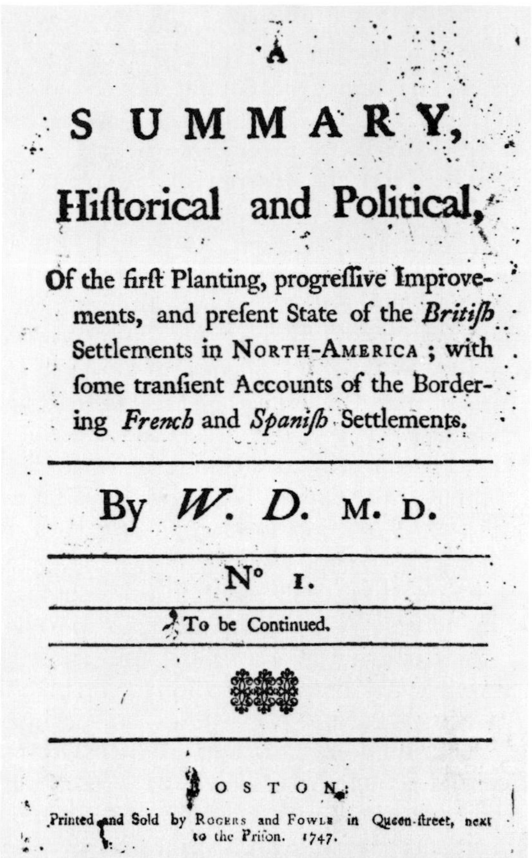

A

SUMMARY,

Hiſtorical and Political,

Of the firſt Planting, progreſſive Improvements, and preſent State of the *Britiſh* Settlements in NORTH-AMERICA ; with ſome tranſient Accounts of the Bordering *French* and *Spaniſh* Settlements.

By *W. D.* M. D.

N° I.

To be Continued.

BOSTON:

Printed and Sold by ROGERS and FOWLE in Queen-ſtreet, next to the Priſon. 1747.

Title page for the first part of Douglass's history, said to be the first work "to present the American colonies as a unity" (John Carter Brown Library, Brown University)

fellow historians; he referred to the work of Cotton Mather and other New England historians as "beyond all excuse intolerably erroneous" and to Daniel Neal's *History of New England* (1720) as "a tedious silly ridiculous conjectural account." The fact that he wrote at odd times stolen from his professional work is obvious—his work is badly organized and seems more like a mass of pungent, ill-digested notes than a finished history. Frequently, for example, he drifted into lengthy "digressions," many on medicine and currency, of course, and with good information, but others were on subjects which simply seemed to interest him at the moment and were not at all relevant to the story he was telling. "The following digression may perhaps be an agreeable amusement to some readers," he might say, or sometimes he simply inserted the blunt heading "A DIGRESSION." This trait, among others, led Hawke to conclude that Douglass's history "resembles no other work in the English language so much as Laurence Sterne's

Tristram Shandy. . . . Compared with Sterne, Douglass was an artless writer, yet the two men shared a strikingly similar approach to their material. Each knew where he was going and took an incredibly circuitous route to get there."

Finally, and most seriously, Douglass was extremely careless about his sources. He denied the necessity of using original sources: "This is a laborious affair, being obliged to consult MSS records." And he gathered material to support his views from the reports of unreliable correspondents. "Historians, like sworn Evidences in Courts of Law, ought to declare the WHOLE TRUTH (so far as comes to their knowledge) and nothing but the TRUTH." So proclaimed Douglass at the beginning of his second volume, but his work fell far short of that ideal, partly because Douglass died before he was able to complete it.

In many ways, Douglass's work is comparable to John Oldmixon's *The British Empire in America* . . . (1708); both wrote of the colonies in general rather than of a particular colony, and they are sometimes regarded as early "imperialist" historians. But Oldmixon's work, with all its flaws, is superior to Douglass's—even though Douglass did refer to Oldmixon as "an erroneous Scribbler." Certainly Oldmixon would have agreed with Douglass that "It is a common but mistaken notion, that sending abroad colonists weakens the mother-country. . . . The people sent from Great-Britain and their progeny made vastly more profitable returns, than they could possibly have done by their labour at home."

Douglass began his history with a short survey of ancient and modern colonization and then went on to the settlement of North America, including Canada. The materials on the colonies outside of New England, however, are comparatively scanty. Clearly, despite the mass of misinformation Douglass supplied, his volumes do possess value. A section entitled "Loose proposals towards regulating the British colonies" contains interesting material on imperial reorganization and shows Douglass to be—despite his deploring such abuses of England's power as impressment of colonial seamen by the Royal Navy and the sending of colonial troops to fight outside the colonies—essentially a defender of the royal prerogative. Douglass's work includes far more economic and social history than the books of most of his contemporaries. For the most part, though, posterity has been less impressed by Douglass's history than were his contemporaries, especially in Great Britain. The *Monthly Review*, in England, praised it highly, saying it contained a "fuller and more circumstantial account of North America, than is anywhere else to be met with." Perhaps that statement is more a commentary on the lack of information readily available on the colonies than it is legitimate praise for Douglass's history.

References:

David Freeman Hawke, "William Douglass's *Summary*," in *The Colonial Legacy, Volume II: Some Eighteenth Century Commentators*, edited by Lawrence H. Leder (New York: Harper & Row, 1971), pp. 43-74;

Michael Kraus, *The Writing of American History* (Norman: University of Oklahoma Press, 1953), pp. 55-56;

Max Savelle, *Seeds of Liberty: The Genesis of the American Mind* (New York: Knopf, 1948);

George H. Weaver, "Life and Writings of William Douglass," *Bulletin of the Society of Medical History of Chicago*, 2 (1921): 229-259.

Jonathan Edwards

Mason I. Lowance, Jr.
University of Massachusetts, Amherst

Portrait by Joseph Badger (Yale University Art Gallery)

BIRTH: East Windsor, Connecticut, 5 October 1703, to Timothy and Esther Stoddard Edwards.

EDUCATION: B.A., Yale College, 1720.

MARRIAGE: July 1727 to Sarah Pierpont; children: Sarah, Jerusha, Esther, Mary, Lucy, Timothy, Susannah, Eunice, Jonathan, Elizabeth, Pierpont.

DEATH: Princeton, New Jersey, 22 March 1758.

SELECTED BOOKS: *God Glorified in the Work of Redemption, By the Greatness of Man's Dependence upon Him* . . . (Boston: Printed by S. Kneeland & T. Green for D. Henchman, 1731);

A Divine and Supernatural Light, Immediately imparted to the Soul by the Spirit of God, Shown to be both a Scriptural, and Rational Doctrine . . . (Boston: Printed by S. Kneeland & T. Green, 1734);

The Duty and Interest of a People, Among Whom Religion has been planted, to Continue Stedfast and Sincere In The Profession and Practice of it . . . (Boston: Printed & sold by S. Kneeland & T. Green, 1736); revised as *A Faithful Narrative Of The Surprizing Work of God In The Conversion of Many Hundred Souls in Northampton, and the Neighbouring Towns and Villages* . . . (London: Printed for John Oswald, 1737; Boston: Printed & sold by S. Kneeland & T. Green and by D. Henchman, 1738);

A Letter To The Author Of the Pamphlet Called An Answeer to the Hampshire Narrative . . . (Boston, 1737);

Discourses on Various Important Subjects, Nearly concerning the great Affair of the Soul's Eternal Salvation . . . (Boston: Printed & sold by S. Kneeland & T. Green, 1738); enlarged as *Sermons on Various Important Subjects* (Edinburgh: Printed for M. Gray, 1785);

The Distinguishing Marks Of a Work of the Spirit of God . . . (Boston: Printed & sold by S. Kneeland & T. Green, 1741; London: Printed by S. Mason, 1742);

The Resort and Remedy of those that are bereaved by the Death of an eminent Minister . . . (Boston: Printed by G. Rogers for J. Edwards, 1741);

Sinners in the Hands of an Angry God . . . (Boston: Printed & sold by S. Kneeland & T. Green, 1741; Edinburgh: Printed & sold by T. Lumisden & J. Robertson, 1745);

Some Thoughts Concerning the present Revival of Religion In New-England . . . (Boston: Printed & sold by S. Kneeland & T. Green, 1742; Edinburgh: Printed by T. Lumisden & J. Robertson, 1743);

The great Concern of a Watchman for Souls . . . (Boston: Printed by Green, Bushnell & Allen for N. Proctor, 1743);

The true Excellency of a Minister of the Gospel . . .

(Boston: Printed by Rogers & Fowle for W. McAlpine, 1744);

Copies of the Two Letters Cited by The Rev. Mr. Clap, Rector of the College of New-Haven . . . (Boston: Printed & sold by S. Kneeland & T. Green, 1745);

An Expostulatory Letter From the Rev. Mr. Edwards of Northampton, To The Rev. Mr. Clap, Rector of Yale College in New Haven . . . (Boston: Printed & sold by Kneeland & Green, 1745);

The Church's Marriage to her Sons, and to her God . . . (Boston: Printed & sold by S. Kneeland & T. Green, 1746);

A Treatise Concerning Religious Affections . . . (Boston: Printed for S. Kneeland & T. Green, 1746; abridged edition, London: Printed for T. Field, 1762; unabridged edition, Edinburgh: Printed by John Gray for E. & C. Dilly in London and for J. Wood in Edinburgh, 1772);

True Saints, when absent from the Body, are present with the Lord . . . (Boston: Printed by Rogers & Fowle for D. Henchman, 1747);

An Humble Attempt To promote Explicit Agreement and Visible Union of God's People in Extraordinary Prayer for the Revival of Religion and the Advancement of Christ's Kingdom on Earth, pursuant to Scripture-Promises and Prophecies concerning the last Time . . . (Boston: Printed for D. Henchman, 1747; Northampton, England: Printed by T. Dicey, 1789);

A Strong Rod broken and withered . . . (Boston: Printed by Rogers & Fowle for J. Edwards, 1748);

An Humble Inquiry Into The Rules of the Word of God Concerning The Qualifications Requisite to a Compleat Standing and full Communion In the Visible Christian Church . . . (Boston: Printed & sold by S. Kneeland, 1749; Edinburgh: Printed for William Coke, 1790);

Christ the great Example of Gospel Ministers . . . (Boston: Printed & sold by T. Fleet, 1750);

A Farewel-Sermon Preached at the first Precinct in Northampton, After the People's publick Rejection of their Minister, and renouncing their Relation to Him . . . (Boston: Printed & sold by S. Kneeland, 1751);

Misrepresentations Corrected, And Truth vindicated, In A Reply to the Rev. Mr. Solomon Williams's Book, intitled, The True State of the Question concerning the Qualifications necessary to lawful Communion in the Christian Sacraments . . . (Boston: Printed & sold by S. Kneeland, 1752);

True Grace, Distinguished from the Experience of Devils . . . (New York: Printed by James Parker, 1753);

A careful and strict Enquiry Into The modern prevailing Notions Of That Freedom of Will, Which is supposed to be essential To Moral Agency, Vertue and Vice, Reward and Punishment, Praise and Blame (Boston: Printed & sold by S. Kneeland, 1754; London: Printed for Thomas Field, 1762);

The Great Christian Doctrine of Original Sin defended . . . (Boston: Printed & sold by S. Kneeland, 1758; London: Printed for G. Keith & J. Johnson, 1766);

Remarks On The Essays, On The Principles of Morality, And Natural Religion . . . (Edinburgh, 1758);

The Life and Character Of The Late Reverend Mr. Jonathan Edwards, President of the College at New-Jersey. Together with a Number of his Sermons On Various important Subjects, edited by Samuel Hopkins (Boston: Printed & sold by S. Kneeland, 1765; Glasgow: Printed by David Niven for James Duncan, Jr., in Glasgow & for John Brown in Dunce, 1785);

Two Dissertations, I. Concerning the End for which God created the World. II. The Nature of True Virtue. (Boston: Printed & sold by S. Kneeland, 1765; Edinburgh: Printed by William Darling for W. Laing, 1788);

A History Of the Work of Redemption . . . (Edinburgh: Printed for W. Gray in Edinburgh & for J. Buckland & G. Keith in London, 1774; Boston: Printed by Draper & Folsom, 1782);

Sermons, On The Following Subjects; The Manner in which Salvation is to be sought. The unreasonableness of Indetermination in Religion. Unbelievers contemn the glory of Christ. The folly of looking back in fleeing out of Sodom. The Warnings of Scripture in the best Manner adapted to the awakening and conversion of Sinners. Hypocrites deficient in the Duty of Prayer. The future Punishment of the wicked unavoidable and intolerable. The eternity of hell torments. The Peace which Christ gives his true Followers. The perpetuity & change of the Sabbath (Hartford: Printed by Hudson & Goodwin, 1780); enlarged as *Twenty Sermons, On Various Subjects* (Edinburgh: Printed for M. Gray, 1789);

The Eternity of Hell Torments, revised and corrected by C. E. DeCoetlogon (London: Printed by W. Justins for R. Thomson, 1788);

Practical Sermons, Never Before Published (Edinburgh: Printed for M. Gray, 1788);

Miscellaneous Observations On Important Theological Subjects, Original and Collected (Edinburgh: Printed for M. Gray in Edinburgh & for Vernor & Hood and Ogilvie & Speare in London, 1793);

Remarks on Important Theological Controversies (Edinburgh: Printed for J. Galbraith & Arch. Constable & sold by T. Longman & by Vernor & Hood in London, 1796);

Advice to Young Converts. A Letter From The Late Rev. Jonathan Edwards Of Northhampton, To A Young Lady At Suffield, Conn. To Which Is Added, A Discourse, Recommending Religious Conversation; And An Extract From A Sermon On Christian Conversation (Northampton: Printed & sold by Thomas Pomroy, 1807);

The Theological Questions Of President Edwards, Senior, And Dr. Edwards, His Son . . . (Providence: Printed by Miller & Hutchens, 1822);

Charity And Its Fruits; Or, Christian Love As Manifested In The Heart And Life . . ., edited by Tryon Edwards (New York: Carter, 1852; London: Nisbet, 1852);

Observations Concerning The Scripture Oenomy Of The Trinity And Covenant of Redemption, edited by Egbert C. Smyth (New York: Scribners, 1880);

An Unpublished Essay Of Edwards On The Trinity With Remarks On Edwards and His Theology By George P. Fisher (New York: Scribners, 1903).

COLLECTIONS: *The Works of President Edwards*, Leeds Edition, 8 volumes (Leeds: Printed by Edward Baines, 1806-1811); London Edition, 8 volumes (London: Printed for James Black & Son, 1817); supplement to the London Edition, 2 volumes (Edinburgh: Robert Ogle and Oliver & Boyd / Glasgow: M. Ogle & Son and William Collins / London: Hamilton, Adams, 1847);

The Works of President Edwards, First American Edition, 8 volumes (Worcester: Isaiah Thomas, Jr., 1808-1809);

The Works Of President Edwards: With a Memoir of His Life, 10 volumes (New York: S. Converse, 1829-1830);

The Works of Jonathan Edwards, John E. Smith, general editor, 7 volumes to date (New Haven & London: Yale University Press, 1957-).

Jonathan Edwards has usually been regarded as belonging more to the Puritan New England ministry than to a circle of early American writers. However, an examination of his career will show that he was far less successful as a parish minister in the early eighteenth century than he eventually became as a prose stylist and author of sermons, treatises, and even history. It is ironic, then, that Edwards is often depicted in the popular imagination as a staunch Calvinist minister, a "fire and brimstone" preacher closely associated with the Great Awakening, and a persecutor of wrongdoers. A more accurate picture of the real Edwards would reveal one who lost control of his congregation so completely that by 1748, he was the object of an inquisition and was subsequently dismissed from his pulpit and sent into virtual exile in Stockbridge, Massachusetts, where he spent almost ten lonely years as a missionary-minister to the Indians, who would hardly have understood his language, let alone his metaphysics. As a parish minister, he was successful only so long as he worked closely in the shadow of his grandfather, Solomon Stoddard, the powerful and liberal "bastard of the [Connecticut River] valley," with whom Edwards shared the Northampton pulpit for several years and whose practices of liberal admissions to the sacrament he continued even after assuming the pulpit on his own.

Edwards's career follows the parabolic curve of a tragic drama. His ministry was initially responsible for the vast emotional upheaval that disturbed New England during the 1730s and 1740s and was later known as the Great Awakening. As a preacher known to the general population of his time, Edwards was immensely successful. But as a parish minister, his life was agonizing and frustrating, ending ultimately in what amounts to a church trial and dismissal, as Patricia Tracy's excellent book on the subject makes clear. He had extremely poor relations with his congregation in Northampton, resulting in petty squabbles over the cost of his meager clothing (the price of a hat, in one instance) and his more extensive quarrel in 1744 that was based on his tactless and unfortunate public reading of a list of persons from his congregation involved in immoral practices, such as the use of foul language and the reading of a prohibited book, *Midwifery Rightly Represented.* Having secured the congregational authority to investigate these young people, he proceeded to read, from the pulpit, a long list that included many of the more prominent children of the town, without bothering even to distinguish between those children who were being accused of bad practices and the accusers themselves. Later, in 1748, when many of these humiliated young people had reached voting age in the church, Edwards recanted his ministry-long practice of admitting anyone of good moral character to the Lord's Supper, one of only two sacraments retained by the Puritans, and he asserted that only those who had made public professions of faith would hereafter be admitted.

Church admission and full or partial membership had always been a problem in Massachusetts, and the Half-Way Covenant of 1662 made clear the urgent need for some kind of compromise with the staunch principles of Dortian Calvinism that the early settlers brought with them from Holland and England. It provided that the children of nonregenerate members who owned the Covenant might receive baptism, but they were not to receive the Lord's Supper, nor were they to be allowed to vote in church affairs. The Half-Way Covenant and its widespread adoption clearly indicated the liberal direction of change in New England theology before Edwards's ministry, and his cooperation with Solomon Stoddard, who loosened the requirements for church participation even further, tested Edwards's Calvinist principles and in the end precipitated his confrontation with the Northampton congregation. By the adoption of the Half-Way Covenant, unawakened persons were thus permitted to become "half-way" church members, and there came to be large numbers of people in every church whose relation was merely formal. In his bold assertions of 1748, Edwards not only offended nearly everyone in sight by excluding all but a few of his parishioners from the Lord's Supper, but he also espoused a theology of the sacrament that had been superseded during the middle decades of the previous century, nearly one hundred years earlier. As in all congregational matters, Edwards's timing was dreadful. The following two years were fraught with controversy, Edwards attempting to state his case from the pulpit and his parishioners refusing to listen. Finally, he was reduced to publishing his views in a long defense that bore an equally laborious title, *An Humble Inquiry Into The Rules of the Word of God Concerning The Qualifications Requisite to a Compleat Standing and full Communion In the Visible Christian Church* . . . (1749). For those parishioners who had already been refused the sacrament, having once enjoyed full privileges of the Northampton church, being asked to read Edwards's defense was the ultimate imposition, and few bothered even to cut the pages open, as many extant copies of this dull volume clearly show. As a minister, Edwards was finished long before he penned his defense, but from a historical point of view, it is important that he fully expressed his views, since the congregation in 1748 and 1749 was so hostile that they refused to allow him to defend himself verbally, and his sermons in manuscript from this period do not fully reflect the growing tensions over the communion issue.

As a public figure Edwards represents the last vestiges of New England Puritanism in its early form, and his chronological life closely paralleled that of Benjamin Franklin, born only a few years later and throughout the eighteenth century a rival in thought to the Edwardsean Puritanism in his insistence that the only true oracle was man's reason. In this larger arena, it could easily be argued, Edwards lost out to more modern and progressive forces, just as he appeared to be an anachronism to his congregation, who preferred to destroy their minister rather than suffer his Calvinist upbraidings. What did he ever do that would lead twentieth-century Americans to celebrate his leadership, to study his work in college and university courses?

The answer to this question is elusive, because it lies somewhere between Edwards's importance as a thinker (he was perhaps the most original philosophical mind in American history) and his distinction as a prose stylist (he was one of the most creative figures in eighteenth-century America). His many works are all written in prose; he was not a poet nor did he attempt, as had Cotton Mather, to imitate classical models in the exercise of his imagination in verse. His prose, on the other hand, is almost poetic at times, and much of his writing was generated out of the creative force of a powerful intellect that applied its genius to the observation of nature. To understand properly the importance of Jonathan Edwards in the history of American culture, it is necessary to examine him as a writer in a variety of prose genres—sermons, treatises, discourses, and histories—all of which in some way establish for Edwards an original place in American literary history.

For the student familiar with English literary history, this task is not so imposing, for Edwards wrote a kind of prose that would have appealed to Jonathan Swift as he sought to establish an academy to "regularize" the English language. Edwards was not an "imitator" of Swift, or Addison and Steele, or Samuel Johnson. It is doubtful that he knew their works well; he rarely took note of anything that was not philosophical—especially metaphysical—or theological. Unlike his English contemporaries, Edwards was not a student of manners or of social behavior. But it is clear from the results produced that Edwards was just as concerned as Johnson with the development of a concise, definitive prose style, one that would enable him to communicate to himself and to his readers his own inner perceptions of God's revealed will. While at Yale College he had read and been influenced strongly by John Locke's *An Essay Concerning Human Understanding* (1690); he is described as having consumed it with more delight "than the most greedy miser finds when gathering up handfuls of silver and gold, from some newly discovered treasure." And most of his youthful or collegiate writings belong more to the realm of natural science than theology. Even his "Notes on the Scriptures" betray a catholic interest in the world of nature and the world of scientific discovery, and he left an intriguing record of his youthful inquiries from such essays as "Of Insects," where at the age of twelve he investigated the behavior of spiders, to more complex studies of the phenomena of light and geometric vectors, which are accompanied by diagrams Edwards drew. Like Isaac Newton, Edwards was immensely interested in the properties of bodies and the forces of universal gravity; like John Locke, he was compelled to discover the ways in which the senses relate to our ideas about things and how the mind ultimately relates to the external world by which it is surrounded. In his "Notes on the Mind," Edwards attempted to state principles on which the mind itself operates, and, like many other college students of his day, his theological and classical training was complemented by wide-ranging reading in the scientific philosophy of the day, writers such as John Locke, John Norris (*An Essay towards the Theory of the Ideal or Intelligible World*, 1701-1704), and the French philosopher Nicolas Malebranche. Recent studies have shown that Edwards owed as much to Malebranche and Norris as to Locke, and it is clear that he cared intensely for a proper understanding of God's revelation not only through scripture but also through the revealed forces of nature. Nature, Edwards believed, was a complementary source of understanding to scripture, and he differed greatly from his Puritan predecessors and some of his contemporaries in asserting the importance of nature as a source for understanding God.

Throughout his early writing a pattern emerges that would remain constant throughout his career as a thinker and writer. He always seemed to give prominence to the pursuit of excellence, and ultimately, he would declare that God himself was a form of divine excellence expressed in the perfection of natural and supernatural beauty. The orderly patterns of nature so evident through the recent discoveries of science led Edwards to praise the God of Nature in ways that some earlier Puritans had been unable to do. In a thoroughly Platonic manner, Edwards early declared that our senses perceive the universe imperfectly and that the ideas generated through sense impressions must ultimately be correlated with the perfect images that can be supplied only by God, and then only to the regenerate and elect intellect. For example, he said that color exists only in the mind and cannot be understood independent of its existence in God: "The secret lies here: that which truly is the substance of all Bodies, is the infinitely exact, and precise, and perfectly stable Idea, in God's mind, together with his stable Will, that the same shall gradually be communicated to us, and to other minds, according to certain fixed and exact established Methods and Laws." Edwards was to observe this personal law throughout his writing, and in many respects, his best works are a consistent attempt to reconcile natural and scriptural revelation.

We must therefore parallel Edwards's chronological life with an examination of the life of his mind, and many of the titles of studies of Jonathan Edwards imply just that, for example, Edward Davidson's *Jonathan Edwards: The Narrative of a Puritan Mind* (1966). His personal life is intriguing and fully revealed through his *Personal Narrative*, first published in *The Life and Character Of The Late Reverend Mr. Jonathan Edwards . . .* (1765), though not so fully as Cotton Mather's in his diary. But the outward circumstances of Edwards's existence imperfectly show the strength and development of his extraordinary mind.

Jonathan Edwards was born at East Windsor, Connecticut, 5 October 1703, to Timothy Edwards and Esther Stoddard Edwards, daughter of Solomon Stoddard of Northampton, Massachusetts, with whom Jonathan would later share the pulpit. Edwards was married in July 1727 to Sarah Pierpont of New Haven, Connecticut, a young woman of tremendous emotional fervor. Edwards's only marriage was to Sarah, mother of his less famous but equally pious son Jonathan Edwards, Jr. This marriage rivals that of Abigail and John Adams for fervor and commitment.

Edwards was tutored at home during his early years, a usual custom for young children of Puritan families in New England. In 1716, at the age of thirteen, Edwards entered Yale College, then located in Saybrook, Connecticut, but to be moved for a time to Wethersfield, where Edwards was again tutored but by members of the Williams family. About one year before Edwards's graduation in 1720, the college was permanently established in New Haven.

He graduated from Yale in September 1720, then spent two additional years in New Haven reading theology. In August 1722 he became a minister at a Presbyterian church in New York City, a position from which he withdrew after only nine months. On 21 May 1724, he was offered the post of tutor at Yale, and he taught there until 1725, when his teaching career was interrupted by illness. In 1726, he resigned his post at Yale to become assistant minister in Northampton to Solomon Stoddard, who controlled much more than a church in the Connecticut River Valley.

Edwards's death was tragic by any account. In 1757, he was living in Stockbridge, Massachusetts, serving as a missionary to the Indians there, following his dismissal from his Northampton pulpit. Late in the year, he was called to the presidency of the College of New Jersey at Princeton (now Princeton University) and soon after his arrival was inoculated against smallpox with a primitive vaccination which caused his death on 22 March 1758. He is buried in Princeton, New Jersey.

In the 1730s, Edwards began to preach a theology of faith and justification by faith that was to be fulfilled only through a personal experience of regeneration. The originality and uniqueness of Edwards's position was not that he preached a "born again" theology for the first time. Puritans had always stressed the importance of conversion and the value of transformation from a hardened heart of stone to the full measure of God's divine grace. But for Edwards, this transforming experience was recalled and expressed in the language of sensory experience, so that his writings and preaching during the decades of the Great Awakening show the power of God as revealed in the beauty and perfection of the natural universe, as it, in turn, is perceived by the regenerate and elect saint. From Edwards's view of divine immanence emerged an undistinguished mingling of the human and divine in the action of the moral conscience. However, the vision of divine beauty, which for Edwards meant salvation, came only by supernatural illumination and was sensibly perceived, by the saint, in natural experiences. The Great Awakening was an enthusiastic movement of the 1730s and 1740s which recognized a new departure in the means of religious conversion. Calvinism had long required a relation of the conversion experience as a sign of salvation and election; however, the New Lights and Edwards argued that there were certain natural means which might be used to put the soul in position to receive the regenerating touch of God's spirit. Thus a new doctrine of conversion evolved which laid increasing emphasis on human responsibility and emotional response to the callings of God, whether they came from scripture or nature. It was the combination of these influences—a fear among the people of the coming judgment and a new emphasis on individual responsibility in the conversion process—that largely accounts for the great revival which began in central Massachusetts in the fourth decade of the eighteenth century as a direct response to the preachings of Jonathan Edwards and the Reverend George Whitefield, a visitor from Scotland who preached a gospel of enthusiasm and emotional commitment to Christ.

This facet of Edwards's mind should be understood in examining his writing. His prose style is stimulating and powerful. What emerges from a study of Edwards's sermons is evidence of a conscious commitment to imagery, to word pictures, so that God may be communicated through the senses as well as through the language of scripture. It is not accidental, therefore, that Edwards is best remembered in the popular imagination for a single sermon, *Sinners in the Hands of an Angry God. . . .* This Enfield Sermon, first preached in 1741 (he gave it again in Northampton, having realized its success as a model sermon in the Enfield delivery), is the work by Edwards most often included today in anthologies of American literature. The sermon is representative of Edwards as a literary stylist, but not because it represents him as a "fire and brimstone" minister, regardless of the effect that this sermon and others like it may have had during the Great Awakening. As a social force in the 1730s and 1740s, Jonathan Edwards and his New Light followers were indeed an important aspect of the evolving American culture; in addition, as a literary artist, Edwards was careful and meticulous in his sermon writing, a minister who chose each word for the ultimate effect it might produce on his audience or congregation. When Edwards is taught today, it should be as much for his contributions to the evolution of American letters as for his importance in shaping the movement we now call the Great Awakening.

Since much early American culture was founded on English models, it might be expected that Edwards would model his sermons on English Puritan antecedents. To some extent he did. Like many Puritan sermons, *Sinners in the Hands of an Angry God* is divided into three separate, rationally divided parts. First, a *text* was declared, in this case Deuteronomy 32:35, "Their foot shall slide in due time." Generally, the minister would explain the scriptural context for the text and might even resort to exegesis by invoking the original biblical languages, Hebrew or Greek, depending on whether the text was taken from the Old or New Testament. Second, a suitable doctrine was derived from the text, and Edwards's doctrine is clear: "There is nothing that keeps wicked men at any one moment out of hell, but the mere pleasure of God." The doctrinal sections of most Puritan sermons, however, were heavy theological arguments, divided into several "reasons," and it is likely that in most cases this section of the sermon would do little to arouse enthusiasm. Finally, each minister would appeal to his particular congregation in the application section of the sermon, which attempted to make both the text and the doctrine relevant to the group before which the sermon was being preached.

The genius of Jonathan Edwards was that he moved right from the text into a form of exegesis which left his listeners spellbound. But it is important to note that he did not accomplish this through an extravagant waving of the arms or an exaggerated caricature of the minister's authority. Rather, he read his sermons from small note cards, many of which are still preserved in Beinecke Library of Yale University, and he read with a quiet passion that relied heavily on his *choice* of words and use of a particular style. For example, the doctrine of *Sinners in the Hands of an Angry God* is expanded in the following way, showing little regard for the text on which it is based: "Thus it is that natural men are held in the hand of God, over the pit of hell; they have deserved the fiery pit, and are already sentenced to it; and God is dreadfully provoked, his anger is as great towards them as to those that are actually suffering the executions of the fierceness of his wrath in hell, and they have done nothing in the least to appease or abate that anger, neither is God in the least bound by any promise to hold them up one moment; the devil is waiting for them, hell is gaping for them, the flames gather and flash about them, and would fain lay hold on them, and swallow them up; the fire pent up in their own hearts is struggling to break out; and they have no interest in any Mediator, there are no means within reach that can be of any security to them. In short, they have no refuge, nothing to take hold of; all that preserves them every moment is the mere arbitrary will, and uncovenanted, unobliged forbearance of an incensed God." Edwards's sermon has come a long way from "Their foot shall slide in due time," though the theme of doom and destruction is common to the several sections of the piece. What Edwards was able to do was unusual because he fused the doctrinal themes of his sermons with a new approach to style in the writing and delivery of his messages.

Earlier Puritan writing had not always been so accommodating to flourishes of literary style. It has recently been shown that Puritans were indeed aware of beauty in writing and that they used conventional seventeenth-century imagery freely; however, in its early decades the movement considered purely decorative images to be seductive and intrinsically deceptive. All human activity was believed to reflect the will of God, and, if writing was to delight at all, it should delight in order to instruct the reader in doctrinal truths. The complex symbolism of the medieval church had already been rejected by the Protestant mind of the reformed tradition in Europe, and the New England Puritans were the legatees of English Protestantism. Thus the real power of the sermon in New England in the seventeenth century came not from the pleasure or artistic satisfaction it provided but from the truth it contained. In keeping with such a generally accepted literary philosophy was the development of the "plain stile" in some Puritan writing. In his preface to *Of Plimouth Plantation,* William Bradford remarks that he has attempted to write "a plaine stile; with a singuler regard unto the simple trueth in all things." Both the style and the form of the sermon were facets of the Puritan belief in the logical accommodation of divine mysteries to the human mind. More specifically, plainness in delivery and logical procedures of form were developed in order to render the complex theological problems posited by scripture intelligible to the congregational regenerate.

Ultimately the sermon was preached by God, who sought to use the minister's talents in an effort to reveal himself to his moral followers. John Milton, in the *De Doctrina Christiana,* states the theory behind Puritan sermonizing in this way: "Our safest way is to form in our minds such a conception of God as shall correspond with his own delineation and representation of himself in the sacred writings. For granted that both in the literal and figurative descriptions of God, he is exhibited not as he really is, but in such a manner as may be within the scope of our comprehensions, as he, in condescending to accommodate himself to our capacities, has shown that he desires we should conceive. For it is on this very account that he had lowered himself to our level, lest in our flights above the reach of human understanding, and beyond the written word of Scripture, we should be tempted to

In this letter to the Reverend Joseph Bellamy, one of his followers, Edwards reports on the progress of the Great Awakening (Princeton University Library).

indulge in vague cogitations and subtleties." The sermon formula, therefore, was restricted initially because its expansion might invite the ingenious participation of man in a process that belonged essentially to God. The sermon, after all, was regarded as not only a source of divine revelation but also a means of conversion. Although the sermon structure had its foundation in the logical propositions of the anti-Catholic, anti-Aristotelian Peter Ramus, its adoption by the seventeenth-century Puritans as a practical method for delivering the revealed truths of scripture came to be its crucial function in Puritan society.

From the beginning of the concern over the form and style of Puritan sermonizing, as expressed in William Perkins's *The Arte of Prophesying* (1607), to Edwards's 1741 Enfield Sermon, the form remained essentially the same. The varied employments of the sermon during those years, however, occasioned the development of special kinds of sermons that were more suitable for one kind of function than another. An extreme case is the funeral sermon, designed to eulogize the departed saint and to give the life some meaning in the larger context of God's providential dispensation. The election sermon, another specialized example, was designed to encourage the pious behavior of God-fearing men such as the magistrates of the colony, although most election sermons were preached after the election had already taken place so that they would not influence voters. No sermon genre, however, developed so precise a relationship between form and content as did the jeremiad, of which *Sinners in the Hands of an Angry God* . . . is one of the finest examples.

The jeremiad (so-called because its approach originated with the biblical prophet Jeremiah) was a type of sermon that arose out of the tensions between secular and sacred fulfillment that characterized much of New England life in the last decades of the seventeenth century. By the 1730s and 1740s, the monolithic culture of the previous century had been challenged severely, and the Great Awakening itself grew out of a perceived need to reorient the society to God's original calling. Increase Mather preached many jeremiads, calling, as he did in *Ichabod, or, the Glory has Departed* . . . (1702), for a restoration of the original impulses that led the Puritans on their "errand into the wilderness." So Jonathan Edwards was preaching to a sensitized audience, if not always to the converted, when he attacked contemporary behavior and morality and sought to bring the sinner before him to the experience of conversion, as he himself had known it. The denunciatory sermon, or jeremiad, generally offered little hope that there existed an alternative to the doom it foreshadowed. For Edwards and his followers, the New Lights, the jeremiad formula was a useful tool for bringing the sinners to the point of conversion. It was more than "fire and brimstone"; it was a means by which the penitent soul might dramatically know the will of God and might, under the right circumstances, perceive a "new sense of things" and enjoy the intervention of grace.

The jeremiad had its origins in the General Court of Massachusetts Bay Colony, which in 1652 declared an annual fast day during which the plight of the colony might be catalogued and lamented. It was a kind of communal purgation in which the whole Puritan tribe focused attention on its moral progress and lamented its deviation from a predetermined standard. Implicit in its structure was a dangerous corollary: the rhetorical power that was inevitably to result from this practice would be lost if ever perfection were attained. The jeremiad formula, therefore, was successful only so long as there were sins and calamities to support it. A variation on the standard Puritan sermon formula, the jeremiad has been described by Perry Miller in *The New England Mind: from Colony to Province*: "The structure of the jeremiad was prescribed by the theory of the external covenant. Perforce it addressed mankind not as beings of a complicated psychology, but as creatures governed by a simple calculus. The 'doctrine' must be some proposition that they are pertinaciously pursued for their sins; any of a hundred verses in the Old Testament would supply the text, especially Isaiah or Jeremiah. The 'reasons' would then become expositions of the national covenant, its terms, conditions and duties. But the real substance of the discourse came at the end, in the 'applications' or 'uses,' where the preacher spelled out the significance of the situation. Here he enumerated, in as much detail as he had courage for, the provocations to vengeance, proposed a scheme for reformation, and let his imagination glow over the still more exquisite judgments yet in store unless his listeners acted upon his recommendations." This formula, of course, depended on a uniform interpretation of history by the Puritans who responded to its warnings, both collectively and individually. The numerous analogies to the Old Testament found in Edwards's sermons and other warnings of the same type are not accidental. It was earnestly believed that New England enjoyed a privileged relationship to God, just as the Israelites had been chosen to settle in the "promised land." This relationship existed in legal form, established in the various covenants between God and his people: the Covenant of Grace, the Church Covenant, and the Social Covenant. Therefore, violations of this standard could easily be measured in terms of the standard itself. No one would contest the challenges of the jeremiad because the evidence was overwhelming against New England's apostasy and the sins of her individual citizens. For the second and third generations, the jeremiad was a suitable convention because it made sense out of their unique experience of apostasy from a divinely imposed standard. Thus it served a useful social function, explaining contemporary history, as it were. The New England Puritans of the late seventeenth and early eighteenth centuries were a lot like the communitarian experiments of the nineteenth century: they were judged by their own previously articulated standards.

For Edwards, the ultimate objective of the sermon's power was to bring about a wrenching conversion in his listener. Language and thought worked together to *affect* the senses and to alter the will through an appeal to the understanding. Brought thus to the anguished conviction that God was absolutely just in their condemnation, and made completely submissive to divine sovereignty, the hearers passed from depth of terror and despair to a calm acquiescence, with a bare hope of possible divine mercy. Eventually, regeneration might emerge from this moment of truth, and a regenerated heart might actually *feel* a joyful adoration in contemplation of the unmerited mercy that would elect so reprobate an individual as the worthless self to eternal glory. It was Edwards's task to *persuade*, through speech, his changing congregation and his audiences elsewhere that God actually would work in this strange and wonderful way.

We are fortunate that Edwards recorded much of his experience in his *Personal Narrative*, which is less a chronology of his life's activities than it is a record of the inner life, that habit of mind by which the reader may eventually know Edwards as a thinker and individual Puritan preacher. He says, in the *Personal Narrative*, that his own conversion led to a new way of perceiving the universe around him: "After this [experience of conversion] my sense of divine things gradually increased, and became more and more lively, and had more of that inward sweetness. The appearance of everything was altered, there seemed to be, as it were, a calm, sweet cast, or appearance of divine Glory, in almost everything. God's excellency, his wisdom, his purity and love, seemed to appear in everything; in the sun, moon, and stars; in the clouds, and blue sky; in the grass, flowers, trees; in the water, and all nature; which used greatly to fix my mind. I often used to sit and view the moon for continuance; and in the day, spent much time in viewing the clouds and sky, to behold the sweet glory of God in these things. . . . And scarce anything among all the works of nature was so sweet to me as thunder and lightning, formerly, nothing had been so terrible to me. Before, I used to be uncommonly terrified with thunder, and to be struck with terror when I saw a thunder storm rising; but now, on the contrary, it rejoiced me. I felt God, so to speak, at the first appearance of a thunder storm; and used to take the clouds, and see the lightnings play, and hear the majestic and awful voice of God's thunder, which oftentimes was exceedingly entertaining, leading me to sweet contemplations of my great and glorious God." The notion that conversion prompted a "new sense of things" is at the heart of the New Light conception of regeneration or transformation. The "new beginning," or the "fresh start" so commonly associated with immigration to America from Europe in the nineteenth century, actually had its origins in the Puritan notion that conversion led to such a total transformation of the individual that each regenerated person would have the opportunity to start all over again, so to speak, leaving the "old man," or old world, behind.

Stylistically, this forceful message is presented in Edwards's writings by such passages as the one quoted above, where a regenerated Edwards takes full joy in the natural universe of his creator. Edwards left little to guesswork, and he presents in the *Notes on Natural Science* (first published in the 1829-1830 edition of Edwards's works), ironically a very likely place, some of his rules for literary style. Although his style was to be much, much more complex than these rules suggest, they are a good place to begin in the study of Edwards as a literary figure. He listed several principles:

> —To give but few prefatorial admonitions about the style and method. It doth an author much hurt to show his concern in these things. . . .
>
> —Let much modesty be seen in the style [of one's writing]. . . .
>
> —The world will expect more modesty because of my circumstances in America . . . yet the models ought not to be affected and foolish but decent and natural. . . .
>
> —To be very moderate in the use of terms of art. Let it not look as if I was much read, or was conversant with books, or with the learned world. . . .

> —In writing, let there be much compliance with the reader's weakness, and according to the rules in the Ladies Library, Vol. 1, p. 340, and sequel. . . .
>
> —Before I venture to publish in London to make some experiment in my own country to play at small games first. That I may gain some experience in writing first to write letters to some in England and to try my hand in these lesser matters before I venture in great.

These preliminary self-admonitions were followed throughout Edwards's life by occasional reminders that he should remain always a conscious artist, a writer who had a powerfully compulsive inner message to communicate to those who read his works. In 1738, in the five *Discourses on Various Important Subjects,* he wrote: "And have we not reason to think, that it ever has been, and ever will be God's manner, to bless the foolishness of preaching to save them that believe, lest the elegance of language and excellency of style be carried to never so great a height, by the learning and wit of the present and future ages?"

One does not expect to find references to the *Ladies' Library* in the writings of Jonathan Edwards; this book was merely a collection of rules for style set down by contemporary grammarians. However, it is clear that Edwards was at least aware of the stylistic theories practiced by the essayists and often repeated in the pages of the *Guardian,* the *Tatler,* and the *Spectator,* contemporary journals that were influential models for others if not for the Puritan sermon writers. Nevertheless, both the essayists and the sermon writers were concerned to develop clear, concise, logical styles (for wholly different purposes), and it is clear that Edwards was part of a much larger movement designed to give prominence to the way in which truth was expressed, in short, to show a concern for style in writing as well as for content and form.

From 1731 to his death in 1758, Edwards wrote profusely. It is remarkable that, as he composed throughout the years, he seems to have evolved a theory of perception and understanding that aided him in writing for individual readers whose perceptions were similarly affected. There were, in Edwards's world, two classes of people: the regenerate and the unregenerate. For the unregenerate, the natural universe was a blank stone, an uninspiring environment from which little could be learned beyond a literal appreciation of things transmitted to the senses. But for the regenerate one who had experienced the transformation of conversion and the "new sense of things" that followed—the same universe opened up new vistas of understanding and new ways of expressing that understanding to others. It is this cumulative effect of the transformation that caused Edwards's writings to develop toward what must be his most profound statement on the matter of style, the 1746 document called *A Treatise Concerning Religious Affections*. . . , a book that had its beginning as a series of sermons in 1742 and 1743. This method of composition was not uncommon practice for Edwards and his contemporaries; "treatises" often had their beginnings in this way, and Edwards's own *A History of the Work of Redemption* . . . , not published until 1774, after his death, had its origin as a series of sermons preached in 1739 and 1740.

A Treatise Concerning Religious Affections has been the subject of much debate over whether Edwards was indeed influenced in his youth more by John Locke's *Essay Concerning Human Understanding,* which he is known to have read, or by Nicolas Malebranche's *The Search for Truth* or by John Norris's *An Essay towards the Theory of the Ideal or Intelligible World.* Each of these works speaks to the very matter which concerned him most throughout his life: whether or not the natural man understood truth and perceived his environment any differently from the saint, or regenerate elect individual. For Edwards, the answer was simple. The saint had special powers of perception made available through grace, which must separate him from the unregenerate or damned. In *A Treatise Concerning Religious Affections,* and in *A Divine and Supernatural Light* (1734), he makes clear that for him the soul "receives light from the Sun of Righteousness, in such a manner that its nature is changed, and it becomes properly a luminous thing; not only does the sun shine in the saints, but they also become little suns, partaking of the nature of the fountain of their light. In this respect, the manner of their derivation of light, is like that of the lamps in the tabernacle, rather than that of a reflecting glass; which though they were lit up by fire from heaven, yet thereby became, themselves burning shining things. The saints don't only drink the water of life, that flows from the original fountain; but this water becomes a fountain of water in them, springing up there, and flowing out of them. Grace is compared to a seed implanted, that not only is in the ground, but has hold of it, has root there, and grows there, and is an abiding principle of life and nature there . . ." (*A Treatise Concerning Religious Affections*). Saints are indeed special people, not because they have been saved or predestined to eternal lives of glory, but because they have special powers of perception and special features of the imagination, not unlike those of writers whose sensitivities are greater than those of men who lead lives of quiet desperation: "The Spirit of God acts in a very different manner in the one case, from what he doth in the other. He may indeed act upon the mind of a natural man, but he acts in the mind of a saint as an indwelling vital principle. He acts upon the mind of an unregenerate person as an extrinsic, occasional agent; for in acting upon them, he doth not unite himself to them; for notwithstanding all his influences that they may be the subjects of, they are still sensual, having not the Spirit. . . . This spiritual and divine light does not consist in any impression made upon the imagination. It is not impression upon the mind, as though one saw any thing with the bodily eyes; it is no imagination or idea of an outward light or glory, or any beauty of form or countenance, or a visible lustre or brightness of any object. The imagination may be strongly impressed with such things; but this is not spiritual light. Indeed, when the mind has a lively discovery of spiritual things, and is greatly affected by the power of divine light, it may, and probably very commonly doth, much affect the imagination; so that the impressions of an outward beauty or brightness may accompany those spiritual discoveries. But spiritual light is not that impression upon the imagination, but an exceeding different thing from it. Natural men may have lively impressions on their imaginations; and we cannot determine but the devil, who transforms himself into an angel of light, may cause imaginations of an outward beauty, or visible glory, and of sounds and speeches, and other such things; but these are things of a vastly inferior nature to spiritual light" (*A Divine and Supernatural Light*). For Edwards and his New Light followers, the "spiritual light" not only guided the saint in his life on this earth, but it also made his natural powers greater so that his perceptions compounded and quickened.

Another characteristic of the saint's transformation is that he was endowed with a sense of the presence of God everywhere, so that he could communicate directly and intimately with the "Divine Being," and thus become one with God. From this union spring such strong assurances of being loved that the joy and security seem to go beyond anything found in mere human relations. Yet the New Lights' taste of the heavenly Canaan did not make them dissatisfied with human relationships; on the contrary, the surrender to the divine only intensified people's desires for a "Reign of Love," a marriage of heaven and earth that would manifest itself in more loving unions among men and the arrival of the "peaceable kingdom" promised in scripture. Edwards and the New Lights of the Great Awakening realized that man's life after rebirth was like a vessel to be used by the indwelling spirit. Inward thoughts and outward actions converge and are a testimony to the presence of the spirit and a realization that the Word has been made Flesh. Christ by his spirit is not only in the saints but actually and really lives in them. They do not just "drink living water," but this water becomes a well or fountain of water in the soul, springing up into spiritual and everlasting life. Thus all of nature, all of the created universe, becomes a medium of communication for Edwards, a language in which words live and have actual being. If words served as forms to initiate the process of rebirth and conversion, as in the hearing of a sermon, the "new sense of things" enjoyed by the saint was also the introduction to a new language of saintly discourse, so that the New Lights urged everyone to come into the Heavenly/Earthly Kingdom, where the presence of God would be felt in a joyous communion of hearts in union with each other.

While the writers and preachers of the last half of the seventeenth century regarded it as a primary task to defend what the first generation had created and while they used the language of the jeremiad to preserve the old order and to lament the state of the present, in the language of the New Lights of the Great Awakening, there is less lamentation of the passing of the old order and more emphasis on the coming of a new order. A new, millennial impulse is born of the promise that Christ will come again and that all peoples will speak a common language of the heart. As Sydney Ahlstrom has pointed out in *A Religious History of the American People* (1972), "although Jonathan Edwards was surprised in 1734 when a revival of religion became manifest in Northampton, that event was neither accidental nor strange; the soil had in many ways been prepared. In the first place, Puritanism was itself, by expressed intention, a vast and extended revival movement. Few of its central spirits had wandered far from a primary concern for the heart's inward response, and its laity inwardly knew that true religion could never be equated with dutiful observance. Even in years of most lamented declension the churches were informed by a carefully reasoned theology and warmed by a deeper faith than the jeremiads acknowledge." The New Lights who did make the fearful leap, and who found that they had been reborn, became convinced that whole societies might do the same. Just as they had been severed from their own individual pasts, so, they believed, an entire nation might shed its former self and surrender to the future, trusting it would find joy and fulfillment. This conviction that their present lives prophesied future fulfillments was the deepest impulse of the New Light movement, and it is represented in Edwards's works in the posthumous *A History of the Work of Redemption*. . . . New Lights read their Bibles to understand what future realities God had revealed in the words and lives of His chosen peoples. And they used sermons, histories, poetry, autobiographies, and biographies, not to lament the present order as much as to propel their audiences toward a realization of the New Jerusalem.

Edwards's life was at one level a social tragedy, but as a writer and thinker, he was clearly the most important figure in the eighteenth century, perhaps even more critical to the development of American thought than his contemporary Benjamin Franklin. It is irrelevant to debate this point, however, because both men were vitally important in different ways. Franklin's political thinking far exceeded Edwards's, and he was able to negotiate internationally where Edwards was unsuccessful locally in human relationships. However, Edwards's writing has had far greater influence on later American authors, such as the transcendentalists, than has Franklin's. Edwards left not only reams of prose in his own energetic style; he also left models of prose writing that today provide a crucial link between the sermons of the seventeenth-century Puritans and the poems and essays of Emerson and Thoreau.

Bibliographies:

Thomas H. Johnson, *The Printed Writings of Jonathan Edwards, 1703-1758: A Bibliography* (Princeton: Princeton University Press, 1940);

M. X. Lesser, *Jonathan Edwards: A Reference Guide* (Boston: G. K. Hall, 1981).

Biographies:

Ola E. Winslow, *Jonathan Edwards, 1703-1758: A Biography* (New York: Macmillan, 1940);

Perry Miller, *Jonathan Edwards* (New York: Sloane, 1949);

Edward Griffin, *Jonathan Edwards* (Minneapolis: University of Minnesota Press, 1971).

References:

Alfred O. Aldridge, *Jonathan Edwards*, Great American Thinkers Series (New York: Washington Square Press, 1964);

Paul R. Baumgartner, "Jonathan Edwards: The Theory Behind His Use of Figurative Language," *PMLA*, 78 (1963): 321-325;

Sacvan Bercovitch, "The Typology of America's Mission," *American Quarterly*, 30 (Summer 1968): 135-155;

Conrad Cherry, *The Theology of Jonathan Edwards: A Reappraisal* (Garden City: Doubleday, 1966);

Edward H. Davidson, "From Locke to Edwards," *Journal of the History of Ideas*, 24 (1963): 355-372;

Davidson, *Jonathan Edwards: The Narrative of a Puritan Mind* (Boston: Houghton Mifflin, 1966);

James West Davidson, *The Logic of Millennial Thought: Eighteenth-Century New England* (New Haven & London: Yale University Press, 1977), pp. 150-221;

Douglas J. Elwood, *The Philosophical Theology of Jonathan Edwards* (New York: Columbia University Press, 1960);

David Laurence, "John Locke and Jonathan Edwards," *Early American Literature*, 15 (Fall 1980): 1-35;

Mason I. Lowance, Jr., *The Language of Canaan: Metaphor and Symbol in New England from the Puritans to the Transcendentalists* (Cambridge & London: Harvard University Press, 1980), pp. 178-207, 249-295;

Lowance, "Typology and Millennial Eschatology in Early New England," in *Literary Uses of Typology from the Late Middle Ages to the Present*, edited by Earl Miner (Princeton: Princeton University Press, 1977), pp. 228-273;

Daniel Shea, "Jonathan Edwards, Historian of Consciousness," in *Major Writers of Early American Literature*, edited by Everett Emerson (Madison: University of Wisconsin Press, 1972), pp. 179-204;

Stephen Stein, "Providence and Apocalypse in the Early Writings of Jonathan Edwards," *Early American Literature*, 13 (Winter 1978): 250-267;

Patricia Tracy, *Jonathan Edwards, Pastor* (New York: Hill & Wang, 1981);

John Wilson, "Jonathan Edwards as Historian," *Church History*, 46 (March 1977): 5-18.

Papers:

The Beinecke Library at Yale University and Andover-Newton Theological Seminary in Boston have collections of Edwards's papers.

John Eliot

Jane Donahue Eberwein
Oakland University

BIRTH: Widford, England, August 1604, to Bennett and Lettese Eliot.

EDUCATION: B.A., Jesus College, Cambridge, 1622.

MARRIAGE: October 1632 to Hanna Mumford; children: Hannah, John, Joseph, Samuel, Aaron, Benjamin.

DEATH: Roxbury, Massachusetts, 20 May 1690.

BOOKS: *The Whole Booke of Psalmes Faithfully Translated into English Metre,* by Eliot, Thomas Welde, Richard Mather, and others (Cambridge: Printed by Stephen Daye, 1640);

Tears of Repentence: or, A Further Narrative of the Progress of the Gospel amongst the Indians in New-England . . . , by Eliot and Thomas Mayhew (London: Printed by P. Cole, 1653);

A Primer or Catechism in the Massachusetts Indian Language . . . (Cambridge: Printed by Samuel Green, 1654?);

The Book of Genesis, Translated into the Massachusetts Indian Language (Cambridge: Printed by Samuel Green, 1655);

The Gospel of Matthew, translated into the Massachusetts Indian Language (Cambridge: Printed by Samuel Green, 1655);

A Late and Further Manifestation of the Progress of the Gospel amongst the Indians in New-England (London: Printed by M.S., 1655);

A Few Psalmes in Meeter, translated into the Massachusetts Indian Language (Cambridge: Printed by Samuel Green, 1658);

The Christian Commonwealth: or, The Civil Policy of the Rising Kingdom of Jesus Christ . . . (London: Printed for L. Chapman, 1659);

A Further Accompt of the Progresse of the Gospel amongst the Indians of New-England . . . (London: Printed by M. Simmons for the Corporation of New-England, 1659);

The New Testament of Our Lord and Saviour Jesus Christ. Translated into the Indian language and Ordered to be Printed by the Commissioners of the United Colonies in New-England . . . [Algonquian title: *Wusku Wuttestamentum Nul-Lordumun Jesus Christ Nuppoquoh-Wussaueneumun*] (Cambridge: Printed by Samuel Green & Marmaduke Johnson, 1661); revised edition, *Wusku Wuttestamentum Nul-Lordmun Iesus Christ Nuppoquoh-wussuae-Neumun* (Cambridge: Printed for the Right Honorable Corporation in London, 1680);

Etching based on the portrait by William Whiting

The Assembly's shorter catechism translated into the Massachusetts Indian language (Cambridge?, 1663?);

The Holy Bible: Containing the Old Testament and the New. Translated into the Indian Language, and Ordered to be Printed by the Commission-

ers of the United Colonies in New-England . . . [Algonquian title: *Mamusse wunneetupanatamwe Up-Biblum God Naneeswe Nukkone Testament Kah Wonk Wusku Testament*] (Cambridge: Printed by Samuel Green & Marmaduke Johnson, 1663); revised edition, *Mamusse Wunneetupanatamwe Up-Biblum God Naneeswe Nukkone Testament Kah Wonk Wusku Testament* (Cambridge: Printed by Samuel Green, 1685);

Up-Bookum Psalmes (Cambridge: Printed by Samuel Green & Marmaduke Johnson, 1663);

Wame Ketoohomae uketoohomaongash David [Eliot's complete translation of the metrical psalms] (Cambridge: Printed by Samuel Green & Marmaduke Johnson, 1663);

Wehkomaonganoo asquam peantogig Kah asquam Quinnuppegig . . . [Eliot's translation of Richard Baxter's *Call to the Unconverted*] (Cambridge: Printed by Samuel Green & Marmaduke Johnson, 1664);

Manitowompae pomantamoonk . . . [Eliot's translation of Lewis Bayly's *Practice of Piety*] (Cambridge: Printed by Samuel Green, 1665);

Communion of Churches: Or, the Divine Management of Gospel Churches by the Ordinance of Councils, Constituted in Order according to the Scriptures . . . (Cambridge: Privately printed by Marmaduke Johnson, 1665);

The Indian Grammar begun: or, an Essay to bring the Indian Language into rules, For the Help of such as desire to Learn the same, for the furtherance of the Gospel among them (Cambridge: Printed by Marmaduke Johnson, 1666);

The Indian Primer; or, The Way of training up of our Indian youth in the good Knowledge of God, in the knowledge of the Scriptures and in an ability to Reade [Algonquian title: *Qut ken nagwutteansh nish nahtuhtauanish kah pohkontamanish, Waheadt noh nahtuhtauonadt . . .*] (Cambridge: Printed by Marmaduke Johnson, 1669; Edinburgh: A. Elliot, 1877);

A Brief Narrative of the Progress of the Gospel amongst the Indians in New-England in the Year 1670 (London: Printed for J. Allen, 1671; Boston: J. K. Wiggin & W. P. Lunt, 1868);

Indian Dialogues, for their Instruction in that Great Service of Christ, in Calling Home their Countrymen to the Knowledge of God and of Themselves, and of Jesus Christ (Cambridge: Printed by Marmaduke Johnson, 1671);

The Logic Primer. Some Logical Notions to initiate the Indians in Knowledge of the Rule of Reason; and to know how to make use thereof (Cambridge: Printed by Marmaduke Johnson, 1672);

The Harmony of the Gospels in the Holy History of Humiliation and Sufferings of Jesus Christ, from His Incarnation to His Death and Burial (Boston: Printed by John Foster, 1678);

A Brief Answer to a Small Book written by John Norcot, against Infant Baptisme . . . (Boston: Printed by John Foster, 1679);

The Dying Speeches of Several Indians (Cambridge: Printed by Samuel Green, 1683?);

Sampwutteahae quinnuppekompauaenin . . . [Eliot and Grindal Rawson's translation of Thomas Shepard's *Sincere Convert*] (Cambridge: Printed by Samuel Green, 1689).

John Eliot, traditionally remembered as "the Apostle to the Indians," remains one of the most distinctive figures among the first-generation New England ministers, although his stature rests more on the magnitude of his undertakings and the qualities of his character as reported by others than on the books he left behind him. His greatest undertaking, the Indian Bible (1663), is written in a language no living American can read. *The Christian Commonwealth . . .* (1659), his most important speculative book, was publicly condemned, and copies were destroyed. For Eliot, the central book in human history was the Bible: the source of his evangelical vision, the grounding for his theory of governance, and the essential foundation of any Christian life. Even though a bibliographer can list many books written or translated by Eliot, he was essentially a man of this one book, and his faith in its power led to one of the most remarkable life stories among the Puritan clergy.

The son of Bennett and Lettese Eliot, John was baptized (appropriately, as it turned out) at the church of St. John the Baptist in Widford, England, and grew up in the neighboring Essex village of Nazeing as part of a large, religious family. He seems to have attended a local grammar school in preparation for his entry to Jesus College, Cambridge, as a pensioner in 1618. Graduating from the university in 1622, he may have continued his studies for the ministry before applying for ordination in 1625. No record of his ordination has been found, but he had established himself as a minister in Essex before immigrating to America. In Essex Eliot associated with the nonconforming clergy at a time of tension with the bishops, and he lived with Thomas Hooker's family while teaching at his school in Little Baddow until Hooker's flight to Holland in 1630. After the closing of the school, Eliot sailed for Massachusetts Bay in 1630 aboard the *Lyon*, the same ship that carried Governor John Winthrop's wife.

Accepting the position that Roger Williams had refused, Eliot served as a substitute pastor for the Boston church while its pastor, John Wilson, visited England on family business. Eliot resisted entreaties of the congregation to remain at that church as teacher upon Wilson's return. He chose instead to settle in Roxbury and serve as teacher to the newly gathered church of Essex neighbors from 1632 to 1636 and then as pastor until his death. In October 1632, he married Hanna Mumford to whom he had become engaged in England; they had six children.

Eliot's Roxbury ministry proved a long and apparently happy one, leaving few church records of special interest. As none of Eliot's sermons (including the Election Sermon of 1659) has been preserved, readers must turn to anecdotal records of his pastorate, substantially preserved in Cotton Mather's *The Triumphs of the Reformed Religion in America: or The Life of the Renowned John Eliot* . . . (1691), which was reprinted in *Magnalia Christi Americana* (1702). There one reads of Eliot's profound kindliness, his meekness, his gentle teaching, and his habitual good works. "He that will write of Eliot," Mather wrote, "must write of charity, or say nothing." A famous anecdote recounted by Samuel Eliot Morison in *Builders of the Bay Colony* (1930) tells how the church leaders once attempted to preserve their minister's salary intact by tying the money in a handkerchief fastened by tight knots, so that the charitable man would be protected from giving much of it to needy people on his way home. Stopping to visit a poor family, however, Eliot was frustrated by his inability to untie the knots and simply handed the pouch to the mother, saying, "Here, my dear, take it! I believe the Lord designs it all for you." One of Eliot's principal local achievements was the founding in 1645 of a grammar school, later known as the Roxbury Latin School.

As a minister, Eliot found himself occasionally active in colonial affairs. In 1634 he publicly protested Governor Winthrop's concluding a treaty of peace with the Pequot Indians (then at war with the Narragansets) without asking the consent of the people. After a visit from a committee of ministers sent to dissuade him from his position, Eliot acknowledged his error in the particular case without rejecting the general value of democratic consultation. Later he held to the orthodox clerical-magisterial alliance when he participated in Anne Hutchinson's trial during the Antinomian controversy of 1637-1638. Eliot's first literary venture came in 1640 when he, as a "good Hebrician," joined Thomas Welde and Richard Mather as principal poet-translators for *The Whole Book of Psalmes Faithfully Translated into English Metre*, better known as the *Bay Psalm Book*. This book was a translation of the Hebrew psalms into metered English suitable for congregational singing in the New England churches. Concurring with John Cotton's prefatory statement that "God's altar needs not our polishing," the writers valued accuracy above poetry and strove for plainness in their verses. The writing was deliberately impersonal, and Eliot's direct contribution cannot be established. The importance of this project for his career must be measured by the experience it offered him in translation and the encouragement it provided for making biblical literature widely accessible—eventually to Indians in the forests as well as to his own congregation in their new meetinghouse at Roxbury.

Eliot's Indian apostolate began in the 1640s, actuated by several strong motives. Late in life he recalled inspiration from the colonial seal of Massachusetts Bay, which showed an Indian with outstretched arms calling for help—a symbol supposed to represent Puritan commitment to evangelization. He spoke also of his "pity for the poor Indian," a pity intensified by his reading of scripture which persuaded him that these American natives were the lost tribe of Israel. Eliot's chiliastic interpretation of biblical prophecies led him to hope that conversion of the Indians would be one of the decisive points in salvation history as it reached fulfillment with the Second Coming of Christ. Christianization of the Indians had been one of the original goals of the Massachusetts settlers, but John Eliot was the first of the Boston colonists to attempt it. Two centuries later, Hawthorne would characterize him as the "single man, among our forefathers, who realized that an Indian possesses a mind, and a heart, and an immortal soul." With some help and considerable monitoring from other Massachusetts clergy, many of whom distrusted Indian converts, and evangelical support from Thomas Mayhew (whose family carried on missionary efforts among the Indians of Martha's Vineyard over a span of four generations), Eliot took upon himself responsibility for ministering to the Algonquian tribesmen of eastern Massachusetts even while continuing his pastoral responsibilities in Roxbury. Financial support came mainly from English Puritans through the Society for Promoting and Propagating the Gospel of Jesus Christ in New England (founded in 1649).

After the Pequot War of 1637, Eliot had begun studying the Algonquian language with Indian tutors, chiefly Job Nesutan, who became his assistant for many years. By 1646, he was ready to preach; and he traveled to the Indian village of Nonantum to present a sermon and introduce himself to the inhabitants, followers of a chief named Waban. More such visits followed throughout a wide region, and in 1647 Eliot was able to gather an impressive group of Indians in Cambridge to hear his preaching and respond loudly to catechetical questions, thus demonstrating the success of his experiment and building support for establishing the Indian College at Harvard, for importing a printing press to publish scriptural translations in the Algonquian tongue, and for mobilizing support efforts in England. Several of his books described this missionary work: *Tears of Repentence* . . . (1653); *A Late and Further Manifestation* . . . (1655); *A Further Accompt of the Progresse of the Gospel* . . . (1659); *A Brief Narrative of the Progress of the Gospel* . . . (1671); and *Indian Dialogues* . . . (1671). Other accounts of Eliot's apostolate appear in letters and reports by Massachusetts ministers who visited his Praying Indians and examined their progress in Christianity—one of the first being John Wilson's tract *The Day-Breaking, if not the Sun-Rising of the Gospell with the Indians in New England* (1647).

Preaching and catechizing, however, were not enough. Eliot held that the Indians must be able to read the Bible if they were to be Christians. As there was no written form of the Algonquian language, he set himself the task of transcribing its grammar and vocabulary and the equally ambitious task of teaching people to read who had no tradition of writing. *The Indian Grammar begun* . . . (1666), *The Indian Primer* . . . (1669), and *The Logic Primer* . . . (1672) demonstrate his commitment to literacy and systematic thinking. His main endeavor, however, was to translate scripture into the Indian language, a process he undertook in stages. First came the Psalms, Genesis, and Matthew. *The New Testament* . . . appeared in 1661 and in 1663 the complete Holy Bible, a copy of which was presented to King Charles.

In translating the Bible, as he had with the Psalms in the *Bay Psalm Book*, Eliot worked for accuracy rather than poetic grace. There were linguistic hurdles to be overcome, like the absence of the verb *to be* in all its forms. His preaching efforts had also demonstrated difficulties in accustoming his Indian auditors to unfamiliar concepts basic to biblical metaphor. A people with no tradition of animal herding found the Good Shepherd a strange concept. Nor did the Indians number among their previous gods any who judged human behavior and punished sin. Forgiveness of enemies seemed a puzzling expectation. For his Bible, Eliot resorted to English words where the Algonquian language offered no equivalents. When Indian equivalents departed from the literal meaning of scripture, he sometimes followed native usage, as in the substitution of ten chaste young men for the virgins awaiting the bridegroom in Christ's parable. (The Indians regarded chastity as a male virtue and female virginity as comparatively unimportant.) Eliot emphasized the Ten Commandments and the habit of prayer in his teaching; the Lord's Prayer had been one of his first translations. Here is the Algonquian wording from his 1663 Bible, with English lines grammatically rearranged to follow Indian syntax provided as an interlinear gloss:

Nushun *kesukqut;* *Quttianatamunach*
Our father heaven in hallowed

koowesuonk; *Peyaumootch* *kukketossutamoonk;*
thy name come thy kingdom

Kuttenantamoonk *nen nach ohkeit*
thy will done earth on

neane kesukqut; *Nummeetsuongash*
as heaven in our food

asekesukokish *asamaiinean* *yeuyeu* *kesukod;*
daily give us this this day

Kah *ahquontamaiiunnean* *nummatch*
and forgive us our

eseongash *neane* *matchenekuk queagigu*
sins as wicked-doers

nutahquontamounnonog; *Ahque* *sagkom—*
we forgive them also lead

pagunaiinnean *en* *qutchhuaonganit;*
us not temptation in

Wehe *pohquohwussinnean* *wutch match*
Oh deliver us evil

itut;	*New wutche*	*kutahtaun*	*ketassootamoonk*
from	for	thine	kingdom
kah	*menukesuonk*	*kah*	*sohsumoonk*
and	power	and	glory
nicheme.	*Amen.*		
forever	Amen		

This Bible, known in its Algonquian title as *Mamusse wunneetupanatamwe Up-Biblum God . . .*, was still used by Indians on Martha's Vineyard in the early decades of the nineteenth century. Surviving copies of both the 1663 and 1685 editions appear worn from heavy use. The translation remains an extraordinary example of linguistic and anthropological effort, admired by ethnographic scholars, though resistant to literary criticism.

Christianization, for Eliot, meant civilization. He organized his approximately four thousand converts into fourteen towns of Praying Indians. Each town was to have its church—duly gathered according to Congregational usage, its school, and its government modeled on biblical directives. From his experience of forming Indian towns, Eliot envisaged a governance structure based on Jethro's advice to Moses in Exodus 18:17-26, which he recommended for general Christian use. Each ten men in the towns would have a leader, each hundred a council of leaders of ten, each thousand a council of leaders of hundreds. He developed his premillennial model around 1649 and had it printed ten years later in England as *The Christian Commonwealth . . .*, only to have it banned by the General Court of Massachusetts after the Restoration of the British monarchy in 1660 for its antimonarchical sentiments. Eliot publicly recanted its republicanism, although he maintained, "Much is spoken of the rightful heir of the crown of England, and the unjustice of casting out the right heir; but Christ is the only right heir of the crown of England and all other nations also." Copies of *The Christian Commonwealth . . .* were ordered defaced or turned over to the magistrates within fourteen days of the ban voted on 30 May 1661. A slightly better fate awaited *Communion of Churches . . .*, privately printed four years later, in which Eliot adapted Jethro's advice to church governance by calling for a series of church councils from local to ecumenical levels (the ecumenical councils to be conducted in Hebrew). This work was largely ignored or dismissed lightly as an example of its

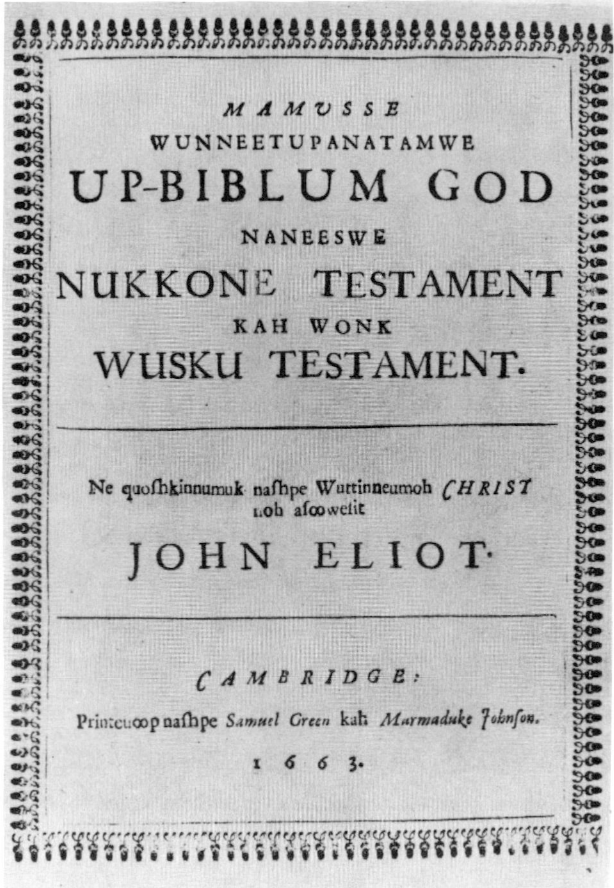

MAMVSSE
WUNNEETUPANATAMWE
UP-BIBLUM GOD
NANEESWE
NUKKONE TESTAMENT
KAH WONK
WUSKU TESTAMENT.

Ne quoshkinnumuk nashpe Wuttinneumoh *CHRIST* noh asoowesit

JOHN ELIOT.

CAMBRIDGE:
Printeuoop nashpe *Samuel Green* kah *Marmaduke Johnson.*
1663.

Algonquian title page for Eliot's translation of the Bible

author's well-intended but already outdated scriptural literalism.

The Indian towns, where Eliot's theories were put into practice, were intended as stable communities for their native inhabitants. Previously migrant tribesmen settled into English-style villages with roads, bridges, frame houses, and centrally located churches. Eliot worked to teach the men farming skills and to provide them with tools for agriculture and marketable handcrafts. The women learned spinning. Men cut their hair in the roundhead style that Eliot favored. Native magistrates attempted to enforce sabbath-keeping laws and edicts against drunkenness. Several of these communities flourished until they, like *The Christian Commonwealth . . .*, fell victim to historical forces.

When King Philip's War erupted in 1675, English colonists suspected Eliot's converts of disloyalty. To protect the Praying Indians from massacre, the Massachusetts government exiled them to Deer Island in Boston Harbor, driving them hastily and brutally from their villages. The towns

Letter from Eliot to the Reverend Jonathan Hammer in England. Hammer had written to Eliot expressing interest in his work with the Indians and asking what goods he should buy with money donated to aid the Christian Indians in building a new town.

themselves were destroyed in the war, with most copies of the Indian Bible burned. Eventually some of the Praying Indians fought with their white fellow Christians, providing decisive aid in the overthrow of King Philip by their skill in Indian warfare. When the fighting ended in 1676, however, many Indians had died in exile and others had been seduced from their Christian practices. Only four villages were rebuilt, including Natick, which Eliot continued to visit regularly as long as he could make the trip on horseback. Eliot, who had struggled during the war to protect Indians against cruel treatment, even West Indian slavery, was seventy-four years old when he began the process of biblical translation over again—this time helped somewhat by John Cotton of Plymouth. The revised New Testament was printed in 1680, the whole Bible in 1685.

In his later years, Eliot wrote a book of biblical reflection on Christ's sufferings, *The Harmony of the Gospels* . . . (1678), and a defense of infant baptism, *A Brief Answer to a Small Book written by John Norcot* . . . (1679). His wife died in 1687; four sons also preceded Eliot in death. Although he offered to resign his pastorate when declining health made it difficult to climb Meetinghouse Hill, Eliot's congregation continued him in his office. Confined to his home in Roxbury, he tutored black slaves so that they could read the Bible. Eliot died in 1690, almost the last of the first-generation ministers.

From Mather's biography to the present, Eliot's reputation has rested on his actions more than his authorship. It is the fact itself of his having mastered the Algonquian language and having translated the whole Bible into it—twice—that commands attention rather than the literary merit of his translations, catechisms, textbooks, and devotional writings. Evaluations of his achievement have varied in proportion to authors' sympathy with his missionary purpose. Cotton Mather, for instance, admired Eliot as an example of ministerial piety but held his Indians in contempt: "To think on raising a number of these hideous creatures unto the elevations of our holy religion, must argue more than common or little sentiments in the undertaker; but the faith of an Eliot could encounter it." He doubted Eliot's linkage between Indians and the Jews, but mythologized the conflict between gospel light and devilish darkness until Eliot's success in establishing towns of Praying Indians became a prelude to Armageddon. After the Revolution, Timothy Dwight praised Eliot and Mayhew as Puritan missionaries representing the religious ideal of colonial settlement and anticipating the millennium. In the romantic era, with its rediscovery of New England antiquities, Eliot became a sentimental hero, esteemed for his kindliness toward a doomed race and for his commitment to books. Emerson, Whittier, and Longfellow mentioned him approvingly in their writings. Hawthorne treated him as a Puritan saint in *The Scarlet Letter* (1850), *The Blithedale Romance* (1852), and most extensively in *Grandfather's Chair* (1841). Twentieth-century historical responses (more common lately than literary ones) vary according to anthropological and political judgments of Eliot's Indian evangelizing, with Francis Jennings presenting him as an imperialist profiteer in *The Invasion of America: Indians, Colonialism, and the Cant of Conquest* (1975) and Alden T. Vaughan taking a more favorable view in *New England Frontier: Puritans and Indians 1620-1675* (1965). Recent scholarship in millennial thought focuses attention on Eliot's chiliasm and sets his endeavors in a theological context which shows him, in David D. Hall's words, as "*sui generis*, isolated from the rest of his colleagues by an unquenchable millenarianism." He stands apart in the American memory as a representative of that racial tolerance that might have bettered the course of our nation's history. And he is esteemed by bibliophiles, who place exceptional value on the *Bay Psalm Book* and the Indian Bible for their very scarcity. Eliot's fame, however, depends less on the few volumes now reposing in libraries as mementoes of a language no one reads than on the tradition of his many Algonquian books that burned in the frontier warfare or, as he would have wished it to happen, disintegrated from constant use.

Other:

"The Learned Conjectures touching the Americas," in *Jews in America, or, Probabilities that those Indians are Judaical*, by Thomas Thorowgood (London: Printed for H. Brome, 1660).

Biographies:

Convers Francis, *Life of John Eliot, the Apostle to the Indians* (New York: Harper, 1854; republished, New York: Garrett, 1969);

Ola Elizabeth Winslow, *John Eliot: "Apostle to the Indians"* (Boston: Houghton Mifflin, 1968).

References:

Sydney E. Ahlstrom, *A Religious History of the American People* (New Haven: Yale University Press, 1972), pp. 103, 157, 219, 251;

Ezra H. Byington, "John Eliot, the Puritan

Missionary to the Indians," *Papers of the American Society of Church History*, 8 (1897), 109-145;

Peter N. Carroll, *Puritanism and the Wilderness: The Intellectual Significance of the New England Frontier, 1629-1700* (New York & London: Columbia University Press, 1969), pp. 53, 79, 80, 123, 163, 170, 205, 212;

David D. Hall, *The Faithful Shepherd: A History of the New England Ministry in the Seventeenth Century* (Chapel Hill: University of North Carolina Press, 1972), pp. 139, 154, 262;

Francis Jennings, *The Invasion of America: Indians, Colonialism, and the Cant of Conquest* (Chapel Hill: University of North Carolina Press, 1975), pp. 228-253, 277, 286-287, 294;

Cotton Mather, "The Triumphs of the Reformed Religion in America: or The Life of the Renowned John Eliot," in his *Magnalia Christi Americana* (London: Printed for T. Parkhurst, 1702; republished, New York: Russell & Russell, 1967);

Samuel Eliot Morison, "John Eliot, Apostle to the Indians," in his *Builders of the Bay Colony* (Boston: Houghton Mifflin, 1930), pp. 289-319;

James Constantine Pilling, *Bibliography of the Algonquian Languages*, Smithsonian Institution Bureau of Ethnology (Washington: U.S. Government Printing Office, 1891), pp. 127-184;

Alden T. Vaughan, *New England Frontier: Puritans and Indians 1620-1675* (Boston: Little, Brown, 1965), pp. 245-321;

Larzer Ziff, *Puritanism in America: New Culture in a New World* (New York: Viking, 1973), pp. 173-174, 290, 322.

Papers:

Eliot's letters and other documents are scattered through British and American libraries. The most substantial holdings may be found at Harvard University, the Archives of the Massachusetts Secretary of State, the Massachusetts Historical Society, the Historical Society of Pennsylvania, and the American Philosophical Society. Occasional materials are at Yale University, the Boston Public Library, Boston University, the Pierpont Morgan Library, and Dartmouth College.

Giles Firmin

(1615-1697)

Max Rudin
Columbia University

SELECTED BOOKS: *A Serious Question Stated; viz. Whether Ministers of England Are Bound by The Word of God to Baptize the Children of All Such Parents Which Say they Believe in Jesus Christ but . . . Refuse to Submit to Church Discipline? The Negative . . . is Moderately Defended* . . . (London: Printed by R. I. for S. Bowtell, 1651);

Separation Examined: or, a Treatise Wherein the Grounds for Separation from the Ministry and Churches of England are weighed, and found too Light . . . (London: Printed by R. I. for Stephen Bowtell, 1652);

A Sober Reply to the Sober Answer of Reverend Mr. Cawdry, to A Serious Question Propounded . . . (London: Printed by J. G. & sold by R. Littlebury, 1653);

Stablishing against Shaking: Or, a Discovery of the Prince of Darknesse (Scarcely) Transformed into an Angel of Light, powerfully now Working in the Deluded People Called, Quakers . . . (London: Printed by F. G. for Nathanael Webb & for William Grantham, 1656);

Of Schism. Parochial Congregations in England, and Ordination by Imposition of Hands . . . (London: Printed by T. C. for Nathanael Webb & William Grantham, 1658);

Tythes Vindicated From Anti-Christianisme And Oppression . . . (London: Printed for Nathanael Webb & William Grantham, 1659);

Presbyterial Ordination Vindicated . . . (London: Printed for Nathanael Webb, 1660);

The Liturgical Considerator Considered; Or, A Brief

View of Dr. Gauden's Considerations Touching the Liturgy of the Church of England... (London: Printed for Ralph Smith, 1661);

The Real Christian; Or a Treatise of Effectual Calling... (London: Printed for Dorman Newman, 1670; Boston: Printed by Rogers & Fowle for J. Edwards & for J. Blanchard, 1742);

Meditations upon Mr. Baxter's Review of His Treatise on the Duty of Heavenly Meditations . . . (London, 1672);

The Questions between the Conformists and Nonconformists . . . (London?, 1681);

Scripture-warrant sufficient Proof for Infant Baptism . . . (London: Printed for Tho. Parkhurst, 1688);

The Answer of Giles Firmin, to the Vain and Unprofitable Question Put to Him and Charged Upon Him by Mr. Grantham, in His Book, Entituled, The Infants Advocate: viz. Whether the Greatest Part of Dying Infants Shall Be Damned? . . . (London: Printed for J. Lawrence, 1689);

Weighty Questions Discussed . . . (London: Printed for the Author, 1692);

Ilanergia a Brief Review of Mr. Davis's Vindication... (London: Printed for J. Lawrence, 1693).

Giles Firmin, known to medical history as the first colonial physician to prepare a skeleton and to lecture on anatomy, was a Puritan minister whose writings, while upholding the New England Way as a model of church government, criticized some of its more rigid doctrines in ways that foreshadowed the liberal attitudes of the eighteenth century. Born in England at Ipswich, son of Giles Firmin, an apothecary, Firmin matriculated at Emmanuel College, Cambridge, in 1629 and studied medicine. Before taking a degree he left with his father for New England in 1632. Firmin was admitted a member of the First Church in Boston, where his father was ordained deacon, and then he sailed for London in 1633 to finish his medical training. He returned to Boston in 1637 at the height of the Antinomian controversy, in which certain members of the colony challenged the authority of the Puritan ministry, and was present at the synod which condemned Anne Hutchinson for such beliefs. His later allusions to the proceedings, his attacks on schismatics and on toleration, his defenses of strict church discipline and the use of civil authority in combating heresy all reflect his approbation of the synod's actions. In 1638 Firmin was granted 100 acres of land in Ipswich (formerly called Agawam), Massachusetts, where Nathaniel Ward had recently resigned as pastor, and in 1639 Firmin married Ward's daughter Susan. In this year he wrote John Winthrop that his medical practice afforded him but "meene help," and he intended to study divinity. In 1644 Firmin returned to England to stay. His family and father-in-law joined him in 1646. Two years later he was appointed to a vicarage in Shalford, Essex.

It was in Shalford, at the age of thirty-five, that Firmin began his writing career, entering into controversies on many of the issues that were dividing Presbyterians and Independents at the time—such as whether all infants should be baptized, or only those of the church members in good standing; whether laymen may preach; whether ministers should be ordained by their congregations or other ministers—and especially separatism and the enforcement of church discipline. Although a Congregationalist in principle, and thus believing in theory that there is no religious authority higher than an individual congregation, Firmin virulently attacked the separatist independents as schismatics, defended the use of civil magistrates to prosecute heretical individuals and congregations, and worked for a voluntary association of Essex ministers rather than an institutionalized "synod" to help maintain orthodoxy. While holding that the Church of England was a true church and defending the parochial system, he favored restricting church membership to "visible saints" and baptism to their children. These views, illustrated by Firmin's frequent references to his New England experiences and buttressed by citations from New English divines such as Thomas Hooker, Thomas Shepherd, and John Norton, demonstrate the continuing influence on him of the New England Way of "non-separating congregationalism." His more moderate spirit, however, is evident in a comparatively lenient definition of visible sainthood which emphasized upright behavior and knowledge of doctrine over conversion experience.

But Firmin did not by any means denigrate the importance of conversion. His Puritan concern for charting the phases and qualities of saving faith is apparent in his best-known work, *The Real Christian* . . . (1670), a treatise on the preparatory stages through which a believer moves toward faith. This book was written after Firmin had been ejected from Shalford for nonconformity in 1662 and had resumed the practice of medicine in nearby Ridgewell, where in 1672 he was licensed to hold Presbyterian conventicles in his home. In *The Real Christian* . . . , which Cotton Mather called "that

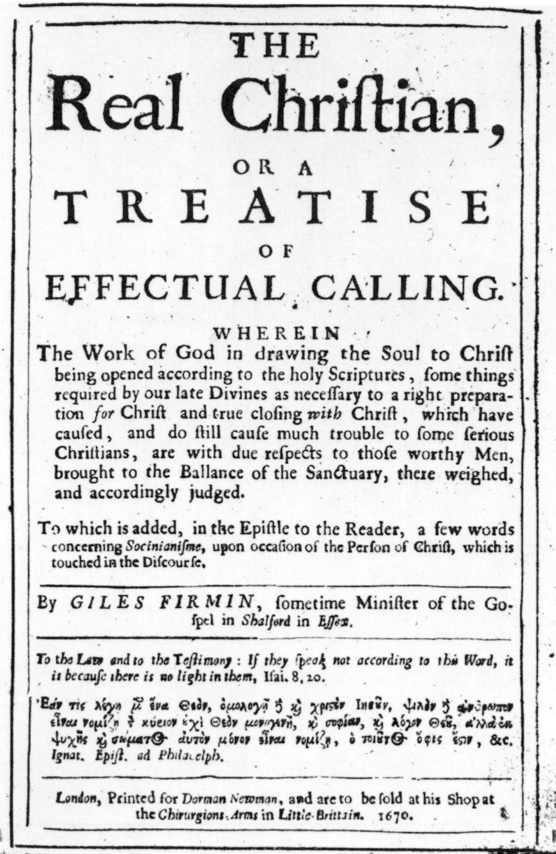

THE
Real Chriſtian,
OR A
TREATISE
OF
EFFECTUAL CALLING.

WHEREIN
The Work of God in drawing the Soul to Chriſt being opened according to the holy Scriptures, ſome things required by our late Divines as neceſſary to a right preparation *for* Chriſt and true cloſing *with* Chriſt, which have cauſed, and do ſtill cauſe much trouble to ſome ſerious Chriſtians, are with due reſpects to thoſe worthy Men, brought to the Ballance of the Sanctuary, there weighed, and accordingly judged.

To which is added, in the Epiſtle to the Reader, a few words concerning *Socinianiſme*, upon occaſion of the Perſon of Chriſt, which is touched in the Diſcourſe.

By *GILES FIRMIN*, ſometime Miniſter of the Goſpel in *Shalford* in *Eſſex*.

To the Law and to the Teſtimony: If they ſpeak not according to this Word, it is becauſe there is no light in them, Iſai. 8, 20.

Ἐάν τις λέγῃ μὲν ἕνα Θεόν, ὁμολογῇ δὲ καὶ Χριστὸν Ἰησοῦν, ψιλὸν δὲ ἄνθρωπον εἶναι νομίζῃ τὸν κύριον οὐχὶ Θεὸν μονογενῆ, καὶ σοφίαν, καὶ λόγον Θεοῦ, ἀλλὰ ἐκ ψυχῆς καὶ σώματος αὐτὸν μόνον εἶναι νομίζῃ, ὁ τοιοῦτος ὄφις ἐστιν, &c. Ignat. *Epiſt. ad Philadelph.*

London, Printed for *Dorman Newman*, and are to be ſold at his Shop at the *Chirurgions-Arms* in Little-Brittain. 1670.

Title page for Firmin's best-known work, written after he had been ejected from his English pastorate for nonconformity with the doctrines of the Church of England (John Carter Brown Library, Brown University)

golden" book, Firmin criticizes Hooker and Shepherd, among others, for their too rigid and schematic accounts of preparation and faith. In their attempt to keep out hypocrites, Hooker and Shepherd raised the standards of church membership so high that they caused needless anxiety in many members of their congregations and in fact scared many real believers away. Moreover, since God works grace in different ways, no one schema can adequately describe the experience of all converts. Most significantly, Firmin objects to the New Englanders' definition of faith as assurance of election and to their doctrine of humiliation, or the necessity of the believer's absolute denial of any concern for himself in seeking salvation. Such a definition of faith, he argues, is too much to ask of sinners only too aware of their sinful nature, and could lead to the false assurance of the Antinomians. The doctrine of humiliation, furthermore, is contrary to human nature, since all action is motivated by some form of self-love: men come to Christ not only because it is their duty but also because they make a rational decision for their own future well-being.

This man-centered argument from a reasonable human nature rather than an inscrutable Divine Will, along with Firmin's emphasis on God's Mercy and Goodness rather than His Sovereignty, look forward to future developments in religious thought. But the fundamental orthodoxy of *The Real Christian* . . . is attested by the fact that when it was reprinted in 1742 in Boston during the Great Awakening (the only one of Firmin's works published in America), its doctrines were defended by the moderate New Light minister Solomon Williams. Firmin died at Ridgewell. A park in Ipswich, Massachusetts, bears his name.

References:

John Ward Dean, "A Brief Memoir of Rev. Giles Firmin," *The New England Historical and Genealogical Register*, 20 (1866): 47-58;

James W. Jones, *The Scattered Synthesis* (New Haven & London: Yale University Press, 1973), pp. 32-53;

George H. Moore, "Giles Firmin and His Various Writings," *Historical Magazine*, second series 3 (1868): 146-151.

John Fiske

(circa 20 March 1608-14 January 1677)

Wesley T. Mott
University of Wisconsin

BOOKS: *The Watering of the Olive Plant in Christs Garden* (Cambridge: Printed by Samuel Green, 1657);

Appendix of Catechism . . . (Cambridge: Printed by Samuel Green, 1668);

Extracts from the Note-Book of the Rev. John Fiske, 1637-1675 (Cambridge: Wilson, 1898);

The Notebook of the Reverend John Fiske, 1644-1675, edited by Robert G. Pope (Boston: Colonial Society of Massachusetts, 1974).

John Fiske, schoolmaster, physician, and minister, has only recently emerged as an important Puritan poet. Baptized at St. James' parish in South Elmham, Suffolk, England, on 20 March 1608, the son of John and Anne Fiske, he graduated from Peterhouse College, Cambridge, in 1628 and preached for several years before persecution for nonconformity led him to turn to the practice of medicine.

Fiske sailed for New England in 1637. On board ship he and John Allin preached so zealously that one passenger claimed *"That he did not know when the Lord's Day was; he thought every Day was a Sabbath Day; for,"* he said, *"they did nothing but pray and preach all the Week long."* Fiske's faith was undaunted by the death of his mother during the voyage and the loss of his infant soon after landing. His wife, Anne, was disinherited by her parents, who disapproved of her emigration, but Fiske farmed, practiced medicine, and taught at Salem, Massachusetts, where he also assisted the Reverend Hugh Peter. And in 1641 Fiske removed to Wenham, Massachusetts, where on 8 October 1644 he was ordained pastor of the newly gathered church and began the valuable notebook on matters of church discipline and ecclesiastical affairs which he kept almost to the end of his career.

Fiske's extant verse, written from 1652 to 1655, was discovered in a neglected commonplace book at Brown University and published by Harold Jantz in 1943. The verses, most of them funeral elegies, are anagrammatic. No mere acrostics, Fiske's anagrams rearrange the letters of his subject's name into phrases or paired nouns that, through rich metaphorical associations, reveal the person's godly qualities, which in turn reinforce the values of the Puritan community. Fiske's finest poem is generally considered to be his elegy on John Cotton, "O, Honie knott." He praises Cotton as an epitome of the Puritan leader, "A gurdeon knot of sweetest graces as / He who set fast to Truths so clossly knitt / as loosen him could ne're the keenest witt," a divine "who the knotts of Truth, of Mysteries / sacred, most cleerely did ope' fore our eyes." Cotton is depicted as tough-minded yet meek ("as in a honi-comb a knott / of Hony sweete"), harmonizing in his life the seeming contradictions of experience that Fiske yokes and reconciles in his verse. Though strange to the modern sensibility, Fiske's verse has won critical praise for its "contrapuntal," "polyphonic technique," which places it in the Baroque tradition.

In 1655 Fiske, along with the majority of his Wenham congregation, removed to Chelmsford, Massachusetts, where he served as minister until his death. Cotton Mather recorded that in Chelmsford "none of [Fiske's] Labours were more Considerable than his *Catechetical*." New England was becoming increasingly concerned about what to do with children of baptized parents who could not give the profession of saving grace necessary for full church membership. Concerned with nurturing the children of these "half-way members" long before the Bay Colony ministers institutionalized the Half-Way Covenant in 1662, Fiske wrote his own catechism for the children of his church, *The Watering of the Olive Plant in Christs Garden* (1657). In later years afflicted by "the *Stone*, and then the *Gout*," he had himself "carried unto the Church in a Chair, and preached . . . sitting." Though Fiske's ministerial labors have long been forgotten, his recently published notebook gives a rare full record of the daily affairs of a seventeenth-century church. And his verse, never intended for wide distribution, has established his reputation as a skillful poet.

Other:

Harold S. Jantz, ed., "The First Century of New England Verse," includes poems by Fiske,

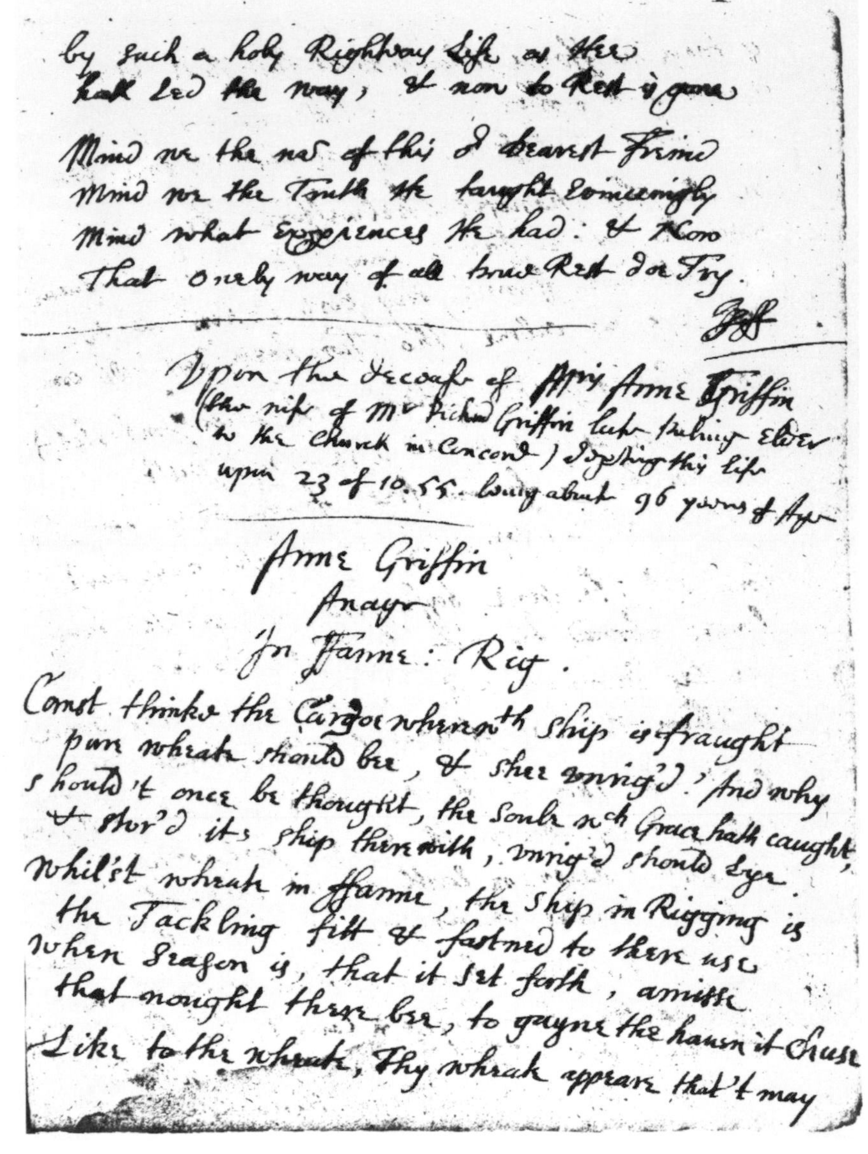
by such a holy Righteous Life as Shee
hath led the way; & now to Rest is gone

Mind we the use of this our dearest Friend
Mind we the Truth she taught Convincingly
Mind what Experiences she had: & How
That onely way of all true Rest doe Try.

J F

Upon the decease of Mris Anne Griffin
(the wife of Mr Richard Griffin late ruling Elder
to the Church in Concord) departing this life
upon 23 of 10. 55. being about 96 yeares of Age

Anne Griffin
Anagr
In Fanne: Rig.

Canst thinke the Cargoe wherewth ship is fraught
pure wheate should bee, & shee unrig'd? And why
should't once be thought, the Soule wch Grace hath caught
& stor'd its ship therewith, unrig'd should Lye.
Whil'st wheate in ffanne, the Ship in Rigging is
the Tackling fitt & fastned to there use
when Season is, that it set forth, amisse
that nought there bee, to gayne the haven it Chuse
Like to the wheate, thy wheate appeare that't may

Page from Fiske's commonplace book (Harris Collection of American Poetry and Plays, Brown University)

Proceedings of the American Antiquarian Society, new series 53 (October 1943): 219-508; republished as a book (Worcester, Mass.: American Antiquarian Society, 1944).

References:

James Bray, "John Fiske: Puritan Precursor of Edward Taylor," *Early American Literature,* 9 (Spring 1974): 27-38;

Harold S. Jantz, "American Baroque: Three Representative Poets," in *Discoveries & Considerations,* edited by Calvin Israel (Albany: State University of New York Press, 1976), pp. 3-23;

Jantz, Introduction to his *The First Century of New England Verse* (Worcester: American Antiquarian Society, 1944), pp. 30-34;

Cotton Mather, *Magnalia Christi Americana* (London: Printed for Thomas Parkhurst, 1702), III: 141-143;

Astrid Schmitt-v. Mühlenfels, "John Fiske's Funeral Elegy on John Cotton," *Early American Literature,* 12 (Spring 1977): 49-62.

Papers:

Fiske's commonplace book is at Brown University. His notebook is at the Essex Institute in Salem, Massachusetts.

William Fitzhugh

(circa 1651-21 October 1701)

Michael A. Lofaro
University of Tennessee

BOOK: *William Fitzhugh and His Chesapeake World, 1676-1701: The Fitzhugh Letters and Other Documents,* edited by Richard Beale Davis (Chapel Hill: Published for the Virginia Historical Society by The University of North Carolina Press, 1963).

William Fitzhugh's significance derives from his 215 letters, some speeches, his will, and a few miscellaneous documents, which together yield a wealth of information on seventeenth-century Virginia. His letters reflect his interlocking occupations of lawyer, businessman, and gentleman-farmer, and, as a group, parallel and may surpass those of William Byrd I, the only other extensive epistolary collection of that time and place, in giving a detailed picture of day-to-day plantation life. In addition to presenting the best physical description of a seventeenth-century plantation, these letters tell the story of the growth of the early economic and governmental systems of Virginia and document as well Fitzhugh's emergence as a local leader and his founding of a prominent Virginia family.

William, the youngest child of Henry Fitzhugh, a wealthy woolen draper, was born in Bedford, England, and baptized on 10 January 1651. Little is known of his early life. Already a lawyer when he arrived in Virginia about 1670, he either purchased lands in the Northern Neck or received them on 26 August 1674 as a partial dowry for Sarah Tucker. Family tradition holds that Sarah, the eleven-to-thirteen-year-old daughter of an influential Virginia family, was sent to Europe for two years before the marriage was consummated. Within these two years, Fitzhugh became a prosperous grower and exporter of tobacco and the Stafford county representative to the House of Burgesses. A known authority on colonial law, Fitzhugh came to legal prominence through his defense of Robert Beverley against the Crown (1682-1685) after Beverley refused to supply the royal governor with copies of the House of Burgesses's journals without that body's permission. By 1684 Fitzhugh had become both lieutenant colonel of the militia and justice of the peace. A supporter of the Stuarts and accused of

John Hesselius's 1751 copy of a portrait of William Fitzhugh (Virginia Historical Society)

papistry, Fitzhugh was ordered to take the Oath of Allegiance and complied on 26 May 1693. In that year he completed a brief history of Virginia as a preface to his edition of its laws, which was never published and is no longer extant, and in 1697 he projected a longer history to encourage settlement. After returning from a trip to England (1699?-1701?), Fitzhugh died on 21 October 1701 of a bloody flux which he contracted from the French Huguenot refugees whom he had befriended and encouraged to settle upon his Ravensworth tract on the upper Potomac.

Without question William Fitzhugh was best known among his contemporaries for his legal expertise, a reputation gained from his career as a lawyer's lawyer and his service in the House of Burgesses, but his activities as a businessman and farmer also placed him in the first rank of the leading Virginians of his day. His tobacco farming made him a voracious acquirer of land. He was able to leave 54,054 acres to his descendants despite his having failed in his bid to buy his entire parish and a tract of 100,000 acres. Fitzhugh was the first to employ large-scale slave labor in Stafford County, the first to establish a central trading town in Virginia (an act directly in opposition to the wishes of the powerful English merchants who wished to monopolize the profit resulting from the exchange of American tobacco for English goods), and, as one of the two resident agents for the Culpeper heirs and Lord Fairfax in the Northern Neck Proprietary, he helped to set the pattern of land grants and patenting for future American land speculation and development.

Fitzhugh led a sophisticated social life for the time, and his love of the good life evidently matched his desire for the wealth which supported it. His description of his "own Dwelling house" as "furnished with all accommodations for comfortable & gentile living . . ." underscored his preferences. Ample testimony to verify Fitzhugh's view of his life-style is found in the 1686-1687 travel account of a Frenchman named Durand. With no previous announcement of his intentions and but two days before Christmas, Durand and a party of his friends "rode twenty strong to Colonel Fichous', but he has such a large establishment that he did not mind. We were all of us provided with beds, one for two men. He treated us royally, there was good wine & all kinds of beverages, so there was a great deal of carousing. He had sent for three fiddlers, a jester, a tight-rope dancer, an acrobat who tumbled around, & they gave us all the entertainment one could wish for. It was very cold, yet no one ever thinks of going near the fire, for they never put less than a cartload of wood in the fireplace & the whole room is kept warm. . . ."

Such lordly festivals are neither denied nor recorded in Fitzhugh's correspondence, which portrays a busy, practical man. His numerous requests for silver stem more from sound investment than from a wish for self-aggrandizement or love of craftsmanship. Purchase orders given to the English merchants who received his tobacco highlighted his refusal to spend beyond his means with stipulations such as "but let me not be a farthing in Debt. . . ."

His business communications consistently provide personal insight as well as historical data. Trial shipments of ore and black walnut timber to England and his attempt to grow olives in Virginia were speculative ventures which hint at his dissatisfaction with his dependence upon tobacco. Combine these attempts with his negative refrain concerning uncertain tobacco prices, the vagaries of shipping, and dealings with unreliable merchants, and one of the reasons behind his emphasis upon personal control and his pursuit of the *via media* as the most suitable philosophy for a man whose fortunes are never completely secure becomes clear. Enforced overproduction and consequent lack of demand for tobacco, quickly exhausted lands, Indian uprisings, and political upheaval are matters over which he can exert little influence. But he can give a certain order to his life through a stress upon moderation, an emphasis which permeates his letters and leads as well to some of his more literary comments. Consider, for example, the reasons for his resilient constitution: "I never much frequented Bacchus Orgyes, & always avoided Adoration to Ceres shrine, & never was one of Venus Votarys: To speak plainly to you, I never courted unlawfull pleasures with women, avoided hard drinking as much as lay in my power, & always avoided feasting & consequently the surfeits occasioned thereby. . . ." The same method makes for a peaceful mind. He praises his uncle's "contented Condition, which in my opinion far exceeds the other, for its the mark that all drive at from the Monarch on the Throne, to the lowest Tradesman, without which the Riches of Croesus are not satisfactory, & with it the lowest Degree passes his time away here pleasantly. Sr. My Condition here is in a very equal temper, I neither abound nor want. . . ." Even his metaphors evince support of the middle way. In regard to the choice between conciseness and perfect clarity through repetition, he elects the latter, despite the perception of his correspondent's taxed patience, explaining, "I am more afraid of falling upon Scylla to avoid Charybdis. . . ."

Holding the view typical of his day, Fitzhugh regards the letter as a literary form of which, at his best, he is an able practitioner. Though he once says "I must confess I want abilitys, to polish & adorn my expressions . . . ," his modesty and literary convention cause him to underestimate the effectiveness of prose such as: "Necessity as 'tis the Mother of Invention, so it is the Nurse of Industry . . ."; "with the same Content & satisfaction as wearyed travellers take up their Inn, or weather beaten Voyagers their desired Port, after a long tedious & stormy Voyage, so did I the most welcome joyfull, & glad news of your health, welfare, & prosperity . . ."; "you are not Yorkshire enough, to set the Course of your advice by the Compass of your Interest"; and "what a hard Game we have to play the contrary party that is our Opposers, having the best Cards & the Trumps to boot especially the Honor[.] Yet would my Lord Fairfax there, take his turn in Shuffling & Dealing the Cards & his Lordship with the rest see that we were not cheated in our game, I question not but we should gain the sett, tho' the game is so far plaid. . . ."

Such is the literary quality of Fitzhugh's letters. His correspondence remains important for the valuable portrait of his time which it provides and as an indispensable point of reference for the correct evaluation of the life and mind of William Fitzhugh. To appreciate the gentle art of his letters is indeed to understand more fully both the age and the man.

Other:

"William Fitzhugh and the Northern Neck Proprietary: A Letter," edited by Richard Beale Davis, *Virginia Magazine of History and Biography*, 89 (January 1981): 39-43.

References:

Philip A. Bruce, *Institutional History of Virginia in the Seventeenth Century*, 2 volumes (New York & London: Putnam's, 1910);

Richard Beale Davis, "Chesapeake Pattern and Pole-Star: William Fitzhugh in his Plantation World, 1676-1701," *Proceedings of the American Philosophical Society*, 105 (1961): 525-529;

Davis, *Intellectual Life in the Colonial South, 1585-1763*, 3 volumes (Knoxville: University of Tennessee Press, 1978);

Davis, Introduction to *William Fitzhugh and His Chesapeake World, 1676-1701* (Chapel Hill: Published for the Virginia Historical Society by the University of North Carolina Press, 1963);

Davis, *Literature and Society in Early Virginia, 1608-1840* (Baton Rouge: Louisiana State University Press, 1973);

Durand de Dauphiné, *Voyages D'un François exilé pour la Religion, Avec Une description de la Virgine & Marilan dans L'Amerique* (The Hague, 1687); republished as *A Huguenot Exile in Virginia, or Voyages of a Frenchman exiled for his Religion, with a Description of Virginia & Maryland*, edited by Gilbert Chinard (New York: Press of the Pioneers, 1934);

Howard Mumford Jones, *The Literature of Virginia in the Seventeenth Century* (Charlottesville: University Press of Virginia, 1968), pp. 79-85;

Bishop William Meade, *Old Churches, Ministers and Families of Virginia*, 2 volumes (1857; Philadelphia: Lippincott, 1885);

Louis B. Wright, *The First Gentlemen of Virginia: Intellectual Qualities of the Early Colonial Ruling Class* (San Marino, Cal.: Huntington Library, 1940).

John Foster

(December 1648-9 September 1681)

James Lawton

BOOKS: *1675. An Almanack of Coelestial Motions for the Year of the Christian Aera, 1675 . . .* (Cambridge: Printed by Samuel Green, 1675);

1676. An Almanack of Coelestial Motions for the Year of the Christian Aera 1676 . . . (Boston: Printed by John Foster, 1676);

1677. An Almanack of Coelestial Motions for the Year of the Christian Aera 1677 . . . (Boston: Printed by John Foster, 1677);

1678. An Almanack of Coelestial Motions for the Year of the Christian Epoca 1678 . . . (Boston: Printed by John Foster for John Usher, 1678);

1679. An Almanack of Coelestial Motions for the Year of the Christian Epocha 1679 . . . (Boston: Printed by John Foster & sold by Henry Phillips, 1679);

MDCLXXX. An Almanack of Coelestial Motions

for the Year of the Christian Aepocha, 1680 (Boston: Printed by John Foster, 1680);
MDCLXXXI. An Almanack of Coelestial Motions for the Year of the Christian Epocha, 1681 . . . (Boston: Printed by John Foster, 1681).

John Foster, first American wood engraver and Boston's first printer, was born in Dorchester, Massachusetts, and baptized on 10 December 1648 in Richard Mather's church. He was the son of Hopestill Foster, a brewer and representative in the General Court, and Mary Foster, the daughter of James Bates, who was a Dorchester Selectman and later General Court representative from Hingham, Massachusetts. John Foster graduated from Harvard College in the class of 1667. In 1669 Foster was receiving a salary from the town of Dorchester for teaching Latin scholars in his father's house. By 1674, he is recorded as receiving recompense for teaching grammar scholars English, Latin, and writing at the schoolhouse in Dorchester.

In May 1674 the General Court decided to end the prohibition that had restricted printing at Cambridge. This action enabled Marmaduke Johnson to move his press to Boston, but he died on Christmas day 1674, without printing any work that bore a Boston imprint. At this point, Foster purchased Johnson's press and, in 1675, opened the first Boston printing office at the Sign of the Dove. Foster was probably encouraged in this enterprise by Increase Mather, who wrote at least fifteen of fifty or so works printed by Foster during his six years at business. Although Isaiah Thomas says that Foster did not appear to be acquainted with the art of printing, he must have had at least a passing familiarity with the presses operating in Cambridge during his student days. A sermon by Increase Mather, *A Wicked Mans Portion . . .* (1675), was the first work printed on Foster's press, and the quality of the work equaled that produced at Cambridge. Over the next six years Foster printed about fifty works, including Thomas Thacher's 1677 broadside *A Brief Rule to Guide the Common People of New-England how to Order Themselves and Theirs in the Small Pocks, or Measles,* the first medical treatise printed in British North America. Also in 1677, Foster printed William Hubbard's *A Narrative of the Troubles with the Indians in New-England . . . ,* in which he included a woodcut "Map of New England," the first map of any kind to be printed in the English colonies. In 1678, he printed Anne Bradstreet's *Several Poems Compiled with a Great Variety of Wit and Learning . . . ,* the first American edition of *The Tenth Muse lately sprung up in America* (published in London in 1650) and believed to be the first book by a woman to be published in America.

Foster appears to have taken up wood engraving as an avocation in college. Some crude relief cuts used as ornaments on broadsides printed at Cambridge by Samuel Green as early as 1667 may have been cut by Foster. The first substantial engraving attributed to Foster is a woodcut portrait of his pastor, Richard Mather, made about 1670 probably as a frontispiece for Increase Mather's *The Life and Death of that Reverend Man of God, Mr. Richard Mather . . . ,* printed by Samuel Green and Marmaduke Johnson in 1670. A cut of the Seal of Massachusetts which appeared in 1672 has been attributed to Foster, although some authorities attribute it to English origins. A later cut of the seal which first appears on a broadside of the *Severall Lawes and Ordinances of War* (1675), printed by Foster, is almost certainly his work.

Foster compiled almanacs for the years 1675-1681. The first, printed by Samuel Green, contains diagram cuts by Foster of the sun, moon, stars, and lunar eclipse. In his almanac for 1678, Foster included the first human anatomical chart published in this country. His last almanac (1681) includes his article "Comets, their Motion, Distance, and Magnitude," with "Observations of a Comet seen this last Winter 1680."

Foster died of tuberculosis on 9 September 1681 at Dorchester, age thirty-two. The last work Foster printed was, like the first, by Increase Mather, *Heavens Alarm to the World . . .* (1681). Two poems on Foster's death were printed in 1681. One of these, by Joseph Capen, concludes with the following lines:

> Thy body, which no activeness did lack
> Now's laid aside like an old Almanack;
> But for the present only's out of date—
> 'Twill have at length a far more active state.
>
> Yea, though with dust thy body soiled be,
> Yet at the Resurrection we shall see
> A fair Edition and of matchless worth,
> Free from Erratas, new in Heaven set forth:
> 'Tis but a word from God the great Creatour,
> It shall be done when He saith Imprimatur.

An epitaph not unlike this one was written for himself by another Boston printer, Benjamin Franklin, one hundred years later.

References:

Samuel A. Green, *John Foster: The Earliest*

American Engraver and the First Boston Printer (Boston: Massachusetts Historical Society, 1909);

John Langdon Sibley, Biographical Sketches of *Harvard Graduates,* volume 2 (Cambridge: Charles William Sever, 1881), pp. 222-228;

Isaiah Thomas, *The History of Printing in America* (1810; republished, New York: Weather Vane Books, 1970), pp. 79-81.

Benjamin Franklin

Richard E. Amacher
Auburn University

BIRTH: Boston, Massachusetts, 17 January 1706, to Josiah and Abiah Folger Franklin.

MARRIAGE: 1 September 1730 to Deborah Read; children: William (born out of wedlock), Francis Folger, Sarah.

DEATH: Philadelphia, Pennsylvania, 17 April 1790.

Portrait by Joseph-Siffred Dupplessis, 1778 (Metropolitan Museum of Art, Michael Friedsam Collection, 1931)

SELECTED BOOKS: *A Dissertation on Liberty and Necessity, Pleasure and Pain* . . . (London, 1725);

A Modest Enquiry into the Nature and Necessity of Paper-Currency . . . (Philadelphia: Printed & sold at the New Printing-Office, 1729);

Poor Richard, 1733. An Almanack. . . , as Richard Saunders, Philom. (Philadelphia: Printed & sold by B. Franklin, 1732);

Poor Richard, 1734. An Almanack. . . , as Saunders (Philadelphia: Printed & sold by B. Franklin, 1733);

Poor Richard, 1735. An Almanack. . . , as Saunders (Philadelphia: Printed & sold by B. Franklin, 1734);

Some Observations on the Proceedings against The Rev. Mr. Hemphill; with a Vindication of His Sermons (Philadelphia: Printed & sold by B. Franklin, 1735);

A Letter to a Friend in the Country, Containing the Substance of a Sermon Preach'd at Philadelphia, in the Congregation of The Rev. Mr. Hemphill, Concerning the Terms of Christian and Ministerial Communion (Philadelphia: Printed & sold by B. Franklin, 1735);

A Defense Of the Rev. Mr. Hemphill's Observations: or, An Answer to the Vindication of the Reverend Commission . . . (Philadelphia: Printed & sold by B. Franklin, 1735);

Poor Richard, 1736. An Almanack..., as Saunders (Philadelphia: Printed & sold by B. Franklin, 1735);

Poor Richard, 1737. An Almanack..., as Saunders (Philadelphia: Printed & sold by B. Franklin, 1736);

Poor Richard, 1738. An Almanack..., as Saunders (Philadelphia: Printed & sold by B. Franklin, 1737);

Poor Richard, 1739. An Almanack..., as Saunders (Philadelphia: Printed & sold by B. Franklin, 1738);

Poor Richard, 1740. An Almanack..., as Saunders (Philadelphia: Printed & sold by B. Franklin, 1739);

Poor Richard, 1741. An Almanack..., as Saunders (Philadelphia: Printed & sold by B. Franklin, 1740);

Poor Richard, 1742. An Almanack..., as Saunders (Philadelphia: Printed & sold by B. Franklin, 1741);

Poor Richard, 1743. An Almanack..., as Saunders (Philadelphia: Printed & sold by B. Franklin, 1742);

Poor Richard, 1744. An Almanack..., as Saunders (Philadelphia: Printed & sold by B. Franklin & Jonas Greene, 1743);

An Account Of the New Invented Pennsylvanian Fire-Places... (Philadelphia: Printed & sold by B. Franklin, 1744);

Poor Richard, 1745. An Almanack..., as Saunders (Philadelphia: Printed & sold by B. Franklin, 1744);

Poor Richard, 1746. An Almanack..., as Saunders (Philadelphia: Printed & sold by B. Franklin, 1745);

Poor Richard, 1747. An Almanack..., as Saunders (Philadelphia: Printed & sold by B. Franklin, 1746);

Plain Truth: or, Serious Considerations On the Present State of the City of Philadelphia, and Province of Pennsylvania, as a Tradesman of Philadelphia (Philadelphia: Printed by B. Franklin, 1747);

Poor Richard improved: Being an Almanack and Ephemeris... for the Bissextile Year, 1748..., as Saunders (Philadelphia: Printed & sold by B. Franklin, 1747);

Poor Richard improved: Being an Almanack and Ephemeris... For the Year of Our Lord 1749..., as Saunders (Philadelphia: Printed & sold by B. Franklin & D. Hall, 1748);

Proposals Relating to the Education of Youth in Pensilvania (Philadelphia, 1749);

Poor Richard improved: Being an Almanack and Ephemeris... For the Year of Our Lord 1750..., as Saunders (Philadelphia: Printed & sold by B. Franklin & D. Hall, 1749);

Poor Richard improved: Being an Almanack and Ephemeris... For the Year of Our Lord 1751..., as Saunders (Philadelphia: Printed & sold by B. Franklin & D. Hall, 1750);

Experiments and Observations on Electricity, made at Philadelphia in America..., part 1 (London: Printed & sold by E. Cave, 1751);

Poor Richard improved: Being an Almanack & Ephemeris... For the Year of Our Lord 1752, as Saunders (Philadelphia: Printed & sold by B. Franklin & D. Hall, 1751);

Poor Richard improved: Being an Almanack and Ephemeris... For the Year of Our Lord 1753..., as Saunders (Philadelphia: Printed & sold by B. Franklin & D. Hall, 1752);

Supplemental Experiments and Observations on Electricity, Part II. Made at Philadelphia in America... (London: Printed & sold by E. Cave, 1753);

Poor Richard improved: Being an Almanack and Ephemeris... For the Year of Our Lord 1754, as Saunders (Philadelphia: Printed & sold by B. Franklin & D. Hall, 1753);

Some Account of the Pennsylvania Hospital... (Philadelphia: Printed by B. Franklin & D. Hall, 1754);

New Experiments and Observations on Electricity. Made at Philadelphia in America..., part 3 (London: Printed & sold by D. Henry & R. Cave, 1754);

Poor Richard improved: Being an Almanack and Ephemeris... For the Year of Our Lord 1755..., as Saunders (Philadelphia: Printed & sold by B. Franklin & D. Hall, 1754);

Poor Richard improved: Being an Almanack and Ephemeris... For the Year of Our Lord 1756..., as Saunders (Philadelphia: Printed & sold by B. Franklin & D. Hall, 1755);

Poor Richard improved: Being an Almanack and Ephemeris... For the Year of Our Lord 1757..., as Saunders (Philadelphia: Printed & sold by B. Franklin & D. Hall, 1756);

Poor Richard Improved: Being an Almanack and Ephemeris... For the Year of Our Lord 1758..., as Saunders (Philadelphia: Printed & sold by B. Franklin & D. Hall, 1757);

Father Abraham's Speech To a great Number of People, at a Vendue of Merchant-Goods; Introduced to The Publick By Poor Richard (A famous Pennsylvanian Conjuror and Almanack-

Maker)... (Boston: Printed & sold by Benjamin Mecom, 1758); republished as *The Way to Wealth, as clearly shewn in the Preface of An Old Pennsylvania Almanack, Intituled, Poor Richard Improved* (London: Printed & sold by M. Lewis, 1774; London: Printed & sold by R. Snagg, 1774);

The Interest of Great Britain Considered, With Regard to her Colonies, And the Acquisitions of Canada and Guadaloupe. To which are added, Observations concerning the Increase of Mankind, Peopling of Countries, &c. (London: Printed for T. Becket, 1760; Boston: Printed by B. Mecum, 1760);

A Narrative of the Late Massacres, in Lancaster County, of a Number of Indians, Friends of this Province, By Persons Unknown . . . (Philadelphia: Printed by Anthony Armbruster, 1764);

Cool Thoughts on the Present Situation of Our Public Affairs . . . (Philadelphia: Printed by W. Dunlap, 1764);

Remarks on a late Protest Against the Appointment of Mr. Franklin an Agent for this Province (Philadelphia: Printed by B. Franklin & D. Hall, 1764);

Oeuvres de M. Franklin, 2 volumes, edited by Jacques Barbeu-Duborg (Paris: Quillau, 1773);

Political, Miscellaneous, and Philosophical Pieces..., edited by Benjamin Vaughan (London: Printed for J. Johnson, 1779);

Observations on the Causes and Cure of Smokey Chimneys (London: Printed for J. Debrett, 1787);

Philosophical and Miscellaneous Papers. Lately written by B. Franklin, LL.D., edited by Edward Bancroft (London: Printed for C. Dilly, 1787);

Rules for Reducing a Great Empire to a Small One (London: Printed for James Ridgway, 1793);

Autobiography of Benjamin Franklin, first complete edition, edited by John Bigelow (Philadelphia: Lippincott / London: Trübner, 1868);

Benjamin Franklin Experiments. A New Edition of Franklin's Experiments and Observations on Electricity, edited by I. Bernard Cohen (Cambridge: Harvard University Press, 1941);

Benjamin Franklin's Autobiographical Writings, edited by Carl Van Doren (New York: Viking, 1945);

Benjamin Franklin's Memoirs. Parallel Text Edition, edited by Max Farrand (Berkeley: University of California Press, 1949);

Benjamin Franklin: His Contribution to the American Tradition, edited by Cohen (New York: Bobbs-Merrill, 1953);

Franklin's Wit and Folly: The Bagatelles, edited by Richard E. Amacher (New Brunswick: Rutgers University Press, 1953);

The Autobiography of Benjamin Franklin, edited by Leonard W. Labaree, Ralph L. Ketcham, and others (New Haven: Yale University Press, 1964);

The Political Thought of Benjamin Franklin, edited by Ketcham (Indianapolis: Bobbs-Merrill, 1965);

The Bagatelles from Passy by Benjamin Franklin, Text and Facsimile (New York: Eakins Press, 1967);

The Autobiography of Benjamin Franklin, A Genetic Text, edited by J. A. Leo Lemay and P. M. Zall (Knoxville: University of Tennessee Press, 1981).

COLLECTIONS: *The Works of Dr. Benjamin Franklin*, 6 volumes, edited by William Duane, (Philadelphia: Duane, 1808-1818);

Memoirs of the Life and Writings of Benjamin Franklin, 3 volumes, edited by William Temple Franklin (London: Henry Colburn, 1817-1818);

The Works of Benjamin Franklin, 10 volumes, edited by Jared Sparks (Boston: Hilliard, Gray, 1836-1840);

The Writings of Benjamin Franklin, 10 volumes, edited by Albert Henry Smyth (New York: Macmillan, 1905-1907);

The Papers of Benjamin Franklin, edited by Leonard W. Labaree, Whitfield J. Bell, Jr., and others, 23 volumes to date (New Haven: Yale University Press, 1959-);

The Complete Poor Richard Almanacs published by Benjamin Franklin, edited by Bell (Barre, Mass.: Imprint Society, 1970).

As author of one of the most famous autobiographies ever written and publisher of the Poor Richard almanacs, Benjamin Franklin holds forever a firm place in the hearts and minds of Americans (and, indeed, of all people) who honor good humor, common sense, and wisdom—traits in his writing for which he is best known. Less well known but still of great historical importance are his scientific writings on electricity and his voluminous contributions to political satire—pamphlets, letters, essays—which, along with the powerful rhetoric of Thomas Paine, Philip Freneau, and others, shaped the public opinion that gave birth to the American republic. In addition, Franklin wrote skillful personal essays; and his three series of works in this genre—the Dogood essays, the Busy-Body essays, and the Bagatelles—are models of grace and charm.

Primarily a nonfiction writer, Franklin's appealing style (which he modeled after the examples of Addison, Defoe, and Swift) proved effective in a great variety of short literary forms. His writings were addressed to American, English, and French audiences and gained popularity by reason of his simple diction, convincing arguments, native humor, and secular spirit. If Jonathan Edwards was, as some contend, the greatest theological writer ever produced in America and thus represents the religious spirit of the eighteenth century in America, Franklin's life and writings are important as typifying the other great movement of the American Enlightenment—its secular spirit, the rise of the self-made man.

Franklin was born in humble circumstances in Milk Street in Boston. His mother was the second wife of an English silk dyer who had emigrated (for reasons of religious freedom) from Banbury in Oxfordshire to the New World, where he had set up as a tallow chandler and soap boiler. In his autobiography (the main source for most of our knowledge about his early life) Franklin explains that he was the youngest son of the youngest son for five generations. As the tenth son of a devout Congregationalist, he had at one point been thought of by his father as a tithe to the ministry. Eventually Franklin did become a minister, but not in the sense his father had intended.

Of formal education Franklin had little, despite his early fondness for reading. (In the *Autobiography* he mentions being put into grammar school at age eight and staying there for "not quite one Year," after which his father put him in a school for learning writing and arithmetic.) When he was ten he began work in his father's shop. Two years later (at the customary age) he was apprenticed to his brother James to learn the printing trade.

The office of James Franklin's newspaper, the *New-England Courant*, turned out to be a propitious environment for Benjamin Franklin's development as a writer. The presence there of a group of young writers of satire (whom the Mathers had dubbed the Hell-Fire Club because of their opposition) stimulated young Ben to try his hand at this kind of writing. The resulting Dogood essays, which he wrote over the pseudonym of Silence Dogood, a young widow, satirized from her point of view such varying subjects as extravagant female dress, moonlight strolling, religious hypocrisy in government office, bad verse obituaries (the famous recipe for a New England elegy, attacking sentimentalism), alcoholism, Harvard education, and the expulsion of Timothy Cutler, the rector of Yale College, for his Arminian and Anglican views. In all there were fourteen of these popular personal essays, which appeared every fortnight (from 2 April to 8 October in 1722) when Franklin was only sixteen years old.

During part of this time his brother had been jailed for criticizing the Massachusetts authorities' failure to provide defense against a pirate ship reported off the coast. From 12 June, when his brother went to jail, until the end of the legislative session (so the brother's sentence read) Franklin acted as manager of the paper. Dogood number 8, dated 9 July 1722, stands out from the other essays. Its tone is more militant, and its subject was certainly timely—freedom of speech and freedom of the press. Two other Dogoods representative of this period show his early concern for the public good. In numbers 10 and 11, less satiric in tone, he advocates social security for widows and elderly spinsters.

These familiar or personal essays took their name from an earlier "dogood" series by Cotton Mather (*Bonifacius*, 1706), which Franklin probably had read. But their flavor to a certain degree recalls Addison and Steele's *Spectator*, which also endeavored to correct the follies of the age by means of its Latin mottoes, lay sermons, allegorical visions or dreams, characters of eavesdroppers and street strollers, and by its letters from correspondents. (In the third Dogood, for example, Franklin in his role as a young widow invites correspondence from his female readers, saying that he will look on such letters as favors and will acknowledge them "accordingly.") Showing the influence of Addison and Steele again, the fourteenth Dogood is in part a verbatim extract of *Spectator* number 185 and *The Guardian* number 80. But there were differences, too. Although he used a similar colloquial manner, Franklin discarded their learned allusions and literary anecdotes, replacing them with homely sayings (Dogood number 5) and with comic and sometimes earthy stories (number 13) and, in general, with a new brand of lively native humor.

The Dogood papers were obviously very important in Franklin's development as a writer of satire. At a relatively early age, he says in the *Autobiography*, he had achieved a reputation as "a young Genius that had a Turn for Libelling and Satyr." Thomas Goddard Wright concludes that the Dogood papers were "among the most literary essays which that period published."

The following year (1723) Franklin enjoyed another opportunity to act as manager of the *Courant*. This time his name appeared on the masthead as publisher, a scheme whereby his brother—again under arrest—attempted to evade a court order obliging him to submit to censorship by the Secretary of the Province. (The scheme permitted the paper to continue publication.) But since it was known in Boston that Franklin was still an apprentice, his brother and others on the *Courant* staff contrived the plan of publicly announcing the breaking of his indentures, or contract of apprenticeship, so that it might appear that the paper had a new publisher. Secretly new indentures were signed. Ultimately this arrangement led to a quarrel between the two brothers—Franklin also claimed that his brother had beaten him—and this new outbreak precipitated the younger brother's escape to New York and finally to Philadelphia in search of work.

During the period 11 February-7 May, when his brother was under arrest, Franklin not only managed the paper but continued writing the kind of entertaining satires he had done the previous year as Silence Dogood. This time, however, he presented a new character, that of an elderly two-faced "Inhabitant of this Town of Boston, whom we honour as a Doctor in the Chair, or a perpetual Dictator," modeled after the Roman deity Janus, "a Man of such remarkable *Opticks*" that he can "look two ways at once," a man "of good Temper, courteous Deportment, sound Judgment; a mortal Hater of Nonsense, Foppery, Formality, and endless Ceremony." The postscript to this essay makes clear that Dr. Janus "can say all the Greek Letters by heart." A week later (18 February 1723) he again alludes to Dr. Janus's habit of "looking *two ways at once*," which he says reminds him of "lawyers who with equal Force of Argument, can plead either for the *Plaintiff* or *Defendant*." The postscript of this essay, like the earlier Dogoods, welcomes correspondence with "old Janus," but its most noteworthy feature is an attack on titles of honor by a member of Dr. Janus's club: "In Old Time it was no disrespect for Men and Women to be call'd by their own Names: Adam, was never called *Master* Adam; we never read of Noah, *Esquire*, Lot *Knight* and *Baronet*, nor the *Right Honourable* Abraham, *Viscount Mesopotamia, Baron of Carran* [*sic*]; no, no, they were plain Men, honest Country Grasiers, that took great Care of their Families and their Flocks. . . . we never read of the *Reverend* Moses, nor the *Right Reverend Father in God*, Aaron, by Divine Providence, *Lord Arch-Bishop of Israel*: Thou never sawest *Madam* Rebecca in the Bible, my *Lady* Rachel, nor Mary . . . call'd the *Princess Dowager of Nazareth*; no, plain Rebecca, Rachel, Mary . . . It was no Incivility then to mention their naked Names as they were expressed."

Possibly, write the Yale editors of the Franklin papers, the pseudonymous essays written under the personae of Timothy Wagstaff and Abigail Twitterfield and one or two others that appeared in the *Courant* before 16 September 1723 (the last date Franklin is believed to have worked on the *Courant*) were also composed by Franklin. At any rate, soon afterward he ran away to Philadelphia, where he began working as a journeyman for Samuel Keimer.

In Philadelphia he began to entertain notions of setting himself up as an independent printer. Since his childhood, however, he had "always had a strong Inclination for the Sea." On 5 November 1724, therefore, at the age of eighteen he sailed for England, his ostensible purpose being to acquire a set of type and other printing paraphernalia—offered to him by Governor William Keith's letters of credit to influential persons in London. Discovering himself hoodwinked by Keith, who had no credit, Franklin, now thrown on his own resources, found work with Palmer's, a well-known London printing house. During his stay there, which lasted nearly a year, he became interested in Deism and wrote what he referred to as "a little metaphysical piece," *A Dissertation on Liberty and Necessity, Pleasure and Pain* . . . (1725), which he inscribed to his erstwhile friend James Ralph.

Employed as a compositor at Palmer's, Franklin's interest in Deism had grown out of his disagreement with some of the ideas of the third edition of William Wollaston's work entitled *The Religion of Nature Delineated* (first published in 1722), which had been assigned him as a typesetting job. In answer to Wollaston, an Anglican clergyman, Franklin wrote and printed 100 copies of his dissertation, which raised his prestige with Palmer, who nevertheless objected to its line of reasoning. In later life Franklin referred to this little pamphlet as an "Erratum."

Franklin's *A Dissertation on Liberty and Necessity, Pleasure and Pain* . . . is exactly what its title says, a discussion of freedom of the will in a universe governed by the pleasure-pain principle. With some ingenious syllogizing he disposes of the entire problem of evil in the universe, something which he says had long perplexed "many of the Learned." Starting from the proposition that God is all-wise, all-good, and all-powerful, he infers that everything God creates must be good, since to create anything evil would be logically opposite to his nature; therefore "Evil doth not exist." Franklin readily admits that "there are both Things and

A

DISSERTATION

ON

Liberty and *Neceſſity*,

PLEASURE *and* PAIN.

Whatever is, is in its Cauſes juſt
Since all Things are by Fate; but purblind Man
Sees but a part o'th' Chain, the neareſt Link,
His Eyes not carrying to the equal Beam
That poiſes all above.

Dryd.

LONDON:
Printed in the Year MDCCXXV.

Title page for Franklin's first book, which he printed in Samuel Palmer's London shop

Actions to which we give the Name of *Evil.*" But these, he contends, are really explainable as *pain*—such matters as sickness, want, theft, and murder. (At one point he carries his refutation of Wollaston so far as to defend horse stealing, but his common sense quickly asserts itself: he throws logic overboard and states that "The Order and Course of Things will not be affected by Reasoning of this Kind.") If God is all-powerful, man is only able to do such things as God would have him do. Free will ceases to exist. If there is no such thing as free will, then it follows that there can be no such thing as "Merit or Demerit in Creatures." All are "esteemed" equally by the creator. In the second part of the dissertation, his ingenious albeit somewhat mechanistic definitions of pain and pleasure permit him to conclude that all creatures are "equally used" by their creator. Hence *justice* exists in the universe, and there is consequently no need of an afterlife in which to correct the injustices of the present. Every creature obtains as much pleasure as pain because both have been defined as related in terms of exact proportions—every pain being balanced by an equal amount of pleasure when the pain is relieved. Thus even the experience of dying painfully is attended by an equal amount of pleasure at the relief of death.

We must remember that Franklin was only nineteen years old when he wrote this dissertation. His failure to offer more profound answers to these endless puzzling philosophic problems some might censure. But his logic is irrefutable—once his basic premises have been accepted. At the beginning of the letter, too, in his address to Ralph, he stresses that the hypothetical parts of the argument are to be distinguished from the conclusive. "You will easily perceive," he adds, "what I design for Demonstration, and what for Probability only." Besides the two main divisions of this pamphlet in letter form, the dissertation contains a clear and well-ordered recapitulation at its close and an excellent sketch of the Deist view of the universe as a beautifully ordered clock or "curious Machine." ("An Arabian Tale," an essay believed by A. O. Aldridge to have been written toward the end of Franklin's life, offers another Deist view, that of the great chain of being.)

The style of *A Dissertation on Liberty and Necessity, Pleasure and Pain* . . . is lightened by Franklin's characteristic humor—a quality so often lacking in philosophical discourses; and his broad sense of man's position and equality of membership in the unity of all life shows the early turn of his mind toward science. The dissertation also reflects his reading of Locke, Shaftesbury, Anthony Collins, and the Port-Royal *Logic, or the Art of Thinking* by Antoine Arnauld and Pierre Nicole. He is known to have possessed Ozell's 1717 translation of *Logic, or the Art of Thinking*.

On his return from London in 1726 Franklin worked first as a clerk for a businessman by the name of Denham, then took work again with Keimer, his old employer, who hired him as his manager in order that he (Keimer) might devote himself to his stationery shop. During 1727 Franklin also kept his literary interests alive by forming the Junto, a club which stipulated that each member was to read an essay of his own "on any Subject he pleased" once every three months. (Franklin himself drew up the rules for this club, one of which was that every member should produce "one or more Queries on any Point of Morals, Politics or Natural

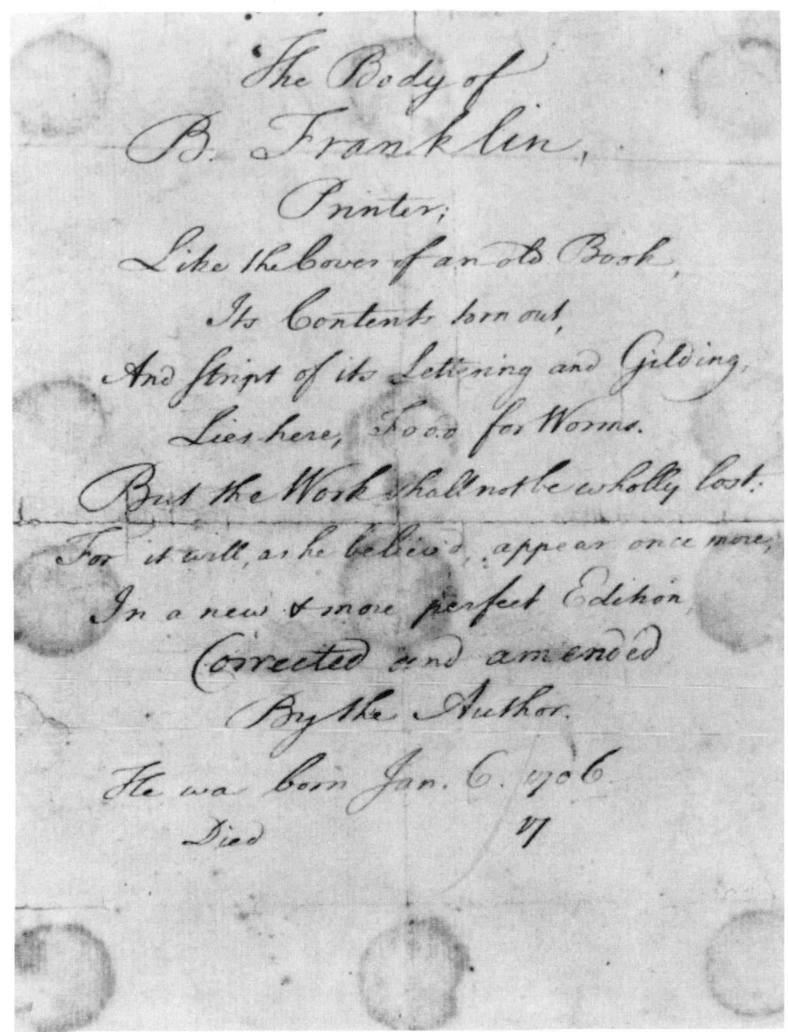

The Body of
B. Franklin,
Printer;
Like the Cover of an old Book,
Its Contents torn out,
And stript of its Lettering and Gilding,
Lies here, Food for Worms.
But the Work shall not be wholly lost:
For it will, as he believ'd, appear once more,
In a new & more perfect Edition,
Corrected and amended
By the Author.
He was born Jan. 6. 1706
Died 17

A fair copy of Franklin's epitaph, which he wrote circa 1728 (Yale University Library)

Philosophy [science]." Thus the discussions and readings in the Junto reflected his own strong interest in such matters.)

By 1728 Franklin's business relations with Keimer had deteriorated greatly. In London he had learned of Keimer's unscrupulous character. Now, therefore, when Keimer threatened to reduce his wages and on one occasion embarrassed him by a public scolding and then continued to quarrel with him in the print shop, Franklin quit and organized his own print shop with Hugh Meredith, a fellow Junto member, as his partner. The two planned to start a newspaper, but Keimer learned of this plan and beat them into print with his own *Universal Instructor in all Arts and Sciences: and Pennsylvania Gazette* on 24 December 1728. Franklin retaliated with a short series of essays—the Busy-Body papers—designed to discredit Keimer.

The Busy-Body papers were only partly written by Franklin. He is thought to have written the first four numbers; parts of numbers 5 and 8, however, were the work of another member of the Junto, Joseph Breintnall, who continued the series. The termination of Franklin's interest in this series coincided with his purchase of Keimer's bankrupt paper on 25 September 1729, a striking instance of his utilitarian spirit as a writer.

The Busy-Body essays appeared in Andrew Bradford's *American Weekly Mercury*, the only real rival publication to Keimer's. The first Busy-Body explains the narrator's character as a meddler, saying that "out of zeal for the Public Good" he has designed to make himself a kind of Censor of Morals. The "growing Vices and Follies" of his countrymen, he writes, have determined him on this course. His aim, however, is to entertain as well as to instruct—

in morality, philosophy, and politics. Busy-Body number 2 treats the general topic of *ridicule,* which Franklin dramatizes by means of two characters, Ridentius (a fool) and Eugenius, "who never spoke yet but with a Design to divert and please." Busy-Body number 3 also sets up two characters to personify the subject under discussion—*virtue,* this time. Virtue is represented by Cato, a humble American farmer. His counterpart, Cretico, a "sowre Philosopher," possesses cunning and craft but is far from being wise. Keimer apparently thought the portrait of Cretico applied to him, because he warned in the *Universal Instructor* (25 February 1729) that Busy-Body might be making himself liable to charges of scandal and defamation. The fourth Busy-Body is about the proper regulation of social visits. Part of it takes the form of an amusing letter wherein a female shopkeeper, Patience, complains that her neighbor's children, on the occasion of their bothersome social visits to her shop, disrupt the entire store, mixing up the assortments of nails, urinating on the dry goods, making "a terrible Din upon my Counter with a Hammer," no matter how many customers are in the shop. The mother of these mischievous little children takes the view that no great damage has been done. "*Let them play a little,*" she says; "*I'll put all to rights my self before I go.*" But of course she never does. Busy-Body then lectures his audience on how the Turks handle the problem of guests who stay too long and how he himself adopted a modification of this custom in order to have time for his studies relating to the public good. Part of number 5 is a long serious defense of Busy-Body against Keimer's attack on Cretico in the *Universal Instructor.* In number 8 Franklin satirizes get-rich-quick schemes.

The Busy-Body persona has been likened to Silence Dogood in breeches. The Busy-Body papers bear a remarkable resemblance to commonplace books because of their loose structure, their use of Latin epigraphs and letters. There is a workaday, didactic quality about them, reminiscent of talk in the print shop. In Franklin's development as a writer they might also be thought of as a slightly retrograde motion, but they nevertheless succeeded in their purpose—the destruction of competition from Keimer—and enlarged Franklin's experience as a writer of rhetoric, one who could more than hold his own in a paper war. After buying out Keimer's paper, he shortened its title to *Pennsylvania Gazette.*

After dissolving his partnership with the alcoholic Hugh Meredith on 14 July 1730, Franklin continued from time to time to write familiar essays for his paper. Among these were a work entitled "On Conversation" (15 October 1730) and a brilliant but neglected masterpiece of humor in the manner of a hoax or a burlesque, entitled "A Witch Trial at Mount Holly" (22 October 1730). This satire pokes fun at contemporary suspicions of witchcraft among the Quakers along with the foolish methods of so-called trial by water employing the ducking stool and weighing the witch against the weight of the Bible. (The Yale editors of the Franklin papers point out that in 1731 the English *Gentleman's Magazine* printed a brief account of the trial in Franklin's satire, accepting it as fact.)

In the year 1732 Franklin continued the pseudonymous kind of writing he had done in the Dogood and Busy-Body papers. Three of these 1732 essays may be of more than passing interest: his essay, as Anthony Afterwit, on married couples who live beyond their means; that on domestic quarrels between husbands and wives, written under the pseudonym Celia Single; and the indirect attack on scandal presented by Alice Addertongue. In the same vein (and genre) "A Scolding Wife" (*Pennsylvania Gazette,* 5 July 1733), in which the anonymous author says he "speaks from Experience," presents an argument for scolding as "*Musick*"—carrying rhetoric some distance. (Deborah Read was known for her hot temper.) Franklin carries the fun, and the metaphor, to Homeric proportions by quoting a translation of a slightly altered sonnet by Jean Passeret (a sixteenth-century poet and friend of Ronsard's). An idea of Franklin's flair for satire and humor during this period of his early married life may be seen in his presentation of the speaker in the essay: "For my own Part, I sincerely declare, that the meek whining Complaints of my first Wife, and the silent affected Discontent in the Countenance of my second, gave me (either of them) ten Times the Uneasiness that the Clamour of my present dear Spouse is capable of giving." The essay ends with the author's desire to turn polygamist by marrying two young women widely known for their ability to scold. This, he maintains, would complete his musical "Consort."

A few details on the reason for Franklin's common-law marriage to Deborah Read may shed some light on the state of his relations with her at this time. Deborah's mother had earlier objected to Franklin's desire to marry her daughter, and during the nearly two years that Franklin spent in England (1724-1726) Deborah, thinking that he was no longer interested in her, had married John Rogers, who subsequently contracted numerous debts and abandoned her. (It was reported that he had a wife in

England and also rumored that he had died.) Pennsylvania law at that time did not permit Deborah to divorce Rogers. If she and Franklin had undergone a legal marriage (after his return to Philadelphia) and if Rogers had then returned alive, both Franklin and Deborah might have been convicted of bigamy, the punishment for which was extreme—"thirty-nine lashes on the bare back and imprisonment at hard labor for life." Franklin mentions in his autobiography his "Intrigues with Low Women," which may account for the birth of his illegitimate son William before 1 September 1730, the date when he says he took Deborah as his wife. Luckily Rogers did not turn up, and Franklin's common-law marriage endured for forty-four years until Deborah's death in 1774.

The texture of this marriage is explored in *The Private Franklin: The Man and His Family* (1975) by Claude-Anne Lopez and Eugenia W. Herbert, who say that Deborah was "warmly appreciated" by Franklin "during their two decades in business," then "coolly left to age and die alone as history swept him on" to spend long years abroad away from her. There is "no evidence," they add, that Franklin "ever thought he should have behaved differently toward Deborah," and he continued to speak of his dead wife "with the comfortable affection one feels for a valiant comrade." Deborah's fear of ocean travel had kept her from joining him during his years in England. In any case she could hardly have played a distinguished role in the intellectual milieu in which he moved. Lopez and Herbert do not present Franklin as the libertine some have implied he became. There is more evidence, says Herbert, that Franklin exhibited a "kind of emotional promiscuity in creating familial surroundings wherever he happened to be." As for Franklin's late-in-life proposal of marriage to Madame Helvétius in his bagatelle *The Elysian Fields*, Lopez and Herbert characterize it as "tongue-in-cheek" (though he did want to marry her). Strangely, David Schoenbrun describes this bagatelle as "mordant, bitter and spiteful."

As the proprietor of a new print shop Franklin soon considered the possibility of increasing his income by means of an almanac. Other printers had found almanacs lucrative, starting with William Price's *Almanack for New-England for the Year 1639*. Among Franklin's contemporaries Nathaniel Ames's *Astronomical Diary and Almanack*, published in Dedham, Massachusetts, was one of the best, beginning in 1726 and lasting until 1764. Back home in Boston Franklin's brother James had begun *Poor Robin's Almanack* in 1728. In that same year in Philadelphia, Andrew Bradford, Franklin's rival, was printing four almanacs. Franklin printed two others, Godfrey's *Pennsylvania Almanack* and Jerman's *American Almanack*. In 1732 when Godfrey and Jerman took their almanacs away from him and gave them to his competitor Bradford, Franklin formed his own almanac, advertising it in the *Pennsylvania Gazette* for 28 December 1732 as "JUST PUBLISHED, FOR 1733." Evidence exists that he had toyed with the idea of printing almanacs some six or eight years earlier during his stay in England, for he had ordered sent to Philadelphia the kind of type (weather and astronomical figures) commonly used in almanacs.

The first edition of *Poor Richard* was sold out in one month. He brought out two more editions during the first year and sold the almanac as far north as Rhode Island and as far south as the Carolinas. For many years thereafter *Poor Richard* sold ten thousand copies annually. It was much imitated—in England as well as at home. This almanac was his first great success, and it not only put his printing house on a sound financial basis but it also made him known as a writer throughout the colonies.

The *Poor Richard* sayings, embodying the wisdom of the ages, were rarely original with Franklin himself. He merely rewrote them in such a way as to give them currency for his time; they were used as filler in between more important matters—such as weather reports, astronomical notices of the different phases of the moon, eclipses, tides, tables of English kings, dates of court terms, announcements of Quaker meetings, town and city fairs, tables of distances between various towns, and, of course, the almanac or calendar itself (one month per page). The sayings include short, witty, epigrammatic verses, proverbs, aphorisms (which differ from proverbs in being by known authors), and maxims or rules of conduct.

With one or two exceptions, most of the compendia Franklin used were published in London during the second quarter of the eighteenth century. But these volumes were not generally available to his large audience of American readers. Among the sources he used, according to Robert Newcomb's excellent detective work, are: James Howell's *Lexicon Tetraglotton* (1659-1660); Thomas Fuller's *Gnomologia* (1732), *Introductio ad Prudentiam* (1726-1727), and *Introductio ad Sapientiam* (1731); George Herbert's *Outlandish Proverbs* (1640); George Savile, Lord Halifax's *A Character of King Charles the Second: and Political, Moral, and Miscellaneous Thoughts* (1750); Charles

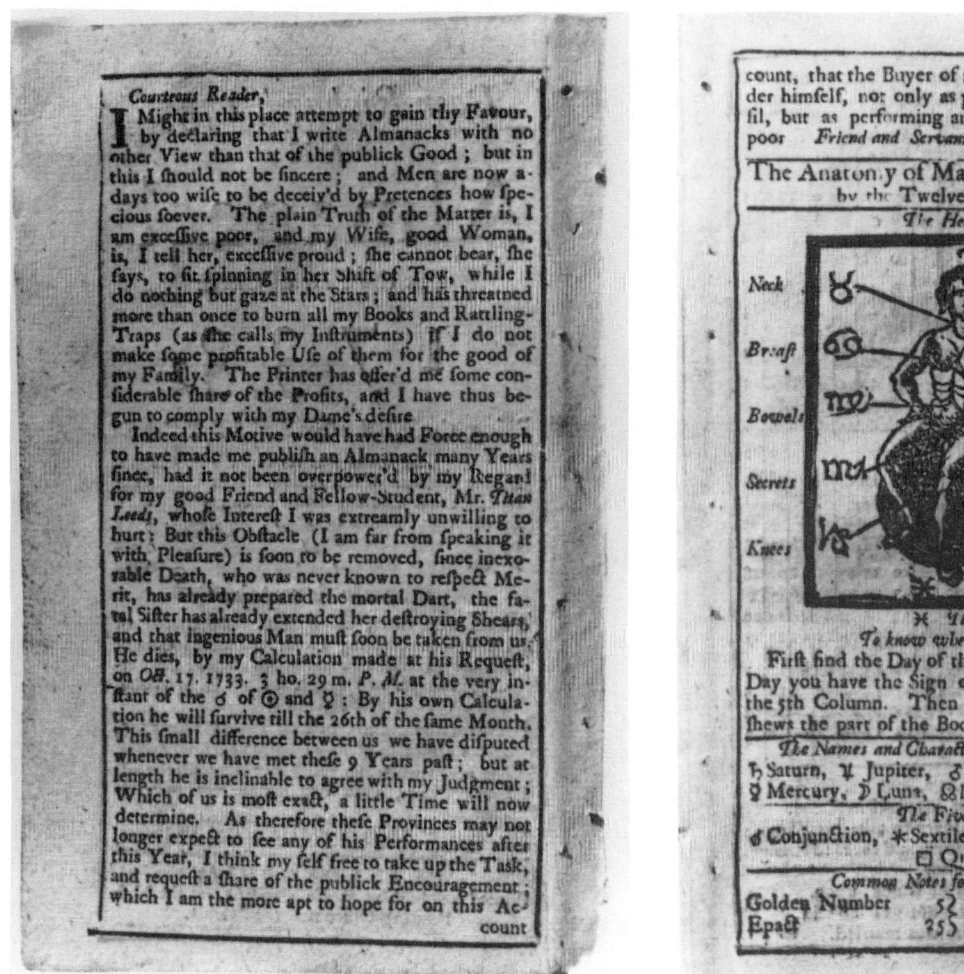

Courteous Reader,

I Might in this place attempt to gain thy Favour, by declaring that I write Almanacks with no other View than that of the publick Good ; but in this I ſhould not be ſincere ; and Men are now a-days too wiſe to be deceiv'd by Pretences how ſpecious ſoever. The plain Truth of the Matter is, I am exceſſive poor, and my Wife, good Woman, is, I tell her, exceſſive proud ; ſhe cannot bear, ſhe ſays, to ſit ſpinning in her Shift of Tow, while I do nothing but gaze at the Stars ; and has threatned more than once to burn all my Books and Rattling-Traps (as ſhe calls my Inſtruments) if I do not make ſome profitable Uſe of them for the good of my Family. The Printer has offer'd me ſome conſiderable ſhare of the Profits, and I have thus begun to comply with my Dame's deſire

Indeed this Motive would have had Force enough to have made me publiſh an Almanack many Years ſince, had it not been overpower'd by my Regard for my good Friend and Fellow-Student, Mr. *Titan Leeds*, whoſe Intereſt I was extreamly unwilling to hurt : But this Obſtacle (I am far from ſpeaking it with Pleaſure) is ſoon to be removed, ſince inexorable Death, who was never known to reſpect Merit, has already prepared the mortal Dart, the fatal Siſter has already extended her deſtroying Shears, and that ingenious Man muſt ſoon be taken from us. He dies, by my Calculation made at his Requeſt, on *Oct.* 17. 1733. 3 ho. 29 m. *P. M.* at the very inſtant of the ☌ of ☉ and ☿ : By his own Calculation he will ſurvive till the 26th of the ſame Month. This ſmall difference between us we have diſputed whenever we have met theſe 9 Years paſt ; but at length he is inclinable to agree with my Judgment ; Which of us is moſt exact, a little Time will now determine. As therefore theſe Provinces may not longer expect to ſee any of his Performances after this Year, I think my ſelf free to take up the Task, and requeſt a ſhare of the publick Encouragement ; which I am the more apt to hope for on this Account, that the Buyer of my Almanack may conſider himſelf, not only as purchaſing an uſeful Utenſil, but as performing an Act of Charity, to his poor *Friend and Servant* *R. SAUNDERS.*

The Anatomy of Man's Body as govern'd by the Twelve Conſtellations.

To know where the Sign is.

Firſt find the Day of the Month, and againſt the Day you have the Sign or Place of the Moon in the 5th Column. Then finding the Sign here, it ſhews the part of the Body it governs.

The Names and Characters of the Seven Planets.

♄ Saturn, ♃ Jupiter, ♂ Mars, ☉ Sol, ♀ Venus, ☿ Mercury, ☽ Luna, ☊ Dragons Head and ☋ Tail.

The Five Aſpects.

☌ Conjunction, ⚹ Sextile, ☍ Oppoſition, △ Trine, □ Quartile.

Common Notes for the Year 1733.

Golden Number	5	Cycle of the Sun	6
Epact	25	Dominical Letter	G

Franklin's address to the reader in his first almanac

Palmer's *A Collection of Select Aphorisms and Maxims* (1748); Sir John Mennes and Rev. James Smith's *Wit's Recreations* (1640); and an anonymous *Collection of Epigrams* (1735-1737). He also used some of John Gay's poems and his *Fables* (1727), Francis Quarles's *Enchiridion* (1640), and works by several other writers—among them Pope, Dryden, Swift, and Edward Young.

The cultural impact of the *Poor Richard* almanacs and sayings on Franklin's contemporaries and on the later development of the native American tradition was immense. Walter Blair and Hamlin Hill's *America's Humor: From Poor Richard to Doonesbury* emphasizes the historical progress of this tendency to value common sense and good judgment, especially that gained from experience, more than "book larnin'."

But *Poor Richard* (and the other almanacs) obviously did perform a "book larnin' " function, too. As a Deist, Franklin included written tributes to Newton, Locke, Bacon, and Robert Boyle. He also defended in his almanac theories of astronomy that seemed to run counter to the Bible. Thus *Poor Richard* introduced to the common people scientific and philosophical information not otherwise obtainable; for, as G. Browne Goode maintained, the colonists bought scarcely any books *but* almanacs. They were the one form of literature read in every family. By means of its sayings and essays *Poor Richard* provided both horse sense and book learning. No other almanac has ever been so famous or influential.

Not all of the ninety sayings included in Franklin's essay *The Way to Wealth* (first published in the 1758 almanac and published separately the same year as *Father Abraham's Speech . . .*) came from earlier *Poor Richard* almanacs. Most of them, however, were gleaned from these almanacs. By 1890 this particular essay had undergone seventy editions in English and numerous foreign ones. Goode has called this essay "probably the most printed and translated work in all American literature." Newcomb points out that *The Way to Wealth* compares favorably in genre and economic philosophy with such works as Defoe's *The Complete English Tradesman*, (1726), *The Trades-man's Calling* (1684) by Richard Steele (1629-1692), John Sowter's *The Way to Be Wise and Wealthy* (1716), and the anonymous *Pleasant Art of Money Catching* (1684). Key terms in Franklin's *The Way to Wealth* are *industry, frugality*, and *prudence*, prudence being the result of *experience*. These terms follow logically from one another in his carefully ordered presentation. The essay may possibly have been intended for his son William, since they were both on board ship bound for England from 20 June to 17 July 1757 when Franklin composed the preface.

In connection with *Poor Richard* and *The Way to Wealth* it is well to remember that from 1732 to 1758 Franklin was exercising great versatility as a writer. He used his pen during the Great Awakening to defend Rev. Mr. Samuel Hemphill's practical kind of religion (in 1735) and to describe the opinions and activities of that wide-ranging revivalist George Whitefield. He explained popular science in *An Account of the New Invented Pennsylvanian Fire-Places . . .* (1744). In *Plain Truth . . .* (1747) he alerted his readers to the danger of French and Spanish privateers on the lower Delaware River. He urged higher education in *Proposals Relating to the Education of Youth in Pensilvania* (1749). And he pioneered in the new science of electricity, which he had dramatized by his kite experiment, in *Experiments and Observations on Electricity* (1751) and in two further volumes published in 1753 and 1754. His involvement in projects for the public good (such as the Union Fire Company, which he helped found in 1736, the Pennsylvania Hospital, and the American Philosophical Society), his appointment as clerk of the Pennsylvania Assembly, his position as Philadelphia postmaster and increasing participation in politics generally, his short-lived *General Magazine* (which Moses Coit Tyler says aimed at, but did not achieve, "a more explicit literary intention" than his *Pennsylvania Gazette*, for which he meanwhile continued to write)—all these made great demands on his ability as a writer in many different forms and on a great variety of subjects.

As a writer Franklin's penchant for simple diction, order, method, and formal plan helped immeasurably to win him the gratitude of his readers. Also, as an aid to easy readability, he insisted (in his essay "On Literary Style," published in the *Pennsylvania Gazette*, 2 August 1733) that writing to be good should be "smooth, clear and short." He especially enjoyed satirizing long-winded lawyers and preachers. (See his entertaining essay "On Amplification," published in the *Pennsylvania Gazette*, 17 June 1736.) But he also thought good writing should benefit the reader, "*either by improving his Virtue or his Knowledge*," as he says in "On Literary Style." This moralizing or didactic bent sometimes tended (for example, in parts of the *Autobiography* and in the bagatelle entitled *The Handsome and the Deformed Leg*, written circa 1780) to mar the enjoyable quality of his writing.

Portrait of Franklin circa 1738-1746, attributed to Robert Feke (Harvard University)

During this period Franklin's powerfully persuasive style or rhetoric manifested itself again and again in his pleas for his projects. His pamphlet *Plain Truth . . .* (1747), for example, embroiled him in controversy with Quakers and German pacifists and drew the opposition of the wealthy proprietor Thomas Penn. In this pamphlet, which underwent at least two editions, translation into German, and circulation in other colonies, Franklin emerged as the spokesman and defender of those "most unhappily circumstanced," "the middling People, the Tradesmen, Shopkeepers, and Farmers of this Province and City." The rich, he argues in this pamphlet, could shift for themselves on short notice from the invaders, but "we," the defenseless poor, "must bear the Brunt." His remedy? A proposal for a military defense association of "60,000 Fighting Men, acquainted with Fire-Arms, many of them Hunters and Marksmen, hardy and bold."

Earlier in the same year that Franklin formed his association for the defense of Pennsylvania (1747) his interest in electrical experiments became apparent. By 1748, when he formed his partnership with David Hall, he had prospered sufficiently in business to enable him to think of devoting the remainder of his life to "philosophical" (scientific) interests. "I proceeded in my Electrical Experiments with great Alacrity," he writes in the *Autobiography*. But "the Publick now considering me as a Man of Leisure, laid hold of me for their Purposes. . . . The Governor put me into the Commission of Peace; the Corporation of the City chose me of [*sic*] the Common Council, and soon after an Alderman; and the Citizens at large chose me a Burgess to represent them in [the] Assembly." In the midst of all this political activity Franklin yet found time to help found and manage the Pennsylvania Hospital and to carry on his work in electricity, which culminated in the publication of his letters on this subject to his friend Peter Collinson in London (*Experiments and Observations on Electricity*, part one, 1751). The famous kite experiment is thought to have been performed in early June of 1752. With the publication of parts two and three in 1753 and 1754 the almost entirely self-educated Franklin began to receive notice from the academies. Harvard conferred an honorary A.M. degree upon him on 25 July 1753, just two weeks before his appointment as Deputy Postmaster General of North America, an office he shared with William Hunter. Yale gave him an honorary M.A. on 12 September 1753. On 30 November of that year the Royal Society awarded him the Copley Medal. Within ten days of the time he received another M.A. (from William and Mary, 20 April 1756), he was elected a fellow of the Royal Society, a signal honor (29 April 1756). Honorary doctorates followed—the LL.D. from the University of St. Andrews in 1759 and an honorary D.C.L. from Oxford in 1762—after which, despite his early remonstrance against titles, he was known as "Doctor Franklin," one of the world's most honored men.

From here on Franklin's private life and public career may be thought of as comprising three important political missions abroad—two trips to England (1757-1762 and 1764-1775), and one to France (1776-1785)—plus his remaining years at home in America (1785-1790). These missions involved considerable travel and life in urban centers. Franklin spent a total of twenty-five years in London and Paris. He also traveled in Germany with Sir John Pringle, the Queen's physician, during the summer of 1766, when he was elected to the Royal Society of Göttingen. (Earlier he had toured Holland and Belgium with his son William.) If we would understand Franklin's cosmopolitan background as a well-traveled writer, we must also consider the fact that he was mainly an urban dweller, one who had earlier lived in the two principal American literary centers.

Franklin's first mission to England was less important than the second so far as our interest in his ability as a writer is concerned. During this first political mission he corresponded with numerous persons on both sides of the Atlantic, but his main order of business was to represent the Pennsylvania Assembly in the dispute with the proprietaries, who as descendants of the original landowners (the Penn family) claimed continuance of their tax-exempt status. In effect, the wealthy Penn family paid no taxes while every poor farmer and tradesman in Pennsylvania shouldered the tax burden of the rich as well as their own. The long-protracted adjudication of this dispute occupied most of Franklin's time during this first mission to England. (His success as negotiator led to increased responsibilities during his second mission, when he served as agent not only for Pennsylvania but also for New Jersey, Massachusetts, and Georgia, who were plagued with similar conflicts with their proprietaries.) Little wonder, then, that Franklin's writing from 1757 to 1762 consists mainly of letters to his family, to his printing partner David Hall, and to friends on social, business, political, and scientific matters. Those he corresponded with at this time include his political partner Joseph Galloway, Isaac Norris, Israel Pemberton, Ebenezer Kinnersley, Ezra Stiles, Cadwallader Colden, Josiah Quincy, Lord Kames, Sir Alexander Dick, and David Hume, who wrote to him, "America has sent us many good things, Gold, Silver, Sugar, Tobacco, Indigo, &c.: But you are the first Philosopher, and indeed the first Great Man of Letters for whom we are beholden to her" (letter to

Portrait of Benjamin Franklin by Benjamin Wilson, painted in London in 1759. Like Franklin, Wilson experimented with electricity (The White House Collection).

Portrait of Deborah Franklin attributed to Benjamin Wilson, painted in London in 1758-1759 from a miniature Mrs. Franklin sent to her husband (American Philosophical Society)

Franklin, Edinburgh, 10 May 1762).

Probably the most important of his works apart from his voluminous correspondence during this first session was that known as the Canada pamphlet, published in London (17 April 1760) under the title *The Interest of Great Britain Considered, With Regard to her Colonies, And the Acquisitions of Canada and Guadaloupe. To which are added, Observations concerning the Increase of Mankind, Peopling of Countries, &c.* The editors of the Yale edition of the Franklin papers regard this long rhetorical work as one of Franklin's most important pamphlets. It deals with the problem of what to do with mainly French Canada after the defeat of the French at the Battle of Quebec in 1759. Earlier, in the *London Chronicle* (25-27 December 1759), Franklin had written a highly humorous and ironical letter, offering eleven "reasons" for giving Canada back to the French just after it had been won from them. "We should restore it," he wrote, "lest, thro' a greater plenty of beaver, broad-brimmed hats become cheaper to that unmannerly sect, the Quakers." "We should restore Canada, that we may *soon* have a new war . . . there being great danger of our growing too rich, our European expences not being sufficient to drain our immense treasures."

> We should restore it, that we may have occasion constantly to employ, in time of war, a fleet and army in those parts; for otherwise we might be too strong at home. . . . We should restore it, that the French may, by means of their Indians, carry on . . . a constant scalping war against our colonies, and thereby stint their growth; for, otherwise, the children might in time be as tall as their mother.
>
> . . . .
>
> . . . Should we not restore Canada, it would look as if our statesmen had *courage* as well as our soldiers; but what have statesmen to do with *courage*? . . .
>
> . . . What can be *braver*, than to show all Europe we can afford to lavish our best blood as well as our treasure, in conquests we do not intend to keep? Have we not plenty of Howe's and Wolfe's, &c. &c. &c. in every regiment?

Finally, he recommends the restoration on grounds of consistency of character, it always having been "the character of the English to fight strongly, and negotiate weakly."

This little satire, which was immediately reprinted in the *Grand Magazine* (December 1759) under the title of "Humorous Reasons for Restoring Canada," served as a preliminary sketch or outline for the longer pamphlet. In *The Interest of Great Britain* . . . Franklin argued that the interest of Great Britain concerned more the security of Canada and the West than the sugar islands of Guadaloupe in the West Indies. Although one of his friends—one William Burke (no relative)—had taken an opposing view, Edmund Burke praised Franklin's writing in this pamphlet, saying that he was "clearly the ablest, most ingenious, and the most dextrous" of those who had written on the controversy, and that he had said "everything in the best manner."

Back home between missions Franklin first tended to his post-office duties during most of 1763. Then he encountered political difficulties. Although he had been elected Speaker of the Pennsylvania Assembly, his career there lasted only from April to October of 1764, when he was defeated for reelection to the assembly itself. This was his first defeat in fourteen elections. According to the Yale editors, this defeat was caused by a "scurrilous campaign" on the part of his opponents. Fortunately for him, the proprietary issue was still alive. And since he had published a plan calling for indemnifying the proprietaries and the king's assuming control of the government of the colony (*Cool Thoughts on the Present Situation of Our Public Affairs*. . . , 12 April 1764), the Assembly again selected him (by a narrow margin of 19 to 11) to return to England as their agent.

One of Franklin's most unusual pamphlets—from the standpoint of tone and style—was written in the early part of 1764. Massacres of friendly Indians at Conestoga Manor and Lancaster, the episode in American history known as the "Paxton Boy" attack, provoked some of his most virulent writing. The attack had grown out of the Paxton Boys' feeling that the assembly had failed to provide adequate defense against less friendly Indians along the frontier. Consequently they demanded from the assembly security from these attacks, abolition of the property qualification for voting, revision of the apportionment system that gave most of the voting power to the wealthy eastern counties of Pennsylvania—in short, they wanted greater political power for the Scotch-Irish Presbyterian group which they represented and which opposed the Quakers. The pamphlet that Franklin penned in response to this episode, known as *A Narrative of the Late Massacres*. . . (1764), can be likened to a seventeenth-century jeremiad in tone and to a Ciceronian oration in structure. It contains some of the most powerful indignation ever expressed in any of his writings, including a blistering attack on racial prejudice, as he threatens the Paxton Boys with having broken the laws of king, country, and God. An "infamous Death" hangs over their heads, he says. "Justice, though slow, will come at last. All good People everywhere detest your Actions. You have imbrued your Hands in innocent Blood; how will you make them clean? The dying Shrieks and Groans of the Murdered, will often sound in your Ears: Their Spectres will sometimes attend you, and affright even your innocent Children! Fly where you will, your Consciences will go with you." Thus he turns the ghosts of their murdered victims into Furies, to pursue and drive insane the "unhappy Perpetrators of this horrid Wickedness!" The conclusion, however, pleads more temperately for support of law and government, so that "justice may be done, the Wicked punished, and the Innocent protected," warning, however, that there will be no security for anyone if anarchy, confusion, and "Violence without Judgment" "prevail over all."

The period 1765-1775—from the passage of the Stamp Act to the Second Continental Congress—gave Franklin frequent opportunity to engage in satire. Verner W. Crane thinks "that his English political journalism," most of which dates from 1765 to 1775, was "the largest body of his contemporaneously published writings." Arguing against the Stamp Act, the Townshend Acts, the Tea Act, and the Punitive Acts, Franklin now turned zealous propagandist for the rights of the American colonies. Crane cites thirty-three essays in H. S. Woodfall's *Public Advertiser*, thirty-two in William Strahan's *London Chronicle*, and eighteen in Charles Say's *Gazeteer and New Daily Advertiser*. These anonymous and pseudonymous letters to the editor employed a variety of forms—such as fable, hoax, allegory, satiric essay, and Socratic dialogue—and were written under a great variety of pseudonyms (Crane mentions approximately forty). Obviously the effect Franklin aimed at was a widespread opposition to the British government. Franklin's friendships with London printers such as Strahan and Woodfall permitted him easy access to publication in these dailies. Although by modern standards the circulation of these newspapers was relatively small (about three thousand for the *Public Advertiser* and about five thousand for the *Gazeteer*), Franklin's satires were often reprinted in the monthlies, too, giving them wider currency. Moreover, according to F. X. Davy, the fact that writers for the British ministry took note of them and replied against the man they dubbed "Dr. Doubleface" and "The Judas of Craven St."—where Franklin lived—called extra attention to them.

Among Franklin's satires at this time a resemblance to Swift may be seen in such works as *Rules by Which a Great Empire May be Reduced to a Small One* (*Public Advertiser*, 11 September 1773; separately published in 1793), "An Edict by the King of Prussia" (*Public Advertiser*, 22 September 1773), and "*Pax Quaeritur Bello*" ("Peace Sought by War"). "*Pax Quaeritur Bello*," written over the signature of Pacificus, appeared on 26 January 1766 in the *Public Advertiser* in connection with the controversy over the Stamp Act. Like Swift in *A Modest Proposal*, Franklin proposes that a British expeditionary army, well reinforced by Indians, burn "all the Capitals of the several [American] Provinces . . . cut the Throats of all the Inhabitants, Men, Women, and Children, and scalp them to serve as an Example," and destroy "all the Shipping," which would prevent smuggling and the expense of guarding the coasts against pirates. He then writes, "No Man in his Wits, after such terrible Military Execution, will refuse to purchase stamp'd Paper. If any one should hesitate, five or six Hundred Lashes in [*sic*] a cold frosty Morning would soon bring him to Reason."

"An Edict by the King of Prussia" closely parodies British mercantile regulations on the American colonists' manufacture of iron and steel, the export of wool, the manufacture of beaver hats, the ad valorem tax, and the expatriation of British convicts to America. (In an earlier satire—in the *Pennsylvania Gazette* for 9 May 1751—Franklin had suggested sending a shipload of rattlesnakes to England as an appropriate return for such dumping of British felons on the colonies.) In the form of a letter or royal edict by the King of Prussia proclaiming the justice of these measures already imposed on England (since England might be regarded as a colony of Prussia, no formal separation ever having been declared), Franklin ridicules these English trade regulations as capricious and tyrannical. Evidence exists that some English readers of this hoax at first believed that it came directly from the King of Prussia and that he actually intended an invasion of England. Franklin's use of nearly the exact legal language of the trade regulations contributed to the deception of such readers. George Simson regarded this "edict" as Franklin's most successful political satire.

But Franklin himself thought the *Rules by Which a Great Empire May be Reduced to a Small One* was his finest satire. It takes the form of a list of some twenty arguments or rules whereby the British empire, like a large cake, might first be diminished at its edges and ultimately reduced to a very small empire indeed. The list embodies the injustices suffered by the colonists, ordered climactically and also from general to specific, and amounts to a summary justification of the American Revolution. (In general, the list corresponds to the list of grievances in the Declaration of Independence, which Franklin was later to help draw up.) These rules are presented through Franklin's persona of a "modern simpleton" who thinks the colonial policies of the Earl of Hillsborough are deliberately aimed at "reducing" or completely destroying the British empire. In each of the rules the good conduct of the colonists is weighed against the stupid administrative policies of the minister for colonial affairs with a gradual but very powerful arousal of indignation in terms of the effect on the reader. Thus Franklin served warning on the British government as to what might be expected if the grievances were not redressed.

Not long after this witty ultimatum he also served warning in the press on his lifelong friend Will Strahan, a member of parliament and the King's printer, who had turned Tory. In his well-known letter of 5 July 1775, which he never sent to Strahan, Franklin concluded: "You and I were long Friends:—You are now my Enemy,—and I am, Yours, B. Franklin." Two days later Franklin sent a friendly letter to Strahan, to which he received a personal answer. Their correspondence was interrupted during the war but was revived after it.

Franklin's activities during the Revolutionary War are well known. With the death of his wife in 1774 he was free to devote all his energies to the American cause, and he proceeded to do so. Sent as the senior of three commissioners to France (along with Arthur Lee and Silas Deane), he was charged by Congress with the task of negotiating a treaty of "amity and commerce" with the French, a treaty which mainly he had drafted. By skillful diplomacy he eventually succeeded in negotiating this treaty and a treaty of alliance (1778) with France. Indirectly he was responsible by reason of his popularity for the considerable sums of money and numbers of ships, war supplies, and fighting recruits that accrued to the Americans. As the most "political" of the three commissioners—he had been so dubbed by Deane—he cultivated assiduously the sympathetic but slippery French foreign minister, Vergennes (without whose aid the American cause would have suffered), holding out to him the prospect of future American commerce and the humiliation of

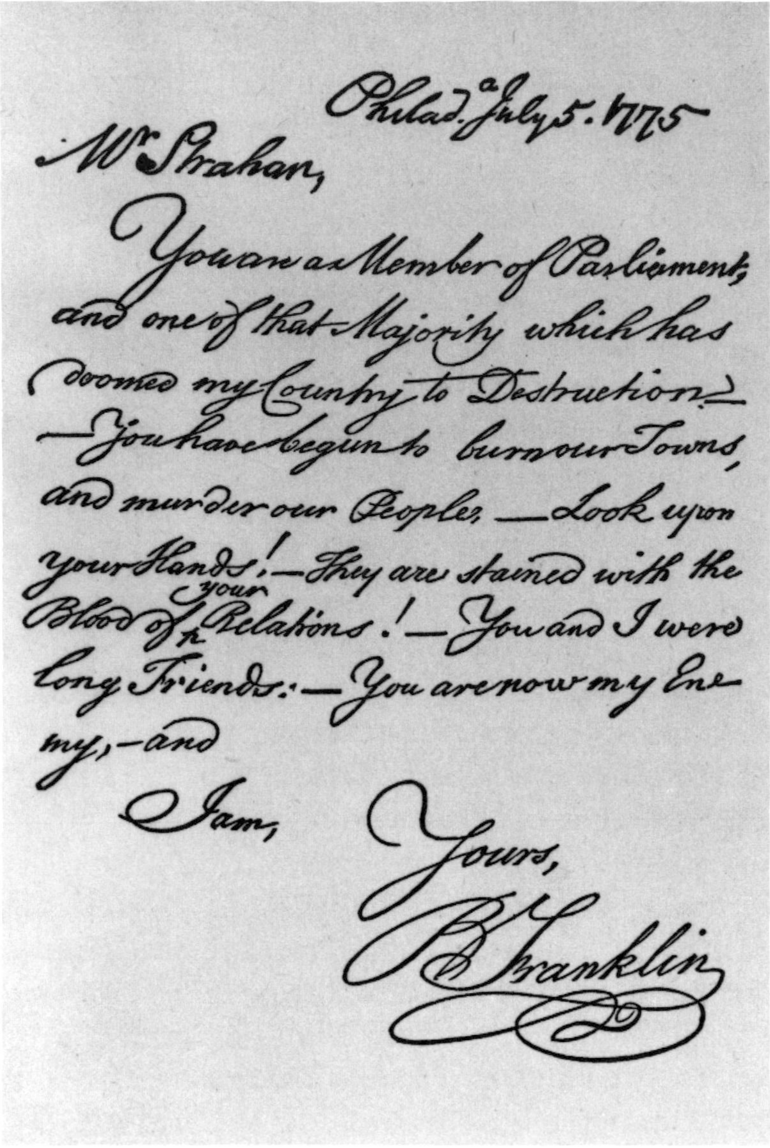

Philada. July 5. 1775

Mr. Strahan,

You are a Member of Parliament, and one of that Majority which has doomed my Country to Destruction. — You have begun to burn our Towns, and murder our People. — Look upon your Hands! — They are stained with the Blood of your Relations! — You and I were long Friends: — You are now my Enemy, — and

I am,

Yours,

B Franklin

The letter Franklin did not send to William Strahan, his Tory friend in the British Parliament (Library of Congress)

England. Socially he cultivated the wealthy and the aristocracy, failing to win the favor of one of the most prominent, the Marquise de Deffand, but attracting the attention of a former prime minister of the king, the Duc de Choiseul, who was intent on recouping his former position, the wealthy Jacques-Donatien Leray de Chaumont, who offered him an ideal hideaway and spying post in a wing of his chateau in Passy on the road to Versailles, and the young Marquis de Lafayette, who defied his uncle the Duc de Noailles, the French ambassador to England, with his enthusiasm for the colonial cause. His pen, too, was rarely idle; he attacked the British use of German mercenaries with his Swiftian satire "The Sale of the Hessians." According to Durand Echeverria, the first publication of this work occurred in French in the 10 March 1777 issue of the weekly *Correspondance littérature secrète* in the German town of Neuwied.

Franklin's relationship with his son William during the period 1775-1785 also deserves some comment. In the late spring of 1775 he met William, then Governor of New Jersey, at Joseph Galloway's estate in Bucks County, Pennsylvania. During this meeting he was unsuccessful in persuading either William or Galloway, who had been his former political partner in the Pennsylvania legislature, to join him against the mother country. Thus began a long separation between father and son.

During the Revolution, William was arrested as a Tory. At first he was kept under a kind of parole in private homes in various Connecticut towns, but later he was jailed by Washington for violating parole. (He had been issuing secret pardons in the name of the king to Tories in Connecticut and New Jersey.) His wife died while he was in jail. When he was exchanged as a prisoner, he moved to New York, where he became, as president of the Board of Associated Loyalists, "the most influential loyalist in America."

Not until after the war, on his return from Paris in 1785 to Southampton (prior to his last voyage home to Philadelphia), did Franklin again see or speak to William and then only to arrange a deed of transfer of the remainder of William's unconfiscated land in New Jersey in return for paying off some of William's debts. (Franklin apparently planned to settle his grandson Temple on this land.) Part of this four-day negotiation at the Star Tavern in Southampton concerned his granting William power of attorney to recover certain debts owed to Franklin by the British government. (Half of what William might recover was to go to Franklin's daughter, Sarah Bache.)

During the Revolution while Franklin was in France, he set up a printing press at Passy, where he was then living in a wing of the Hotel de Valentinois, owned by Jacques-Donatien Leray de Chaumont. On this press he printed propaganda, passports, and other official business. Here, too, he struck off for the small circle of his friends the little letters and essays known as the bagatelles. These light, humorous essays sometimes took the form of playful lovemaking to Mme Anne-Louise d'Hardancourt Brillon and Mme Anne-Catherine de Ligniville Helvétius, the two outstanding leaders of this circle, which also included intellectuals such as the Abbé Morellet, the Abbé de la Roche, and Pierre-Georges Cabanis, a young physician who was interested in poetry.

Some of Franklin's bagatelles were in French, some in English, some in both languages. Despite two earlier visits to France—both of short duration in 1767 and 1769—Franklin's French was not very good, and his friends sometimes had to help him. Cabanis, for example, is known to have translated *The Handsome and the Deformed Leg*. Lopez thinks that Mme Brillon, de la Roche, and possibly Le Veillard (the mayor of Passy) worked over and improved the French versions of some of the other bagatelles. All but one of the bagatelles in the unique copy in the William Smith Mason collection at Yale University have been translated into French, the *Letter to the Royal Academy* being the only exception. The *Letter to the Royal Academy* was intended for Franklin's scientific friends in England—Dr. Richard Price and Dr. Joseph Priestley, among others.

The bagatelles are important in Franklin's career as a writer because they represent one of his most delightful excursions into belles lettres. Almost all of his writing has a utilitarian cast, but such items as *The Dialogue between Franklin and the Gout, The Whistle, The Ephemera, The Elysian Fields,* and *The Flies* show him at work as an artist. In the bagatelles the essay is no longer a means to an end but an end in itself.

These little classics, of course, had their predecessors—or near relatives—the playfully reasoned defense of illegitimacy in "The Speech of Polly Baker" (*General Advertiser,* 15 April 1747), for example, the *Old Mistresses Apologue* (written on 25 June 1745), *The Craven Street Gazette* (which he wrote on 22 September 1770 to entertain Polly Stevenson, the daughter of his London landlady), and *An Economical Project* (*Journal of Paris,* 1784)—a neglected masterpiece of humor dealing with daylight saving and solar energy. All of these were remarkable for humor, wit, style, and good sense. One of the bagatelles, in the form of an allegory, *The Ephemera,* is notable for the charm with which Franklin in his guise as an old insect handles serious themes—the brevity of life, the origin and end of the world, the true values of time and life. Of this work Theodore Hornberger writes, "Pathos has seldom been more delicately sustained."

Back home in Philadelphia, after a sad departure from his French friends, Franklin continued to enjoy, despite failing health, his well-deserved celebrity. Also, the time had come to put the finishing touches on his *Autobiography*.

Franklin had begun his *Memoirs,* as he called his autobiography, during the first two weeks in August of 1771 while visiting the home of his friend Bishop Jonathan Shipley at Chilbolton near Twyford. Encouraged by other friends (Benjamin Vaughan, Le Veillard, and Abel James), he had continued it, some thirteen years later, in Passy during the year 1784. Four years later in Philadelphia, now aged eighty-two, he took up once more his task of reminiscence. He had intended to finish this work during his voyage home in 1785 but had penned three essays instead: *Maritime Observations*; *Observations on the Causes and Cures of Smokey Chimneys*; and *Description of a New Stove for Burning of Pitcoal, and Consuming all Its Smoke*

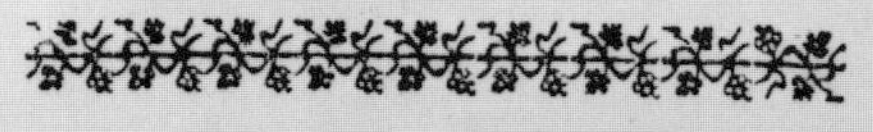

DIALOGUE

ENTRE

LA GOUTTE ET M. F.

à Minuit le 22 Octobre 1780.

M. F.

EH ! oh ! eh ! Mon Dieu ! qu'ai-je fait pour mériter ces ſouffrances cruelles ?

LA GOUTTE.

Beaucoup de choſes. Vous avez trop mangé, trop bu, & trop indulgé vos jambes en leur indolence.

M. F.

Qui eſt-ce qui me parle ?

LA GOUTTE.

C'eſt moi-même, la goutte.

M. F.

Mon ennemie en perſonne !

LA GOUTTE.

Pas votre ennemie.

A ij

First page for one of the bagatelles that Franklin printed on his press at Passy (Yale University Library)

(all published in *Transactions of the American Philosophical Society*, 1786). Having made out his will (17 July 1788), he wrote a hundred more pages in the autobiography, progressing as far as the year 1756. In a letter to Le Veillard (24 October 1788) he wrote: "I have lately made great progress in the work you so urgently demand, and have come as far as my fiftieth year. Being now free from public business, as my term in the Presidentship [of the Supreme Executive Council of Pennsylvania, which ended on October 14] is expired and resolving to engage in no other public employment, I expect to have it finished in about two months, if illness or some unforeseen interruption does not prevent." On the same day he wrote to Vaughan in England, saying that he had advanced to 1756, the year he was elected to the Royal Society. Since the autobiography brings Franklin's life only to July 1757, Carl Van Doren assumes that this part was then nearly complete. Probably sometime between 13 November 1789 and 17 April 1790, the date of his death, he wrote seven and one-half pages more. J. A. Leo Lemay and P. M. Zall point out that ink and handwriting evidence show that he also revised part one (written in 1771) "several times" between the summer of 1788 and the day he died. (The same holds true for the part written at Passy, except that the terminal date for these revisions was the fall of 1789.) One might conclude that since the autobiography was written in four sittings over a period of more than eighteen years, it lacks unity; but the fact that Franklin worked from the same outline and that he followed it rather faithfully with few significant changes negates this view.

The contents of the four parts of the autobiography may be described as follows: Part one, unified by his rise from a poor apprentice to a master printer, contains, according to Zall's analysis, three main divisions—(1) his early life in Boston and his trip to Philadelphia, (2) his trip to London and return to Philadelphia, and (3) thereafter, his early married life, including the start of his public projects—the Junto and the Library Company. Part two stresses his bourgeois virtues of *industry* and *frugality*, which he would have his reader believe contributed to his rise as a printer as well as to his success in later life. This part includes his "bold and arduous [but unsuccessful] Project of arriving at moral Perfection." The third part emphasizes primarily the growth of his public projects but also includes his part as organizer of supplies and paymaster in the disastrous Braddock expedition, a project that nearly caused his financial ruin. Part four centers on the dispute between the Proprietaries and the Pennsylvania Assembly and its eventual resolution (with the help of Lord Mansfield) in favor of the Assembly.

The history of the manuscript of Franklin's autobiography before its publication by John Bigelow in 1868 is, as the Yale editors say, a "strange and complicated story." Although Franklin had completed only three of the four parts by November 1789, he nevertheless had his grandson Benjamin Franklin Bache make two fair copies of the original manuscript. These fair copies were then sent to his friend Benjamin Vaughan in England and to Le Veillard, both of whom had been urging him to complete his work. When Franklin died on 17 April 1790, William Temple Franklin, his other grandson, fell heir to the original manuscript, which by now included the additional seven and one-half pages of the fourth and last part. William Temple Franklin apparently intended to publish the manuscript; but before he could do so a French translation of part one appeared in Paris over the imprint of Jacques

Buisson and dated 1791. Displeased by this event, William Temple Franklin wrote to Le Veillard, saying that he hoped to block the English translation of this Buisson edition. Supposedly sometime late in 1791 (according to the Yale editors) William Temple Franklin exchanged the original manuscript in his possession for the fair copy of Le Veillard (probably because it was easier to read). Through a descendant of Le Veillard, John Bigelow, American minister to France (1865-1866), finally managed to buy and publish the original manuscript in 1868.

The complications that ensued as a result of William Temple Franklin's exchanging the more valuable original manuscript for the less valuable fair copy were manifold. He was not able, as he had hoped, to block the English translations of Buisson's edition (believed to be the French translation of Dr. Jacques Gibelin)—two of which appeared in 1793. One of these translations, which appeared in installments beginning in January in the *Lady's Magazine*, was reprinted by the same publishers, G. G. J. & J. Robinson, in the two-volume *Works of the late Doctor Benjamin Franklin* (1793). This translation has been attributed to Vaughan and is superior to that which turned up in *The Private Life of the Late Benjamin Franklin. . .*, published in London by J. Parsons in 1793. The Yale editors report that this Vaughan translation in the Robinson edition then became the version reprinted more than 150 times throughout the world during the next seventy years.

When William Temple Franklin finally had an edition of the autobiography published by Henry Colburn in London in volume three of *Memoirs of the Life and Writings of Benjamin Franklin LL.D., F. R. S. . . .* (1817-1818), he had to use the fair copy, which contained only the first three parts of the original manuscript. This version was translated into French and published in Paris in the two-volume *Mémoires sur la vie de Benjamin Franklin, écrits par lui-meme* (1828), to which was added Le Veillard's translation of part four. (Le Veillard had translated his fair copy and then corrected it against the original manuscript he had received from William Temple Franklin. His publication plans were "cut short" by the guillotine in 1794, but part of his translation—most of Franklin's part two—did appear after his death in *La Décade Philosophique, Litterature et Politique* for 18 February 1798.)

All this translation and retranslation of fair copy and incomplete texts of the autobiography resulted in the greatest possible confusion. Even the original manuscript is not completely unassailable, since Franklin may have intended corrections of it, and, indeed, may possibly have dictated some changes to Benjamin Bache—or authorized him to make some—while Bache was making the two fair copies. Max Farrand, Lemay, and Zall have attempted to discover as nearly as possible the exact nature of Franklin's text.

Franklin's autobiography is undoubtedly his best-known single work, and part one, which reads like an eighteenth-century picaresque narrative, is undoubtedly its most interesting part. What better example of the American dream, the great archetypal American success story, could one point to? Farrand regards the autobiography as "an unsurpassed story of how a printer and shopkeeper in Philadelphia rose to be one of the world's great figures, and the most complete representative of his century that any nation can point to." Farrand also reminds us that Franklin's autobiography was only one of many of its kind and that it probably withstood the competition of a "flood of memoirs deluging the eighteenth century" because of its simpler style and greater clarity. Its greatest influence, however, was not as a work of style but rather as "a source book and text in the education of youth." Clinton Rossiter writes that it has been "translated and retranslated into a dozen languages, printed and reprinted in hundreds of editions, read and reread by millions of people, especially by young and impressionable Americans." "The influence of these few hundred pages," he concludes, "has been matched by that of no other American book."

In the closing period of his life, Franklin also wrote one of his most brilliant satires. This work is dated 23 March 1790—only twenty-four days before his death. Published on 25 March 1790 in the form of a letter to the *Federal Gazette* and signed Historicus, it is anthologized in Mott and Jorgenson's *Benjamin Franklin: Representative Selections* (1936) under the title "On the Slave-Trade." It parodies Congressional debate—especially the proslavery remarks of Congressman James Jackson of Georgia—on a petition which had been presented to Congress on 12 February 1790, from the Pennsylvania Society for Promoting the Abolition of Slavery. (Franklin, as president of that society, had signed the petition—his last public document.)

In his letter to the *Federal Gazette*, Franklin says he has read Congressman Jackson's speech as reported on the previous night in that newspaper and is struck by the similarity of the arguments to those of a certain Sidi Mehemet Ibrahim, who justifies Moslem kidnapping of Christians along the African coast and selling them into slavery. With reasoning—or, rather, with bad logic—paralleling that which Jackson and other Congressmen used in Congressional debate (12 February and 17-23 March 1790) to support black slavery and to discredit the Pennsylvania Society's petition (as well as another antislavery petition), Ibrahim justifies his rejection of a petition to abolish the enslavement of white Christians.

Paul Conner and others have noted that Franklin himself once owned slaves, that the *Pennsylvania Gazette* sometimes carried an advertisement for the sale of slaves, and that he was lukewarm on the abolition issue before the year 1772. But such critics have also had to admit that as early as 1729 non-Quaker Franklin was publishing Quaker Ralph Sandiford's antislavery pamphlet and that he later published similar pamphlets by other Quakers such as Benjamin Lay (1737) and John Woolman (1762). In 1764, too, Franklin belonged (along with Dr. Samuel Johnson) to Dr. Thomas Bray's Associates, a London philanthropical group organized to promote Negro education in the colonies. Verner W. Crane and the Yale editors have attributed an antislavery work printed in the *Public Advertiser* (30 January 1770) to Franklin. In "A Conversation between an Englishman, a Scotchman, and an American on the Subject of Slavery" he argued in answer to Granville Sharp's *A Representation of the Injustice and Dangerous Tendency of Tolerating Slavery* (1769) that the English working-class poor and the English sailors and soldiers were little better off than the Negro slaves in America. (Franklin also protested the dumping of British felons on the colonies in this work.) Later he corresponded with Anthony Benezet. In his 22 August 1772 letter to Benezet he refers to slavery as "a detestable commerce" and says that he has made an extract of Benezet's antislavery letter and published it in the *London Chronicle* of the previous June and that he will also publish Benezet's Virginia address with some remarks of his own. In this same letter he writes, "I am glad to hear that the disposition against holding negroes grows more general in North America." Similar in tone and substance is his letter to his London friend Dean Woodward, dated 10 April 1773. There were ambiguities in Franklin's attitude toward blacks and slavery—ambiguities documented by Lopez and Herbert. They were the ambiguities of an age whose ideals were expressing themselves in the not always reconcilable terms of business and humanitarianism, of prudence and altruism.

The fact that Franklin came to his abolitionist position late in life might well be considered as less a denial of his eminent humanity than a proof of his status as representative man during the radical changes of the American Enlightenment. Involved as he was in the forefront of political, scientific, religious, educational, municipal, and international projects for the well-being of his fellow man, what eighteenth-century American—with the possible exception of Thomas Jefferson—can rival the multifarious accomplishments of this most interesting founding father? Thomas Paine and Philip Freneau were also powerful propagandists for the American cause, but they lacked Franklin's sense of humor, his human touch, his simplicity, his sophisticated but charming magnanimity. Also, Franklin's versatility as a writer made him the great and enduring champion, both at home and abroad, of the native American pragmatic tradition as it unfolded during the course of almost a century, the century known as the Age of Reason.

Early in life Franklin had attempted to model his thinking along the lines of a modern Socrates, who pursued truth disinterestedly as a humble inquirer, asking questions, the answers to which he often pretended not to know. We have seen him playing this rhetorical role in the *Rules by Which a Great Empire May be Reduced to a Small One*. He used the same method in "The Speech of Polly Baker," in "On the Price of Corn, and Management of the Poor" (*London Chronicle*, 27-29 November 1766), and in the brilliant list of twenty-nine "Queries Addressed to a Friend of Lord Baltimore" (see "To the Printer" in the *London Chronicle*, 19 September 1758). It is no exaggeration to say that in the person of Franklin the spirit of Socrates lived again in a new Age of Reason.

Today, sparked by the 1976 bicentennial and the publication of Franklin papers at Yale, scholarly interest in Franklin runs high. There seems to be no lessening of interest in this perennial favorite, albeit a perhaps more realistic picture of Franklin the man emerges from studies such as Lopez and Herbert's *The Private Franklin*. To be sure, Franklin was not above sometimes resorting to trickery and expedience in rhetorical situations. And certain aspects of his bourgeois philosophy are not popular today. But wherever common sense and humor and the inquiring mind are valued, wherever good judgment and political justice are honored, Franklin will continue to live and be read with enjoyment.

Letters:

Les Amitiés américaines de Madame d'Houdetot, d'après sa correspondance inèdite avec Benja-

min Franklin et Thomas Jefferson, edited by Gilbert Chinard (Paris: E. Champion, 1924);

"My Dear Girl": The Correspondence of Benjamin Franklin, Polly Stevenson, Georgiana and Catherine Shipley, edited by James M. Stifler (New York: Doran, 1927);

The Letters and Papers of Benjamin Franklin and Richard Jackson, 1753-1785, edited by Carl Van Doren (Philadelphia: American Philosophical Society, 1947);

Benjamin Franklin and Catherine Ray Greene: Their Correspondence, edited by William G. Roelker (Philadelphia: American Philosophical Society, 1949);

Benjamin Franklin's Letters to the Press, 1758-1775, edited by Verner W. Crane (Chapel Hill: University of North Carolina Press, 1950);

"Franklin's Letters on Indians and Germans" and "Franklin and Jackson on the French War," edited by A. O. Aldridge, in American Philosophical Society *Proceedings*, 94 (August 1950): 391-395 and 396-397;

The Letters of Benjamin Franklin and Jane Mecom, edited by Carl Van Doren (Princeton: Princeton University Press, 1950);

" 'All Clear Sunshine!' New Letters of Franklin and Mary Stevenson Hewson," edited by Whitfield J. Bell, Jr., in American Philosophical Society *Proceedings*, 100 (December 1956): 521-536;

Mr. Franklin: A Selection from his Personal Letters, edited by Leonard W. Labaree and Bell (New Haven: Yale University Press, 1956).

Bibliographies:

Paul Leicester Ford, *Franklin Bibliography: A List of Books Written by, or Relating to, Benjamin Franklin* (Brooklyn: Historical Printing Club, 1889);

I. Minis Mays, *Calendar of the Papers of Benjamin Franklin in the Library of the American Philosophical Society*, 6 volumes (Philadelphia: University of Pennsylvania Press, 1908);

C. William Miller, *Benjamin Franklin's Philadelphia Printing, 1728-1766. A Descriptive Bibliography* (Philadelphia: American Philosophical Society, 1974).

Biographies:

James Parton, *Life and Times of Benjamin Franklin*, 2 volumes (Boston: Mason Brothers, 1864);

Carl Van Doren, *Benjamin Franklin* (New York: Viking, 1938);

Carl L. Becker, *Benjamin Franklin, A Biographical Sketch* (Ithaca: Cornell University Press, 1946);

A. Owen Aldridge, *Benjamin Franklin: Philosopher and Man* (Philadelphia: Lippincott, 1965);

Claude-Anne Lopez, *Mon Cher Papa: Franklin and the Ladies of Paris* (New Haven: Yale University Press, 1966);

Lopez and Eugenia W. Herbert, *The Private Franklin: The Man and His Family* (New York: Norton, 1975);

David Freeman Hawke, *Franklin* (New York: Harper & Row, 1976);

Ronald W. Clark, *Benjamin Franklin: A Biography* (New York: Random House, 1983).

References:

F. B. Adams, Jr., "Franklin and his Press at Passy," *Yale University Library Gazette*, 30 (April 1956): 133-138;

A. O. Aldridge, *Benjamin Franklin and Nature's God* (Durham: Duke University Press, 1967);

Aldridge, *Franklin and his French Contemporaries* (New York: New York University Press, 1957);

Aldridge, "Franklin's Deistical Indians," American Philosophical Society *Proceedings*, 94 (August 1950): 398-410;

Aldridge, "A Religious Hoax by Benjamin Franklin," *American Literature*, 36 (May 1964): 204-209;

Richard E. Amacher, *Benjamin Franklin* (New York: Twayne, 1962);

Amacher, "Humor in Franklin's Hoaxes and Satires," *Studies in Humor*, 2 (April 1975): 4-20;

Brian M. Barbour, ed., *Benjamin Franklin: A Collection of Critical Essays* (Englewood Cliffs, N. J.: Prentice-Hall, 1979);

Frances M. Barbour, *A Concordance to the Sayings in Franklin's "Poor Richard"* (Detroit: Gale Research, 1974);

Philip D. Beidler, "Franklin's and Crevecoeur's 'Literary Americans,' " *Early American Literature*, 13 (Spring 1978): 50-63;

Robert Bell, "Metamorphoses of Spiritual Autobiography," *English Literary History*, 44 (Spring 1977): 108-126;

Whitfield J. Bell, Jr., "Benjamin Franklin and the German Charity Schools," American Philosophical Society *Proceedings*, 99 (December 1955): 381-387;

Bell, "Benjamin Franklin As an American Hero," *Association of American Colleges Bulletin*, 43 (March 1957): 121-132;

Ernst Benz, "Franklin and the Mystic Rocket," *American-German Review*, 29 (June-July 1963): 24-26;

Walter Blair and Hamlin Hill, *America's Humor: From Poor Richard to Doonesbury* (New York: Oxford University Press, 1978);

Stanley Brodwin, "Strategies of Humor: The Case of Benjamin Franklin," *Prospects*, 4 (1979): 122-167;

Melvin M. Buxbaum, *Benjamin Franklin and the Zealous Presbyterians* (University Park: Pennsylvania State University Press, 1975);

Gilbert Chinard, "Abbé Lefebvre de la Roche's Recollections of Benjamin Franklin," American Philosophical Society *Proceedings*, 94 (June 1950): 214-221;

Chinard, "Benjamin Franklin and the mysterious Madame G---," American Philosophical Society *Library Bulletin* (1946): 49-72;

Chinard, "Benjamin Franklin et la Muse Provinciale," American Philosophical Society *Proceedings*, 97 (October 1953): 493-510;

Chinard, "Random Notes on Two Bagatelles," American Philosophical Society *Proceedings*, 103 (December 1959): 740-760;

I. Bernard Cohen, *Franklin and Newton: An Inquiry into Speculative Newtonian Experimental Science and Franklin's Work in Electricity as an Example Thereof* (Philadelphia: American Philosophical Society, 1956);

Paul W. Conner, *Poor Richard's Politics: Benjamin Franklin and his New American Order* (New York: Oxford University Press, 1965);

Hugh J. Dawson, "Fathers and Sons: Franklin's 'Memoirs' as Myth and Metaphor," *Early American Literature*, 14 (Winter 1979-1980): 269-292;

Dawson, "Franklin's 'Memoirs' in 1784: The Design of the *Autobiography*, Parts I and II," *Early American Literature*, 12 (Winter 1977-1978): 286-293;

Norman Fiering, "Benjamin Franklin and the Way to Virtue," *American Quarterly*, 30 (Summer 1978): 199-223;

Edward J. Gallagher, "The Rhetorical Strategy of Franklin's 'Way to Wealth,' " *Eighteenth-Century Studies*, 6 (Summer 1973): 475-485;

Bruce I. Granger, *Benjamin Franklin, An American Man of Letters* (Ithaca: Cornell University Press, 1964);

Max Hall, *Benjamin Franklin and Polly Baker* (Chapel Hill: University of North Carolina Press, 1960);

William S. Hanna, *Benjamin Franklin and Pennsylvania Politics* (Palo Alto: Stanford University Press, 1964);

Richard Boyd Hauck, "Benjamin Franklin: Man of Confidence, Confidence Man," in his *A Cheerful Nihilism* (Bloomington: University of Indiana Press, 1971), pp. 32-39;

Ralph W. Ketcham, *Benjamin Franklin* (New York: Twayne, 1965);

Adrienne Koch, "Franklin and Pragmatic Wisdom," in her *Power, Morals, and the Founding Fathers* (Ithaca: Cornell University Press, 1961), pp. 14-22;

Betty Kushen, "Three Earliest Published Lives of Benjamin Franklin, 1790-93: The *Autobiography* and Its Continuations," *Early American Literature*, 9 (Spring 1974): 39-52;

J. A. Leo Lemay, "Benjamin Franklin, Universal Genius," in *The Renaissance Man in the Eighteenth Century* (Los Angeles: William Andrews Clark Memorial Library, University of California, 1978), pp. 1-44;

Lemay, "Franklin's Suppressed 'Busy-Body,' " *American Literature*, 37 (November 1965): 307-311;

Lemay, ed., *The Oldest Revolutionary: Essays on Benjamin Franklin* (Philadelphia: University of Pennsylvania Press, 1976);

David Levin, "The Autobiography of Benjamin Franklin: The Puritan Experimenter in Life and Art," *Yale Review*, 43 (December 1963): 258-275;

William E. Lingelbach, "B. Franklin, Printer—New Source Material," American Philosophical Society *Proceedings*, 92 (May 1948): 79-100;

Luther D. Livingston, *Franklin and his Press at Passy* (New York: Grolier Club, 1914);

Frank Lawrence Lucas, *The Art of Living: Four Eighteenth-Century Minds—Hume, Horace Walpole, Burke and Benjamin Franklin* (New York: Macmillan, 1959);

Dorothy Medlin, "Benjamin Franklin and the French Language," *French-American Review*, 1 (Fall 1977): 232-239;

Medlin, "Benjamin Franklin's Bagatelles for Madame Helvétius: Some Biographical and Stylistic Considerations," *Early American Literature*, 15 (Spring 1980): 42-58;

Richard D. Miles, "The American Image of Benjamin Franklin," *American Quarterly*, 9 (Summer 1957): 117-143;

Frank L. Mott and Chester E. Jorgenson, Introduction to *Benjamin Franklin: Representative Selections* (New York: American Book Company, 1936), pp. xiii-cxli;

Benjamin H. Newcomb, *Franklin and Galloway: A Political Partnership* (New Haven: Yale University Press, 1972);

Robert Newcomb, "Poor Richard's Debt to Lord Halifax," *PMLA*, 70 (June 1955): 535-539;

Antonio Pace, *Benjamin Franklin and Italy* (Philadelphia: American Philosophical Society, 1958);

Vernon L. Parrington, "Benjamin Franklin: Our First Ambassador," in his *Main Currents in American Thought: The Colonial Mind, 1620-1800* (New York: Harcourt, Brace, 1927), I: 164-178;

Clinton Rossiter, "Benjamin Franklin," in his *Seedtime of the Republic* (New York: Harcourt, Brace, 1953), pp. 281-312;

Charles L. Sanford, ed., *Benjamin Franklin and the American Character* (Boston: Heath, 1955);

Robert F. Sayre, *The Examined Self: Benjamin Franklin, Henry Adams, Henry James* (Princeton: Princeton University Press, 1964);

David Schoenbrun, *Triumph in Paris: The Exploits of Benjamin Franklin* (New York: Harper & Row, 1976);

Charles Coleman Sellers, *Benjamin Franklin in Portraiture* (New Haven: Yale University Press, 1962);

Jayme A. Sokolow, " 'Arriving at Moral Perfection': Benjamin Franklin and Tolstoy," *American Literature*, 47 (November 1975): 427-432;

Gerald Stourzh, *Benjamin Franklin and American Foreign Policy* (Chicago: University of Chicago Press, 1954);

Arthur B. Tourtellot, *Benjamin Franklin: The Shaping of Genius, The Boston Years* (Garden City: Doubleday, 1977);

Mark Twain, "The Late Benjamin Franklin," *Galaxy*, 10 (July 1870): 138-140;

Carl Van Doren, ed., *Meet Dr. Franklin* (Philadelphia: Franklin Institute, 1943);

Daniel Walden, "Benjamin Franklin's Deism; A Phase," *Historian*, 26 (May 1964): 350-361;

Toshio Watanabe, "Benjamin Franklin and the Younger Generation in Japan," *American Studies International*, 18 (Winter 1980): 35-49;

Karl J. Weintraub, "The Puritan Ethos and Benjamin Franklin," *Journal of Religion*, 56 (July 1976): 223-237;

Stephen J. Whitfield, "Three Masters of Impression Management: Benjamin Franklin, Booker T. Washington, and Malcolm X as Autobiographers," *South Atlantic Quarterly*, 77 (Fall 1978): 399-417;

Reiner Wild, "Benjamin Franklin in der deutschen Literature des 18ten Jahrhunderts," *Amerika Studien/America Studies*, 23 (1978): 30-39;

Louis B. Wright, "Franklin's Legacy to the Gilded Age," *Virginia Quarterly Review*, 22 (Spring 1946): 268-279.

Papers:

The American Philosophical Society Library in Philadelphia is the largest repository of Franklin manuscripts, numbering over 14,000 items. The Library of Congress contains in its Stevens Collection the mostly public and scientific papers that William Temple Franklin, Franklin's literary executor, took to London for the 1817-1818 edition of his grandfather's works. Much of Franklin's official correspondence is in the National Archives. Collections numbering more than 500 manuscripts include the following: Pennsylvania Historical Society, University of Pennsylvania, Yale University, Massachusetts Historical Society, and the French Foreign Office. Other sizeable collections are housed in the Harvard College Library, the William L. Clements Library at the University of Michigan, the New York Public Library, the Henry E. Huntington Library, the Library Company of Philadelphia, the British Museum, the Royal Society, the Bibliothèque Nationale, and various other libraries and collections scattered widely in this country and abroad.

Ebenezer Gay

(15 August 1696-18 March 1787)

Jeffrey M. Jeske
University of California at Los Angeles

BOOKS: *Ministers are Men of Like Passions with Others. A Sermon Preach'd at Barnstable, May 12. 1725* . . . (Boston: Printed by B. Green, 1725);

A Discourse on the Transcendent Glory of the Gospel . . . (Boston: Printed for D. Henchman, 1728);

Zechariah's Vision of Christ's Martial Glory . . . (Boston: Printed for J. Eliot, J. Phillips & B. Love, 1728);

The Duty of People to Pray for and Praise their Rulers. A Sermon at the Lecture in Hingham, August 12, 1730, On Occasion of the Arrival of His Excellency Jonathan Belcher, Esq.; to His Government . . . (Boston: Printed by Thomas Fleet, 1730);

Well-Accomplish'd Soldiers, A Glory to Their King, and a Defence to Their Country. A Sermon Preach'd at Hingham, on a Training-Day, there May 10, 1738 . . . (Boston: Printed by T. Fleet for Daniel Henchman, 1738);

Ministers Insufficiency for Their Important and Difficult Work, Argued from the Opposite Eternal Events of It. A Sermon Preach'd at the Ordination of The Rev. Mr. Ebenezer Gay, Junior . . . (Boston: Printed by D. Fowle for S. Eliot, 1742);

The Untimely Death of a Man of God Lamented. In a Sermon Preach'd at the Funeral of The Reverend Mr. John Hancock . . . (Boston: Printed by S. Kneeland & T. Green, 1744);

The Character and Work of a Good Ruler, and the Duty of an Obliged People. A Sermon Preach'd Before His Excellency William Shirley, Esq; The Honourable His Majesty's Council, and House of Representatives of the Province of Massachusetts-Bay in New-England . . . (Boston: Printed for Daniel Gookin, 1745);

The True Spirit of a Gospel-Minister Represented and Urged. A Sermon Preach'd Before the Ministers of the Province . . . (Boston: Printed by D. Gookin, 1746);

The Alienation of Affections from Ministers Consider'd and Improv'd. A Sermon Preach'd at the Ordination of the Reverend Mr. Jonathan Mayhew . . . (Boston: Printed by Rogers & Fowle, 1747);

Portrait of Gay by John Hazlett

The Mystery of the Seven Stars in Christ's Right Hand: Open'd and Apply'd in a Sermon Preached at the Ordination of the Reverend Mr. Jonathan Dorby . . . (Boston: Printed & sold by J. Draper, 1752);

Jesus-Christ the Wise Master-Builder of His Church. A Sermon Preached at the Installment of the Reverend Mr. Ezra Carpenter . . . (Boston: Printed & sold by S. Kneeland, 1753);

The Work of a Gospel-Minister, and the Importance of Approving Himself to God in It. A Sermon Preached at the Ordination of Rev. Cotton Mather Smith . . . (New Haven: Printed & sold by James Parker, 1755);

The Levite Not to Be Forsaken. A Sermon Preach'd at the Instalment of the Rev. Mr. Grindall Rawson . . . (Boston, 1756);

Natural Religion, as Distinguish'd from Revealed: A Sermon Preached at the Annual Dudleian-Lecture at Harvard-College . . . (Boston: Printed & sold by John Draper, 1759);

The Evangelical Preacher. A Sermon Delivered at the Ordination of the Rev'd Mr. Bunker Gay . . . (Boston: Printed by Richard & Samuel Draper, 1763);

A Beloved Disciple of Jesus Christ Characterized. In a Sermon Preached at the West-Church in Boston, July 27, A.M. 1766. The Third Lord's-Day from the Decease of the Reverend Pastor Jonathan Mayhew . . . (Boston: Printed by R. & S. Draper, T.& J. Fleet, and Edes & Gill, 1766);

St. John's Vision of the Woman Cloathed with the Sun &c. in Rev. XII. 1-5. Explained and Improved in a Discourse Had at the West Church of Christ in Boston, July 27, P.M. 1766. The Third Lord's-Day after the Decease of the Reverend Pastor Jonathan Mayhew . . . (Boston: Printed by R. & S. Draper, 1766);

The Sovereignty of God, in Determining Man's Days, or the Time and Manner of His Death: Illustrated and Improved, in a Sermon . . . (Hartford: Printed by Thomas Green, 1767);

A Call from Macedonia. A Sermon Preached at Hingham, in New-England, October 12, 1768, at the Ordination of the Reverend Mr. Caleb Gannett . . . (Boston: Printed by Richard Draper and Thomas & John Fleet, 1768);

The Devotions of God's People Adjusted to the Dispensations of His Providence . . . (Boston: Printed by Richard Draper, 1771);

The Old Man's Calendar. A Discourse on Joshua XIV. 10 . . . (Boston: Printed by John Boyle, 1781; London: Printed by H. Goldney for J. Buckland, 1781).

Ebenezer Gay, son of Nathaniel and Lydia Gay, was born and raised in Dedham, Massachusetts. After graduating from Harvard College in 1714, he studied for the Congregational ministry while teaching at schools in Hadley and Ipswich. In 1718 he was ordained minister of the First Church at Hingham, Massachusetts, a position he maintained for three months short of seventy years. During this time he married Jerusha, a great-granddaughter of Governor William Bradford, and with her raised eleven children.

During the Revolution, his political sympathies were Tory. In theology, however, he was noted for his Arminianism, a liberal and democratic intellectualism in religious doctrine. This stance, condemned by his Calvinist contemporaries because of its opposition to the doctrine of absolute predestination, was expressed in Gay's emphasis on the efficacy of free will, his forceful opposition to creeds, and in the rationalist and progressive ideas which appear throughout his sermons. In *Natural Religion, as Distinguish'd from Revealed* . . . (1759), for example, Gay postulates a Newtonian universe from which man's unaided natural reason can deduce ethical principles and the attributes of deity. Other published sermons include *A Beloved Disciple of Jesus Christ Characterized* . . . (1766), preached on the death of Jonathan Mayhew, whose liberal views Gay helped shape, and another, preached on the text "And now, lo, I am four score and five years old" (1781), which was published repeatedly as *The Old Man's Calendar* . . . (1781). Gay died at Hingham in 1787.

Gay is considered to be the founder of American Unitarianism because of his influential leadership in the establishment of free inquiry and a set of opinions distinct from Calvinism.

References:

George Willis Cooke, *Unitarianism in America* (Boston: American Unitarian Association, 1902);

Solomon Lincoln, Jr., *History of the Town of Hingham, Plymouth County, Massachusetts* (Hingham: Caleb Gill, Jr., 1827);

Conrad Wright, *The Beginnings of Unitarianism in America* (Boston: Starr King Press, 1955).

Daniel Gookin

(1612-19 March 1687)

Richard Cogley

WORKS: *Historical Collections of the Indians in New England Of Their Several Nations, Numbers, Customs, Manners, Religion and Government Before the English Planted There. Also a True and Faithful Account of the Present State and Condition of the Praying Indians . . . ,* in Massachusetts Historical Society *Collections,* first series 1 (1792): 141-227;

An Historical Account of the Doings and Sufferings of the Christian Indians in New England in the Years 1675, 1676, 1677, in American Antiquarian Society *Transactions,* 2 (1836): 423-534.

Daniel Gookin of Cambridge, Massachusetts, is the author of two narratives about the Indians, *Historical Collections of the Indians in New England . . . ,* first published in Massachusetts Historical Society *Collections* in 1792, and *An Historical Account of the Doings and Sufferings of the Christian Indians in New England in the Years 1675, 1676, 1677,* first published in American Antiquarian Society *Transactions* in 1836.

Gookin, whose place of birth is unknown, spent his childhood in County Cork, Ireland. In 1621, he moved to Newport News, Virginia, where his father, Daniel, a merchant adventurer originally from Canterbury, Kent, had established a plantation. A committed Puritan, the younger Gookin left Virginia in 1643, shortly after the General Assembly began to persecute Nonconformists. In May 1644, following a year's residence in Annapolis, Maryland, he settled in Massachusetts and became a prominent figure in that state's affairs, serving as a deputy (1649, 1651-1652) and as an assistant (1653-1675, 1677-1687) in the General Court; as sergeant major (1676-1680) and as major general (1680-1687) in the militia; and as Indian Superintendent (1656-1657, 1661-1687) in the Massachusetts Bay Colony.

During his long tenure as Indian Superintendent, Gookin acquired considerable knowledge about the Indians. His *Historical Collections of the Indians . . . ,* which he completed in 1674, is the best source of information written by a Massachusetts Puritan about traditional Indian religion, political organization, dress, agriculture, commerce, and domestic relations. It also contains an important account of the efforts of John Eliot and other New England missionaries to convert the natives to the Christian faith. *An Historical Account of the Doings and Sufferings of the Christian Indians . . . ,* written in 1677, focuses on the shameful treatment that Eliot's converts received during King Philip's War at the hands of an Indian-hating populace. Gookin wrote this poignant narrative in reaction to Increase Mather and William Hubbard, whose histories of the war had slighted the Christian Indians.

Gookin wrote about the New England Indians with a sensitivity rare among Massachusetts Puritans. His writings are characterized by their careful organization and lucid syntax. "I have endeavoured all plainness that I can, that the most vulgar capacity might understand," he explained. Two unpublished works, a history of New England and an account of the Mohawk Indians of New York, are not extant.

References:

Frederick William Gookin, *Daniel Gookin, 1612-1687: Assistant and Major General of the Massachusetts Bay Colony: His Life and Letters and Some Account of His Ancestry* (Chicago: Privately printed, 1912);

Moses Coit Tyler, *A History of American Literature, 1607-1765* (1878; republished, Williamstown, Mass.: Corner House Publishers, 1973), I: 151-157.

John Hammond

(birth date unknown-1663)

Daniel E. Williams
Universität Tübingen

BOOKS: *Hammond versus Heamans. Or, An answer To an audacious Pamphlet published by an Impudent and ridiculous Fellow, named Roger Heamans* . . . (London: Printed for the author & sold at Royall Exhange in Cornhill, 1655);

Leah and Rachel, or The two fruitfull sisters Virginia and Mary-land: Their Present Condition, Impartially Stated and Related . . . (London: Printed by T. Mabb, 1656); republished in *Tracts*, edited by Peter Force, volume 3, number 14 (Washington, D.C.: Peter Force, 1844); and in *Narratives of Early Maryland*, edited by Clayton C. Hall (New York: Scribners, 1910).

John Hammond attempted to describe Virginia and Maryland honestly at a time when honest descriptions were rare. In mid-seventeenth-century England, where both pamphlets and rumors proliferated, the New World was either extravagantly praised or bitterly damned. Glowing promotional tracts promised paradise, while early reports depicted hell. Published in London in 1656, Hammond's *Leah and Rachel, or The two fruitfull sisters Virginia and Mary-land* disputed many of "the odiums and cruell slanders cast on those two famous Countries . . . ," but in doing so he neither overpraised nor overpromised. Ultimately, according to Hammond's articulate and balanced view based on over two decades of residence, the New World promised nothing more than opportunity—a new beginning in a fertile country. Like many later American writers, he placed the burden of success or failure squarely on the individual. Those coming to the New World determined, self-reliant, and willing to work would prosper.

Nothing is known for certain about Hammond's early life. In *Leah and Rachel* . . . he stated that he had spent nineteen years in Virginia and two years in Maryland. If so, then he immigrated to Virginia sometime in 1633 or 1634. He settled in Isle of Wight County and remained there until swept up by political controversy and conflict. In 1652 he was elected a burgess, but the Assembly of Virginia immediately dismissed him, citing his bad character and scandalous reputation as reasons for the dismissal. A more likely reason, however, was that Hammond's fierce loyalties and bluntness had already gotten him in trouble. Sixteen fifty-two was a year of political upheaval and shifting allegiances in Virginia. The assembly, previously loyal to the Crown, was forced to recognize Cromwell's victory and authority. The royal governor was dismissed, and a new one was appointed by Parliament. Evidently Hammond was unable to make the same sudden shift in loyalty.

After his abrupt dismissal, Hammond and his family left Virginia and moved to Maryland, settling in St. Mary's County. In 1654 he was granted two licenses by the county, one for selling liquor and one for establishing a ferry, in return for allowing the county court to meet at his inn. But, again overtaken by controversy and conflict, Hammond did not remain long in the role of a quiet innkeeper. Maryland at this time was torn by bitter factionalism and political uncertainty. Maryland's proprietor, Lord Baltimore, had attempted to prevent repercussions of the English Civil War from erupting into open conflict in Maryland by urging the passage of the Toleration Act, which formally recognized his earlier policy of religious freedom in the colony, and by appointing Protestants to the colonial government. Despite these efforts, a group of Maryland Puritans, distrusting Baltimore's Catholicism and jealous of his powers, used lies and vilification in order to discredit Baltimore and take control of the colony. Sides were quickly taken, and Maryland was soon divided between those supporting Baltimore and those wishing to see his proprietorship revoked. Hammond supported Lord Baltimore's forces against the Puritans, and, according to his own statements, took an active part in the struggle for possession of the colony. On 25 March 1655 the Puritans soundly defeated Baltimore's forces in the Battle of the Severn, thereby firmly gaining control of the colony. William Stone, Baltimore's Protestant governor, was wounded and imprisoned, and several of his followers were executed. The Puritans immediately attempted to arrest Hammond, also a follower of Stone. Fearing for his life, he disguised himself and fled to Virginia, leaving his wife, Ann, with power of attorney for him. Under an assumed name, Hammond gained passage to England on board the *Crescent*, whose captain, Thomas Thoroughgood, was later indicted by the Virginia Assembly for aiding his escape.

In England Hammond continued to fight, but now with a pen instead of a sword. The Maryland conflict had broken out in print as well as in battle, and several inflammatory pamphlets had already been written. Hammond's first published work, *Hammond versus Heamans* . . . (1655), came about as a direct result of this pamphlet war. In particular, he wrote in response to Roger Heaman's *An Additional Brief Narrative of a late design against the Protestants in Ann Arundel County Severn in Maryland* . . . (1655). Heaman, whose participation in the Battle of the Severn had greatly aided the Puritan victory, had (among other accusations) accused the Maryland Catholics of plotting with the Indians to destroy the Protestants of the colony. In his pamphlet Hammond employed a clever and capable mixture of sarcasm, ridicule, invective, and execration in order to rebuke Heaman and to defend Baltimore. Heaman was characterized as "an Impudent and ridiculous Fellow" whose perfidy both in person and in print had nearly caused the "utter ruine" of Maryland. Aside from vilification and rebuttal, Hammond described his actions during the Maryland hostilities, particularly his mission to fetch the colony's records for Governor Stone.

Leah and Rachel, or The two fruitfull sisters Virginia and Mary-land . . . (1656) followed soon after *Hammond versus Heamans* but exhibited far less bitter factionalism. Instead, Hammond wrote (according to most literary historians) one of the finest and earliest celebrations of "the American Dream." In this pamphlet the most significant confrontation was not between the Maryland factions but between England and America. In his subtitle, Hammond stated that he intended "A Removal of such Imputations as are scandalously cast on those Countries [Virginia and Maryland], whereby many deceived Souls, chose rather to Beg, Steal, rot in Prison, and come to shamefull deaths, then to better their being by going thither." Shocked by the misery of the poor in England and affronted by the poor reputation of the American colonies in England, he set about to describe the many favorable opportunities for "pleasure and plenty" in the two colonies. He began by establishing his own honesty and love for America: "It is not long since I came from thence (God knows sore against my will) having lived there upward of one and twenty years; nor do I intend (by Gods assistance) to be long out of it again: and therefore can by experience, not hearsay . . . but truly let ye know, what they are, and how the people live." Hammond was careful throughout never to overpraise or to make America appear like a paradise, as early writers had done: "I affirme the Country to be wholesome, healthy and fruitfull; and a model on which industry may as much improve itself in, as in any habitable part of the World; yet not such a Lubberland as the Fiction of the land of Ease is reported to be, nor such a Utopian as Sr. Thomas Moore hath related to be found out."

Attempting an honest appraisal, Hammond admitted the failures and the incredibly high mortality of early Virginia but attributed them to misrule, corruption, and poor diet. In order to counter the belief that America was a death trap, he came closer to the actual causes of the mortality than

LEAH and RACHEL,
OR,
the Two Fruitfull Sisters
VIRGINIA,
AND
MARY-LAND:
Their Present Condition, Impartially stated and related.
WITH
A Removall of such Imputations as are scandalously cast on those Countries, whereby many deceived Souls, chose rather to Beg, Steal, rot in Prison, and come to shamefull deaths, then to better their being by going thither, wherein is plenty of all things necessary for Humane subsistance.

By *John Hammond.*

Eccles. 21. v. 8.
If children live honestly and have wherewith, they shall put away the shame of their Parents.

LONDON,
Printed by *T. Mabb*, and are to be sold by *Nich. Bourn*, neer the Royall Exchange, 1656.

Title page for Hammond's book about Virginia and Maryland. At a time when honest descriptions of the New World were rare, Hammond attempted to be objective (John Carter Brown Library, Brown University).

most previous writers. "I believe (and that not without reason) it was only want of such diet as best agreed with our English natures, good drinks and wholesome lodgings were the cause of so much sicknesses, as were formerly frequent . . . that change of ayre does much alter the state of our bodies: by which many travellers thither may expect some sickness, yet little danger of mortality." Hammond also advised prospective colonists to expect unscrupulous colonial agents, difficult voyages, and hard work upon arrival. Specifically he cautioned that those interested in emigration should "not rashly throw themselves upon the voyage" but should prepare as much as possible and expect some setbacks.

Following the format of all previous promotional tracts, Hammond described the many benefits of the land: fertility, plentiful crops, temperate weather, and an endless variety of fish, game, and domestic animals. But unlike most previous promotional tracts, his stressed determination, honesty, and hard work as the keys to success, thus offering the same promise of prosperity celebrated by Franklin over a century later: "Those Servants that will be industrious may in their time of service gain a competent estate before their Freedomes, which is usually done by many, and they gaine esteeme and assistance that appear industrious . . . and by that time as he is for himself, he may have Cattel, Hogs and Tobacco of his own, and come to live gallantly; but this must be gained (as I said) by Industry and affability, not by sloth nor churlish behavior." After further advice on the problems of settlement, he again emphasized the rags to riches theme; America offered a new beginning: "It is knowne (such preferment hath this Country rewarded the industrious with) that some from being woolhoppers and of as mean and meaner imployment in England have there grown great merchants, and attained to the most eminent advancements the Country afforded. If men cannot gaine (by diligence) states in those parts . . . it will hardly be done. . . ." The new beginnings offered in America, however, were not only economic but spiritual as well. In order to counter the view that morality and soul degenerated in America, Hammond stated "that many who in England have been lewd and idle, there in emulation or imitation . . . of the industry of those they finde there, not onely grow ashamed of their former courses, but abhor to hear of them, and in a small time wipe off those stains they have formerly been tainted with."

With such great opportunities, Hammond was amazed that so many in England preferred to live there in misery and drudgery than to immigrate to America: "And therefore I cannot but admire, and indeed much pitty the dull stupidity of people necessitated in England, who rather then they will remove themselves, live here a base, slavish, penurious life; as if there were a necessity to live and to live so, choosing rather then they will forsake England to stuff New-Gate, Bridewell, and other Jayles with their carkessies, nay cleave to tyburne it selfe, and so bring confusion to their souls, horror and infamie to their kindred or posteritie, others itch out their wearisom lives in reliance of other mens charities, an uncertain and unmanly expectation; some more abhoring such courses betake themselves to almost perpetuall and restlesse toyle and druggeries out of which (whilst their strength lasteth) they (observing hard diets, earlie and late houres) make hard shift to subsist from hand to mouth, untill age or sicknesse takes them off from labour and directs them the way to beggerie. . . ." Hammond concluded that "their manner of living was degenerate and base, and their condition to be far below the meanest servant in Virginia." In order to illustrate his point, he described his encounter with a man "heavily loaden with a burden of Faggots on his back, crying, Dry Faggots, Dry Faggots." After watching the man struggle under his load for three hours without selling anything, Hammond stopped him to inquire how much the man made each day, and "he replyed, some dayes nothing some dayes six pence; some times more, but seldome; me thought it was a pittiful life, and I admired how he could live on it."

Hammond's final section described his experiences in Maryland, which, he said, offered even brighter promises than Virginia. "Having for 19 yeare served Virginia the elder sister, I casting my eye on Mary-land the younger, grew in amoured on her beauty, resolving like Jacob when he first served for Leah, to begin a fresh service for Rachell." Hammond was not, however, able to complete his service to the younger sister. Maryland's beauty offered too many promises, "so that its extraordinary goodnes hath made it rather desired then envied, which hath been fatall to her (as beauty is often times to those that are endued with it)." Hammond then described the hostilities in Maryland as resulting from greed rather than from purely religious differences: "But it was not religion, it was not punctilios they [the Puritan faction] stood upon, it was that sweete, that rich, that large Country they aimed at." According to Hammond, the Puritans living in Maryland conspired to incite and then to exploit a quarrel with Baltimore's followers. He again mentioned Heaman and his treachery during the Battle of the Severn. But Hammond's last remarks again express his love for America: "I know no country (although I have travelled many) that I more affect, more esteem; that which profits delights, and here is both absolute profit, reall delight . . . it is that Country in which I desire to spend the remnant of my dayes, in which I covert to make my grave."

Hammond was able to fulfill this last desire. After the Restoration he returned to Maryland and died there sometime early in the year 1663. Typically, Hammond spent his last years in conflict, being involved in several legal disputes. During his stay in England, his wife, Ann, had lost several court battles trying to protect her husband's estate. Upon returning, Hammond petitioned for the "Reheareings" of these cases. Hammond's last court action grew out of a conflict with Jacob Lumbroso, a Portuguese Jew, who charged Hammond with failing to pay for some goods. In the rather bitter dispute which followed, Lumbroso attempted to slander Hammond's wife by stating that she had been offered in lieu of other payment. The case was decided in October 1662, against Lumbroso. His charges were dropped, and he was forced to pay considerable damages for defaming Hammond and his wife. Hammond's last battle was a victory.

With the exception of the works of Captain John Smith, Hammond's *Leah and Rachel* . . . is the best-known and most admired promotional tract dealing with the early South. In particular, literary historians, beginning with Moses Coit Tyler and most recently J. A. Leo Lemay, have praised the American qualities of the book. Certainly their views are justified. Hammond celebrated self-reliance, initiative, determination, hard work, honesty, charity, the rejection of rigid social hierarchy, and the desire to better one's life—all the ingredients that went into the creation of the American Dream. His American farmer in many ways resembled the sturdy yeoman later extolled by both Crevecoeur and Jefferson. His view of America as a refuge is also central to American thought. Overall, his description of America as a land of opportunity and his emphasis on individual effort mark not only a significant development in American promotional literature but also in the development of American identity.

References:

Robert D. Arner, "A Note on John Hammond's *Leah and Rachel*," *Southern Literary Journal*, 6 (Fall 1973): 77-80;

Jay B. Hubbell, *The South in American Literature* (Durham: Duke University Press, 1954), pp. 22-23;

J. A. Leo Lemay, *Men of Letters in Colonial Maryland* (Knoxville: University of Tennessee Press, 1972), pp. 28-47;

Montrose J. Moses, *The Literature of the South* (New York: Crowell, 1910), pp. 39-41;

Kenneth B. Murdock, "Early Travellers and Observers," in *Literature of the American People*, edited by Arthur Hobson Quinn (New York: Appleton-Century-Crofts, 1951), pp. 17-34;

Moses Coit Tyler, *A History of American Literature 1607-1765* (New York: Putnam's, 1878; reprinted, Ithaca: Cornell University Press, 1949), pp. 53-57;

Louis B. Wright, "Writers of the South," in *Literary History of the United States*, volume 1, edited by Robert E. Spiller and others (New York: Macmillan, 1948), pp. 40-53.

Daniel Henchman

(21 January 1689-25 February 1761)

James Lawton

Daniel Henchman, the most enterprising bookseller in colonial America, was born in Boston, the son of Hezekiah and Abigail Henchman. His grandfather, for whom he was named, served with distinction in the militia during King Philip's War and was a founder of Worcester, Massachusetts.

Nothing is known about Henchman's formative years. He presumably served the normal seven-year apprenticeship, perhaps with the bookseller Samuel Phillips, and he became an independent bookseller about 1710. A substantial number of his business ledgers and journals are extant and provide a detailed picture of commerce in colonial America. In 1713 Henchman opened a shop at the south corner of King and Cornhill Streets (now State and Washington) and married Elizabeth Gerrish, the daughter of a prominent general merchant; they had one child, Lydia, who married Thomas Hancock. Starting with a simple range of books and stationery, Henchman expanded his stock rapidly. He handled both new and used books and was soon wholesaling to booksellers outside Boston in an ever-widening circle which eventually included Great Britain and the West Indies.

Not satisfied with expanding his market, Henchman also turned his attention to the production of books and in so doing may have become the closest eighteenth-century equivalent of a twentieth-century publisher. He imported leather and tools and established a bindery at his shop. (A number of books bound there, including his own ledgers, are still extant in New England libraries today.) He commissioned various printers in Boston to produce numerous books and pamphlets, which he marketed, and occasionally he would have books printed in London or Scotland and sent over in sheets to be bound at his bindery. Among the books he imported in sheets were large numbers of the English Bible, which by English law could not be printed in the colonies. According to Isaiah Thomas in *The History of Printing in America* (1810), Henchman was principally responsible for a pirated edition of the Bible reputed to be the first Bible in English to be printed in America. Thomas said that it was printed at Boston about 1752 by Kneeland and Green but carried the imprint "London: Printed by Mark Baskett, Printer to the King's Most Excellent Majesty." Although Thomas claims to have apprenticed with printers who worked on it, no authentic copy of this Bible has been located. Indeed, the story of this Bible may have been a myth created by older printers as a joke on a young apprentice.

Danl Henchman

In 1728 Henchman, in partnership with Benjamin Faneuil, Gillam Phillips, and Thomas Hancock, set out to establish a paper mill near Boston. At that time the only paper mills in America were at Philadelphia, and Boston had to import most of its paper from Britain. Henchman acquired real estate in Dorchester, hired a manager and laborers, and kept the accounts. The mill was soon supplementing Boston's paper needs, but due to a chronic shortage of rags and of skilled labor, it did not generate the profits Henchman would have liked. The last of the original partners, Henchman sold his share of the mill to the manager in 1748. The mill continued to be marginally profitable for another fifteen years, finally becoming a successful enterprise after 1763.

Bookselling and related fields remained the mainstay of Henchman's business throughout his life. However, like most merchants of the time, he found it necessary to be involved in other commodities and enterprises. He held various parcels of real estate which he rented, and he owned shares in a substantial number of ships. The lack of hard currency in the colonies forced colonial merchants to engage in barter and to deal in the commodities which they received as payment for their primary merchandise. Henchman was no exception, and his accounts indicate that he dealt in Bibles, buckles, and butter with equal facility. Henchman died in 1761 and left the bulk of his substantial estate to Thomas and Lydia Hancock. After Thomas Hancock died in 1764, most of Henchman's estate passed into the hands of John Hancock and eventually helped to finance the beginnings of the American Revolution.

References:

W. T. Baxter, "Daniel Henchman, a Colonial Bookseller," *Essex Institute Historical Collections*, 70 (1934): 1-30;

Isaiah Thomas, *The History of Printing in America* (1810; republished, New York: Weathervane Books, 1970), pp. 103-104, 195-196.

Papers:

The Baker Library, Harvard Business School, has ledgers, business journals, correspondence, and bills; Boston Public Library has a business journal, correspondence, and bills; additional manuscript material is at the Massachusetts Historical Society and the New England Historic Genealogical Society.

Thomas Hooker

Sargent Bush, Jr.
University of Wisconsin, Madison

BIRTH: Markfield, Leicestershire, England, circa 7 July 1586, to John Hooker (mother's name unknown).

EDUCATION: Queen's College, Cambridge, 1604; Emmanuel College, Cambridge, 1604-1618. B.A., 1608; M.A., 1611.

MARRIAGE: 3 April 1621 to Susanna Garbrand; children: Joanna, Anne, Sarah, Mary, Sarah, John, a son (name unknown), Samuel.

DEATH: Hartford, Connecticut, 7 July 1647.

BOOKS: *The Soules Preparation for Christ. Or, A Treatise of Contrition* . . . (London: Printed for Robert Dawlman, 1632);

The Poore Doubting Christian Drawne to Christ . . . (London: Printed for R. Dawlman & L. F., 1635; Boston: Printed by Green, Bushell & Allen for D. Henchman, 1743);

The Soules Humiliation (London: Printed by I. L. for Andrew Crooke, 1637);

The Soules Ingrafting into Christ (London: Printed by J. H. for Andrew Crooke, 1637);

The Soules Effectuall Calling to Christ (London: Printed by J. H. for Andrew Crooke, 1637); republished as *The Soules Vocation* . . . , as T. H. (London: Printed by John Haviland for Andrew Crooke, 1638);

The Soules Implantation . . . (London: Printed by R. Young, sold by Fulke Clifton, 1637); corrected and enlarged as *The Soules Implantation into the Naturall Olive* (London: Printed by R. Young, sold by Fulke Clifton, 1640);

Foure Learned and Godly Treatises . . . (London: Printed by Tho. Cotes for Andrew Crooke, 1638);

The Soules Exaltation . . . (London: Printed by John Haviland for Andrew Crooke, 1638);

The Soules Possession of Christ . . . (London: Printed by M. F. for Francis Eglesfield, 1638);

The Unbeleevers Preparing for Christ . . . (London: Printed by Tho. Coates for Andrew Crooke, 1638);

The Sinners Salvation . . . (London: Printed for Robert Dawlman, 1638);

Spiritual Munition . . . (London: Printed for Robert Dawlman, 1638);

Spiritual Thirst . . . (London: Printed for Robert Dawlman, 1638);

The Stay of the Faithfull: Together With the Properties of an Honest Heart . . . (London: Printed by M. F. for R. Dawlman, sold by Thomas Nichols, 1638);

Three Godly Sermons . . . (London: Printed by M. P. for John Stafford, 1638); revised and expanded as *The Saints Guide, In Three Treatises*. . . , (London: Printed for John Stafford, 1645);

The Christians Two Chiefe Lessons . . . (London: Printed by T. B. for P. Stephens & C. Meredith, 1640);

The Pateme of Perfection: Exhibited in Gods Image on Adam . . . (London: Printed for R. Y. & F. Clifton, 1640); republished as *Gods Image on Man* . . . (London: Printed by A. M. for John Browne, 1653);

The Danger of Desertion: Or a Farwell Sermon of Mr. Thomas Hooker . . . (London: Printed by G. M. for George Edwards, 1641);

The Faithful Covenanter . . . (London: Printed for Christopher Meredith, 1644);

A Briefe Exposition of the Lords Prayer... (London: Printed by Moses Bell for Benjamine Allen, 1645); revised as *Heavens Treasury Opened in a Fruitful Exposition of the Lords Prayer* . . . (London: Printed for R. Dawlman, 1645);

An Exposition of the Principles of Religion (London: Printed for R. Dawlman, 1645);

A Survey of the Summe of Church-Discipline . . . (London: Printed by A. M. for John Bellamy, 1648);

The Covenant of Grace Opened . . . (London: Printed by G. Dawson, 1649);

The Saints Dignitie, and Dutie... (London: Printed by G. D. for Francis Eglesfield, 1651);

The Application of Redemption . . . The First Eight Books (London: Printed by Peter Cole, 1656);

The Application of Redemption . . . The Ninth and Tenth Books (London: Printed by Peter Cole, 1656);

A Comment upon Christ's Last Prayer in the Seventeenth of John . . . (London: Printed by Peter Cole, 1656).

COLLECTION: *Thomas Hooker: Writings in England and Holland, 1626-1633*, edited by George H. Williams, Norman Pettit, Winfried Herget, and Sargent Bush, Jr., Harvard Theological Studies, no. 28 (Cambridge: Harvard University Press, 1975).

When Thomas Hooker died in Hartford, Connecticut, in the summer of 1647, his congregation and colleagues mourned the loss of an exceptional preacher and pastor. Two prominent members of his congregation called him "one of a thousand, whose diligence and unweariednesse (besides his other endowments) in the work committed to him, was almost beyond compare." John Cotton wrote in couplets: "Prudent in Rule, in Argument quick, full: / Fervent in Prayer, in Preaching powerfull." Later in the century a younger clergyman remembered him as "that great Elijah, that renowned man of God in his generation." And Cotton Mather, in 1702, called him the "Light of the Western Churches." Modern scholars consider him one of the best preachers of his generation in New England; he may have been the very best. His prominence as a leader during troubled times in England and New England was owing primarily to his power as a preacher. In an age when the sermon was the preeminent form of discourse in his milieu, he was a master of the form.

T. Hooker

He was born in Markfield, Leicestershire, probably in July of 1586, one of the six children of a yeoman, Thomas Hooker, and his wife, whose name is unknown. He went to school in the neighboring town of Market Bosworth, eventually going up to Queen's College, Cambridge, where he matriculated on 27 March 1604. In October of the same year he transferred to Emmanuel College, which had been founded exactly twenty years earlier with a decidedly Puritan orientation. He remained there as Dixie Fellow, tutor, and catechist until 1618, earning his B.A. in 1608 and his M.A. in 1611. His fourteen years at Emmanuel brought him into contact with many other scholars of strong Puritan conviction, including John Cotton, Nathaniel Rogers, John Dod, Zechariah Symmes, Anthony Tuckney, and Simeon Ashe. Sometime during his stay there he experienced the conversion which determined the course his life would follow.

On leaving Cambridge in the fall of 1618, he probably went directly to the village of Esher in Surrey, outside London, to become rector of St. George's and chaplain to the family of one Sir Francis Drake. For at least part of his time in Esher he spent much of his energy counseling Sir Francis's wife, Joan, who was emotionally and spiritually disturbed, convinced she had committed the sin against the Holy Ghost. After Hooker's help and that of several other ministers, Mrs. Drake was converted and died content in 1625. It was during his stay at Esher that Hooker met and married Susanna Garbrand, a member of Mrs. Drake's household staff. The wedding took place on 3 April 1621 in Amersham, Buckinghamshire. Their first child, Joanna, was probably named after Joan Drake; she later married Thomas Shepard, her father's successor as minister at Cambridge in Massachusetts Bay, in 1638, and she died in 1646, the year before her father. We know of seven other Hooker children: Anne (born and died 1625), Sarah (1628-1629), Mary (who married Roger Newton in 1645), Sarah (who married John Wilson), John (who returned to England to attend Oxford University), a son whose name is unknown, and Samuel (circa 1633-1697, who became well known as the minister at Farmington, Connecticut).

Exact dates of Hooker's moves are often uncertain, but it was apparently sometime in 1625 that he took a new position as lecturer at Chelmsford in Essex county, a hotbed of Puritanism. He was an outspoken advocate of Puritan ways, insistently espousing the importance of maintaining the "purity of the ordinances," which meant opposing such outward and "idolatrous" signs (which were insisted upon by the Church of England's hierarchy and conformist ministry) as genuflecting, making the sign of the cross, and wearing the surplice. Although he had had a lengthy apprenticeship as a preacher in Cambridge, it was probably in Esher and especially in front of the large audiences at Chelmsford that Hooker refined his preaching to the degree of sharpness and to the level of power which eventually earned the wrath of the English church hierarchy.

In the very year in which Hooker went to his position at Chelmsford, the British monarchy passed from James I to Charles I, who very quickly began to encourage tighter control over the public lecturers, a group which tended to be strongly populist and Puritan and was thus in King Charles's view a threat to the stability of the established form of religion in the kingdom. From the beginning of his preaching at Chelmsford, Hooker was aware of the political ramifications of his message. Although he surely preached in various tones and on a full range of scriptural texts, four of the sermons which have survived from this period—through the careful transcription of sermons by auditors and later publication of the texts from these listeners' copies—demonstrate dramatically the degree to which Hooker, in supporting the Puritan stand on the "purity" of the ordinances and in opposing governmental repression of preachers, was engaging enthusiastically in a very serious struggle.

The earliest datable sermon is entitled *Spiritual Munition. . . .* It was preached at the funeral of a young minister, Robert Wilmot, on 22 June 1626 and published in 1638. Here, in a refrain that would very soon become more pronounced in his and other Essex Puritans' sermons, Hooker insists that loyalty to God must come before loyalty to an earthly king. Ideally, there is no conflict in these loyalties, but even in 1626 it was already clear that the English king and his church leaders were not very friendly to nonconformists of the Puritan stripe. Hooker boldly asserted, therefore, that "those which are the enemies to God's faithful ministers are the greatest adversaries that the Church or State hath." Persecutors of faithful ministers, he insisted, are "traitors" to England. It was a refrain to which he would return in more directly political sermons in the next three years.

Hooker's *The Stay of the Faithfull. . .*, a sermon published in 1638, deals specifically with the central Puritan issue of purity in the forms of worship. Not overtly radical, the book nevertheless confronts a highly political subject, citing as it does typological examples of good kings such as Hezekiah and Jehoshaphat who set the "Ordinances of God in their purity," and whose kingdoms thereby prospered. The comparison with England in the present day was implicit but clear. Hooker became more explicit, however, in two other sermons preached in the late 1620s at Chelmsford. "The Churches Deliverance" (published in *Foure Learned and Godly Treatises. . .* , 1638) and *The Danger of Desertion* (published in 1641) are Hooker's most thoroughgoing jeremiads. In each of them he again stresses the danger in a nation's persecuting its godly people. He affirms the idea which had been traditional since the preceding century, that England was a favored nation of God, but he also warns that this is not a condition which will necessarily continue in the face of corruptions and persecutions. The increasing repression of nonconformist ministers is clearly on his mind as he says, "When corruptions are grown so strong that good men are defiled and their hearts tainted and their mouths stopped, woe to that kingdom and people."

By the autumn of 1629 Hooker's arousing preaching and insistent nonconformity had clearly made him a controversial figure. In November some ninety Essex clergy divided about equally in filing two petitions with the Bishop of London, William Laud, asking in one case that Hooker be allowed to continue his ministry at Chelmsford and in the other that he be made to conform. The latter group clearly wanted this dangerous preacher removed from his position. They ultimately won out. On 10 July 1630 Hooker was cited to appear before the Court of High Commission, whereupon he resolved to escape from England. The ecclesiastical repressions at the time were resulting in imprisonment and even mutilation of some of the most forceful Puritan preachers. For some months, however, Hooker apparently remained more or less "underground" in England, probably meeting with younger Puritan ministers and conducting a school from his home, Cuckoos Farm at Little Baddow.

In the spring of 1631 Hooker was encouraged to flee to Holland, where he expected a call to the pulpit of the English Reformed Church in Amsterdam. His departure from England, which meant leaving his wife and children behind, produced his famous jeremiad *The Danger of Desertion*, which, scholars have concluded, may have been preached on Maundy Thursday, 17 April 1631. His "farewell sermon" was thus preached from the knowledge that the repressions by the English church hierarchy had made him an exile and deprived him both of his family's unity and of his vocation as God's "messenger."

It was clearly with a certain bitterness, therefore, that he composed and preached *The Danger of Desertion,* which is one of our best surviving examples of the jeremiad in its premigration British form. Here, as in his other political sermons, Hooker is playing the role of prophet to his nation. Speaking on the text in Jeremiah 14:9 Hooker warns of the danger that God will turn his back on England, even in spite of his partiality to the English people. "God may leave a nation, and his elect may suffer, and why may not England?" The nation that rejects God, in other words, can in turn expect to be rejected by him. He presses the point to the extent of saying that even the King of England is not exempt from God's wrath. Lest some may think the King is safe, Hooker relentlessly applies his theology's leveling tendency: "God will say, be he a King that rules or reigns, yet as he hath rejected God, so God will reject him. He is a King of Kings and Lord of Lords, and therefore such a one as will laugh at thy destruction." Elsewhere in this sermon, Hooker's character painting is dramatic and his rhetoric worthy of tragic actors on the Jacobean stage. He plays the role of the sad English subject, terror stricken at the loss of God's presence and pleading for his constancy in the present need: "Oh, therefore my brethren, lay hold on God, and let him not go out of your coasts. . . . Look about you, I say, and stop him at the town's end, and let not thy God depart! Oh England, lay siege about him by humble and hearty closing with him." But in the end the dominant refrain is a lament over the nation's infidelity. He mourns the fact that "the gospel is going, Christ is departing, he is going to seek better entertainment." England's best days are past, he says. God is headed west, where "New England shall be a refuge for his Noahs and Lots, a rock and a shelter for his righteous ones to run unto." Like Hooker himself, God is no longer welcome in England. The sermon is packed with dramatic lines and gestures, replete with typological analogies and even includes references to the audience's responses, or lack of them. It represents Hooker's impassioned prophetic manner as well as any sermon he ever preached.

His sojourn of nearly two years in Holland did not bring release from controversy. On arriving in Amsterdam, he found a congregation and their pastor divided over the question of whether to invite Hooker to become a minister to the congregation. The people were impressed by his preaching, but the pastor, John Paget, disliked Hooker's Congregationalist notions of church polity. Paget accordingly put twenty questions in writing and required Hooker to write out his answers to them. It was a test of Hooker's position on matters such as membership and baptism, where the independent, or Congregationalist, ministers were in disagreement with traditional Church of England conformist pastors. When he saw the questions, Hooker knew very well he could not answer them honestly and "pass" the test, so he was reconciled to the need to leave Amsterdam. He did, however, provide straightforward answers which define in writing the precise nature of his commitment to Congregationalist polity more fully than he had done before. The document, "Mr. Paget's 20 Propositions to Mr. Hooker with his Answers Thereto," became a significant one for the history of Congregationalism, though it was not published in full until 1940. Hooker was subsequently called to join John Forbes, a Scottish minister in exile, at the English Merchant Adventurers' Church at Delft.

Sometime in late 1632 Hooker apparently wrote a lengthy preface to *A Fresh Suit against Humane Ceremonies* (1633), William Ames's final installment in a lengthy controversy with John Burgess. Hooker's preface was published anonymously, as was the book itself. Hooker's contribution is mainly an attack on Burgess for his conversion from a nonconformist to a conformist position in regard to English ecclesiastical matters, and for Burgess's argument that it is better to obey the authority of the church and to continue to preach the Word than to disobey authority and thus be prevented from preaching. Hooker expresses firm belief in the responsibility of the individual to search for Truth regardless of what he is told by the hierarchical officers of the church. As he puts it, the authority of the Word of God is a higher authority than that of the Church, which is after all subject to human corruption. And on the other issue, Hooker and nearly all other clergy who immigrated to New England in the first generation of colonization believed it is better *not* to continue to lead worship if corrupt, "unlawful" ceremonies must be practiced in order to do so. The central question, as he said, was "whether we may come to do lawful things by unlawful means, to sin that we may do service." Hooker and Ames were both willing to be exiled, if necessary, to maintain the purity of church services as they understood that purity to be described in the Bible. The preface to *A Fresh Suit . . .* is not great writing. But, together with the answer to Paget's "20 Propositions," this piece of controversial writing represents the further refinement of Hooker's commitment to Congregationalist principles which occurred during his stay in Holland. When he returned, probably secretly, to England in the spring of 1633, he knew that his next stop would be New England, where he could not only minister to God's word and His people, but where he could also live together with his family.

Two of Hooker's earliest publications appeared before his departure for New England. *The Poore Doubting Christian* . . . (first published in Richard Sibbes's *The Saints Cordials* . . . , 1629, and separately published in 1635) and *The Soules Preparation for Christ* . . . (1632) were important writings on what was to become the central achievement of his career as preacher and author. *The Poore Doubting Christian* . . . is an example of Hooker's pastoral concern for the more timid, reticent believers in his congregation. It argues for the importance of perseverance in one's faith and encourages the "poor, doubting" soul. It has been suggested that this work is based on the lessons he learned about pastoral encouragement while dealing with Joan Drake. In any case, this work, which was reprinted more than any other Hooker book, represents the compassionate side of Hooker's temperament. *The Soules Preparation for Christ* . . . is in the end perhaps a more important work. Published in London while he was still in Holland, probably without his knowledge or consent—as was the case with the great majority of his books—it is a description of the first stage in the progress of the soul from damnation to salvation and glorification, a dramatic progression which Hooker described in lengthy sermon series at least three times in the course of his career—at Cambridge, at Chelmsford, and at Hartford. It was the essential story of his ministry and was present as an issue in all of his preaching. How the soul, in the face of such realities of Hooker's Calvinistic theology as innate human depravity and the eternal election of predestined souls to salvation or damnation, can ever be assured of God's grace was the great challenging question for his congregations and for him as their spiritual shepherd. *The Soules Preparation for Christ* . . . was apparently printed from the enlarged notes of an auditor at one of his early offerings of this sermon series on contrition. It represents extremely well the liveliness of Hooker's oral style. Later in New England Hooker rewrote this work, which was published posthumously as *The Application of Redemption . . . The Ninth and Tenth Books* (1656). The later version doubtless satisfied Hooker more in the matter of logical and theological precision and thoroughness, but the earlier version remains valuable for the immediate sense which it conveys of Hooker's pulpit presence and power.

Hooker, together with his family and two other prominent ministers, John Cotton from Boston in Lincolnshire and Samuel Stone from Hertford in Hertfordshire, arrived in the Massachusetts Bay Colony in September of 1633. A group of colonists whom John Winthrop described as "Mr. Hooker's Company" had preceded Hooker a year earlier and settled in what was then called Newtown (later Cambridge). Hooker and Stone became the first two ministers in the church there while Cotton went to the church in Boston, joining John Wilson. These acquaintances from Cambridge days were thus all established within a short distance of each other and of others who either were already in New England or soon would be—such prominent figures as Roger Williams, Richard Mather, John Eliot, and John Norton. Within two years, however, there was talk in Newtown of departure. Lack of adequate land was the ostensible and probably a real reason, though it has traditionally been supposed that friction between Cotton and Hooker, perhaps the two most prominent clerics in the colonies, led Hooker to want more elbow room. It was probably a combination of these economic and political causes which in 1636 motivated Hooker, Stone, and much of their congregation to migrate to the western bank of the Connecticut River at what they called Hartford. Hartford remained Hooker's home until his death eleven years later.

In 1637 and 1638, shortly after his move to Connecticut, books by Hooker suddenly appeared in startling numbers back in London. Fourteen volumes of his sermons, some large, some small, appeared in these two years alone, probably without his approval or foreknowledge. These books were printings of sermons which he had preached while still in England. In many cases, however, he was repeating versions of them in New England. They are parts of his long series of sermons detailing his understanding of spiritual psychology. The stages of grace, or *ordo salutis*, comprised an immutable sequence of the soul's experiences beginning with contrition and followed by humiliation, vocation, justification, adoption, sanctification, and glorification. Hooker's special insistence on the importance of the first two stages, contrition and humiliation, placed him with a small but important group of "preparationist" preachers. Other ministers, including John Cotton, opposed the notion of preparation for grace, believing that vocation is the first stage in a Christian life. Hooker devoted special

Ink-wash drawing of Hooker's house in Hartford. The room in the projection over the front door was Hooker's study (Connecticut Historical Society).

attention at Hartford to rewriting this series, but got only as far as a volume of theological background (*The Application of Redemption . . . the First Eight Books*), a volume on the first stage of the soul's progress, contrition (*The Application of Redemption . . . The Ninth and Tenth Books*), and another on the last stage, glorification (*A Comment upon Christ's Last Prayer . . .*). All three of these books from his Hartford years were published posthumously in 1656. The entire series is the chief literary accomplishment of Hooker's career, an achievement which Perry Miller described as a "masterpiece."

Perhaps no other Puritan minister explained so fully and so dramatically the adventure of the spiritual life as perceived by English and New English nonconformist Calvinists of the early seventeenth century. Often using metaphors of journeying and always insisting on the difficulty, the strenuousness of the journey, Hooker preached with a full engagement of his creative imagination, giving sensory vitality to what in the hands of less resourceful writers and speakers could seem an intangible experience of such airy concepts as soul, spirit, grace, and redemption. Hooker moulded these notions into understandable and realizable entities by associating them with such well-known aspects of earthly life as manual labor, physical love, farming, and traveling. His sermons are full of the tools of figurative language—images, tropes, analogies, metaphors, symbols—as well as imagined dialogues, character portraits, and typological storytelling. All of this is entirely consistent with Hooker's use of the plain style, which avoids difficult words, ornate style, foreign terminology, and other distractions from the message. He despised preaching which was merely a series of weak generalizations; he called such sermons "roving reproofes, toothless, powerless dispensations" which "profit no man at all." "General truths," he punned, "generally do little good. That which is spoken to all, is spoken to none at al." It is "sharp reproofs," he believed, which make "sound Christians." At its best—in such books as *The Soules Preparation for Christ. . .* , *The Soules Humiliation* (1637), and *The Soules Effectuall Calling to Christ* (1637), for instance—Hooker's preaching shows how the plain style could be an engaging, colorful, dynamic style.

The secret of his chief success as speaker and

writer is in his merging of theology and style. He was profoundly convinced that, within the terms of Calvinist theology, grace and salvation are available to the simple folks as well as the learned, to the poor as well as the wealthy, but that one must be committed to engaging in an active, spiritually oriented life, perhaps for a long period of time, before becoming assured of God's grace. This meant that he preached a theology of activism in one's spiritual life. As he moved from mood to mood in his preaching, he would threaten, cajole, terrify, comfort, inform, exhort, encourage, but he always returned to the choric admonition to "labor," insisting that the earnest seeker of grace would not give himself or God rest until he had assurance. This emphasis, together with his realistic recognition of both the power of sin and corruption in the world and the ultimate power of God to decide one's spiritual destiny, created a dynamic tension in his work between his sense of what ought to be and his awareness of what is. He taught his congregations that this tension is a constant fact of life which one must both live with and struggle to resolve. Preaching on the central importance of a sound faith, Hooker insisted, "You must labour to get faith, we ought to make it our daily taske and study, the aime of a man's desire, the main white and mark that we should shoot at in all our labours." Laboring to "get" faith of course involves prayer, worshipful listening to the minister, and diligence in reading of scripture. In this laboring, Hooker's congregations became, as he said, "wildering . . . travelers, . . . sea-faring men, that are tossed up and down the waters of the world." But such people did not sit on their hands. They were up and doing if they had a spark of spiritual life in them. And in the end, with the help of their inspired guide, they arrived at a firm assurance of the soundness of their faith.

While Hooker was refining this story of the great adventure for his people at Hartford, on the edge of the wilderness, he was sometimes still needed back in Massachusetts Bay. He returned, for instance, to serve with Peter Bulkeley as a moderator in the three-week formal inquiry into the spread of Antinomian opinions in September of 1637, the inquiry which eventually led to the trial of Anne Hutchinson. The seven sermons in Hooker's *The Saints Dignitie, and Dutie* . . . (1651) may have been preached during and after this period, since they all deal with issues, political and theological, which have immediate relevance to the Antinomian controversy.

Five years later, when the English Church was convening the Westminster Assembly, Hooker, Cotton, and John Davenport of New Haven were invited by the Assembly to be New England's representatives. Hooker, knowing the Congregationalist point of view was decidedly in the minority in that gathering, declined to attend, as did the other two for somewhat different reasons. But Hooker's writings in the 1640s were in some instances on issues of direct relevance to the assembly, notably his catechism, *An Exposition of the Principles of Religion* (1645), and his *A Briefe Exposition of the Lords Prayer* . . . (1645). A far more important work, however, was also a product of the mid-1640s. His *A Survey of the Summe of Church-Discipline* . . . (1648) was one of several books written by New England divines in answer to inquiries from English and Scottish clergymen regarding "the New England way" of church polity. Hooker's book was a direct reply to Samuel Rutherford, a Scottish Presbyterian whose *Peaceable and Temperate Plea for Pauls Presbyterie* (1642) and *The Due Right of Presbyteries* (1644) challenged the congregational system which was followed in New England. Hooker's long study of the Congregational polity was completed by mid-1645 and approved by the New England ministers, but it had to be rewritten from notes when the ship carrying it to England sank with its whole cargo. This learned work has been a standard inquiry into essential points of Congregationalist polity ever since.

When Hooker died of an "epidemical sickness" at the age of sixty-one in July of 1647, he was a widely revered and respected man. His reputation was based largely on his power as a preacher, a power still evident in the published versions of many of his sermons. In the earliest biography of Hooker, first published in 1695, Cotton Mather tells of a comment by the Reverend Henry Whitfield, who knew Hooker in Connecticut and who described him as "incomparable," "a man in whom learning and wisdom were . . . tempered with zeal, holiness, and watchfulness." Hooker had, according to Whitfield, a "cholerick disposition, and . . . a mighty vigor and fervor of spirit, which as occasion served, was wondrous useful to him, yet he had ordinarily as much government of his choler, as a man has of a mastiff dog in a chain; *he could let out his dog, and pull in his dog, as he pleased.*" Another who knew him said simply that Hooker "was a person who while doing his Master's work, would put a king in his pocket." He was, in short, a man of passion and discretion, of eloquence and compassion, well suited for his ultimate ministry in New England's "howling wilderness," where his spiritual guidance and his ability as a practical leader were both of great value to his fellow settlers. He was a man at home in a time when the sermon was the dominant form of literature and in a place where spiritual faith and worldly wisdom were equally valuable. In both his idealism and his symbolic imagination, he anticipates later American writers such as Edwards, Thoreau, Emerson, and Eliot, but he was decidedly a man of his own time—both a product and a shaper of it, a voice of the utmost importance to the first generation of New England life.

Other:

"To the Reader," in *The Doctrine of Faith . . .*, by John Rogers (London: Printed for Nathanael Newbery & William Sheffard, 1627);

"The Praeface," in *A Fresh Suit against Humane Ceremonies in Gods Worship*, by William Ames (Rotterdam?, 1633);

"Abstracts of Two Sermons by Rev. Thomas Hooker. From the Shorthand Notes of Mr. Henry Wolcott," *Collections of the Connecticut Historical Society*, 1 (1860): 19-21;

"Touching ye Crosse in ye Banners," *Proceedings of the Massachusetts Historical Society*, third series 42 (April 1909): 272-280;

"Mr. Paget's 20 Propositions to Mr. Hooker with his Answers Thereto," in *Congregationalism in the Dutch Netherlands: The Rise and Fall of the English Congregational Classes, 1621-1635*, by Raymond Phineas Stearns (Chicago: American Society of Church History, 1940), pp. 105-113;

"A Thomas Hooker Sermon of 1638," edited by Everett Emerson, *Resources for American Literary Study*, 2 (Spring 1972): 75-89.

Bibliography:

Sargent Bush, Jr., "A Bibliography of the Published Writings of Thomas Hooker," in *Thomas Hooker: Writings in England and Holland, 1626-1633*, edited by George H. Williams, Norman Pettit, Winfried Herget, and Sargent Bush, Jr., Harvard Theological Studies, no. 28 (Cambridge: Harvard University Press, 1975), pp. 390-425.

References:

Sydney E. Ahlstrom, "Thomas Hooker—Puritanism and Democratic Citizenship," *Church History*, 32 (December 1963): 415-431;

Sargent Bush, Jr., "Four New Works by Thomas Hooker: Identity and Significance," *Resources for American Literary Study*, 4 (Spring 1974): 3-26;

Bush, "The Growth of Thomas Hooker's *The Poor Doubting Christian*," *Early American Literature*, 8 (Spring 1973): 3-20;

Bush, "Thomas Hooker and the Westminster Assembly," *William and Mary Quarterly*, 29 (April 1972): 291-300;

Bush, *The Writings of Thomas Hooker: Spiritual Adventure in Two Worlds* (Madison: University of Wisconsin Press, 1980);

Everett H. Emerson, "Thomas Hooker: The Puritan as Theologian," *Anglican Theological Review*, 49 (April 1967): 190-203;

Winfried Herget, "Preaching and Publication: Chronology and the Style of Thomas Hooker's Sermons," *Harvard Theological Review*, 65 (April 1972): 231-239;

Herget, "The Transcription and Transmission of the Hooker Corpus," in *Thomas Hooker: Writings in England and Holland, 1626-1633*, edited by George H. Williams, Norman Pettit, Winfried Herget, and Sargent Bush, Jr., Harvard Theological Studies, no. 28 (Cambridge: Harvard University Press, 1975), pp. 253-270;

Cotton Mather, "Piscator Evangelicus, or The Life of Mr. Thomas Hooker," in his *Johannes in Eremo* (Boston: Printed for & sold by Michael Perry, 1695); republished, with minor revisions, as "The Light of the Western Churches; or, The Life of Mr. Thomas Hooker," in his *Magnalia Christi Americana* (London: Printed for T. Parkhurst, 1702);

Norman Pettit, *The Heart Prepared: Grace and Conversion in Puritan Spiritual Life* (New Haven: Yale University Press, 1966), pp. 86-101;

Pettit, "Hooker's Doctrine of Assurance: A Critical Phase in New England Spiritual Thought," *New England Quarterly*, 47 (1974): 518-534;

Pettit, "Lydia's Conversion: An Issue in Hooker's Departure," Cambridge Historical Society *Proceedings*, 40 (1964-1966): 59-83;

Pettit, "The Order of Salvation in Thomas Hooker's Thought," in *Thomas Hooker: Writings in England and Holland, 1626-1633*, pp. 124-139;

Clinton Rossiter, "Thomas Hooker," *New England Quarterly*, 25 (December 1952): 459-488;

Frank Shuffelton, *Thomas Hooker, 1586-1647* (Princeton: Princeton University Press, 1977);

Keith L. Sprunger, "The Dutch Career of Thomas Hooker," *New England Quarterly*, 46 (March 1973): 17-44;

George L. Walker, *Thomas Hooker: Preacher, Founder, Democrat* (New York: Dodd, Mead, 1891);

George H. Williams, " 'Called by Thy Name, Leave us Not': The Case of Mrs. Joan Drake, a Formative Episode in the Pastoral Career of Thomas Hooker in England," *Harvard Library Bulletin*, 16 (1968): 111-128, 278-300;

Williams, "The Life of Thomas Hooker in England and Holland, 1586-1633," in *Thomas Hooker: Writings in England and Holland, 1626-1633*, pp. 1-35;

Williams, "The Pilgrimage of Thomas Hooker (1586-1647) in England, The Netherlands, and New England," *Bulletin of the Congregational Library*, 19 (October 1967/January 1968): 5-15, 9-13.

Papers:

Very few manuscripts in Hooker's hand have survived. Those known to be extant are in the Hutchinson Papers in the Massachusetts State Archives, Boston; the Winthrop Papers at the Massachusetts Historical Society, Boston; the Yale University Library; and the Connecticut Historical Society, Hartford.

William Hubbard

(circa 1621-14 September 1704)

Alasdair Macphail
Connecticut College

BOOKS: *The Happiness of a People In the Wisdome of their Rulers Directing And in the Obedience of their Brethren Attending Unto what Israel ought to do* (Boston: Printed by John Foster, 1676);

Narrative of the Troubles with the Indians in New-England, from the First Planting Thereof in the Year 1607, to this Present Year 1677... (Boston: Printed by John Foster, 1677); republished as *The Present State of New-England. Being a Narrative of the Troubles with the Indians in New-England, from the first Planting Thereof in the Year 1607, to this Present Year 1677*... (London: Printed for Tho. Parkhurst, 1677);

The Benefit of a Well-Ordered Conversation, As It Was Delivered in a Sermon Preached June 24th 1682 . . . (Boston: Printed by Samuel Green, 1684);

A Testimony, To The Order of the Gospel, In the Churches of New England. Left In The Hands of The Churches; By the Two Most Aged Ministers Of The Gospel; Yet Surviving In the Countrey, by Hubbard and John Higginson (Boston: Printed by T. Green, 1701);

A General History of New England from the Discovery to MDCLXXX, Collections of the Massachusetts Historical Society, second series 5-6 (1815).

In the course of a long and distinguished ministry in Ipswich, Massachusetts, the Reverend William Hubbard published two sermons, jointly authored a tract in defense of orthodox Congregational church polity, and wrote in quick succession two books of history. The first of these, *Narrative of the Troubles with the Indians in New-England* . . . (1677), deals primarily with King Philip's War of 1676-1677, the most recent New World crisis and a matter of grave curiosity on both sides of the Atlantic. This book was republished six times before Samuel Drake's "definitive" edition of 1865, and it was dubbed "an American classic" by Moses Coit Tyler in 1878. Hubbard's second and more ambitious work, *A General History of New England from the Discovery to MDCLXXX*, which remained unpublished until 1815 (133 years after Hubbard is thought to have finished it), purportedly illuminates the whole of New England's past but actually focuses only on the years from 1630 to the death of Governor John Winthrop in 1649. The work is pedestrian and, as scholars discovered in 1825, less than original. Yet ironically it was *A General History of New England*..., rather than his often-reprinted volume on King Philip's War, that established Hubbard's prominent place among the early historians of New England. The importance placed on *A General History of New England* . . . is due in part to the acknowledged reliance of such eighteenth-century New England historians as Cotton Mather, Thomas Prince, and

Thomas Hutchinson upon Hubbard's manuscript for their own histories of New England, all of which were highly successful publications.

Hubbard, after all, had been an original settler. As "a Compiler" of facts, he claimed in the preface to *A General History of New England*... that "he hath not wanted the best advantages to be acquainted with all such matters as may be thought were worthy to be communicated to posterity, either by the original manuscripts of such as had the managing of those affairs under their hands, or were related by the persons themselves concerned in them . . . and so were eyewitnesses thereof." It was not until the belated publication in 1825 of Governor John Winthrop's journal, *The History of New England*, that scholars came to appreciate that Hubbard's best "advantage" in the early 1680s had been his personal access to the late governor's version of events. James Savage, the editor of the 1825 edition of Winthrop's history, charged that "more than seven eighths" of Hubbard's work "is borrowed" from Winthrop. It should now be noted that this copying, often verbatim, contributed significantly to the authoritative tone which distinguishes *A General History of New England* . . . and had much enhanced Hubbard's reputation prior to 1825. Indirectly, therefore, his "precious relick" of a manuscript (as Thomas Prince once called it) was even more of a primary source of information than numerous historians had supposed. Its perspective is, indeed, that of the founders of the Bay Colony.

Listed as a thirteen-year-old on the roster of passengers aboard the *Defence*, which sailed from London on 1 July 1635 for Boston, where it landed on 8 October, Hubbard and his five siblings, ages four to twenty-two, came with their parents, William and Judeth Hubbard, from Little Clacton in Essex. There his father had been a husbandman, and as such he prospered in Ipswich, Massachusetts, where he accumulated many parcels of land and served his neighbors well before removing to Boston in 1662: he contributed one acre of land toward the founding of the Ipswich Grammar School in 1650 and was elected Deputy to the General Court (or legislature) of Massachusetts six times between 1638 and 1646. When William Hubbard, Sr., died in 1670, he was remembered for his commitment to learning and to the commonweal.

William, the second son and fourth child of Judeth and William Hubbard, graduated from Harvard College in the first class (1642) and may have practiced medicine for several years. About 1646 he married Margaret, the only daughter of the Reverend Nathaniel Rogers of Ipswich, whose fifth son, Ezekiel, had already married or was soon to marry Hubbard's older sister Margaret, the widow of Thomas Scott. Margaret and William Hubbard raised three children to adulthood. John, the eldest, was born in 1648; Nathaniel and Margaret had arrived before 3 July 1655, when all three children were left legacies in the nuncupative will of their maternal grandfather, then dying of "the epedemic cough."

Within a year of Nathaniel Rogers's death, William Hubbard entered the ministry. He was called to be Thomas Cobbett's colleague in the same church where Rogers had been pastor and where he himself was ordained as its teacher in 1658. There Hubbard remained for forty-five years with a succession of colleagues including his brother-in-law John Rogers, who, as an assistant, was responsible primarily for the Thursday lecture from 1656 until he became Harvard's fifth president in 1683. (Because of Rogers's sudden illness on Commencement Day, 1 July 1684—he died the next day—Hubbard obliged the overseers of Harvard College by officiating as acting president during the ceremonies.) John Rogers's son and namesake assisted Hubbard from 1686 until 1692, when he too was ordained and became Hubbard's colleague in Ipswich's First Church. William Hubbard relinguished his charge on 6 May 1703. According to John Eliot (1754-1813), "Certainly [he] was for many years the most eminent minister in the county of Essex, equal to any in the province for learning and candour; and superior to all his contemporaries as a writer." Scant wonder, then, that a grateful congregation voted Hubbard a retirement gift of £60, a generous sum equal to his annual stipend as agreed upon in 1656.

Like many clergymen Hubbard always found it difficult to make ends meet, and he may have been less provident than most of those who lived on fixed incomes. (Since his historical works were written during the years of what appears to have been his direst financial crisis, it is possible to speculate that Hubbard may have hoped to write his way to solvency.) Where his money went, however, remains something of a mystery. It is known that his wine cellar was amply stocked, but not so well supplied that he failed to miss the "more than five gallons" which his servant Peter Leycross and two accomplices carried off on their third, and final, nightly raid. Hubbard saw to it that the trio were whipped and fined for this offense and for previously stealing "his fat sheep" and selling them for personal gain. Losses of this sort no doubt contributed to the minister's woes, as did the additional burden of a guardianship, made official in 1678, of two of his older sister's children after she was widowed for the second time by the sudden death of Ezekiel Rogers on 5 July 1674. By then his own wife's £200 dowry must have been quite exhausted, and on 20 July Hubbard was driven to mortgage the greater part of his personal inheritance—that is, his house in Ipswich and two lots totaling forty-two acres—to John Richards of Boston, all for £324. Ten years later he was forced to part with the last seven acres of orchard, garden, and pasturelands that still remained from his father's legacy. In the interval between these two transactions Hubbard had prevailed upon John Hull, Boston goldsmith, diarist, and the colony's mint-master, to loan him £300. He had then defaulted on both the interest and the loan and owed Hull £347.5.0 when Hull wrote a dunning letter on 5 March 1680. Three years later Hull passed away. Two years after that his heirs were willing to settle amicably for £210. Eventually they got nothing at all and never sued—a response that redounds to their family's credit and God's honor, perhaps, but was much to Hubbard's advantage.

The townspeople of Ipswich were deeply upset when Hubbard, age seventy-three, chose to marry the thirty-seven-year-old widow of Samuel Pearce, Mary, who had been Hubbard's housekeeper. Her prior status, rather than his seniority, appears to have given the offense, "for though she was a serious, worthy woman, she was rather in the lower scenes of life, and not sufficiently fitted, as they thought, for that station." Be that as it may, she had entered this union with the proceeds of the sale on 10 April 1694 of her first husband's modest homestead.

When Hubbard died peacefully at home, having supped at a friend's house after the Thursday lecture on 14 September 1704, he left his widow in indigence. His people may have foreseen that embarrassing possibility the year before when they voted him the retirement gift, but it was not until March 1710 that they came specifically to his widow's aid by voting in a town meeting to add £20 to the town rates "for suppling Mrs. Hubbard in her distressed condition." Their concern previously had been with Hubbard's needs and, indirectly, with Ipswich's reputation as when, for example, the town voted in October 1704 to use the £20 from the sale of the Old Meeting House "towards ye defraying Mr. Hubbard's funeral." Only belatedly did the second Mrs. Hubbard win public sympathy.

Clearly the Hubbard household was inept in marshaling its financial resources. Yet the remarks of John Dunton, an English traveler who visited Hubbard in 1686 and was given "a very handsome Entertainment," suggest that the minister possessed an open, engaging personality: "The benefit of nature and the fatigue of study have equally contributed to his eminence . . . he freely communicates of his learning to all who have the happiness to share his converse. In a word, he is learned without ostentation and vanity, and gives all his productions such a delicate turn and grace, that the features and lineaments of the child make a clear discovery and distinction of the father; yet he is a man of singular modesty, of strict morals, and has done as much for the conversion of the Indians as most men in New-England." Even if we allow that most Puritans did little for the conversion of the Indians, this surely is the portrait of an approachable New Englander.

Less than exemplary, perhaps, in financial affairs, William Hubbard stood his ground firmly but inoffensively on public issues. A conscientious, calm, and courageous minister, he did not yield to every passion of the age or truckle to those who overstepped their legal authority. In the midst of the public hysteria over witchcraft in 1692, he wrote a strongly worded character reference for Mrs. Sarah Buckly of Salem, which evidently kept her accusers at bay. Five years previously during the constitutional crisis of the Dominion of New England, he had joined John Wise in Ipswich's defiance of the arbitrary tax levied by the royal governor Sir Edmund Andros. And long before that confrontation, he was one of fifteen ministers who protested publicly in 1671 against the General Court's blanket censure of "the generality of ministers" for alleged innovations and apostasy with respect to the founding of the Old South Church in Boston. Such visible stances go far to explain the high regard in which many members of the rising generation held William Hubbard. In old age he was, in Thomas Prince's words, one of the few "ancient Witnesses, who brought up the rear of the first generation that came from England." The respect of his contemporaries was just as forthcoming, as is evident by the invitation to preach the election sermon before the General Court in 1676. This honor quickly led to Hubbard's first publication, a sermon which the historian Perry Miller once singled out as "the finest prose of the decade, which rises to a lofty hymn to order."

In *The Happiness of a People In the Wisdome of their Rulers Directing And in the Obedience of their Brethren Attending Unto what Israel ought to do* (1676), Hubbard comes across as a politically orthodox Puritan who nevertheless inclines toward a moderate, tolerant, and optimistic point of view. He strongly reiterates the traditional call for more order in both church and state as the only way to quell dissension and restore harmony, but he also urges "Christian Prudence" upon the magistrates, whom he cautions against overzealousness and a counterproductive adherence to Old Testament precedents that no longer are appropriate. The times, he observes, with a keen sense of history's flow, are "curious" and changing. Disagreements abound precisely because "neither wise nor good men are all of one mind" about religious doctrine and other issues, and thus the magistrates must appreciate that "it can be no part of wisdome to be eager or rigorous" in the cause of uniformity. In a decidedly commonsense way he therefore seeks to sever the alleged continuity between Old Testament rulers and those of the Bible Commonwealth. Four decades earlier this undertaking would have required sustained, sophisticated, and (in Massachusetts) suspect biblical exegesis of the disjunctive typological sort in which Roger Williams alone was adept in the whole of New England. By comparison, Hubbard's approach is empirical rather than intellectual, and pragmatic rather than exegetical, so that his stance on intolerance has everything to do with the observed facts of the matter but little if anything to do with the matter of conscience which had so inspired Williams. Hubbard's sermon is a plea not for religious toleration but for a revision in the way a necessary intolerance should be demonstrated by the civil authorities. Thus one decade after Quakers were being executed in Massachusetts and at a time when Baptists and other dissenters were still the objects of Puritan harassment, Hubbard repeatedly advises only that "It is better sometimes to march about to gain the wind than to fall directly upon the Enemy." Given England's resentment over the colony's more direct approach in previous years, this advice was good indeed, except to the ears of diehards who supposed Massachusetts could defy the Crown indefinitely.

To Hubbard's calm admonition on behalf of moderation in 1676 is added his faith in the new generation of colonists then coming of age and, in some cases, gaining influence. This optimism is unusual. The collective and individual inferiority complex of the sons and grandsons of the "Founding Fathers" is known to have contributed to a pervasive sense of "degeneracy" by the end of the seventeenth century. Hubbard, it seems, was initially immune to its excesses. Whereas others prophesied doom on account of an alleged "declension" of piety associated with the liberalization of church polity with respect to baptism that is known as the Half-Way Covenant (1662), Hubbard refuses in this sermon to make a causal link between the shortcomings of the younger generation and his own admission that God "hath a controversy with New England." He attributes contemporary problems to "some secret heart evil" in the population at large and well beyond the rhetorical reach of mere civil or ecclesiastical "censure." He acknowledges the shortcomings but does not fall into step behind the doomsayers since he is convinced that there are "many hopeful buds springing up amongst the rising Generation." In summary, Hubbard expresses confidence that Massachusetts will hold to the Covenant (and prosper as well) provided the people practice "sweet subordination," provided the electorate votes into office only those who are "understanding of the times" both at home and in England, and provided these same magistrates recognize the fiduciary nature of that which qualifies them for high office—not their social standing so much as their "understanding," for understanding, too, is a God-given distinction. Thus even the "best and most prudent" magistrates are not independent agents but "instruments" of a higher will who at all times must be "guided by Divine Providence." The presumption is that such guidance will indeed be sought by all concerned with Massachusetts's welfare.

A comparable refreshing optimism is found in Hubbard's *The Benefit of a Well-Ordered Conversation . . .*, the 24 June 1682 fast-day sermon which he published in 1684 with his funeral discourse on Major General Denison and Denison's noticeably moderate farewell tract, *Irenicon . . .* . The sermon comes dangerously close to Arminianism in its main assertion: namely, that individuals can so order their lives according to God's precepts that he will "show" them salvation. "The way [of life] which we have designed to ourselves, and persist in," he declares, "will certainly in the issue bring us to the good which is promised, or the evil threatened in the Word of God." The choice clearly rests with individual men and women since God made "The way of his Precepts plain before his Servants" and endowed them with the rationality to follow his directions. Allowing that "it is as natural for man to breed himself trouble, as for sparks to fly upwards," Hubbard is nevertheless convinced that "it is the property of all rational Agents, to act for some end . . . [and] those who are guided by the principle of Reason can aim at no lower end, than God himself." Thus with right reason, faith, willpower, and "the affection to embrace and desire that way which is the most necessary and excellent," people can almost expect the salvation which "is from God only." Most of the sermon delineates the path of righteousness in typical fashion, but it ends with an unusually comforting declaration for those "real and sincere Christians" who still "know not how to perform." Says Hubbard, "if we be found sincere in our endeavours, our Saviour Christ will put the best construction upon our wayes. . . ."

Early in the eight years separating the publication of these two sermons, New England narrowly survived the ravages of King Philip's War, and Hubbard was inspired by this further proof of God's overruling providence to become a chronicler. Money problems may well have been an additional incentive, as he wrote his two histories in an uncharacteristic burst of literary activity. His work is representative of the age. In everything except the issue of causation, Hubbard's treatment of people and events is quintessentially Puritan. His *Narrative of the Troubles with the Indians in New-England*... is rich in invective toward the satanic enemies of God's elect. Throughout his discursive account of the fighting and in a supplemental chapter on the Pequot War of 1636-1637, Hubbard gives vent to all the ethnocentric bias that was common to settlers already convinced that it was not themselves but those "ungrateful, perfidiously False and Cruel" Indians who were the real aggressors. Similarly, the central point and didactic purpose of the book is orthodox: Indian atrocities are God's way of humbling New Englanders and teaching them true obedience. Thus their sore affliction is really his tender mercy since he reminds them with this scourge that their sole hope of earthly security and heavenly salvation lies with him.

That point of view was, of course, prerequisite for the Covenant theology of the day. Furthermore, this total reliance upon God rather than upon oneself or the community to overcome adversity required that the Puritan hero be passive—someone who waited for the Lord to reveal his will before springing into action, and then only as his temporal agent in the cosmic drama of redemptive history. Such are the personae in the version of the war which Hubbard recorded for the edification of posterity. His leading actors are merely the servants of the Lord. Consequently, the glory of their victory over the "savage miscreant," King Philip, belongs entirely to the King of Kings. The *Narrative of the Troubles with the Indians in New-England*... deviates from the normative portrayal of events only

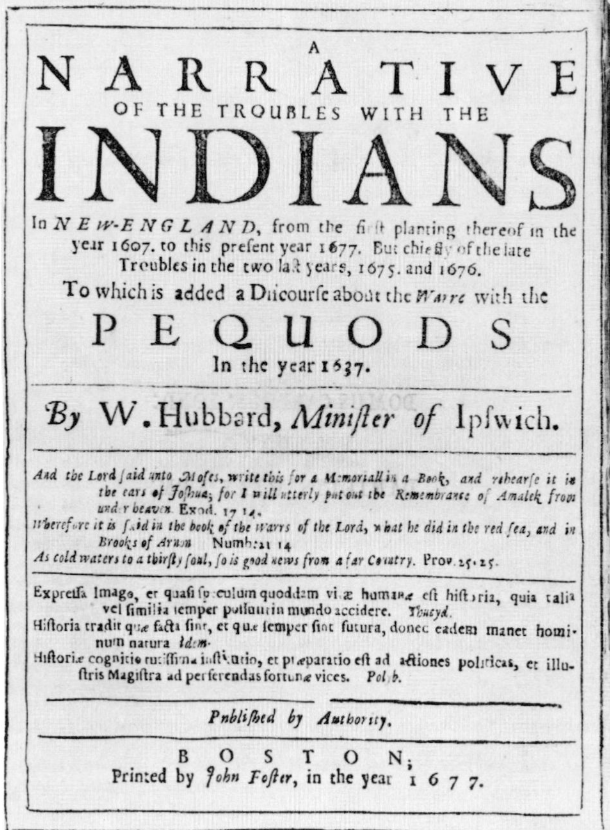
A
NARRATIVE
OF THE TROUBLES WITH THE
INDIANS
In *NEW-ENGLAND*, from the first planting thereof in the year 1607. to this present year 1677. But chiefly of the late Troubles in the two last years, 1675. and 1676.
To which is added a Discourse about the *Warre* with the
PEQUODS
In the year 1637.

By W. Hubbard, *Minister of* Ipswich.

And the Lord said unto Moses, write this for a Memoriall in a Book, and rehearse it in the ears of Joshua; for I will utterly put out the Remembrance of Amalek from under heaven. Exod. 17 14.
Wherefore it is said in the book of the warrs of the Lord, what he did in the red sea, and in Brooks of Arnon Numb: 21 14
As cold waters to a thirsty soul, so is good news from a far Coutry. Prov. 25. 25.

Expressa Imago, et quasi speculum quoddam vitæ humanæ est historia, quia talia vel similia semper possunt in mundo accidere. *Thucyd.*
Historia tradit quæ facta sint, et quæ semper sint futura, donec eadem manet hominum natura *Idem.*
Historiæ cognitio rectissima institutio, et præparatio est ad actiones politicas, et illustris Magistra ad perferendas fortunæ vices. *Polyb.*

Published by Authority.

BOSTON;
Printed by *John Foster*, in the year 1677.

Title page for Hubbard's account of the Puritans' relationship with the Indians (John Carter Brown Library, Brown University)

with respect to the imputed cause behind minor developments and isolated incidents in the war. The grand design behind New England's travail is God's alone, but still, the author notes, "Time and Chance hath strangely interposed to the prolonging of our Miseries." Comments of this sort suggest a mind groping for a new perspective, for a way of enfolding a natural interpretation of mundane incidents within the larger fabric of the doctrine of providence. Hubbard was openly exploring the boundaries of orthodoxy when he suggested a role for accident in the affairs of God's chosen people, and not all who were alert to this departure in his first book would have approved. Herein, one suspects, lay part of the problem he encountered when the time came to publish his second, and larger, manuscript.

The genesis of this work remains a bit obscure. Hubbard probably began to compile his notes for *A General History of New England from the Discovery to MDCLXXX* soon after the colony's licensers permitted the publication of his first work of history. He or his friends then approached the legislature for a sizable commission to be paid in advance, it seems, of the book's completion. On 11 June 1680, the General Court of Massachusetts set up a committee headed by Governor Simon Bradstreet to "peruse" the work and "make returne of their opinion thereof to the next session, that the Court may then, as they shall then judge meete, take order for the impression [printing] thereof." No commission was yet forthcoming, and two years passed before the Court again took up this matter. On 11 October 1682 it was ordered: "Whereas it hath been thought necessary and a duty incumbent on us to take due notice of all occurrences and passages of God's Providence towards the people of this jurisdiction since their first arrival in these parts, which may remain to posterity, and that the Rev. Wm. Hubbard hath taken pains to compile a History of this nature, which the court doth with thankfulness acknowledge, and as a manifestation thereof, do hereby order the treasurer to pay unto him the sum of fifty pounds in money, he transcribing fairly into a book that it may be more easily perused in order to the satisfaction of this Court." Evidently the hitch at this juncture was Hubbard's poor handwriting. The court was withholding his commission until the manuscript of more than 300 pages had been tidied up. Hubbard presumably busied himself in rendering a better copy during the next six months, but the legislators remained only partially satisfied. On 30 March 1683 they resolved that the "Treasurer pay him or his order half of the said sume as soone as money comes into his hands." Why they did not pay him the full commission or agree to publish the book remains conjectural. Current speculation is that Increase Mather's opposition was cause enough, in this critical decade, to suppress a work which embodied some ambivalence toward the belief that God's intervention even in mundane affairs alone determines their outcome. In the wake of the Indian war and at a time when the colony's charter, its social fabric, and its very purpose were in jeopardy (the charter was actually revoked in 1684), orthodox minds could not entertain a rational, natural explanation of events alongside the

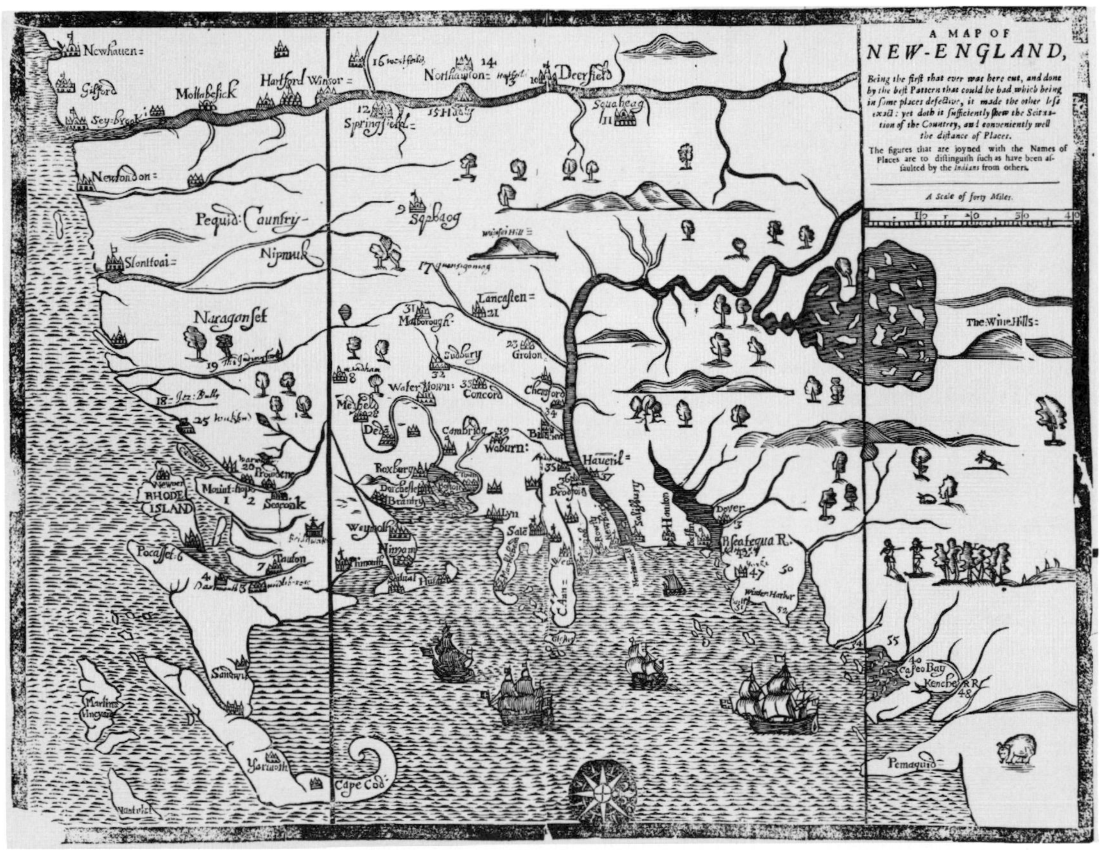

Map by John Foster that appeared in the Boston edition of Narrative of the Troubles with the Indians in New-England. *Because Foster had trouble reading Hubbard's poor handwriting, the White Hills are labeled the "Wine Hills." The map was corrected for the London edition (John Carter Brown Library, Brown University).*

supernatural one that was central to the Puritan's view of history. For what would it mean to be the chosen people if all secular history were not ultimately a manifestation of God's cosmic plan, or if all reality were not an emanation of the divine mind? The orthodox had no answer, but they were still in control of the legislature.

What the colonial lawmakers shunned in 1683 others preserved, and eventually *A General History of New England* . . . was published by the Massachusetts Historical Society in 1815. It was not, however, the original manuscript that went so belatedly to the printers, for that had been lost sometime in the eighteenth century. It was, instead, a copy which had been in the possession of Lieutenant Governor Thomas Hutchinson, the historian and Chief Justice, until the night of 26 August 1765 when the Boston mob sacked his home during the Stamp Act crisis. Tossed from a window along with other papers, this copy was retrieved from the mud by Hutchinson's neighbor, the Reverend Andrew Eliot, whose son gave it to the Library of the Massachusetts Historical Society in about 1791. Because of this abuse at the hands of the mob, the copy was incomplete and defective at both the beginning and the end of Hubbard's book. The society therefore tried to obtain access to a second copy of the original manuscript, one that had been owned by Judge Peter Oliver, author of the most telling (but only recently published) Tory account of the Revolution, *The Origin and Progress of the American Rebellion* (1967), and a participant in the exodus of Loyalists for England in 1776. Oliver's heirs would not comply in 1814, so the society was constrained to use the American copy of *A General History of New England* . . . for the first printing in 1815. When William Thaddeus Harris edited a second edition in 1848, it remained difficult to tell just how much was lost in the missing leaves before page 9 and after page 338 of Hutchinson's copy. There were, moreover, many places in the text where the handwriting was illegible or obscure. With useful notes appended, Harris's edition became the more informative and authoritative version of the original manuscript. The Arno Press edition of 1972 is a reprint of the Harris edition lodged in the State Historical Society of Wisconsin. That it is no more than that testifies to the diminished reputation of William Hubbard as a historian ever since James Savage pointed out the derivative nature of *A General History of New England* . . . in 1825, for the Arno Press could have included the missing pages, which came to light in the 1870s.

What Peter Oliver's English descendants had been reluctant to share early in 1814, when the War of 1812 was not yet over, they provided the Massachusetts Historical Society after the Civil War. The society's *Proceedings* of 1878 described this happy "opportunity of perfecting" the 1815 and 1848 editions of Hubbard's posthumous work. The title page and short preface, "by far too interesting to be lost," were now declared available, and it was also noted that "Of the text, less is shown to have been wanting in the beginning of the Society's printed volume than had been supposed." Charles Dean, for the society, then had the nine pages of the preface as well as the other previously missing or damaged pages printed in 1875 as a "replacement part" to be inserted in the 100 copies of the 1815 edition still in stock. Other copies of this insert were sent to major libraries; yet it did not come to the attention of more recent bibliographers. Consequently, no definitive edition of *A General History of New England* . . . has been published, and it is unlikely that any will be forthcoming until there is a revival of interest in the work of William Hubbard. His history of New England will do little in that regard. In addition to its lack of originality and the thinness of its discussion of what ensued after Governor Winthrop's death in 1649, *A General History of New England* . . . suffers from structural defects and stylistic inadequacies. The prose falls short of what Hubbard achieved in his two published sermons, and neither of his histories supports the claim, so often heard before 1825, that he was an inspired and polished writer. In his hands the mytho-historical depiction of New England as the New Israel is perfectly conventional. Indeed, his wayfaring / seafaring imagery (for example, settlers = pilgrims; magistrates = helmsmen) is such standard fare in the spiritual biographies of the age as to be a form of literary cliché. Thus in retrospect it is tempting to see some literary justice in the General Court's decision in 1683 to pay Hubbard only half of his commission and not to authorize publication. On the other hand it was meet, in 1814, for the legislature of the Commonwealth of Massachusetts to agree to take 600 copies "at two dollars for each volume" of the tardily published book.

How Hubbard took the personal disappointments of 1683 remains unknown, but an optimistic disposition in the sermons he published both before and after he tried his hand at writing history has already been noted. During the tumultuous years from 1676 to 1682 he was wont, it seems, to put the best possible construction on the age in which he lived. Despite his conventional reference in *A General History of New England* . . . to the era of

John Winthrop as "the golden age," the Ipswich minister had not yet begun to doubt the future or those who would fulfill it. In the 1670s while watching young men muster alongside their elders to do battle with the Indians, he had caught a glimpse of what many another clergyman failed to believe: the fine potential of "the rising generation, on whom that blessed promise, Isa: 44.3 begins to take place, 'I will pour my spirit upon thy seed, and my Blessing upon thy offspring.' Is there not found in them," he asked rhetorically in 1676, "a great readiness to give up themselves to the work and service of their generation[,] Such as have offered themselves willingly . . . to the death."

The ready optimism that distinguishes the tone and even the theology of Hubbard's published sermons is nowhere evident in his last work. Written jointly with John Higginson of Salem, *A Testimony, To The Order of the Gospel, In the Churches of New England. Left In The Hands of The Churches; By the Two Most Aged Ministers Of The Gospel; Yet Surviving In the Countrey* (1701) is filled with foreboding and reproach. It is a defense of the New England way of Congregationalism as delineated in 1648 by the Cambridge Platform of Church Discipline. The authors decry Solomon Stoddard's defection from orthodoxy and, by extension, the desertion of all who support both the Presbyterian tendencies and the misuse of the Lord's Supper as a device to promote conversion—the two hallmarks of Stoddardeanism. With what amounts to a filiopietistic regard for the insight and inspiration of the first generation of New England ministers, the authors assert that those who follow in the footsteps of the founders are far less qualified to judge on matters of church polity. Consequently, "we that are Old Men must confess ourselves Ashamed, when we see after what manner some of our Youth, have expressed and behaved themselves and with what Scoffs they have assaulted the Order of the Gospel, in some things lately Published, and scattered about the Countrey." This defection, the two ancients believe, is the undoing of New England because it threatens piety itself, the sine qua non of Christian fellowship and cohabitation: "It is too observable, that the Power of Godliness, is exceedingly Decaying and Expiring in the Countrey; and one great point in the Decay of the Power of Godliness, is mens growing weary of the Congregational Church-Discipline, which is evidently Calculated for to maintain it." The authors then expand upon the presumed connection between church polity and public piety in order to promote the only cure for what ails New England that their logic will allow. Their prognosis for a full recovery is, at best, guardedly optimistic: "If that Congregational Church-Discipline were more thoroughly and vigorously kept alive, even by those that make profession of it, it might be hoped, that the Lord would Sanctify it, for the Revival of all Godliness in the Land."

This work was Hubbard's farewell message. His last memorable action, however, was the petition which he, John Rogers, John Wise, and nine other Essex County ministers forwarded to the General Court in July 1703 to clear formally the names of all who had been accused of witchcraft a decade earlier and who still suffered, technically, under legal disabilities. He died the following year at the age of eighty-three, and his townspeople had to defray the cost of his funeral and pay later for the support of his widow. Little wonder, then, that his reputation locally was not what it formerly had been. As John Eliot sadly recorded, "a generation in the town of Ipswich rose up, who only were witnesses of his infirmities," and, Eliot generalized, "I believe in every instance where a young minister grows old, and people are put to expense to maintain him, they will treat him with neglect."

References:

Charles E. Banks, *The Planters of the Commonwealth* (Boston: Houghton Mifflin, 1930);

John Dunton, "Extracts From the Life, etc. of John Dunton," *Collections of the Massachusetts Historical Society*, second series 2 (1814): 97-124;

Dunton, *John Dunton's Letters from New-England* (Boston: Printed by T. R. Marion & Son for the Prince Society, 1867);

John Eliot, *A Biographical Dictionary* (Boston: Printed by Oliver for Cushing & Appleton of Salem, 1809);

Emory Elliott, *Power And The Pulpit in Puritan New England* (Princeton: Princeton University Press, 1975);

"Genealogical Memoir of the Family of Rev. Nathaniel Rogers," by a Descendant, *New England Historical and Genealogical Register*, 5, 2 (1851): 105-152;

David D. Hall, *The Faithful Shepherd: A History of the New England Ministry in the Seventeenth Century* (Chapel Hill: University of North Carolina Press, 1972);

Abraham Hammatt, *The Hammatt Papers: Early Inhabitants of Ipswich, Massachusetts, 1633-1700* (Baltimore: Genealogical Publishing, 1980);

John Hull, *The Diaries of John Hull, Mint-Master and Treasurer of the Colony of Massachusetts Bay* (Boston: Printed by J. Wilson & Son, 1857), in *Archaeologia Americana,* 3 (Worcester: American Antiquarian Society, 1857), pp. 109-316;

Perry Miller, *The New England Mind: From Colony to Province* (Cambridge: Harvard University Press, 1953);

Miller, *The New England Mind: The Seventeenth Century* (New York: Macmillan, 1939);

Samuel Eliot Morison, *The Puritan Pranaos: Studies in the Intellectual Life of New England in the Seventeenth Century* (New York: New York University Press, 1936);

Kenneth B. Murdoch, "William Hubbard and the Providential Interpretation of History," *Proceedings of the American Antiquarian Society,* 52 (1941): 15-37;

F. E. Oliver, "Prefatory Note to the Recently recovered pages of Hubbard's History," *Proceedings of the Massachusetts Historical Society: 1878,* 16 (1879): 12-13, 38-41;

Nathaniel B. Shurtlett, ed., *Records of the Governor and Company of the Massachusetts Bay in New England,* 5 volumes (Boston: W. White, 1853-1854);

John L. Sibley, *Biographical Sketches of Graduates of Harvard University,* volume 1 (Cambridge: Charles William Sever, 1873);

Thomas F. Waters, *Ipswich in the Massachusetts Bay Colony* (Ipswich: Ipswich Historical Society, 1905).

John James

(circa 1633-1729)

Robert W. Hill
Clemson University

BOOKS: "On the Decease of the Religious & Honourable Jno Haynes Esqr, Who made his Exit off the Stage of this world—1713," in Connecticut Historical Society *Annual Report* (1908): 20-21;

"Of John Bunyans Life &c," in *The First Century of New England Verse,* edited by Harold S. Jantz (Worcester, Mass.: American Antiquarian Society, 1944), p. 150.

John James, born in London, immigrated to America in about 1657 and served as pastor first in Derby, Connecticut, and then in Brookfield, Massachusetts. He later became the first minister of Haddam, Connecticut, where he remained from 1686 until 1689; and in 1693 he was called to Wethersfield, Connecticut, where, as well as being minister, he served as town clerk and schoolmaster. Although, according to Harold Jantz, James stood "somewhat apart from the university group" and was "eccentric and rather unstable," he was nonetheless awarded an honorary M.A. from Harvard College in 1710.

James's body of poetry is small, part of it found only in manuscript, written in the margins and on blank pages of a 1616 edition of the poetry of William Drummond. One work, *On the Death of the very Learned, Pious and Excelling Gershom Bulkley Esq. M.D.* (1714) was published as a broadside by Timothy Green in New London. Other surviving manuscripts include "On the Decease of the Religious & Honourable Jno Haynes Esqr, Who made his Exit off the Stage of this world—1713"; elegies on an unnamed infant who died in 1696; on Grace Nichols, who died in 1702; and on Esther Buckinghame and Esther Beaumont, a mother and daughter who died in 1702. An epitaph on Noadiah Russell is mentioned in the 1908 *Annual Report* of the Connecticut Historical Society (some scholars believe that it was published).

Probably James's best-known work is the taut, ten-line memorial "Of John Bunyans Life &c," anthologized in Harold S. Jantz's *The First Century of New England Verse* (1944) and Harrison T. Meserole's *Seventeenth-Century American Poetry* (1968). Characteristically, the poem displays James's use of images from alchemy, but here the allusion to Bunyan's occupation as a tinker reinforces the

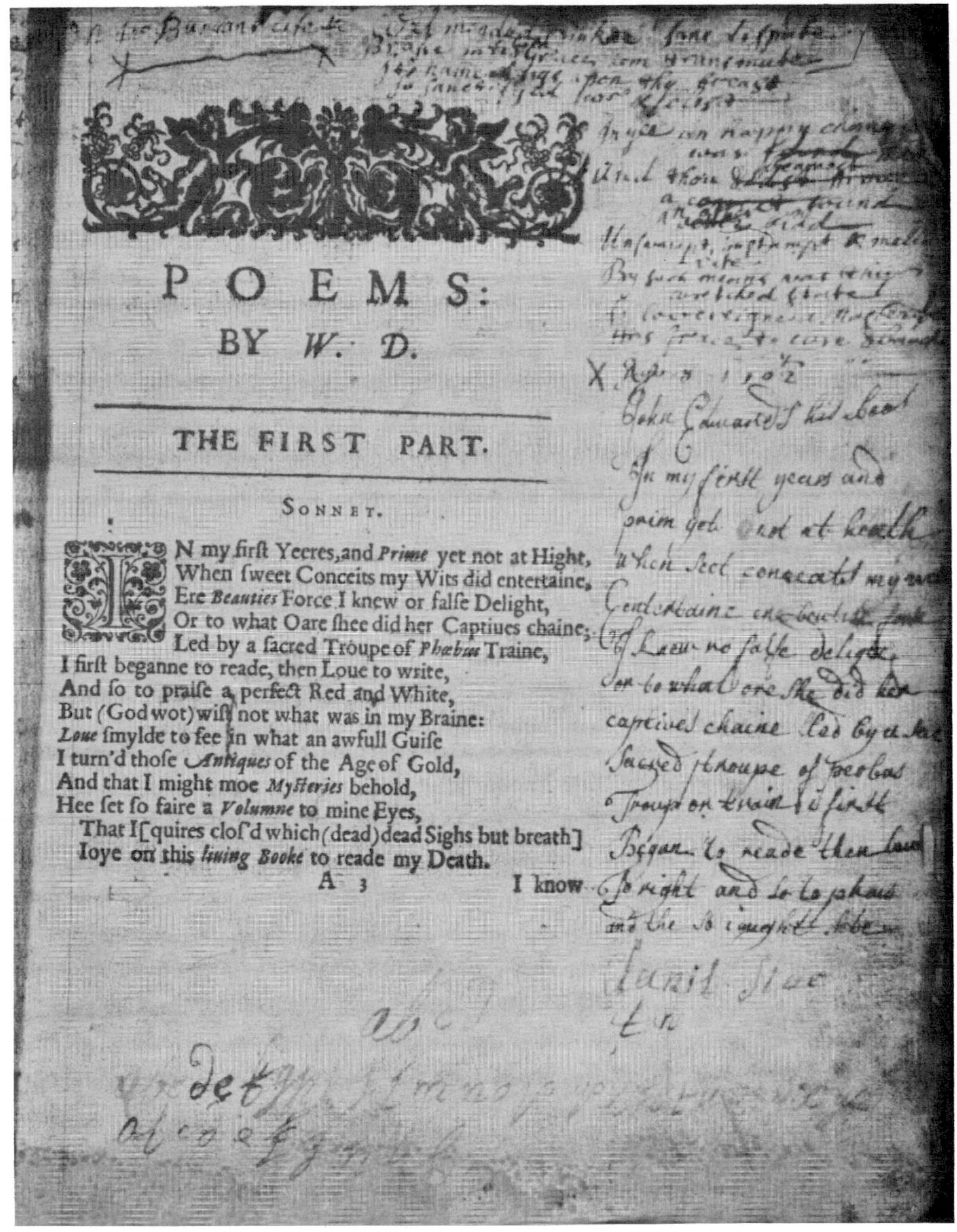

POEMS:

BY *W. D.*

THE FIRST PART.

SONNET.

IN my firſt Yeeres,and *Prime* yet not at Hight,
When ſweet Conceits my Wits did entertaine,
Ere *Beauties* Force I knew or falſe Delight,
Or to what Oare ſhee did her Captiues chaine,
Led by a ſacred Troupe of *Phœbus* Traine,
I firſt beganne to reade, then Loue to write,
And ſo to praiſe a perfect Red and White,
But (God wot) wiſt not what was in my Braine:
Loue ſmylde to ſee in what an awfull Guiſe
I turn'd thoſe *Antiques* of the Age of Gold,
And that I might moe *Myſteries* behold,
Hee ſet ſo faire a *Volumne* to mine Eyes,
That I [quires cloſ'd which (dead) dead Sighs but breath]
Ioye on this *liuing Booke* to reade my Death.

A 3 I know

A page from James's copy of the 1616 large paper edition of William Drummond's poems, with James's marginalia (Harris Collection of American Poetry and Plays, Brown University)

metallurgical concreteness. As the force of Grace moved upon the "brass" of Bunyan's life to make it gold, God's hammer fashioned of Bunyan "an other blad / Unswaupt, instampt and meliorate"; that is, he is redeemed (and not to be swapped), stamped or engraved with the sign of grace, and made better, as base metal may be transformed into precious and as amorphous substance may be made into art.

Papers:

The only extant copy of James's broadside elegy for Gershom Bulkley is at the Boston Athenaeum. James's copy of William Drummond's poems is in the Harris Collection at Brown University, and the manuscript for his elegy on John Haynes is at the Connecticut Historical Society.

Edward Johnson

Ursula Brumm
Freie Universität Berlin

BIRTH: In or near Canterbury, England, circa 16 September 1598 to William and Susan Porredge Johnson.

MARRIAGE: Circa 1618 to Susan Munnter; children: Edward, William, George, Susan, William, Martha, Matthew, John.

DEATH: Woburn, Massachusetts, 23 April 1672.

BOOKS: *Good news from New-England . . . ,* attributed to Johnson (London: Printed by Matthew Simmons, 1648);

A History of New-England. From the English Planting in the Yeere 1628. Until the Yeere 1652 . . . (London: Printed for N. Brooke, 1654); republished as *Wonder-working Providence of Sions Saviour in New-England . . . ,* edited by William Frederick Poole (Andover, Mass.: Warren F. Draper, 1867); republished as *Johnson's Wonder-working Providence, 1628-1651,* edited by J. Franklin Jameson (New York: Scribners, 1910).

Edward Johnson was known to his contemporaries in the Massachusetts Bay Colony as a man of many skills. A respected member of the commonweal, experienced in the tasks which were essential to the young colony's survival, he was one of the capable and energetic rank-and-file immigrants who helped to build the colony and who, by their dedication, insured its growth and success as a self-administrative commonwealth. To some of his contemporaries he was also known as the author of the first published account of the early history of New England.

Edward Johnson was born in England as the son of a parish clerk and was baptized at St. George's Church, Canterbury, on 16 or 17 September 1598. Around 1618 he married Susan Munnter, with whom he had eight children, one of whom died in infancy. He owned property in and around Canterbury, and it appears that in England he was engaged in trading and in military activities, in which he attained the rank of captain. He put this experience to good use in America. In the Massachusetts records his name appears with his military rank or with the title Mr., an indication that he was considered a man of good standing.

When in 1636 Johnson embarked from England with his wife, seven children, and three servants, he was registered as a joiner (as he was also in his home parish), although he may at the time have been a carpenter and shipbuilder, who, like other emigrants of the time, downgraded his professional skills in order to escape detention. This journey was Johnson's second and final passage to New England. His first had been in 1630 with John Winthrop and his group, perhaps even on Winthrop's flagship, the *Arbella.* The first visit was a short one: Johnson was admitted a freeman in 1631 but did not join a church. He was licensed to do some trading with the Indians and probably returned to England in 1631.

While it seems that on his first visit Johnson was mainly interested in trading, he returned in 1636 with the intention of becoming a settler. When Johnson arrived at Boston in 1636, the town was disturbed by the Antinomian controversy. He moved to Charlestown with his family, where he acquired property but did not join the church. In 1640 he was appointed to a committee formed for erecting a new church and town at Woburn. (He seems to have planned for some time to participate in the settling of a town.) The founding of Woburn enabled Johnson to apply his abilities and energy both to his own advantage and to the common good, and he turned out to be a major force in the development of the new community.

During the rest of his life, for more than thirty years, Johnson was active in the affairs of the town of Woburn and of the Massachusetts Bay Colony at large. As one of the original founders of Woburn, he was appointed town clerk and served his community as selectman (at one point he was their chairman), as militia captain, and as deputy to the General Court, which appointed him frequently to important committees. He was thus engaged in such diverse duties as surveying boundaries and the supervision and inspection of munitions and fortifications. Also

An excerpt from Johnson's records for the town of Woburn

he was an active member of a committee appointed "for perfecting the laws" of the young colony. It is evident that his legal knowledge and good sense were highly regarded, for he was subsequently called to serve in other such matters. In Woburn he was appointed as one of the three "Commissioners for ending small causes," that is, cases involving petty quarrels which did not exceed the value of twenty (later forty) shillings. Early in his American career, Johnson attained the reputation of being proficient in difficult missions. In 1643 he was sent with two other officers and forty men to apprehend the "blasphemous" and "seditious" Samuel Gorton and his company of dissenters. When after the restoration royal interference in colonial affairs was foreseen, Johnson was made a member of a committee which was to consider the problems attached to the colony's patent and privileges. He was, in short, throughout his American existence, a prominent citizen, a public servant highly respected for his abilities, dedication, and achievements.

No portrait of Edward Johnson is known to have survived, yet his handwriting survives in the records he kept as recorder or town clerk of Woburn, two sections of which are reproduced in Poole's 1867 edition of *Wonder-working Providence*. . . . In giving a "True Relation of the proceedings" of erecting a church and town at Woburn, Johnson illustrated his literary skill by including a birthday poem on the new town:

Its Rare to see how this poore Towne did rise
By weakest means, two [too] weake in great ons [ones'] eys.
And sure it is that mettells cleere exstraction
Had never share in this Poore Towns erextion;
Without which metall and sum fresh suplys
Patrons conclud she never upp wold rise.
If ever she mongst ladys have a station,
Say twas ffrom Parentes, not har education,
And now conclud the lords owne hand it wase
That with weak means did bring this work to pass,
Not only Towne but Sistor church to ade
Which out of dust and Ashes now is had.
Then all Inhabit woburne Towne, stay make
The lord, not means, of all you undertake.

His report indicates that he was serving not only as a recorder but also as an active participant in the practical labors of establishing a town: "Edward Johnson was appointed Recorder, who drew a plot of the town," he reports. It is more than likely that he had also his share in formulating the strict rules of "orders" which all future inhabitants of the town had to subscribe to.

Johnson was the author of one, perhaps even of two works published anonymously around the middle of the seventeenth century. His authorship of *Wonder-working Providence . . .* is firmly established; some scholars believe that he also wrote *Good news from New-England . . .* (1648), yet in this case his authorship remains uncertain.

Wonder-working Providence . . . illuminates Johnson's personality and his convictions and makes him an important if somewhat controversial Puritan writer. It was published in London in 1654 as *A History of New-England*; six years later, under circumstances still obscure, it was inserted into a series of tracts published under the title *America Painted to the Life* and attributed falsely to Sir Ferdinando Gorges, an archenemy of the American Puritans. It seems certain that the title *A History of New-England* was chosen by the printer or publisher, while Johnson considered the title of his work to be *Wonder-working Providence of Sions Saviour in New-England,* the title used in the running heads and often repeated in the text. It is under this title that modern editions of the work have appeared.

Johnson's authorship was established beyond doubt by William Frederick Poole, who in 1867 edited the book and included a lengthy introduction in which he provided abundant proof of Johnson's authorship and a thoroughly researched biographical sketch. Although Johnson is not known to have acknowledged his authorship, a tradition about it is reported to have existed in New England. There is also much internal evidence, which reflects Johnson's interest in military affairs and in the founding of churches and towns. The events he is known to have participated in are described in detail, above all the founding of the church and town of Woburn, which is made to stand as a model "Of the manner of planting Towns and Churches in N.E. . . ," and is reported with particular familiarity and engagement.

Wonder-working Providence . . ., the first full-scale historical report of the early years in New England published before Cotton Mather's *Magnalia Christi Americana* (1702), was known to, and used by, such early New England historians as John Josselyn, Increase Mather, William Hubbard, Joshia Scottow, and Cotton Mather. After *Wonder-working Providence . . .* was edited by James Savage and published in five volumes of the *Collections of the Massachusetts Historical Society* (1814-1819),

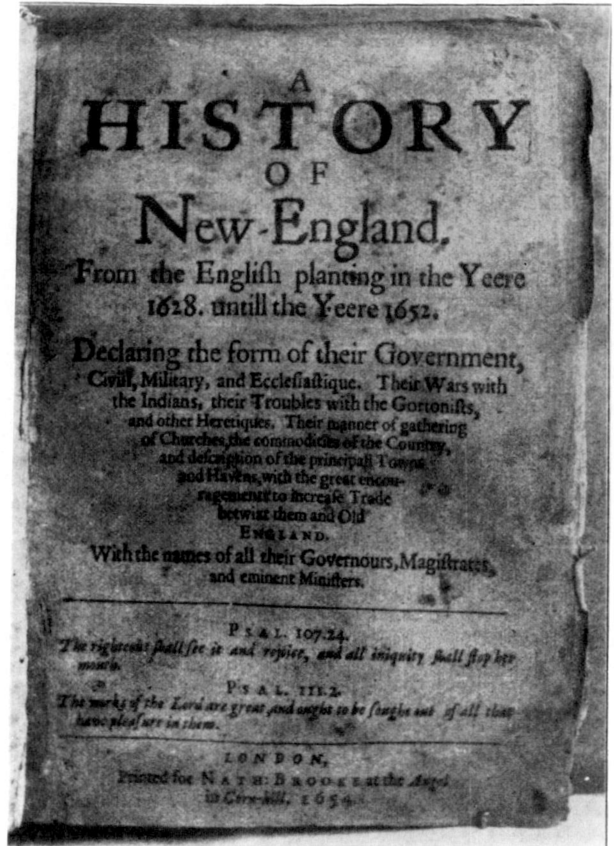

A
HISTORY
OF
New-England.
From the English planting in the Yeere 1628. untill the Yeere 1652.
Declaring the form of their Government, Civill, Military, and Ecclesiastique. Their Wars with the Indians, their Troubles with the Gortonists, and other Heretiques. Their manner of gathering of Churches, the commodities of the Country, and description of the principall Towns and Havens, with the great encouragement to increase Trade betwixt them and Old England.
With the names of all their Governours, Magistrates, and eminent Ministers.

Psal. 107.24.
The righteous shall see it and rejoice, and all iniquity shall stop her mouth.

Psal. 111.2.
The works of the Lord are great, and ought to be sought out of all that have pleasure in them.

LONDON,
Printed for Nath: Brooke at the *Angel* in *Corn-hill*, 1654.

Title page for the book Johnson called Wonder-working Providence of Sions Saviour in New-England. *The title for this first edition was probably supplied by the printer or the publisher.*

Johnson was quoted, cited, or commented upon by such major New England writers as Emerson (in his "Historical Discourse," the speech he gave at the bicentennial celebration of the founding of Concord in 1836), Thoreau (in *Week on the Concord and Merrimack Rivers* and in *Walden*), and Whittier (in *Margaret Smith's Journal*). He was probably known to Hawthorne, who seems to have used Johnson's history as a source for some of his stories.

Edward Johnson is a truly Puritan and American phenomenon: a seventeenth-century writer who was neither a clergyman nor university-educated, yet who was not afraid to express his convictions in a forceful way. His *Wonder-working Providence . . .* is an interesting, even fascinating book, though its hotheaded rhetoric and its high-flying religious visions make at times difficult reading. Although occasionally inaccurate in regard to dates or numbers, it is a valuable source for the social, economic, and intellectual history of New England, a report about the first two and one-half decades of the New England settlement (1628-1651), which is framed by passionate religious convictions, bold appeals, proclamations, and fervent admonitions. As an active member of the New England venture and as a man who was vitally concerned with the success of the undertaking, Johnson wrote with deep involvement and concern. It seems likely that reports spread in England by enemies of the American Puritans and criticism from Presbyterians in England had challenged him to defend the New England system and proclaim its achievements to skeptical English readers. *Wonder-working Providence* ... displays Johnson's practical mind and energy, yet it also demonstrates that his energy was essentially visionary: the author of *Wonder-working Providence* . . . testifies to the spiritual force behind the colonization of New England.

Most of Johnson's early interpreters disapproved of what they considered the "crudities" or the "bombast" of his style; the jogging and chopped meter of the poems which Johnson inserted into his narrative suggested to them that, as a carpenter and a captain, he used the pen as he would a gun, a sword, an adze, or a broadax. Johnson was censured by his descendant J. Franklin Jameson, the editor of the 1910 edition of *Wonder-working Providence* . . . , who saw in him "a striking example of the hot zealotry, the narrow partisanship, the confident dogmatism, which characterized so much of Puritanism." To some liberal historians and critics of the nineteenth and early-twentieth century, Johnson's stern rebuke of Anne Hutchinson and other sectarians proved him to be a Puritan "zealot"—yet these critics had no concept of how zealous and hotly partisan the sectarians themselves were in their beliefs. Johnson was certainly partisan and much vexed by these "erronists," as he called them. In chapter forty-one of book one he gives a specimen of his narrative talent and also of his caustic humor when he describes how the Antinomian followers of Anne Hutchinson operated among the colonial populace: "Come along with me, sayes one of them, i'le bring you to a Woman that Preaches better Gospell then any of your black-coates that have been at the Ninneversity, a Woman of another kinde of spirit, who hath had many Revelations of things to come, and for my part, saith hee, I had rather hear such a one that speakes from the meere motion of the spirit, without any study at all, then any of your learned Scollers, although they may be fuller of Scripture (I) [ay] and admit they may speake by the helpe of the spirit, yet the other goes beyond them." Johnson was indeed a stalwart Puritan who wholly supported the orthodox clergy and the administration of the Massachusetts Bay Company. He was deeply worried by the portents of religious heterodoxy or by any deviation from what he considered the truth of Christian faith. His concern about sectarianism is apparent throughout *Wonder-working Providence* . . . , and Johnson expresses graphically the fear of many Puritan immigrants that they, who had given up their status and belongings in England and had left friends and relatives behind, might find in the New World the same confusions and problems they had hoped to escape.

Internal evidence suggests that Johnson began to write his book in 1649 and finished it, with additions and alterations, in 1651. Book one mainly concerns the seven years from 1630 to 1637, book two the next seven years, from 1637 to 1644, and book three the last seven years, of which Johnson writes toward the end: "and that as this in three seven years is comprised, though very weakly, in this little book, there's in one seven years would require volumes. . . ."

Wonder-working Providence . . . begins with a kind of prologue of six chapters which contain a proclamation: Christ summons his people to attend to their "commission," and, "This Proclamation being audibly published through the Ile of Great Brittaine by sundry Herraulds, which Christ had prepared for that end: the rumour ran through Cities, Townes and Villages. . . ." It is in these religious visions that Johnson's rhetoric takes its most flamboyant strides and his bent toward military pomp and circumstance asserts itself. Yet the military embellishments are well chosen to express the urgency and the strictness of Christ's orders, which are conveyed with detailed and precise instructions. The meaning of this "commission" is spiritual as well as practical, its practical significance being derived from the conviction that "the Reader may behold Government both in Churches and Common-wealth, to be an institution of the Lord, and much available through his blessing for the accomplishment of his promises to his people." The founding of churches and towns and the establishment of rightful government in them is the fulfillment of Christ's commission, a religious as well as a political mission, an endeavour "to keepe the truths of Christ pure and unspotted." Descriptions of the founding of the first thirty churches in New England and of almost as many towns, as well as the establishment of a government for the colony, are the main component of *Wonder-working Providence* . . . , and Johnson reports these events with clarity and apparent enjoyment. Speaking as a surveyor and an expert in the business of settlement, he notes a town's location, the lay of the land, the availability of timber and springs with potable water. He reports how a town is laid out, how many families live there, and how much cattle they own, and also, quite often, how "comly and faire" a town presents itself with its fine houses, beautiful gardens and orchards, its pleasant marketplace and meeting-house.

Wonder-working Providence . . . also reveals Johnson to be a man of feeling, of kindness and nobility. Of the Indians he speaks with fairness, sometimes even with compassion, as when he reports the ravages done by smallpox. We do have some unique accounts by Johnson which indicate what was involved in settling New England. Among them are dramatic descriptions, with dialogue, of the sorrow of leave-taking before the settlers embarked for the New World and of the dangers, anxieties, and hardships of the sea voyage. Johnson pays tribute to the sufferings endured by the women: "Here also might you see weakly Women, whose hearts have trembled to set foote in Boate, but now imboldened to venter through these tempestuous Seas with their young Babes, whom they nurture up with their Breasts, while their bodies are tossed on the tumbling Waves; also others whose Wombes could not containe their fruit, being ready for the Worlds-light, travailed and brought forth upon this depthlesse Ocean in this long Voyage, lively and strong Children yet living, and like to prove succeeding Instruments in the Hands of Christ, for furthering this worke. . . ."

Chapter thirty-six of book one describes *"the laborious worke Christ's people have in planting this wilderness, set forth in the building the Towne of Concord, being the first in-land Towne"*: "the land they purchase of the Indians, and with much difficulties traveling through unknowne woods, and through watery scrampes [swamps], they discover the fitnesse of the place, sometimes passing through the Thickets, where their hands are forced to make way for their bodies passage, and their feete clambering over the crossed Trees, which when they missed they sunke into an uncertaine bottome in water, and wade up to the knees, tumbling sometimes higher and sometimes lower, wearied with this toile, they at end of this meete with a scorching plaine, yet not so plaine, but that the ragged Bushes scratch their legs fouly, even to wearing their stockings to their bare skin in two or three houres; if they be not otherwise well defended with Bootes, or Buskings, their flesh will be torne: (that some being forced to passe on without further provision) have had the bloud trickle downe at every step, and in the time of Summer the Sun casts such a reflecting heate from the sweet Ferne, whose scent is very strong so that some herewith have beene nere fainting, although very able bodies to undergoe much travell. . . ." This passage is only part of a precise and compassionate description which impressively documents the frontier experience.

Book three of *Wonder-working Providence* . . . contains a number of poems which are more carefully executed than most of the biographical poetic tributes in earlier parts. They are elegiac in mood; in chapter nine of book three Johnson mourns "all our miscariages" and some of the recently deceased leaders of the colony, such as John Winthrop and Thomas Hooker. Warnings are included against earthly mindedness, coveting of land and possessions:

Lord stay thy hand, and stop my earthly mind,
Thy Word, not world, shall be our sole delight,
Not Medow ground, but Christs rich pearl wee'l find,
Thy Saints imbrace, and not large lands down plight.
Murmure no more will we at yearly pay,
To help uphold our Government each way;

Not strive who least, but who the most shall give,
Rejoyce will we, our hearts inlarged are,
Those wait on th' Altar, shall on Altar live,
Nor shall our riches their good doctrine mar;
Our pride of parts in thought of clear discerning,
No longer shall disgrace their godly learning.

The book ends with a meditative poem beseeching the further assistance of Christ, the "King of Saints." These poems are written, like the meditations of Edward Taylor, in ten-syllable, six-line stanzas. Judging by the achievement of these poems, it seems possible that Johnson also wrote the readable and entertaining verse of *Good news from New-England*. . . . There are some characteristics and themes which support this theory: *Good news from New-England* . . . displays a similar interest in the founding of towns and gives the names of some of the military leaders of the colony. It also includes an homage to Thomas Shepard, whom Johnson revered. On the other hand, emphasis throughout is on material benefits, while the religious fervor, the absolute devotion to Christ, and the dedication to the great design of the colony that characterize *Wonder-working Providence* . . . are missing from *Good news from New-England*. . . . While the question of Johnson's authorship remains inconclusive, he must certainly have at least known this work, for he occasionally quotes from it in *Wonder-working Providence*. . . .

Recent scholarship has considerably enhanced Johnson's rank among early Puritan writers, and his *Wonder-working Providence* . . . has been more readily understood. For example, instead of complaining about the crudeness of Johnson's style, Harold Jantz has praised "his magnificent command of prose rhythm, his amazing sense of the truly epic: the elevation of a set of local events into the universal under the span of a great unifying idea." Intellectually Johnson was heir to a typological understanding of the Bible and the world, and he applied his typology in much the same way as other more learned Puritans. (He was not an uneducated man; he seems to have known Vergil and other classical authors.) As a Puritan, he was imbued by the same hopes and visions which guided more intellectual minds, such as Winthrop or John Cotton, whom he refers to, and quotes, frequently.

Johnson projected onto his work a prophetic conception of history which, as is suggested by his striking use of the present tense, interpreted historical events as under the eternal and ever-present providence of Christ and as fulfillments of prophecies and commands. At the same time, he shared the millenarian convictions of many American Puritans. His vision of the colonists as soldiers of Christ, commissioned to fight the Antichrist and to prepare themselves for the imminent final battle by erecting in the New World, in church and civil government, the Kingdom of Christ, must be seen as one of the earliest conceptions of an American national destiny. Johnson often alerts his reader to this destiny, as in this account of the year 1642: "Here the Reader is desired to take notice of the wonderful providence of the most high God toward these his new-planted Churches, such as was never heard of . . . that in ten or twelve years there should be such wonderful alteration, a Nation born in a day, a Commonwealth orderly brought forth from a few fugitives."

Bibliography:

Edward J. Gallagher and Thomas Werge, "Writings About Edward Johnson, 1814-1975," in their *Early Puritan Writers: A Reference Guide* (Boston: Hall, 1976), pp. 127-148.

References:

Sacvan Bercovitch, "The Historiography of Johnson's *Wonder-working Providence*," *Essex Institute Historical Collections*, 104 (April 1968): 138-161;

Ursula Brumm, "Edward Johnson's *Wonder-working Providence* and the Puritan Conception of History," *Jahrbuch für Amerikastudien*, 14 (1969): 140-151;

Edward J. Gallagher, "The Case for the *Wonder-working Providence*," *Bulletin of the New York Public Library*, 77 (Autumn 1973): 10-27;

Gallagher, "An Overview of Edward Johnson's *Wonder-working Providence*," *Early American Literature*, 5 (Winter 1971): 30-49;

Gallagher, "The *Wonder-working Providence* as Spiritual Biography," *Early American Literature*, 10 (Spring 1975): 75-87;

Harold Jantz, "The First Century of New England Verse," *Proceedings of the American Antiquarian Society*, 53 (1943): 239-245, 436-440;

Cecelia Tichi, "Edward Johnson and the Puritan Territorial Imperative," in *Discoveries & Considerations: Essays on Early American Literature and Aesthetics Presented to Harold Jantz*, edited by Calvin Israel (Albany: State University of New York Press, 1976), pp. 152-188.

Samuel Johnson

(14 October 1696-6 January 1772)

R. C. Gordon-McCutchan
University of California, Santa Barbara

Portrait of Johnson by John Smibert, 1730s (Columbia University Libraries)

BOOKS: *A Letter from a Minister of the Church of England to His Dissenting Parishioners . . .* (New York: Printed by John Peter Zenger, 1733);

A Second Letter from a Minister of the Church of England to His Dissenting Parishioners . . . (Boston, 1734);

A Third Letter from a Minister of the Church of England to the Dissenters . . . (Boston, 1737);

An Introduction to the Study of Philosophy . . . (New London: Printed & sold by T. Green, 1743; London: J. Rivington, 1744);

A Letter from Aristocles to Authades, Concerning the Sovereignty and the Promises of God . . ., as Aristocles (Boston: Printed & sold by T. Fleet, 1745);

Ethices Elementa. Or the First Principles of Moral Philosophy. And Especially that Part of It Which Is Called Ethics . . ., as Aristocles (Boston: Printed & sold by Rogers & Fowle, 1746); republished as *Ethica . . .* in *Elementa Philosophica* (1752);

A Sermon Concerning the Obligations We Are Under to Love and Delight in the Public Worship of God . . . (Boston: Printed & sold by Rogers & Fowle, 1746);

A Letter to The Rev. Jonathan Dickinson in Defence of Aristocles and Authades . . . (Boston: Printed & sold by Rogers & Fowle, 1747);

Elementa Philosophica: Containing Chiefly, Noetica, or Things Relating to the Mind or Understanding: And Ethica, or Things Relating to the Moral Behaviour (Philadelphia: Printed by B. Franklin & D. Hall, 1752); corrected and enlarged as *The Elements of Philosophy . . .* (London: Printed for A. Millar, 1754);

A Short Catechism for Young Children . . . (Philadelphia: Printed for Ant. Armbruster, 1753);

A Demonstration of the Reasonableness, Usefulness, and Great Duty of Prayer . . . (New York: Printed & sold by W. Weyman, 1760);

A Sermon of the Beauty of Holiness in the Worship of the Church of England . . . (New York: Printed & sold by James Parker, 1761);

The First Easy Rudiments of Grammar, Applied to the English Tongue . . . (New York: Printed by J. Holt, 1765);

An English and Hebrew Grammar, Being the First Short Rudiments of Those Two Languages, Taught Together (London: Printed for W. Faden, 1767; revised 1771);

The Christian; Explained, In Two Sermons, of Humility and Charity . . . (New Haven: Printed by Thomas & Samuel Green, 1768).

COLLECTION: *Samuel Johnson, President of King's College: His Career and Writings*, 4 volumes, edited by Herbert and Carol Schneider

(New York: Columbia University Press, 1929).

Samuel Johnson, educator and Anglican minister, is today remembered chiefly for his attempt to reconcile enlightenment philosophy and science with the basic teachings of reformed Christianity. He is also significant for having been (along with Jonathan Edwards) one of North America's first philosophical idealists.

Born in Guilford, Connecticut, the son of Samuel II and Mary Sage Johnson, Johnson attended the Collegiate School at Saybrook, Connecticut (soon to become Yale College after its removal to New Haven in 1716), and delivered the valedictory address for the class of 1714. Shortly after Johnson's graduation, the school received from an English benefactor, Jeremiah Dummer, a large collection of the newest works on Baconian science and empirical philosophy (now called the Dummer collection). Johnson was among the first to make use of it. He read in these books enthusiastically and began revising his theology in terms of the "new learning."

In 1716 Johnson accepted the post of tutor at Yale College and quickly modernized the curriculum for his courses along recently inspired enlightenment lines. Forced out of Yale in 1719 because the trustees objected to his deviation from the traditional curriculum, he accepted a ministerial post at nearby West Haven in 1720. His parish duties did not keep Johnson from deeper theological study, however, study which began to raise questions in his mind about the authenticity of the Puritan way in New England. To sort out these questions, Johnson immersed himself in the biblical accounts of the early church as well as Anglican literature such as William Sclater's *Original Draught of the Primitive Church* (1691) and John Potter's *Discourse on Church Government* (1701). He also had a series of earnest discussions with George Pigot, a missionary sent from England by the Anglican Society for the Propagation of the Gospel in Foreign Parts. These investigations convinced Johnson that the chain of apostolic succession for Puritan ministers in New England had been broken at key points. His deep concern over the validity of the ordination of the Puritan clergy occasioned Johnson's conversion to Anglicanism. This apostasy from the New England way deeply shocked Johnson's Calvinistic teachers and friends.

Shortly after his religious reorientation Johnson set sail for England, where in 1723 he received ordination in his new faith from the Archbishop of Canterbury. Appointed as a colonial missionary by the Society for the Propagation of the Gospel in Foreign Parts, he returned to Stratford, Connecticut, to minister to the Anglican families there.

On 26 September 1725 Johnson married recently widowed Charity Nicoll, daughter of a socially prominent New York family. They had two sons—William Samuel (born 1727) and William (born 1731). But domestic happiness did not protect Johnson from religious strife with his Calvinistic critics. Regarded by them as a traitor, Johnson suffered bitter denunciations from his former co-religionists. He responded by setting forth his Anglican ecclesiastical views in *A Letter from a Minister of the Church of England to His Dissenting Parishioners . . .* , which was published in 1733. Johnson expanded on these thoughts in two later pamphlets (also epistolary in style) which saw print in 1734 and 1737. For the next thirty years Johnson was embroiled in the religious conflicts of the colonies. Especially noteworthy was his work attacking Calvinistic predeterminism and championing free-will Arminianism.

If empiricism was one important influence on Johnson's philosophical development, idealism was the other. It was inspired by direct contact with the great English thinker Bishop George Berkeley, whom Johnson visited frequently during the bishop's stay in Newport, Rhode Island, from 1729 to 1731. Under Berkeley's influence, Johnson produced *An Introduction to the Study of Philosophy*, first published in the London journal *Present State of the Republic of Letters* in 1731. An enlarged edition was published in New London in 1743.

Of greater intellectual significance was the compendium of moral philosophy which Johnson titled *Ethices Elementa. Or the First Principles of Moral Philosophy* (1746). He summed up his mature views in the revised version of this book, titled *Ethica* and published in 1752. Johnson's *Ethica* lays strong claim to being the first true philosophical textbook published in America. His only other publication of note was a Hebrew-English grammar which appeared in 1767 as *An English and Hebrew Grammar, Being the First Short Rudiments of Those Two Languages, Taught Together.*

Johnson's efforts on behalf of Anglicanism led to his receipt of an honorary D.D. from Oxford in 1743. His work as a scholar made him an attractive academic figure, and he received an invitation (in 1749) to become president of the nascent college in Philadelphia. Although he declined this offer (made

Johnson about the time he became president of King's College (Columbia University Libraries)

at the urging of Benjamin Franklin), he accepted the one made him by the recently formed King's College (now Columbia) in New York, and he became president in 1754.

An ongoing fight between the college trustees and the state assembly over the policies at King's marred Johnson's presidency. Led by prominent attorney William Livingston, the assembly insisted that the college ought to be governed by all of the people and not by one religious denomination (as the Anglicans wanted). The assembly wanted a strictly secular, nonsectarian college controlled by the representatives of the community, that is, the members of the assembly. Johnson and his supporters wanted the college under Anglican guidance. They firmly opposed separation of religious and temporal power. They wanted the civil magistrates, in the name of domestic tranquility, to promote and establish the Anglican church over others. Stridently objecting to practices which furthered the Anglican religion, the assembly-backed trustees of the college drove Johnson out in 1763. This strife increased the woe Johnson felt as the result of the death of his second wife. Johnson had married Sarah Beach in 1761 only to have her die a year later in an epidemic which swept New York. Considerably saddened by these problems, Johnson returned to his old parish at Stratford.

In 1766 Johnson passed his mantle of colonial Anglican leadership to T. B. Chandler and turned his attention to political affairs. He was at the heart of the agitation for an Anglican bishop in the colonies, a considerable factor in the growing alienation between the mother country and her colonial offspring. In "Raphael of the Genius of English America" (written circa 1765-1766), Johnson analyzed the reasons for the breakdown of relations between England and America. He concluded that the imperial crisis stemmed from moral laxity on both sides of the Atlantic. True to his lifelong principles, he felt that the solution to hostilities lay in a more thorough and effective moral and general education. But before hostilities became armed conflict Johnson died as he had hoped—peacefully like his mentor Berkeley.

Biographies:

Thomas Bradbury Chandler, *The Life of Samuel Johnson, D.D.* (New York: Printed by T. & J. Swords, 1805);

E. Edwards Beardsley, *Life and Correspondence of Samuel Johnson* (New York: Hurd & Houghton, 1874);

Joseph J. Ellis, *The New England Mind in Transition: Samuel Johnson of Connecticut, 1696-1772* (New Haven & London: Yale University Press, 1973).

Papers:

Johnson's papers are at Columbia University.

Hugh Jones

(circa 1692-September 1760)

Randall M. Miller
Saint Joseph's University

BOOKS: *An Accidence to the English Tongue, Chiefly for the Use of such Boys and Men, as have never Learnt Latin perfectly, and for the Benefit of the Female Sex: Also for the Welch, Scotch, Irish, and Foreigners. Being a Grammatical Essay Upon Our Language, Considering the True Manner of Reading, Writing, and Talking proper English* (London: Printed for John Clarke, 1724);

The Present State of Virginia. Giving A Particular and short Account of the Indian, English, and Negroe Inhabitants of that Colony. Shewing their Religion, Manners, Government, Trade, Way of Living, &c., with a Description of the Country. From whence is inferred a short View of Maryland and North Carolina . . . (London: Printed for J. Clarke, 1724);

A Protest Against Popery, Showing, I. The Purity of the Church of England. II. The Errors of the Church of Rome. And III. The Invalidity of the Most Plausible Objections, Proofs and Arguments of the Roman Catholics . . . (Annapolis: Printed & sold by Jonas Green, 1745);

The Pancronometer, or Universal Georgian Calendar; Adjusted to the Gregorian and Julian Accounts... (London: Printed by E. Cave & sold by J. Payne & by W. Clarke, 1753).

Hugh Jones, an Anglican clergyman, mathematician, and historian, is primarily remembered for his vigorous promotion of colonial Virginia. Born in the county of Hereford, the son of Richard Jones of Little Dewchurch, Jones earned his bachelor's (1712) and master's degrees (1716) at Oxford, and upon the recommendation of the Bishop of London, he received the first appointment to the chair in mathematics in the College of William and Mary. Jones arrived in Virginia in 1717 and quickly gained the confidence of Governor Alexander Spotswood, through whom he became the chaplain of the House of Burgesses, a minister in Jamestown, and a lecturer at Bruton Church in Williamsburg, all while continuing at the college. In colonial politics his alignment with Spotswood brought about Jones's clash with Commissary James Blair in 1719 over ministerial appointments, with Jones supporting the governor's claim to appoint ministers to all ecclesiastical benefices in the colony and challenging Blair's Episcopal ordination. Blair's victory in the contest made Jones's position uncomfortable, and he left Virginia for England in 1721.

Before leaving, Jones had composed three treatises: an "Accidence to Christianity," an "Accidence to the Mathematicks," and *An Accidence to the English Tongue. . .* , the first English grammar written in America, which Jones had published upon his return to England. A combination of grammar and rhetoric, *An Accidence to the English Tongue, Chiefly for the Use of such Boys and Men, as have never Learnt Latin perfectly, and for the Benefit of the Female Sex: Also for the Welch, Scotch, Irish, and Foreigners. Being a Grammatical Essay Upon Our Language, Considering the True Manner of Reading, Writing, and Talking proper English* (1724) reflected Jones's practical and liberal ideas on education nurtured in Virginia and his interest in bringing greater mathematical precision to language. He proposed an alphabet of nineteen letters, the education of women, and the reading of "correct modern authors" to develop widespread use of proper written and spoken English. While in England, Jones also completed his book *The Present State of Virginia. Giving A Particular and short Account of the Indian, English, and Negroe Inhabitants of that Colony. Shewing their Religion, Manners, Government, Trade, Way of Living, &c., with a Description of the Country. From whence is inferred a short View of Maryland and North Carolina* . . . (1724), designed to update and supplement previous histories, particularly Robert Beverley's *History and Present State of Virginia* . . . (1705). Jones also sought to correct British misconceptions about the colonies and, incidentally, to promote Virginia's interests. Typical of other Southern colonial histories, Jones's book was descriptive, factual, and without rhetorical adornment. It was also unabashedly provincial, as Jones celebrated Virginia's bounty and religious orthodoxy and

THE
PRESENT STATE
OF
VIRGINIA.
GIVING
A particular and ſhort Account of the *Indian*, *Engliſh*, and *Negroe* Inhabitants of that Colony.
Shewing their Religion, Manners, Government, Trade, Way of Living, *&c.* with a Deſcription of the Country.
From whence is inferred a ſhort VIEW of
MARYLAND *and* NORTH CAROLINA.
To which are added,
Schemes and Propoſitions for the better Promotion of Learning, Religion, Inventions, Manufactures, and Trade in *Virginia*, and the other *Plantations*.
For the Information of the *Curious*, and for the Service of ſuch as are engaged in the *Propagation of the Goſpel* and *Advancement of Learning*, and for the Uſe of all Perſons concerned in the
Virginia *Trade and Plantation.*

GEN. ix. 27.
God ſhall enlarge JAPHETH, *and he ſhall dwell in the Tents of* SHEM, *and* CANAAN *ſhall be his Servant.*

By *HUGH JONES*, A. M. Chaplain to the Honourable Aſſembly, and lately Miniſter of *James-Town*, &c. in *Virginia*.

LONDON:
Printed for J. CLARKE, at the *Bible* under the *Royal-Exchange*. M DCC XXIV.

Title page for Jones's history of Virginia, intended to update Robert Beverley's history and to correct British misconceptions about the New World (John Carter Brown Library, Brown University)

denigrated the sister colonies for their religious diversity. Jones's efforts to show the mildness of Virginia's treatment of her slaves and indentured servants aside, the 150-page book offers a revealing social, economic, and religious portrait of Virginia—an account that continues as an important primary source for historians. Particularly noteworthy were Jones's suggestions for curriculum improvements at William and Mary and his appeal for a less restrictive mercantile policy toward the colonies.

In 1725 Jones returned to Virginia. Commissary Blair assigned Jones to "a notoriously difficult" parish, St. Stephens, in King and Queen County, which was near one of Jones's large tracts of land in Essex County. A dispute with the vestry forced Jones to seek a new cure in William and Mary Parish, Charles County, Maryland, about forty miles away. In 1731, through the influence of his friend and political ally Governor Benedict Leonard Calvert, Jones settled in North Sassafras (now St. Stephens) Parish, Cecil County, Maryland, where he remained as rector until a few months before his death. There the vigorous Anglican exhibited the complete devotion to the Church of England and hostility toward religious enthusiasm or deviations of any kind, the mathematical skills, and the pecuniary success that marked his entire life. From the pulpit he railed especially against papists and nonconformists. At least one of his sermons, *A Protest Against Popery . . .* (1745), attracted wide attention. He also added to his personal estate, pressing for larger clerical emoluments and even arranging with Benjamin Franklin to publish his brief account of a mill claim. During his Maryland years he remained a firm supporter of the Calvert family, serving Lord Baltimore as chief mathematician for Maryland in the boundary dispute with Pennsylvania.

Jones's interest in scientific observation and measurement led to several essays and his final significant work. In 1745 Jones published an "Essay on the British Computation of Time, Coin, Weights, and Measures," over the signature Hirossa Ap-Iccim, in the July 1745 number of the *Gentleman's Magazine*, and he promised to send a fuller account of his proposals for calendar revision upon request. In 1751, Edward Cave, editor of the magazine, invited Jones to do so, and in 1753, after some delay, Cave printed Jones's pamphlet under the title *The Pancronometer, or Universal Georgian Calendar; Adjusted to the Gregorian and Julian Accounts. Shewing the Day of the Year, Month and Week, With the Fixt and Moveable Feasts and Festivals, and Terms for Any Time Past, Present, and Future, and Explanations and Directions. Also the Fundamental Hypotheses, Reasons and Uses of This Calendar. And the Reasons, Rules, and Uses of Octave Computation, or Natural Arithmetic*. In *The Pancronometer . . .* Jones attempted to reconcile theology and natural science. Among his suggestions were a calendar of thirteen months with fixed dates for Easter, Christmas, and the beginnings of the seasons, and an elaborate argument for an octave system as the base for arithmetic, geometry, and natural philosophy. The pamphlet conformed to both scripture and natural history as they were understood in the eighteenth century. For example, Jones argued that the Great Flood caused the earth's slippage from a perfect orbit into an elliptical one. Neither Parliament nor the public embraced Jones's recommendations. Jones resumed his religious and temporal duties in Maryland, continuing his lifelong struggle for precision and orthodoxy in all manners of expression and observation and contributing pieces to the *Maryland Gazette.* He died in Cecil County sometime in early September 1760.

References:

Richard Beale Davis, *Intellectual Life in the Colonial South, 1585-1763,* volume 1 (Knoxville: University of Tennessee Press, 1978), pp. 91-96;

Richard L. Morton, Introduction to *The Present State of Virginia,* edited by Morton (Chapel Hill: University of North Carolina Press, 1956);

John Davenport Neville, "The Reverend Hugh Jones and His Universal Georgian Calendar," *Virginia Cavalcade,* 26 (Winter 1977): 134-143.

John Josselyn

(birth date unknown-1675)

Robert D. Arner
University of Cincinnati

BOOKS: *New-Englands Rarities Discovered: in Birds, Beasts, Fishes, Serpents, and Plants of that Country . . .* (London: Printed for G. Widdowes, 1672); republished in American Antiquarian Society, *Transactions and Collections,* 4 (1860): 130-238;

An Account of Two Voyages to New-England . . . (London: Printed for Giles Widdows, 1674); republished in Massachusetts Historical Society, *Collections,* third series 3 (1833): 211-354.

John Josselyn, Gent., is remembered as the author of two brief and entertaining accounts of his travels to New England, the first of which, *New-Englands Rarities Discovered . . . ,* was published in 1672 and favorably noted in the *Philosophical Transactions* of the Royal Society on 15 July 1672. Quite likely this attention inspired the second book, *An Account of Two Voyages to New-England . . . ,* which was published in 1674 but went unnoticed even though it was dedicated to the Fellows of the Royal Society. The two voyages upon which Josselyn based his books had been undertaken first in 1638, when the author paid a visit to his brother Henry at "*Black-point,* otherwise called *Scarborow*" in Maine, and again in July 1663, a visit that lasted until August of 1671. During his second visit, Josselyn ran afoul of the Puritan authorities for failing to attend church on a regular basis, and it was probably this experience, together with prevailing Restoration feelings against the Puritans, that lay behind the anti-Puritan remarks that enliven *An Account of Two Voyages to New-England . . . .* Though Josselyn is alleged to have had a hand in the first edition of the Bay Psalm Book, the facts that his brother served as an agent of the heirs of Sir Fernando Gorges in seeking to establish the Gorges's title to New England and that the two were descended from aristocratic stock suggest that the Josselyns as a family had little natural sympathy for the Puritans even in the best of times.

The evidence of *New-Englands Rarities Discovered . . . ,* which displays a scientific curiosity about the New World, indicates that Josselyn may have been educated as a surgeon and physician. Yet he was also something of a poet, interspersing among his observations verses of considerable quality, the best of which are descriptions of an Indian woman to whose charms he is frankly responsive and a brief account of a storm at sea as viewed from the coast. The most striking quality of Josselyn's writing, however, is the man's seemingly limitless capacity for awe and wonder before the mythical possibilities of the New World. Whether such a capacity argues more than an ordinary degree of gullibility is debatable, but it is certain that, by his own account, Josselyn's passage to America was attended with more wonders and near-wonders than other seventeenth-century travelers, including Captain John Smith, appear to have encountered: St. Elmo's fire, a ghostly school of whales, and, in Boston harbor, a merman who suddenly seized the gunwale of Josselyn's boat but was driven off by a blow from a sharp hatchet. For Josselyn the very gateway of America was guarded by fabulous beings. Henry Josselyn, knowing his brother's predelection for the marvelous, must have encouraged his Scarborough neighbors to make sure that the

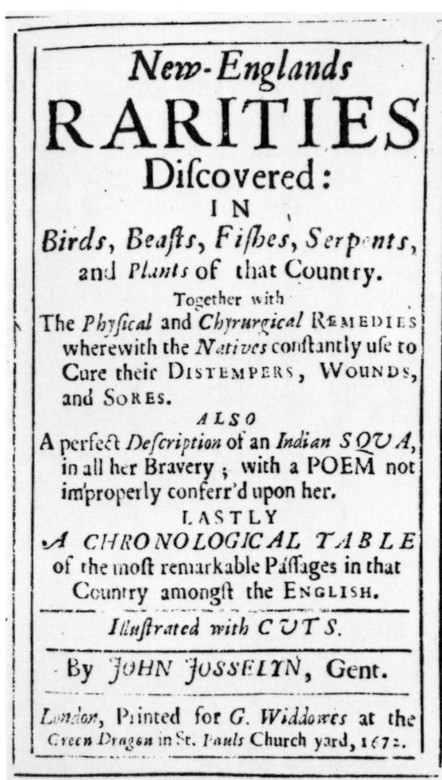
New-Englands
RARITIES
Diſcovered:
IN
Birds, Beaſts, Fiſhes, Serpents,
and Plants of that Country.
Together with
The Phyſical and Chyrurgical REMEDIES
wherewith the Natives conſtantly uſe to
Cure their DISTEMPERS, WOUNDS,
and SORES.
ALSO
A perfect Deſcription of an Indian SQUA,
in all her Bravery; with a POEM not
improperly conferr'd upon her.
LASTLY
A CHRONOLOGICAL TABLE
of the moſt remarkable Paſſages in that
Country amongſt the ENGLISH.
Illuſtrated with CUTS.
By JOHN JOSSELYN, Gent.
London, Printed for G. Widdowes at the
Green Dragon in St. Pauls Church yard, 1672.

Title page for Josselyn's first account of his voyages to New England (John Carter Brown Library, Brown University)

traveler heard every local legend, tales of strange beasts and haunted islands—Josselyn tells perhaps the first ghost story in American literature—which were dutifully transcribed in Josselyn's wonder book. About some of these tales Josselyn himself expressed deep reservations, but he apparently swallowed others that were equally incredible, thereby appearing in his own narrative as both a victim of the comic exaggeration of other yarn spinners and a victimizer of his own audience in England, all too ready to believe any terrific tale about a land they had never seen.

In *New-Englands Rarities Discovered* . . . , Josselyn lavishes careful attention on the flora and fauna of New England, even drawing the delicate hummingbird with a genuine appreciation of the scientific marvel of the thing. But he also tells his readers, without additional comment, that New England Indians always speak "perfect *Hexamitre* Verse" in their extemporaneous orations in their assemblies, and his account of the "Troculus," a small black and white bird, has been sired by the bestiary on the beast fable and emerges finally as a full-fledged tall tale about a mythical animal who, like the hoop snake, frequents the forests and hillsides of the American imagination and lives in no other locale. The Troculus, it seems, always nests in chimneys and always throws one of its own young down the flue as a token of its gratitude toward its hospitable human hosts; the feathers of the Troculus form sharp points, which the birds "stick into the sides of the Chymney (to rest themselves, their legs being exceedingly short)." Wild turkeys weighing sixty pounds, wobbles ("an ill shaped Fowl . . . not much unlike the *Penqwin*"), jackals, lions, and "Caribo" with horns growing backwards to their rumps, then turning again to protrude "a handful beyond the Nose," and yet another "Horn in the middle of their Forehead, . . . wreathed like an *Unicorns* Horn" also inhabit the New England of which Josselyn writes.

As a counterpoint to *New-Englands Rarities Discovered* . . . , with its praise and overpraise of American nature, *An Account of Two Voyages to New-England* . . . offers readers some anti-Puritan satire especially focused on the Puritans' pretense of otherworldliness while they keep their eyes squarely on the main chance. Josselyn's jokes distinctly anticipate a good bit of American humor aimed at Yankees as pious frauds, including Irving's portrait of Ichabod Crane and James Russell Lowell's caricature of Emerson as a man with one eye on heaven and the other on the stock exchange. The principal value of Josselyn's two thin books lies in such comic moments and in their revelation of the moral ambiguity compelled by the American wilderness, which is so vast and various that even a well-intentioned traveler could not resist, solely for the fun of it, weaving in a "stretcher" or two and thus lending the authority of an eyewitness to the most extravagant hyperboles about the New World.

References:

H. W. Felter, *The Genesis of American Materica Medica, Including a Brief Sketch of "John Josselyn, Gent.,"* (Cincinnati, 1927);

Philip F. Gura, "Thoreau and John Josselyn," *New England Quarterly,* 48 (December 1975): 503-518;

Karl Josef Höltgen, "Francis Quarles, John Josselyn, and the Bay Psalm Book," *Seventeenth-Century News,* 34 (Summer-Fall 1976): 42-46;

Fuller Mood, "Notes on John Josselyn, Gent.," *Colonial Society of Massachusetts Publications,* 30 (1933);

Moses Coit Tyler, *A History of American Literature* (New York: Putnam's, 1878), I: 180-185.

Sarah Kemble Knight

(19 April 1666-25 September 1727)

Ann Stanford
California State University, Northridge

BOOK: *The Journals of Madam Knight, and Rev. Mr. Buckingham. From the Original Manuscripts Written in 1704 & 1710,* by Knight and Thomas Buckingham, edited by Theodore Dwight, Jr. (New York: Wilder & Campbell, 1825).

Sarah Kemble Knight's account of her journey on horseback from Boston to New York in the early eighteenth century ranks as one of the finest and earliest examples of witty prose and the sort of broad humor and characterization that would be typical of later American writers. Her journal gives intimate details of travel in early America, as well. Her work is secular, in an age when most published writing was done by ministers, and her attitude toward religion, though pious, marks the change in her time from an earlier, more somber view. Finally she reveals herself as a resourceful woman, an entrepreneur well able to handle matters of business.

Sarah Kemble was a third-generation American, daughter of Thomas Kemble, a Boston merchant, and Elizabeth Trerice, whose family settled in Charlestown in the 1630s. Sometime before 1689 she married Richard Knight, who by some accounts was a sea captain, by others a publican. In either case he seems to have been often away from home. Madam Knight occupied a large house on Moon Street in Boston. A vigorous woman, she conducted a writing school; according to an early biographer, one of her pupils may have been Benjamin Franklin, although this has never been verified. She was frequently a witness for legal documents and probably also owned a stationery shop on the ground floor of her house. She kept lodgers as well, and it was on a legal matter involving one of her lodgers that she rode on horseback to New Haven, Connecticut, and then on to New York, keeping a journal of her travels.

The journal begins with her leaving Boston on the afternoon of 2 October 1704 and ends with her return to the busy household on Moon Street on 3 March 1705. It was a time when overland travel between the colonies was difficult; the roads were not marked, and it was necessary to secure local guides or to accompany the post from one town or wayside inn to another. The colonies differed in customs, government, and forms of religion, almost as separate countries would today. Between Rhode Island and Connecticut lay a tract called the Narragansett Country, sometimes affiliated with one colony, sometimes with another, and sometimes a separate entity. Heavy woods overhung the trails, and the numerous rivers and streams that mark every few miles of the coast of Rhode Island and Connecticut needed to be crossed by fording, by ferry, or by narrow bridges.

There is a dichotomy in the journal in that the customs of towns in which Madam Knight stayed are carefully set down, while passages involving actual travel are quick-moving narratives. Her descriptions of places and customs are often amusing. She tells us that in Connecticut "Their Cheif Red Letter day is St. Election" and that in Fairfield "They have aboundance of sheep, whose very Dung brings them great gain, with part of which they pay their Parsons sallery, And they Grudg that, prefering their Dung before their minister."

In describing manners, Madam Knight sometimes shows the prejudices of an upper-class Bostonian. She was racially biased and held rigid ideas of social class. Her description of a country "bumpkin" is one of her most famous passages. Bumpkin Simper is the precursor of such tobacco-chewing Americans as Yankee Doodle and a long line of country yokels. He was "a tall country fellow, with his alfogeos full of Tobacco; . . . he advanc't to the midle of the Room, makes an Awkward Nodd, and spitting a Large deal of Aromatick Tincture, he gave a scrape with his shovel like shoo, leaving a small shovel full of dirt on the floor, made a full stop, Hugging his own pretty Body with his hands under his arms, Stood staring rown'd him, like a Catt let out of a Baskett." Madam Knight here shows her belief in education, remarking that such a people have as large a portion of "mother witt" as others, simply needing education and improvements. Again, while she found the Indian "Natives of the Country" the most savage she had ever seen, it was because there was "little or no care taken (as I heard upon enquiry) to make them otherwise."

In the narrative portions of the journal Madam Knight made much of her fears, especially in night riding and in the crossing of rivers. Her comment on crossing by canoe is typical of her joking at her own expense: "The Cannoo was very small and shallow, so that when we were in she seem'd redy to take in water, which . . . caused me to be very circumspect, sitting with my hands fast on each side, my eyes stedy, not daring so much as to lodg my tongue a hair's breadth more on one side of my mouth then tother."

Her sharp wit lit upon others as well as herself. Her feet had hardly "saluted" the shore after the canoe ride when her guide began to talk of the fierce river they would shortly have to ford. She rode thus entertaining her imagination, "Sometimes seing my self drowning, otherwhiles drowned, and at best like a holy Sister Just come out of a Spiritual Bath in dripping Garments," a reference to the Anabaptists.

Madam Knight did not write for publication; it is probable she intended that her journal keep her memory fresh for recounting her travels to those relations and friends who would come "flocking in" to welcome her on her return. This was a time before the advent of newspapers, when news and stories and knowledge of other places passed most often by word of mouth. Madam Knight was well acquainted with such oral forms as sermons, myths, and folktales, and refers to several mythical characters and a folktale in her narrative. That she had also read widely seems probable; she refers to two romances by the sixteenth-century author Emmanuel Ford, still being reprinted in her day, and she interpolated short poems in the journal using stanza forms popular at the time.

One scholar, Robert O. Stephens, has suggested that she treated her journey in a mock-heroic fashion with the travels of Odysseus in mind. As a Bostonian, she represents a Greek among barbarians, taking hospitality as a measure of civilization. Her stop at Mr. Devil's resembles a journey to the underworld, and the games she describes at New Haven are a parallel to the epic games practiced by the Greeks. Thus she mingles the Greek and Puritan world views in a mythic narrative.

The realism of the narrative, however, shows her as a writer in the picaresque fashion, according to Peter Thorpe. As do other picaresque writers, she casts her narrative in the first person, makes much of the element of traveling, which divides the narrative into separate episodes; she comments on the morals and manners of a wide spectrum of social classes; and, though she often treats her subject comically, the close of the journal is serious.

There is also in the journal a resemblance to certain scenes and characters from folktales, for example, the animallike creature who guides her across a river, the humble cottages where she seeks refuge. The journal too contains Gothic effects in the passages in which she recounts the terrors of the night similar to those later used by Washington Irving. And she is romantic in her elation upon seeing the rising of Cynthia, the goddess of the moon, under whose spell she looks on the forest as a vision of the castles and panoply of Europe. Thus she displays that longing for European civilization that recurs through a long line of American authors to Henry James and beyond.

We have no writing by Madam Knight after her return to Boston. Of her husband there is no record after 1706, and following her daughter's marriage to John Livingston of New London, Connecticut, in 1713, Madam Knight moved to the vicinity of Norwich and New London, becoming the owner of several farms and an inn. Her business acumen is attested to by the fairly large estate of £1800 left at her death.

Madam Knight's journal remains as a testimony to the keen observation of one woman and to her sensitivity to literary and idealistic currents that would long continue in America: the humorous view of typically American characters; an eclectic use of materials from European literature and oral traditions; a belief in education as a means of helping people rise to their potential; and a feeling of attraction toward a European civilization ever lost.

Filled as it is with such nuances, its less than seventy-five pages are all too few to have attracted much attention from scholars. But modern readers, once directed to the journal, find it a rewarding interlude in an age of more somber writing.

References:

Malcolm Freiberg, Introductory note to *The Journal of Madam Knight* (Boston: Godine, 1972);

Jacqueline Hornstein, "Comic Vision in the Literature of New England Women before 1800," *Regionalism and the Female Imagination*, 3 (Fall 1977 and Winter 1977-78): 11-19;

Alan Margolies, "The Editing and Publication of 'The Journal of Madam Knight,'" *Papers of the Bibliographical Society of America*, 58 (first quarter 1964): 25-32;

Ann Stanford, "Images of Women in Early American Literature," in *What Manner of Woman*, edited by Marlene Springer (New York:

New York University, 1977), pp. 184-210;
Robert O. Stephens, "The Odyssey of Sarah Kemble Knight," *College Language Association Journal,* 7 (March 1964): 247-255;
Peter Thorpe, "Sarah Kemble Knight and the Picaresque Tradition," *College Language Association Journal,* 10 (December 1966): 114-121;
Rev. Anson Titus, "Madam Sarah Knight: Her Diary and Her Times, 1666-1726," Bostonian Society *Publications,* 9 (1912): 99-126;
George Parker Winship, Introductory note to *The Journal of Madam Knight* (Boston: Small Maynard, 1920);
Erastus Worthington, "Madam Knight's Journal," *Dedham Historical Register,* 1 (1890): 36-39.

Papers:

The New England Historic Genealogical Society, Boston, has a collection gathered by William R. Deane including papers relating to Madam Knight's career and one autograph.

John Lawson

(birth date unknown-September 1711)

Homer D. Kemp
Tennessee Technological University

BOOK: *A New Voyage to Carolina; Containing the Exact Description and Natural History of That Country. . . ,* in *A New Collection of Voyages and Travels. . . ,* edited by John Stevens, volume 1 (London: J. Knapton, 1708; republished separately, London, 1709); republished as *The History of Carolina; Containing the Exact Description and Natural History of That Country . . .* (London: Printed for W. Taylor and J. Baker, 1714; Raleigh, N.C.: Printed by Strother & Marcom, 1860).

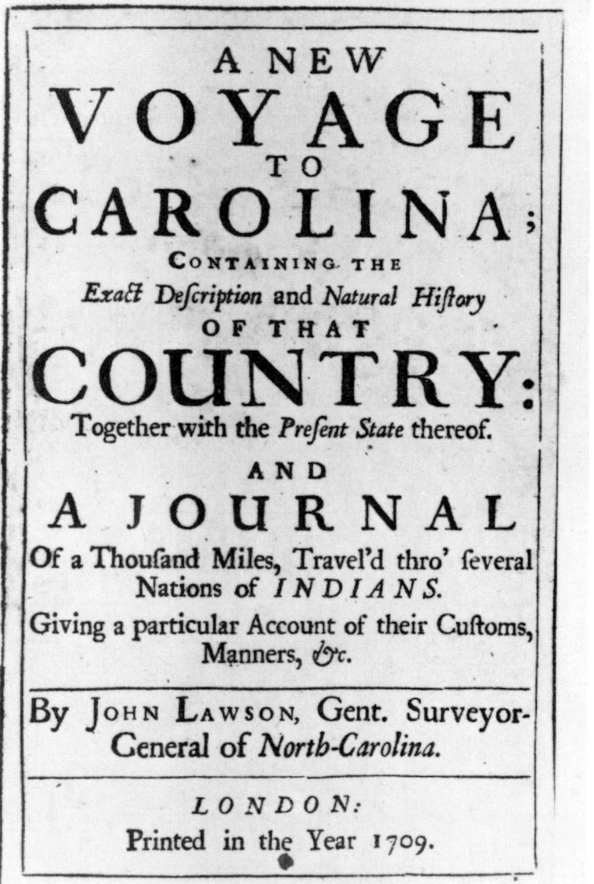

A NEW
VOYAGE
TO
CAROLINA;
CONTAINING THE
Exact Description and *Natural History*
OF THAT
COUNTRY:
Together with the *Present State* thereof.
AND
A JOURNAL
Of a Thousand Miles, Travel'd thro' several Nations of *INDIANS.*
Giving a particular Account of their Customs, Manners, &c.

By JOHN LAWSON, Gent. Surveyor-General of *North-Carolina.*

LONDON:
Printed in the Year 1709.

Title page for the first separate publication of Lawson's description of North Carolina

John Lawson—surveyor, traveler, natural historian, and author—was a dominant figure in North Carolina during the first decade of the eighteenth century. During a surveying career, which included his appointment as surveyor-general of North Carolina, Lawson conducted the first survey of the interior of Carolina and participated as cofounder and planner of Bath and New Bern, North Carolina's two oldest towns. His *A New Voyage to Carolina; Containing the Exact Description and Natural History of That Country . . .* (published separately in 1709) was the only book to come out of proprietary North Carolina and has been cited variously as "one of the best travel accounts of the early eighteenth-century colonies" (Hugh T. Lefler), "the most accurate and detached of the early natural histories of America" (U. P. Hedrick), and the "only great book on the Indians" from colonial North Carolina (Richard Beale Davis).

Nothing for certain has been documented about Lawson's life before 1700. It was thought for many years that he was probably from Yorkshire; however, the most recent authorities feel that he was a Londoner and an apothecary by training. Lawson's only explanation for going to America in 1700 was that he "accidentally met with a Gentleman" who assured him "that Carolina was the best country I could go to," but recent scholars feel that he may well have been sent by James Petiver, the greatest collector of botanical specimens of his day and a correspondent of many colonial Americans. Lawson was in Charleston in 1700 and was commissioned to make a reconnaissance survey of the interior of Carolina. An adventurous man with an insatiable curiosity, Lawson conducted the survey between December 1700 and late February 1701 in uncharted country among Indians about whom virtually nothing was known. After the survey Lawson became a significant landowner, later drawing plans for Bath, North Carolina's oldest town (1706). Although the date of his appointment is uncertain, Lawson was appointed surveyor-general of North Carolina before 1709.

Probably on 6 January 1709, Lawson left for England primarily, it seems, to direct the separate publication of his book, *A New Voyage to Carolina . . .* , which had already been published in the first volume (December 1708) of John Stevens's *A New Collection of Voyages and Travels . . .* (1708-1710). While in England from spring 1709 through January 1710, Lawson was paid by the Lords Proprietors of Carolina to prepare a "Map of Carolina" and was appointed on 21 July 1709 as a commissioner for the settlement of the boundary line dispute between North Carolina and Virginia. Lawson's efforts on behalf of *A New Voyage to Carolina . . .* proved successful. Subsequent editions of the work after 1709 were misleadingly titled *The History of Carolina; Containing the Exact Description and Natural History of That Country . . .* (London, 1714 and 1718; Raleigh, North

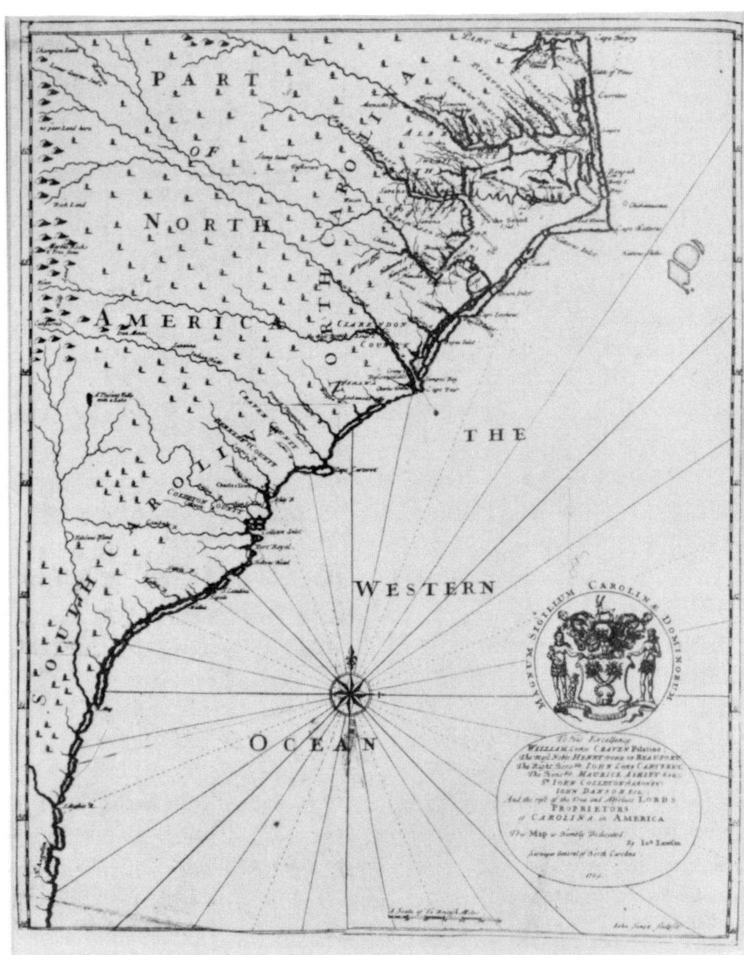

Map from the 1709 edition of A New Voyage to Carolina

"The Beastes of Carolina," from the 1709 edition of A New Voyage to Carolina

Carolina, 1860; Charlotte, Virginia, 1903; Richmond, Virginia, 1937). During the eighteenth century two editions of Lawson's work were also published in Hamburg (1712 and 1722).

Essentially a promotion-discovery tract, *A New Voyage to Carolina* . . . has been treated as serious history, natural history, travel literature, and anthropology. In addition to its importance in several areas of content, Lawson's work is also of interest to the student of colonial Southern literature for its originality, its lively writing style, and its brand of earthy humor and delight in good stories of life in the woods that were to become so prominent in Southern writing.

The first of the five divisions of *A New Voyage to Carolina* . . . , "A Journal of a Thousand Miles Travel Among the Indians from South to North Carolina," describes the 1700-1701 survey trip, which was actually only about 550 miles but a remarkable accomplishment for having taken place over fifty-nine days in winter. In "A Description of North Carolina," the second division, Lawson treats such matters as history, topography, geology, economic products, and flora and fauna. Part three, "The Present State of Carolina," describes current settlement and its relation to Virginia and has the typical promotion tract's emphasis on abundance and ease of living. Perhaps the fourth part, "The Natural History of Carolina," has been the most useful for its detailed descriptions of the flora and fauna and its comparative treatment of European and American wildlife. For example, Lawson's bird list is one of the most complete from the first century of Carolina settlement.

Throughout his career in North Carolina Lawson studied the Indians closely, defended them as a mild and gentle people, and pictured them sympathetically in descriptions that are still useful to anthropologists. In "An Account of the Indians of North Carolina," part five of *A New Voyage to Carolina* . . . , Lawson presents a wealth of data about the Indians, including a comparative dictionary of several hundred English words and their parallels in three Indian languages as well as valuable information on Indian medicine. Unlike many other Englishmen of his day, Lawson asserted that the Indians were happier and healthier before the white man came. Moreover, he suggested intermarriage between whites and Indians as a means of Christianizing them, a point made by at least two other early eighteenth-century Southern observers, Robert Beverley and William Byrd II.

By the time he left England to return to America in January 1710, Lawson had spent a great deal of time with James Petiver and his friends in the Temple Coffee House Botany Club and had entered into an agreement with Baron Christoph von Graffenried to help a group of Palatines to settle in North Carolina. Lawson's correspondence with Petiver suggests that it was during the period between his return to North Carolina and his death in late 1711 that Lawson engaged in his most productive botanical collecting. A letter written to Petiver on 30 December 1710 outlines Lawson's plans for a complete collection of scientific specimens of North Carolina, a project whose completion his untimely death prevented. Much of Lawson's time during the last year and one-half of his life was devoted to the Palatine settlement at New Bern; he drew the plans for the town and participated in its founding in 1710.

Unfortunately, his participation in the New Bern settlement and his other surveying activities probably contributed to his death. In September 1711, Lawson set out with Von Graffenried on an expedition to find a new, more convenient route to Virginia. The Tuscarora Indians and their allies, upset over white encroachments on their lands and encouraged by the weakness of the colony of North Carolina after three years of division in the "Cary Rebellion," launched an attack against the white settlements during the month of Lawson's trip. Efforts to establish the Church of England and legal discriminations against Quakers and other dissenters had stirred up reactions which finally resulted in 1710 in widespread opposition to Thomas Cary, president of the council. The controversy came to an end in the early summer of 1711, when Cary fled to Virginia and Edward Hyde became governor of North Carolina. These troubles, coupled with a series of bad crops, left the colony demoralized and weak, giving the Indians an excellent opportunity for attacking the whites. Probably identifying Lawson's surveying activities as the cause of their troubles, the Indians attacked Lawson's party, tortured and killed Lawson, but allowed Von Graffenried to live. In his accounts of the incident, Von Graffenried devoted many pages to explaining his own escape from death and to shifting the blame for Lawson's death onto Lawson's surly and arrogant behavior toward the Indians. This description of Lawson does not agree with Lawson's previous defense of and admiration for the Indians; indeed, the great irony of Lawson's life is that he died in a most cruel manner at the hands of the Indians whom he had defended.

References:

Percy G. Adams, "John Lawson's Alter Ego—Dr. John Brickell," *North Carolina Historical Review*, 34 (July 1957): 313-326;

Matt H. Allen, "John Lawson, Gentlemen [*sic*]," *Address to the North Carolina Society of Colonial Dames of America, 1900-1926* (Wilmington, n.d.), pp. 170-179;

Richard Beale Davis, *Intellectual Life in the Colonial South, 1585-1763* (Knoxville: University of Tennessee Press, 1978), I: 56-58, 135-136; II: 840-844;

Francis Latham Harriss, ed., Introduction to *Lawson's History of North Carolina* (Richmond, Va.: Garrett and Massie, 1937), pp. ix-xvii;

U. P. Hedrick, *A History of Horticulture in America to 1860* (New York: Oxford University Press, 1950), pp. 122-124;

Hugh T. Lefler, ed., Introduction to *A New Voyage to Carolina by John Lawson* (Chapel Hill: University of North Carolina Press, 1967), pp. xi-liv;

Raymond Phineas Stearns, "James Petiver, Promoter of Natural Science, c. 1663-1718," *Proceedings of the American Antiquarian Society*, 62 (16 April 1952-15 October 1952): 243-365;

V. H. Todd and Julius Goebel, eds., *Christoph Von Graffenried's Account of the Founding of New Bern, with an Historical Introduction and an English Translation* (Raleigh, N.C.: Edwards and Broughton Printing Co., 1920);

Stephen B. Weeks, "John Lawson," in *Biographical History of North Carolina from Colonial Times to the Present*, edited by S. A. Ashe (Greensboro, N. C.: C. L. Van Noppen, 1905-1917): II, 212-218.

Richard Lewis

(circa 1700-March 1734)

Robert Micklus
State University of New York at Binghamton

BOOKS: *The Mouse-Trap, or the Battle of the Cambrians and Mice,* Lewis's translation of *Muscipula,* by Edward Holdsworth (Annapolis: Printed by William Parks, 1728);

Carmen Seculare, for the Year M, DCC, XXXII (Annapolis: Printed by William Parks, 1732);

A Rhapsody (Annapolis: Printed by William Parks, 1732).

Richard Lewis was the foremost poet of American nature before Philip Freneau. But even today Lewis's works remain nearly as obscure as the details surrounding his early life. Lewis was perhaps the son of Richard Lewis of Llanfair, Montgomeryshire, Wales; perhaps the same Richard Lewis who matriculated at Balliol College, Oxford, on 3 April 1718, at the age of nineteen, staying only thirteen weeks before leaving for Maryland in the same year; and probably the same Richard Lewis who married Elizabeth Batee in January 1719, at All Hallows Parish, Anne Arundel County, Maryland. But the earliest positive identification of Lewis as a Marylander was his own report to the Royal Society in October 1725 on an explosion of air at Patapsco (near present-day Baltimore). And in a letter from Benedict Leonard Calvert, governor of Maryland, to the antiquarian Thomas Hearne, dated 18 March 1728/9, Lewis is identified as a schoolmaster in Annapolis.

The first writing attributed to Lewis is his translation of Edward Holdsworth's Latin poem, *Muscipula,* or *The Mouse Trap . . .* (1728), an extensively annotated edition in which Lewis's translation appears side by side with the Latin original. By the early 1730s Lewis was writing some first-rate poetry of his own, including several occasional pieces but especially his three finest poems, "A Journey from Patapsco to Annapolis" (published in the *Pennsylvania Gazette* for 20 May 1731, but probably published in the *Maryland Gazette* earlier in 1731), "Food for Criticks" (*Maryland Gazette,* probably by May 1731), and "Upon Prince Madoc's Expedition to the Country now called America, in the 12th Century" (*American Weekly Mercury,* 26 February 1733/4).

"A Journey from Patapsco to Annapolis" is one of the best nature poems in colonial literature. The poem begins with Lewis's idyllic portrayal of the lush Maryland countryside awakening at the dawn of a beautiful April morning. This section ends with Lewis's vivid description of the hummingbird:

> He takes with rapid Whirl his noisy Flight,
> His gemmy Plumage strikes the Gazer's Sight;
> And as he moves his ever-flutt'ring Wings,
> Ten thousand Colours he around him flings.
> Now I behold the Em'rald's vivid Green,
> Now scarlet, now a purple Die is seen;
> In brightest Blue, his Breast *He* now arrays,
> Then strait his Plumes emit a golden Blaze.
> Thus whirring round he flies, and varying still
> He mocks the *Poet's* and the *Painter's* Skill;
> Who may forever strive with fruitless Pains,
> To catch and fix those beauteous changeful Stains;
> While Scarlet now, and now the Purple shines;
> And Gold, to Blue its transient Gloss resigns.
> Each quits, and quickly each resumes its Place,
> And ever-varying Dies each other chase.
> Smallest of birds, what Beauties shine in thee!
> A living Rainbow on thy Breast I see.

In a poem whose primary purpose is to establish the place of that diminutive speck, man, in the universe, this diminutive but splendid bird achieves symbolic significance; but even without the symbolism, this passage, coming as it does at the end of a crescendoing list of nature's wonders, is especially moving as pure nature poetry.

During the second section of the poem, Lewis leaves the open countryside and journeys through the woods, offering a hearty description of the surrounding oaks, hickories, and pines, and forebodingly noting that "The tender Leaves in downy Robes appear, / Trembling, they seem to move with cautious Fear." Again, Lewis builds the reader's emotions to the perfect climax for this section of his journey:

> Hark how the *Thunder* rolls with solemn Sound!
> And see the forceful *Lightning* dart a Wound
> On yon tall Oak!—Behold its Top laid bare!
> Its Body rent, and scatter'd thro' the Air
> The Splinters fly!—Now—now the *Winds* arise,
> From different Quarters of the low'ring Skies;
> Forth issuing fierce, the *West* and *South* engage,
> The waving Forest bends beneath their Rage:

But where the winding Valley checks their Course,
They roar and ravage with redoubled Force;
With circling Sweep in dreadful Whirlwinds move
And from its Root tear up the gloomy Grove,
Down rushing fall the Trees, and beat the Ground
In Fragments flie the shatter'd Limbs around;
Tremble the Underwoods, the Vales resound.

In the third section Lewis leaves the "plain" and travels up a mountain. "Now looking round," he says, "I view the outstretch'd *Land, /* O'er which the Sight exerts a wide Command." As night closes in, his prospect broadens even further, now encompassing the heavens:

From earthly Objects I remove mine Eye,
And view with Look erect the vaulted Sky,
Where dimly shining now the Stars appear,
At first thin-scatt'ring thro' the misty Air;
. . . .
Are these bright Luminaries hung on high
Only to please with twinkling Rays our Eye?
Or may we rather count each *Star* a *Sun*,
Round which *full peopled Worlds* their Courses run?
Orb above Orb harmoniously they steer
Their various Voyages thro' Seas of Air.

"Snatch me some *Angel* to those high Abodes," Lewis prays, "The Seats perhaps of *Saints* and *Demi-gods!*," and concludes this section of the poem contemplating all the patriots, priests, poets, and philosophers who have found eternal life.

In the final portion of his poem a falling meteor brings Lewis's vision back to earth, prompting him to turn "inward [his] reflective View" and review his life. After recalling the idyllic days of youth, Lewis emphasizes the allegorical nature of the first three sections of the poem when he writes:

But ah! too soon this Scene of Pleasure flies;
And o'er his Head tempestuous Troubles rise.
He hears the Thunders roll, he feels the Rains,
Before a friendly Shelter he obtains;
And thence beholds with Grief the furious Storm
The *noontide* Beauties of his *Life* deform;
He views the *painted Bow* in distant Skies;
Hence, in his heart some Gleams of Comfort rise;
He hopes the *Gust* has almost spent its Force,
And that he safely may pursue his Course.
Thus far *my Life* does with the *Day* agree,
Oh! may its coming Stage from Storms be free.

Lewis prays for a full life so that he may face death unflinchingly "And to a better World my Soul convey," but then he momentarily wonders whether eternity is not a delusion:

TREMENDOUS GOD! May I not justly fear,
That I, unworthy Object of thy Care,
Into this World from thy bright Presence tost,
Am in th'Immensity of *Nature* lost!
And that my Notions of the *World above*,
Are but Creations of my own *Self-Love*!
To feed my coward Heart, afraid to die,
With *fancied* Feats of Immortality.

But Lewis finally spurns despair, arguing that "These *Thoughts* [of eternity] which in my Bosom roll, / Must issue from a *never-dying Soul*," and ends the poem with an "ardent Prayer" to God that he may find peace with himself and his station in life.

The prayer seems more gratuitous than ardent, and the allegory is a bit heavy-handed at times (fortunately, the most memorable part of the allegory, the connection between man and the hummingbird, is only implied), but "A Journey from Patapsco to Annapolis" works well, not only because of Lewis's superb eye for detail and his ability to describe nature in an unhackneyed way, but because of his adeptness at bringing the reader's emotions to a peak in each of the first three sections of the poem. We need not dub this poem the "first" anything in colonial literature to warrant its reading; it is simply good poetry.

Lewis's other significant nature poem, curiously entitled "Food for Criticks," is less an allegorical application of nature to man than a forthright appreciation of nature and an admonition against its corruption by man. His description of the idyllic scenery lining the Severn River in Maryland (the locale was changed in copies of the poem printed outside Maryland) culminates in his imagining the restless spirit of an Indian who leaves paradise to visit again this better earthly paradise:

During the dark, if poets eyes we trust,
These dawns are haunted by some swarthy ghost.
Some Indian prince, who fond of former joys,
With bow and quiver thro' the shadow flies;
He can't in death his native groves forget,
But leaves elyzium for his ancient seat.

But "the throng of *Harvard*," a newer and more "learned tribe" than that of the reverent Indian, has begun to spoil the land:

Some take the fish with a delusive bait,
Or for the fowl beneath the arbors wait;
And arm'd with fire, endanger ev'ry shade,
Teaching ev'n unfledg'd innocence a dread.
To gratify a nice luxurious taste
How many pretty songsters breath their last:

Spite of his voice they fire the linnet down,
And make the widow'd dove renew his moan.

Lewis ends the poem, as he typically does, on a more optimistic note, grateful that the

more humane seek the shady gloom,
Taste nature's bounty and admire her bloom:
In pensive thought revolve long vanish'd toil,
Or in soft song the pleasing hours beguile;
What Eden was, by every prospect told,
Strive to regain the temper of that age of gold;
No artful harms for simple brutes contrive,
But scorn to take a being they cannot give;
To leafy woods resort for health and ease,
Not to disturb their melody and peace.

The last of Lewis's three major poems, "Upon Prince Madoc's Expedition to the Country now called America. . . ," is an early attempt to create an epic figure associated with America. Lewis's choice of the rugged twelfth-century Welshman, and the unadorned couplets in which he sings his praises, are well suited to the rude new world he celebrates. After a lengthy series of couplets in which he praises Madoc above all other heroes of antiquity, Lewis focuses upon the distinguishing features of this epic figure who dreams of founding "an Empire spacious as his Will":

The Hero thought, and to Perfection brought,
What *only* he could do, that *only* thought.
On like Adventures later Kings have sent;
But *Madoc* would not send to search but went.
The nimble Stag by Hounds and Horn deter'd,
And beat from Shelter by the treach'rous Herd,
Collecting all his Spirits leaps the Pales,
And reigns in safety in the fenceless Dales.
From bit'rest Plants the Bee her Honey stills;
And with rich Stores her new built City fills.
Deep under-ground rich Mines of Gold are laid,
From roughest Stones the polish'd Diamond's made.
The violent Force of harden'd Steel gives vent
To hidden Fires within the Flint-stone pent.
Distress and Toil from *Madoc* thus drew forth
The glorious Treasure of his *innate* Worth.

Despite the tiresome name-dropping in other portions of the poem, passages such as these manage to bring Lewis's noble Welshman to life. These lines, fresh, straightforward, unconfounded by Latinate inversions, typify the best of Lewis's works, including his occasional pieces (especially good is his "An Elegy on the much lamented Death of the Honourable Charles Calvert"), and make his verses well worth reading not merely as historical curiosities, but as exceptionally vigorous neoclassical poetry.

Periodical Publications:

"To Mr. Samuel Hastings, (Shipwright of Philadelphia) on his launching the Maryland-Merchant, a large Ship built by him at Annapolis," *Maryland Gazette*, 30 December 1729;

"A Journey from Patapsco to Annapolis," *Pennsylvania Gazette*, 20 May 1731;

"Food for Criticks," *Maryland Gazette*, circa May 1731;

"Upon Prince Madoc's Expedition to the Country now called America, in the 12th Century," *American Weekly Mercury*, 26 February 1733/4;

"An Elegy on the much lamented Death of the Honourable Charles Calvert," *Maryland Gazette*, 15 March 1733/4.

References:

C. R. Kropf, "Richard Lewis's 'Food for Criticks' as Aesthetic Statement," *Early American Literature*, 15 (Winter 1980-81): 205-216;

J. A. Leo Lemay, *Men of Letters in Colonial Maryland* (Knoxville: University of Tennessee Press, 1972), pp. 126-184;

Lemay, "Richard Lewis and Augustan American Poetry," *PMLA*, 83 (March 1968): 80-101.

James Logan
(20 October 1674-31 October 1751)

Robert P. Winston
Dickinson College

BOOKS: *The Charge Delivered from the Bench to the Grand-Jury, at the Court of Quarter Sessions, Held for the County of Philadelphia, the 2nd. Day of September 1723 . . .* (Philadelphia: Printed & sold by Andrew Bradford, 1723);

The Antidote. In Some Remarks on a Paper of David Lloyd's, Called A Vindication of the Legislative Power . . . (Philadelphia: Printed by Andrew Bradford, 1725);

A Dialogue Shewing, What's Therein to Be Found. A Motto Being Modish, For Want of Good Latin, Are Put English Quotations . . . (Philadelphia: S. Keimer, 1725);

A More Just Vindication of the Honorable Sir William Keith, Bart. Against the Unparalleled Abuses Put Upon Him, In a Scandalous Libel Call'd, A Just and Plain Vindication of Sir William Keith, &c. (Philadelphia: Printed by Andrew Bradford, 1726);

Cato's Moral Disticbes Englished in Couplets, translated by Logan (Philadelphia: Printed & sold by B. Franklin, 1735);

De plantarum generatione experimenta et meletemata (Philadelphia, 1737); republished as *Experimenta et meletemata de plantarum generatione . . .* (Leyden: Lugduni Batavorum, apud C. Haak, 1739; London: Printed for C. Davis, 1747);

Demonstrationes de radiorum lucis in superficies sphaericas . . . (Leyden: Ludguni Batavorum, apud C. Haak, 1741);

To Robert Jordan, and Others the Friends of the Yearly Meeting . . . (Philadelphia: Printed by B. Franklin, 1741);

M. T. Cicero's Cato Major; or, His Discourse of Old Age, translated by Logan (Philadelphia: Printed & sold by B. Franklin, 1744; London: Printed by S. Austen, 1750).

James Logan was an important force in the political and cultural development of colonial Pennsylvania. After an early education in his birthplace, Lurgan, Northern Ireland, and in Edinburgh and Bristol, as well as brief service as a schoolteacher in Bristol, Logan journeyed to Philadelphia in 1699 as William Penn's secretary. Thoroughly dedicated to the interests of the proprietors, Logan remained in the service of Penn and his descendants for the next forty-five years, holding at various times almost all the important political offices of the colony.

Portrait by Gustavus Hesselius, circa 1735-1745 (Historical Society of Pennsylvania)

When Penn left the province in 1701 to return to England, Logan became secretary of the province and commissioner of property as well as clerk of the provincial council. A staunch conservative, he was convinced of the need for an aristocracy to check the lower classes and argued for a government which balanced elements of the monarchy, aristocracy, and democracy. Logan's defense of the interests of the proprietors against Penn's political opponents and those who favored popular rule alienated many, and antiproprietary forces impeached him in 1707, although he was vindicated two years later. Controversy continued to follow him, and in the 1720s his efforts on behalf of the Penns led him to publish *The Charge Delivered from the Bench to the Grand-Jury* . . . (1723) and *The Antidote* . . . (1725), in which he presented his political positions. In 1731 Logan was appointed Chief Justice of Pennsylvania, a position he held until 1736, when he was named president of the provincial council and for two years served as acting governor. Over the years Logan had negotiated with the Indians on behalf of Penn and had established a successful fur trade. By the late 1730s he was aware of the dangers which threatened Pennsylvania, and, though a Quaker, he was convinced that defensive war was justifiable. In his final years of public service, he attempted to persuade his fellow Friends of the necessity of arming the populace and quietly aided Benjamin Franklin's efforts to create a militia.

In addition to his political service, Logan was a major figure in the cultural life of early Pennsylvania. Broadly educated in both the humanities and the sciences, Logan was an indefatigable scholar. He was an accomplished master of Latin, Greek, and Hebrew, as well as Italian and French; later in life he taught himself Spanish and German, and he had a working knowledge of Arabic, Chaldaic, and Syriac. As a classical scholar, his interest in Greek and Roman texts was unflagging, and his correspondence with Johann Albert Fabricius in which Logan offered notes, corrections, and variant readings for Fabricius's monumental *Biblioteca Graeca* was eventually published in Amsterdam in 1740 as *Epistola ad virum clarissimum Joanem Albertum Fabricium.* Logan composed verse in both Latin and Greek, and two of his translations from Latin, *Cato's Moral Disticbes Englished in Couplets* (1735) and *M. T. Cicero's Cato Major; or, His Discourse of Old Age* (1744), were printed by Benjamin Franklin in Philadelphia.

Logan was also a mathematician and scientist of some import, regularly corresponding with members of the Royal Society. His first love was mathematics, and he published a number of works in the field, including comments on Pythagoras (1737) and Euclid (1740), as well as two treatises on optics (1739, 1741). Intrigued by the natural sciences, he conducted experiments on the sexual generation of plants, the results of which were published at Leyden in 1739 as *Experimenta et meletemata de plantarum generatione*; for his investigation Logan was commended in a letter by the great Swedish naturalist, Linnaeus. In addition to his own efforts, Logan also encouraged his fellow colonists in their scientific endeavors. He held long and frequent discussions with Benjamin Franklin on both scientific and civic matters; he tutored John Bartram in Latin and loaned him learned treatises from his personal library, thus assisting him in his botanical studies; and he aided the colonial mathematician Thomas Godfrey, the inventor of an advanced marine quadrant now known as Hadley's quadrant, by tutoring him and loaning him books, including Isaac Newton's *Principia mathematica.*

Logan's library at his country seat, Stenton, was

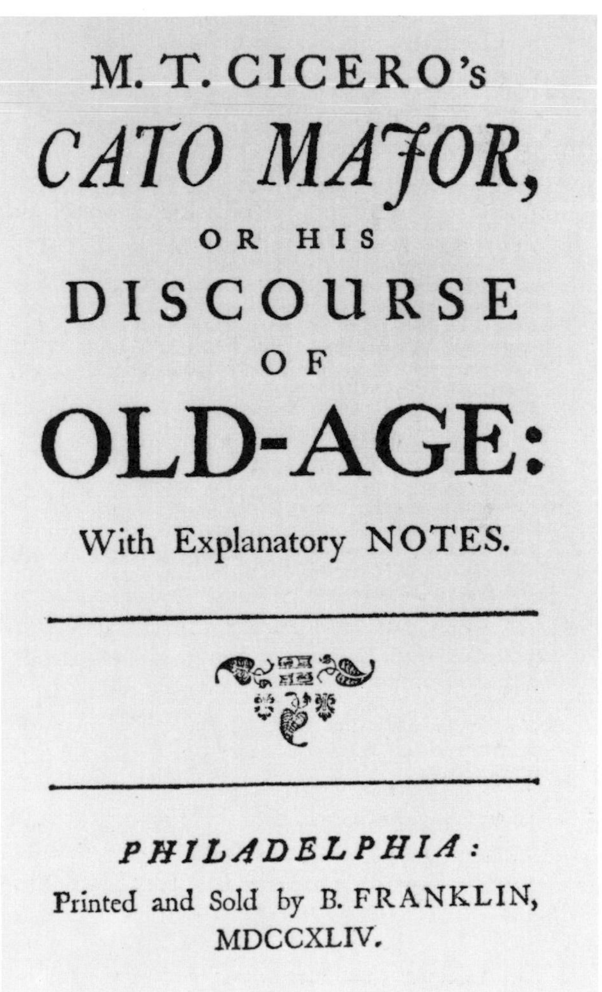
M. T. CICERO's

CATO MAJOR,

OR HIS

DISCOURSE

OF

OLD-AGE:

With Explanatory NOTES.

PHILADELPHIA:

Printed and Sold by B. FRANKLIN,

MDCCXLIV.

This title page for Logan's translation is generally considered the finest example of printing produced by Benjamin Franklin's press.

one of the largest and possibly the most scholarly private library in the American colonies. His collection was unsurpassed both as a repository of classical works and as a scientific collection. While his library did contain some works of modern literature, he focused on classical historians and poets, owning multiple editions of Homer, Horace, Vergil, Plato, Aristotle, Aeschylus, Sophocles, and others. He owned copies of the major works of ancient Greek mathematicians as well as those of their modern counterparts. In all probability Logan brought the first copy of Newton's *Principia* to America; eventually he owned all three editions as well as commentaries on the work. Logan's library also contained a sizable collection of writings by oriental authors, including both literary and scientific works which Logan read, whenever possible, in the original. At James Logan's death, the Loganian Library was set up in Philadelphia; containing over three thousand volumes, it was the first free public library outside Boston.

Other:

Epistola ad virum clarissimum Joanem Albertum Fabricium, in *Miscellaneae observationes criticae novae in auctores veteres et recentiores,* edited by Jacques Phillippe d'Orville (Amsterdam, 1740), pp. 91-112.

References:

E. Gordon Alderfer, "James Logan: Patron and Natural Philosopher," *Pennsylvania History,* 24 (April 1957): 101-120;

Alderfer, "James Logan: The Political Career of a Colonial Scholar," *Pennsylvania History,* 24 (January 1957): 34-54;

Frederick E. Brasch, "James Logan, a Colonial Mathematical Scholar and the First Copy of Newton's *Principia* to Arrive in the Colony," *Proceedings of the American Philosophical Society,* 86 (September 1942): 3-12;

Amelia Mott Gummere, "James Logan as a Poet," *Pennsylvania Magazine of History and Biography,* 27 (July 1903): 337-339;

Richard M. Gummere, *The American Colonial Mind and the Classical Tradition: Essays in Comparative Culture* (Cambridge: Harvard University Press, 1963), pp. 120-138;

L. M. Kaiser, "An Unpublished Latin Poem of James Logan," *Seventeenth-Century News,* 25 (1967): 43;

Roy N. Lokken, "The Social Thought of James Logan," *William and Mary Quarterly,* 27 (January 1970): 68-89;

Ellis Paxson Oberholtzer, *The Literary History of Philadelphia,* volume 1 (Philadelphia: Jacobs, 1906), pp. 10-12;

Frederick B. Tolles, *James Logan and the Culture of Provincial America* (Boston: Little, Brown, 1957);

Tolles, "Philadelphia's First Scientist," *Isis,* 47 (March 1956): 20-30;

Tolles, "Quaker Humanist: James Logan as a Classical Scholar," *Pennsylvania Magazine of History and Biography,* 79 (October 1955): 415-438;

John F. Watson, *Annals of Philadelphia* (Philadelphia: Carey & Hart, 1830), pp. 506-510;

Edwin Wolf II, "The Romance of James Logan's Books," *William and Mary Quarterly,* 13 (July 1956): 342-353;

Albright G. Zimmerman, "James Logan, Proprietary Agent," *Pennsylvania Magazine of History and Biography,* 78 (April 1954): 143-176.

Francis Makemie

(circa 1658-1708)

Jeffrey M. Jeske
University of California at Los Angeles

BOOKS: *A Catechism . . .* (Philadelphia: Printed by William Bradford?, 1691);

An Answer to George Keith's Libel. Against A Catechism Published by Francis Makemie . . . (Boston: Printed by Benjamin Harris, 1694);

Truths in a True Light. Or, A Pastoral Letter, to the Reformed Protestants, in Barbados Vindicating the Non-Conformists . . . (Edinburgh: Printed by the Successors of A. Anderson, 1699);

A Plain and Friendly Persuasive to the Inhabitants of Virginia and Maryland, for Promoting Towns and Cohabitation . . . (London: Printed by J. Humphreys, 1705);

A Good Conversation. A Sermon Preached at the City of New-York, January 19, 1706, 7 (Boston: Printed by B. Green for B. Eliot, 1707);

Letter to Lord Cornbury (Boston: Printed by B. Green, 1707);

A Narrative of a New and Unusual American Imprisonment of Two Presbyterian Ministers, and Prosecution of Mr. Francis Makemie, One of Them, for Preaching One Sermon at the City of New-York, as A Learner of Law, and Lover of Liberty (New York: Printed by William Bradford, 1707; London, 1708).

Francis Makemie, the chief founder of American Presbyterianism, was born near the town of Ramelton in County Donegal, Ireland. After graduating from the University of Glasgow in 1681, he was licensed to preach by the Presbytery of Laggan, and in the following year he was ordained a missionary. For nearly two decades he evangelized along the coasts of North Carolina and Virginia (1684-1685), Maryland (1690-1691), and in Barbados (1696-1698). His writings of this period include *A Catechism . . .* (1691), in which Makemie attacks tenets of the Society of Friends while supporting the Westminster Confession, and *An Answer to George Keith's Libel . . .* (1694), in which he incorporates verbatim Keith's attacks on his catechism and vindicates his doctrinal views. In *Truths in a True Light . . .* (1699), written in 1696, Makemie defends Presbyterianism against charges that its principles deviate too far from those of the Westminster Confession, arguing that the two agree on all significant issues of faith.

Sometime before 1698 Makemie married Naomi Anderson, the daughter of a wealthy Virginia merchant who died in 1699, leaving most of his estate to Makemie, who thereupon settled in Virginia. He then secured from the court of Accomac County a license to preach in his own house and in one other house some miles away, thus becoming the first dissenting minister licensed to preach under the Act of Toleration. Soon after, Makemie also established five churches in Maryland, the best known being at Snow Hill and Reheboth; he was to remain the pastor of the congregation at Reheboth until his death.

H. A. Ogden's 1908 painting of Makemie defending himself before Governor Cornbury during his 1707 trial for preaching in New York without a license

During a 1704 visit to London, Makemie recruited two missionaries, and on their return to America he decided to organize the now widely spread Presbyterian churches under his care. Hence in 1706, at a meeting in Philadelphia, Makemie and six other Presbyterian leaders oversaw the formation of the first presbytery, of which he was appointed moderator. This presbytery was the first systematic, cross-colonial organization of churches free of direct European intervention; its hierarchical system of governance also represented a major alternative to Congregational church polity, in which each local church has free control of its own affairs.

In 1707 an event involving Makemie suddenly brought widespread colonial attention to American Presbyterianism, which had heretofore been developing in relative obscurity. At the invitation of Presbyterians in New York, Makemie traveled to that colony and preached once in New York City and once on Long Island. As a result, he was arrested for preaching without a valid New York license and imprisoned by Governor Cornbury, who challenged his nonconformity and called him "a disturber of governments." At his trial, Makemie was able to argue successfully that his Virginia license was valid anywhere in the realm, and he was acquitted. Cornbury retaliated, however, by fining Makemie the entire cost of the trial, a sum roughly equivalent to a minister's annual salary. The colonists of New York were so incensed by Makemie's treatment that the following year they passed a bill preventing a court from assessing the costs of prosecution against a defendant. Charges were also made in London against Cornbury, who was subsequently recalled. Meanwhile Makemie published *A Narrative of a New and Unusual American Imprisonment . . .* (1707), which recounted his successful defense of the rights of nonconformists. Makemie died in 1708 in Boston.

References:

L. P. Bowen, *The Days of Makemie: Or, the Vine Planted. A.D. 1680-1708* (Philadelphia: Presbyterian Board of Publication, 1885);

Alfred Nevin, *History of the Presbytery of Philadelphia and Philadelphia Central* (Philadelphia: W. S. Fortescue, 1888);

Boyd S. Schlenther, *The Life and Writings of Francis Makemie* (Philadelphia: Presbyterian Historical Society, 1971).

Cotton Mather

Mason I. Lowance, Jr.
University of Massachusetts, Amherst

BIRTH: Boston, Massachusetts, 12 February 1663, to Increase and Maria Cotton Mather.

EDUCATION: A.B., 1678; M.A., 1681; Harvard College.

MARRIAGES: 4 May 1686 to Abigail Phillips; children: Abigail, Katharine, Mary, Increase, Abigail, Mehitabel, Hannah, Increase, Samuel. 18 August 1703 to Elizabeth Clark Hubbard; children: Elizabeth, Samuel, Nathaniel, Jerusha, Eleazar, Martha. 5 July 1715 to Lydia Lee George.

DEATH: Boston, Massachusetts, 13 February 1728.

SELECTED BOOKS: *Military Duties, Recommended to an Artillery Company; At their Election of Officers, in Charls-Town . . .* (Boston: Printed by Richard Pierce for Joseph Brunning, 1687);

Memorable Providences, Relating to Witchcrafts And possessions . . . (Boston: Printed by R. Pierce & sold by Joseph Brunning, 1689); republished as *Late Memorable Providences Relating to Witchcrafts and Possessions . . .* (London: Printed for Thomas Parkhurst, 1691);

Work upon the Ark. Meditations upon the Ark As a Type of the Church . . . (Boston: Printed by Samuel Green, 1689);

The Wonderful Works of God Commemorated. Praises Bespoke for the God of Heaven, In a Thanksgiving Sermon . . . (Boston: Printed by S. Green & sold by Joseph Browning & by Benjamin Harris, 1690);

The Triumphs of the Reformed Religion, in America. The Life of the Renowned John Eliot;

A Person justly Famous in the Church of God, Not only as an Eminent Christian and an Excellent Minister, among the English, But also, As a Memorable Evangelist among the Indians, of New-England... (Boston: Printed by Benjamin Harris & John Allen for Joseph Brunning, 1691);

A Midnight Cry. An Essay For our Awakening out of that Sinful Sleep, To which we are at This Time too much disposed: and For our Discovering of what peculiar things there are in This Time, That are for our Awakening . . . (Boston: Printed by John Allen for Samuel Phillips, 1692);

Preparatory Meditations upon the Day of Judgement, published with *The Great Day of Judgement,* by Samuel Lee (Boston: Printed by Bartholomew Green for Nicholas Buttolph, 1692);

The Wonders of the Invisible World. Observations As well Historical as Theological, upon the Nature, the Number, and the Operations of the Devils . . . (Boston: Printed by Benj. Harris for Samuel Phillips, 1692); republished as *The Wonders of the Invisible World: Being an Account of the Tryals of Several Witches, Lately Executed in New-England...* (London: Printed for John Dunton, 1692);

Early Religion, Urged in a Sermon, Upon The Duties Wherein, and the Reasons, Wherefore, Young People Should Become Religious . . . (Boston: Printed by Benjamin Harris for Michael Perry, 1694);

Brontologia Sacra: The Voice of the Glorious God in the Thunder Explained and Applyed . . . (London: Printed by John Astwood, 1695);

Johannes in Eremo. Memoirs, Relating to the Lives, of the Ever-Memorable Mr. John Cotton, Who Dyed, 23.d. 10.m. 1652. Mr. John Norton, Who Dyed, 5.d. 2.m. 1663. Mr. John Wilson, Who Dyed, 7.d. 6.m. 1667. Mr. John Davenport, Who Dyed, 15.d. 1.m. 1670 . . . (Boston: Printed for & sold by Michael Perry, 1695);

Piscator Evangelicus. Or, The Life of Mr. Thomas Hooker . . . (Boston, 1695);

Humiliations follow'd with Deliverences. A Brief Discourse On the Matter and Method Of that Humiliation which would be an Hopeful Symptom of our Deliverance from Calamity. Accompanied and Accommodated with A Narrative Of a Notable Deliverance lately Received by some English Captives From the Hands of Cruel Indians . . . (Boston: Printed by B. Green & J. Allen for Samuel Phillips, 1697);

Pietas in Patriam: The Life of His Excellency Sir William Phips, Knt. Late Captain General, and Governour in Chief of the Province of the Massachusetts-Bay, New England . . . (London: Printed by Sam. Bridge for Nath. Hiller, 1697);

Peter Pelham mezzotint of Cotton Mather, 1727 (American Antiquarian Society)

The Bostonian Ebenezer. Some Historical Remarks, On the State of Boston, The Chief Town of New-England, and of the English America . . . (Boston: Printed by B. Green & J. Allen for Samuel Phillips, 1698);

Eleutheria: Or, An Idea of the Reformation in England: And a History of Non-Conformity in and since that Reformation, With Predictions of a more glorious Reformation and Revolution at hand . . . (London: Printed for J. R., 1698);

Decennium Luctuosum. An History of Remarkable Occurrences, In the Long War, which New-England hath had with the Indian Salvages, From the Year 1688 To the Year 1698 . . . (Boston: Printed by B. Green and J. Allen for Samuel Phillips, 1699);

Pillars of Salt. An History of Some Criminals Executed in this Land for Capital Crimes. With some of their Dying Speeches; Collected and

Published, For the Warning of such as Live in Destructive Courses of Ungodliness... (Boston: Printed by B. Green & J. Allen for Samuel Phillips, 1699);

A Pillar of Gratitude . . . (Boston: Printed by B. Green & J. Allen, 1700);

The Religious Marriner. A Brief Discourse Tending to Direct the Course of Sea-Men, In those Points of Religion, Which may bring them to the Port, of Eternal Happiness... (Boston: Printed by B. Green & J. Allen for Samuel Phillips, 1700);

Magnalia Christi Americana: Or, the Ecclesiastical History of New-England, from Its First Planting in the Year 1620, unto the Year of our Lord, 1698... (1 volume, London: Printed for Thomas Parkhurst, 1702; 2 volumes, Hartford: Published by Silas Andrus, printed by Roberts & Burr, 1820);

Family Religion Excited And Assisted . . . (Boston, 1705); republished with an Algonquian translation by Experience Mayhew (Boston: Printed by B. Green, 1714);

The Negro Christianized. An Essay to Excite and Assist that Good Work, The Instruction of Negro-Servants in Christianity . . . (Boston: Printed by B. Green, 1706);

The Best Ornaments of Youth. A Short Essay, on the Good Things, Which are found in Some, and should be found in All, young people . . . (Boston: Printed & sold by Timothy Green, 1707);

A Memorial Of the Present Deplorable State of New-England, With the many Disadvantages it lyes under, by the Male-Administration of their Present Governour, Joseph Dudley . . . (London: Printed by Benjamin Harris & sold by S. Phillips, N. Buttolph & B. Elliot in Boston, 1707);

Corderius Americanus. An Essay upon The Good Education of Children, And what may Hopefully be Attempted, for the Hope of the Flock, in a Funeral Sermon upon Mr. Ezekiel Cheever... (Boston: Printed by John Allen for Nicholas Boone, 1708);

The Deplorable State of New-England, By Reason of a Covetous and Treacherous Governour, and Pusillanimous Counsellors . . . (London: Printed by Benjamin Harris, 1708; Boston: Printed by Samuel Kneeland?, 1721);

Bonifacius. An Essay Upon the Good, that is to be Devised and Designed, By Those Who Desire to Answer the Great End of Life, and to Do Good While they Live . . . (Boston: Printed by B. Green for Samuel Gerrish, 1710);

Nehemiah. A Brief Essay on Divine Consolations... (Boston: Printed by Bartholomew Green, 1710);

Theopolis Americana. An Essay on the Golden Street Of the holy City: Publishing, A Testimony against the Corruptions of the Market-Place. With Some Good Hopes of Better Things to be yet seen in the American World... (Boston: Printed by B. Green & sold by Samuel Gerrish, 1710);

Perswasions from the Terror of the Lord. A Sermon Concerning The Day of Judgement; preached on a solemn occasion . . . (Boston: Printed by Timothy Green, 1711);

Duodecennium Luctuosum: The History of a Long War With Indian Salvages, And their Directors and Abettors: From the Year, 1702. To the Year, 1714... (Boston: Printed by B. Green for Samuel Gerrish, 1714);

Psalterium Americanum. The Book of Psalms, In a Translation Exactly conformed unto the Original; But All in Blank Verse . . . (Boston: Printed by S. Kneeland for B. Eliot, S. Gerrish, D. Henchman & J. Edwards, 1718);

A Voice from Heaven. An Account Of a Late Uncommon Appearance in the Heavens. With Remarks upon it. Written for the Satisfaction of One that was desirous to know the meaning of it. By One of the Many who observed it. (Boston: Printed for Samuel Kneeland, 1719);

The Christian Philosopher: A Collection of the Best Discoveries in Nature, with Religious Improvements (London: Printed for Eman. Matthews, 1720; Charlestown, Mass.: Published at the Middlesex Bookstore, printed by J. M. M'Kown, 1815);

India Christiana. A Discourse, Delivered unto the Commissioners, for the Propagation of the Gospel among the American Indians . . . (Boston: Printed by B. Green, 1721);

The Angel of Bethesda, Visiting the Invalids of a Miserable World (New London: Printed & sold by Timothy Green, 1722);

Coelestinus. A Conversation in Heaven, Quickened and Assisted, With Discoveries Of Things in the Heavenly World . . . (Boston: Printed by S. Kneeland, 1723);

A Father Departing. A Sermon On the Departure of the Venerable and Memorable Dr. Increase Mather, Who Expired Aug. 23. 1723. In the Eighty Fifth Year of his Age . . . (Boston: Printed by T. Fleet for N. Belknap, 1723);

The Voice of God in a Tempest. A Sermon Preached in the Time of the Storm; Wherein many and heavy and unknown Losses were Suffered at

Boston . . . (Boston: Printed by S. Kneeland, 1723);

Parentator. Memoirs of Remarkables in the Life and the Death of the Ever-Memorable Dr. Increase Mather . . . (Boston: Printed by B. Green for Nathaniel Belknap, 1724);

The Palm-Bearers. A brief Relation of Patient and Joyful Sufferings; and of Death Gloriously Triumphed over; In the History of the Persecution which the Church of Scotland Suffered, from the Year 1660, to the Year 1688 . . . (Boston: Printed by T. Fleet for S. Gerrish, 1725);

Manuductio ad Ministerium. Directions For a Candidate of the Ministry . . . (Boston: Printed for Thomas Hancock, 1726); republished with *Gratulatio* . . . by Samuel Mather, as *Dr. Cotton Mather's Student and Preacher* . . . (London: Printed for Charles Dilly, 1781);

Ratio Disciplinae Fratrum Nov Anglorum: A Faithful Account of the Discipline Professed and Practised in the Churches of New-England . . . (Boston: Printed for S. Gerrish, 1726);

The Vial poured out upon the Sea. A Remarkable Relation Of certain Pirates Brought unto a Tragical and Untimely End . . . (Boston: Printed by T. Fleet for N. Belknap, 1726);

Agricola. Or, The Religious Husbandman: The Main Intentions of Religion, Served in the Business and Language of Husbandry . . . (Boston: Printed by T. Fleet for D. Henchman, 1727);

Boanerges. A Short Essay to preserve and strengthen the Good Impressions Produced by Earthquakes . . . (Boston: Printed for S. Kneeland, 1727);

The Terror of the Lord. Some Account of the Earthquake That Shook New-England In the Night, Between the 29 and the 30 of October. 1727 . . . (Boston: Printed by T. Fleet for S. Kneeland, 1727);

Diary, edited by Worthington Chauncey Ford, Massachusetts Historical Society *Collections*, seventh series 7 (1911), 8 (1912).

Cotton Mather was born in Boston on 12 February 1663, the eldest child of Increase Mather and Maria Cotton Mather, who was the daughter of John Cotton, an elder statesman of the first generation of settlers in the Massachusetts Bay Colony. He lived most of his life in the Boston area, always in the shadow of his more illustrious father, with whom he shared the pulpit of the Old North Church. Unlike his father, he was never to be chosen the president of Harvard College, a post he would have liked very much, but his reputation today exceeds that of his father, perhaps because he wrote so voluminously, having published some 444 works during his lifetime and leaving large volumes of work in manuscript, such as the learned and lengthy "Biblia Americana," a translation of the Bible from Greek and Hebrew with full annotation and commentary that fills several folio volumes. This document and many other Mather manuscripts and books are housed in the Massachusetts Historical Society library in Boston.

Cotton Mather's early education was in the classical tradition, and he was educated at Boston Latin School and Harvard College. He was a melancholy child and suffered from a stammer that plagued him throughout his life as a minister. He was apparently never very popular with his peers at school or with his congregations, and he was thought by most to be a pedant and a self-righteous prig, the modern stereotype of the New England Puritan. All of the Mathers are unfortunately (and often inaccurately) identified with a false image of New England Puritanism and its harsher doctrines, but Increase and Cotton Mather were unusually enlightened colonists and were responsible for the acceptance of the smallpox vaccination in New England when it was introduced in the early eighteenth century. Cotton Mather was married three times, and he was the father of a large family of children, most of whom he buried as the result of loss to disease or tragedy. He lived an extremely full and varied life and was hardly, in an intellectual or historical context, a biblical fundamentalist or pulpit-thumping revival minister.

A citizen of the world and man of his time, he was visited by Benjamin Franklin, and Cotton Mather was always considered a leading intellectual in New England, Old England, and on the Continent. His personal life was strained, however, and his public career was often successful when his personal suffering was greatest. In 1713 alone, he was elected a fellow of the Royal Society of London, and became father to his tenth and eleventh children, the twins Martha and Eleazar, who were born on 30 October. However, his losses that year were equally great. During an epidemic of measles, his second wife, Elizabeth, died on 9 November; Eleazar died at midnight on 18 November; Martha followed on 20 November; and another child, Jerusha, died on 21 November. Even in a time when colonists were rather used to infant mortality, these were staggering statistics, and Cotton Mather's own suffering has been partially recorded in his *Diary*, so that modern readers may glimpse the personal agony that attended most of his adult years.

The extraordinary strength and character required to sustain such losses are also reflected in Mather's *Diary*, where the details of his daily life are less important than the sense of divine purpose that always seemed to guide his daily affairs. He always seemed convinced that he was spiritually destined to play an important role in the evolution of the New English Israel, and his life of extremely hard work, harsh personal discipline, and personal commitment to his calling supported this vision.

In 1702, he had the pleasure of seeing his magnum opus, the *Magnalia Christi Americana*, an ecclesiastical history of New England, published in London, having taken the risk of sending his only copy of this document, the product of many years of work, to London with a friend who had been delegated to have it printed there. He was an extremely complex person, politically and publicly involved in the affairs of Massachusetts Bay Colony and his church but deeply introspective and given to brooding self-examination. Mather's complexity is nowhere better demonstrated than in his actions during the Salem witchcraft trials of 1692, where he engaged in the controversy more intellectually than politically, writing *The Wonders of the Invisible World* . . . (1692), a study of the trials, their effects, and the implications of evidence introduced in the trial of a witch, while warning the world of the dangers of judging too hastily and condemning witches without sufficient evidence. The book nevertheless reflects Mather's consistent belief that the authorities should be allowed to deal with the very real presence of witchcraft in Massachusetts Bay.

Despite his tragic personal life, he was a prolific author and was possessed of a powerful mind, especially as a historian. On the personal side, he lost his first wife, Abigail, in 1702 and his second, Elizabeth, in 1713. His third wife, Lydia, became mentally unbalanced. Of his fifteen children, nine died while very young and only two survived him. He was the minister at the many funerals of his wives and children, and if these losses were not enough, three sisters who had lost their husbands became financially dependent on Mather.

His intellectual complexity is often elusive, because in some respects it is more inconsistent than the various movements of his personal and public careers. It is clear from his *Diary* that he was morbidly introspective and at times the victim of hallucinations. His belief that an angel appeared to him has been the subject of much recent scholarly debate, and it is clear from a modern psychological perspective that Cotton Mather strained himself with overwork, the exploitation of an excess of nervous energy, and the continuous struggle to set his own ideals against the tide of the times. Moreover, he was vain and self-important, though some scholars feel that his ambition for power and rank may have been determined at least in part by his desire to preserve orthodoxy and piety as he conceived them, as well as by love of worldly position for its own sake. Ironically, Mather is viewed by historians as having been increasingly tolerant of opposing views as he grew older. Some of his nervous disorders were clearly the result of these personal and professional pressures, and Mather suffered more domestic tragedy than most modern fathers, perhaps more than any of his contemporaries. But curiously, this suffering was not a Job-like anguish over the injustice of God's ways to man, the problem of theodicy that had pervaded Hebrew literature and was Milton's most prominent concern. Rather, his *Diary* records the anguish Mather felt because he was insecure in his religious and spiritual commitments, and it reveals that he was tormented by temptations from the evil one. The records of his marriages and the deaths of his children show a pattern of spiritual testing known only to the mythical, biblical Job figure. And yet, throughout Mather's writings, we find an image of a strong, centrally sound faith in God's providence and in his own personal destiny. His writings are a chronicle of a spiritual odyssey, a pilgrimage from Babylon to Jerusalem that only a person as learned and intense as Cotton Mather could have traveled. In late 1727, only five years after the death of his illustrious father, who always outshone him as a minister and as a political figure, Cotton Mather became seriously ill, and he died on 13 February 1728. He is buried in the family tomb at Copp's Hill, Boston.

Mather's writings are so varied and extensive that summary judgments hardly do them justice. He wrote and analyzed poetry without much success, as in his blank-verse translation of the Psalms, the *Psalterium Americanum* . . . (1718); however, his understanding of contemporary poetics is richly learned even if his own efforts at verse were pathetic. He was at the forefront of some of the more creative and original scientific movements of his day, and he was elected a fellow of the Royal Society of London primarily for these achievements but also for writing *The Angel of Bethesda* . . . (1722). The manuscript subtitle of this document is "An Essay upon the

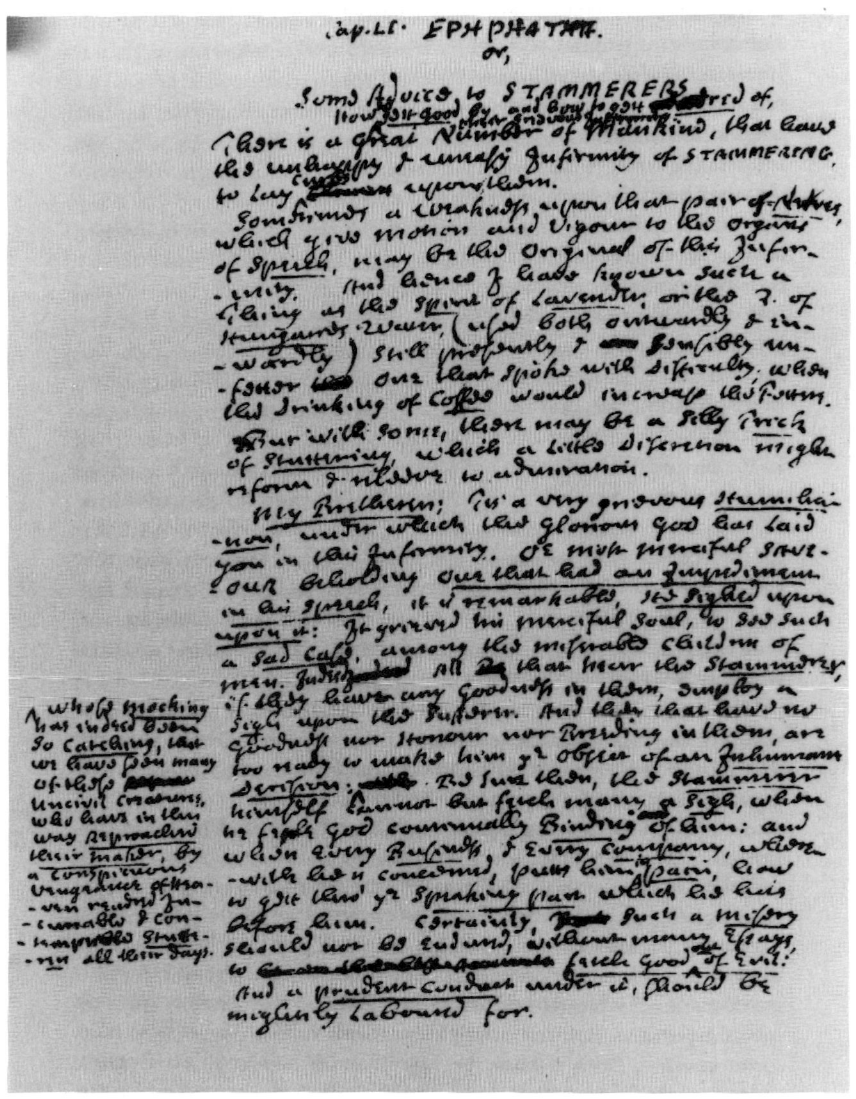

Cap. LI. EPHPHATHA.
or,
Some Advice to STAMMERERS.

A page from the chapter on stammering in the manuscript for The Angel of Bethesda *(American Antiquarian Society)*

Common Maladies of Mankind. Offering . . . Approved Remedies for the Maladies, Accompanied with many very practicable directions for the PRESERVATION of HEALTH, to such as enjoy a good measure of so great a Blessing. . . ," and the title gives clear indications of the subject of this important book. Though the book was published anonymously, its author was known to the public, and Mather achieved a reputation in science as well as theology.

He was also the author of numerous pieces such as *Bonifacius. An Essay Upon the Good* . . . (1710), and he actively attempted to reconcile theological structures inherited from the seventeenth-century Puritans with the discoveries about nature embraced by the new, rationalist, and deistic thinkers of the eighteenth century. Other works by Cotton Mather that reflect this tension in natural theology include *The Christian Philosopher: A Collection of the Best Discoveries in Nature, with Religious Improvements* (1720) and *Agricola. Or, The Religious Husbandman* . . . (1727). Of these, *Bonifacius*... proved to be Mather's most popular work, and it provided the substantive backdrop for Benjamin Franklin's imitation in the Silence Dogood essays. There were eighteen editions of *Bonifacius* . . . and a modern revision edited by David Levin in the twentieth century. *Bonifacius* . . . has been called Mather's most representative work because it is not only a book for saints and deeply religious persons, but for the common man, a handbook of human behavior to which Benjamin Franklin paid the highest tribute, saying that it had largely directed his conduct through life and had done much to make him a useful citizen of the world. Ironically, in view of our modern assessment of Mather as a pedantic and vain prude, *Bonifacius* . . . was also published anonymously, and yet its author was soon known to the public.

The *Magnalia Christi Americana* (1702), *Bonifacius, The Christian Philosopher*, and the *Manuductio ad Ministerium* . . . (1726) are probably Mather's most important published books, though his manuscripts include numerous pieces which are equally important in assessing the quality of his mind and the value of his writing. *The Christian Philosopher*, clearly Mather's most important single scientific writing, exhibits the beginnings of American scientific and philosophical liberalism. This statement is a large claim, and yet it is one which the book itself substantiates. Mather needed to reconcile revelation in scripture—the truth as the Puritans had known it—with the new sources of truth found in the natural world, a world early Puritans had considered to be fallen and corrupt. The first eleven essays of *The Christian Philosopher* are dominantly astronomical, dealing with light, the stars, the sun, the planets, comets, and other heavenly bodies such as the moon. Mather displays a knowledge of contemporary astrophysics, and, under the title *Miscellaneous Curiosa*, it quotes such sources as Derham's *Astro-Theology* (1715) and papers published as *Philosophical Transactions* in London in 1705-1707. A second section of the work is primarily concerned with physics, meteorology, geography, geology, and mineralogy, and the essay titles themselves are a table of contents for the section. Like Jonathan Edwards, Cotton Mather wrote pieces on such subjects as "Of the Rain," "Of the Rainbow," "Thunder and Lightning," "Of the Terraqueous Globe," "Of Gravity," and "Of Minerals," each an introductory study of the subject and a summary of contemporary knowledge in the field. Similarly, in the final section of *The Christian Philosopher*, Mather treated such subjects as vegetables, insects, reptiles, fishes, quadrupeds, and man—essentially a treatise on the biological sciences where the second section had grouped together the physical sciences. Again, the book is derivative, and Mather quotes Derham's *Physico-Theology* and Ray's *Wisdom of God Manifested in the Works of the Creation*. He also used classification systems that appear in Newton's *Principia* (1687), so it is clear that Mather was extremely thorough in his immersion in contemporary science, and that his interest was more profound than that of a theologian simply attempting to bolster the tenets of his faith with idly gathered scientific facts. *The Christian Philosopher* was natural theology at its inception, and the attempted reconciliation would continue to dominate writing throughout the intellectually charged eighteenth century.

By contrast, *Agricola. Or, The Religious Husbandman* . . . (1727), which is subtitled *The Main Intentions of Religion, Served in the Business and Language of Husbandry* . . . , is a work that attempts no genuine reconciliation between nature and spirit but uses the analogies of nature to prove spiritual truths. In the prefatory material, Mather makes clear that he intends "to Spiritualize the common Actions of Life, and [to] make a religious Improvement of worldly Affairs," a phrase applied to the work by the eleven ministers who signed their recommendation for *Agricola*. . . . Although this book, like many of his works, was also published anonymously, everyone in Boston knew that the author was Cotton Mather when it appeared in 1727. Although it does not rank with the other volumes discussed here in historical importance, it is crucial to an understanding of Mather as a writer because it shows him in a consistently literary frame of mind, in which his "truth" is metaphorically developed allegory, using the traditional symbols of husbandman and plow to signify the sowing of the seeds of divine truth and the reaping of a harvest of spiritual plenty.

Moreover, some of Mather's unpublished writings, such as the monumental "Biblia Americana," his translation of the entire Bible with extensive annotations and other exegetical apparatus, show the deep commitment he had to discovering truth in whatever form he found it, whether in the revelation of God through the natural world or in scripture. Mather's association with the rigid and harsh doctrines of Puritanism often obscures the sheer strength of his mind and the range of his intellectual abilities, but his writings reveal both. His style is often wooden, and his approach to his subjects is rather humorless and single-minded, but his analytical skills were keen, and his contributions to such fields as literature, theology, and history are unquestioned. Mather's supreme achievement as a writer and thinker is found in his histories, or, perhaps, in his "theory of history" (or historiography), as it emerges from Mather's sermons that speak to contemporary events and in the superbly crafted *Magnalia Christi Americana*, which registers Mather as one of the most brilliant historians to have written in English. It is important when considering Mather as a writer

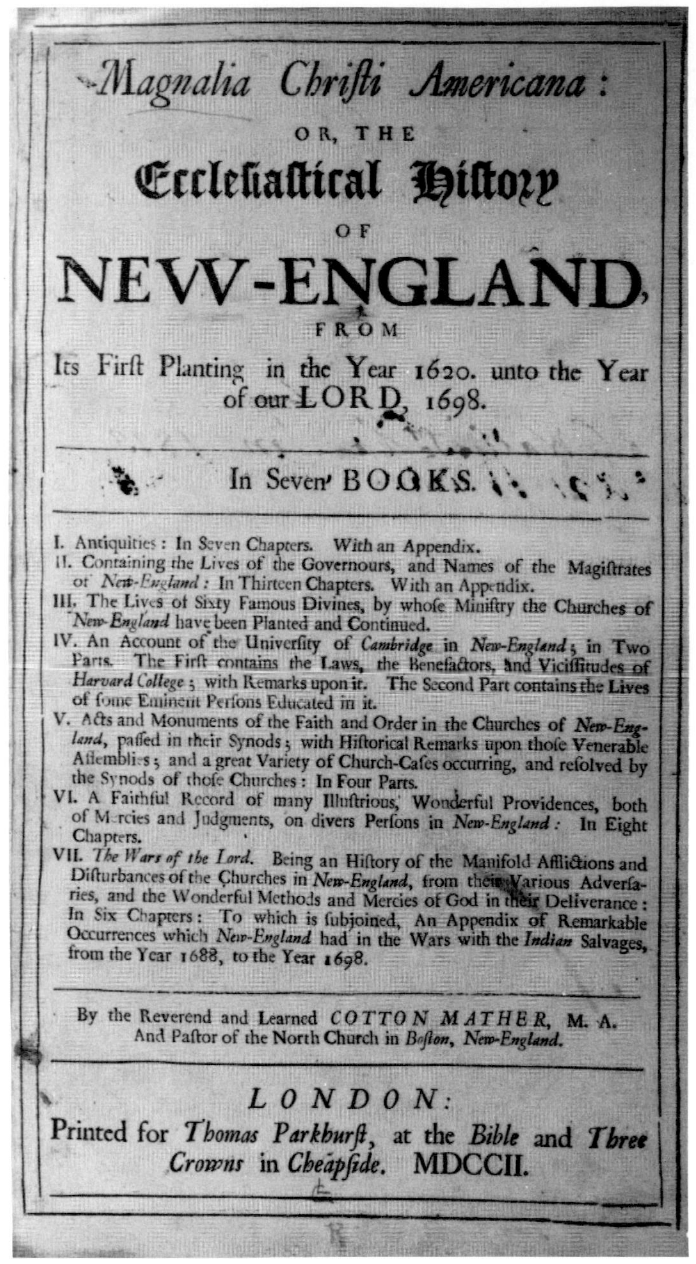

Magnalia Chriſti Americana:

OR, THE

Eccleſiaſtical Hiſtory

OF

NEW-ENGLAND,

FROM

Its Firſt Planting in the Year 1620. unto the Year of our LORD, 1698.

In Seven BOOKS.

I. Antiquities: In Seven Chapters. With an Appendix.
II. Containing the Lives of the Governours, and Names of the Magiſtrates of *New-England*: In Thirteen Chapters. With an Appendix.
III. The Lives of Sixty Famous Divines, by whoſe Miniſtry the Churches of *New-England* have been Planted and Continued.
IV. An Account of the Univerſity of *Cambridge* in *New-England*; in Two Parts. The Firſt contains the Laws, the Benefactors, and Viciſſitudes of *Harvard College*; with Remarks upon it. The Second Part contains the Lives of ſome Eminent Perſons Educated in it.
V. Acts and Monuments of the Faith and Order in the Churches of *New-England*, paſſed in their Synods; with Hiſtorical Remarks upon thoſe Venerable Aſſemblies; and a great Variety of Church-Caſes occurring, and reſolved by the Synods of thoſe Churches: In Four Parts.
VI. A Faithful Record of many Illuſtrious, Wonderful Providences, both of Mercies and Judgments, on divers Perſons in *New-England*: In Eight Chapters.
VII. *The Wars of the Lord.* Being an Hiſtory of the Manifold Afflictions and Diſturbances of the Churches in *New-England*, from their Various Adverſaries, and the Wonderful Methods and Mercies of God in their Deliverance: In Six Chapters: To which is ſubjoined, An Appendix of Remarkable Occurrences which *New-England* had in the Wars with the *Indian* Salvages, from the Year 1688, to the Year 1698.

By the Reverend and Learned *COTTON MATHER*, M. A. And Paſtor of the North Church in *Boſton*, *New-England*.

LONDON:
Printed for *Thomas Parkhurſt*, at the *Bible* and *Three Crowns* in *Cheapſide*. MDCCII.

Title page for Mather's monumental church history, which he began in July 1693 and completed about five years later (Thomas Cooper Library, University of South Carolina)

to look carefully at the *Magnalia Christi Americana* and surrounding historical documents and sermons in order to understand the sophisticated literary techniques employed in his writing.

Like other Puritan historians, Mather considered his own time to be an analogue to the period in Old Testament history when the Israelites enslaved in Egypt (analogous to England) were liberated by Moses (who was often compared to William Bradford, John Winthrop, or even the Mathers themselves). Some historians employed this analogy more directly than others. For example, in the *Wonder-working Providence of Sions Saviour in New-England* (1654), Edward Johnson used a straightforward allegorical method to portray the New England Puritans as being prepared for the spiritual struggle of the New World by Christ himself, who armed them and provided them with the breastplate of righteousness for protection. But for all Puritan historians, the underlying motif was the analogy between New England and Israel, the comparison of the mission of those persecuted souls in the early biblical narratives with the providential operations of God in supporting the earthly wanderings of the New English Israel, that elect group of saints selected for the extension of God's kingdom on earth into the newly discovered world. This central analogy, which governs *Magnalia Christi Americana*, is consistent with the view of history that Mather inherited from first-generation Puritan historians such as William Bradford, but he extended and perfected the analogy as a highly specialized literary tool.

The New England Puritans made metaphor out of nearly every experience they had. Thus the suffering of the Israelites on their journey through the wilderness became a paradigm for the Puritans' arduous crossing of the Atlantic, and like the ancient Israelites, the Puritans were moving in a linear fashion from Babylon, or the earthly and corrupt city, to the "City on a Hill," Jerusalem, or the City of God. Ultimately, they were destined for the Heavenly City, for which the earthly "City on a Hill" was but a preparation.

However, it is crucial to realize some distinctions that operate between the biblical metaphors and those employed by Mather and the Puritan historians. The "City on a Hill" that God had prepared for his New Testament saints differs from that prepared for Abraham and the ancients, and the Puritans sought the New Testament fulfillment of earlier scriptural promises. Christ's kingdom is not the land between the Jordan and the Mediterranean but the heavenly kingdom. Nevertheless, the Puritan historians could identify profoundly with both Moses's and the New Testament's references to the "heavenly city" because the life and spirit of faith were the same for Old and New Testament believers. Though outwardly the promised lands are very different, they were, the Puritans thought, manifestations of the same divinity, revealed more perfectly to some than to others. All visions of the "City on a Hill" were seen as symbolic or representative of the ultimate spiritual kingdom of God in heaven, and because they found Christ revealed in the entire history of redemption, the Puritans trusted that the New Testament promises of the New Jerusalem would flower into fact in the same way that Abraham had faith that the Old Testament prophecies of Canaan would be fulfilled in visible form. Thus the oneness of old and new believers would extend their earthly lives into a spiritual and future fulfillment, timeless and yet future in time. Ancient Israel and New England were united in the process of history, which would reach its fulfillment only when all the saints were gathered in the heavenly kingdom at the end of human time.

Both the "Biblia Americana" and the *Magnalia Christi Americana* reflect this pattern of history, and both are saturated with the symbolic analogies drawn between ancient Israel and the New England Puritan migrations of the first and second generations. One feature of the "Biblia Americana" that reveals much about Mather's literary technique is his pervasive interest in biblical typology, that inexact science by which Old Testament figures were assigned value in terms of the New Testament as prefigurations of events in the life of Christ and the early church. These analogies between the two testaments of scripture were by Mather and other Puritan intellectuals, extended into parallels between the life of ancient Israel and the life of the New English Israel, so that both groups were perceived to be foreshadowings of the coming of Christ. Thus Old Israel prefigured the first dispensation, and the New English Israel would prefigure the second dispensation. The Puritan analogy of New England with ancient Israel thus has important contemporary meaning, and the "Biblia Americana" should be read in conjunction with the *Magnalia Christi Americana* by students who are interested in Mather's philosophy of history or historiography.

In the *Magnalia Christi Americana*, these parallels and correspondences are elevated to artistic controls for the work, and throughout the history, the sense of providential destiny is extremely strong. It is important to realize that Mather's insistence that New England was on an "errand into the wilderness" like that of ancient Israel was an important statement about his view of New England, since by 1700 many communities had abandoned the original errand idea for more secular pursuits, such as the development of natural resources or commerce and trade. In the *Magnalia Christi Americana*, Mather not only turns to the past to find meaning for the present, but he also celebrates the founders of New England and creates a mythological framework for the writing of history as biography. The *Magnalia Christi Americana* is written in the tradition of the medieval saint's life, but it is constructed with the underlying support of the Israel/Puritan analogy so that the entire document is a carefully wrought literal and metaphorical (or spiritual) statement at once.

Not only was the *Magnalia Christi Americana*

designed to glorify the founders of New England; it was also conceived with an awareness of the mission that New England had been assigned by providence and with a concern for her late seventeenth-century apostasy from that original calling. Mather seems concerned to establish the analogy between New England and the Israel of old as a way of redeeming New England, but he stops short of insisting that New England is a fulfillment of the Old Testament promises concerning Israel. Rather, New England is viewed as a reconfirmation of the original design, and as such, the two "dispensations" in human time, that of Old Israel and New England, become analogous to one another in a pattern of history that moves from the beginning of time to the final fulfillment of scriptural promises. While John Cotton literally regarded New England as the spiritual fulfillment of Old Israel and expected the imminent return of Christ to happen in New England, Mather established the analogy between New England and Israel but did not insist so strongly that Massachusetts Bay was to be transformed into the millennial kingdom. Therefore, his use of scriptural metaphors in the *Magnalia Christi Americana* is conservative, and he shows that the moral parallels between the two times are only illustrative and should not be interpreted as literal evidence of Christ's coming kingdom in Massachusetts Bay, which by 1700 was a far cry from any biblical commonwealth.

But for Cotton Mather, the extension of the Protestant Reformation into New England history was the highest form of providential expression, and the seven separate books of the *Magnalia Christi Americana* are all gathered around a central theme: God's divine plan for the world being worked out through the experience of the New English Israel, a group chosen for the special "errand into the wilderness" through which the entire world would eventually be transformed. Mather perceived the Protestant Reformation to be the ultimate expression of God's divine will, and in its earthly manifestations the extension of this reformation movement into New England was the climax of Judeo-Christian history, so that the book is resonant with allusions to the earlier stages of the movement, particularly the life of ancient Israel.

Mather's method is to associate specific details of the ancient world with contemporary events and persons from his own period. He writes history as Emerson would have liked it—as a mixture of current events and detailed biographical sketches of eminent persons who exemplify the best qualities of New England's divine calling. "The leader of a People in a Wilderness had need been a Moses," he declares, "and if a Moses had not led the people of Plymouth Colony, when this worthy person [Bradford] was their governour, the people had never with so much unamity and importunity still called him to lead them." Prominent leaders of the New English Israel are compared to the leaders of ancient Israel, and in several instances, Mather uses the same Biblical precedent to correspond to several Puritan leaders. History thus becomes reconstructed mythology, using analogies from the Bible and from ancient history to reinforce the moral value of contemporary historical experience. The Moses analogy is the most frequently employed parallel, and of John Winthrop, leader of the Massachusetts Bay Colony, Mather writes, "Accordingly, when the noble design of carrying a colony of chosen people into an American wilderness was, by some eminent persons undertaken, this eminent person was, by the consent of all, chosen for the Moses, who must be the leader of so great an undertaking; and indeed, nothing but a Mosaic spirit could have carried him through the temptations, to which either his farewel to his own land, or his travel in a strange land, must needs expose a gentleman of his education."

Obviously, Mather is not attempting to reconstruct the exact history of ancient Israel in New England. Rather, he uses these examples from ancient history as moral exemplar, whose value reinforces the divine characteristics of his own contemporaries and gives to the history the aura of a divinely sanctioned document, such as the book of Exodus or one of the Gospels. The Israel / New England analogy is everywhere present, and in the chapter on the life of John Cotton, one of the early ministers of the Massachusetts Bay Colony, the Moses analogue is given a new twist, when Mather quotes John Woodbridge's elegy on the death of Cotton, in which John Norton, Cotton's successor, is compared to Joshua, Moses's successor:

> Though Moses be, yet Joshua is not dead;
> I mean renowned Norton; worthy he,
> Successor to our Moses, is to be.
> O happy Israel in America,
> In such a Moses, such a Joshua.

These analogies are easy associations to make, but their pervasive use throughout the work makes myth of contemporary history more simply than any doctrinal statements would have done. By relying on the assumptions of his contemporaries about the moral and didactic value of the Bible, he grafted the narrative of his own time onto the record everyone knew of those times of old, when divine inspiration guided the Israelites on their own version of the "errand into the wilderness."

It is important to keep clearly in mind that Mather was not attempting to reincarnate ancient Israel through these analogies and through the many biographical parallels. Rather, he uses the biblical figures metaphorically and morally to organize the *Magnalia Christi Americana* around prominent themes that were shared by the biblical and the contemporary situations. In one specific instance, he declares that "the most crooked way that was ever gone, that of Israel's perigrination through the wilderness, may be called a right way, such was the way of this little Israel, now gone into the wilderness." He has here used the parallel between Israel and New England to demonstrate and illustrate how God is as concerned for his new chosen people as he was for the earlier version of these people in the history of the world of redemption, in which both ancient and new Israel were participants.

Mather, like most of his Puritan contemporaries, perceived the history of the world to be a divine drama, in which the eternal conflict between good and evil was continuously being worked out. Like Increase Mather, he wrote a history of relations with the Indians, who were commonly regarded to be descendants of Satan and the enemies of God—*Decennium Luctuosum. An History of Remarkable Occurrences, In the Long War, which New-England hath had with the Indian Salvages, From the Year 1688 To the Year 1698* (1699). Although his view of Indians and Negroes was not as liberal as that of his contemporary Samuel Sewall, he did write a document entitled *The Negro Christianized. An Essay to Excite and Assist that Good Work, The Instruction of Negro-Servants in Christianity . . .* (1706), and he wrote eloquently of the Rev. John Eliot, a pioneer not only in the settling of New England but also in the translation of the Bible into the Algonquian language and an early missionary to the Indian tribes. Indeed, it is through the lives of these eminent men—Bradford, Winthrop, Cotton, and Eliot—that the history of New England emerges as divine history. Even Sir William Phips, the royal governor of Massachusetts Bay, fits the providential pattern. Mather thus transforms history into biography, or biography into history, and the myth that results is timeless, divinely inspired art. In the introduction to a biographical account of his father, Increase Mather, Cotton Mather stated a method for historical writing that would essentially be a biographical accounting of the lives of saints: "I know not how the Pen of an Historian can be better Employ'd than in reporting the vertuous tempers and actions of the men that have therein shown forth the vertues of our blessed redeemer, and been the epistles of Christ unto the rest of mankind. Nor indeed has mankind generally found any sort of history to be more useful and more grateful than what has been given in the lives of men that have been distinguished by an excellent spirit. The best of books does very much consist of such an history." The allusion here, of course, is to the Bible, that "best of books" on which Mather has based his own historical methodology. He does use other ancient models, such as Plutarch's *Lives*, but it is the Bible that gives his history its power and scope, its mythological dimension. History is for Mather a spiraling process of progressive regeneration, leading up to the ultimate redemption of the elect saints who are placed on this earth to perform God's will. After all, Christ's first coming to earth was a fulfillment of promises made in the Old and some portions of the New Testaments; the world Mather inhabited was eagerly awaiting the Second Coming, and in that sense, the New English Israel stood analogous to Old Israel in preparing the way for the millennium kingdom. His purpose was to prove to posterity that New England was continuously under the providential guidance of God, and the parallels with Greece, Rome, and even the Bible were illustrations of this pattern. His belief that all history was a spiraling line of divinely guided episodes, some of which were recapitulations of earlier models, emerged as a method for his own historical account.

Mather's historical writing was, of course, only one outlet for his inexhaustible energy for literary composition. The sheer volume of his writing from the hour of his first publication insured that he was able to see something of his own freshly printed about once every five weeks. He seemed to argue through his energetic and prolific documents that the more one composed, the better it would become. He seemed to see a correlation between moral piety and literary composition. For an author of his persuasion to enjoy seeing his work in print as often as Mather was able to do must have provided the most fulfilling and satisfying sense of God's pleasure. He left little unsaid and recorded all his moments of weakness, his possible sins, always with regret and, as Babette Levy has shown, always with sufficient ambiguity to arouse a question of just how severe the fall from virtue had been. He also listed, on the opposite side of the ledger, like Benjamin Franklin, the positive intentions he had to do good works. Not exactly a listing of virtues contrasted with sins, Mather's early diary entries show that he was a typical Puritan caught in the dilemma of earthly habits and desires tempting his soul away from its spiritual purpose, known to him through biblical revelation and through more personal meditative contact with God.

This tension in his personal life had important implications for his writing style. Mather never fully resolved his doubts, and his writing is always overstylized, excessive, and occasionally morbid. His histories are his best literature because they do not permit the intrusion of personality in the way that sermons and diary writing do. More restrictive and more formulaic, the histories succeed because they have been wrought with a careful eye to the use of words in an artistic framework, whereas many of his other works are tedious and repetitious. Some of his philosophical writings, such as *The Christian Philosopher,* also adhere to a more disciplined style of writing, which Mather adapted from contemporary writers. His sermons are a mixed group. For the most part they follow the basic pattern of the Puritan sermon form. In that sense, he was employing a style or a form that he had inherited, just as he had inherited and borrowed some features of the historical form. But his sermons offer opportunity for a more intense and personal treatment of theme than the histories, and, where the histories are notable as collections of analogies and saints' lives, many of the sermons obscure Mather's reputation as a writer because they exhibit the ponderous and more self-righteous aspects of the author's character. It is to Mather's historical writing, then, and especially to his superb *Magnalia Christi Americana,* that students of his style and craft must turn for the most satisfying glimpse of Cotton Mather as a seventeenth- and eighteenth-century writer in the English language.

Bibliography:

Thomas J. Holmes, *Cotton Mather: A Bibliography of His Works,* 3 volumes (Cambridge: Harvard University Press, 1940).

Biographies:

Otho T. Beall, Jr., and Richard Shryock, *Cotton Mather: First Significant Figure in American Medicine* (Baltimore: Johns Hopkins Press, 1954);

Barrett Wendell, *Cotton Mather: the Puritan Priest,* edited by Alan Heimert (New York: Harcourt, Brace & World, 1963);

David Levin, *Cotton Mather* (Cambridge: Harvard University Press, 1978).

References:

Sacvan Bercovitch, "Cotton Mather," in *Major Writers of Early American Literature,* edited by Everett Emerson (Madison: University of Wisconsin Press, 1972), pp. 93-149;

Bercovitch, "New England Epic: Cotton Mather's *Magnalia Christi Americana," Journal of English Literary History,* 33 (1966): 337-350;

Peter Gay, *A Loss of Mastery: Puritan Historians in Colonial America* (Berkeley: University of California Press, 1966);

Babette Levy, *Cotton Mather* (Boston: Twayne, 1979);

Mason I. Lowance, "Cotton Mather's *Magnalia* and the Metaphors of Biblical History," in his *The Language of Canaan: Metaphor and Symbol in New England from the Puritans to the Transcendentalists* (Cambridge: Harvard University Press, 1980), pp. 160-177;

William R. Mannierre, "Cotton Mather and the Biographical Parallel," *American Quarterly,* 13 (1961): 153-160;

Robert Middlekauf, *The Mathers: Three Generations of Puritan Intellectuals, 1596-1728* (New York: Oxford University Press, 1971);

Perry Miller, *The New England Mind: From Colony to Province* (Cambridge: Harvard University Press, 1953);

John Sibley, *Biographical Sketches of Graduates of Harvard University,* volume 3 (Cambridge, Mass.: Charles William Sever, 1885), pp. 6-158;

Peter H. Smith, "Politics and Sainthood: Biography by Cotton Mather," *William and Mary Quarterly,* 20 (1963): 186-206;

Larzer Ziff, *Puritanism in America: New Culture in a New World* (New York: Viking, 1973).

Papers:

The major collections of the Mathers' papers are at the American Antiquarian Society and the Massachusetts Historical Society.

Increase Mather

Mason I. Lowance, Jr.
University of Massachusetts, Amherst

BIRTH: Dorchester, Massachusetts, 23 June 1639, to Richard and Katherine Holt Mather.

EDUCATION: B.A., Harvard College, 1656; M.A., Trinity College, Dublin, 1658.

MARRIAGES: March 1662 to Maria Cotton; children: three sons and seven daughters, including Cotton, Samuel, Elizabeth, Maria, Nathaniel, Sarah. 1715 to Ann Lake Cotton.

DEATH: Boston, Massachusetts, 23 August 1723.

SELECTED BOOKS: *The Mystery of Israel's Salvation, Explained and Applyed*... (London: Printed for John Allen, 1669);

The Life and Death of That Reverend Man of God, Mr. Richard Mather... (Cambridge: Printed by S. Green & M. Johnson, 1670; London: Printed for Thomas Simmons, 1683);

Wo to Drunkards. Two Sermons Testifying against the Sin of Drunkenness... (Cambridge: Printed by Marmaduke Johnson & sold by Edmund Ranger, 1673);

The Day of Trouble is Near. Two Sermons Wherein is Shewed, What are the Signs of a Day of Trouble being near... (Cambridge: Printed by Marmaduke Johnson, 1674);

Some Important Truths About Conversion, Delivered in Sundry Sermons (London: Printed by Richard Chiswell, 1674); republished as *Some Important Truths Concerning Conversion, and the Improving Seasons of Grace*... (Boston: Printed by Samuel Green for John Griffin, 1684);

A Discourse Concerning the Subject of Baptisme Wherein the present Controversies, that are agitated in the New English Churches are from Scripture and Reason modestly enquired into (Cambridge: Printed by Samuel Green, 1675);

The First Principles of New-England, Concerning The Subject of Baptisme & Communion of Churches... (Cambridge: Printed by Samuel Green, 1675);

The Wicked mans Portion. Or A Sermon (Preached at the Lecture in Boston in New-England the 18th day of the I Moneth 1674, when two men were executed, who had murthered their Master.)... (Boston: Printed by John Foster, 1675);

Increase Mather in London, 1688. Portrait by Van Der Spriett (Massachusetts Historical Society).

A Brief History of the Warr With the Indians in New-England, (From June 24. 1675. when the first English-man was murdered by the Indians, to August 12. 1676. when Philip, alias Metacomet, the principal Author and Beginner of the Warr, was slain.)... (Boston: Printed & sold by John Foster, 1676; London: Printed for Richard Chiswell, 1676);

An Earnest Exhortation To the Inhabitants of New-England, To hearken to the voice of God in his late and present Dispensations. As every they desire to escape another Judgement, seven times greater than any that has yet hath been (Boston: Printed by John Foster, 1676);

A Relation Of the Troubles which have hapned in New-England, By reason of the Indians there. From the Year 1614. to the Year 1675 . . . (Boston: Printed & sold by John Foster, 1677);

Renewal of Covenant the great Duty incumbent on decaying or distressed Churches . . . (Boston: Printed by John Foster for Henry Phillips, 1677);

Pray for the Rising Generation, or a Sermon Wherein Godly Parents are Encouraged, to Pray and Believe for their Children . . . (Cambridge: Printed by Samuel Green & sold by Edmund Ranger, 1678);

A Call from Heaven To the Present and Succeeding Generations . . . (Boston: Printed by J. Foster, 1679);

The Divine Right of Infant-Baptisme Asserted and Proved from Scripture and Antiquity (Boston: Printed by John Foster, 1680);

Heavens Alarm to the World. Or A Sermon Wherein is Shewed, That fearful Sights and Signs in Heaven are the Presages of great Calamities at hand (Boston: Printed by John Foster, 1681); republished in *Heaven's Alarm to the World; and the Latter Sign* . . . (London: Printed by Dean & Schulze, 1812);

Practical Truths Tending to Promote the Power of Godliness . . . (Boston: Printed by Samuel Green for Samuel Sewall, 1682);

Kometographia. Or A Discourse Concerning Comets . . . (Boston: Printed by S. Green for S. Sewall & sold by J. Browning, 1683); republished as *A Discourse Concerning Comets* . . . (London: Printed by W. Stratford for J. Stratford, 1811);

The Doctrine of Divine Providence Opened and Applyed . . . (Boston: Printed by Richard Pierce for Joseph Brunning, 1684);

An Essay For the Recording of Illustrious Providences, Wherein an Account is given of many Remarkable and very Memorable Events, which have happened in this last Age; Especially in New-England (Boston: Printed by Samuel Green for Joseph Browning, 1684; London: Sold by George Calvert, 1684);

An Arrow Against Profane and Promiscuous Dancing Drawn out of the Quiver of the Scriptures . . . (Boston: Printed by Samuel Green & sold by Joseph Brunning, 1684);

The Mystery of Christ Opened and Applyed . . . (Boston: Printed by Richard Pierce, 1686);

A Sermon Occasioned by the Execution of a Man found Guilty of Murder . . . (Boston: Printed for Dunton, 1686; Boston: Printed for Joseph Brunning, 1686); republished in part with *The Wonders of Free-Grace* . . . , anonymous (London: Printed for John Dunton, 1691);

A Testimony Against Several Profane and Superstitious Customs, Now Practised by some in New-England . . . (London, 1687; Boston: Printed by Richard Pierce, 1688);

A Narrative of the Miseries of New-England, By Reason of an Arbitrary Government Erected there under Sir Edmund Andros . . . (London: Printed for Richard Baldwin?, 1688; Boston: Printed by Richard Pierce, 1688);

A Brief Relation of the State of New England, From the Beginning of that Plantation To this Present Year, 1689 . . . (London: Printed for Richard Baldwin, 1689);

New-England Vindicated, From the Unjust Aspersions cast on the former Government there . . . (London, 1689);

Cases of Conscience Concerning evil Spirits Personating Men, Witchcraft, infallible Proofs of Guilt in such as are accused with that Crime . . . (Boston: Printed & sold by Benjamin Harris, 1692); republished and augmented as *A Further Account of the Tryals of the New-England Witches* (London: Printed for J. Dunton, 1693);

The Great Blessing, of Primitive Counsellours . . . (Boston: Printed & sold by Benjamin Harris, 1693);

Angelographia, or A Discourse Concerning the Nature and Power of the Holy Angels, and the Great Benefit which the True Fearers of God Receive by their Ministry . . . (Boston: Printed by B. Green & J. Allen for Samuel Phillips, 1696);

A Case of Conscience Concerning Eating of Blood, Considered and Answered (Boston: Printed by B. Green & J. Allen, 1697);

David Serving His Generation . . . (Boston: Printed by B. Green & J. Allen, 1698);

The Folly of Sinning, Opened & Applyed . . . (Boston: Printed by B. Green & J. Allen for Michael Perry and for Nicholas Buttolph, 1699);

The Surest Way to the Greatest Honour . . . (Boston: Printed by Bartholomew Green & John Allen for Samuel Phillips, 1699);

The Order of the Gospel, Professed and Practiced by the Churches of Christ in New England, Justified, by the Scripture, and by the Writings of many Learned men, both Ancient and Modern Divines . . . (Boston: Printed by B. Green & J. Allen, 1700; London: Printed & sold by A. Baldwin, 1700);

A Discourse Proving that the Christian Religion Is the only True Religion . . . (Boston: Printed &

sold by the Booksellers, 1702);

The Excellency of a Publick Spirit Discoursed . . . (Boston: Printed by B. Green & J. Allen for Nicholas Boone, 1702);

Ichabod. Or, A Discourse, Shewing what Cause there is to Fear that the Glory Of the Lord, is Departing from New-England . . . (Boston: Printed by Timothy Green, 1702);

The Duty of Parents to Pray For their Children, Opened & Applyed in a Sermon . . . (Boston: Printed by B. Green & J. Allen, 1703);

Soul-Saving Gospel Truths . . . (Boston: Sold by Eleazer Phillips, 1703);

The Voice of God, in Stormy Winds . . . (Boston: Printed by T. Green, 1704);

Meditations on the Glory of the Lord Jesus Christ... (Boston: Printed by Bartholomew Green, 1705);

A Discourse Concerning Earthquakes. Occasioned by the Earthquakes which were in New-England... (Boston: Printed by Timothy Green for Benjamin Eliot, 1706);

Meditations on Death... (Boston: Printed & sold by Timothy Green, 1707);

A Dissertation, Wherein the Strange Doctrine Lately Published in a Sermon, The Tendency of which, is, to Encourage Unsanctified Persons (while such) to Approach the Holy Table of the Lord, is Examined and Confuted . . . (Boston: Printed by B. Green for Benj. Eliot, 1708);

A Dissertation Concerning the Future Conversion of the Jewish Nation... (London: Printed by R. Tookey for Nath. Hillier, 1709);

Awakening Truth's Tending to Conversion . . . (Boston: Printed by B. Green for Benj. Eliot, 1710; Boston: Sold by Timothy Green, 1710);

Meditations on the Glory of the Heavenly World... (Boston: Sold by Benjamin Eliot, 1711; Boston: Sold by Timothy Green, 1711);

A Discourse Concerning the Existence and the Omniscience of God . . . (Boston: Printed by John Allen, 1716);

Practical Truths, Plainly Delivered . . . (Boston: Printed by B. Green for Daniel Henchman, 1718);

Several Reasons Proving that Inoculating or Transplanting the Small Pox, is a Lawful Practice, and that has been Blessed by God for the Saving of many a life, published with *Sentiments on the Small Pox Inoculated,* by Cotton Mather [single sheet] (Boston: Printed by S. Kneeland & J. Edwards, 1721);

A Dying Legacy of a Minister To his Dearly Beloved People . . . (Boston: Printed by S. Kneeland for J. Edwards, 1722);

A Call to the Tempted. A Sermon On the horrid Crime of Self-Murder... (Boston: Printed by B. Green, sold by Samuel Gerrish, 1724).

Increase Mather's son Cotton Mather was much better known to succeeding generations of New Englanders than was the father, perhaps because he published much more than Increase Mather, and because he made the transition into the eighteenth century more easily. Cotton Mather's bibliography runs to some four hundred and forty-four printed items, with additional manuscript volumes such as the yet unpublished "Biblia Americana." By comparison, Increase Mather published some one hundred and two histories, tracts, treatises, and autobiographical fragments, some of which were printed from transcriptions made by persons who heard Mather preach them.

Increase Mather is an excellent representative of early New England Puritan writers because he wrote in nearly all of the available genres, except poetry, and while he did not freely experiment with form, he developed characteristically original approaches to the recording of his own times through historical narratives such as *A Brief History of the Warr With the Indians in New-England*... (1676); he moved to the forefront of scientific challenges to accepted and traditional ways in his advocacy of inoculation against smallpox in *Several Reasons Proving that Inoculating or Transplanting the Small Pox, is a Lawful Practice* (1721); and in *Cases of Conscience Concerning evil Spirits* (1692), he was eloquent in his analysis of the many problems surrounding the Salem witchcraft episode in 1692. As a craftsman or chronicler, he is perhaps overlooked because of modern aversion to the style of seventeenth-century New England Puritan writing. But in his own time, Increase Mather was the most prominent representative of the Mather dynasty, originally established by his father, Richard Mather, when he immigrated to Boston from England in 1635. Neither Richard Mather nor Cotton Mather ever assumed the presidency of Harvard College, a post occupied by Increase Mather from 1685 to 1701. If Cotton Mather has inspired regard for the breadth and vigor of his dynamic and varied intellect, Increase Mather should command respect as a rigorous intellectual, as a principled Christian and Calvinist theologian, as a compulsive defender of the orthodox faith by pen and pulpit, and as one of Harvard's outstanding presidents. His ministry in the Old North Church, Boston, extended over nearly a sixty-year period, from 1664 to 1723, and, while ministering to God's chosen "New English Israel" on the banks of the Charles, he was quite active politically, serving in 1688 as agent of the colonies to the King of England after the charter, originally granted in 1628, was revoked in 1684. In contemporary terms, his life of political negotiation and travel, his Harvard post, and his simultaneous control of the New England Way through his ministry at the Old North Church represent a more varied career than that of his son, whose writings leave the incorrect impression that it was he, not Increase Mather, who broadened the spectrum of Calvinist Puritanism to embrace tenets of science and theology that were everywhere challenging accepted notions of orthodoxy in the late seventeenth century. Increase Mather was very much involved in bringing about these changes, and his writings demonstrate that in a number of the central controversies both men faced together, he was more disciplined in his approach to orthodoxy, but no less innovative in his way of dealing with the thorny questions of transition in an age beset with theological and intellectual strife.

In 1639, the youngest son of Richard Mather and Katherine Holt Mather was born in Dorchester, Massachusetts, and was christened Increase. Mather wrote freely about his father in *The Life and Death of . . . Mr. Richard Mather* (1670), a characteristically Puritan biographical study that develops the life of a saint rather than an accurate portrait faithful to the facts of the evolving narrative. Similarly, in his own manuscript *Autobiography*, edited recently by M. G. Hall for the American Antiquarian Society, Mather portrays his mother, Katherine Holt Mather, generously as a woman whose exemplary life taught fundamental Christian precepts: "She was a Woman of Uncommon Devotion, and in her Importunate Prayers for this her Son, she became twice a mother to him. She sometimes told her Son, while he was yet scarce more than an infant . . . that she desired of the Glorious God only two things on his behalf: the one was, the Grace to fear and love God; the other was, the Learning that might accomplish him to do Service for God . . . said she, if God make thee a Good Christian and a Good Scholar, thou hast all that ever thy Mother Asked for thee." Parental influences on Increase Mather were undoubtedly strong from the beginning, and in the *Autobiography*, Mather's depiction of his mother complements the portrait of Richard Mather written by the son in *The Life and Death of . . . Mr. Richard Mather*.

Increase Mather's early education was primarily tuition at home, but he also studied at a free school in Boston. In 1651 he entered Harvard College, at the age of twelve, and continued to enjoy a personal tutorial relationship with the Reverend John Norton, whose home he shared. He graduated from Harvard in 1656. The following year, on 23 June, his eighteenth birthday, he preached his first sermon. Shortly after, he sailed from Boston for Ireland and England. In Ireland, he visited his brother Samuel Mather, a Puritan minister in Dublin, and he entered Trinity College, Dublin, from which he received the Master of Arts degree in 1658. He was offered a post as tutor at Trinity but refused it and returned to England, where he accepted a ministerial position at Great Torrington, Devonshire.

Mather's experience with English churches was mixed; at first, he was a Puritan preaching during the Cromwell interregnum; however, in 1660, with indications that the Anglican persuasion might soon regain control in England, Mather accepted a post as chaplain to the garrison at Guernsey, where he hoped to avoid the repercussions of the Puritans' fall from power. Mather went to Guernsey in April, and Charles II was proclaimed King of England in May, commencing the Restoration of Anglicanism as the official religion of England and signaling trouble for all Puritans and dissenters, who had enjoyed a brief, twelve-year respite from persecution and disapprobation.

In 1661, Mather served briefly at Weymouth and Dorchester in Dorset, and, although he enjoyed these posts it became clear to him that he would flourish in New England, but he would have to conduct underground ministeries against the Anglicans in England. He returned to his father's church in Dorchester, Massachusetts, although he had been called to preach at a number of other churches in Massachusetts Bay Colony. Shortly after his return, in March 1662, he married Maria Cotton, his stepsister, the daughter of the Reverend John Cotton and his stepmother; they later had three sons and seven daughters, one of whom died young. (In 1714, Maria Cotton died, and in 1715 he married Ann Lake Cotton, his nephew's widow.)

Sixteen sixty-two was an important year, not only for Increase Mather but also for the colony and for the New England Way. The ministers were divided on the issue of church membership, on what should constitute an appropriate procedure for determining the requirements of church affiliation, whether or not a public confession of faith should precede induction to membership and enjoyment of the only two sacraments acknowledged by the Puritans, baptism and the Lord's Supper. Initially, Increase Mather took an extremely conservative stand, against his own father, who aligned with a group of ministers supporting the Half-Way

Covenant of 1662, an important political, social, and theological measure which would have allowed the baptism of children of uncovenanted church affiliates who had not made public professions of the experience of saving grace but would not allow these uncovenanted halfway members to take the Lord's Supper. Increase Mather rightly perceived that this measure would diminish the strength of orthodoxy, but practical experience soon convinced him that the churches could not prosper unless their standards made possible large numbers of new members, and he changed his mind and became a promoter of the Half-Way Covenant. In 1675, he wrote two books defending it (*A Discourse Concerning the Subject of Baptisme* and *The First Principles of New-England*), both important more for their contributions to the intellectual history of New England than for any literary value.

Most of Increase Mather's writings exhibit more historical value than literary merit; however, his own compositions reflect a rigorous and disciplined mind, an intellectual rather than purely aesthetic perception of people and situations, and a consistent effort to develop each work within the larger framework of his pervasive concern with the glorification of God. In his major writing, Mather employed three important genres, each of which had rich association with contemporary literature, both in England and in America. He gathered folklore and factual narratives from Old and New England in books such as *An Essay For the Recording of Illustrious Providences* (1684), a pseudoscientific attempt to show how the world of nature reflected the wisdom if not the beauty of God; he wrote numerous historical treatises and summaries, of which several, such as his Indian histories, were cultural and even anthropological rather than political and purely social; and he spent much of his creative energy in the composition of sermons, the most representative of which is a jeremiad from 1702, *Ichabod*.

By 1683, Mather had published more than twenty-five books and pamphlets and had established himself as one of the foremost Puritan thinkers of his time; however, his first work of literary significance is *An Essay For the Recording of Illustrious Providences*, a masterpiece of its genre.

Attempting to illustrate the principle of God's providence at work in the world of nature, it was an early exploration of the relationship between natural revelation and scriptural revelation, a subject that would occupy many writers during the eighteenth century. Mather's aim in pursuing this project was stated in the preface: "to publish a

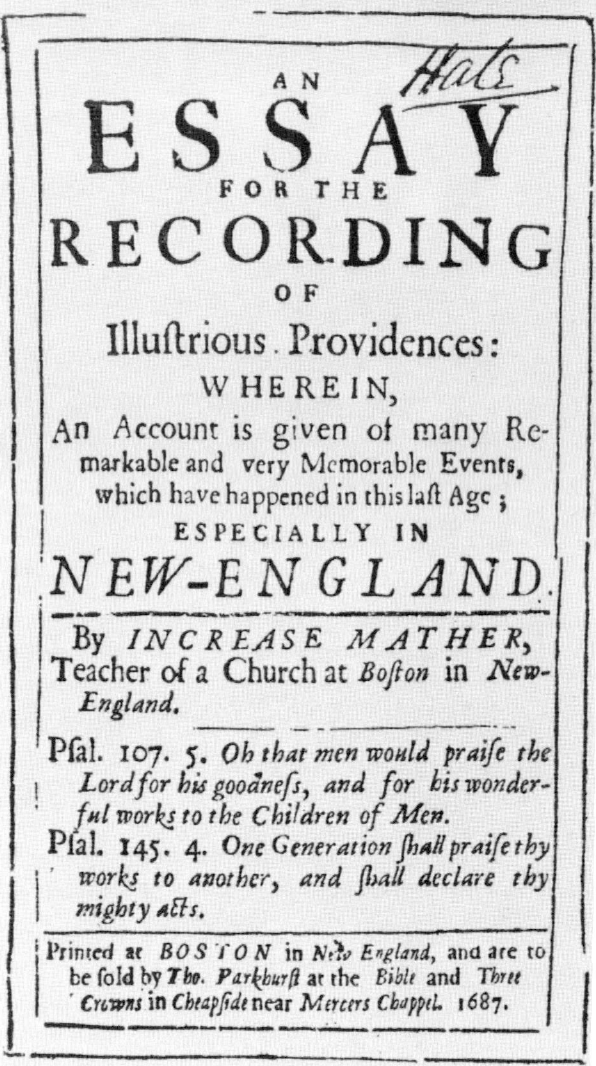
AN ESSAY FOR THE RECORDING OF Illuſtrious Providences: WHEREIN, An Account is given of many Remarkable and very Memorable Events, which have happened in this laſt Age; ESPECIALLY IN NEW-ENGLAND.

By *INCREASE MATHER*, Teacher of a Church at *Boſton* in *New-England.*

Pſal. 107. 5. *Oh that men would praiſe the Lord for his goodneſs, and for his wonderful works to the Children of Men.*
Pſal. 145. 4. *One Generation ſhall praiſe thy works to another, and ſhall declare thy mighty acts.*

Printed at *BOSTON* in *New England*, and are to be ſold by *Tho. Parkburſt* at the *Bible* and *Three Crowns* in *Cheapſide* near *Mercers Chappel.* 1687.

Title page for Mather's attempt to employ scientific method to illustrate the intervention of divine providence in human affairs

Discourse of Miscellaneous observations, concerning things rare and wonderful; both as to the works of Creation and Providence." While the book is a collection of seemingly scientific narratives about natural and apparently supernatural events, Mather seems concerned that the natural phenomena should represent theological truth. He may have wished to think of it as scientific or natural history, but its frame of reference is clearly that of natural science in the service of theology.

An Essay For the Recording of Illustrious Providences is crucial to understanding Mather's role as a writer because he successfully and artistically develops the genre of the providential narrative. Legends and tales like these had supplied the folklore of religious belief for centuries, but in the hands of the Puritans of the seventeenth century, the providential narrative came to have a very special meaning because the Puritans not only had to justify their theological positions in the face of harsh judgment from the Anglicans and Roman Catholics who controlled the political and social order, but they were also asked to accommodate their theology to the scientific discoveries of the day. Although *An Essay For the Recording of Illustrious Providences* is not a scientific document, even when assessed by seventeenth-century standards, it has scientific significance in that it uses a primitive scientific method to reach a theological conclusion; Mather was attempting to follow an elementary scientific procedure in assembling his evidence for the manifestation of God's glory in the works of nature.

Throughout this fascinating collection of narratives, Mather follows a systematic method of classification, an imitation of the scientific divisions of genus and species. Titles provided each section suggest the work of God's providence in the events of nature: "Remarkable Sea Deliverances," "Remarkable Preservations," "Remarkables About Thunder and Lightening," and "Things Preternatural which have happened in New-England" accompany "Remarkable Tempests in New England" to suggest a collection of historical, New England experiences all governed by the intervening power of God. Obviously these are not empirical narratives with evidence gathered inductively so that the conclusions reached arise entirely from the evidence presented as fact. However, as a methodology for presenting information, Mather laid a primitive groundwork for such an empirical investigation in each chapter, and, because he makes careful note of each source he employs, the reader senses authority in the document rather than the pedestrian collection of trivia that sometimes characterizes purely religious miracle accounting. Mather was extremely careful in his elaborate efforts to establish credibility, and he took some of his stories from eyewitness accounts or from letters sent to him by persons he considered trustworthy and reliable.

The stories themselves are often preposterous to a modern reader. Our own perspectives will not allow us to draw the same conclusion Mather's early readers would have reached, and we are inclined to be suspicious of providential accounts that are resolved entirely in the favor of God's justice and mercy. But what stands out about *An Essay For the Recording of Illustrious Providences* is the sheer narrative power of Increase Mather as a storyteller. Most of the episodes are narrated in the third person with a concluding assessment where he indicates the role God plays in bringing events to a spiritual rather than earthly conclusion. Because all these episodes are concluded through the intervention of divine providence, they assume the character of miracle narratives and, as such, represent an unsuccessful attempt by Mather to reconcile religion and science, an experience with which his son Cotton Mather and his successor Jonathan Edwards would have greater success in the following century. However, we must not hastily dismiss this document as primitive Puritan theological misperception of the natural world. Storytellers and folklorists have always relied on the vivid imaginations of their audiences, and *An Essay For the Recording of Illustrious Providences* much appeals to the literary imaginations of a reading audience. Mather has ingeniously transformed some natural and some abnormal phenomena into a curious combination of episode and interpretation through a process of careful editing and selective adaptation. The book is one of his most careful literary works, and it relies heavily on the fanciful imagination of its author and the imaginative response of its readers. Mather clearly knew how to control the reader's imaginative responses by invoking the techniques of contemporary literary art. Like John Bunyan's *Pilgrim's Progress,* Mather's narratives draw heavily upon the reader's imagination, through which he then is able to develop concluding theological principles.

Another genre through which Increase Mather's extraordinary writing skills were displayed is his New England histories. Both Increase and Cotton Mather were historians, and Cotton Mather's *Magnalia Christi Americana* (1702) is probably the best-known historical document to emerge from Puritan New England. For these writers, history and biographical writing were inseparable; as the biography illustrated the life of a Puritan saint, the history was designed to illustrate the communal life of the gathered saints of the New English Israel. The Increase Mather documents most prominent in any study of Puritan historiography (or, the theory of history writing) relate invariably to his interest in recording examples, as we have seen in *An Essay For the Recording of Illustrious Providences.* Mather's Indian histories are also filled with examples of providential deliverances, but these are viewed in the context of a larger drama, the eternal war between good and evil, that struggle which began with creation and will end with the judgment. In between, the saints are pitted against the forces of

Satan, and in New England most nearly suited to represent Satan's forces were the Indians, those tribal groups present when the New English Israel entered their land of milk and honey. Like the Canaanites of old, they had to be dealt with, either through a long, tedious process of religious assimilation, or through extermination, or some combination of the two. In these histories, the Indians are regarded to be descendants of Satan and the Puritans, of course, are presented as on a divine errand into the wilderness, always carrying the banner of Christianity and wearing the breastplate of righteousness. The title alone of Increase Mather's second history of Indian warfare suggests this clear polarization: *A Relation Of the Troubles which have hapned in New-England, By reason of the Indians there. From the Year 1614. to the Year 1675* (1677). Mather's hostility to the Indians is implied in the title, and the narrative bears witness to a predisposition toward the native Americans which is inconsistent with modern, anthropological interest in the process of assimilation and acculturation. We are led through accounts of Indian atrocities and betrayals of the Puritans and are told that the loyal or good Indians were those who, like a few of the guides, betrayed their tribal bonds and came over to the Puritan side.

The Mather Indian histories reinforce and extend the providential approach to the Puritan experience, and the two primary documents in this genre, *A Brief History of the Warr With the Indians in New-England* . . . and *A Relation Of the Troubles* . . . both were designed to portray relationships between the Puritans and the Indians in the larger context of the eternal Holy War between the forces of good and evil. Both histories expand the evolving Puritan mythology by which the New English Israel was a contemporary manifestation of the chosen people of God. But the Indian histories are more metaphorical and mythical than factual; they are fascinating reading and, studied in the appropriate context, can offer valuable insight into the Puritan mind of the seventeenth century.

Increase Mather also wrote brief accounts of specific historical moments, and because they tend toward factual reconstruction of contemporary events, they are much less interesting, on the whole, than the Indian histories. Documents such as *The First Principles of New-England* (1675); *A Narrative of the Miseries of New-England, By Reason of an Arbitrary Government Erected there under Sir Edmund Andros* (1688); *A Brief Relation of the State of New England* (1689); and both *New-England Vindicated* . . . (1689) and a broadside, *The Present State of New English Affairs* (1689), are really political essays as much as they are historical accounts. Basically, they attempt a defense of the New England Way in the face of threats such as the revocation of the charter for the Massachusetts Bay Colony, and their purely factual nature renders them dull reading. None exhibits the literary skill or imagination characteristic of the Indian stories.

In recounting this early period of Indian relations with the Puritans, Mather relied heavily on Captain John Smith's record books, particularly *A Generall Historie of Virginia, New-England, and the Summer Isles* . . . (1624) and on *A Relation or Journal of the beginning and proceedings of the English Plantation setled at Plimoth* . . . (1622), the latter commonly known as *Mourt's Relation* and attributed largely to Edward Winslow, and on an edition of *Purchas His Pilgrimage, or Relations of the World and the Religions Observed in All Ages* (1613), by Samuel Purchas. These early histories cover events in a straightforward, factual manner, but they cannot always be counted reliable accounts and in some cases are inaccurate chronologically. It is clear that Increase Mather was a skillful editor, but that his historiographical method led him to manipulate the facts toward an ideological interpretation or myth of New England which he and other Puritan historians developed as they mixed ancient history, the record of Israel from the Bible, and contemporary events in the evolution of an ecclesiastical record of God's providential guidance of His New English Israel. Mather follows *Mourt's Relation* in his account of the events at Plymouth colony for the year 1620, but his rendering of the facts shows the evangelical force of his metaphorical shaping of those events to fit a prescribed formula for historical writing. He says, "Anno 1620: A Company of Christians belonging to the northern parts of England, who proposed no so much worldly as spiritual ends in their undertaking, ayming at the conversion of the Indians, and the establishment of the worship of God in purity, did therefore transport themselves and familyes into this howling wilderness." The original source for this narrative is much less forceful in its development of ideology. Mather weaves episodes from these earlier histories together in such a way that the Indian histories, even where there are dated entries, contain a new kind of historical evidence, that God was always guiding the destiny of his chosen people as they continued in their errand into the wilderness.

The depth of this conviction is also found in Mather's *Autobiography*, circulated in manuscript during his lifetime and only recently published in the twentieth century. It would be impossible, however, to discuss Increase Mather as a literary figure without paying significant attention to his most prominent literary achievement and his most prolific form of literary discourse, the sermon. Literary historians have determined four primary groups of Mather's sermons. The first group includes "Moral or Persuasive Sermons," especially documents that were designed for the edification of listeners and readers toward a more wholesome and moral way of everyday living. These sermons are usually ethical treatises that show the practical measures a wayward Christian must take for returning to God's divine plan. Sermons in this category would include: *Practical Truths Tending to Promote the Power of Godliness* (1682); *Wo to Drunkards* (1673); *The Wicked mans Portion* (1675); *A Testimony Against Several Profane and Superstitious Customs . . .* (including health drinking, dicing, cards, Christmas-keeping, New Year's gifts) (1687); and *The Folly of Sinning, Opened & Applyed* (1699). Instruction characterizes these dull sermons, and the "doctrine" in each case is both biblical and Puritan.

The second group of sermons includes the vast number of Mather's works about specific doctrinal matters. During his long career as a minister, he was always concerned to develop state of the art interpretations of thorny doctrinal points, and he was thrust into the role of a defender of traditional values at a time when the winds of change were constantly shifting. Many of these so-called "doctrinal" sermons are attempts to clarify the problems of changing theology that the Mathers sought to hold in place for three successive generations, represented by the grandfather, Richard Mather, the son, Increase Mather, and the grandson, Cotton Mather. Included in this group of Increase Mather sermons would be *A Discourse Concerning the Subject of Baptisme* (1675), *Renewal of Covenant the great Duty* (1677), *The Doctrine of Divine Providence Opened and Applyed* (1684), and several longer works that exhibit Mather as utopian believer in the imminent arrival of the Kingdom of Christ, for example, *The Mystery of Israel's Salvation* (1669).

In addition, Increase Mather was called upon to preach four election sermons, each of which was delivered on the special occasion of the election of leaders for the colony, and each of which required a special invitation by the General Court of the Massachusetts Bay Colony. These are formulaic and occasional sermons, but, taken as a group, they indicate the changing rhetorical strategies Mather employed throughout his long career. They are: *A Discourse Concerning the Danger of Apostacy*, which was preached in 1677 and printed in *A Call from Heaven To the Present and Succeeding Generations* (1679); *The Surest Way to the Greatest Honour* (1699); and finally *The Excellency of a Publick Spirit . . .* (1702).

The last group of sermons is small, but it is perhaps the most significant. Increase Mather perfected a sermon form known as the jeremiad, named after the great Biblical prophet Jeremiah, who often lashed out at the corrupt practices of his own day and deplored the departure of ancient Israel from the original calling to God's divine errand. Most prominent in the Mather canon of jeremiads are *The Day of Trouble is Near* (preached and

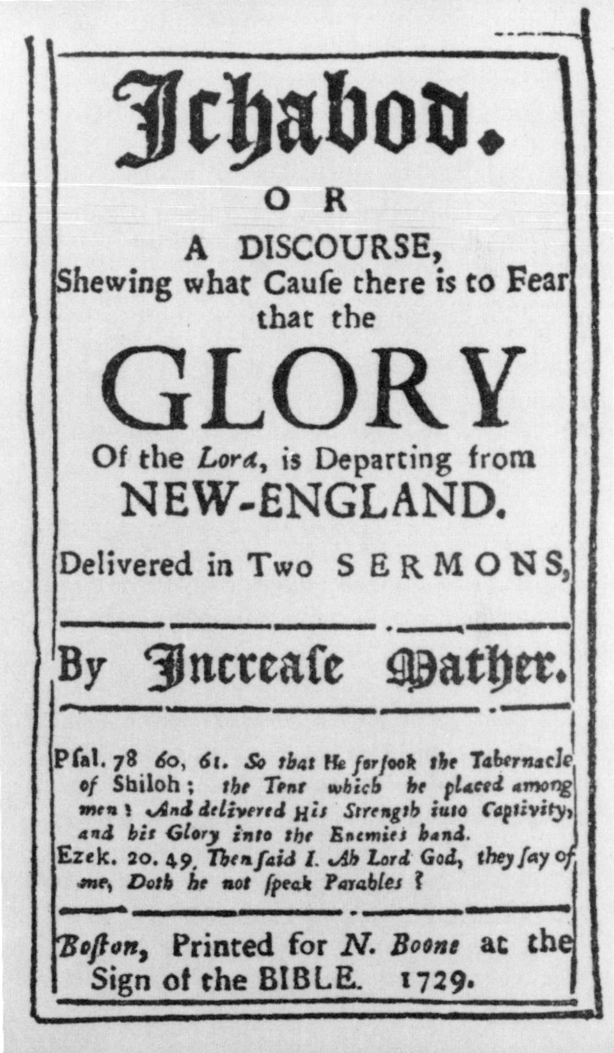

Ichabod.

OR

A DISCOURSE,
Shewing what Cause there is to Fear
that the

GLORY

Of the *Lord*, is Departing from
NEW-ENGLAND.

Delivered in Two SERMONS,

By Increase Mather.

Psal. 78 60, 61. *So that He forsook the Tabernacle of* Shiloh; *the Tent which he placed among men: And delivered His Strength into Captivity, and his Glory into the Enemies hand.*
Ezek. 20. 49. *Then said I. Ah Lord God, they say of me, Doth he not speak Parables?*

Boston, Printed for *N. Boone* at the Sign of the BIBLE. 1729.

Title page for one of Mather's most powerful jeremiads, in which he asks his listeners, "How many Churches, how many towns are there in New-England, *that we may Sigh over them, and say,* The Glory is Gone!"

printed in 1674), whose title speaks volumes about the prophecy contained in its text, and *Ichabod. Or . . . the Glory Of the Lord, is Departing from New-England* (1702), in which Mather's rhetorical flourishes are perhaps among his finest writing. Consider this passage, for example, where Mather is attempting to call attention to the loss of spiritual nerve at the end of the seventeenth century in New England: "Look into the Pulpits, and see if there is such a Glory there, as once there was? *New-England* has had Teachers very Eminent for Learning, & no less Eminent for Holiness, & all Ministerial accomplishments. When will *Boston* see a COTTON, & a NORTON, again? When will *New-England* see a HOOKER, a SHEPARD, a MITCHEL, not to mention others? No little part of the Glory was laid in the Dust, when those Eminent Servants of Christ were laid in their Graves. Look into our Civil State: does Christ reign there as once He did? Is there that Glory in Courts as once there was? Is not our House in diverse parts of this Land, in some danger of falling for want of Pillars to support it? . . . How many Churches, how many towns are there in *New-England,* that we may Sigh over them, and say, *The Glory is Gone!*" *Ichabod* is possibly Mather's finest sermon, and it is certainly one of his most powerful jeremiads. Not only does it contain the rhetorical strategies commonly used in the denunciatory jeremiad; it also exhibits clearly the three divisions of the Puritan sermon form—the text, the doctrine, and the application—so that the modern reader is able to understand the seventeenth-century minister's method of composition in preparing a sermon.

Increase Mather's one hundred-odd publications were overshadowed by Cotton Mather's four-hundred and forty-four, but Increase Mather has been long regarded to have been the more contemporary Puritan of the two. He was complex, ideological, and certainly controversial. He was devoted to God, to his calling as a minister, and he demonstrated an intellectual and psychological rigor which was extraordinary for his times. Like the structure of the Puritan sermon, Mather's career was one of devotion to the scriptural text, from which he always was able to derive a suitable doctrine or idea which would, in turn, be applied or enforced rigorously in his life. He was a "Puritan's Puritan," and his life was an example of the effectiveness with which Puritan precepts might be developed in human or earthly society. With his death and with the death of Cotton Mather a very few years later, Puritanism entered a new phase. Puritanism was no longer the pure orthodoxy established by the first generations and carried forward by the Mathers, and the century that followed their deaths would witness an accommodation of doctrine and practice to the new forces of science and capitalism. The Mather "dynasty," as Robert Middlekauf calls it, was held in place more firmly by Increase Mather than by any other members of the clan.

Other:

Autobiography, edited by M. G. Hall, American Antiquarian Society *Proceedings,* 71, part 2 (1962): 271-360.

Bibliography:

Thomas James Holmes, *Increase Mather: A Bibliography of His Works,* 2 volumes (Cleveland: Privately printed, 1931).

Biography:

Kenneth B. Murdock, *Increase Mather: The Foremost American Puritan* (Cambridge: Harvard University Press, 1925).

References:

Peter Gay, *A Loss of Mastery: Puritan Historians in Colonial America* (Berkeley: University of California Press, 1966);

Mason I. Lowance, Jr., *Increase Mather* (New York: Twayne, 1974);

Robert Middlekauf, *The Mathers: Three Generations of Puritan Intellectuals* (New York: Oxford University Press, 1971);

John L. Sibley, *Biographical Sketches of Graduates of Harvard University,* volume 3 (Cambridge, Mass.: Charles William Sever, 1885);

Larzer Ziff, *Puritanism in America* (New York: Viking, 1973).

Papers:

The major collections of the Mathers' papers are at the American Antiquarian Society and the Massachusetts Historical Society.

Richard Mather

(1596-22 April 1669)

Nancy Craig Simmons
Virginia Polytechnic Institute

BOOKS: *The Whole Book of Psalmes Faithfully Translated into English Metre,* by Mather, John Eliot, Thomas Mayhew, and others (Cambridge: Printed by Stephen Daye, 1640);

An Apologie of the Churches in New-England for Church-Covenant... (London: Printed by T. P. & M. S. for B. Allen, 1643);

Church-Government and Church Covenant Discussed; in an Answer of the Elders of the Severall Churches in New England to Two and Thirty Questions Sent Over to Them by Divers Ministers in England . . . (London: Printed by R. O. & G. D. for B. Allen, 1643);

A Modest & Brotherly Answer to Mr. Charles Herle His Book, Against the Independency of Churches . . . , by Mather and William Tompson (London: Printed for H. Overton, 1644);

A Reply to Mr. Rutherfurd; or, A Defense of the Answer to Reverend Mr. Herles Booke Against the Independency of Churches . . . (London: Printed for J. Rothwell & H. Allen, 1647);

A Platform of Church Discipline Gathered Out of the Word of God, by Mather, John Cotton, and others (Cambridge: Printed by Samuel Green, 1649);

An Heart-Melting Exhortation Together With a Cordiall Consolation . . . , by Mather and Tompson (London: Printed by A. M. for I. Rothwell, 1650);

A Catechisme, or the Grounds and Principles of the Christian Religion (London, 1650);

The Summe of Certain Sermons Upon Genes: 15.6 . . . (Cambridge: Printed by Samuel Green, 1652);

A Farewel-Exhortation to the Church and People of Dorchester in New-England . . . (Cambridge: Printed by Samuel Green, 1657);

A Disputation Concerning Church-Members and Their Children, in Answer to XXI Questions... (London: Printed by J. Hayes for Samuel Thomson, 1659);

Massachusetts Election Sermon (Cambridge: Printed by Samuel Green, 1660);

A Defence Of The Answer and Arguments Of The Synod Met at Boston in the Year 1662. Concerning the Subject of Baptism, And Consociation of Churches. . . , by Mather and Jonathan Mitchel (Cambridge: Printed by S. Green & M. Johnson for Hezekiah Usher, 1664);

An Answer to Two Questions: Question I. Whether Does the Power of Church Government Belong to All the People, or to the Elders Alone? Question II. Whether Does Any Church Power, or Any Power of the Keys Belong to the People . . . (Boston: Printed by B. Green, 1712).

John Foster's woodcut of Richard Mather. As the frontispiece to Increase Mather's 1670 biography of his father, it was the first engraving to be published in America (The Society for the Preservation of New England Antiquities).

Richard Mather, founder of the Mather dynasty in New England, was an active preacher and writer whose published works help to focus the issues faced by the first generation of Massachusetts Bay Puritans in their effort to establish a biblical commonwealth in the New World. Although Mather's pulpit oratory is generally conceded to lack both artistry and power, he developed a vigorous and often heated argumentative style in his polemical writing—a series of rebuttals, definitions, explanations, and statements of church doctrine and government. In his own day, Mather lived in the shadow of his more brilliant contemporaries, especially John Cotton and Thomas Hooker. Subsequently, the roles of his sixth son, Increase, and grandson Cotton as defenders and chroniclers of the faith have eclipsed Richard Mather's position as definer and codifier of that remarkable system known as New England Congregationalism, the federalist theocracy promulgated at Massachusetts Bay in the first half of the seventeenth century.

Mather was not a member of the original settlement, the 1630 expedition led by John Winthrop. Instead, Mather arrived at Boston five years later, disembarking on 17 August 1635 after an uneventful voyage aboard the *James*. (His journal of this voyage was first published in 1850.) Little in his background had prepared him for his new world.

The son of Thomas and Margrett Mather, Richard was born in Lowton, Lancashire, England. His yeoman-class parents, apparently ambitious for their son, encouraged his liberal education at the local grammar school; a university education, however, was deferred when, at the age of fifteen, Mather began teaching at Toxteth Park, near Liverpool. Though his family seems to have had little interest in religious matters, at Toxteth Mather boarded with a strongly nonconformist family. In 1614, after three years at Toxteth, Mather experienced a religious awakening that changed the direction of his life. Assured through his experience that he was one of the elect, Mather began immediately to prepare for the ministry, while he continued to teach Greek and Latin as master of the Toxteth School.

In 1618 Mather entered Brasenose College, Oxford, to complete his studies. After only a few months, however, he left Oxford in response to a call from the people of Toxteth to return as their minister. Ordained in the Church of England, Mather enjoyed several successful years at Toxteth before his nonconformity became a liability. In 1624, after a courtship of several years (extended, the story goes, by her father's dislike of nonconformists), Mather married Katherine Hoult; while they remained in England, the couple had four sons: Samuel (born in 1625), Timothy (born in 1628), Nathaniel (born in 1630), and Joseph (born in 1632?). By the end of 1633 Mather's refusal to accede to new demands for conformity to official Anglican practices led to his permanent removal from his pulpit. Out of a living, with no prospects for the future, and fearing, above all, persecution, by 1635 Mather had decided to emigrate. (A recent biographer, B. R. Burg, believes Mather was particularly influenced by the agonizing martyrdoms recounted in John Foxe's *Acts and Monuments of the Christian Religion*.)

For Mather, arrival in Boston was a sudden plunge into the realities and peculiarities of the New England system, a unique attempt to found a society on the principles prescribed in the Bible. First he learned the meaning of church membership in the colony: he was refused membership in the Boston church because his answers to some questions about ordination suggested an unregenerate nature. Unlike the English system, where everyone was expected to subscribe to the official religion and thus was automatically admitted to the church whether "saved" or not, in New England church membership was awarded only to those who presented visible proof of their election—approximately one-fifth of those residing in the colony under its first charter, Perry Miller estimated.

For several months, Mather experienced the terrors of one who is not assured of his election. Having corrected his beliefs, Mather was later admitted to the church; soon afterwards (1636) he accepted a call to the church at Dorchester. Here Mather skirmished with another of the peculiarities of the New England system, the method of establishing churches. Upon arriving at Dorchester, Mather discovered he did not really have a church; the body of believers would have to "gather" together and receive permission from the magistrates and clergy of the colony to incorporate—or "covenant," as this practice of voluntarily binding themselves to each other and to God was called—themselves into a church. Because his new parishioners showed little evidence of regeneration, Mather's initial application for permission to covenant was refused. Only after months of reeducation by their chastened minister was the Dorchester congregation able to convince the authorities that they were indeed of the "elect." Mather's efforts to understand this feature of the New England system are reflected in the labyrinthine reasoning of his later explanations of the church covenant; and his sense of outrage at civil interference in the matter of covenanting led to his strong advocacy of separation of secular and religious authority.

After he had managed to gather his church at Dorchester in August 1636, Mather continued as preacher and teacher to the community of this small farming village for the remainder of his life. Here were born his last two sons, Eleazar in 1637 and Increase in 1639. Mather's primary responsibility was pastoral: unassisted for most of his tenure, he preached several times every week, a three-to-four-hour Sunday "sermon" and weekday "lectures." From this large output, Mather published only one collection of sermons, *The Summe of Certain Sermons Upon Genes: 15.6* (1652), on the doctrine of justification by faith. As these and other sermons (which survive in manuscript) suggest, to his congregation Mather was a practical teacher and moralist, little concerned to embellish his sermons with the metaphysical exuberances of some of his contemporaries or to employ the close reasoning of his polemical writing. His preaching style was plain, as his grandson Cotton Mather explains in the *Magnalia Christi Americana* (1702); he avoided foreign phrases and the like, "aiming to shoot his *Arrows*, not over the *Heads*, but into the *Hearts* of his Hearers." One of his early tasks involved preparing, with John Eliot, Thomas Mayhew, and others, *The Whole Book of Psalmes Faithfully Translated into English Metre* (1640), more commonly known as the *Bay Psalm Book*. Although Mather has traditionally been considered the author of the preface to this volume, in 1956 Zoltán Haraszti presented compelling evidence—including consideration of style, handwriting, and a parallel work—that it was instead the work of John Cotton.

Mather had arrived in New England at a time when its peculiar practices were under increasing scrutiny by conformists and nonconformists alike. Having done some theological writing before he left England, in 1639 Mather was chosen by his fellow clerics to compose answers to two separate criticisms of the system: an English cleric named Bernard had objected to the New England method of gathering churches, and some Lancashire clergy had heard tales of a number of unusual practices in the colony. Mather's answers to these critics of the New England system make him an important spokesman: the two works that circulated first in manuscript and then were published in 1643 provide the first extensive statement of the Bay Colony's doctrinal and political framework. The answer to Bernard, *An Apologie of the Churches in New-England for Church-Covenant*... was, according to B. R. Burg, a "much-needed justification for the colonists' use of covenanting in organizing their churches," in which Mather provided the definition of the term *covenant* that is most often cited today: "A solemne and publick promise before the Lord, whereby a company of Christians, called by the power and mercy of God to fellowship with Christ, and by his providence to live together . . . in the unitie of faith, and brotherly love . . . bind themselves to the Lord, and to one another. . . ." The second work, *Church-Government and Church Covenant Discussed; in an Answer of the Elders of the Severall Churches in New England to Two and Thirty Questions* . . . (1643) is a more comprehensive statement of church government and procedures. In 1643 Mather was selected to deliver the annual election sermon for the colony, an honor indicative of both the esteem with which he was regarded and his "doctrinal correctness."

A combination of zeal and what Burg calls a "quixotic determination to be a leader among his ministerial colleagues" probably led to Mather's continued defense of the New England system in the 1640s. With William Tompson, pastor at Braintree, he wrote *A Modest & Brotherly Answer to Mr. Charles Herle* . . . (1644) in response to the English Presbyterian who had attacked the Congregational pattern; *A Reply to Mr. Rutherfurd* . . . (1647) was a response to a Scottish argument for presbyteries; and for two years Mather labored to answer a third Presbyterian, William Rathband, in "A Plea for the Churches of Christ in New England," a monumental work combining defense with a statement of faith. (This last effort was never published.) In 1645 Mather and Tompson wrote *An Heart-Melting Exhortation* . . . (1650), a jeremiad in the form of a letter addressed to Mather's former Lancashire neighbors. About 1650 Mather submitted two catechisms to the Westminster Assembly, and long after his father's death Increase Mather had printed another work on the power of church government, *An Answer to Two Questions* . . . (1712). No believer in complete democracy, Mather had written that the people should submit to their elders.

Mather is usually credited with chief authorship of the Cambridge Platform of 1648, the major doctrinal statement of New England Congregationalism (published as *A Platform of Church Discipline* . . . , 1649). A concerted response to mounting criticism and attack, the platform stated and defended the basic tenets and practices of the faith. Against increasing sentiment for a Presbyterian form of strict church organization, the platform insisted on the congregational system of

An 1895 photograph of Richard Mather's birthplace

organization and government. Each covenanted church was an independent unit, loosely joined in fellowship with the other churches. The platform specified the criteria for church membership, retaining the hard line on baptism: the first sacrament was reserved for children whose parents were full church members, who had, that is, undergone the required religious experience that signified salvation. The platform also firmly limited the power of civil authority over religious matters.

These questions had been among those discussed at a synod convened at Cambridge in 1646 to deal with issues of doctrinal deviation and baptism. At the end of that two-week session, Mather (as well as Ralph Partridge, pastor at Duxbury), was asked to draw up a model of church government to be considered the next year. An epidemic in 1647 postponed final consideration of the document until 1648, when Mather presented his weighty, eighteen-chapter "Modell of Church Government," a comprehensive, carefully constructed, and often impassioned statement of doctrine and practice. The synod, however, wanted a more direct statement of policy, and in the course of its revision and condensation of Mather's "Modell of Church Government," it also altered some of his ideas, particularly his more liberal view that baptism should be available to children of unregenerate but baptized parents. The platform's limitation of the authority of courts and magistrates over church matters, however, clearly reflects Mather's insistence on greater separation between church and state.

The baptism question was again the issue a decade later when Mather represented his church at the synod of 1657 which revised the stand taken in the Cambridge Platform by endorsing the Half-Way Covenant, which allowed children of baptized but unconverted Christians to be baptized. Soon Mather was attempting to explain these actions to his more conservative congregation in *A Disputation Concerning Church-Members and Their Children, in Answer to XXI Questions . . .* (1659). They refused, however, to follow their minister on this matter. At the synod of 1662 Mather again supported the redefined covenant (while his son Increase opposed it) and explained his position in *A Defence Of The*

Answer and Arguments Of The Synod Met at Boston in the Year 1662. Concerning the Subject of Baptism, And Consociation of Churches . . . (1664).

In his last years, Mather remained remarkably active for a man of his age, continuing to work for almost twelve years after writing *A Farewel-Exhortation to the Church and People of Dorchester*... (1657), a sort of jeremiad in which the old preacher lamented the decline of religion and urged his people not to lose sight of godliness in the midst of the world. The death of his wife in 1655 left Mather alone only a short time: the next year he married Sarah Cotton, the widow of his friend John Cotton, who had died in 1652. Six years later his son Increase married Sarah's daughter Maria. Increase Mather assisted his father with his pastoral duties, but Richard Mather continued his prodigious activity until his death in Dorchester at the age of seventy-three.

Other:

Journal of Richard Mather, in *Collections of the Dorchester Antiquarian and Historical Society,* no. 3 (Boston: David Clapp, 1850).

Bibliography:

Edward J. Gallagher and Thomas Werge, *Early Puritan Writers: A Reference Guide* (Boston: G. K. Hall, 1976), pp. 149-163.

Biographies:

Increase Mather, *The Life and Death of that Reverend Man of God, Mr. Richard Mather, Teacher of the Church in Dorchester in New England*... (Cambridge: Printed by S. Green & M. Johnson, 1670);

Walker Williston, *Ten New England Leaders* (New York & Boston: Silver, Burdett, 1901), pp. 97-134;

Robert Middlekauff, *The Mathers: Three Generations of Puritan Intellectuals, 1596-1728* (New York: Oxford University Press, 1971), pp. 3-75;

B. R. Burg, *Richard Mather of Dorchester* (Lexington: University of Kentucky Press, 1976).

References:

B. R. Burg, *Richard Mather* (Boston: Twayne, 1982);

Zoltán Haraszti, *The Enigma of the Bay Psalm Book* (Chicago: University of Chicago Press, 1956);

Cotton Mather, *Magnalia Christi Americana* (London: Printed for Thomas Parkhurst, 1702), III: 122-133.

Papers:

The Mather Family Papers, 1613-1819, at the American Antiquarian Society in Worchester, Massachusetts, include drafts of several of Mather's published writings as well as of "A Modell of Church Government" and drafts of the "Cambridge Platform," an indexed volume of sermon notes for 1646-1650, and other papers. The Mather Collection in the Alderman Library at the University of Virginia, Charlottesville, includes Mather's draft of his *Church-Government and Church Covenant Discussed*... and three unpublished sermons. Some other manuscripts are scattered in various repositories.

Jonathan Mitchel

(1624-9 July 1668)

Jane Gold
George Washington University

BOOKS: *Propositions concerning the subject of Baptism and Consociation of Churches, collected and confirmed out of the word of God, by a Synod of Elders and Messengers of the Churches in Massachusets-Colony in New-England . . .* , by Mitchel and others (Cambridge: Printed by Samuel Green for Hezekiah Usher, 1662);

A Defence of the Answer and Arguments of the Synod met at Boston in the year 1662. Concerning The subject of Baptism, and Consociation of churches . . . , by Mitchel and Richard Mather (Cambridge: Printed by S. Green & M. Johnson for Hezekiah Usher, 1664);

Nehemiah on the Wall in Troublesom Times; or, A Serious and Seasonable Improvement of that great Example of Magistratical Piety and Prudence, Self-denial and Tenderness, Fearlessness and Fidelity, unto Instruction and Encouragement of present and succeeding Rulers in our Israel . . . (Cambridge: Printed by S. Green & Marmaduke Johnson, 1671);

A Discourse of the Glory to which God hath called believers by Jesus Christ . . . (London: Printed for Nathaniel Ponder, 1677; Boston: Printed by B. Green, 1721).

Jonathan Mitchel, among the most prominent of the second-generation Puritan ministers, is best known as the chief architect of the Half-Way Covenant. Born in Halifax, Yorkshire, to Matthew and Susan Butterfield Mitchel, wealthy Puritans who fled to America in August 1635, Mitchel entered Harvard in 1645 to be trained for the ministry, earned his A.B. in 1647, and in 1649 became one of the first fellows of Harvard. He preached a well-received sermon at Cambridge in August 1649, and, when Thomas Shepard died shortly after, Mitchel was unanimously chosen to succeed him as pastor to the Church of Cambridge, where he served for eighteen years. To honor Shepard, he edited Shepard's sermons on the parable of the ten virgins, adding his own preface and having the work printed in London in 1660. He was ordained on 21 August 1650, and on 19 November 1650, he married Shepard's young widow, Margaret Boradel. Although they had several children, only their daughter Margaret married and bore descendants.

When Henry Dunster, his old preceptor and the president of Harvard, publicly embraced Anabaptism, Mitchel opposed him in a controversy which cost Dunster his office but did not alter the friendship between the two men. This dispute led Mitchel into a study of the doctrine of infant baptism and a defense of "the *visible interest* of the *children* of the faithful in the *covenant of grace*." When the Synod of 1662 met in Boston to combat declining religious enthusiasm and to relax partially the strict standards for church membership established earlier, Mitchel was the leading advocate and chief author and defender of the Half-Way Covenant, which proposed that children of noncommunicants who lived without scandal and in accordance with church doctrine could be baptized. Although Mitchel's arguments eventually persuaded Increase Mather, who originally sided with Charles Chauncy against him, the compromise was later struck down by Jonathan Edwards.

Widely respected by friends and opponents alike for his brilliance, piety, and wisdom, Mitchel was an exceedingly modest man of a moderate and judicious nature. To Nathaniel Morton, "he was a man whom God had richly furnished, and eminently fitted for his Work." But although Mitchel's chief aim was always the preservation of the church, he also took an active role in public affairs. When the regicides Edward Whalley and William Goffe (one of the judges who condemned Charles I) arrived in Cambridge in July 1660, after the restoration of the British monarchy, Mitchel hospitably received them and gave them communion. On 8 October 1662, the General Court appointed Mitchel and Capt. Daniel Gookin the first licensers of the press in Massachusetts, and in August 1664, it named Mitchel and two others to draw up a petition to Charles II regarding the colony's charter. Mitchel wrote the petition himself. He sought tirelessly to promote the prosperity and excellence of Harvard; he visited churches throughout the neighboring towns, often proposing

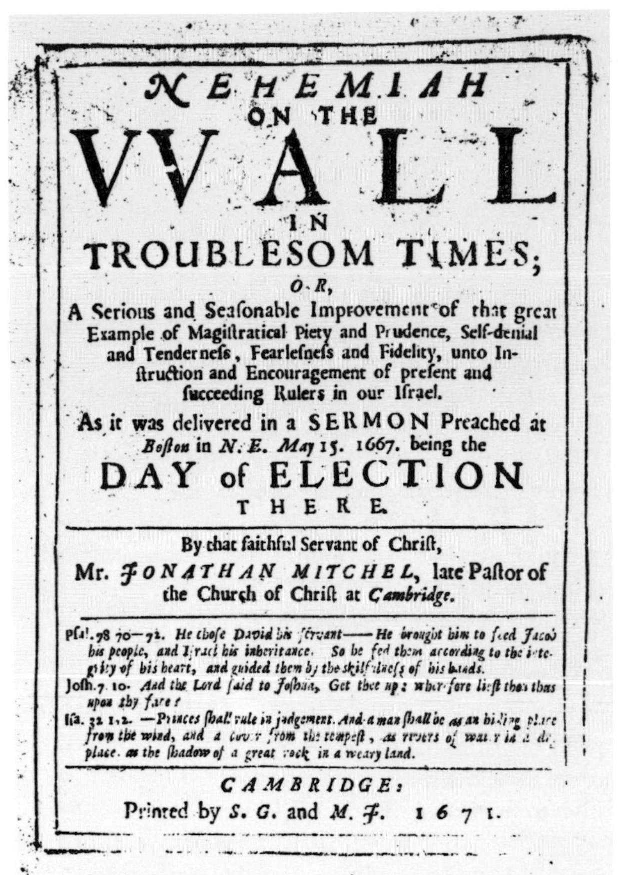

NEHEMIAH
ON THE
VVALL
IN
TROUBLESOM TIMES;
OR,
A Serious and Seaſonable Improvement of that great Example of Magiſtratical Piety and Prudence, Self-denial and Tenderneſs, Fearleſneſs and Fidelity, unto Inſtruction and Encouragement of preſent and ſucceeding Rulers in our Iſrael.

As it was delivered in a SERMON Preached at Boſton in N. E. May 15. 1667. being the
DAY of ELECTION
THERE.

By that faithful Servant of Chriſt,
Mr. JONATHAN MITCHEL, late Paſtor of the Church of Chriſt at Cambridge.

Pſal. 78 70—72. He choſe David his ſervant—He brought him to feed Jacob his people, and Iſrael his inheritance. So he fed them according to the integrity of his heart, and guided them by the skilfulneſs of his hands.
Joſh. 7. 10. And the Lord ſaid to Joſhua, Get thee up: wherefore lieſt thou thus upon thy face?
Iſa. 32 1, 2. —Princes ſhall rule in judgement. And a man ſhall be as an hiding place from the wind, and a cover from the tempeſt, as rivers of water in a dry place, as the ſhadow of a great rock in a weary land.

CAMBRIDGE:
Printed by S. G. and M. J. 1671.

Title page for Mitchel's election sermon exhorting civil rulers to glorify God by seeking the welfare of their people (John Carter Brown Library, Brown University)

improvements for the general advantage of the church, and both ecclesiastical councils and the General Court consulted him often, since his judgments were always tempered with reason and served the best advantage of all.

Several of Mitchel's numerous sermons and treatises were published posthumously under the title *A Discourse of the Glory to which God hath called believers by Jesus Christ* . . . (1677). Affixed to this work is his "Letter to his Brother" (written in May 1649), a response, from his own experiences, to his brother's plea for spiritual advice. Mitchel's letter explores the question of how to live in the world so as to live in heaven, and, according to Cotton Mather, it "has been reckoned one of the most *consummate pieces,* in the methods of addressing a *troubled mind.*" Mitchel's sermons, which reveal his humanism and scholasticism in their allusions to Vergil and Aquinas, demonstrate the basic formula of the seventeenth-century Puritan jeremiad, first interpreting man's afflictions as punishments occasioned by sin and then prescribing recovery through reformation and faith in Christ. His 1667 election-day sermon, *Nehemiah on the Wall* . . . (1671), exhorting civil rulers to glorify God by seeking the welfare of their people, exemplifies this pattern. Although his pulpit style was characteristically plain, his delivery was powerful, and Mather writes that "the people . . . would often *shake* under his dispensations, as if they had heard the *sound* of the *trumpets* from the burning mountain. . . ." The tutor and mentor of Increase Mather, Mitchel was so greatly revered that Cotton Mather considered his life exemplary of Puritan ideals and included a biographical chapter about him in the *Magnalia Christi Americana* (1702).

Other:

Thomas Shepard, *The Parable of the Ten Virgins, Opened & Applied* . . . , edited, with a preface by Mitchel (London: Printed by J. H. for John Rothwell and Samuel Thomson, 1660);

"The Great End and Interest of New-England," in *Elijah's Mantle. A Faithful Testimony, To the Cause and Work of God, in the Churches of New-England* . . . , edited by Cotton Mather and William Cooper (Boston: Printed by S. Kneeland for S. Gerrish, 1722).

References:

Cotton Mather, "Ecclesiastes.—*Or the* Life *of Mr.* Jonathan Mitchel," in *Magnalia Christi Americana* (London: Printed for Thomas Parkhurst, 1702);

Perry Miller, *The New England Mind from Colony to Province* (Cambridge: Harvard University Press, 1953), pp. 27-29, 93-96;

Samuel Eliot Morison, *The Intellectual Life of Colonial New England* (Ithaca: Cornell University Press, 1956), p. 32;

Nathaniel Morton, *New Englands Memoriall* . . . (Cambridge: Printed by S. Green & M. Johnson for John Usher, 1669);

James Savage, *A Genealogical Dictionary of the First Settlers of New England,* volume 3 (Boston: Little, Brown, 1861), pp. 220-221;

J. L. Sibley, *Biographical Sketches of the Graduates of Harvard University,* volume 1 (Cambridge: Charles William Sever/University Bookstore, 1873), pp. 141-157;

Williston Walker, *The Creeds and Platforms of Congregationalism* (Boston: Pilgrim Press, 1960), pp. 238-339.

Joshua Moody

(circa 1633-4 July 1697)

Peter L. Rumsey
Columbia University

BOOKS: Souldiery Spiritualized, or the Christian Souldier Orderly and Strenuously Engaged in the Spiritual Warre, and so Fighting the Good Fight . . . (Cambridge: Printed by Samuel Green, 1674);

A Practical Discourse Concerning the Choice Benefit of Communion with God in His House . . . (Boston: Printed by Richard Pierce for Joseph Brunning, 1685);

The Great Sin of Formality in God's Worship; Or, the Formal Worshipper Proved a Lyar and Deceiver . . . (Boston: Printed by Benjamin Harris & J. Allen, 1691);

The Believers Happy Change by Dying as It Was Recommended in a Sermon Preached, On the Occasion of the Death of Capt. Thomas Daniel... (Boston: Printed by B. Green & J. Allen, 1697).

Joshua Moody (or Moodey), probably born at Ipswich in England, was brought to New England in 1634 by his father, William, one of the first settlers of Newbury, Massachusetts. Moody graduated from Harvard in 1653 and went on to take an M.A. In February of 1655, he was chosen a fellow of Harvard College, where he remained almost three years before taking up ministerial duties at Portsmouth in 1658. During the next thirteen years, Moody labored as a frontier minister, supported by the voluntary subscription of some eighty-six persons, until he was able to organize a church in 1671. While at Portsmouth, Moody showed himself a staunch supporter of Harvard College, for in response to a government appeal for funds, he and his followers pledged £60 per annum for a period of seven years for "the advancement of good litterature there."

Throughout his life, Moody never hesitated to speak freely about sin in high places or to voice his opinions when he felt that public behavior did not measure up to the standards which God had set for his people. Moody's forthrightness brought him into open conflict with the authorities upon a number of occasions. In 1682, an animosity which had developed between Moody and Governor Cranfield because of the former's outspokenness came to a head over the case of a smuggler. The case had come to trial, but the smuggler had managed mysteriously to spirit his impounded vessel out of the harbor, having reached a compromise with Cranfield and the revenue collector. Moody was furious at this obvious flouting of the law, and, since the smuggler was a member of his congregation, he approached Cranfield for copies of the evidence presented at the trial. Cranfield refused Moody's request on the grounds that neither the church nor its minister should meddle with him. When Moody went ahead and publicly disciplined the smuggler in church, Cranfield was enraged at being thus defied and determined to have revenge upon the minister. Since Cranfield could do nothing directly in the case in question, he decided to even the score with Moody by devious means. In England at the time, penal laws against nonconformists were being vigorously enforced. Cranfield issued an order that any person desiring baptism or any other sacrament was entitled to have it administered according to the liturgy of the Church of England. With his trap set, Cranfield and four others who were Anglicans presented themselves at Moody's church and demanded to be served communion. Moody, who refused on the grounds of his nonconformist convictions, was tried, found guilty, imprisoned, and then barred from preaching in the province.

Obtaining his release after thirteen weeks in confinement, Moody moved to Boston and became assistant to James Allin at the First Church. Shortly thereafter, he was called to a ministry at New Haven and, a few months later, was offered the presidency of Harvard, but he declined both positions. In 1689, when news of the Glorious Revolution reached New England and the citizens staged one of their own by arresting and deposing Edmund Andros, who had been appointed governor by James II and who had ruled the colonies by virtual fiat, Moody was among the ringleaders.

During the Salem witch trials in 1692, Moody again came to public prominence when he aided Philip English and his wife, members of a respected Salem merchant family who had been accused and imprisoned, to flee the colony. Moody also preached a public sermon on the text—"If they persecute you in one city, Flee to another." This stand brought condemnation upon him and may have prompted his return to his former congregation at Portsmouth in 1693. In 1697, Moody went to Boston in search of medical advice and died there on 4 July.

Although only five of Moody's sermons were published, they demonstrate his range and his control of the sermonic form. The most ambitious of Moody's sermons, *Souldiery Spiritualized*... (1674), contains one of the most extended metaphors in seventeenth-century Puritan writing. In it, the human condition is portrayed as an ongoing spiritual battle, and Moody skillfully works most of the military terminology of his day into the text of this artillery-day sermon. Moody's execution sermon, *An Exhortation to a Condemned Malefactor*, published with another sermon on the same subject by Cotton Mather (1686), is as stinging a denunciation of a murderer as may be found in New England literature at the time, while *A Practical Discourse Concerning the Choice Benefit of Communion* . . . (1685) and *The Great Sin of Formality in God's Worship*... (1691) show Moody to be adept at expounding matters of religious orthodoxy to a general audience. Finally, *The Believers Happy Change by Dying*. . . (1697), a funeral sermon, demonstrates that Moody was able to convey compassion as well as to take harsh, unremitting stands against evildoers. In this sermon, Moody builds a metaphor from the equation of the scriptures with an apothecary's shop. As a spiritual physician, Moody goes on to dispense soothing doses from the heavenly pharmacy, and he suggests that the Lord has been pleased "to find out the most sweet, pleasant and alluring *Metaphors*" to remove the "Sting of Death." Ultimately, Moody presents death as analogous to a prescription of rest and sleep for the weary traveler.

Moody adhered to the Puritan principle of using the plain style in his sermons. As a result, his homilies are tightly organized compositions in which the chosen texts are carefully and simply improved upon. His frequent use of metaphors in his work is typical of sermons of the day, since the aim of the plain style was to render points of theology in a manner easily understood by a general audience.

Other:

An Exhortation to a Condemned Malefactor, in *The Call of the Gospel Applyed unto all Men in General, and Unto a Condemned Malefactor in Particular*. . . , by Cotton Mather (Boston: Printed by R. Pierce, 1686).

Letters:

Collections of the Massachusetts Historical Society, fourth series 5 (1861): 73, 116; 8 (1868): 357-373.

References:

Nathaniel Adams, *Annals of Portsmouth* (Exeter, N.H.: Printed by C. Norris, 1825);

Ralph May, *Early Portsmouth History* (Boston: Goodspeed, 1926), pp. 167-168, 170, 190-197;

John L. Sibley, *Biographical Sketches of Graduates of Harvard University*, volume 1 (Cambridge: Charles William Sever, 1873), pp. 367-379.

Papers:

A volume of Moody's sermon manuscripts is preserved in the library of the Massachusetts Historical Society.

Nathaniel Morton

(1613-29 June 1685)

Thomas P. Slaughter
Rutgers University

BOOK: *New-Englands Memoriall: or, A Brief Relation of the most Memorable and Remarkable Passages of the Providence of God, manifested to the Planters of New-England in America* . . . (Cambridge: Printed by S. Green & M. Johnson for John Usher, 1669).

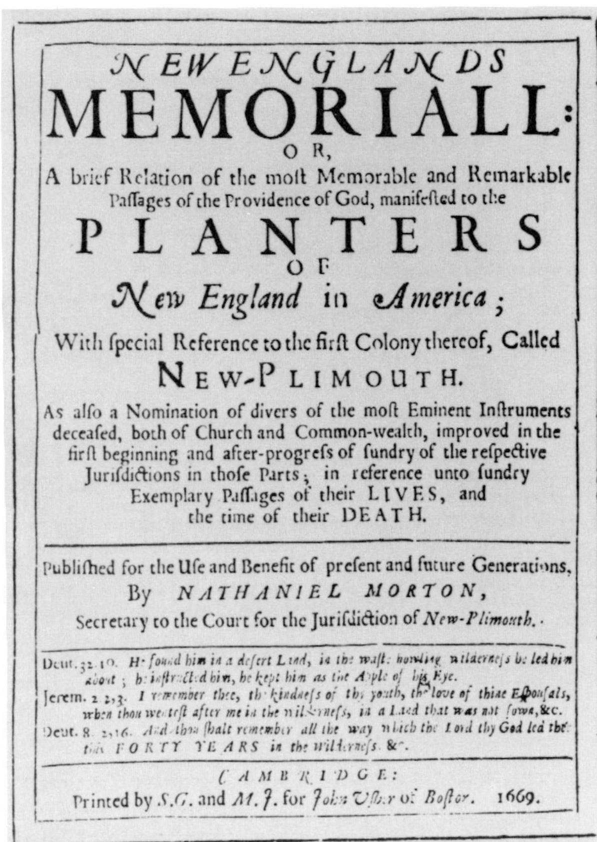

NEW-ENGLANDS
MEMORIALL:
OR,
A brief Relation of the most Memorable and Remarkable Passages of the Providence of God, manifested to the
PLANTERS
OF
New England in *America;*
With special Reference to the first Colony thereof, Called
NEW-PLIMOUTH.
As also a Nomination of divers of the most Eminent Instruments deceased, both of Church and Common-wealth, improved in the first beginning and after-progress of sundry of the respective Jurisdictions in those Parts; in reference unto sundry Exemplary Passages of their LIVES, and the time of their DEATH.

Published for the Use and Benefit of present and future Generations,
By *NATHANIEL MORTON*,
Secretary to the Court for the Jurisdiction of *New-Plimouth.*

Deut. 32. 10. *He found him in a desert Land, in the waste howling wilderness he led him about; he instructed him, he kept him as the Apple of his Eye.*
Jerem. 2. 2, 3. *I remember thee, the kindness of thy youth, the love of thine Espousals, when thou wentest after me in the wilderness, in a Land that was not sown,* &c.
Deut. 8. 2, 16. *And thou shalt remember all the way which the Lord thy God led thee this FORTY YEARS in the wilderness.* &c.

CAMBRIDGE:
Printed by *S.G.* and *M.J.* for *John Usher* of *Boston*. 1669.

Title page for Morton's history, which served as the standard account of the Plymouth colony's early years for nearly two centuries

Nathaniel Morton, one of the early Pilgrim settlers of Plymouth Colony, arrived from Leyden on the *Anne* with his family in 1623 and upon the death of his father, George Morton, in 1624 was taken into the household of his uncle, Governor William Bradford. He later served as the governor's clerk, amanuensis, and agent in public and private transactions, and from 1647 to 1685 he was secretary of the colony and keeper of the records. During the last forty-five years of his life, Morton was one of the wealthiest and most influential men in the colony. Largely responsible for drafting most of the colony's laws, he served the town of Plymouth, the colony, and his church in numerous capacities.

Morton's *New-Englands Memoriall* . . . (1669) was the second and most important history of the colony to be published during the seventeenth century. (*Mourt's Relation*, largely the work of Edward Winslow with contributions by William Bradford and published under the direction of George Morton in 1622, was the first.) Until the discovery of the manuscript for Bradford's *Of Plimmoth Plantation* in 1855, Morton's book was the major history of the colony's settlement, but it is now largely superseded by Bradford's work, which is far richer in observation and detail, especially about the earliest period of the colony's settlement. About one-third of Morton's *New-Englands Memoriall*. . ., which was prepared from Bradford's papers, is drawn directly from Bradford's *Of Plimmoth Plantation*. Morton's attempt at a fuller account was accidentally burned in 1676. He completed yet another version which was published along with a dialogue of Bradford's and numerous commemorative verses in 1680. The major contribution of Morton's *New-Englands Memoriall* since the recovery of Bradford's *Of Plimmoth Plantation* lies in historical facts which are available from no other contemporary source. For example, it is the only account that lists the signers of the compact in 1620 and the name of the ship that set out with the *Mayflower* but had to turn back: *Speedwell*.

When Morton began writing *New-Englands Memoriall* and upon whose initiative is unknown. His reasons for writing and publishing the book were similar to those which impelled Cotton Mather to write the *Magnalia Christi Americana* (1702). Both books were didactic records for later generations, who would need to be reminded of the marvelous providences of God that had led their forefathers in their hazardous endeavors to colonize the New World. Morton's account should also be classed with such books as Edward Johnson's *Wonder-Working Providence of Sion's Saviour in New-England* (1654) as a spiritual defense of the much-maligned Puritan movement. The book served its purposes well, providing a plain, concise, authoritative account of the physical and spiritual tasks of the founding fathers. To five or six generations of New England schoolboys, *New-Englands Memoriall* served as the standard history of the first settlement of New England, and its four new editions (1721, 1722, and two in 1826) stand as evidence of steady demand for the account during the colonial years and the early years of the republic.

References:

John K. Allen, *George Morton of Plymouth Colony and Some of His Descendants* (Chicago: Privately printed, 1908);

Howard J. Hall, Introduction to *New Englands Memoriall . . .* , edited by Hall (New York: Scholars' Facsimiles & Reprints, 1937).

Thomas Morton

(circa 1579-circa 1647)

Alan Axelrod
Henry Francis du Pont Winterthur Museum

BOOK: *New English Canaan or New Canaan. Containing an Abstract of New England, Composed in three Books . . .* (Amsterdam: Printed by Jacob Frederick Stam, 1637); republished in *Tracts*, edited by Peter Force, volume 2, number 5 (Washington, D.C.: Peter Force, 1838).

Thomas Morton (British Museum)

Thomas Morton was the author of a single, though remarkable, book. His *New English Canaan...* (1637) is an account of Indian life and manners, a history of early New England told from an unusual non-Puritan perspective, a tract promoting settlement of the region, and, most memorably, the story of bitter rivalry between the saintly settlers of Plymouth and the reveling Morton of Merry Mount. This tale, at once charming and acidly satiric, dramatizes conflicting values—the "righteous" versus the "wild"—at the heart of American experience and identity.

Morton was born about 1579 possibly in the West Country of England. He became an attorney, and his marriage in 1621 to a widow named Alice Miller almost immediately embroiled him in a series of lawsuits over property rights. Shortly after the termination of litigation, in 1624, he left for New England, establishing a fur-trading post at Mount Wollaston (modern Quincy), Massachusetts, which he renamed Ma-re-Mount or Merry Mount. In 1627, with the trading post prospering, Morton invited the

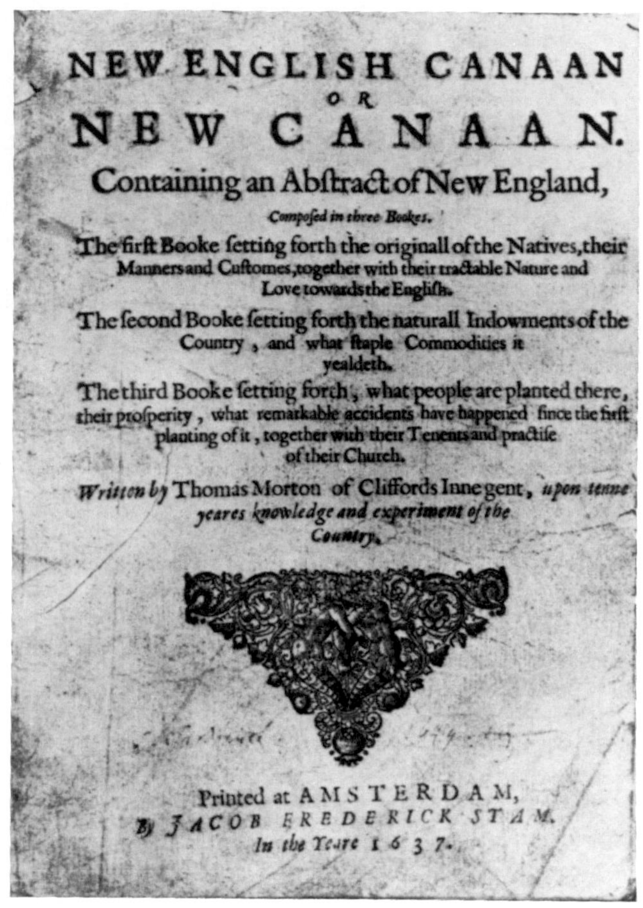

NEW ENGLISH CANAAN
OR
NEW CANAAN.
Containing an Abſtract of New England,
Compoſed in three Bookes.
The firſt Booke ſetting forth the originall of the Natives, their Manners and Cuſtomes, together with their tractable Nature and Love towards the Engliſh.
The ſecond Booke ſetting forth the naturall Indowments of the Country, and what ſtaple Commodities it yealdeth.
The third Booke ſetting forth, what people are planted there, their proſperity, what remarkable accidents have happened ſince the firſt planting of it, together with their Tenents and practiſe of their Church.
Written by Thomas Morton of Cliffords Inne gent, *upon tenne yeares knowledge and experiment of the Country.*

Printed at AMSTERDAM,
By JACOB FREDERICK STAM.
In the Yeare 1637.

Title page for Morton's history, written as part of the campaign to nullify the Massachusetts Bay Company patent

local Indians, lads as well as "Lasses in beaver coats," to dance around the maypole he had erected. This symbol and the revelry associated with it galled the Pilgrims of Plymouth (according to Morton) almost as bitterly as did the financial success of the Merry Mount trading post. In the spring of 1628 Plymouth and other plantations charged Morton with selling guns to the Indians; he was arrested in June by Miles Standish, tried, and shipped back to England in August. Acquitted there, he returned to Merry Mount in 1629. John Endecott, who had chopped down the offending maypole while Morton was abroad, arrested the reveler again in 1630 and, again, banished him to England, also confiscating his goods and burning his house.

This time Morton worked with the anti-Puritan Anglican Archbishop William Laud to nullify the Massachusetts Bay Company patent. From instigation to the final judgment of the Court of King's Bench, nullification proceedings spanned 1632-1637. The judgment, however, proved unenforceable, and the company maintained control of the territory.

As part of the campaign against the company, Morton wrote his *New English Canaan. . . .* Book one treats the Indians of New England, finding them noble, ripe for conversion to Christianity, and, in ironic contrast to the white settlers of Plymouth, "most full of humanity." Though some historians (most notably Charles Francis Adams, Jr.) have disputed the accuracy of Morton's portrayals, his vivid sketches of individual Indians appear to have a firsthand authenticity.

Book two is an example of that popular colonial literary genre, the promotion tract. Morton writes of New England's natural resources, drawing on his own observations as well as on John Smith's *A Description of New England* (1616) and blending biblical and Renaissance traditions to depict the new land as both Canaan and Arcadia. But it is for book three that *New English Canaan* . . . is best known. A product of Renaissance literary conventions, this section combines arcane verse, prose satire—at first lighthearted and then scathing—with the revelry of a Jonsonian antimasque to relate Morton's sad adventures among the Plymouth Separatists.

Thomas Morton ended his second exile in 1643, returning to America after an absence of thirteen years. Upon his arrival, he wintered in Plymouth and traveled in the wilderness. He was arrested by Boston authorities in September of 1644. Convicted of slander partly because of his agitation against the Massachusetts Bay Company and partly on evidence in his own book, he was imprisoned during the winter of 1644-1645. Released, he settled in Agamenticus (modern York), Maine, where he died about 1647.

As history, *New English Canaan* . . . is suspect. Morton's biases need to be checked against those of his Pilgrim counterpart, William Bradford. Nevertheless, witty, ribald, and occasionally obscure beyond penetration, Morton's book records the working of a cultivated European sensibility in an American wilderness. As comedy (rare in early American literature) and as an early articulation of enduring cultural stereotypes, the book has influenced at least eleven later American writers—among them Washington Irving, Nathaniel Hawthorne, John Greenleaf Whittier, Henry Wadsworth Longfellow, Stephen Vincent Benét, and Robert Lowell.

References:

Charles Francis Adams, Jr., Introduction to *The New English Canaan of Thomas Morton* (Boston: Prince Society, 1883);

Donald F. Connors, *Thomas Morton* (New York: Twayne, 1969).

John Norton

(6 May 1606-5 April 1663)

Michael P. Kramer
University of California, Davis

BOOKS: *Responsio ad Totam Quaestionum Syllogen à clarissimo Viro Domino Guilielmo Apollonio, Ecclesiae Middleburgensis Pastore, propositam* . . . (London: Typis R. B. impensis Andreae Crook, 1648); republished as *The Answer to the Whole Set of Questions of the Celebrated Mr. William Apollonius,* translated by Douglas Horton (Cambridge: Harvard University Press, 1958);

A Brief and Excellent Treatise containing the Doctrine of Godliness or Living unto God . . . (London: Printed by John Field for Edmund Paxton, 1648); republished as *A Brief Catechisme Containing The Doctrine of Godlines. Or Of Living Unto God* (Cambridge: Printed by S. Green & M. Johnson, 1660);

A Discussion of that Great Point in Divinity, the Sufferings of Christ . . . (London: Printed by A. M. for Geo. Calvert & Joseph Nevill, 1653);

The Orthodox Evangelist . . . (London: Printed by John Macock for Henry Cripps & Lodwick Lloyd, 1654);

The Life and Death of the Deservedly Famous Mr. John Cotton, The Late Reverend Teacher of the Church of Christ at Boston in New England (Cambridge, 1657); republished as *Abel being Dead yet speaketh; or the Life & Death of that deservedly Famous Man of God, Mr. John Cotton* (London: Printed by T. Newcomb for L. Lloyd, 1658); republished as *Memoir of John Cotton,* edited by Enoch Pond (Boston: Perkins & Marvin / Philadelphia: H. Perkins, 1834);

The Heart of N-England rent at the Blasphemies of the present Generation. Or a brief Tractate concerning the Doctrine of the Quakers . . . (Cambridge: Printed by Samuel Green, 1659; London: Printed by J. H. for J. Allen, 1660);

Three Choice and Profitable Sermons Upon Severall Texts of Scripture . . . and *A Copy of the Letter Returned by the Ministers of New-England to Mr. John Dury about his Pacification* . . . (Cambridge: Printed by S. Green & M. Johnson for Hezekiah Usher, 1664).

Renowned for his erudition and forensic skills, John Norton was one of the most respected figures among the first generation of New England Puritans. As minister, theologian, and polemicist, he placed himself at the service of the Puritan colony and played a major role in its religious and political life. His writings eloquently and forcefully defend the unique brand of theology and politics that define the early decades of the Massachusetts orthodoxy.

He was born in Stortford, Hertfordshire, England, the eldest son of a respectable family. His parents, William and Alice Norton, placed the boy under the tutelage of Alexander Strange in Buntingford, where he distinguished himself in his studies, especially Latin. At fourteen he entered Peterhouse, Cambridge University, where he received his B.A. in 1623 and his M.A. in 1627. Norton was apparently forced to leave the university (it is unclear exactly when), due to financial setbacks suffered by his father, to accept a position as usher at Stortford Grammar School and to become as well curate of the local church. During this period, he frequented lectures by several dissenting ministers, in particular, the Reverend Jeremiah Dyke. He had already been exposed to Puritan ideas at Cambridge, but it was at Stortford that he experienced conversion. Because of his newly heightened religious convictions, he refused both a lucrative benefice from his uncle and a fellowship at Cambridge in favor of an appointment as private chaplain to Sir William Mashaw of High Lever, Essex.

As religious tensions grew in England in the early 1630s, Norton grew discouraged about fulfilling his ministerial calling in his native land and decided to immigrate to the new Puritan colony in New England. In the winter of 1634, he and his new wife (her name is unknown, but, according to Cotton Mather, she was "a gentlewoman of good estate and good esteem") joined the Reverend Thomas Shepard aboard the *Good Hope*, bound for the New World. Soon out of port the ship was caught in a violent storm, and its master, losing hope of saving the vessel, asked the two ministers on board to pray. Shepard describes the event in his autobiography: "So Mr. Norton in one place and myself in another part of the ship, he with the passengers, and myself with the mariners above decks, went to prayer and committed our souls and bodies unto the Lord that gave them. Immediately after prayer the wind began to abate, and the ship stayed. . . ." The *Good Hope* was nevertheless unable to complete the voyage, and Norton's passage was delayed for a year, when, with Edward Winslow, he sailed for Plymouth, arriving there October 1635 and remaining to preach through the winter. Although urged to stay on at Plymouth, he preferred the nonseparating Congregationalism of their northern neighbors to the Pilgrims' Separatism, and early in 1636 he removed to Boston. Soon he accepted a call from the church at Ipswich, joining as a freeman on 17 May 1637 and preaching as an assistant to Nathaniel Ward. On 20 February 1638 he became ordained teacher, with Nathaniel Rogers as pastor.

Norton quickly became a powerful advocate of the Middle Way of New England Congregationalism, warding off attacks on all religious fronts. Even before he moved to Ipswich he defended his Protestantism against Roman Catholicism in a public debate with a French friar, and, when Antinomianism threatened to tear the colony apart, he played an important role in the synod which dealt with the questions raised by Anne Hutchinson and her followers. Before too long, his fellow ministers put Norton's literary skills to public use. (To Thomas Shepard, he was "the *master of sentences*.") In 1644, when a series of questions raised by the Dutch minister William Apollonius about Congregational polity arrived in New England, the task of formulating an answer devolved, by unanimous request, upon the teacher from Ipswich. The work, *Responsio ad Totam Quaestionum* . . . , was completed in 1645 and published in 1648: it was the author's first publication and the first Latin work to be written in New England. As an exposition of the New England Way ("between compromise on the left and separation to the right") the book was praised not only by Puritan divines but by the Anglican church historian Thomas Fuller, who wrote: "Of all the authors I have perused concerning the opinions of these dissenting brethren, none to me was more informative than Mr. John Norton (one of no less learning than modesty), minister in New England, in his answer to Apollonius. . . ." Another Latin work composed during this period was a letter to John Dury regarding his efforts toward the pacification and unification of the various Protestant churches. The letter, published in English in 1664, was signed by Norton and forty-three other ministers and is remarkable for its conciliatory tone in a time of vociferous sectarian controversy: "in whatever Assemblies amongst us the whole Company of them that profess the Gospel, the Fundamentals of Doctrine, and Essentials of Order are maintained, although in many niceties of controversial Divinity they are at less Agreement with us, we do hereby make it manifest . . . that we do acknowledge them all, and every one for Brethren; and that we shall be ready to give unto them the right hands of fellowship in the Lord, if in other things they be peaceable, and walk orderly." Norton's inclination,

RESPONSIO
AD
Totam Quæſtionum Syllogen à clariſsimo Viro Domino GUILIELMO APOLLONIO, Eccleſiæ *Middleburgenſis* Paſtore, propoſitam.

Ad componendas Controverſias quaſdam circa *Politiam Eccleſiaſticam* in *Anglia* nunc temporis agitatas ſpectantem.

Per IOHANNEM NORTONUM Miniſtrum Eccleſiæ quæ eſt *Ipſuici* in *Nova Anglia*.

Ezechiel. 43.11. *Quumque pudore ſuffuſi fuerint propter omnia quæ fecerunt, tum notifica eis formam illius domus, & conſtitutionem ejus, & exitus ejus, & introitus ejus, & omnes formas ejus, & omnia ſtatuta ejus, & omnes formas ejus, & omnes leges ejus; & deſcribe illam ante oculos eorum; ut obſervent omnem formam ejus, & omnia ſtatuta ejus, & faciant ea.*

LONDINI,
Typis R.B. impenſis *Andreæ Crook*, ad Inſigne Draconis viridis in Cœmiterio *D.Pauli*.1648.

Title page for Norton's first book, the first Latin work written in New England (John Carter Brown Library, Brown University)

expressed in these early Latin works, to steer between extremes and to preserve peaceableness and order would inform much of his later writing, even his harshest polemics.

The Puritan magistrates, too, often had recourse to Norton's talents. In 1645 he was called upon to preach an election sermon before the General Court, and the following year he and John Winthrop were appointed agents of the colony to England, a commission which was subsequently abandoned because of the still volatile state of the Puritan revolution there. In part as a response to the struggles between Presbyterians and sectarians across the Atlantic, the magistrates called for a synod to prepare an official declaration of the New England Way, and when several churches, including John Cotton's influential Boston church, balked at what they felt was a threat to congregational autonomy, Norton was called in. At the weekly lecture in Boston he preached a sermon which, according to Winthrop, recalled the biblical account of "Moses and Aaron meeting on the mount and kissing each other" and defended "the power of the civil magistrates in calling such assemblies, and the duty of the churches in yielding obedience to the same." The lecture was considered integral in bringing about the relenting of the Boston church. Norton also played an important role in the synod itself, which produced the central document of New England Puritanism, the Cambridge Platform. Once again, in 1650, the General Court called upon Norton when William Pynchon, a Springfield, Massachusetts, magistrate, published *The Meretorious Price of Our Redemption,* a tract which denies that God literally imputed the sins of mankind upon Christ and caused him to suffer in hell in order to redeem them—an essential aspect of the drama at the center of Puritan theology. Norton refuted this heresy in *A Discussion of that Great Point in Divinity, the Sufferings of Christ . . .* (1653), for which he received the substantial sum of £20 (about three months' salary). Pynchon's book was committed to the flames by the magistrates.

Norton published his first work not written upon official request in 1654. *The Orthodox Evangelist . . .*, a major, systematic reexamination of early Puritan theology, exemplifies the blend of conservatism and emotionalism that characterized the teachings of the emigrant clergy. "As a spouse is first married to the person, i.e. her Husband, before she enjoyeth any conjugal communion with him," Norton explains, "so, we first by faith receive the person of Christ before we are made partakers of the benefits of Christ bestowed upon Believers." As the analogy suggests, the pietistic love at the core of Puritan religiosity had to be expressed within the bounds of the saints' covenanted lives. Perhaps the most significant issue in the work is preparation for salvation, the question of man's role in the process of conversion. Norton wanted to maintain the strict Calvinist principle of the inefficacy of man's thought and action before receiving Christ. In his view, grace did not come gradually, as some Puritan theologians believed. "In the moment of Conversion," he argues, "God workes that blessed work . . . in an instant." But neither does it come unawares, and Norton elaborates a long series of preparatory experiences that the soul must undergo before the efficacious influx of God's spirit occurs. So conceived, conversion is both spontaneous and controlled, and Norton is able to pave a theological middle way between Antinomianism on the one hand and Arminianism on the other. Of *The Orthodox Evangelist . . .* John Cotton wrote, "Clusters of ripe grapes passing under the press, are fit to be transported unto all nations; thus, such gifts and labours passing under the press, may be fitly communicated to all churches."

When Cotton was near death in the winter of 1652, his congregation asked him to suggest who might succeed him as teacher in the church at Boston. The eminent minister named Norton, whom he saw in a dream riding into Boston, messiahlike, upon a white horse. Norton had then been contemplating a return to England, but he conditionally accepted the call to Boston, where, he said, he would await God's will in the matter. Two years later, Nathaniel Rogers died, and the Ipswich church demanded their teacher's return. After considerable bickering between the two congregations—bickering that almost persuaded Norton to pursue his plans to return to England—the General Court appointed a council of twelve churches to intervene. His former church was persuaded to drop its demands, and Norton was installed in Boston on 23 July 1656. In an elegy for Cotton, Benjamin Woodbridge, Harvard's first graduate, applied biblical parallels to the succession, reaffirming New England's sense of its divine mission in the face of its loss:

> Though *Moses* be, yet *Joshua* is not dead;
> I mean Renowned NORTON, worthy hee
> Successor to our MOSES is to bee,
> O happy Israel in AMERICA,
> In such a MOSES such a JOSHUA.

On the day of his installation, Norton married his second wife, Mary Mason. (It is not known when his first wife died.)

The following year, Norton published what is credited as being the first American biography—a memoir of his predecessor, best known by the title of the 1658 London edition: *Abel being Dead yet speaketh. . . .* For the author, to record Cotton's life was a moral imperative: "they who have known his doctrine, manner of life, purpose, faith, long suffering, love, patience, persecution, and affliction, [should] not suffer such a light to be hid under a bushel, but put it on a candlestick, that it may give light to them that are in the house." Drawing upon information provided by Cotton's widow and upon memorial sermons by ministers John Davenport and Samuel Whiting, Norton weaves the events of Cotton's career together with skeins of classical, biblical, and ecclesiastical history to produce an elaborate literary fabric, both biography and hagiography, an inspiring model for the individual faithful and an intricate defense of their corporate enterprise in New England.

In Boston, Norton maintained the position of political influence he had secured while at Ipswich. He was appointed an overseer of Harvard College in 1654 and was frequently called upon to advise the magistrates in matters of public policy. In one instance, he performed the signal service of preventing an outbreak of hostilities during a territorial dispute between English and Dutch settlers. He continued to command the respect and admiration of his fellow clergy; Richard Mather entrusted him with the education of his gifted son, Increase. And he remained as well an effective minister, notably instrumental in expanding the importance of public prayer in the Puritan church service. According to Cotton Mather, "It even transported the souls of his hearers to accompany him in his devotions, wherein his *graces* would make wonderful *salleys* into the vast field of *entertainments*, and *acknowledgements*, with which we are furnished in the *new-covenant*, for our *prayers*." It is reported that one of his former parishioners would regularly walk the thirty miles from Ipswich to Boston to partake in Norton's prayers.

But, toward the end of his life, Norton's stand in the community was weakened, and his reputation seriously soiled, by the confluence of two events that shook the Puritan colony—the Quaker persecutions and the Stuart restoration. On both theological and political grounds, Norton had long opposed the Quakers, along with other sects of enthusiasts, and in 1659, at the request of the General Court, he published *The Heart of N-England rent at the Blasphemies of the present Generation . . .*, a refutation of Quaker doctrine and a defense of the punitive measures taken by the magistrates against the sect. It was the year that two of its members, William Robinson and Marmaduke Stevenson, were hanged in Boston. Norton's enmity may be seen in the context of his larger, persistent concern with communal order. "Formes are essential without which things cannot be," he argues, depicting the unruly Quakers as a serious threat to political, religious, and social stability. To Norton, "madmen acting according to their frantick passions, are to be restrained with chaines, when they cannot be restrained otherwise." But to the Quakers, as well as to many of his more liberal countrymen, Norton's name became a byword for intolerance. Two centuries later, Longfellow would have Norton characterize himself as

> A terror to the impenitent, and Death
> On the pale horse of the Apocalypse
> To all the accursed race of heretics.

When Charles II ascended the British throne the following year, New England faced a political crisis. With the fall of the Commonwealth, the American Puritans had to redefine their relationship to the mother country and to reshape their corporate self-image. To complicate matters, King Charles, upon learning of the Quaker executions, ordered a suspension of the death penalty for religious dissension. Many colonists feared for their liberties. Norton's Election Sermon of 1661, "Sion the Outcast healed of her Wounds," called for political reconciliation with the Crown but left ambiguous the religious and ecclesiastical aspects of the relationship: "In matters of State-Civil, and of the Church, let it be shewn that we are his Disciples, who said, 'Give unto Caesar the things that are Caesars, and give unto God the things that are God's; and in matters of Religion, let it be known, that we are for Reformation, and not for Separation." It was certainly no call for surrender. Faced with threats from the Quakers on the one hand and the Stuart monarchy on the other, Norton refused to acknowledge the defeat of the Puritan errand. He interpreted the current crisis as evidence of God's displeasure toward a backsliding people; the Puritans were "out-casts" and had reason to lament. But he found in the outpouring of divine wrath a cause for celebration, too. "If we look at Sion in the glass of the Promise," he declared before the General Court, "the Out-cast is both Marah [bitter] and Hepzibah [joyful], both a widow and Beulah [married]." The divine message was clear: "God's touching an impenitent Out-cast with repentance, is a signal of God's having mercy thereon."

The General Court decided to send Norton and Simon Bradstreet as agents to answer the king's complaints and to obtain a renewal of the Massachusetts charter. They left in February 1662. Charles agreed to ratify the charter but demanded that religious toleration be instituted. Norton's conciliatory position had not rested well with many of his fellow citizens, even among some of his own congregation. Rumblings of dismissal had been heard. When the agents returned from England in September, Norton was greeted, after a quarter-century of public service, with cries of treason. He died suddenly of apoplexy the following spring, after delivering a Sunday morning sermon. At his death, he left a library of 729 volumes and a number of unfinished writings, including a "Body of Divinity." In 1664, a posthumous collection of sermons ("Sion the Out-cast," "The Believer's Consolation," and "The Evangelical Worshipper") was published under the title *Three Choice and Profitable Sermons* . . . and was printed together with Norton's own translation of his Latin letter to John Dury. He was survived by his wife. He left no children.

Nathaniel Morton gives this account of John Norton in *New-Englands Memoriall* . . . (1669): "He was singularly endowed with the tongue of the learned, enabled to speak a word in due season, not only to the wearied soul, but also a word of counsel to a people in necessity thereof, being not only a wise steward of things of Jesus Christ, but also a wise statesman; so that the whole land sustained a great loss of him." Over the years, Norton's reputation among scholars has risen and fallen with the stock of his fellow Puritans. There are as yet no modern biographies nor any extended analyses of his thought and writings.

References:

Sacvan Bercovitch, *The American Jeremiad* (Madison: University of Wisconsin Press, 1978);

Bercovitch, *The Puritan Origins of the American Self* (New Haven: Yale University Press, 1975);

David D. Hall, *The Faithful Shepherd: A History of the New England Ministry in the Seventeenth Century* (Chapel Hill: University of North Carolina Press, 1975);

Cotton Mather, *Johannes in Eremo, Memoirs Relating to the Lives of the Ever-Memorable Mr. John Cotton, Mr. John Norton, Mr. John Wilson, and Mr. John Davenport* (Boston: Printed by Michael Perry, 1695), pp. 1-39;

Dana K. Merrill, "The First American Biography," *New England Quarterly*, 11 (March 1938): 152-154;

Norman Petit, *The Heart Prepared: Grace and Conversion in Puritan Spiritual Life* (New Haven: Yale University Press, 1966), pp. 177-184;

William B. Sprague, *Annals of the American Pulpit* (New York: Carter, 1857), I: 54-59.

Papers:

Norton's manuscript "Body of Divinity," as well as other manuscripts, are in the Massachusetts Historical Society.

Nicholas Noyes

(22 December 1647-13 December 1717)

Peter L. Rumsey
Columbia University

BOOK: *New-Englands Duty and Interest, To Be an Habitation of Justice, and Mountain of Holiness . . .* (Boston: Printed by Bartholomew Green & John Allen, 1698).

Nicholas Noyes, son of Nicholas and Mary Cutting Noyes, was born at Newbury, Massachusetts. He graduated from Harvard in 1667, and shortly thereafter he was called to preach at Haddam, Connecticut. In 1675 Noyes was appointed to go forth with the army during King Philip's War and was at the Swamp Fight at South Kingston, Rhode Island. Six years later, the General Court granted him 200 acres for good service during the war, upon the condition that he agree to settle or stay in Connecticut for four years, but instead in October 1682 Noyes answered the call of the First Society at Salem, Massachusetts, to become the assistant to their pastor, John Higginson. Noyes was installed as minister after Higginson's death in December 1708 and remained in Salem for the rest of his life.

As a minister of Salem Town, Noyes took an active part in the prosecution of the so-called witches in 1692. He apparently acted in good faith, and there is no evidence that he ever experienced a change of heart over his part in the trials even after the proceedings were overturned. A lifelong bachelor, Noyes is described in contemporary accounts as a corpulent man devoted to scholarship. At his death in 1717, he left behind one of the largest libraries in New England, valued at £88.

Noyes's primary literary interest was his poetry, which is composed mainly of rhyming epitaphs and elegies in which puns, quibbles, and conceits abound. He was a belated practitioner of verse-making in the metaphysical style, exhibited in his works by extended plays on words, and analogies between sacred and secular, high and low experiences, in a mixture of traditionally elevated and humble diction. Noyes's broadside "To my worthy Friend, Mr. James Bayley. . . ," printed in Boston in 1707, is representative of Noyes's poetry. In the poem, which is an encomium of sorts on his friend Bayley's fortitude in suffering with a chronic case of kidney stones, Noyes rings seemingly endless

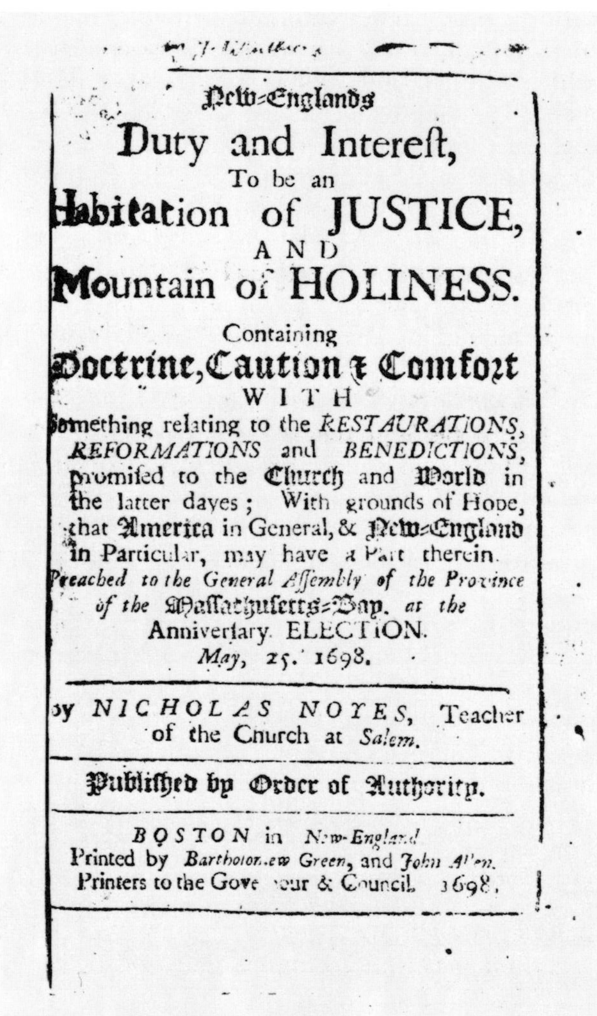

New-Englands
Duty and Interest,
To be an
Habitation of JUSTICE,
AND
Mountain of HOLINESS.
Containing
Doctrine, Caution & Comfort
WITH
Something relating to the *RESTAURATIONS, REFORMATIONS* and *BENEDICTIONS*, promised to the Church and World in the latter dayes; With grounds of Hope, that America in General, & New-England in Particular, may have a Part therein.
Preached to the General Assembly of the Province of the Massachusetts-Bay, *at the* Anniversary ELECTION. *May*, 25. 1698.

By *NICHOLAS NOYES*, Teacher of the Church at *Salem*.

Published by Order of Authority.

BOSTON in *New-England*
Printed by *Bartholomew Green*, and *John Allen*.
Printers to the Governour & Council, 1698.

Title page for the election sermon that Noyes preached before the General Assembly of the Massachusetts Bay Colony on 25 May 1698 (John Carter Brown Library, Brown University)

changes on the name of his friend's disease. If Bayley "shouldst be Stoned to death," then he will "like Stephen fall asleep, / And free from pain forever keep." Later in the poem Noyes exhorts Bayley, advising him to "think what Christ for thee hath done, / Who took an harder, heavier, Stone / Out of thine heart" and reminding him that his earthly pains are as nothing when compared with those of some in hell who "roll the Sisyphean Stone."

In addition to the obviously humorous intent of much of his poetry, Noyes's poems seem to have been motivated by a desire to give the same importance and dignity to his New England contemporaries that English metaphysical verses typically gave to their subjects. Noyes's poems, which lack the compression and inventiveness of their best English counterparts, share the didactic and hortatory qualities and extensive use of biblical allusions which characterize other New England poetry of his day.

Other:

Biographical sketch and "A Prefatory Poem . . . ," in *Magnalia Christi Americana,* by Cotton Mather (London: Printed for Thomas Parkhurst, 1702);

"A Praefatory Poem . . . ," in *Christianus Per Ignem. . . ,* by Cotton Mather (Boston: Printed by B. Green and J. Allen for Benjamin Eliot, 1702);

"A Consolatory Poem Dedicated unto Mr. Cotton Mather . . . ," in *Meat Out of the Eater . . . ,* by Cotton Mather (Boston: Printed for Benj. Eliot, 1703);

"An Elegy upon the Death of the Reverend Mr. John Higginson . . . ," in *Nunc Dimittis, Briefly Decanted On . . . ,* by Cotton Mather (Boston: Printed by B. Green for Eleazar Phillips, 1709);

"An Elegy on the Much Lamented Death of the Reverend Mr. Joseph Green . . . ," in *The deaths of eminent men, and excellent friends, very distressing to the survivors . . . ,* by Thomas Blowers (Boston: Printed by B. Green for Samuel Gerrish, 1716).

References:

Joseph B. Felt, *The Annals of Salem* (Salem: W. & S. B. Ives, 1827);

Sidney Perley, *The History of Salem, Massachusetts,* volume 3 (Salem: Privately printed, 1928);

Richard D. Pierce, ed., *The Records of the First Church in Salem, Massachusetts, 1629-1736* (Salem: Essex Institute, 1974);

John Langdon Sibley, *Biographical Sketches of Graduates of Harvard University,* volume 2 (Cambridge: Charles William Sever, 1881), pp. 239-246;

Town Records of Salem, Massachusetts, volume 3 (Salem: Essex Institute, 1934).

Urian Oakes

(circa 1631-25 July 1681)

Catherine Rainwater
University of Texas at Austin

BOOKS: *MDCL. An Almanack for the Year of Our Lord 1650 . . .* (Cambridge: Printed by Samuel Green, 1650);

New-England Pleaded With, and Pressed to consider the things which concern her peace . . . (Cambridge: Printed by Samuel Green, 1673);

The Unconquerable, All-Conquering & More-Then-Conquering Souldier: Or, the Successful Warre Which a Believer Wageth with the Enemies of His Soul . . . (Cambridge: Printed by Samuel Green, 1674);

An Elegie upon the Death of the Reverend Mr. Thomas Shepard, Late Teacher of the Church at Charlestown in New-England . . . (Cambridge: Printed by Samuel Green, 1677);

The Soveraign Efficacy of Divine Providence; Overruling and Omnipotently Disposing and Ordering All Humane Counsels and Affairs . . . (Boston: Printed for Samuel Sewall, 1682);

A Seasonable Discourse Wherein Sincerity & Delight in the Service of God is earnestly pressed upon Professors of Religion . . . (Cambridge: Printed by Samuel Green, 1682).

Urian Oakes is best known for two works, his 1677 elegy on Thomas Shepard of Charlestown (son of the well-known Cambridge divine) and *The Soveraign Efficacy of Divine Providence . . .* (1682), a sermon accounting for the colonists' heavy losses in King Philip's War. These two texts, together with his lesser-known sermons and addresses, reflect the wealth of classical contemporary knowledge for which Oakes was highly acclaimed during his lifetime. Praising Oakes's fluency in classical Latin, Cotton Mather proclaimed in *Magnalia Christi Americana* (1702) that "America never had a greater master of the true, pure, Ciceronian Latin & Language." In fact, Mather declared, "Considered as a *Scholar*, he was a Notable *Critick* in all the Points of Learning." Increase Mather shared his son's opinion, for he called Oakes *"one of the greatest lights, that ever shone in this part of the world, or that is ever like to arise in our* Horizon."

Urian Oakes was born around 1631, probably in London. His parents, Edward and Jane Oakes, arrived at Cambridge, Massachusetts, with young Urian in about 1640. Information about Oakes's early life is scant, but it is probably significant that he grew up in Cambridge while the elder Thomas Shepard was minister there. Oakes's works repeatedly suggest his unbounded respect for such first-generation figures as Shepard and for the religious zeal which these original settlers embodied. In 1649 Oakes graduated from Harvard, and for the next three years he remained there as a fellow of the college. At the age of nineteen he compiled an impressive table of astronomical calculations, published in the Harvard almanac which he prepared for the year 1650. Oakes's interest in astronomy, shared with many of his contemporaries, especially his friend Increase Mather, is also apparent in his later writings (especially his elegy for the younger Shepard), which employ astronomical imagery and metaphors. Eventually, Oakes married Ruth Ames, the daughter of one of the founders of Puritanism in England, the renowned William Ames, whose family came to America shortly after his death in 1633. Before Ruth Oakes died in 1670 or 1671, she gave birth to at least two, possibly three children.

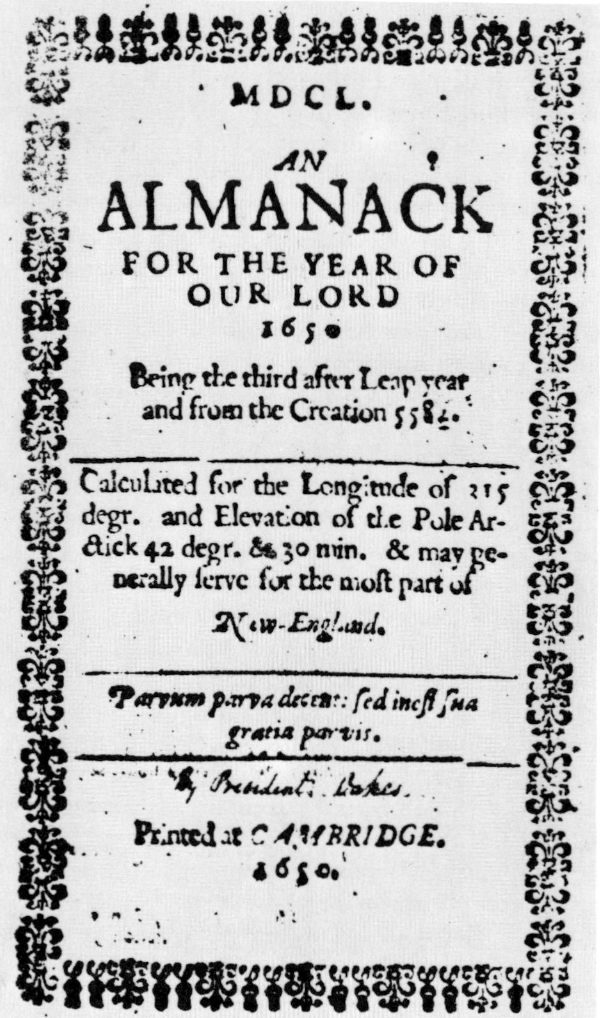
MDCL.

AN
ALMANACK
FOR THE YEAR OF
OUR LORD
1650

Being the third after Leap year
and from the Creation 5582.

Calculated for the Longitude of 315
degr. and Elevation of the Pole Ar-
ctick 42 degr. & 30 min. & may generally serve for the most part of
New-England.

*Parvum parva decent: sed inest sua
gratia parvis.*

By President Oakes.

Printed at CAMBRIDGE.
1650.

Title page for Oakes's almanac (from a facsimile at John Carter Brown Library, Brown University; location of original unknown)

The motto affixed to the 1650 Harvard almanac suggests several of the personal traits for which Oakes was appreciated, a self-effacing sense of humor as well as profound wit and scholarly accomplishment: *"Parvum parva decent, sed inest sua gratia parvis."* This motto may be translated, "Diminutively do diminutives decorate, but their grace pertains to the diminutive." Difficult to translate precisely into English, the motto suggests that small things suitably "decorate" small people, that the "grace" of small things suits small people. The expression refers to Oakes's "diminutive" physical stature and perhaps to his "small" contribution in the almanac, and it displays no small amount of Oakes's wit. The gnomic syntax of his Latin sentence, employing three separate inflections of a single noun, allows Oakes to develop the two halves of the statement as mirror images of one another. Within this eight-word motto Oakes makes a joke and demonstrates his impressive facility with the Latin language. He remains well-known for such masterful verbal effects in both Latin and English.

After about three years as a fellow of Harvard College, Oakes returned to England to become minister of a nonconformist church at Tichfield. However, the Act of Uniformity in 1662 silenced Oakes, and he left Tichfield to become headmaster of Southwark Grammar School. When Jonathan Mitchel died at Cambridge in 1668, Oakes was invited to return to America to take Mitchel's place, but he was detained for three years owing to his own and his wife's illnesses. In 1671, just after Ruth Oakes's death, Oakes arrived in Cambridge where he became minister and, in 1672, a freeman. His ten-year career in America was marked by a recurrent concern with the falling away of the successive generations of Puritans and by continual objections to the sort of religious tolerance which Charles II tried to enforce in the Massachusetts Bay Colony. On this subject of enforced tolerance Oakes proclaimed: "I profess I am heartily for all due moderation. . . . Nevertheless I must adde (as I have great reason) that I look upon an unbounded Toleration as the first born of all *Abominations*. . . . No doubt but it belongs to the *Magistrate* to judge what is *tolerable in his Dominions*. . . . And the Eye of the *Civil Magistrate* is to be the securing of the way of God that is duly established." Doubtless, this conservative stance further endeared him to the Mathers, who devoted much energy to formulating the Bay Colony's position on religious tolerance.

All of Oakes's works display much reverence toward the first generation of New England Puritans and much respect for the virtually infallible authority which they came to represent. Called the "*Moses* among his People" by Cotton Mather in *Magnalia Christi Americana*, Oakes repeatedly likened the New England experience to that of the Canaanites under Moses's charge; time and again he urged the Puritans not to lapse from first-generation principles as the Canaanites lapsed from their original status as the Chosen People. His earliest extant sermon, *The Unconquerable, All-Conquering & More-Then-Conquering Souldier* . . . (1674), delivered on an artillery day in 1672, emphasizes the importance of submission to civil and divine authority, a theme to which Oakes returns in almost all of his subsequent sermons and in his elegy for Shepard. *New-England Pleaded With, and Pressed to consider the things which concern her peace* . . . (1673), an election-day jeremiad delivered at Boston the following year, similarly calls for an end to "rebelliousness" and for submission to established authority. Again citing Moses and the Canaanites as types for the original New England divines and their people, Oakes warns the colonists against the spiritual complacency which brought God's wrath upon those earlier Chosen People. Written in the plain style of the conventional Puritan sermon, both *The Unconquerable, All-Conquering & More-Then-Conquering Souldier* . . . and *New-England Pleaded With* . . . nevertheless reveal Oakes's extensive knowledge of languages and etymology as well as his ability artistically to manage verbal textures even within the constraints imposed by the plain style.

Oakes's pronounced concern with rebelliousness was apparently as much a personal issue as a communal one. His quite pragmatic advice to the soldier in his 1672 artillery-day sermon suggests Oakes's political intelligence, and indeed, for several years he seems to have suffered a dilemma of conscience resulting from his political actions. Between the years 1671 and 1675, together with the Mathers, Oakes was a leader of a faction which eventually ousted Harvard College President Leonard Hoar. Objecting primarily to the chaotic state into which Harvard student life had declined during Hoar's administration, Oakes worked against Hoar because Hoar failed to inspire respect for authority. But paradoxically, Oakes's own resistance to authority may have caused him to do much soul-searching between the years 1675, when he was selected to replace Hoar, and 1680, when he finally agreed. Perhaps he suspected himself of ambition; certainly he wished to avoid looking as if he had been self-serving in his actions against Hoar. In any case, Oakes remained acting president for five years until 1680, when he accepted the presidency. He held the office until his death on 25 July 1681.

Oakes's *An Elegie upon the Death of the Reverend Mr. Thomas Shepard* . . . (1677) reflects some of Oakes's perennial concerns. Outstanding among the many examples of the genre produced during this time, Oakes's elegy examines the meaning of the life and death of Shepard for the Puritan community and concludes that his passing may forbode disaster for the lukewarm rising generation of New Englanders. The elegy is also a sermon in verse. Like the conventional Puritan sermon, its concern is with opening the eye of reason and turning the heart toward God, and it proceeds to do so by evoking the popular memory of the deceased Shepard. Within the fifty-seven six-line stanzas, Oakes examines Shepard's life according to the conventions of Puritan hagiography, and the departed saint's life becomes a metaphor for the collective spiritual state of New England. While Shepard lived he was the soul of the community, an index to the state of grace which New England enjoyed in the past. However, according to Oakes, Shepard's death reflects God's judgment against his chosen New England people, who have failed to live up to God's expectations. Thus, in addition to being a lament for the death of Shepard, the elegy is also an attempt to set the Puritans back onto their original path.

Written in the Augustinian high style, which avoids rhetorical adornments in hope that the loftiness of the subject itself might lend grace to expression, Oakes's verse nevertheless reveals his knowledge of classical rhetoric and his acquaintance with the *metaphysical* style of his contemporaries in England. Although he proclaims that the plain style suits his purpose, Oakes's elegy abounds with rich strains of imagery complexly integrated in the metaphysical fashion. It is also replete with multileveled puns (one on the word *bank* in stanza seventeen yokes his economic imagery with his imagery of flowing water). Furthermore, his astronomical images and his reference to "Magnetick" forces reveal Oakes's familiarity with the New Science informing many metaphysical poems and adumbrate his efforts in *The Soveraign Efficacy of Divine Providence* . . . to reconcile religion and science according to orthodox Puritan principles. Considered one of the finest examples of elegiac verse to emerge from the Puritan era, Oakes's elegy suggests his knowledge of classical and Renaissance rhetorical practices, which he tempers with plain style and the Puritan emphasis upon "fettered" grief. While it derives its structure from the scriptural image of Israel and the story of David and Jonathan, the elegy simultaneously reveals Oakes's familiarity with contemporary *belles-lettres*; among other influences, it displays those of Jonson and Milton.

The Soveraign Efficacy of Divine Providence... and his last printed sermon, *A Seasonable Discourse Wherein Sincerity & Delight in the Service of God is earnestly pressed upon Professors of Religion* . . . (1682), were published posthumously, the latter through the offices of Increase Mather, whose lengthy preface extols Oakes as a divine and as a scholar. *The Soveraign Efficacy of Divine Providence* . . . , an artillery-day sermon, discloses much about Oakes's scholarly nature, for besides being an attempt to renew a Calvinistic faith in God's undeniable providence, the sermon is also an indirect attempt to reconcile science and religion (which, in light of the Copernican New Science, often appeared at odds). Written in an essentially eighteenth-century philosophical mode, Oakes's sermon explains how the laws of nature are only secondary causes within God's system. God allows these secondary laws to govern until he chooses to operate providentially through the seemingly random agents of "time" and "chance." God controls ostensible randomness, Oakes explains; thus, despite all apparent logic and principles of justice, the colonists almost lost King Philip's War. Rife with military metaphors, the sermon proclaims that God's judgment against New England came in the form of its near defeat at the hands of the Indians, God's instruments of providence. Explaining both natural and human events in terms of such primary and secondary causes, Oakes's sermon anticipates eighteenth-century modes of discourse.

Oakes's last sermon, *A Seasonable Discourse* . . . , was never intended for publication, but even in its "unpolished" state it reveals his invariably graceful style and ease with language, as well as his wide range of secular knowledge. His last thoughts apparently still centered around the laxity of the successive generations of Puritans, whose enthusiasm and religious zeal could never equal that of the first generation, by the 1680s doubtless already heavily mythologized. In this sermon, Oakes castigates his people for exhibiting too much outward, ritualistic show of religion and too little of the inner intensity of spirit which galvanized the original settlers of the American wilderness.

Oakes's reputation, celebrated in his own era, has hardly diminished. He is acclaimed today for many of the same reasons as he was in his own time. During the 1970s, several critics such as T. G. Hahn, William J. Scheick, and Edwin T. Bowden devoted special attention to *An Elegie upon the Death of the Reverend Mr. Thomas Shepard* . . . , proclaiming it among the best of its genre and discovering in it many levels of aesthetic richness. The Latin texts of Oakes's Harvard addresses have also recently been examined and evaluated as among the most brilliant of their kind. Certainly Urian Oakes emerges as an important literary figure in America's colonial past.

Other:

"To the Christian Reader," in *The Cry of Sodom Enquired Into: Upon Occasion of the Arraignment and Condemnation of Benjamin Goad, For His Prodigious Villainy* . . . , by Samuel Danforth (Cambridge: Printed by Marmaduke Johnson, 1674);

"To the Christian Reader," in *The Day of Trouble is Near* . . . , by Increase Mather (Cambridge: Printed by Marmaduke Johnson, 1674);

"The *Oratio Quinta* of Urian Oakes, Harvard, 1678," Latin text, edited by Leo M. Kaiser, *Humanistica Lovaniensis,* 19 (1970): 485-508;

"The Unpublished *Oratio Secunda* of Urian Oakes, Harvard, 1675," Latin text, edited by Kaiser, *Humanistica Lovaniensis,* 21 (1972): 385-412;

"Tercentary of an Oration: The 1672 Commencement Address of Urian Oakes," Latin text, edited by Kaiser, *Harvard Library Bulletin,* 21 (January 1973): 75-87.

References:

Joseph L. Blau, Introduction to *The Soveraign Efficacy of Divine Providence* (Los Angeles: William Andrews Clark Memorial Library, 1955);

Edwin T. Bowden, "Urian Oakes' 'Elegy': Colonial Literature and History," *Forum* (Houston), 2 (1972): 2-8;

T. G. Hahn, "Urian Oakes's 'Elegie' on Thomas Shepard and Puritan Poetics," *American Literature*, 45 (1973): 163-181;

Leo M. Kaiser, "On the Epitaph of Thomas Shepard II and a Corrigendum in Jantz," *Early American Literature*, 14 (Winter 1979/80): 316-317;

J. A. Leo Lemay, "Jonson and Milton: Two Influences in Oakes's *Elegy*," *New England Quarterly*, 38 (March 1965): 90-92;

Cotton Mather, *Magnalia Christi Americana* (London: Printed for Thomas Parkhurst, 1702);

William J. Scheick, "Standing in the Gap: Urian Oakes's Elegy on Thomas Shepard," *Early American Literature*, 9 (Winter 1975): 301-306;

J. L. Sibley, *Biographical Sketches of Graduates of Harvard University*, volume 1 (Cambridge: Charles William Sever, 1873), pp. 173-185.

Papers:

Oakes's almanac manuscript is in Huntington Library; the manuscript for his elegy on Thomas Shepard is in the Brown University Library; and the manuscripts for the Latin texts of his Harvard addresses are in the Harvard University Archives.

Philip Pain

(birth date unknown-circa 1666)

Frank Shuffelton
University of Rochester

BOOK: *Daily Meditations: or, Quotidian Preparations for, and Considerations of Death and Eternity* (Boston: Printed by Marmaduke Johnson, 1668).

Philip Pain may well be the most shadowy figure in all of American literature; nothing is known of his birth, his family, or his place of residence, and all we know of his death comes from the title page of his only book, where we are told that he "lately suffering Shipwrack, was drowned." Leon Howard found no evidence that he was even an American, although he discovered no trace of him in England either and surmised that he might possibly have been the son or nephew of Capt. Philip Payne of St. Christopher in the West Indies. All we have finally is his one slim book containing sixty-four six-line meditations on death, one of the more unusual examples of poetry from early New England and for one brief moment one of the best.

The six-line poems in *Daily Meditations* . . . are printed four to a page with a separate couplet at the foot, and each page is dated, beginning with 19 July 1666 and proceeding a page a day to 3 August 1666. The whole is preceded by a twenty-two line poem which, because it is titled "The Porch," calls attention to the influence of George Herbert, particularly to "The Church-porch," a prefatory poem in *The Temple* (1633). A final postscript, not by Pain, closes the volume. The evocation of Herbert in the opening poem is important in a number of ways, for Pain is arguably the most Herbertian poet to appear in seventeenth-century New England (although that, in the circumstances, is not much of a claim). There is reason to doubt that Pain was an orthodox Calvinist in the New England fashion; Howard points to meditations 30 and 32, the one claiming "every soul in this world hath its day / Of grace, and if he will improve it may" and the other suggesting the damned are in hell for "Mispence of Time." These universalist and Arminian sentiments, however, are merely touched on, and Pain overall displays, like Herbert, a kind of sober, reformed protestantism that would be unobjectionable to established churchman and dissenter alike. Furthermore, Pain's meditations have more in common with the mood of Herbert's poems, or those of Francis Quarles, than with the kind of meditation recommended by a New England minister as an aid to preparation for salvation. When Thomas Hooker

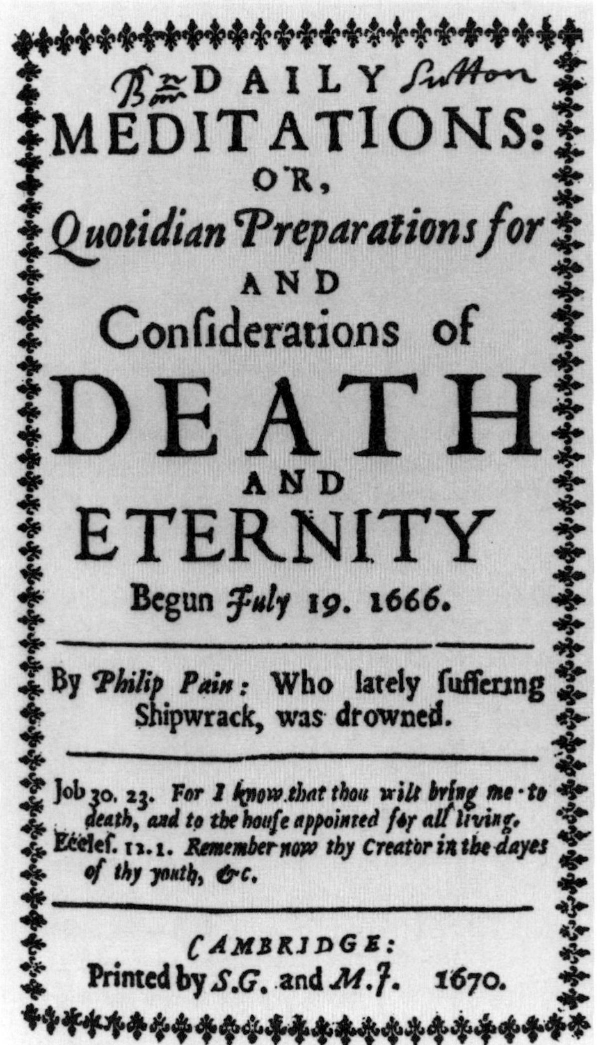
The DAILY
MEDITATIONS:
OR,
Quotidian Preparations for
AND
Considerations of
DEATH
AND
ETERNITY
Begun *July* 19. 1666.

By *Philip Pain*: Who lately suffering Shipwrack, was drowned.

Job 30. 23. *For I know that thou wilt bring me to death, and to the house appointed for all living.*
Eccles. 12.1. *Remember now thy Creator in the dayes of thy youth, &c.*

CAMBRIDGE:
Printed by *S.G.* and *M.J.* 1670.

Title page for the second edition of Pain's book, to which printer Marmaduke Johnson added a postscript praising the young poet for turning away from youth's customary concerns and "prizing high / A place i' th' Mansions of Eternity" (Massachusetts Historical Society)

urged his listeners to meditate, he wanted them to search their hearts in order to discover the necessity of divine grace in this world, but Pain thinks both abstractly and emblematically about the world in order to detach himself from it. As Robert Daly points out, the "unqualified rejection of the world and a yearning for death in his poetry" distinguish him from Puritan poets such as Anne Bradstreet, Edward Johnson, and Richard Steere.

"The Porch" asks, "O where's the man or woman that can say, / Lord, I desire my dissolution day" and claims that "nought but the sense / Of guilt & sin" make death terrible. The individual meditations, however, address not sin and guilt but death itself, each one being a kind of willed acceptance and embrace of mortality. The meditations relentlessly observe the prosodic form of three iambic-pentameter couplets, but a use of enjambment and weak and strong stresses gives them some of the suppleness required to carry the repetitive message, stated in meditation 58 as "The day of death's a coming." Within the narrow range of his concern, Pain is able to rise to wit—"O my Soul, must I / Go from PAIN here to Pain eternally?" (no. 50)—to use a repeated, antiphonal line ending (no. 56), and to ask, a bit like Edward Taylor, "Lord, grant that I may praise thee, whiles that I / Have time to live" (no. 15).

The poems are often clumsy, not always quite at ease with syntax and tending to close with a tacked-on, prayerful couplet, but they nevertheless have their moving and graceful moments, a line here, a phrase there. Yvor Winters was surely right in judging meditation 8 to be one of the finest achievements of Puritan poetry in New England:

> Scarce do I pass a day, but that I hear
> Some one or other's dead; and to my ear
> Me thinks it is no news: but Oh, did I
> Think deeply on it, what it is to dye,
> My Pulses all would beat, I should not be
> Drown'd in this Deluge of Security.

Here Pain's emotional control and mastery of his language and technique come together to produce a genuinely fine poem. With the paradoxical irony of the enlivening perception of being trapped in a deadening security, an unawareness of the need for saving grace, Pain is here most orthodoxly Puritan, and at the same time his skillful use of alliteration, both internally (day, dead, did, deeply, dye, Drown'd) and for closure (*Scarce*, *Security*), give this poem an almost Dickinsonian force. Meditation 6 refers to "The Passing-bell," and in meditation 8 the news tolling the death of others echoes in the beating pulses of the poet who is "Drown'd in this Deluge of Security." Pain will always be considered a minor poet, but his place is secure in any history of poetry in New England.

References:

Robert Daly, *God's Altar: The World and the Flesh in Puritan Poetry* (Berkeley: University of California Press, 1978), pp. 136-138;

Norman Farmer, Jr., "The Literary Borrowings of Philip Pain," *Notes and Queries*, new series 11 (1964): 465-467;

Theodore Grieder, "Philip Pain's 'Daily Meditations' and the Poetry of George Herbert," *Notes and Queries*, new series 9 (1962): 213-215;

Leon Howard, Introduction to *Daily Meditations by Philip Pain* (San Marino: Huntington Library, 1936), pp. 5-12;

Donald E. Stanford, "The Imagination of Death in the Poetry of Philip Pain, Edward Taylor, and George Herbert," *Studies in the Literary Imagination*, 9, no. 2 (1976): 53-67.

Francis Daniel Pastorius

(1651-circa 1720)

Rosamond Rosenmeier
University of Massachusetts, Boston

BOOKS: *Vier kleine doch ungemeine Trachtätlein* (Germanopoli, 1690);

Kurtze Geographische Beshreibung der lentzmahls erfundenen Americanischen Landschafft Pennsylvania, appendix to *Kurtze Beschreibung der H. R. Reichs Stadt*, by Melchior Adam Pastorius (Windsheim, 1692); published separately as *Umständige Geographische Beschreibung Der zu allerletzt erfundenen Provintz Pennsylvaniae . . .* (Frankfurt & Leipzig: Zu finden bey Andreas Otto, 1700); republished as *A Particular Geographical Description of the Lately Discovered Province of Pennsylvania . . . ,* translated by Lewis H. Weiss, *Memoirs of the Historical Society of Pennsylvania*, 4, part 2 (1850): 83-104;

Henry Bernhard Koster, William Davis, Thomas Rutter & Thomas Bowyer. Four Boasting Disputers of This World Briefly Rebuked . . . (New York: Printed & sold by William Bradford, 1697);

A New Primmer of Methodical Directions to Attain the True Spelling, Reading & Writing of English (New York: Printed by William Bradford, 1698).

Francis Daniel Pastorius had many vocations: lawyer, statesman, geographer, master of eight to ten languages, theologian, teacher, historian, poet. One of the most learned people in Colonial America, he wrote constantly and left a rich and diversified literary legacy, much of it in German, still untranslated and unpublished.

Pastorius was born in 1651 in Sommerhausen, Franconia, Germany, where his father, Melchior Adam Pastorius, was a prosperous city official. Francis Daniel's mother was Magdalena Dietz, Melchior Adam Pastorius's first wife. In 1676 Pastorius completed seven years of university study (at a variety of universities) with a degree in law from the university at Altdorf. He practiced law briefly in Windheim but soon moved to Frankfort-au-Main, where he met Jacob Spener, the founder of Pietism. Pastorius's father had left Roman Catholicism for Lutheranism, and the son moved even further away from Roman Catholic orthodoxy. Even before his acquaintance with pietists and Quakers in Frankfort, the young Pastorius's Lutheranism had a pietistic cast. He was not enthusiastic about a law career, and in association with a group of pietistic sectarians he began to envision a new life in the New World. He joined with thirteen families from Crefeld (some Mennonites, some Quakers) and, acting as agent of the Frankfort Land Company, sailed in 1683 to Pennsylvania, where he negotiated the purchase from William Penn of 15,000 acres for settlement in the area later called Germantown.

First mayor of Georgetown, Pastorius quickly became the principal spokesman for the rapidly growing German population of Pennsylvania. He used his extensive knowledge of English and German law in a variety of capacities—as bailiff for Germantown, as scrivener, and as a member of the Provincial Assembly (1687-1691). In 1688 he married Ennecke Klostermanns (born 1658). They had two sons, Johann and Heinrich, for whom Pastorius would later compose his compendious "Bee-hive," from which only selections have been published. In 1688, too, Pastorius and others sent the first public Colonial protest against slavery to the Friends Meeting. Pastorius is credited with the authorship of this protest. Pastorius was not a Quaker, but he attended their meeting and was closely allied with Quakers throughout his life. He even joined them in a theological dispute with the Keithian radicals, who later left the Society of Friends to form the Christian Quakers. He taught in the Quaker school of Philadelphia from 1698 to 1700, and in 1702 he founded the first Germantown school, where he taught until 1718. His school was innovative in several respects: it was coeducational and had classes in the evening as well as during the day. Moreover, some of the study materials, which Pastorius developed and wrote, were bilingual.

Pastorius used his literary talents and energies in the service of his community—friends, neighbors, and family. He acted as a scribe for those who could not write, detailed the history of the settling of Germantown, and kept the public records and documents. His unpublished "Grund-und Lager Buch" illustrates one of his characteristic purposes for writing. In it the literal record of the immovable property in Germantown is embellished with exhortations to the German settlers and their descendants to take pride in their nationality and culture. In another work, *Vier kleine doch ungemeine Trachtätlein* (1690), Pastorius, ever mindful of the dangers of cultural and spiritual deterioration, compiled and translated models of literary merit for the edification of his fellow countrymen.

Pastorius was the first Colonial writer to make extensive use of the adage or aphorism, one of the principal devices of Pennsylvania German literature. In 1696, Pastorius began "Bienenstock or Melliotrophium . . ." ("Bee-hive"), an encyclopaedic compendium of wise sayings and observations intended as a legacy for his sons. In "Bee-hive" his preferred form of expression is the adage, which provides, as well, a controlling rhetorical strategy for his poetry. The simple pietistic turns of phrase in the poetry from the "Bee-hive" are designed to bring home lessons and to assure that his children keep the faith. John Greenleaf Whittier observed in the title poem of *The Pennsylvania Pilgrim and Other Poems* (1872) that Pastorius held fast to "plain and sober maxims" as a way of reminding others of his dream of a future world, a dream that was born in the Old World and that Pastorius feared would lose some of its vitality in the actualities of the New.

Pastorius's clear and concise style suited the range of scholarly projects he undertook. His "geographical" description of Pennsylvania is regarded as his most important published work. In seventeen short chapters Pastorius comments on the place of the province in world history. Written

Umständige Geographische
Beschreibung
Der zu allerletzt erfundenen
Provintz
PENSYLVANIÆ,
In denen End-Gräntzen
AMERICÆ
In der West-Welt gelegen/
Durch
FRANCISCUM DANIELEM
PASTORIUM,
J.V. Lic. und Friedens-Richtern
daselbsten.
Worbey angehencket sind einige notable Begebenheiten / und
Bericht-Schreiben an dessen Herrn
Vattern
MELCHIOREM ADAMUM PASTORIUM,
Und andere gute Freunde.
Franckfurt und Leipzig/
Zufinden bey Andreas Otto. 1700.

Title page for the first separate publication of Pastorius's description of Pennsylvania (John Carter Brown Library, Brown University)

essentially for a European audience, the work describes the native people, flora and fauna of Pennsylvania, the history of European settlement, the government of the province, and its religious denominations. Pastorius makes recommendations for industry and commerce, presenting Pennsylvania as attractive to potential immigrants, despite the hardships of passage. Some of the most remarkable commentary concerns the Native Americans, whom Pastorius finds superior to "ourselves, so-called Christians" in their simplicity, contentment, and temperance. He predicts that many of these "poor American savages" will "in the great day rise up in judgment against our own wicked and perverse generations." Throughout the volume the literal landscape visible to the "outward eye" is not his only or even his principal focus. Pastorius had a millennarian vision which he expressed through his description of Pennsylvania.

In its intention, Pastorius's description of Pennsylvania calls to mind William Bradford's *Of Plimmoth Plantation.* Certainly Pastorius shares with many of his contemporaries in New England a concern about the continuity between generations and anxiety over the evidence of backsliding. In "Hail to Posterity," a poem Pastorius wrote in Latin for the "Grund-und Lager Buch," he called on "men of coming years" to "follow our footsteps." (Whittier used his own translation of this poem to preface *The Pennsylvania Pilgrim and Other Poems.*) Yet Pastorius was not successful at preventing the degeneration of the faith by "weak disciples." Perhaps he did not influence future generations more strongly because of the self-effacing quality of his personality. He said of himself that he had a "melancholy-cholerick complexion" and that he was therefore "gentle, given to sobriety, solitary, studious, doubtful, shame-faced, timorous, pensive, constant and true in action" and "of a slow wit."

Pastorius was, both by temperament and by religious belief, inward, reflective, and pacifistic. Perhaps the ineffableness of his faith, a faith virtually without doctrine, made his a difficult example for future generations to grasp and to follow. Perhaps the sheer virtuosity of his talents made his life seem impossible to emulate. The fact that Pastorius wrote most often in languages other than English is a problem for American-born readers. Pastorius's work and many-sided career have received little critical attention.

Other:

Marion Dexter Learned, ed., "From Francis Daniel Pastorius' Bee-hive or Bee-stock," *American Germanica*, 1, no. 4 (1897): 67-110;

Protest of the German Quakers of Germantown against Negro Slavery in 1688, in *The Life of Francis Daniel Pastorius, The Founder of Germantown, Pennsylvania,* by Learned (Philadelphia: William J. Campbell, 1908), pp. 261-262;

Albert C. Myers, ed., *Narratives of Early Pennsylvania, West New Jersey, and Delaware (1630-1707),* includes an English translation of part of Pastorius's history of Pennsylvania (New York: Scribners, 1912), pp. 353-448;

Harrison T. Messerole, ed., *Seventeenth-Century American Poetry,* includes poems in English from Pastorius's "Bee-hive" (New York: New York University Press, 1968), pp. 293-304.

Biography:

Marion Dexter Learned, *The Life of Francis Daniel Pastorius, The Founder of Germantown, Pennsylvania* (Philadelphia: William J. Campbell, 1908).

References:

Albert A. Faust, *Francis Daniel Pastorius and the 250th Anniversary of the Founding of Germantown* (Philadelphia: Carl Schurz Memorial Foundation, 1934);

Julius Frederic Sachse, *The German Sectarians of Pennsylvania,* 2 volumes (Philadelphia: Privately printed, 1899-1900);

Oswald Seidensticker, *The First Century of German Printing in America, 1728-1830 . . .* (Philadelphia: Schaefer & Koradi, 1893), pp. 1-5;

John Greenleaf Whittier, *The Pennsylvania Pilgrim and Other Poems* (Boston: James Osgood, 1872).

Papers:

The largest collection of Pastorius's papers is at the Historical Society of Pennsylvania.

Deuel Pead

(birth date unknown-12 January 1727)

Michael A. Lofaro
University of Tennessee

SELECTED WORKS: *Jesus is God: or, The Deity of Jesus Christ Vindicated . . .* (London: Printed for George Conyers, 1694);

A Practical Discourse Upon the Death of Our Late Gracious Queen . . . (London: Printed for Abel Roper, E. Wilkinson & Roger Clavel, 1695);

A Word in Season: Being a Sermon Preach'd In the Parish-Church of St. James Clarkenwell, on Wednesday the 11th. of December, 1695. Being the Fast-Day (London: Printed for Roger Clavel, 1695);

The Protestant King Protected: The Popish Kings Detected and Defeated. In a Sermon Preach'd At St. James Clarkenwell, April 16, 1696. being the Day of Public Thanksgiving for the Deliverance of His Majesty K. William III. from Assassination, and His Kingdoms from Invasion by the French (London: Printed for T. Parkhurst, 1696);

Sheba's Conspiracy, and Amasa's Confederacy: Or, A Modest Vindication of the National Association Entered into by the Honorable House of Commons Feb. 25th. 1695 (London: Printed for T. Parkhurst, 1696);

The Wicked Man's Misery and the Poor Man's Hope and Comfort. Being a Sermon Upon the Parable of Dives and Lazarus . . . (London: Printed & sold by J. B., 1699);

The Converted Sinner: Or, An Account of the wonderful Mercy of God recalling James Woossencraft, With Seven of his Companions, who had for many Years, led a most Prophane and Ungodly course of Life . . . (London: Printed & sold by J. Nutt, 1701);

Greatness and Goodness Reprieve Not from Death. A Sermon Occasion'd by the Death Of that Glorious Monarch William the Third, King of England, Scotland, France, and Ireland, &c. . . . (London: Printed for the author, 1702);

England's Present Duty. A Sermon Preached On January the 19th. 1703/4, Being the Day appointed for Fasting and Prayer, By means of the Dreadful Storm of Wind, Which was on the 26 and 27 of November last (London: Printed by J. Heptinstall & sold by A. Baldwin, 1704);

Annus Victoriis Mirabilis. A Thanksgiving Sermon Preach'd on Tuesday, Dec. 31. 1706. At St. James's Clerkenwell. Occasion'd by the Signal Victories Obtain'd Over the French, by the Duke of Marlborough and the rest of the Confederate Forces (London: Printed & sold by H. Hills, 1706?);

Good News for Repenting Sinners, but Ill Tidings for Hypocrites, and Pharisaical Professors of Religion. In Two Familiar Dialogues . . . (London: Printed & sold by H. Hills, 1707);

The Honour, Happiness, and Safety of Union, Or, A Sermon Upon the Uniting of England and Scotland . . . (London: Printed by W. Downing & sold by Benj. Bragge, 1707);

Paturiunt Montes, &c. Or, Lewis and Clement Taken in Their Own Snare. A Sermon Preach'd in the Parish Church of St. James Clarkenwell, On Thursday February the 17th, 1708/9. being The Day of Thanksgiving Appointed by Her Majesty for the Glorious Successes of the last Campaign (London: Printed for E. Curll, 1709);

"A Sermon Preached at James City in Virginia the 23D of April Before the Loyal Society of Citizens born in and about London and inhabiting in Virginia," edited by Richard Beale Davis, *William and Mary Quarterly*, series 3, 17 (July 1960): 371-394.

So few seventeenth-century Southern sermons survive that each is a significant historical document. Only three dated works are extant: Alexander Whitaker's *Good Newes from Virginia . . .* (1613), Gov. William Joseph's lay "sermon" to the General Assembly of Maryland (1688), and Deuel Pead's "A Sermon Preached at James City . . . ," delivered in 1686. (A few manuscripts of Jesuit sermons from the late seventeenth- or early eighteenth-century South also exist but are undated.)

Little is known of Pead's early life. He was admitted to Cambridge as a pensioner in 1664, served as a chaplain in the British navy in 1671, and settled in Anne Arundel County, Maryland, in about 1682. By November of 1683 he had become the minister of

Christ Church, Middlesex County, Virginia, and remained in this post until returning to England some seven years later. In 1691 Pead was appointed minister of St. James, Clerkenwell, London, a position which he held until his death, and in 1707 he was also given the rectorship of Newland St. Lawrence, Essex.

Pead's reputation as a popular and respected preacher of occasional sermons in England was foreshadowed by his James City address, a thanksgiving sermon preached upon the first anniversary of the coronation of James II. He was likely brought from Middlesex to Jamestown to preach this sermon by Francis Howard, Lord Effingham, the current governor of Virginia, who was also Pead's patron and the person to whom the sermon was dedicated. Pead's lifelong loyalty to established authority was evident in his choice of text (Psalm 122:6, "Pray for the peace of Jerusalem/They shall prosper that love thee") and in his sermon's content, which largely ignored the complaints that led to the Revolution of 1688 in England and to various minor uprisings in America. It was not surprising, therefore, that in speaking before his friend and patron, the King's appointed governor, Pead chose to end the sermon proper by sounding notes of English pride and of the ties that should bind the Londoners of Virginia to their brothers, and more important, to their ruler, across the sea: "my bretheren that are citizens by your birth, it lys in some measure within your power to advance the honour of the city by your devotion to God, loyalty to your Prince, your sobriety of conversation, your reall courtesy to all persons and your brotherly love and affection to one another. . . . For it can be noe shame for Virginia to take pattern from whence they received their first inhabitants."

Pead's only surviving American sermon is of literary as well as historical interest since it documents a change in sermonic style from the time of Whitaker's work seven decades earlier. While Pead shares the use of the plain style with Whitaker, he exhibits a more expansive field of allusion which includes mention of Rabbi David Kimhi (circa 1160-1235, the distinguished Jewish grammarian and commentator upon the psalms), of Empedocles, and of the Stoics. He also uses nautical metaphors which are gleaned, no doubt, from his naval service. Although it is impossible to discern what proportion of this display of learning was due to his awareness of the literacy of his audience, to the presence of his patron, or to his own predilections in oration at this stage of his career, Pead's sermon, despite its learned allusions, testifies in the main to the survival of the plain style of preaching in the Southern colonies.

References:

George Maclaren Brydon, *Virginia's Mother Church* (Richmond: Virginia Historical Society, 1947), I: 282;

Richard Beale Davis, *Intellectual Life in the Colonial South, 1585-1763* (Knoxville: University of Tennessee Press, 1978), II: 582, 716-720;

Davis, Introduction to "A Sermon Preached at James City . . . ," *William and Mary Quarterly*, series 3, 17 (July 1960): 371-394;

Edward Lewis Goodwin, *The Colonial Church in Virginia* (Milwaukee: Morehouse Publishing, 1927; London: A. R. Mowbray, & Co., 1927), pp. 297-298;

Bishop William Meade, *Old Churches, Ministers and Families of Virginia* (Philadelphia: Lippincott, 1885), I: 358-359.

William Penn

Harald Alfred Kittel
Freie Universität Berlin

BIRTH: London, 14 October 1644, to Sir William and Lady Margaret Jasper Vanderschuren Penn.

EDUCATION: Christ Church College, Oxford, 1660-1662; Lincoln's Inn, London, 1665.

MARRIAGES: 4 April 1672 to Gulielma Maria Springett; children: Gulielma Maria, William, Mary Margaret, Springett, Laetitia, William, Gulielma Maria, one infant. 5 March 1696 to Hannah Callowhill; children: John, Thomas, Hannah Margaret, Margaret, Richard, Dennis, Hannah.

DEATH: Ruscombe, England, 30 July 1718.

William Penn, circa 1666 (Historical Society of Pennsylvania)

SELECTED BOOKS: *The Sandy Foundation Shaken; or, Those so Generally Believed and Applauded Doctrines of One God, Subsisting in Three Distinct and Separate Persons, the Impossibility of God's Pardoning Sinners, without a Plenary Satisfaction, the Justification of Impure Persons by an Imputative Righteousness, Refuted . . .* (London, 1668);

Truth Exalted, in a Testimony against all those Religions, Faiths and Worships, that have been formed and followed in the Darkness of Apostacy.---And for that Glorious Light which is now Risen, and Shines forth in the Life and Doctrine of the despised Quakers . . . (London, 1668);

Innocency with her Open Face, Presented, by way of Apology for the Book entituled, The Sandy Foundations Shaken . . . (London, 1669);

No Cross, No Crown: Or, Several Sober Reasons against Hat-Honour, Titular-Respects, You to a Single Person, with the Apparel and Recreations of the Times; Being Inconsistent with Scripture, Reason, and the Practice, as well as the Best Heathens, as the Holy Men and Women of All Generations; And Consequently Fantastick, Impertinent and Sinfull . . . (London, 1669); revised and enlarged as *No Cross, No Crown. A Discourse Shewing the Nature and Discipline of the Holy Cross of Christ, and That The Denyal of Self, and daily Bearing of Christ's Cross, is the Alone Way to the Rest and Kingdom of God. To which are added, The Living and Dying Testimonies of Divers Persons of Fame and Learning, in favour of this Treatise* (London: Printed for Mark Swanner & sold by A. Sowl, B. Clark & J. Bringhurst, 1682; Boston: Printed by Rogers & Fowle, 1747);

A Seasonable Caveat against Popery. Or A Pamphlet, Entituled, An Explanation of the Roman-Catholic Belief, Briefly Examined (London, 1670);

The Great Case of Liberty of Conscience Debated and Defended by the Authority of Reason, Scripture and Antiquity . . . (London, 1670);

The People's Ancient and Just Liberties Asserted, in the Trial of William Penn and William Mead . . ., attributed to Penn and others (London, 1670);

Quakerism A New Nick-Name for Old Christianity: Being an Answer to a Book, Entituled, Quakerism No Christianity; Subscribed by J. Faldo . . . (London, 1672);

The Christian-Quaker, and His Divine Testimony Vindicated by Scripture, Reason and Authorities . . . , part 1 by Penn, part 2 by George Whitehead (London, 1673);

England's Present Interest Discover'd with Honour to the Prince, and Safety to the People . . . (London, 1675);

A Treatise of Oaths Containing Several Weighty Reasons Why the People Call'd Quakers Refuse to Swear . . . (London, 1675);

The Continued Cry of the Oppressed for Justice . . . (part 1, London, 1675; part 2, London, 1676);

The Description of West New Jersey, attributed to Penn (London, 1676);

Englands Great Interest in the Choice of This New Parliament . . . , as Philanglus (London, 1679);

One Project for the Good of England: That is Our Civil Union is Our Civil Safety . . . , as Philanglus (London, 1679);

An Address to Protestants upon the Present Conjuncutre . . . (London, 1679); republished as *An Address to Protestants of All Perswasions* . . . (London: Printed & sold by T. Sowle, 1692);

Some Account of the Province of Pennsilvania in America; Lately granted under the Great Seal of England to William Penn, &c. Together with Privileges and Powers Necessary to the Well Governing Thereof . . . (London: Printed & sold by B. Clark, 1681);

A Brief Account of the Province of Pennsilvania in America, Lately Granted under the Great Seal of England to William Penn (London, 1681);

The Frame of the Government of the Province of Pennsilvania in America: Together with certain Laws Agreed upon in England . . . (London, 1682);

A Letter from William Penn, Proprietary and Governour of Pennsylvania in America, to the Committee of the Free Society of Traders of the Province, Residing in London. Containing a General Description of the Said Province . . . (London: Printed & sold by A. Sowle, 1683);

A Further Account of the Province of Pennsylvania and Its Improvements . . . (London, 1685?);

A Perswasive to Moderation to Dissenting Christians, in Prudence and Conscience Humbly Submitted to the King and His Great Council . . . (London: Printed & sold by Andrew Sowle, 1685);

An Essay Towards the Present and Future Peace of Europe, by the Establishment of an European Dyet Parliament, or Estates . . . (London, 1693);

A Key Opening a Way to Every Common Understanding, How to Discern the Difference Betwixt the Religion Professed by the People Called Quakers, and the Perversions, Misrepresentations and Calumnies of their Several Adversaries . . . (London: Printed for Thomas Northcott, 1693; Philadelphia: Printed by Andrew Bradford, 1717);

Some Fruits of Solitude, in Reflections and Maxims Relating to Conduct of Human Life (London: Printed for Thomas Northcott, 1693; Newport: Printed by James Franklin, 1749);

An Account of W. Penn's Travails in Holland and Germany. Anno MDCLXXVI . . . (London: Printed & sold by T. Sowle, 1694);

A Brief Account of the Rise and Progress of the People Called Quakers (London: Printed & sold by T. Sowle, 1694);

A Call to Christendom, in an Earnest Expostulation with Her to Prepare for the Great and Notable Day of the Lord . . . (London: T. Sowle, 1694);

Primitive Christianity Revived, in the Faith and Practice of People Called Quakers . . . (London: T. Sowle, 1696);

An Account of the Blessed End of Gulielma Maria Penn, and of Springet Penn . . . (London?, 1696);

More Fruits of Solitude: Being The Second Part Of Reflections And Maxims, Relating to the Conduct of Humane Life (London: Printed & sold by T. Sowle, 1702; Newport: Printed by James Franklin, 1749);

My Irish Journal (N.p.: Privately printed, 1910); republished as *My Irish Journal, 1669-1670*, edited by Isabel Grubb (London: Longmans, Green, 1952).

COLLECTIONS: *A Collection of the Works of William Penn in two volumes, To which is prefixed a Journal of his life with many original Letters and Papers*, 2 volumes, edited by Joseph Besse (London: Assigns of J. Sowle, 1726);

The Witness of William Penn, edited by Frederick B. Tolles and E. Gordon Alderfer (New York: Macmillan, 1957);

The Papers of William Penn, edited by Mary Maples Dunn, Richard S. Dunn, Richard A. Ryerson, Scott M. Wilds, and Jean R. Soderlund, 2 volumes to date (Philadelphia: University of Pennsylvania Press, 1981-).

Contrary to his popular image, William Penn

was an unusually complex, energetic, versatile, and creative man: mystic and religious activist, political theorist and practical politician, administrator and author. His writings—more than 130 books, pamphlets, broadsides, and numerous letters—reflect the tensions, challenges, and tragedy of his life as well as the political and ideological turmoil of his times.

Shortly after entering Christ Church College, Oxford, on 26 October 1660 as a gentleman commoner, he composed "Verses on the Death of Henry, Duke of Gloucester," a Latin tribute of scant literary merit published in *Epicedia Academiae Oxoniensis, in Obitum Celesissimi Principis Henrici Ducis Glocestrensis* (1660), a collection of sixty-seven memorial poems. When, in the winter of 1661-1662, he was expelled from Christ Church for religious nonconformism, his appalled father, the admiral Sir William Penn, sent him to France. However, Paris and the court of Louis XIV attracted the young man only briefly. He retired to the Huguenot academy of Saumur, where he studied divinity under Moses Amyraut for more than a year. Returning to London in 1664, Penn was a man of the world in outward appearance. Yet the poem "Ah Tyrant Lust," written in the same year, reveals his inner struggle for a sober Christian life. In 1665 he began the study of law at Lincoln's Inn, attended Court, and briefly joined his father and the English fleet in their preparations to fight the Dutch. He acted as a messenger between his father and Charles II and pressed with the King and his officials his father's claim to contested Irish lands. During this period he also formed a lasting friendship with the Duke of York, the future James II. Early in 1666 Penn was sent by his father on business to Ireland, where he took an active part in quelling a mutiny at Carrickfergus and stayed at the viceregal court in Dublin. His interest in religion remained untempered, and he apparently sought out the Quaker Thomas Loe in Cork, fell under his influence, and became a Quaker, probably in the late summer or early autumn of 1667. He suffered his first imprisonment for attending a Quaker meeting in Cork, but he was quickly released. Although the admiral vehemently resented his son's joining the despised sect, rendered conspicuous by his adoption of simple dress and plain speech, father and son were reconciled shortly before the elder Penn's death in 1670, and Penn inherited the major share of his father's estate. In 1672 he married Gulielma Springett, with whom he had eight children. Only three of these children, Springett (1676-1696), Laetitia (1679-1746), and William (1681-1720), lived to adulthood.

During the years 1668-1679 Penn became one of the most vocal and prominent leaders of the Society of Friends. He served the Quaker cause by traveling extensively in England, Ireland, and on the Continent and was repeatedly jailed for preaching. His first imprisonment in the Tower of London from December 1668 until July 1669 was prompted by the publication of a tract, *The Sandy Foundation Shaken* . . . (1668), which the authorities considered a blasphemous attack on the doctrine of the Trinity. Despite his refusal to recant, he was eventually released after explaining his beliefs more fully in the cleverly reasoned tract *Innocency with her Open Face* . . . (1669). In fact, some of Penn's best known religious and political tracts were written in jail, including, for example, the 1669 version of *No Cross, No Crown*. . . . As suggested by the subtitle, the three chapters of this pamphlet reflect the Quaker views passionately embraced by the youthful

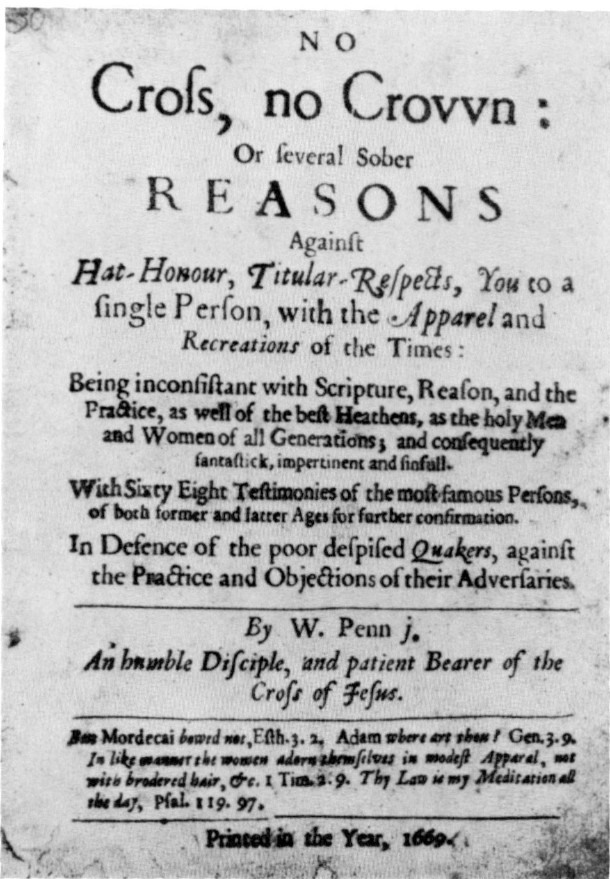

NO

Crofs, no Crovvn:

Or feveral Sober

REASONS

Againft

Hat-Honour, Titular-Refpects, You to a fingle Perfon, with the *Apparel* and *Recreations* of the Times:

Being inconfiftant with Scripture, Reafon, and the Practice, as well of the beft Heathens, as the holy Men and Women of all Generations; and confequently fantaftick, impertinent and finfull.

With Sixty Eight Teftimonies of the moft famous Perfons, of both former and latter Ages for further confirmation.

In Defence of the poor defpifed *Quakers*, againft the Practice and Objections of their Adverfaries.

By W. Penn *j.*

An humble Difciple, and patient Bearer of the Crofs of Jefus.

Mordecai *bowed not*, Efth. 3. 2. Adam *where art thou?* Gen. 3. 9. *In like manner the women adorn themfelves in modeft Apparel, not with brodered hair, &c.* 1 Tim. 2. 9. *Thy Law is my Meditation all the day*, Pfal. 119. 97.

Printed in the Year, 1669.

Title page for the first edition of Penn's defense of the Quakers, written while he was imprisoned for his beliefs in the Tower of London

Penn concerning hat wearing, titles, language, stage plays, waste, and amusements. As in his early broadsides and pamphlets, such as the prophetic *Truth Exalted . . .* (1668), the language chosen is that of judgment and thundering apocalyptic warning. The concluding parade of sixty-eight "testimonies" of heathen and Christian personages does not so much prove the young author's deep learning as the availability to him, even in prison, of Sir Thomas Stanley's 1655 *History of Philosophy*, Sir Samuel Morland's *The History of the Evangelical Churches in the Valleys of Piemont . . .* (1658), and the 1624 English translation of Jean-Paul Perrin's history of the Waldensians and Albigensians.

Shortly after his release from the Tower, Penn traveled to Ireland on his father's business. However, as *My Irish Journal* (written 1669) reveals, for Penn the primary purpose was a spiritual one. He acted, in particular, as a lobbyist with the political authorities, negotiating with limited success for the release of imprisoned Friends. *My Irish Journal* affords intriguing sights into Penn's personal life as well as his religious and political activities, and his social attitudes. Significantly, his contacts were mainly with colonists of English origin, Quaker and non-Quaker. The plight of the oppressed native, mostly Catholic population left him unmoved, and his manifest contempt for their allegedly barbarous religious practices stands in marked contrast to his later efforts at safeguarding the rights of the Indians of Pennsylvania and to his sympathetic appreciation of their customs. During his Irish sojourn Penn also wrote *A Seasonable Caveat against Popery . . .* (1670) in response to *An Explanation of the Roman Catholic Belief* (1659, reprinted 1670), perhaps by Christopher Davenport, who played down doctrinal differences between Catholics and English Protestants. Insisting on the differences, Penn commented critically on such points of Roman Catholic belief as transubstantiation, prayer in Latin, ecclesiastical hierarchy, and civil disobedience. Among other things, this tract reveals its author's ambivalent attitude toward Catholics. While demanding toleration for all religious denominations, including Catholics, he feared that, if they obtained civil power, their allegiance to the Church of Rome would commit them to the persecution of non-Catholics. At a time when Catholic influence was widely feared to be increasing in the royal court and Quakers, too, were often persecuted under laws against Catholics, Penn was particularly anxious to demonstrate the depth of the gulf separating the Quakers from Rome.

The Great Case of Liberty of Conscience . . ., also written in Ireland in 1670, asserts Penn's absolute commitment to freedom of conscience. Facing up to the horrors of religious persecution in Restoration England, *The Great Case of Liberty of Conscience . . .* develops the remarkable theory that conscience is a part of property. Penn's wide-ranging argument for religious freedom transcends the specific historical situation. He rejects persecution not only on theological, religious, and spiritual but also on secular grounds. Insisting that persecution contradicts nature and reason, he anticipates the spirit of Thomas Jefferson's Virginia statute of religious freedom. According to Penn persecution and good government are irreconcilable.

Shortly after his return to London in August 1670 he was once again arrested for nonconformist preaching. However, instead of simply fining Penn for preaching contrary to the Conventicle Act of 1670, the Lord Mayor of London chose to try Penn for conspiring to incite a riot. During the week of 1-5 September 1670 the trial of Penn and his fellow Quaker William Mead, a wealthy London merchant tailor, took place. It was a milestone in Penn's development both as a defender of the Society of Friends and as a champion of religious freedom for all Englishmen. The courtroom drama is vividly captured in the famous pamphlet *The People's Ancient and Just Liberties Asserted, in the Trial of William Penn and William Mead . . .* (1670), which was probably written by Penn and other Quaker leaders. During the trial Penn and William Mead successfully defended themselves against the serious charges of conspiracy to incite a riot. According to the pamphlet, Penn repeatedly appealed to the rights and privileges guaranteed by the Great Charter of 1225 and its earlier version, the Magna Carta. During the trial the jury set a legal precedent. Following Penn's reasoning and urgent appeals, and in defiance of the magistrate's direction, the jury declared the defendants innocent of the charges, thus asserting their right to decide in matters of law as well as of fact. Nevertheless, Penn and Mead were fined for contempt of court because they refused to take off their hats. At that time it was not unusual for courts of law to take advantage of the fact that Quakers would remove their hats only before God in prayer, but never in deference to any man or worldly authority. In February 1671 Penn was, for the second time within a year, arrested for preaching and for refusing to swear an oath. He was incarcerated for six months at Newgate prison. On this occasion he and several fellow Quakers turned directly to Parliament in an effort to prevent further repressive legislation affecting Quakers. There is no recorded evidence, however, that Parliament considered this, or any other Quaker petition, during the 1670s. After his release from Newgate he spent the closing months of 1671 in missionary travel through Holland and Germany, thus avoiding further confrontation with the London authorities. Subsequently, he addressed himself to the Quaker problem of how to avoid imprisonment for refusing to swear loyalty oaths.

Between 1672 and 1675 Penn published numerous tracts, many of them written in direct response to critics of the Society of Friends. In these pamphlets, which are often distinguished by their abusive language, he asserted the right to religious freedom and explained Quaker thought and practice, such as their habits, plain language, hat wearing, refusal to take oaths, their interpretations of the doctrine of the Trinity, of the scripture as the rule of faith, and their belief in the Inner Light. Quakers believe in the equality of all men. One testimony of this belief was the early Quakers' use of *thou* and *thy* and *thee* in addressing an individual regardless of social status. This idiosyncrasy caused a great deal of irritation among non-Quakers. Even more trouble was caused by their refusal to swear oaths. They based this attitude on biblical authority and on their conviction that every man owed it to himself to speak only the truth. However, their refusal to swear oaths was arbitrarily interpreted by the authorities as proof of their lack of loyalty to King and country. Consequently, the laws which had been designed to ensnare Catholics also served to discriminate against Quakers.

The strong physical-spiritual dualism permeating Quaker thought in general, and their testimony to the inner light in particular, accounted for their view of scripture as merely an outward or visible means of grace which, they asserted, had become the main object of puritan idolatry. More specifically, they did not reject the doctrine of the Trinity as such. They did, however, object to orthodox theological terminology and its tendency to anthropomorphize the divine. They were particularly suspicious of the concept of one divine essence in three persons because in their interpretation *person* did not signify a separate consciousness but an "outward" or "human" embodied being. Their own emphasis on the eternal activity of Christ, on the other hand, left little room for the identifiable functions of the Father and the Spirit, and thus made it difficult for Quakers to affirm the traditional doctrine of the Trinity. Quaker writers referred to the divine power that dwelt in men as "Spirit," "Light," and "Christ within." Once the inner light became a powerful presence involving the whole of a person's being, it caused a personal rebirth involving a complete break with the former life. Hence, it was not unusual for Children of the Light to take on new names for their lives as saints.

Penn was also involved in bitter struggles within the Society of Friends, rebutting in letters and pamphlets challenges to the allegedly authoritarian leadership of George Fox. With George Fox, Penn shared the conviction that the Society of Friends could not survive without formal organization and a certain degree of supervision, as distinct from the individualistic character of early Quakerism.

The year 1675 marked the beginning of a new phase in Penn's life. Drawn into the settling of a dispute between two Quakers over land in New Jersey, he became involved in the colonization of America almost by accident. His letters of the time show him in the role of arbitrator and reveal the frustration that dispute caused Penn. They also reflect his concern, shared by other Quaker leaders, that any dispute among Friends in public court would be detrimental to the society. On 10 February 1675 he became a trustee proprietor. He helped arrange for the division of New Jersey in east and west parts, for the settlement of West New Jersey, and he probably wrote *The Description of West New Jersey* (1676). Despite Penn's original view of colonization as a dubious road to wealth, this tract enthusiastically encouraged colonization and brought upon its author the charge from fellow Quakers of tempting Friends to escape from persecution at home, thus shirking their Christian duty. In the summer of 1676 Penn signed the *West New Jersey Concessions and Agreements*, one of the most innovative political documents of the seventeenth century. Edward Byllynge, the author of *A Mite of Affection* (1659), probably made the greatest contribution. However, several chapters of the *West New Jersey Concessions and Agreements* echo themes in Penn's *England's Present Interest Discover'd . . .* (1675), such as the abolition of imprisonment for debt, the increased judicial power of juries, and the involvement of all inhabitants in the making of laws. On the other hand, early drafts of his later *The Frame of the Government of the Province of Pennsilvania . . .* (1682) were closer to the *West New Jersey Concessions and Agreements* than the final document.

From July to October 1677 a healthy and vigorous Penn, accompanied by a group of prominent Quakers, made his second journey into Holland and Germany. His detailed journal account of this religious mission was first published in London in 1694 under the title *An Account of W. Penn's Travails in Holland and Germany. . . .* His exalted spiritual state, his intensive seeking for spiritual communion in long hours of prayer and preaching, the examination of his own religious life and that of others whom he encountered, distinguish this remarkable record. There are also several accounts of his conversion, and some light is shed on his relationship with his family after this event. Characteristically, his dealings were mainly with Quakers and with Protestants of pietist temperament, with the well-born and the well-connected whose "worth" was manifest in their religious outlook and social status. The Princess Elizabeth of Palatine, abbess at Herford, was the most prominent of several upper-class women with whom he shared spiritual experiences and exchanged letters. During this journey he also made contacts with wealthy individuals who would later invest in Pennsylvania.

After his return from the Continent, Penn took an even greater interest in politics than before his departure, lobbying Parliament for religious toleration. In two speeches to a committee of Parliament on 22 March 1678 he pointed out that Quakers "suffered not only by Laws made against them, but by the Laws made against Papists," and he demanded "a discrimination of themselves from Papists." While complaining of being branded "an Emissary of Rome & in pay from the Pope," he nevertheless upheld the principle that neither Catholics nor Quakers ought to be persecuted for matters of conscience.

In the aftermath of the Popish Plot, invented by the perjurer Titus Oates, who charged that the Roman Catholics were planning to assassinate King Charles II and put the Duke of York (later James II) on the throne, the King was forced to dissolve the Cavalier Parliament in 1679 and call for new elections. His brother James, Duke of York, went briefly into exile. Apparently, Penn accepted fully Oates's charges against Catholics in general and the Jesuits in particular. Despite his close personal relationship with the Stuarts, he was prepared to follow the dictates of his conscience and join their political enemies, the Whigs. Penn shared the principles for which conservative Whigs stood: dedication to Protestantism, to toleration for Protestant dissenters, and to the supremacy of Parliament. However, in spite of his support in two elections for the abortive campaigns of the radical republican Algernon Sidney (who was later executed for treason for his alleged complicity in another plot to assassinate Charles II), there was no room in Penn's republicanism for rebellion against tyrants or for a warlike state. During the election campaigns of 1679, Penn, under the pseudonym "Philanglus," wrote two tracts. *Englands Great Interest in the Choice of This New Parliament . . .* is a short piece attacking corruption on all levels of government. It outlines standards of integrity for both the governed and those who govern and states the three fundamental rights of Englishmen: to property, to participation in and consent to legislation, and to a share in the judicatory power. *One Project for the Good of England . . .* expresses Penn's preference for being governed not by men but by laws which serve the civil interest and which respect the integrity of the individual nonconformist. These publications are of particular interest since they unequivocally document their author's political opposition to the Crown just before he petitioned Charles II for the grant of a colony in America and before he asked the Duke of York to support and promote his new colony of Pennsylvania.

Penn's yearning for a safe haven for Quakers and other persecuted groups and individuals had gradually evolved into a concrete vision. Some time before June 1680 he asked the King for a specific piece of land lying west of the Delaware and north of Maryland, in lieu of a large sum of money the Crown owed to his father. Penn thus provided the King with an officially presentable reason for a land grant. At the same time, he knowingly satisfied the King's desire to rid himself of large numbers of political enemies by offering them the opportunity of immigrating to America. The Royal Charter, dated 4 March 1681, names Penn as absolute proprietary of a tract of land in America, thus granting him the power to make and publish laws with the assent of the freemen or their delegates, the power to establish judges and other legal officers, and the power to pardon and abolish crimes, provided these measures were not contrary to the laws of England.

In a letter dated 8 April 1681, Penn assured the inhabitants of Pennsylvania of their personal liberties and of his own benevolent intentions. In other letters, written at that time, he repeatedly and confidentially pointed out his intention of investing the power of government in the people, thus effectively preventing himself and his heirs from imposing the proprietor's will on them. The granting of the province he considered a sign of the providence and love of God rather than a secular favor. His 18 October 1681 letter to the Indians of

Pennsylvania included the American natives in this scheme. Also, in 1681, he published two accounts, *Some Account of the Province of Pennsilvania . . .* and *A Brief Account of the Province of Pennsilvania . . .*, describing and generally advertising the province of Pennsylvania.

Having sought and received the counsel of learned men, of philosophers and politicians, Penn drew up the first version of *The Frame of the Government of the Province of Pennsylvania. . .* , dated 25 April 1682. The original frame of government consisted of a long preface, followed by the twenty-four sections of the constitution. On 5 May he added the forty *Laws Agreed upon in England.* Penn was convinced that, unlike the ideal states of Thomas More, Francis Bacon, and James Harrington, his own utopia, his Holy Experiment, would not exist only on paper.

The preface states that in any form of government, whether monarchy, aristocracy, or democracy, the people are free as long as laws rule and the people partake in the making of those laws.

SOME
ACCOUNT
OF THE
PROVINCE
OF
PENNSILVANIA
IN
AMERICA;
Lately Granted under the Great Seal
OF
ENGLAND
TO
William Penn, &c.
Together with Priviledges and Powers necessary to the well-governing thereof.
Made publick for the Information of such as are or may be disposed to Transport themselves or Servants into those Parts.

LONDON: Printed, and Sold by Benjamin Clark Bookseller in George-Yard Lombard-street, 1681.

Title page for one of the pamphlets Penn wrote to advertise his recently chartered colony

The twenty-four articles describe the future form of government in Pennsylvania. *The Frame of the Government . . .* provides for a powerful provincial council of seventy-two people elected to serve for three years and for an annually elected two-hundred-man assembly. Both bodies would be elected by the freemen of the colony. The council would advise the governor on matters of government, and it would propose bills. The assembly would approve or reject proposed legislation. The governor would preside over the council with a triple vote. The forty laws, known eventually as the Great Law, realized many of the Whig and other principles for which Penn had publicly voiced his support in the years up to 1679. The freemen were granted such civil rights as free elections, the levying of taxes with the consent of the people, guaranty of trial by jury and of bail, legalization of the Quaker wedding without participation of clergy, replacement of oath by simple affirmation, religious toleration, freedom of conscience and expression, and the individual's sovereignty over his property.

Penn's constitution for Pennsylvania, unlike the *West New Jersey Concessions and Agreements,* was founded on the Royal Charter and, therefore, stipulated very different conditions for colonization, rendering genuine republicanism impossible. Nevertheless, the concept of an essentially republican legislature is inherent to both. However, it is essential to realize that Penn was not republican, egalitarian, or democratic in the modern senses of these terms. The aristocracy in which he believed was distinguished by talent and, possibly, by material affluence. Designed by Penn as a contract of fundamental nature, binding to both the governor and the governed, the main weakness of *The Frame of the Government . . .* was its built-in resistance to change. This inflexibility, shared to some extent by the proprietor, would eventually lead to considerable frictions within the provincial government and between the various factions and the proprietor. On 30 August 1682 Penn departed for America, where he arrived late in October 1682.

Only a few days before his departure Penn signed the preface of the second edition of *No Cross, No Crown . . .*, which is rather more than a corrected and enlarged version of the 1669 publication. The new book is divided in two parts of eighteen and four chapters, respectively, and comprises a greatly increased number of "testimonies." While the 1669 edition reflected its author's youthful radicalism, the 1682 version was the work of the liberal reformer, humanist, and religious thinker, whose primary concern was no longer with hats, titles, and plain

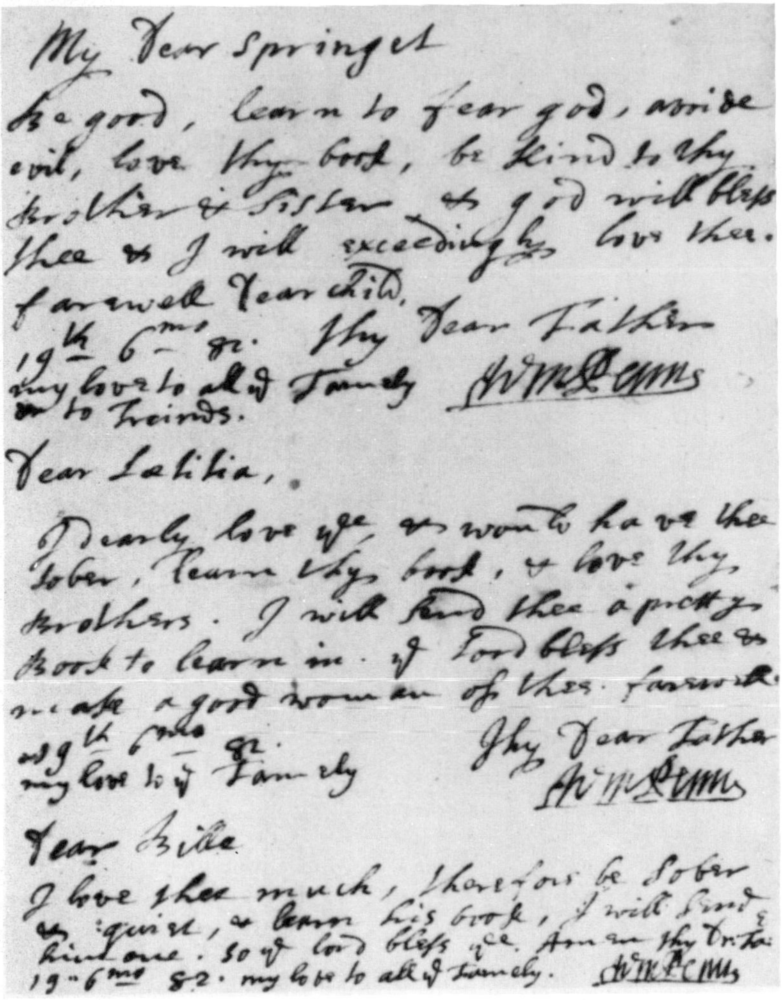
My Dear Springet

be good, learn to fear god, avoide evil, love thy book, be kind to thy brother & Sister & god will bless thee & I will exceedingly love thee. farewell dear child.

19th 6mo 82. thy dear Father

my love to all ye family & to friends. Wm Penn

Dear Letitia,

I dearly love yee, & would have thee sober, learn thy book, & love thy brothers. I will send thee a pretty book to learn in. ye Lord bless thee & make a good woman of thee. farewell.

19th 6mo 82. thy dear Father

my love to ye family Wm Penn

Dear Bille

I love thee much, therefore be Sober & quiet, & learn his book, I will send him one. so ye lord bless yee. Amen thy Dr. Fa:

19-6mo 82. my love to all ye family. Wm Penn

A letter from Penn to his children, written before he left on his first trip to Pennsylvania

language but with man's spiritual life. Appropriately, his language is no longer that of fire and brimstone but of sincere exhortation and firm persuasion. His sentences are classically short and to the point; his arguments relating to the fate of mankind tend to be of a general nature. The preface appeals to the reader, Quaker and non-Quaker alike, "To Retire into Thy Self, and take a View of the Condition of thy Soul; for Christ hath given thee Light with which to do it; Search carefully and thoroughly, thy Life is upon it; thy Soul is at Stake. . . . Ay, and one knowing the Comfort, Peace, Joy and Pleasure of the Ways of Righteousness too, I exhort and invite thee, to embrace the Reproofs and Convictions of Christ's Light and Spirit in thine own Conscience, and bear the Judgment, who hast wrought the Sin." The Christ Penn speaks of is the spiritual light of the world that enlightens everyone. And the cross mystical with which he is concerned is the Divine grace and power which obstructs the carnal wills of men and directs them to meekness, mercy, self-denial, suffering, temperance, justice, and goodness. Whoever wishes to bear Christ's crown must first suffer the pains of the cross of self-denial in the world, not in monastic seclusion. There are two selves in every man that the light may require man to deny. The lawful self comprises the worldly happiness and possessions with which God has blessed man: husband, wife, children, house, liberty, and life. The unlawful self relates, on one hand, to exterior pomp and superstition in religious worship and to worldly affairs and the satisfaction of self-love as manifest in pride, avarice, and luxury, on the other.

In the 1669 version of *No Cross, No Crown . . .* and in other early tracts Penn had already used classical examples to appeal for moral change in humanistic English readers. In his contribution to *The Christian-Quaker, and His Divine Testimony* . . . (1673) he went so far as to claim that even Socrates, like Abraham, was saved by his faith and obedience in following the inner light. Permeated by the Puritan passion for moral righteousness and expressive of its nonconformity to the world, *No Cross, No Crown* . . . was a commentary on and rejection of the worldliness of Restoration England, of its luxury, pride, and corruption.

On this occasion, Penn stayed in Pennsylvania for two years. During that time the frame of government was amended and the laws revised. Philadelphia was declared the permanent capital, and negotiations with the Indians for land were being peacefully and successfully conducted. However, the dispute with Lord Baltimore over the border between Pennsylvania and Maryland forced Penn, at considerable personal risk, to return to England, where liberties had been suspended and prominent Whigs were being mercilessly hounded. Soon after Penn's return, the death of Charles II brought to the throne the Catholic James II, under whom the suffering of dissenters intensified. His close association with the new King placed Penn in an influential, if highly ambiguous, position. Possibly, his tract *A Perswasive Moderation to Dissenting Christians* . . . (1685), which urges the King to exercise his Christian duty and desist from further alienating his dissenting subjects, had some effect, for in the spring of 1686 James issued a pardon to Quakers, followed by two general acts of indulgence in the next two years. However, when in November 1688 William of Orange landed with his forces, James fled to France, and Penn was left in a highly exposed and dangerous position. In February 1689 a warrant was issued for his arrest upon suspicion of high treason. Unable to prove that he was not involved in any conspiracy against the new king and his government, Penn eventually left London. When another warrant was issued for his arrest in February 1691, he went into hiding for a period of about three years. He may briefly have been in France, yet for most of the time he stayed in England, living in places known only to his family and closest friends. His estates in Ireland were appropriated by the Crown.

Strife within the Pennsylvania administration and his own financial difficulties added to his troubles. Pennsylvania failed to respond to his appeals for a loan to defray expenses partly incurred on their behalf. When, as a result of the war between England and France, demands were made on Pennsylvania for troops and supplies, Penn was unable to persuade the predominantly pacifist Pennsylvania administration to comply. Consequently, the Crown took the colony under its protection.

While in hiding, Penn wrote two remarkable, yet very different works. Appalled by the senseless bloodshed on the Continent in the wake of the War of the League of Augsburg, the religious pacifist Penn wrote his treatise in practical statescraft, *An Essay Towards the Present and Future Peace of Europe* . . . , which was published anonymously in two editions in 1693. This essay consists of an address to the reader, followed by ten sections, and a conclusion. Like Dante, Erasmus, Henry IV of France, and Grotius before him, Penn had a vision of a peacefully united world. However, his essay is distinguished by its suggesting the practical application of advanced legal, social, and moral theories toward disinterested ends. In contrast with the preface to his first frame of government, *An Essay Towards the Present and Future Peace of Europe* . . . considers the origin and purpose of covenant in a secular framework. It envisions a parliament of nations, representation being proportioned to economic power. Disarmament is considered the only ultimate guaranty of international peace. Sovereignty in national affairs is to remain intact, while provisions for sanctions against offenders are vaguely suggested.

Some Fruits of Solitude . . . (1693) and its sequel, *More Fruits of Solitude* . . . (1702), are collections of maxims and aphorisms setting down Penn's mature philosophy of life. Written in a manner reminiscent of La Rochefoucauld's *Maximes* and Pascal's *Pensées*, Penn's highly condensed reflections appear, in both style and substance, to have been composed without haste. The loose syntax, rambling wordiness, and complex clauses of his earlier tracts have been replaced by trenchant, precise formulations and carefully structured short periods. Protestant morality and Puritan austerity, while still present, are no longer forced upon the reader with prophetic fervor. Love of religious and political liberty does not preclude conformity in compliance with conscience. Apparently, the Whig's faith in representative institutions has been tempered by his experience with the headstrong, individualistic people of Pennsylvania. There are interesting sections on people's ignorance of the world and on the necessary education of youth both in morality and practical matters. Nature is considered an emanation and mirror of God. To study the world, to read the volume of nature is to decipher the hieroglyphs of a better world. Human history and institutions are to be judged by moral standards.

Pride, luxury, conscience, friendship, piety, and many other topics are being discussed with poignancy. Though less humorous and pungent than Benjamin Franklin, Penn, in his maxims and aphorisms, demonstrates a concern with the bourgeois virtues of diligence and thrift that foreshadows Poor Richard.

Late in 1693 Penn was finally exonerated, and in a royal grant Pennsylvania was once again restored to him under certain conditions. The first one he fulfilled five years later by returning to his colony. The second one he failed to fulfill because the Provincial Council of Pennsylvania refused to furnish men or money for the defense of the province. Due to his having been defrauded by the steward of his Irish estates, as well as to his taste for genteel living and his neglect of his financial affairs, Penn's economic plight had worsened over the years. By the time Gulielma Penn died (23 February 1694), Penn had sold off a considerable part of her large estate. Pennsylvania, now, seemed to offer the only solution to his problems. On 3 September 1699 he sailed to America, accompanied by his new wife, Hannah Callowhill, and his daughter Laetitia. In Pennsylvania he was soon involved in bitter quarrels between the Anglican party, on the one hand, and the Assembly party, on the other. The political antagonists were united, however, in their opposition to the proprietary interests. When serious charges of misdemeanor were leveled against him and there was a possibility of the colony's being taken away from him, Penn decided to return to England, where he arrived early in 1702. In the meantime his financial situation had grown desperate, and he saw no way out of this twofold predicament but to attempt selling his province to the Crown with the provision that the laws and civil rights in the province would be upheld. However, this transfer was never finalized. On 7 January 1708 a sick and financially ruined Penn reported to the Fleet, London's debtor's prison. He was released after several English Friends raised more than £6000 on his behalf. The affluent Pennsylvanians, on the other hand, on whose behalf he had, at least in part, incurred his enormous debts, refused to come to his assistance on this occasion. When the Assembly added insult to injury by attempting to shift the executive powers from the governor to the Assembly, Penn summarized his grievances in "A Serious Expostulation with the Inhabitants of Pennsylvania in a Letter from the Proprietor and Governor" (written in 1710). After suffering his second stroke in October 1712, Penn never fully recovered his mental faculties. He died nearly six years later.

William Penn, circa 1696 (Historical Society of Pennsylvania)

Although Penn failed to transform his vision of a commonwealth founded on love into political reality, liberty of conscience, the ideal central to his political theory, became the mainstay of the growing secular commonwealth of America. Penn, the writer, developed from a fiery religious and political agitator into a mature political innovator and theorist and a thoughtful historian and interpreter of Quakerism. While he strove throughout his career for the separation of Church and State, in his writings religious motives and political purposes are, by necessity, frequently interwoven. Most of his political writings, with the notable exception of the still readable and popular *An Essay Towards the Present and Future Peace of Europe . . .*, were written for the moment and are of greater interest to the student of seventeenth-century history than to the general reader. In contrast, his religious writings, especially *No Cross, No Crown*, *A Brief Account of the Rise and Progress of the People Called Quakers* (1694), and *Primitive Christianity Revived . . .* (1696), are of lasting interest not only to the historian of religion. Though unrelieved by soaring flights of the imagination and lacking Miltonic grandeur of vision, these works still convey effectively their author's passionate concern for the liberties of the individual and his belief that conscience is a reliable guide to moral action.

Biographies:

Samuel M. Janney, *The Life of William Penn* (Philadelphia: Hogan, Perkins, 1852);

William Isaac Hull, *William Penn, A Topical Biography* (London & New York: Oxford University Press, 1937);

Catherine Owens Peare, *William Penn, A Biography* (Philadelphia: Lippincott, 1957).

References:

Edwin B. Bronner, *William Penn's Holy Experiment* (New York: Temple University Publications, 1962);

Mary Maples Dunn, *William Penn, Politics and Conscience* (Princeton: Princeton University Press, 1967);

Melvin B. Endy, Jr., *William Penn and Early Quakerism* (Princeton: Princeton University Press, 1973);

Joseph E. Illick, *William Penn the Politician* (Ithaca: Cornell University Press, 1965);

Gary B. Nash, *Quakers and Politics, Pennsylvania, 1681-1726* (Princeton: Princeton University Press, 1968);

Ian K. Steele, *Politics and Colonial Policy* (Oxford: Clarendon Press, 1968).

Papers:

The Historical Society of Pennsylvania has 1,350 documents, including the manuscripts of greatest individual value and interest, illuminating every aspect of Penn's career. The Public Record Office, London, has some 300 documents illustrating Penn's dealings with the English government as a Quaker activist, as a political ally of James II, and as the proprietor of Pennsylvania. The Friends' Library, London, has approximately 150 documents tracing Penn's activities within the Society of Friends. The Pennsylvania State Archives, Harrisburg, holds a smaller number of documents detailing Penn's relations with his colonists. The British Library, London, also has Penn correspondence, and the Albert Cook Myers Collection of William Penn Materials, Chester County Historical Society, West Chester, Pennsylvania, has a collection of miscellaneous materials.

Thomas Prince

(15 May 1687-22 October 1758)

Ronald A. Bosco
State University of New York at Albany

BOOKS: *God Brings to the Desired Haven. A Thanksgiving-Sermon, Deliver'd at the Lecture in Boston, N.E., on Thursday, September 5, 1717. Upon Occasion of the Author's safe Arrival Thro' Many Great Hazards & Deliverances, Especially on the Seas, in Above Eight Years Absence from his Dear & Native Country* (Boston: Printed by B. Green, 1717);

A Sermon Delivered by Thomas Prince. . . . At his Ordination (Boston: Printed by J. Franklin for S. Gerrish, 1718);

An Account of a Strange Appearance in the Heavens on Tuesday-Night March 6, 1716. As it was seen over Stow-Market in Suffolk in England (Boston: Printed by S. Kneeland for D. Henchman, 1719);

Earthquakes the Works of God, & Tokens of His Just Displeasure. Two Sermons on Psal. XVIII.7. At the Particular Fast in Boston, Nov. 2. and the General Thanksgiving, Nov. 9. Occasioned by the late Dreadful Earthquake . . . (Boston: Printed by D. Henchman, 1727);

Morning Health No Security against the Sudden Arrest of Death before Night. A Sermon Occasioned by the very Sudden Death of Two Young Gentlemen . . . (Boston: Printed for Daniel Henchman, 1727);

A Sermon on the Sorrowful Occasion of the Death of His Late Majesty King George of Blessed Memory, and the Happy Ascension of His Present Majesty King George II to the Throne . . . (Boston: Printed for Daniel Henchman, 1727);

Civil Rulers Raised up by God to Feed His People. A Sermon at the Publick Lectures in Boston, July

Thomas Prince

25. 1728. In the Audience of His Excellency the Governour, His Honour the Lieut. Governour, and the Honorable Council and Representatives . . . (Boston: Printed for Samuel Gerrish, 1728);

The Departure of Elijah Lamented. A Sermon Occasioned by the Great and Publick Loss in the Decease of the Very Reverend & Learned Cotton Mather . . . (Boston: Printed for D. Henchman, 1728);

The Grave and Death Destroyed, and Believers Ransomed and Redeemed from Them. A Sermon at Middleborough East-Precinct July. VII. 1728. Being the Lord's-Day after the Decease & Funeral of Samuel Prince . . . (Boston: Printed for S. Gerrish, 1728);

The People of New-England Put in Mind of the Righteous Acts of the Lord to Them and Their Fathers, And Reasoned With Concerning Them. A Sermon Delivered at Cambridge Before the Great and General Assembly of the Province of Massachusetts May 27th, MDCCXXX. Being the Anniversary for the Election of His Majesty's Council . . . (Boston: Printed by B. Green for D. Henchman, 1730);

A Sermon at the Publick Lecture in Boston January VIII, 1729, 30. Upon the Death of the Honorable Samuel Sewall . . . (Boston: Printed by B. Green, 1730);

The Vade Mecum for America: or a Companion for Traders and Travellers . . . (Boston: Printed by S. Kneeland & T. Green for D. Henchman & T. Hancock, 1731);

The Dying Prayer of Christ, for His People's Preservation and Unity. A Sermon to the North Church in Boston, January XXV, 1731, 2. Being a Day of Prayer for Divine Direction, in their Choice of Another Colleague Pastor to Succeed the Rev. Dr. Cotton Mather . . . (Boston: Printed by S. Kneeland & T. Green for S. Gerrish, 1732);

The Faithful Servant Approv'd at Death, And Entring into the Joy of His Lord. A Sermon at the Publick Lecture in Boston. July XXVII, 1732. Occasion'd by the Much Lamented Death of the Honorable Daniel Oliver . . . (Boston: Printed by S. Kneeland & T. Green for D. Henchman, 1732);

Young Abel Dead, yet Speaketh. A Sermon Occasioned by the Death of Young Mr. Daniel Oliver . . . (Boston: Printed for D. Henchman, 1732; Bungay, England, 1801);

Precious in the Sight of the Lord Is the Death of His Saints . . . A Sermon upon the Death of Mrs. Elizabeth Oliver . . . (Boston: Printed by S. Kneeland & T. Green, 1735);

Christ Abolishing Death and Bringing Life and Immortality to the Light in the Gospel. A Sermon Occasioned by the Death of the Honorable Mary Belcher . . . (Boston: Printed by J. Draper for D. Henchman, 1736);

A Chronological History of New-England in the Form of Annals. Being a Summary and Exact Account of the Most Material Transactions and Occurences Relating to this Country, In the Order of Time Wherein They Happened, From the Discovery by Capt. Gosnold in 1602, to the Arrival of Governor Belcher, in 1730 . . . , volume 1 (Boston: Printed by Kneeland & Green for S. Gerrish, 1736); volume 2, numbers 1-3 published as *Annals of New-England* . . . (number 1, Boston: Printed & sold by S. Kneeland & by J. & T. Leverett, 1754; numbers 2-3, Boston: Printed by B. Edes & J. Gill for S. Kneeland & for T. Leverett, 1755);

A Funeral Sermon on the Reverend Mr. Nathanael

Williams . . . (Boston: Printed by S. Kneeland & T. Green, 1738);

The Sovereign God Acknowledged and Blessed, Both in Giving and Taking Away. A Sermon Occasioned by the Decease of Mrs. Deborah Prince . . . (Boston: Printed by Rogers & Fowle for T. Rand, 1744);

Extraordinary Events in the Doings of God, and Marvelous in Pious Eyes. Illustrated in a Sermon at the South Church in Boston, N.E. On the General Thanksgiving, Thursday, July 18, 1745. Occasion'd by the Taking of the City of Louisbourg on the Isle of Cape-Breton, by New-England Soldiers, Assisted by a British Squadron . . . (Boston: Printed for D. Henchman, 1745; London: Printed & sold by J. Lewis, 1746);

The Pious Cry to the Lord for Help When the Godly and Faithful Fail Among Them. A Sermon Occasion'd by the Great and Public Loss in the Death of the Honorable Thomas Cushing Esq; Speaker of the Honorable House of Representatives . . . (Boston: Printed for T. Rand, 1746);

The Salvations of God in 1746. In Part Set Forth in a Sermon at the South Church in Boston, Nov. 27, 1746. Being the Day of the Anniversary Thanksgiving . . . (Boston: Printed for D. Henchman, 1746; London: Printed & sold by T. Longman & T. Shewell, 1747);

A Sermon Delivered at the South Church in Boston, N.E. August 14, 1746. Being the Day of General Thanksgiving for the Great Deliverance of the British Nations by the Glorious and Happy Victory near Culloden . . . (Boston: Printed for D. Henchman & for S. Kneeland & T. Green, 1746; London: Printed & sold by John Lewis, 1747);

The Fulness ofLife and Joy in the Presence of God. A Sermon Occasion'd by the Decease of Mrs. Martha Stoddard . . . (Boston: Printed by Kneeland & Green, 1748);

The Natural and Moral Government and Agency of God in Causing Droughts and Rain. A Sermon at the South Church in Boston, Tuesday, Aug. 24, 1749. Being the Day of General Thanksgiving in the Province of the Massachusetts for the Extraordinary Reviving Rains . . . (Boston: Printed & sold by Kneeland & Green, 1749; London: Printed & sold by John Lewis, and by R. Hett & J. Oswald, E. Gardner, G. Keith, and P. Russell, 1750);

God Destroyeth the Hope of Man! A Sermon Occasion'd by the Inexpressible Loss in the Death of His Late Royal Highness Frederick, Prince of Wales . . . (Boston: Printed by S. Kneeland for D. Henchman, 1751);

Be Followers of Them who Through Faith and Patience, Inherit the Promises. A Sermon Occasioned by the Decease of Mrs. Hannah Fayerweather . . . (Boston: Printed by Edes & Gill for D. Henchman, 1755);

An Improvement of the Doctrine of Earthquakes, being the Works of God, and Tokens of His Just Displeasure . . . (Boston: Printed & sold by D. Fowle & by Z. Fowle, 1755);

The Case of Heman Considered In a Sermon on Psal. LXXXVIII.15. . . . Occasioned by the Death of Mr. Edward Bromfield . . . (Boston: Printed by S. Kneeland for D. Henchman, 1756);

The Character of Caleb. In a Sermon Delivered at the South-Church in Boston, on the Lord's Day, after the Funeral of the Honorable Josiah Willard, Esq; Secretary of the Province . . . (Boston: Printed & sold by S. Kneeland, 1756).

Twelve years after Thomas Prince died, Charles Chauncy, Prince's frequent ideological adversary, took special notice of him in "Sketch of Eminent Men in New-England": "I do not know any one that had more learning among us, excepting Doct. Cotton Mather; and it was extensive, as was also his genius. He possessed all the intellectual powers in a degree far beyond what is common. He may be justly characterized as one of our great men . . . [and] deserves to be remembered with honour." Chauncy's estimate of Prince was not an exaggeration; as a theologian, bibliophile, historian, scientist, and pastor of the influential Old South Church in Boston, Prince stood out among his contemporaries as an eighteenth-century Puritan-style renaissance man. On the one hand he was an eloquent and persuasive minister who tried to defend the "old New England way" during the time of its greatest (and final) peril; on the other hand he developed his secular talents as means to accommodate Puritanism's harsh doctrines to the increasingly cosmopolitan and rationalistic temper of the age. Although Prince was not always successful in his efforts, in the eyes of his contemporaries and of modern scholars, Prince has been invariably reckoned a central figure in eighteenth-century religious, social, and political developments.

Prince was born in Sandwich, Massachusetts, in comfortable social and economic circumstances. His father, Samuel, was a successful merchant and a Massachusetts Representative, and his mother, Mercy, was the daughter of Governor Thomas Hinckley of Plymouth Colony. As soon as he could read, his parents gave him a copy of Nathaniel Morton's *New-Englands Memoriall . . .* (1670); by the time he was ten, he had read and annotated *The Marrow of Modern Divinity . . .* (1645; attributed by some to Edward Fisher). Wishing to encourage their son's precocity, the Princes sent him to live with his grandfather Hinckley, who oversaw his education until he entered Harvard College in 1703. At Harvard, from which he received his A.B. in 1707 and A.M. *in absentia* in 1710, Prince made a satisfactory academic showing, but more important for his career as a minister and for his contribution to the intellectual life of colonial society, he entered into a close and lasting friendship with Joseph Sewall, and he began to collect books for what would become the "New England Library." After taking his A.B., he kept a school in Sandwich for over a year, but when it became clear that prospects for a teaching career were mixed at best, he decided to travel abroad. On 29 March 1709, he sailed from Boston with the Barbados fleet and spent two years visiting the West Indies and Europe. In 1711 he settled in England, preaching at various times in London, Great Yarmouth, Norwich, and Battisford. Finally, he accepted a partial ministry in Coombs in Suffolk, where he remained from 1714 to 1716. Prince must have impressed his congregation, for when, after an eight-year absence, he decided to return to his native New England, about thirty of the Coombs congregation followed him, including Deborah Denny, a woman ten years his junior, whom he married on 30 October 1719 and who survived him by almost eight years.

According to all accounts, Prince's return to Boston on 21 July 1717 was a cause for celebration. Although other young colonialists had traveled to the Old World, few had remained so long, seen so much, or made so successful a life for themselves while abroad. Within a short time Prince received calls from the churches of Hingham, Massachusetts, and Bristol, Rhode Island, but declined them in favor of occasional preaching engagements at the Old South Church, where his friend Joseph Sewall was pastor. At Sewall's instigation, the elders of the Old South—Judge Samuel Sewall among them—invited Prince to become its copastor on 23 December 1717. Prince happily accepted and was ordained on 1 October 1718 in one of the most lavish and impressive ceremonies on record. Among the participants during that event were Increase and Cotton Mather, Benjamin Colman, Benjamin Wadsworth, and the younger Sewall. Even Governor Dudley put in an appearance.

A favorite (along with Sewall, Thomas Foxcroft, and John Webb) of the conservative Mather faction, Prince quickly rose to a position of prominence and power in Boston's political and ecclesiastic circles. Cotton Mather was particularly doting, and his diary contains several expressions of unqualified admiration for Prince's theological opinions and scientific curiosity. By the mid-to-late 1720s, Prince, Sewall, and Foxcroft had become the unquestioned heirs-apparent to the intellectual and pastoral dynasty nurtured and preserved by three generations of Mathers. At this time Prince's career was developing in three nonexclusive, overlapping directions, which set the tone and context of his public life and writings from 1730 to 1758, the year he died. As theologian, he concentrated on protecting the idealized piety of New England's founders from the rising secularism and seeming irreligion of the age. As historian he looked to New England's past for evidence of God's special attitude toward his latest chosen people, hoping that such evidence might spur his contemporaries to reform and to return to the original covenant terms upon which New England had been established. As scientist, he looked into events and toward the future, seeking in scientific inquiry and discovery examples of God's continued providential intervention in New England's affairs and using the language of empirical science and reason to restate the convictions of seventeenth-century Puritan cosmologists for the edification of the present "enlightened" generation.

In many respects, as perhaps Chauncy intended to suggest, Prince's career bore striking similarity to that of Cotton Mather. Though separated in age from Mather by a generation, Prince was undoubtedly aware that as theologian, historian, and scientist he was extending the principal interests of New England's foremost intellectual into the eighteenth century. Temperamentally and intellectually, Mather and Prince were kindred spirits. For both, the survival of New England as the divinely prophesied and sanctioned seat of the truly Christian "Kingdom of God" in the Western world provided the primary motivation for and served as the hallmark features of all their respective career endeavors. Prince's own lifelong effort to collect all books, pamphlets, maps, and papers—he discovered them in New England or abroad—which pertained to New England history and public affairs and to preserve them in his New England Library is but one sign of his personal dedication to the survival and celebration of New England in idea and in fact. These materials, which he originally bequeathed to the Old South Church and which today are preserved only in part in the Prince Collection at the Boston Public Library, demonstrate a range of interest and erudition unparalleled by any in early New England history save Mather. Another sign of Prince's intellectual kinship with Mather is the use to which he put the extensive collections of the New England Library. Like Mather, Prince used historical materials in his sermons and scientific tracts, but his principal use of them was in *A Chronological History of New-England* (1736-1755), a literary and historical project with which he was concerned for more than twenty years and which might be said to have failed only for lack of subscription support. In *A Chronological History of New-England* Prince enlarged on the didactic purpose of Mather's own *Magnalia Christi Americana; or, the Ecclesiastical History of New England* (1702), relating the history of New England from the beginning of time, through the various ages and stages of human civilization, to, finally, the colony's establishment in the seventeenth century and its historical growth into the eighteenth century, and expressing at each turn the long-standing Puritan conviction that New England represented the fulfillment of all historical and religious assumptions and prophesies concerning the evolution of mankind and the rise in the Western world of a new "People of God."

Prince's many published works, particularly his sermons, provide today's reader with a full measure of the range of his opinions and the extent of his literary ability. *Earthquakes the Works of God, & Tokens of His Just Displeasure* . . . (1727), *The People of New-England* . . . (1730), *A Chronological History of New-England* (1736-1755), *Extraordinary Events in the Doings of God* . . . (1745), *The Natural and Moral Government and Agency of God* . . . (1749), and *Be Followers of Them* . . . (1755) represent his theological, historical, and scientific ideas and his style at their best. In these works there is considerable overlapping of theology, history, and science. Speaking of earthquakes and other natural disasters, for instance, Prince moves between comment on the natural causes of such phenomena (earthquakes originate in the shifting of underground caverns, he says) and comment on the moral purpose behind such phenomena (God uses them variously to warn his people of his displeasure with their present spiritual condition and to punish them for their past transgressions). History too comes into play in these discussions, for Prince is apt to catalogue a specific disaster as one among many through which God has repeatedly spoken. The more spectacular the disaster, the more it is an indication that God's patience is wearing thin.

In these works Prince repeats many of the commonplace convictions of his conservative contemporaries and their Puritan predecessors. Running through each is an assumption of the backsliding of New England's people balanced by a call to return to the errand of New England's fathers. In this context New England's idealized past is often used as a measure of the present, with the present found wanting. None of the sermons is a true jeremiad; however, the presence of themes such as New England's decline, humiliation and punishment, and, finally, its hoped-for rescue by God demonstrates that Prince is dealing with an updated version of that sermonic form. Typically, Prince attempts to make assumptions associated with the jeremiad form palatable to his mid-eighteenth-century audiences by eschewing vitriolic harangues in favor of reasoned, philosophic discourse. Finally, in all there is a pronounced sense of hope. Unlike many of his contemporaries, including Sewall, who believed that New England was on the verge of an irreversible collapse, Prince believed that New England's spiritual troubles were temporary, and he considered them as so many testings of the faith and perseverance of God's people. For Prince, hopeful signs were everywhere to be found: in the survival by many of natural disasters; in the successful rebuff of New England's French foes; in the revival movement led by George Whitefield, of whom Prince was Boston's most outspoken champion; and in the extension of toleration to all religions, which Prince acknowledged as the surest sign of Puritan New England's final power and security.

An important figure in his own day, Prince continues to be regarded by modern historians and students of colonial homiletics as a figure of central importance in mid-eighteenth-century America. In addition to theologial, historical, and scientific writings, Prince also published a companion for traders and travelers in the New World in 1731, a religious periodical entitled the *Christian History* (1744 to 1745), and a scholarly edition of the *Bay Psalm Book* (1758); however, none of these works has ever received critical attention. To be sure, there are some disappointments to be met with in his work. As an historian, for example, Prince is frequently faulted in terms such as those used by Clifford Shipton, who, when speaking of *A Chronological History of New-England* . . . , said that he "was indeed a far better historian than the Mathers, Hubbard, or Niles, but only in promise, not achievement." Others have faulted him for not pursuing far enough the use of scientific and rational language in his sermons as means to accommodate Puritanism to the changing attitudes of his time. Yet most scholars acknowledge his contributions with respect, and one hopes that this respect will lead some of them to write long-overdue biographical and critical studies of Prince.

Other:

The Great and Solemn Obligations to Early Piety..., in *A Course of Sermons on Early Piety. . .* , edited by Cotton Mather (Boston: Printed by S. Kneeland for N. Buttolph, B. Eliot, & D. Henchman, 1721);

Samuel Willard, *A Compleat Body of Divinity . . .* , edited by Prince and Joseph Sewall (Boston: Printed by B. Green & S. Kneeland for B. Eliot & D. Henchman, 1726);

The Psalms, Hymns, & Spiritual Songs of the Old and New Testament, Faithfully Translated into English Metre. Being the New-England Psalm-Book, Revised and Improved . . . , edited by Prince (Boston: Printed & sold by D. Henchman & S. Kneeland, 1758).

References:

Ronald A. Bosco, Introduction to *The Puritan Sermon in America, 1630-1750*, edited by Bosco, 4 volumes (New York: Scholars' Facsimiles & Reprints, 1978), I: xiii-xcv;

Charles Chauncy, "Sketch of Eminent Men in New-England," *Collections of the Massachusetts Historical Society*, first series 10 (1809): 154-170;

Hamilton Andrews Hill, *History of the Old South Church, 1669-1884*, 2 volumes (Boston: Houghton, Mifflin, 1890);

Cotton Mather, *The Diary of Cotton Mather*, edited by Worthington Chauncey Ford, 2 volumes (1911-1912; republished, New York: Ungar, 1957);

Perry Miller, *The New England Mind: From Colony to Province* (Boston: Beacon Press, 1953);

Joseph Sewall, *The Duty, Character, and Reward of Christ's Faithful Servants. A Sermon at the South-Church in Boston on the Lord's Day, after the Funeral of the Reverend Mr. Thomas Prince* (Boston: Printed by S. Kneeland, 1758);

Samuel Sewall, *The Diary of Samuel Sewall, 1674-1729*, edited by M. Halsey Thomas, 2 volumes (New York: Farrar, Straus & Giroux, 1973);

John Langdon Sibley and Clifford K. Shipton, *Biographical Sketches of Those Who Attended Harvard College in the Classes 1701-1712* (Boston: Massachusetts Historical Society, 1937), pp. 341-368;

William B. Sprague, *Annals of the American Pulpit; or Commemorative Notices of Distinguished American Clergymen of Various Denominations* (New York: Carter, 1866), I: 304-307.

Papers:

Fragments of Prince's papers are to be found in three libraries. The American Antiquarian Society has Prince's almanac for 1736-1737. The Boston Public Library, which has preserved remnants of Prince's "New England Library," has a collection of miscellaneous, generally nonpersonal manuscript material. The Massachusetts Historical Society has a log kept by Prince during his voyages in 1709-1711 and several letters preserved in various manuscript collections.

Mary Rowlandson

(circa 1635-circa 1678)

Richard VanDerBeets
San Jose State University

BOOK: *The Soveraignty & Goodness of God, Together with the Faithfulness of His Promises Displayed; Being a Narrative of the Captivity and Restauration of Mrs. Mary Rowlandson* . . . (Boston: Printed by Samuel Green, Jr., 1682); republished as *A True History of the Captivity & Restoration of Mrs. Mary Rowlandson* . . . (London: Printed & sold by J. Poole, 1682).

Mary White Rowlandson holds a secure if modest place in Colonial American literary history as the author of the first and deservedly best-known New England Indian captivity narrative and, except for sixteenth-century Spanish accounts, the first account of captivity published in North America: *The Soveraignty & Goodness of God, Together with the Faithfulness of His Promises Displayed; Being a Narrative of the Captivity and Restauration of Mrs. Mary Rowlandson* ... (1682). While the popularity of her narrative has carried it through some thirty editions since its first publication, little is known of her life beyond the facts contained in her account.

The wife of the Reverend Joseph Rowlandson, pastor of the Puritan church at Lancaster, Massachusetts, Mary Rowlandson was captured during King Philip's War by a Wampanoag war party at the 20 February 1676 attack on Lancaster and was ransomed and freed at Princeton, Massachusetts, on 2 May of the same year. Her ordeal included witnessing the slaughter of relatives and friends during the initial attack, her own wounding by a musket ball, near starvation and physical privation throughout a forced march to some twenty separate campsites, or "removes," and the death of her six-year-old daughter during the march. Yet the significance of her captivity narrative lies not so much in its unfolding tale of ordeal and fortitude as in its expression of profoundly felt religious experience.

Calvinists believing that the Indian inhabitants of the wilderness were often directly the instruments of Satan and indirectly those of God, the Puritan settlers could view the torments of Indian captivity as one of God's ways of testing or punishing his creatures. "God strengthned them [Indians] to be a scourge to His People," Rowlandson writes; "the Lord feeds and nourishes them up to be a scourge to the whole Land." The scriptural citation she uses for support is Hebrews 12:6: "For whom the Lord loveth he chasteneth, and scourgeth every Son whom he receiveth." In the course of her narrative Rowlandson turns to the scriptures for comfort more than sixty-five times, as she reflects on a variety of incidents ranging from the death of her child (Genesis 42:36: "Me have ye bereaved of my Children . . .") to her staying dry while fording a river (Isaiah 43:2: "When thou passeth through the waters I will be with thee . . ."). Most of her citations are strikingly appropriate to her captivity experience—Psalms 106:46, for example: "He made them also to be pitied, of all those that carried them Captives."

Ultimately the experience was a morally instructive one; there were lessons to be drawn. On the first Sabbath of her captivity, Rowlandson recalls "how careless I had been of God's holy time, how many Sabbaths I had lost and misspent. . . . Yet the Lord still shewed mercy and upheld me; and as he wounded me with one hand, so he healed me with the other." When, after her release, she is troubled with small matters ("a shadow, a blast, a bubble, and things of no continuance . . ."), she thinks upon her recent captivity: "It was but the other day that if I had had the world, I would have given it for my freedom . . . I have learned to look beyond present and smaller troubles." Perhaps the chief spiritual significance for both the captive-narrator and her reader lay in interpreting the captivity as an illustration of God's providence. "God was with me, in a wonderfull manner, carrying me along and bearing up my spirit . . . that I might see more of his Power," writes Rowlandson. "One principall ground of my setting forth these lines is to declare the Works of the Lord, and his wonderfull power in carrying us along, preserving us in the Wilderness, while under the Enemies hand, and returning us to safety again."

Thus, as test or punishment by God, as opportunity for redemptive suffering, and as evidence of divine providence, the experience of Indian captivity is viewed as salutary and morally instructive. Explicit in the narrative are the spiritual lessons to be learned, lessons intended as well for the moral edification of the reader. In this mode and by these apprehensions, Mary Rowlandson's Indian captivity narrative serves as an intense and satisfying expression of religious experience. "The portion of some is to have their afflictions by drops, now one drop and then another; but the dregs of the Cup, the Wine of astonishment did the Lord prepare to be my portion," she writes. "Affliction I wanted, and affliction I had . . . And I hope I can say in some measure, as David did, It is good for me that I have been afflicted."

After her redemption and return to her husband, Mrs. Rowlandson spent the winter in Boston. Then the Reverend Mr. Rowlandson secured a church in Wethersfield, Connecticut, and moved his family there in 1677. He died the next year, and the town voted Mary Rowlandson a pension of £30 a year for as long as she remained a widow. Nothing more is known of her after that time.

References:

Roy Harvey Pearce, "The Significances of the Captivity Narrative," *American Literature*, 19 (March 1947): 1-20;

Richard VanDerBeets, *The Indian Captivity Narrative: An American Genre* (Washington, D.C.: University Press of America, 1983);

VanDerBeets, Introduction to *Held Captive by Indians: Selected Narratives, 1642-1836*, edited by VanDerBeets (Knoxville: University of Tennessee Press, 1973).

John Saffin

(circa 1626-1710)

O. Glade Hunsaker
Brigham Young University

BOOKS: *A Brief and Candid Answer to a Late Printed Sheet, Entituled, The Selling of Joseph. Whereunto is Annexed, A True and Particular Narrative by Way of Vindication of the Author's Dealing with and Prosecution of his Negro Man Servant, for his Vile and Exhorbitant Behavior towards his Master, and his Tenant, Thomas Shepard; which hath been Wrongfully represented to their Prejudice and Defamation . . .* (Boston, 1701);

John Saffin, His Book (1665-1708): A Collection of Various Matters of Divinity, Law, & State Affairs Epitomiz'd both in Verse and Prose (New York: Printed at the Harbor Press, 1928).

John Saffin was not only a prominent lawyer and statesman but also a noteworthy poet of New England. The amazing breadth of his interests and the impressive versatility of his style have prompted some critics to insist on his being placed among the ten best poets in America during the seventeenth century.

Born in Devonshire, England, to Simon and Grace Garrett Saffin, Saffin immigrated to Scituate, Massachusetts, at an early age. As a young man he served as a selectman in Scituate. He married Martha Willett (the first of his three wives) in 1658, and in 1660 he moved to Boston, where he became a prominent merchant and public figure, serving at various times as deputy to the General Court, Speaker of the House, and a member of the Governor's Council. In about 1688 he moved to New Bristol and became the first judge of probate for the newly formed county of Bristol (now part of Rhode Island).

Saffin is best known as a writer for his commonplace book, which was published in 1928 as *John Saffin, His Book (1665-1708).* Found in this work are personal letters, scientific examinations, medicinal cures for diseases, historical anecdotes, summaries of his wide reading, ideas for future writing, analyses of moral behavior, philosophical contemplations, and poetry. While some of the prose pieces have a satirical bent, almost all of them reflect his recognition of divine intervention in the events of this world. The finest of the writings in this volume are Saffin's poems, about which he made two important observations: "Good verse ought to be concise and significant, plain yet elegant"; and "He that would write well in verse must observe these rules . . . that it be elegant, emphaticall, metaphoricall, and historicall; running in a fluent, and smooth channell." These rules are carefully observed in "Sayle Gentle Pinnance," a love poem written during his courtship of Martha Willett, which Brom Weber hails as one of the finest American poetic creations of the seventeenth century and Harold S. Jantz calls "a poem of the most artful simplicity and quiet perfection." Although Saffin did not have a university education, his poems indicate that he was well read. Jessie A. Coffee identifies in Saffin's poems seventy-one allusions to Sir Philip Sidney's *Arcadia* (1590), explaining how Saffin changed context and altered words in Sidney's euphuistic prose to make his own concise and plain style. Alyce E. Sands's dissertation, "John Saffin: Seventeenth-Century American Citizen and Poet," is the most comprehensive analysis of his notebook.

Other:

Harrison T. Messerole, ed., *Seventeenth-Century American Poetry*, includes poems by Saffin (New York: New York University Press, 1968);

Kenneth Silverman, *Colonial American Poetry*, includes poems by Saffin (New York & London: Hafner, 1968).

References:

Jessie A. Coffee, "Arcadia to America: Sir Philip Sidney and John Saffin," *American Literature*, 45 (March 1973): 100-104;

Harold S. Jantz, *The First Century of New England Verse* (Worcester, Mass.: American Antiquarian Society,1944);

Alyce E. Sands, "Establishing John Saffin's Birthday," *Early American Literature Newsletter*, 2 (Spring 1967): 12-17;

Sands, "John Saffin: Seventeenth-Century American Citizen and Poet," Ph.D. dissertation, Pennsylvania State University, 1965;

Brom Weber, "A Puritan Poem Regenerated: John Saffin's 'Sayle Gentle Pinnance,' " *Early American Literature*, 3 (Spring 1968): 65-71.

Papers:

The Rhode Island Historical Society has Saffin's commonplace book.

George Sandys

(2 March 1578-4 March 1644)

Homer D. Kemp
Tennessee Technological University

BOOKS: *A Relation of a Journey Begun An: Dom: 1610. Foure Bookes Containing a description of the Turkish Empire, of Aegypt, of the Holy Land, of the Remote parts of Italy, and Ilands adioyning* (London: Printed for W. Barrett, 1615);

The First Five Bookes of Ovids Metamorphosis, translated by Sandys (London: Printed for William Barrett, 1621);

Ovid's Metamorphosis Englished by G. S. (London: Printed by William Stansby, 1626);

Ovid's Metamorphosis Englished, Mythologiz'd, and Represented in Figures. An Essay to the Translation of Virgil's Aeneis (Oxford: Printed by John Lichfield, 1632);

A Paraphrase upon the Psalmes of David And upon the Hymnes Dispersed throughout the Old and New Testaments (London: Printed by John Legatt, 1636);

A Paraphrase upon the Divine Poems (London: Printed by John Legatt, 1638);

Christs Passion. A Tragedie. With Annotations, Sandys's translation of Hugo Grotius's *Christus patiens* (London: Printed by John Legatt, 1640);

A Paraphrase upon the Song of Solomon (London: Printed by John Legatt, 1641).

COLLECTION: *The Poetical Works of George Sandys*, 2 volumes, edited by Richard Hooper (London: J. R. Smith, 1872).

Portrait of Sandys by Cornelius Janssen, 1632

George Sandys—traveler and travel-account writer, poet, classical scholar, civil servant, and courtier—has been called by Richard Beale Davis the author of the "first piece of real literary merit produced on the Atlantic seaboard." As a writer, Sandys produced a prose travel account that was one of the most popular in the seventeenth century, a translation of Ovid's *Metamorphoses* that is still a standard edition, and verse paraphrases of sacred poetry that were widely popular for at least half a century. One of the best-known Caroline poets, Sandys was a member of the Privy Council to Charles I and an intimate of Lord Falkland's Great Tew Circle. Sandys's personal affairs and career as a civil servant were tied to the destiny of the colony of Virginia for most of his adult life—as a Virginia Company stockholder, resident treasurer of the colony, a member of the first Board of Trade and Plantations, and agent at court for the colonial legislature.

Born on 2 March 1578, the ninth child and the seventh son of Edwin Sandys, Archbishop of York, and Cicely Wilford Sandys, daughter of Sir Thomas Wilford of Hartridge in Kent, George Sandys grew up among ambitious, widely influential family members and associates. The archbishop had distinguished himself as a brave man of conviction who had publicly stood up for Protestantism and was imprisoned by the Catholic Queen Mary and as an ambitious man who was criticized for using his position as archbishop to acquire extensive properties. All three of George's oldest brothers—Samuel, Edwin, and Myles—were knighted, and Sir Edwin had a distinguished career, which included his acting as the founding father of both Plymouth and Jamestown in America. A strong influence was exerted on young George by his namesake and godfather, George, Earl of Cumberland, a dashing man of adventure, once described as "one of the Elizabethan symbols of the thirst to do and see the strange and the new."

After attending a school in York (probably St. Peter's), eleven-year-old George Sandys entered St. Mary's Hall, Oxford, on 5 December 1589, but he and his brother Henry transferred within a few days to nearby Corpus Christi College as gentleman commoners. George entered the Middle Temple of the Inns of Court on 23 October 1596, evidently following a long family tradition, for the name *Sandys* is one of the most frequently recurring names in the records of the Middle Temple. There is no record of how long he stayed there, but he did not stay long enough to be called to the bar. He did, however, use his legal training well throughout a life characterized by persistent litigation.

Until the publication of Richard Beale Davis's *George Sandys, Poet-Adventurer* in 1955, it was generally assumed that Sandys never married. Scattered records reveal, however, that the archbishop's ambition generated a marriage for his son that ended unhappily and adversely affected the remainder of George Sandys's life. Evidently in an agreement with Edwin Sandys, John Norton of Ripon, the scion of a wealthy pro-Catholic family, left conditions in his December 1584 will which virtually demanded the future marriage of his four-year-old daughter Elizabeth to George Sandys. George and Elizabeth were married at least before 1602, and the extant records reveal that the marriage was over by 1606, followed by years of legal actions by Elizabeth's relatives, many recriminations, and the loss on George Sandys's part of the wealth which his father had so carefully planned.

Possibly as a result of influences such as his unhappy marriage and his associations with the Earl of Cumberland, Sandys set out in early May

1610 on a tour which included the Continent, Turkey, the Holy Land, and Egypt. Sometime between his return to England in the spring of 1612 and its publication in 1615, Sandys wrote *A Relation of a Journey Begun An: Dom: 1610. . .*, a book which went through nine English editions, two Dutch editions, and one German edition (1669) before 1700, appeared in large part in Samuel Purchas's *Purchas His Pilgrimes . . .* (1625), and served as a principal source book throughout the seventeenth century. Certainly the book occupies an important place in the Elizabethan travel-literature tradition, for the work represents a significant innovation when compared with its immediate English predecessors among travel books. Sandys took the notes of his personal observations and added to them the accounts of ancient geographers, of the church fathers, and of other travelers and historians prior to and contemporary with his age. In addition, Sandys weaved into his account his own translations of passages from a multitude of classical writers, especially poets. Rather than being simply a display of learning, Sandys's quotations constitute a continuous flow of aptly chosen allusions which are carefully woven into the fabric of the travel account. No English predecessor had used quotations to anything like the extent that Sandys did.

With the quotations and other material, Sandys unified his narrative significantly with the recurring themes of the frailty of man and the permanence of God—themes that were to dominate his writings throughout his lifetime. In addition, Sandys differed from his contemporaries in his sensitivity to folk ways and in the muting of his treatment of the Mahometan religion. As Davis has stated, "Sandys brought to maturity the cultivated travel-narrative." The classical erudition of *A Relation of a Journey Begun An: Dom: 1610 . . .* firmly established Sandys's reputation in his own time as a man of learning.

George Sandys's more than twenty years' association with America began early in the development of the Virginia Company, for his name appears among the list of adventurers in 1607. His brother Sir Edwin was powerful in the company from the early days and was elected treasurer (chief executive officer) in 1619. In November 1620, Sir Francis Wyatt, who was married to George Sandys's niece Margaret, was elected resident Governor of Virginia, and George Sandys was elected on 2 May 1621 to the new position of resident treasurer of the colony and to membership on his Majesty's Council of Virginia. These two friends sailed for Virginia shortly before 1 August 1621, destined to serve Virginia both under the Virginia Company and under royal charter making it a Crown colony (after 1624) and to be intimately connected with Virginia for the remainder of their lives. Evidently, Sandys saw his second book through the press just before leaving for Virginia, for his translation *The First Five Bookes of Ovids Metamorphosis* appeared in 1621. Thus, as he left for America, Sandys's reputation as a translator and a poet was established by a book that was well known in literary circles, went through two printings in 1621, and was published in a new edition while Sandys was in Virginia in 1623. He was able to translate two more books of the *Metamorphoses* on board ship to America.

Upon his arrival in Virginia in October 1621, Sandys began nearly four years of active service as a colonial official. His duties included supervising the collection of annual rents, overseeing industry, promoting staple commodities, and hearing civil suits involving land, rent, tobacco, and trade. Hardly five months after his arrival in Virginia, Sandys found himself leading the first column against the Tappahannock Indians in retaliation for the devastating 22 March 1622 massacre. The anonymous broadside poem *Good Newes from Virginia . . .* (published in London in 1623) gives the reader an insight into the active life of this scholar-poet:

> Stout Master *George Sands* upon a night,
> did bravely venture forth;
> And mong'st the savage murtherers,
> did forme a deed of worth.
> For finding many by a fire,
> to death their lives they pay:
> Set fire of a Towne of theirs
> and bravely came away.

In between his duties as a busy civil servant, Sandys found time during his life in Virginia to translate the last eight books of Ovid's *Metamorphoses* and to prepare the whole work for publication. This major English Renaissance translation was the first significant consciously literary work produced in British America. The work was probably nearly ready for the press when Sandys sailed for England on 25 June 1625, as the entire translated *Metamorphoses* appeared in London as *Ovid's Metamorphosis Englished by G. S.* in the spring of 1626. It seems likely that the new book was published at the request of King Charles I, who had long been Sandys's patron and who had been crowned king on 2 February 1626. Over the next fifteen years, Charles was to reward Sandys with several modest appointments and in his last years apparently was to take great comfort in Sandys's translation of the Psalms.

In 1632 was published Sandys's *Ovid's Metamorphosis Englished, Mythologiz'd, and Represented in Figures. An Essay to the Translation of Virgil's Aeneis,* a large folio edition with elaborate prose commentaries and copperplate engravings illustrating each book. This later edition of Ovid differed from the 1626 edition with the addition of prose commentaries that occupy at least as much space as the poetic text, a translation in decasyllabic couplets of the first book of Virgil's *Aeneid,* and the elaborate engraved illustrations. Sandys's translation of Ovid went through at least ten editions in the course of the seventeenth century, influenced many important writers, and is still accepted as the standard edition.

Both in its prose commentaries and in its verse form, the 1632 edition of *Ovid's Metamorphosis*... is a landmark Elizabethan text. Ovid had been perhaps the most read and translated classical writer in England since the Middle Ages, and, according to Davis, Sandys's commentaries are "the last great representative of the tradition of allegorized interpretation which began in the Middle Ages." The meter and language of Sandys's decasyllabic couplets represent a significant contribution to the development of the English heroic couplet of the early eighteenth century. Later seventeenth-century poets outside the satirical and metaphysical groups based their vocabulary on Sandys and his sources, and Alexander Pope owed much of his rhetoric and diction to Sandys. In his notes on the *Iliad,* Pope praised Sandys as one of the "chief refiners of our language." As late as the early nineteenth century, John Keats and his contemporaries were still using Sandys's translation.

During the years after his return from Virginia, Sandys became an intimate of court circles and a favorite friend of Lord Falkland (Lucius Gray, second Viscount Falkland). Falkland's Oxfordshire estate of Tew was the favorite gathering place of the great Caroline intellects, including such poets as Edmond Waller, Sir Francis Wyatt, Thomas Carew, and Sandys. As verse and religion had always been his two most important concerns, Sandys found congenial company in the Great Tew Circle. Members of the group were interested in theology and produced a significant body of theological prose. It is no surprise that Sandys devoted his later poetic energies to religious verse.

Paraphrases of scripture were a popular poetic form in the seventeenth century, a form which consisted of free translation into English verse forms. Sandys's paraphrases of sacred verse from Latin originals during the later years of his life were among the most popular in the century and received critical acclaim from the leading poets of the age. In 1636 Sandys produced *A Paraphrase upon the Psalmes of David And upon the Hymnes Dispersed throughout the Old and New Testaments,* a book containing verse paraphrases of 150 psalms and hymns. The poems of the 1636 volume were also included two years later in *A Paraphrase upon the Divine Poems* (1638) with the addition of paraphrases from Job, Ecclesiastes, and Lamentations of Jeremiah. This volume was prefaced by laudatory poems to Sandys from such well-known figures as Lord Falkland, Sidney Godolphin, Thomas Carew, Sir Dudley Digges, Sir Francis Wyatt, and Edmond Waller. In 1640, Sandys turned his pen to paraphrasing Dutch writer Hugo Grotius's *Christus patiens* (published in Latin in 1608) into *Christs Passion. A Tragedie. With Annotations.* This translation is a further effort in decasyllabic and octosyllabic couplets and is better poetry than the original of Grotius. Sandys's last published work, *A Paraphrase upon the Song of Solomon,* appeared in 1641 but was probably composed at about the same time as *A Paraphrase upon the Divine Poems.*

By the end of his almost thirty-year literary career, Sandys's fame was secure for the remainder of the seventeenth century. John Dryden was to judge Sandys "the best versifier of the former age." In a reassessment of this judgment, later generations have removed Sandys from the canon of major writers; however, Sandys was the ablest poet between Ben Jonson and Dryden and Milton. Sandys's twentieth-century biographer, Richard Beale Davis, has aptly stated that "he preserved much of the ebullient imagination of the Elizabethans in the very forms in which he prepared the way for the neoclassical age."

America continued to be a vital interest of Sandys's throughout the remainder of his life after his service in Virginia. The prose commentaries of the 1632 translation of Ovid, although composed in England, contain constant references to American matters and scenery—such as the southern frogs called Powhatan's hounds because of their constant croaking or yelping and tall tales of marvelous events in America. Sandys served on the first Board of Trade and Plantations, probably as secretary, and acted as agent for the colony in England as late as the early 1640s. Between the hymns in the 1636 *A Paraphase upon the Psalmes of David . . . ,* Sandys printed for the first time his finest original poem, "Deo Opt. Max.," a ninety-line hymn to his redeemer written in decasyllabic couplets. This poem sums up Sandys's life of adventure, his interest in America, and the themes that dominate his writings—man's transience and God's permanence. After much laudation to God and depictions of his many adventures, including many lines on the Virginia experience, Sandys concludes:

> My grateful Verse thy Goodness shall display,
> O thou who went'st along all my way:
> To where the Morning with perfum'd wings
> From the high Mountains of Panchaea springs,
> To that New-found-out World, where sober Night
> Takes from the Antipodes her silent flight:
> . . . .
> Thou sav'dst me from the bloudy Massacres
> Of faith-less Indians; from their treacherous Wars;
> From raging Feavers, from the sultry breath
> of tainted Aire; which cloy'd the jawes of Death.
> . . . .
> Then brought'st me Home in safety, that this Earth
> Might bury me, which fed me from my Birth:
> Blest with a heathfull age; a quiet Mind,
> Content with little. . . .

With his health declining and the Falkland group pretty well broken up after 1639, Sandys spent most of his time in the quiet solitude of the countryside at Boxley in Kent. It was here that he probably translated *Christs Passion . . .* and prepared *A Paraphrase upon the Song of Solomon* for the press; it was here also that he died on 4 March 1644 and was buried on 7 March at Boxley Abbey.

Bibliography:

Fredson Bowers and R. B. Davis, *George Sandys, A Bibliographical Catalogue* (New York: New York Public Library, 1950).

Biography:

Richard Beale Davis, *George Sandys, Poet-Adventurer* (London: Bodley Head, 1955).

References:

J. M. Attenborough, "George Sandys, Traveller and Poet," *Westminster Review,* 153 (June 1905): 643-655;

Russell H. Barker, "George Sandys' *Relation,*" *Transactions of the Wisconsin Academy of Sciences, Arts and Letters,* 30 (1937): 253-273;

C. W. Broadribb, "Ovid, Sandys, and Milton," *Notes and Queries,* 157 (August 1924): 77-78;

Richard Beale Davis, "America in George Sandys' 'Ovid,' " *William and Mary Quarterly,* third series 4 (July 1947): 297-304;

Davis, "The Early Editions of George Sandys' Ovid: the Circumstances of Production," *Papers of the Bibliographical Society of America,* 35 (Fourth Quarter 1941): 255-276;

Davis, "George Sandys and Two 'Uncollected Poems,' " *Huntingdon Library Quarterly,* 12 (November 1948): 105-111;

Davis, "George Sandys, Poet-Adventurer," *Americana,* 33 (April 1939): 180-195;

Davis, "George Sandys v. William Stansby: the 1632 Edition of Ovid's *Metamorphosis,*" *Library,* fifth series 3 (December 1948): 193-212;

Davis, "*In Re* George Sandys' Ovid," *Studies in Bibliography,* 8 (1956): 226-230;

Davis, *Intellectual Life in the Colonial South 1585-1763* (Knoxville: University of Tennessee Press, 1978), pp. 1332, 1338-1344;

Davis, "Sandys' *Song of Solomon,*" *Papers of the Bibliographical Society of America,* 50 (1956): 328-341;

Davis, "Two New Manuscript Items for a George Sandys Bibliography," *Papers of the Bibliographical Society of America,* 37 (Third Quarter 1943): 215-222;

Davis, "Volumes from George Sandys' Library Now in America," *Virginia Magazine of History and Biography,* 65 (October 1957): 450-457;

Edmond S. deBeer, "George Sandys's Account of Compania," *Library,* fourth series 17 (March 1937): 458-465;

James G. McManaway, "The First Five Bookes of Ovids Metamorphosis, 1621, *Englished by Master George Sandys,*" *Papers of the Bibliographical Society, University of Virginia,* 1 (1948): 71-82;

Ruth C. Wallerstein, "The Development of the Rhetoric and Metre of the Heroic Couplet, Especially in 1625-1645," *PMLA,* 50 (March 1935): 166-209.

Joseph Sewall

(15 August 1688-27 June 1769)

Ronald A. Bosco
State University of New York at Albany

BOOKS: *Believers Invited to Come to Christ as the Author of Their Resurrection and Life. In a Sermon at the Lecture in Boston, N.E. Novemb. 10. 1715* (Boston: Printed by B. Green for Samuel Gerrish, 1716);

Desires that Joshua's Resolution may be Revived: Or, Excitations to the Constant and Diligent Exercise of Family-Religion: Being the Substance of Sundry Sermons . . . (Boston: Printed by B. Green for Samuel Gerrish, 1716);

The Certainty & Suddenness of Christ's Coming to Judgment, Improved as a Motive to Diligence in Preparing for it. In a Sermon at the Lecture in Boston, October 6. 1715 (Boston: Printed by B. Green for Samuel Gerrish, 1716);

The Character and Blessedness of the Upright. A Sermon Occasion'd by the Death of the Honorable Wait Winthrop (Boston: Printed by T. Crump, 1717);

Precious Treasure in Earthen Vessels. A Sermon Occasion'd by the Death of the Reverend and Learned Mr. Ebenezer Pemberton . . . (Boston: Printed by B. Green for Samuel Gerrish & Daniel Henchman, 1717);

A Caveat against Covetousness in a Sermon at the Lecture in Boston, N.E. February 20, 1717/18 (Boston: Printed by B. Green for Samuel Gerrish, 1718);

Rulers Must be Just, Ruling in the Fear of God. A Sermon Preach'd before the Honourable, the Lieutenant Governour, the Council & Representatives of the Province of the Massachusetts Bay in New-England, May 27, 1724. Being the Day for the Election of His Majesty's Council . . . (Boston: Printed by B. Green, 1724);

The Duty of Every Man to be Always Ready to Die. A Sermon Occasion'd by the Very Sudden Deaths of Mr. Thomas Lewis Aged 32. And of Samuel Hirst Aged 22. (Boston: Printed by B. Green, 1727);

The Duty of a People to Stand in Aw of God, and Not Sin, when under His Terrible Judgments. A Sermon Preach'd at the South Meeting House in Boston the Evening after the Earthquake . . . (Boston: Printed for D. Henchman, 1727);

Peter Pelham mezzotint of Joseph Sewall in his forties, from a portrait by John Smibert (American Antiquarian Society)

Jehovah is the King and Saviour of His People. A Sermon Preach'd at the Boston Lecture, August 17, 1727. Upon the Awful Tidings of the Death of His Late Majesty King George . . . (Boston: Printed by B. Green, 1727);

Repentance the Sure Way to Escape Destruction. Two Sermons on Jrr. [sic] *18.7.8. Preach'd December 21st, on a Publick Fast Occasioned by the Earthquake, the Night after the Lord's-Day Octob. 29th. And on the Lord's-Day December 24th. 1727 . . .* (Boston: Printed for D. Henchman, 1727);

He that Would Keep God's Commandments Must Renounce the Society of Evil Doers. A Sermon Preach'd at the Publick Lecture in Boston, July 18th. 1728. After a Bloody and Mortal Duel . . . (Boston: Printed by B. Green for D. Henchman, 1728);

The Holy Spirit the Gift of God Our Heavenly

Father, to Them That Ask Him. A Sermon Preach'd on a Day of Prayer with Fasting, Kept by the South Church in Boston to Ask of God the Effusion of His Spirit on the Rising Generation, Novemb. 13th. 1722* . . . (Boston: Printed for D. Henchman, 1728);

The Orphan's Best Legacy; Or God's Parental Care of Bereaved Children: a Discourse Occasion'd by the Death of the Honorable Samuel Sewall . . . (Boston: Printed by B. Green & sold by S. Gerrish & D. Henchman, 1730);

Christ Victorious over the Powers of Darkness, by the Light of His Preached Gospel. A Sermon Preached in Boston, December 12. 1733. At the Ordination of the Reverend Mr. Stephen Parker, Mr. Ebenezer Hinsdell, and Mr. Joseph Seccombe . . . (Boston: Printed & sold by S. Kneeland & T. Green, 1733);

A Faithful Narrative of the Proceedings of the Ecclesiastical Council Convened at Salem in 1734 . . . , by Sewall and others (Boston: Printed for D. Henchman, 1735);

When the Godly Cease and Faithful Fail; We Must Seek to God for Help. A Sermon Preach'd at Cambridge, upon the Death of the Reverend Mr. Benjamin Wadsworth, President of Harvard College . . . (Boston: Printed by S. Kneeland & T. Green for D. Henchman, 1737);

Nineveh's Repentance and Deliverance. A Sermon Preach'd before His Excellency the Governour the Honourable Council and Representatives of the Province of the Massachusetts-Bay in New-England on a Day of Fasting and Prayer in the Council Chamber Dec. 3. 1740 . . . (Boston: Printed by J. Draper, 1740);

All Flesh is as Grass; But the Word of the Lord Endureth For Ever. A Sermon Preached at the Thursday Lecture in Boston, January 1st. 1740. 1 . . . (Boston: Printed & sold by S. Kneeland & T. Green, 1741);

The Holy Spirit Convincing the World of Sin, of Righteousness, and of Judgment; Considered in Four Sermons . . . (Boston: Printed by J. Draper for D. Henchman, 1741);

God's People Must Enquire of Him to Bestow the Blessings Promised in His Word. A Sermon Preach'd February 26. 1741, 2. On a Day of Prayer Observed by the South Church . . . (Boston: Printed by D. Fowle for D. Henchman, 1742);

The First and Great Commandment, to Love the Lord Our God. A Sermon Preach'd at the Thursday-Lecture in Boston January 28. 1741, 2 . . . (Boston: Printed by T. Fleet for D. Henchman, 1742);

The Second Commandment Like to the First: Thou Shalt Love Thy Neighbour As Thyself. A Sermon Preach'd at the Thursday Lecture in Boston May 6, 1742 (Boston: Printed by Tho. Fleet for D. Henchman, 1742);

The Thirsty Invited to Come, and Take the Waters of Life Freely. A Sermon Preached on the Friday Evening Lecture at the South Meeting-House in Boston, March 5. 1741, 2 . . . (Boston: Printed & sold by Rogers & Fowle, 1742);

The Lamb Slain, Worthy to be Praised, as the Most Powerful, Rich, Wise, and Strong. A Sermon Preach'd at the Thursday Lecture in Boston July 11, 1745 . . . (Boston: Printed for D. Henchman, 1745);

A Tender Heart Pleasing to God and Profitable to Man. A Sermon Preached at the South-Church in Boston: on the Lord's Day after the Death of the Honorable Josiah Willard . . . (Boston: Printed by S. Kneeland, 1756);

The Duty, Character, and Reward of Christ's Faithful Servants. A Sermon Preached at the South-Church in Boston: on the Lord's-Day, after the Funeral of the Reverend Mr. Thomas Prince . . . (Boston: Printed by S. Kneeland, 1758);

A Sermon Preached at the Thursday-Lecture in Boston September 16, 1762, Before the Great and General Court of the Province of the Massachusetts-Bay in New-England. On the Joyful News of the Reduction of the Havannah . . . (Boston: Printed by John Draper & by Edes & Gill, 1762);

The Character and Reward of the Faithful Ministers of Christ. A Sermon Preach'd at the South Church in Boston, on the Lord's Day after the Funeral of the Reverend Mr. Alexander Cumming (Boston: Printed by S. Kneeland, 1763).

Friend and patron of Harvard College, pastor of the prestigious Old South Church in Boston, supporter of several missionary societies, and vigorous defender of the "old New England way," Joseph Sewall was a prominent member of the last generation of New England's great Puritan preachers. To that generation fell the impossible task of preserving the idealized faith of New England's founders against the inroads of cosmopolitan taste and enlightenment philosophy made during the eighteenth century. The rising secularism and apparent irreligion of that age, which in the eyes of many of Sewall's contemporaries foreshadowed the complete downfall of New England's mission as the kingdom of God in the New World wilderness, had been preached against by the generation of religious masters which preceded them in their pulpits, and it fell to men such as Thomas Prince, John Webb, Thomas Foxcroft, and Joseph Sewall to continue warning and, as necessary, haranguing against the secular spirit of their time in the sermonic style counseled by their predecessors: the Mathers, the Shepards, John Danforth, Samuel Willard, and others.

Sewall was born in Boston under uniquely privileged social and economic circumstances. His father, Samuel, was New England's famed judge and diarist, and his mother, Hannah, was the daughter of the colony's mint-master, John Hull. During most of his early years he had a firsthand view of colonial history in the making, for whether in his father's chamber or at the family dinner table, where his father regularly entertained New England's leading citizens, Sewall was exposed to all the important social, political, and religious developments of the day. Judge Sewall encouraged his son's precocity, sending the boy to private school before he was three and arranging for private lessons in Latin under Nehemiah Hobart by the time he was five. The diaries of his father and of Cotton Mather offer numerous anecdotes of Sewall's boyhood, including accounts of his swallowing bullets and eating during family prayer. Although both diarists report that the pious disposition which would grace Sewall's career as a preacher was apparent early on, Sewall seems to have kept complete commitment to God at bay for a while. As an adolescent he was interested more in a military career fighting the French and in picnic and hunting expeditions than in preparing for the ministry. Finally, at his father's instigation, in 1703 he entered Harvard College, where under Jonathan Remington, his demanding tutor, he made an impressive showing. Taking his A.B. in 1707 and his A.M. in 1710, Sewall remained at Harvard until 1712 while he preached in and around Boston. Early in 1712 he declined a call to settle at the church in what is now Peabody, Massachusetts, but he happily accepted the call issued on 4 May 1712 to become a pastor of the Old South Church, of which his grandfather Hull was a founder. Because of illness and the turns of a protracted courtship with Elizabeth Walley, whom he eventually married on 29 October 1713, his ordination was delayed until 16 September 1713. A fit beginning for a career that would span the better part of the eighteenth century, Sewall's ordination ceremony included prayers and sermons by Increase and Cotton Mather and by Ebenezer Pemberton, the radically liberal copastor of the Old South Church.

Immediately thrown into the center of colonial affairs by virtue of his position at the Old South Church—not to mention family ties—Sewall soon distinguished himself as a well-spoken champion of the old order. A favorite of the conservative Mather faction, he became a sought-after preacher who could be depended upon to advance the orthodox views that faction held. At the same time, adversaries of that faction appreciated his levelheadedness, as evidenced by an editorial in a 1722 issue of the Franklins' *New-England Courant*, which suggested that if Bostonians "would all take Example by the Rev. Mr. S——l, and let Inoculation and State Affairs alone, there would not be so much Jangling and Contention as there is." As the record of his published sermons indicates, he preached sermons at funerals for Boston's elite, at the regular Thursday lecture in Boston, and during the many fasts called by the churches and provincial government of Massachusetts. His reputation was so secure by the 1720s that, along with the other principal ministers of Boston, he was invited to participate in Cotton Mather's course of lectures on early piety in 1721, and in 1724 he was asked to preach the annual Massachusetts election sermon. Also in 1724, he was invited to succeed John Leverett as president of Harvard College, but he declined the offer when his congregation refused to release him. That invitation sparked some momentary bad feelings between Sewall and Cotton Mather, but Mather, who had spent nearly a quarter-century lobbying for the presidency for himself, had the good manners to confine his jealousy and rage to entries in his diary.

With Cotton Mather's death in 1728, care of the conservative pastoral dynasty that three generations of Mathers had carefully nurtured and preserved was entrusted to Sewall and others of like mind. Although unsuccessful in the final result, Sewall undertook his charge with much energy. Forty years after his death, Sewall was remembered by John Eliot as "a genuine disciple of . . . John Calvin . . . [who] dreaded the propagation of any opinions in this country, which were contrary to the principles of our fathers. . . . [He] was no friend to free inquiries, or to any discussion of theological opinions, which were held true by the first reformers. . . . He never entered into any curious speculations; his object was to impress upon people what they should believe." For four decades Sewall's voice filled the Old South Church with calls for reform and with repeated warnings about the backsliding of New England's people. His favorite sermonic form for this purpose was the jeremiad, and he could speak to the pride, hypocrisy, and worldliness of his contemporaries with the same fervor with which an earlier generation of preachers had lamented such sins in the 1670s and 1680s. As in the sermons of those earlier preachers, the issue of the errand of New England's fathers was addressed repeatedly in Sewall's sermons, and Sewall missed no opportunity to excite in his hearers a desire to carry on that errand. Delighted at the prospect of a revival of religion during the Great Awakening, Sewall and Thomas Prince, his colleague at the time, were among the few Boston ministers who opened their pulpits to George Whitefield, even after the excesses of the evangelical movement were well known and its chances of success thought doubtful.

Although many ministers of Sewall's generation eventually gave in to the expectations of their congregations and tried to accommodate New England Puritanism to the changing attitudes of the time, Sewall is noteworthy for the unwavering consistency with which he held to his opinions. Religion stood first and foremost in his mind, and he was never shy in expressing that view. For instance, at the 1724 election he told the newly elected officials that despite their own political ambitions, "Christ's Kingdom is not of this World, and consequently, our Work is Spiritual, and lies principally with the Souls of Men." When an earthquake struck New England in 1727, Sewall used the occasion to warn young and old not to pay too much attention to the scientific causes of physical phenomena, for they might thereby miss the providential message that God conveyed through events. Contrary to the enlightened opinion of the day, earthquakes, like the passing of godly men, impressed Sewall much as they had the preachers of the seventeenth century, who viewed all such events as visible signs of God's displeasure with and judgment against his people. Thus, in his two sermons published after the earthquake, Sewall cautioned his congregation to "look above Second Causes, and obey that word which God spake to his People" as he exercised his will and "his terrible Majesty in awful Judgments." Sewall depended on this old-style psychology during the Great Awakening and used it to defend the evangelical methods that by the mid-1740s had been called into question by many ministers. Answering critics in *God's People . . .* (1742), his most impressive sermon from this period, Sewall observed, "As for the Out-cries, Tremblings, and Faintings which have been experienced in some Places, I apprehend the cause must be judged of by the Effect. We may not limit the Holy One. . . . If it shall please God to impress such a Sense of Sin, and of his Wrath on Men, that they are forced to cry out under it; they are to be pitied, and proper Means used for their Relief; and [neither their ministers nor they ought] to be censured as mad and outragious."

A crusading spirit marked the later years of his ministry, when "the weeping prophet," as Sewall was by then known, continued to urge piety and reform on New England. Enjoying good health, he survived three colleagues at the Old South Church (besides Pemberton and Prince, Alexander Cumming, and, finally, John Blair served with him), outlived his wife, who died in 1756, and in old age was pleased to have his only surviving child, Samuel (1715-1771), serve as his deacon. During his career he accumulated more of the laurels that had highlighted the opening years of his ministry. For instance, in 1728 he was elected to the Corporation of Harvard College on which he served until 1765; in 1731 he received an honorary S.T.D. degree from the University of Glasgow and was named a corresponding member of the Society in Scotland for Propagating Christian Knowledge; in 1740 he was invited to preach privately for the governor and his council; and late in life he was celebrated for his piety in an ode by Phillis Wheatley. Sporting a proud provincialism that he likely inherited from his father, Sewall was among the early supporters of the patriot cause that surfaced in Boston during the 1750s and 1760s and that long after his death continued to be associated with the congregation and ministers of the Old South Church.

Except for comments about him in large studies of the period, Sewall has received neither critical nor biographical attention in this century. This neglect is undeserved. Respected in his own time for his learning and piety, Sewall represents one of the fairest versions of Puritanism in its last stages. In that respect, Sewall's temperament and ideas may well be worth study by cultural historians, and, though they might as well have been preached in an earlier time, his sermons, which are vigorous and competent examples of the Puritan form of preaching that survived into the late-eighteenth century, are worth the attention of students of literature and native homiletics.

Other:

Sober-Mindedness Explain'd as a Necessary Part of Early Piety . . ., in *A Course of Sermons on Early*

Piety, edited by Cotton Mather (Boston: Printed by S. Kneeland for N. Buttolph, B. Eliot & D. Henchman, 1721);

Samuel Willard, *A Compleat Body of Divinity. . . ,* edited by Sewall and Thomas Prince (Boston: Printed by B. Green & S. Kneeland for B. Eliot & D. Henchman, 1726);

William Shurtleff, *The Labour that Attends the Gospel-Ministry. . . ,* includes material by Sewall (Boston: Printed by B. Green for Eleazer Russell, 1727);

Samuel Wigglesworth, *The Pleasures of Religion. . . ,* includes material by Sewall (Boston, 1728);

John White, *New-England's Lamentations. . . ,* includes material by Sewall (Boston: Printed & sold by T. Fleet, 1734);

Samuel Willard, *Brief Directions to a Young Scholar. . . ,* includes material by Sewall (Boston: Printed by J. Draper for T. Hancock, 1735);

Jonathan Edwards, *A Faithful Narrative of the Suprizing Work of God. . . ,* third edition, includes material by Sewall (Boston: Printed & sold by S. Kneeland, 1738);

William Cooper, *The Doctrine of Predestination. . . ,* includes material by Sewall (Boston: Printed by J. Draper for J. Edwards & H. Foster, 1740);

Joshua Moody, *A Practical Discourse Concerning the Choice Benefit of Communion with God. . . ,* includes material by Sewall (Boston: Printed for D. Henchman, 1746);

Jonathan Edwards, *An Humble Attempt to Promote Visible Union of God's People in Extraordinary Prayer for the Revival of Religion,* preface by Sewall and others (Boston: Printed for D. Henchman, 1747);

William Homes, *The Good Government of Christian Families Recommended. . . ,* preface by Sewall and others (Boston: Printed for D. Henchman, 1747);

Nathaniel Appleton, *How God Wills the Salvation of All Men. . . ,* includes a charge by Sewall (Boston: Printed & sold by S. Kneeland, 1753);

Ebenezer Pemberton, *All Power in Heaven. . . ,* preface by Sewall (Boston: Printed & sold by D. Fowle, 1756);

Alexander Cumming, *A Sermon Preached Feb. 25, 1761. . . ,* includes a charge by Sewall (Boston: Printed & sold by Benjamin Mecom, 1761).

References:

Charles Chauncy, *A Discourse Occasioned by the Death of the Reverend Dr. Joseph Sewall . . .* (Boston: Printed & sold by Kneeland & Adams, 1769);

Hamilton Andrews Hill, *History of the Old South Church, 1669-1884,* 2 volumes (Boston & New York: Houghton Mifflin, 1890);

Cotton Mather, *The Diary of Cotton Mather,* edited by Worthington Chauncey Ford, 2 volumes (1911-1912; republished, New York: Ungar, 1957);

Perry Miller, *The New England Mind: From Colony to Province* (Boston: Beacon Press, 1953), pp. 184, 270, 314ff.;

Samuel Sewall, *The Diary of Samuel Sewall, 1674-1729,* edited by M. Halsey Thomas, 2 volumes (New York: Farrar, Straus & Giroux, 1973);

John Langdon Sibley and Clifford K. Shipton, *Biographical Sketches of Those Who Attended Harvard College in the Classes 1701-1712,* volume 5 (Boston: Massachusetts Historical Society, 1937), pp. 376-393;

William B. Sprague, *Annals of the American Pulpit; or Commemorative Notices of Distinguished American Clergymen of Various Denominations,* 7 volumes (New York: Robert Carter & Brothers, 1866), I: 278-280.

Papers:

Fragments of Sewall's papers are to be found in three libraries. The Boston Public Library has three commonplace books that Sewall kept before 1719 and a diary that covers several months of 1707. The Massachusetts Historical Society has a manuscript volume of notes kept by Sewall during his college years and, among the Trumbull manuscripts, four pages of Latin verse dated 1704. In the Ewer manuscripts at the New England Historic and Genealogical Society are three pages of Latin notes dated 1707.

Samuel Sewall

Richard E. Amacher
Auburn University

BIRTH: Bishop Stoke, Hants, Hampshire, England, 28 March 1652, to Henry and Jane Dummer Sewall.

EDUCATION: A.B., 1671; A.M., 1674; Harvard College.

MARRIAGES: 28 February 1675 to Hannah Hull; children: John, Samuel, Hannah, Elizabeth, Hull, Henry, Stephen, Joseph, Judith, Mary, Jane, Sarah, an unnamed, stillborn son, and Judith. 29 October 1719 to Abigail Tilley. 29 March 1722 to Mary Gibbs.

DEATH: Boston, Massachusetts, 1 January 1730.

SELECTED BOOKS: *Phaenomena quaedam Apocalyptica Ad Aspectum Novi Orbis configurata. Or, some few Lines towards a Description of the New Heaven, As It makes to those who stand upon the New Earth* (Boston: Printed by Bartholomew Green & John Allen, 1697);

The Selling of Joseph, A Memorial (Boston: Printed by Bartholomew Green & John Allen, 1700);

Proposals Touching the Accomplishment of Prophecies, Humbly Offered . . . (Boston: Printed by Bartholomew Green, 1713);

A Memorial Relating to the Kennebeck Indians (Boston, 1721);

Diary of Samuel Sewall, 1674-1729, in *Massachusetts Historical Society Collections*, fifth series 5 (1878), 6 (1879), 7 (1882); revised as *The Diary of Samuel Sewall, 1674-1729, newly edited from the manuscript at the Massachusetts Historical Society*, 2 volumes, edited by M. Halsey Thomas (New York: Farrar, Straus & Giroux, 1973);

Letter-Book of Samuel Sewall, in *Massachusetts Historical Society Collections*, sixth series 1 (1886), 2 (1888).

Portrait of Samuel Sewall by John Smibert, June 1729 (Museum of Fine Arts, Boston)

Samuel Sewall, the author of the most vivid and most entertaining diary written by an American Puritan, also wrote one of the first antislavery tracts in America, *The Selling of Joseph . . .* (1700). As the only judge in the infamous Salem witchcraft trials who publicly recanted his position, he achieved lasting fame as a man of conscience who had higher regard for truth than for his public image. Sewall's writings also include judicial decisions, essays, tracts, translations in English and Latin, and more than fifty poems.

Sewall, born of a well-to-do merchant family at Bishop Stoke in Hampshire, England, was brought to America at the age of nine in 1661. After grammar school and further careful preparation by Oxford-educated Dr. Thomas Parker, he entered Harvard, then presided over by Charles Chauncy. At Harvard (1667-1671) he shared for two years both room and bed with the poet Edward Taylor, his lifelong friend. After taking his A.B. degree in 1671, he continued there in 1673 as tutor, or resident fellow, and received an A.M. in 1674. While at Harvard Sewall met his future wife, Hannah Hull, the only child of John Hull, the colonial treasurer and master of the mint. Married on 28 February 1675, they had fourteen children before her death in 1717. He married twice again—in 1719 to Abigail Tilley, who died the following year, and to Mary Gibbs in 1722. The account of his courtship of Madam Katherine Winthrop, which preceded his marriage to Mary Gibbs, constitutes the most detailed and interesting portion of the diary.

Marriage to John Hull's daughter amounted to a merger of his business interests with those of his prosperous father-in-law. Although he had been trained for the ministry, Sewall fell, after considerable soul searching, into the familial role of wealthy merchant, banker, landowner, and international trader. He loaned money, acted as a trustee, and traded and sold land both on Martha's Vineyard and on the mainland. Sewall's *Letter-Book* reveals his business transactions. He exported fish (mackerel and cod), whale oil, wood products, furs (largely beaver), and cranberries to the West Indies, the Caribbean islands, and London, and he imported cotton, wool, and other fabrics, as well as oranges, sugar, rum, books, and manufactured articles.

One of Sewall's numerous business ventures, a bookshop, may have led to his appointment by the General Court as manager of the Boston printing press, after the death of printer John Foster on 9 September 1681 left Boston without a printer. Sewall took his duties seriously: he hired Connecticut printer Samuel Green, Jr., "learned to set type himself," and, according to Halsey Thomas, did the composing for two of the books printed at the press. During his years as manager, the press produced a great variety of items—including sermons (by Samuel Willard, Urian Oakes, and Increase Mather), court orders, scientific essays such as Increase Mather's *Kometographia . . . A Discourse Concerning Comets* (1683), *The Shorter Catechism* (1683) of the Westminster Assembly, almanacs, and an edition of Bunyan's *Pilgrim's Progress* (1681). Although he gave up the management of the press on 10 September 1684, it is quite likely that he may have had a hand in the publication of the corrected version of John Eliot's Algonquian translation of the Bible, 2,000 copies of which appeared in 1685.

As a result of his management of the printing press and his having been made a freeman of Massachusetts Bay Colony (on 29 April 1679), Sewall found himself advancing rapidly in Boston political life. He was elected Deputy to the General Court from Westfield, Hampden County, in 1683. The following year, when he retired as publisher, he became a member of the council, a position he held until 1686. The revocation of the Massachusetts charter in 1684 meant that boundary lines on properties no longer held, and, since he was a large landowner, Sewall's interests were endangered. Consequently in 1688 he decided to join Increase Mather's mission, already in England, to work for restoration of the old charter, although he would also use the occasion to visit relatives and to attend to other private business.

After a rough six-week voyage, during which the ship *America* was nearly wrecked off the coast of Cornwall, he landed at Dover on Sunday, 13 January 1689. The following day he rode in a coach to Canterbury to visit relatives. In his *Diary* he describes his first impressions of the city: "Getting to Canterbury a little before night view'd the Cathedral, which is a very lofty and magnificent building, but of little use." In London he heard a number of the Puritan clergy preach, visited St. James Park, Gresham College, and the Guild Hall, and heard a concert at Covent Garden. On 12 February he "saw the Princess [of Orange] pass in a Barge" on her way to accept the crown on the very next day. A few days later he was off to Winchester and to Baddesly, where he visited his "Aunt Alice and Cous[in] Nath[aniel]." His "cousin" Jane Holt invited him to dinner, where he enjoyed "Bacon, Veal, and Parsnips, very good shoulder of Mutton and a Fowl rosted, good Currant suet Pudding and the fairest dish of Apples that I have eat in England." No teetotaler, Sewall was not above enjoying "a Cup of Beer at the Angel" on Saturday, 23 February. At Winchester he picked up letters from home and then visited Salisbury cathedral, Stonehenge, old Sarum, Southampton, and Portsmouth, returning on 16 March to London, where he joined Increase and Samuel Mather. In June he visited Cambridge, and in July he rode to Tyburn and witnessed the hanging of eighteen persons, sixteen men and two women. He also toured Oxford and Coventry. Leaving England on 10 October 1689, he arrived, on the same ship on which he had left the colony, the *America*, in Boston on 2 December 1689.

The revolution against the autocratic Governor Andros, which had taken place during his absence, had delighted him when he heard about it in England. But Halsey Thomas argues that the anonymous work entitled *The Revolution in New-England Justified* (1691), long thought to be written by Sewall and Edward Rawson, has been mistakenly attributed to him. (The S. S. signature on the preface could refer to Samuel Shrimpton, and there is no evidence of Sewall's composition in his *Diary*.)

Probably the most significant event in Sewall's life in 1691 was his being named a member of the council in the new charter, which Sir William Phips brought from England in 1692. Sewall was annually elected to this body until June 1725, when he declined further duty.

During the year of the Salem witchcraft trials (1692), Sewall, who played a leading part as one of nine judges appointed by the new Governor Phips, made relatively few entries on witchcraft in his *Diary*. Cryptic earlier entries (for 21 January 1686 and 16 November 1688) show that, like his fellow judges, he believed in the reality of witchcraft. In the margin of his entry for 19 August 1692, he wrote "Doleful! Witchcraft": "This day George Burrough, John Willard, John Proctor, Martha Carrier and George Jacobs were executed at Salem, a very great number of Spectators being present. . . . All of them said they were innocent. . . . Mr. Mather says they all died by a Righteous Sentence. Mr. Burrough by his Speech, Prayer, protestation of his Innocence, did much move unthinking persons, which occasions their speaking hardly concerning his being executed." On 21 September he noted that Dorcass Hoar was the "first condemned person who ha[d] confessed." On 15 October, however, he recorded that he had visited Thomas Danforth, who opposed and spoke openly against the trials, and "discoursed with Him about Witchcraft." On 22 November he prayed God to "save New England as to Enemies and Witchcrafts, and vindicate the late Judges," the court having ceased to meet in October.

Although there were further trials in 1693,

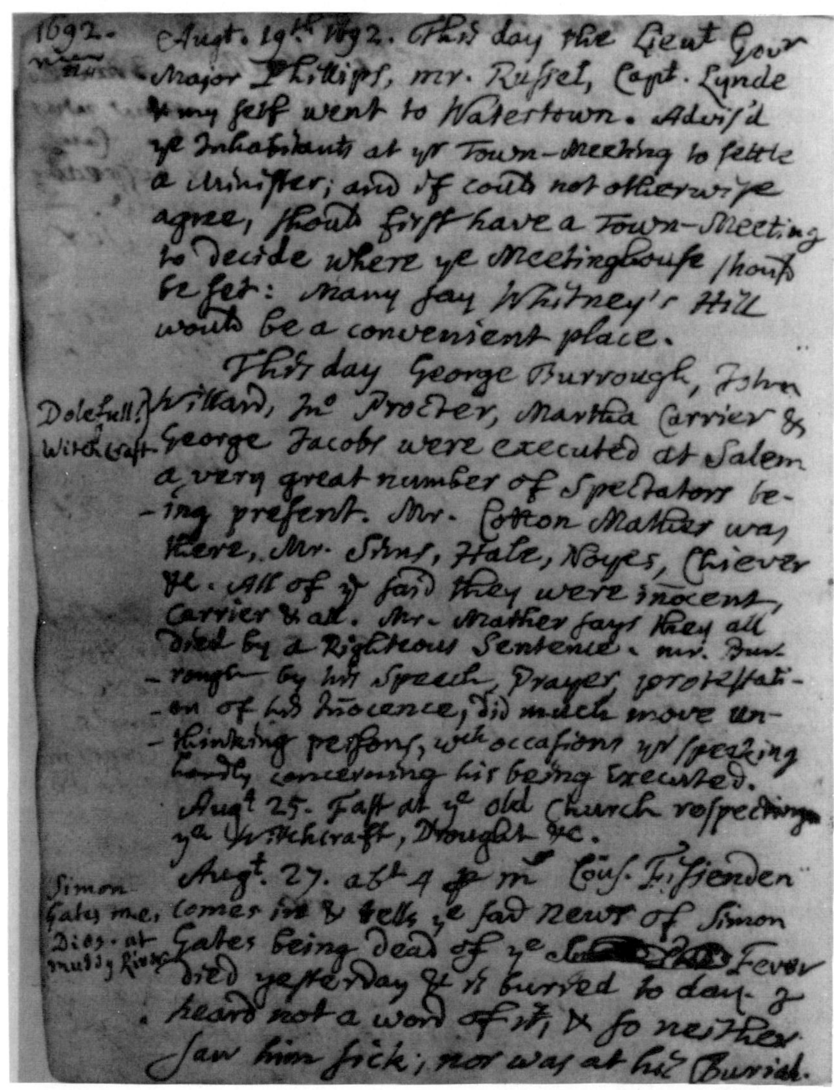

1692. Augt. 19th 1692. This day the Lieut Govr
Major Phillips, mr. Russel, Capt. Lynde
& my self went to Watertown. Advis'd
ye Inhabitants at yr Town-Meeting to settle
a Minister; and if could not otherwise
agree, should first have a Town-Meeting
to decide where ye Meetinghouse should
be set: Many say Whitney's Hill
would be a convenient place.

Doleful! Witchcraft — This day George Burrough, John
Willard, Jno Procter, Martha Carrier &
George Jacobs were executed at Salem
a very great number of Spectators be-
-ing present. Mr. Cotton Mather was
there, Mr. Sims, Hale, Noyes, Chiever
&c. All of ym said they were innocent,
Carrier & all. Mr. Mather says they all
died by a Righteous Sentence. Mr. Bur-
-rough by his Speech, Prayer, protestati-
-on of his Innocence, did much move un-
-thinking persons, wch occasions yr speaking
hardly concerning his being executed.

Augt 25. Fast at ye old Church respecting
ye Witchcraft, Drought &c.

Simon Gates Dies. at Muddy River — Augt. 27. abt 4 p.m. Cous. Fissenden
comes in & tells ye sad news of Simon
Gates being dead of ye [illegible] Fever
died yesterday & is buried to day. I
heard not a word of it, & so neither
saw him sick; nor was at his Burial.

Sewall's diary entry for 19 August 1692, recounting the executions of individuals convicted in the Salem witchcraft trials (Massachusetts Historical Society)

Sewall did not record them in his diary. Not until five years later, after the climate with regard to witchcraft had considerably changed and his minister, Samuel Willard of Old South Church, had begun preaching critically against the Salem trials and—perhaps most important of all—after his daughter Sarah had died, did he stand in his church pew and confess his guilt, asking pardon of God and all men for his part in the Salem episode. The occasion was a public fast day set by the General Court for expiation of the tragic events at Salem. It was the afternoon of 14 January 1697, and he later recorded in his diary the substance of the short note he had handed to Reverend Mr. Willard to be publicly read: "Samuel Sewall, sensible of the reiterated strokes of God upon himself and family; and being sensible, that as to the Guilt contracted, upon the opening of the late Commission of Oyer and Terminer at Salem (to which the order for this Day relates) he is, upon many accounts, more concerned than any that he knows of, Desires to take the Blame and Shame of it, Asking pardon of Men, And especially desiring prayers that God, who has an Unlimited Authority, would pardon that Sin and all other his Sins; personal and Relative: And . . . Not Visit the Sin of him, or of any other, upon himself or any of his, nor upon the Land. . . ."

On 9 November 1697, the publication day for Sewall's first book, he wrote in his diary, "the last half-Sheet is wro't off, and the Book is set to sale in Mr. Wilkins's shop. One is sold." The next day he presented the lieutenant governor with seven copies, and three days later he met Sheriff Bradford on horseback and gave him a copy for his father. A dinner guest, Rev. Mr. John Higginson, minister of Salem, was also given one. Obviously he was proud of *Phaenomena quaedam Apocalyptica Ad Aspectum Novi Orbis configurata. Or, some few Lines towards a Description of the New Heaven, As It makes [sic] to those who stand upon the New Earth,* which ran to sixty pages. Essentially the work is Sewall's interpretation of the Book of Revelation, in which he asks why America may not possibly be the New Jerusalem. Its two prefaces are addressed to Sir William Ashurst and to the lieutenant governor and commander in chief of Massachusetts, William Stoughton.

Sewall's *Phaenomena quaedam Apocalyptica* . . . (which he had reprinted in 1727) is a major rhetorical work, describing the Protestant Reformation and the persecution of the Huguenots in France and arguing that the conversion of the Indians was an accomplishment of glorious prophecies (the conversion is attested to, incidentally, by eighteen signatures of his contemporaries). The brief jottings one finds in Sewall's *Diary* fail to give an adequate idea of the fluid and eloquent style he was capable of and which he reveals in the peroration of this book: "As long as *Plum Island* shall faithfully keep the commanded Post; Notwithstanding all the hectoring Words, and hard Blows of the proud and boisterous Ocean; as long as any Salmon, or Sturgeon shall swim in the streams of *Merrimack*; or any Perch, or Pickeril, in *Crane-Pond*; As long as the Sea-Fowl shall know the Time of their coming, and not neglect seasonably to visit the Places of their Acquaintance; As long as any Cattel shall be fed with Grass growing in the Meadows, which do humbly bow down themselves before *Turkie-Hill*; As long as any Sheep shall walk upon *Old Town Hills*, and shall from thence pleasantly look down upon the River *Parker*, and the fruitful *Marshes* lying beneath; As long as any free and harmless Doves shall find a White Oak, or other Tree within the Township, to perch, or feed, or build a careless Nest upon; and shall voluntarily present themselves to perform the office of Gleaners after Barley Harvest; As long as Nature shall not grow Old and dote; but shall constantly remember to give the rows of Indian Corn their education, by Pairs: So long shall Christians be born there [in Newbury, founded by his father in 1634], and being first made meet, shall from thence be Translated, to be made partakers of the Inheritance of the Saints in Light." He closes this passage with a contractlike benediction that clearly expresses the Puritan idea of the covenant of grace: "Now, seeing the Inhabitants of *Newbury*, and of *New England*, upon the due Observance of their Tenure, may expect that their Rich and Gracious LORD will continue and confirm them in the Possession of these invaluable Privileges: *Let us have Grace, whereby we may serve GOD acceptably with Reverence and godly Fear.*" Robert D. Arner has interpreted these two passages as an early version of the American pastoral.

Sewall's second important rhetorical work, *The Selling of Joseph* . . . (1700), differs from Cotton Mather's *The Negro Christianized* . . . (1706). Mather's concern centered on the spiritual salvation of the blacks; Sewall's concentrated on human liberty as such, although he, too, good Calvinist that he was, buttressed his mainly humanitarian interests with many scriptural quotations. The document falls into three parts. Following the precepts of covenant theology, Sewall argued in the first part that all men were equal heirs of Adam, that God's indulgence to Adam and Eve after the fall took the form of a deed of gift (liberty), and that the deed still

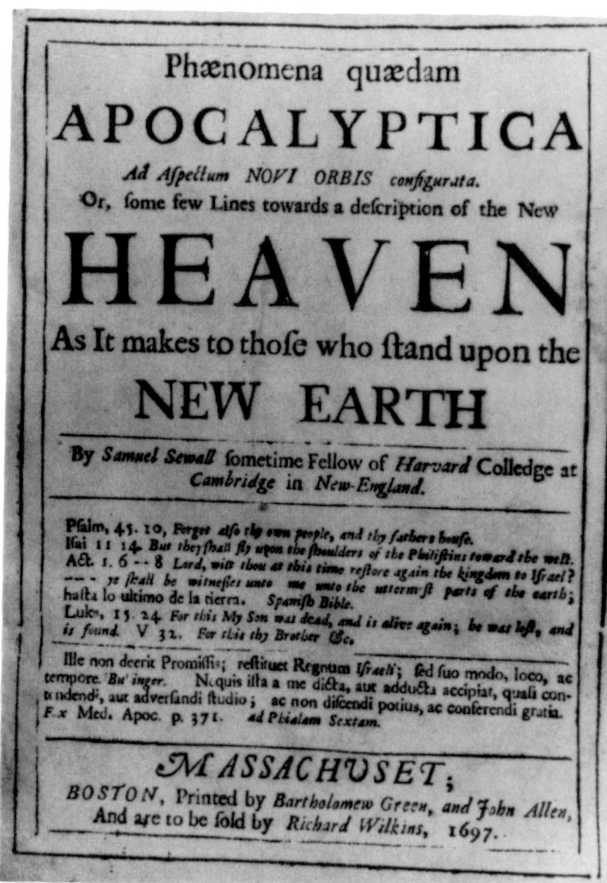

Phænomena quædam

APOCALYPTICA

Ad Aſpectum NOVI ORBIS configurata.

Or, ſome few Lines towards a deſcription of the New

HEAVEN

As It makes to thoſe who ſtand upon the

NEW EARTH

By *Samuel Sewall* ſometime Fellow of *Harvard* Colledge at *Cambridge* in *New-England.*

Pſalm, 45. 10, *Forget alſo thy own people, and thy fathers houſe.*
Iſai 11 14. *But they ſhall fly upon the ſhoulders of the Philiſtins toward the weſt.*
Act. 1. 6 -- 8 *Lord, wilt thou at this time reſtore again the kingdom to Iſrael?* ---- *ye ſhall be witneſſes unto me unto the uttermoſt parts of the earth;* haſta lo ultimo de la tierra. *Spaniſh Bible.*
Luke, 15. 24 *For this My Son was dead, and is alive again; he was loſt, and is found.* V 32. *For this thy Brother &c.*

Ille non deerit Promiſſis; reſtituet Regnum *Iſraeli*; ſed ſuo modo, loco, ac tempore. *Bullinger.* Nequis illa a me dicta, aut adducta accipiat, quaſi contendendi, aut adverſandi ſtudio; ac non diſcendi potius, ac conferendi gratia. Ex Med. Apoc. p. 371. *ad Phialam Sextam.*

MASSACHUSET;

BOSTON, Printed by *Bartholomew Green, and John Allen,* And are to be ſold by *Richard Wilkins,* 1697.

Title page for Sewall's first book, his interpretation of the book of Revelations to suggest that America may be the New Jerusalem

held. Consequently the sale of Joseph by his brothers violated this gift; slavery amounted to "the most atrocious of capital Crimes," and God's word in Exodus 21:16 supported this argument. In the second part Sewall takes up various practical considerations—one of which was that a system of indenturing white servants for a limited number of years might be better than holding black slaves for life. (Yet few emancipated slaves used their freedom well in his opinion.) In the third part he refuted objections of his opponents, especially those based on the Old Testament—for example, that the Blacks as descendants of Cham were under "the Curse of Slavery" and that Abraham "had Servants bought with his Money."

Sewall's *Diary* has been accepted as the principal source book for social history in New England during the fifty-six-year period 1674-1729. Sewall is often remembered only for his humorous courtship of Madam Winthrop—his presents to her of printed sermons and sugar almonds (the price of which he thriftily details down to the penny), their differences over the expenses attendant on his keeping a coach for her, and his asking her to take off her glove because he would sooner caress a live lady than a dead goat. Overlooked by many, however, are his sufferings—such as the deaths of his wives and children; his attempt at mollifying his overheated pastor Ebenezer Pemberton, who had insulted him in his own house for defending the Mathers (Pemberton's enemies) against an attack of libel (see the diary for 28 November 1710); the public humiliation in church following this quarrel when Pemberton had had on the following Sunday the fifty-eighth Psalm (attacking judges) pointedly sung at Sewall; the onslaught of measles, which in January 1688 he and his whole family barely survived; and the frequent deaths of friends.

Many of these events he interpreted as warnings or punishments from his Calvinistic deity. William Matthews has called this work "probably the best American diary." More recent assessments, such as that of Steven Kagle, do not deny the value of the diary for its intrinsic merit as a source book reporting vital events of the period. But Kagle criticizes the style, which he says is readable but has no special literary merit. Furthermore, the reading of the diary imposes a special problem: Sewall's broad interest in both local and faraway happenings, his numerous public offices, and the very detail of the entries tend to fragment the work as a whole. As Kagle says, Sewall "attempted to cover fifty-six years in a fraction of the space that Pepys's covered in ten." (The lacuna for the period 1677-1684 has been explained as due to a lost volume rather than to Sewall's failure to cover these years.) The reader has in many cases to supply the historical context for this great body of atomized events. Despite criticisms such as these, Kagle concludes that "even if the work is not the almost unequalled masterpiece it has often been considered . . . it is still a very fine diary." Few would contest this judgment.

Sewall's life subsequent to 1700 saw him in several different roles. On 2 June 1701 he became Captain of the Ancient and Honorable Artillery Company, which he had joined in 1679. (He had been the captain of two other companies earlier, one of which—the South Company—he resigned from because of an order to put the cross in its flag.) When the old Harvard charter was restored on 6 December 1707, he became an overseer by virtue of his office as a provincial judge. His legal career continued successfully with his appointment as Probate Judge of Suffolk County in 1717—the year his first wife died—and his rise to the position of Chief Judge of the Superior Court, which he held from 1718 to 1728. As a fond father and conscientious Calvinist, he must have felt great satisfaction to see his son Joseph ordained as a pastor of Old South Church. After a rich and full life in which he was permitted to look into the promised land of the Enlightenment, this extraordinary man died at the age of seventy-seven and was buried in the Hull-Sewall family tomb in the Granary Burying-Ground in Boston.

Other:

Talitha Cumi. An Invitation to Women to look after their Inheritance in the Heavenly Mansions, Massachusetts Historical Society *Proceedings,* first series 12 (1873): 380-384.

Letters:

Letters of Samuel Lee and Samuel Sewall Relating to New England and the Indians, edited by George Lyman Kittredge (Cambridge: J. Wilson, 1912).

Biographies:

Nina Moore Tiffany, *Samuel Sewall; A Memoir* (Boston: Houghton, Mifflin, 1898);

Ola Winslow, *Samuel Sewall of Boston* (New York: Macmillan, 1964).

References:

Nathan Henry Chamberlain, *Samuel Sewall and the World He Lived in* (Boston: DeWolfe, Fiske, 1807);

Steven E. Kagle, *American Diary Literature, 1620-1799* (Boston: G. K. Hall, 1979), pp. 147-153;

Sidney Kaplan, "Samuel Sewall and the Iniquity of Slavery," in *Samuel Sewall: "The Selling of Joseph, A Memorial,"* edited by Kaplan (Amherst: University of Massachusetts Press, 1969), pp. 27-63;

Vernon L. Parrington, *Main Currents in American Thought,* volume 1 (New York: Harcourt, Brace, 1927), pp. 85-97;

M. Halsey Thomas, Preface to *The Diary of Samuel Sewall, 1674-1729, newly edited from the manuscript at the Massachusetts Historical Society,* 2 volumes, edited by Thomas (New York: Farrar, Straus & Giroux, 1973);

George Parker Winship, "Samuel Sewall and the New England Company," *Massachusetts Historical Society Proceedings,* third series 67 (1945): 55-110;

Harvey Wish, Introduction to *The Diary of Samuel Sewall,* edited and abridged by Wish (New York: Putnam's, 1967).

Papers:

The largest collections of Sewall papers are in the following libraries: the Massachusetts Historical Society, the Houghton Library at Harvard University, the Boston Public Library, and the Archives Division of Massachusetts in Boston. Smaller collections of letters may be found in the Yale University library, the library of the Pennsylvania Historical Society in Philadelphia, the Rhode Island Historical Society library in Providence, and in the libraries of the University of Virginia and the University of Indiana. The New England Historic Genealogical Society in Boston has a special collection of Sewall papers and related material. Sewall's commonplace book, containing many of his poems, is in the library of the New York Historical Society. His twelve-page pamphlet *Proposals Touching the Accomplishment of Prophecies, Humbly Offered . . .* (1713) is in the Princeton Theological Seminary library.

Thomas Shepard I

(5 November 1604 or 1605-25 August 1649)

Thomas P. Slaughter
Rutgers University

SELECTED BOOKS: *The sincere Convert, discovering the Paucity of True Beleevers; And the great difficulty of Saving Conversion* (London: Printed by Thomas Paine for Matthew Symmons, 1640; Cambridge: Printed by S. Green, 1664);

The Saints Jewell, showing how to apply the promise (Rotterdam?, 1642); republished with *The Sincere Convert . . .* (London: Printed by E. Cotes for John Sweeting, 1655); republished separately (Boston: Printed for & sold by Daniel Gookin, 1743);

New Englands Lamentation for Old Englands present errours, and divisions and their feared future desolations if not timely prevented. Occasioned by the increase of Anabaptists, Rigid Separatists, Antinomians, and Familists. Together with Some seasonable remedies against the infection of those errours . . . (London: Printed by G. Miller, 1645);

The Sound Beleevers. Or, a Treatise of Evangelicall Conversion . . . (Edinburgh: Printed for R. Bryson, 1645; London: Printed for R. Dawlman, 1645; Boston: Printed by J. Draper for D. Henchman, 1736);

Certain Select Cases Resolved. Specially, tending to the right ordering of the heart, that we may comfortably walk with God in our generall and particular callings . . . (London: Printed by M. Simmons for J. Rothwell, 1648);

The Clear Sun-Shine of the Gospel breaking forth upon the Indians in New-England. Or, An Historicall Narration of Gods Wonderfull Workings upon sundry of the Indians . . . (London: Printed by R. Cotes for John Bellamy, 1648); republished in *Massachusetts Historical Society Collections,* third series 4 (1834): 25-67;

Theses Sabbaticae. Or, The Doctrine of the Sabbath . . . (London: Printed by T. R. & E. M. for John Rothwell, 1649);

Four Necessary Cases of Conscience of Daily Use . . . (London: Printed by J. L. for C. Meredith, 1651?);

Subjection to Christ in all His Ordinances and Appointments, the Best Means to Preserve our Liberty . . . (London: Printed for J. Rothwell & sold by T. Brewster, 1652);

Thomas Shepard

The Parable of the Ten Virgins opened & applied: Being the Substance of divers Sermons on Matth. 25.1, . . . 13. . . , edited by Jonathan Mitchel (London: Printed by J. H. for John Rothwell & for Samuel Thomson, 1660);

The Church-membership of Children, and their Right to Baptisme, According to that Holy and Everlasting Covenant of God, Established between Himself, and the Faithfull and their Seed after Them . . . (Cambridge: Printed by Samuel Green, 1663);

Wine for Gospel Wantons: Or, Cautions against Spirituall Drunkenness . . . (Cambridge, 1668);

Two Questions, viz. I. Whether an Account of the Work of Grace is to be Required of Those that are admitted to Full Communion in the Church? II. Whether the Whole Church is to be Judge Thereof? . . . (Boston: Printed & sold by Bartholomew Green & John Allen, 1697);

Three Valuable Pieces, viz. Select Cases Resolved; First Principles of the Oracles of God, or Sum of Christian Religion; Both Corrected by Four Several Editions: And a Private Diary; Containing Meditations and Experiences Never Before Published . . . , edited by Thomas Prince (Boston: Printed & sold by Rogers & Fowle, 1747); part 3 republished as *Meditations and Spiritual Experiences of Mr. Thomas Shepard . . .* (Edinburgh, 1749);

The Autobiography of Thomas Shepard, the Celebrated Minister of Cambridge, N.E. . . . (Boston: Pierce & Parker, 1832).

COLLECTION: *The Works of Thomas Shepard, First Pastor of the First Church, Cambridge, Mass. . . . ,* 3 volumes (Boston: Doctrinal Tract & Book Society, 1853).

Thomas Shepard I was born in Northampton-

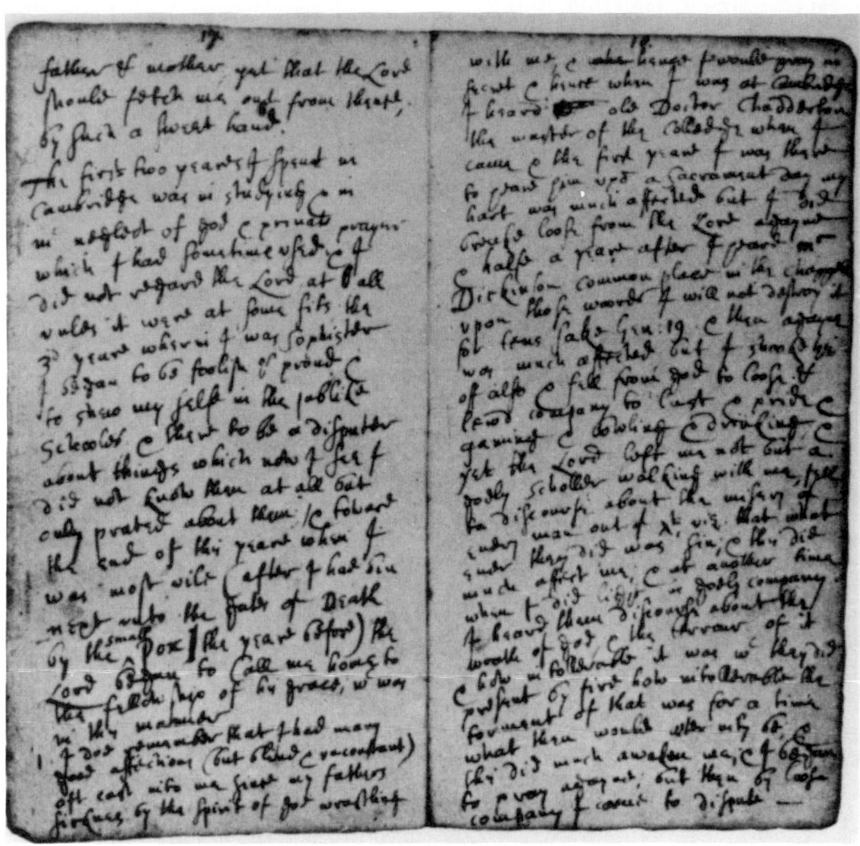

Shepard's account of his days at Emmanuel College, from the manuscript for his autobiography (First Church of Cambridge, Congregational)

shire, the son of a grocer's apprentice and a grocer's daughter, and entered Emmanuel College, Cambridge, as a pensioner, or scholarship student, in 1620. He received his B.A. and M.A. and was ordained there in 1627. Silenced as a lecturer by Bishop Laud for nonconformity in 1630, he immigrated to Massachusetts Bay in 1635. Shepard was chosen pastor at Newtown (later Cambridge), where he remained until his death. He also served as unofficial chaplain of Harvard College, which was located at Newtown partly because of Shepard's presence there.

Shepard's two most significant literary productions are his journal (1747), an immediate recording of his life during the early 1640s, and his *Autobiography* (1832), a retrospective account. Each is a unique document of its kind from the early period of Puritan settlement in New England. Shepard's autobiographical narrative is explicitly teleological and didactic, describing the striking unsettledness of his life with full knowledge that the only significance of his experience lay in its relationship to God's providence. For this reason he stresses episodes of crisis such as the threats of Antinomians and Indians, which plainly display God's hand in deliverances from great dangers.

The only volume of the journal known to exist was written during the early 1640s, after comparative tranquillity had settled on Massachusetts Bay for a time. It was first published in *Three Valuable Pieces*... under the title of *A Private Diary* (1747). The contrast between this outer peace and Shepard's inner chaos is striking. The distinguishing question of the journal is the typically Puritan plaint: "How may I know I am saved?" The log is thus characteristically Puritan and wholly personal, documenting the psychological anguish of devout Puritan life. Shepard's self-examination is a blunt exposition of the terrors of self-doubt and the psychological strategies consciously employed for survival and at least temporary reassurance about personal salvation at the hands of a Calvinist God. Shepard's journal reveals, as well as any other source, the method of maintaining the necessary anxiety of Puritan piety while converting it into assurance of sainthood. Anxiety, he argued, was normal, mandatory, and thus itself reassuring. He displays the continuing experience of assurance drawn from anxiety, which in turn produced anxiety rooted in assurance. Thus, in a dramatic and personalized narrative of one Puritan life, Shepard reveals sainthood as a process rather than a settled condition.

During his lifetime and since, editions of numerous sermons by Shepard have been published. The Puritan divine Jonathan Edwards is reputed to have drawn more than 100 different citations for his sermons from Shepard's *The Parable of the Ten Virgins opened & applied* (1660). Edwards and other Puritan ministers also drew heavily upon Shepard's *The sincere Convert . . .* (1640), which went through twenty editions by 1742. Among the most significant of Shepard's other publications are *Theses Sabbaticae . . .* (1649), *The Church-membership of Children, and their Right to Baptisme* (1663), *The Clear Sun-Shine of the Gospel breaking forth upon the Indians in New-England . . .* (1648), *New Englands Lamentation for Old Englands present errours . . .* (1645), and *Certain Select Cases Resolved . . .* (1648).

The lasting significance of Shepard's writing lies in its epitomization of the Puritan quest. He reveals as well as any writer in the Puritan genre the process of sainthood, the balancing of anxiety and self-assuredness of the most introspective saints. The *Autobiography* documents a Puritan conversion which ran true to expected formula; the journal records the renewals of Shepard's conversion. His other writings, although interesting as literary documents of the times, are mere footnotes or amplifications of this, the central, consuming Puritan experience.

References:

Everett H. Emerson, *Puritanism in America, 1620-1750* (Boston: Twayne, 1977);

Michael McGiffert, Introduction to *God's Plot: The Paradoxes of Puritan Piety, Being the Autobiography & Journal of Thomas Shepard*, edited by McGiffert (Amherst: University of Massachusetts Press, 1972);

Perry Miller, *Errand Into the Wilderness* (Cambridge: Harvard University Press, 1956);

Miller, *The New England Mind: The Seventeenth Century* (New York: Macmillan, 1939).

Thomas Shepard II

(5 April 1635-22 December 1677)

Nancy Craig Simmons
Virginia Polytechnic Institute

BOOKS: *An Almanack for the Year of our Lord 1656 . . .*, as T. S. Philomathemat (Cambridge: Printed by Samuel Green, 1656);

Eye-Salve, Or A Watch-Word From our Lord Jesus Christ unto His Churches: Especially those within the Colony of the Massachusets In New-England, To take heed of Apostacy . . . (Cambridge: Printed by Samuel Green, 1673).

Thomas Shepard II, whom Samuel Eliot Morison called the "beloved son of a beloved father," in many ways fulfills the popular ideal of the second-generation New England Puritan minister. Pious, learned, intelligent, and urbane, he was a gifted preacher who stirred his audiences, but whose life was shadowed by the specter of early death. Though few of his writings have been published, the handful that are available testify to the range of his mind and abilities. And, though little is known of his personal life, evidence of his character and personality is conveyed through the genuine grief of *An Elegie upon the Death of the Reverend Mr. Thomas Shepard* (1677) by his good friend Urian Oakes, then acting president of Harvard College.

The second Thomas Shepard was born in London six months before his father, Thomas Shepard I, immigrated to New England with his wife, Margaret Tauteville Shepard, a cousin of Shepard's former employer, Sir Richard Darley of Yorkshire. That the infant arrived in the New World at all was a miracle, as his father pointed out in the earliest surviving Colonial autobiography, written about 1647. After a dedication to "my dear son Thomas Shepard," the introductory portion of this narrative recounts God's miraculous preservation of the son. Shepard tells of the wreck of the first ship in which he and his wife attempted to flee England in 1634, when the child was in his mother's womb; late in her pregnancy, Margaret Shepard fell down a full flight of stairs. Soon after his birth, young Thomas II (the second child so named by this couple, the first having died in infancy) fell ill to a wasting sickness called a "sore mouth" by his father, who presented the Lord with many "arguments" to spare his child's life. Recovered but still weak, the baby suffered an extremely rough eleven-week Atlantic crossing aboard the *Desire*. Less than five months after disembarking at Boston (in early October 1635), Margaret Shepard died from consumption. The motherless child then suffered a return of the "sore mouth," which made it impossible for him to feed on anything except breast milk; and finally he was struck with the greatest calamity of all, an eye disease, or "humor" as the father calls it, which caused the child to become "stark blind with pearls upon both eyes and a white film." The elder Shepard interpreted his son's recovery as a sign of God's answer to his prayers and "arguments," his confession of his sins and unworthiness, and his acceptance of God's will.

By 1637 Thomas II had a new stepmother, Joanna Hooker, a daughter of the Reverend Thomas Hooker who, along with Thomas Shepard I and John Cotton, made the triumvirate of great preachers in this first generation. The second Mrs. Shepard gave birth to four sons, two of whom survived to adulthood; in 1647 Shepard married for a third time.

The family settled in Cambridge (then called Newtown), where the sophisticated, Cambridge-educated Thomas Shepard I served as pastor of the First Church and quickly established himself as one of the most popular preachers of his day. ("That soule ravishing Minister," he is called in Edward Johnson's *Wonder-working Providence of Sions Saviour in New-England*, 1654.) It was largely due to the elder Shepard's influence that Harvard College came to be located in Cambridge, as Newtown was renamed in honor of its English counterpart. Thomas Shepard II began his studies at Harvard in 1649, the year his father died at the age of forty-four.

During his Harvard career, Shepard earned a reputation as the "choice young man of his generation," according to Morison. After receiving the B.A. degree in 1653, Shepard continued as a tutor and then a fellow at the college while he prepared for the ministry. During this time he married Anna (or Hannah) Tyng in 1656. The couple's first child, Thomas III, was born in the summer of 1658, and by that fall Shepard was admitted to the church at nearby Charlestown. In April 1659 he was ordained teacher and colleague with Zechariah Symmes, pastor of the Church at Charlestown. Here he remained for the rest of his life, a spokesman for the conservative position on such issues as baptism and tolerance. A second child, Anna, was born in 1663; there may have been other children. During his tenure at Charlestown, Shepard remained closely involved in Harvard life, retaining his fellowship until 1673 when he resigned as a protest against the presidency of Leonard Hoar and in support of his friend Urian Oakes, then pastor of the Cambridge church.

Although a large number of Shepard's sermons survive in manuscript, only one has been published: *Eye-Salve, Or A Watch-Word From our Lord Jesus Christ unto His Churches: Especially those within the Colony of the Massachusets In New-England, To take heed of Apostacy* (1673), which Shepard delivered on 15 May 1672 as the Massachusetts election-day sermon for that year. Shepard's selection for this honor suggests his position in the mainstream of prevailing clerical views. In his sermon, Shepard enunciated the second-generation Puritan's sense of decline from the heroism of the founding fathers. The work is remarkable for its extended metaphorical explication of the text "Have I been a wilderness unto Israel" (Jeremiah 2:31). Its title, however, may contain a more personal allusion: after enumerating in his autobiography the disasters suffered by young Thomas, ending with the restoration of his sight, his father had cautioned him not to "make thy eyes windows of lust" but to use them to serve God.

Like many of his class, Shepard also enjoyed writing occasional verse. His earliest surviving work in this vein is some calendar verse. While he was a fellow at Harvard, in 1656, Shepard was appointed to prepare the annual Cambridge almanac, a task that was sweetened by the opportunity to fill the bottoms of the pages with brief poetical passages. For each month Shepard wrote eight lines, a rough "mixture of classical antiquity with the signs of the Zodiac." He also wrote a number of poetic elegies, two of which were preserved in Nathaniel Morton's *New Englands Memoriall* (1669): "An Elegie on the Death of that Eminent Minister of the Gospel, Mr. John Norton" (written in 1663) and "Upon the Death of the most Reverend Man of God, Mr. John Wilson" (written in 1667).

Shepard's most charming writing is a letter to his son on his admission to Harvard in 1672. Combining spiritual admonition with practical advice, Shepard explained that he chose to communicate his thoughts in written form so that they would survive his death, "and that may be sooner than you are aware," he warned. As his father had before him, Shepard reminded his son of his special purpose, his calling to God's "Holy Ministry."

Shepard's thoughts on mortality proved prophetic. Five years later he died of smallpox, contracted while visiting an infected parishioner during the epidemic of 1677-1678. Almost immediately his son succeeded him at Charlestown, where he remained until he died eight years later at the age of twenty-seven.

Shepard's death at the age of forty-two was the stimulus for one of the best Colonial works in a much-practiced genre, the elegy by Urian Oakes. In fifty-two sestets Oakes lamented the "loss of the Glory of our Age" and praised his friend's "solid Judgement, Pregnant Parts, / . . . piercing Wit, and comprehensive Brain; / . . . / . . . Holy Life, and Deeds of Charity, / . . . Grace illustrious . . . / . . . [and] rare Humility." The untimely loss led Oakes to question God, but soon he found significance in his friend's death: God was punishing New England for her sins: "Our sins have slain our *Shepard!* we have bought, / And dearly paid for, our Enormities." The Shepard of Oakes's poem becomes a Christ-figure, a sacrificial lamb rather than a pastor, and his death portends calamity unless the people of New England change their ways.

Although Thomas Shepard II did not achieve the prominence of his father and the other great founding preachers of New England, he remains an outstanding example of a New England type, the Puritan preacher with a special sense of mission, of a calling to serve as an instrument of God, but who was also much endowed (as Simon Bradstreet, son of Gov. Simon Bradstreet and Anne Bradstreet, said of Shepard) with "Piety, meeknesse (eminent charity) Learning and ministeriall gifts."

Other:

"An Elegie on the Death of that Eminent Minister of the Gospel, Mr. John Norton, the Reverend Teacher of the Church of Christ at Boston, who exchanged this life for a better April 5. 1663," in *New Englands Memoriall*, by Nathaniel Morton (Cambridge: Printed by S. Green & M. Johnson, 1669), pp. 166-168;

"Upon the Death of the most Reverend Man of God, Mr. John Wilson, Pastor of the first Church in Boston, in New-England; whose decease was Aug. 7. 1667," in *New Englands Memoriall*, pp. 188-190.

Letters:

"Letter to John Winthrop, Jr., dated 8 March, 1668-9, about the conjunction of the Moone and Venus," *Collections of the Massachusetts Historical Society*, 30 (1849): 70-71;

"A Letter from the Revd Mr Thos Shepard to his Son . . . ," *Publications of the Colonial Society of Massachusetts* (1913), 192-198; republished in Perry Miller and Thomas H. Johnson, eds., *The Puritans: A Sourcebook of Their Writings*, 2 volumes (New York: Harper & Row, 1938), II: 715-720.

Bibliography:

Harold S. Jantz, *The First Century of New England Verse* (Worcester, Mass.: American Antiquarian Society, 1944).

References:

Emory Elliott, *Power and the Pulpit in Puritan New England* (Princeton: Princeton University Press, 1975), pp. 61, 90, 107-109;

Samuel Eliot Morison, *Builders of the Bay Colony* (Boston: Houghton Mifflin, 1930), p. 133;

Morison, *Harvard College in the Seventeenth Century*, part 1 (Cambridge, Mass., 1936), p. 135;

Thomas Shepard I, *God's Plot: The Paradoxes of Puritan Piety, Being the Autobiography & Journal of Thomas Shepard*, edited by Michael McGiffert (Amherst: University of Massachusetts Press, 1972);

John Langdon Sibley, *Biographical Sketches of Graduates of Harvard University*, volume 1 (Cambridge: Charles William Sever, 1873), pp. 327-335.

Papers:

The Shepard Family Papers, at the American Antiquarian Society in Worcester, Massachusetts, include seven volumes of sermons dated 1659 to 1669. Mugar Memorial Library at Boston University is the repository for two notebooks of twenty-three sermons from 1667-1669. The Massachusetts Historical Society in Boston and the Beinecke Library at Yale University are repositories for a few other Shepard manuscripts.

John Smith

Lewis Leary
University of North Carolina at Chapel Hill

BIRTH: Willoughby, Lincolnshire, England, circa 9 January 1580, to George and Ann Smith.

DEATH: London, England, 21 June 1631.

BOOKS: *A True Relation of Such Occurences and Accidents of Noate as Hath Hapned in Virginia since the First Planting of That Collony . . .* (London: Printed for John Tappe, 1608);

A Map of Virginia. With a Description of the Countrey, the Commodities, People, Government and Religion . . . (London: Printed by Joseph Barnes, 1612);

A Description of New England; or, The Observations and Discoveries of Captain John Smith . . . (London: Printed by Humfrey Lownes for Robert Clerke, 1616);

New Englands Trials. Declaring the Successe of 26. Ships Employed Thither within these Six Years . . . (London: Printed by W. Jones, 1620; revised and enlarged, 1622);

The Generall Historie of Virginia, New-England, and the Summer Isles . . ., by Smith and others (London: Printed by I. D. & I. H. for Michael Sparkes, 1624);

An Accidence or The Path-way to Experience. Necessary for all Young Sea-men . . . (London: Printed for Jonas Man & Benjamin Fisher, 1626); enlarged as *A Sea Grammar, With the Plaine Exposition of Smiths Accidence . . .* (London: Printed by John Haviland, 1627);

The true Travels, Adventures, and Observations of Captaine John Smith, in Europe, Asia, Affrica, and America, from Anno Domini 1593. to 1629 . . . (London: Printed by J. H. for Thomas Slater, 1630);

Advertisements for the unexperienced Planters of New-England, Or any where. Or, The Path-way to experience to erect a Plantation . . . (London: Printed by J. Haviland & sold by R. Milbourne, 1631).

COLLECTION: *Travels and Works of Captain John Smith, President of Virginia and Admiral of New England, 1590-1631*, two volumes, edited by Edward Archer, with an introduction by A. G. Bradler (Edinburgh: J. Grant, 1910).

Portrait of Smith from the map of New England in his A Description of New England

John Smith, explorer, colonizer, historian, author, was born in Willoughby, Lincolnshire, England, where he was baptized on 9 January 1580, the son of George and Ann Smith, people of modest means. After brief schooling, he was apprenticed in 1595 to Thomas Sendall, a prominent merchant of nearby King's Lynn. Smith's father's death a year later brought him a modest patrimony, enough apparently to allow him to embark at seventeen on what would become a lifetime of adventuring. After almost four years of soldiering on the Continent, mostly in the Low Countries, which were then part of France, he returned to Lincolnshire by way of Scotland, apparently to recuperate from wounds. But country life seems not to have satisfied him: he spent much of his time in studying Niccolo Machiavelli's *The Art of War* (1521) and practicing horsemanship. By the end of the summer of 1600, he was off again, at the age of twenty, seeking, he said, further "brave adventures" in battle against the Ottoman Turks. Journeying on foot through Europe to the Mediterranean, he took passage for Italy at Marseilles in a vessel containing pilgrims on their way to Rome. When a storm came up, Smith, a mercenary and, what was worse, an English Protestant, was Noah-like thrown overboard to appease the elements. He swam to a nearby deserted island from which he was rescued by a marauding French merchantman, who, with Smith aboard and with his assistance, so successfully attacked and looted rival vessels that when the young adventurer was set ashore some months later, he had a pocketful of gold to help speed him on his adventuresome way. For months he pushed tortuously eastward toward the Hungarian and Transylvanian frontier, where he joined the polyglot forces gathered by Ferdinand, Archduke of Austria, to contain if not overwhelm the Ottoman enemy. Smith's studies in Machiavellian tactics now stood him in good stead as he applied them in setting up signal systems to allow Ferdinand's forces to outmaneuver the Turkish forces. More than that, his strong right arm and invincible courage allowed him on three successive days to slay in single combat, in plain sight of both armies, three lusty Turks, whose heads he presented to his appreciative commander. So impressed was Prince Sigismund Bathori, Prince of Transylvania, that he granted the young Englishman a special coat of arms decorated with three grisly heads and a promised pension of 3000 ducats annually. In a subsequent battle, in November 1603, Smith was taken prisoner and sent to Constantinople as a slave to the Princess Charatza Tragabigzanda, whom Smith described as his captor's "fair Mistresse." She was so attracted to him that to protect him from mistreatment she had him sent northward across the Black Sea to the safekeeping, she thought, of her brother. But the brother turned out to be cruel, so Smith killed him and then beat his way across northern steppes toward England, where after many hardships he arrived at the age of twenty-five with what would seem to be already a lifetime of adventures behind him. Because Smith was to become the sole recorder of these adventures, they have sometimes been suspected to have been inventions of a self-serving person eager for approval. But recent investigation suggests that, barring a stretch of truth here and there, there may be basis in fact for Smith's unashamed recordings of where he adventured and what he did as an adventurer.

After 1605, the record becomes clearer. Restless still and eager for further adventuring, Smith thought of joining the new English plantation in Guiana, where active manpower was badly needed. Instead, however, he took an active part in the promotion and organization of the group of 105 young gentlemen and others who would set sail from Blackwall in three ships on 19 December 1606 to establish a settlement in Virginia. During the voyage, probably for lack of tact in explaining to another seasoned adventurer how this venture should be managed, Smith was placed under arrest. It apparently was not known that in sealed orders, not to be opened until the destination had been reached, he had been appointed one of the council of seven that was to govern the proposed new colony. After a little more than four treacherous months at sea, the ships entered Chesapeake Bay, and a month later the colonists disembarked at what was to be called Jamestown. The long journey was over, but troubles with the Indians, with obtaining food, and with continuing quarrels among the gentlemen settlers had just begun. Denied his place on the council until mid-June 1607, Smith spent much of his time in exploration and in expeditions among the Indians to procure corn and other food for his famished companions, two-thirds of whom are said to have died within the first seven months of settlement. On one of these expeditions he was captured, taken before the Indian chief Powhatan, and sentenced to die, only to be saved, he said, by the intercession of the chief's young daughter, Pocahontas. Returning to Jamestown in January 1608, he was arrested by his enemies and condemned to be hanged but was saved by the arrival, just in time, of new supplies and new colonists from England and the intercession of less harried, less hungry, and cooler heads. In June he sent back to England an account, published in that year as *A True Relation of Such Occurences and Accidents of Noate as Hath Hapned in Virginia since the First Planting of That Collony. . .* , setting forth his side of a story of mismanagement and jockeying for power among the gentlemen settlers. Smith spent much of that summer in further exploration of the Rappahannock and Potomac Rivers and the upper reaches of the Chesapeake Bay, and from his surveys he made a map of those territories. Exploration seemed more agreeable to him than administration, but in

September 1608, the "sickly season" having taken its toll among the people of Jamestown, Smith was elected their president and bent all efforts toward stabilizing the colony, introducing some order among the settlers, who sought more for gold and gems than for food. He saw to the erection of suitable housing, of a church, and of more efficient fortifications, encouraging gardening and fishing to provide foods to supplement what was bartered from the Indians. But quarrels continued among the colonists, and in 1609 Smith, who had been severely burned when his powder bag caught on fire, sailed for England, where he defended himself and the colony against criticism. In 1612 his *A Map of Virginia. With a Description of the Countrey, the Commodities, People, Government and Religion . . .* was published in London.

Smith's role as an actor, and producer also, in the dramatic founding of Virginia was now at an end but not his lust for further adventuring nor his compulsion to set himself forward as a person, qualified by experience, to establish further transatlantic plantations. In March 1614 he sailed with two sloops on a voyage to northern reaches of the western continent, to explore possibilities for the establishment of colonies and profitable fisheries there. He charted the coast carefully, and he named the lands that lay behind it New England. In 1615, he made two more attempts to explore these promising lands. The first failed because of a storm at sea, the second when his vessel was captured by a French ship of war and he was taken captive. When released, he returned to London where in 1616 he published *A Description of New England . . .* , which included a map of its coastline. But he was thirty-six, and his days of adventuring were over. He was not the kind of person wanted by the colonizers of New England, though he offered them his services and hardheaded counsel. The religious folk who would settle in those northern regions had no place for him, though they seem to have made use of his maps, perhaps even of his advice, freely and with great confidence given. So from that time forward, he became a writer, an adviser, and a self-certified expert on adventuring and the successful settlement of new lands. His *New Englands Trials . . .* in 1620 spoke of possibilities for the planting of colonies there; a second edition two years later spoke with little confidence about what the Pilgrims had accomplished, to what extent they had fallen short of expectations, and how, taking instruction from him, they might succeed there.

In 1624, he published *The Generall Historie of Virginia, New-England, and the Summer Isles. . .* , a compendium of his earlier writings and those of other men. *An Accidence or The Path-way to Experience. Necessary for all Young Sea-men. . .* , published in 1626, is a manual of seamanship spiced with incidents and advice based on his own experiences; it was enlarged a year later as *A Sea Grammar, With the Plaine Exposition of Smiths Accidence. . . .* Then in 1630 appeared his masterwork, *The true Travels, Adventures, and Observations of Captaine John Smith, in Europe, Asia, Affrica, and America, from Anno Domini 1593. to 1629,* which includes his "Accidents and Sea-fights. . . , his service and Strategems of warre in Hungary, Transilvania, Wallachia, and Moldavia, against the Turks and Tartans, . . . his description of . . . their strange manners and customs of Religion, Diets, Buildings, Warres, Feasts, Ceremonies and Living," to which were added previously published accounts of the founders of colonies in Virginia and New England. It was a book of marvels with focus unashamedly on its author. Meant to establish John Smith as a worthy man in

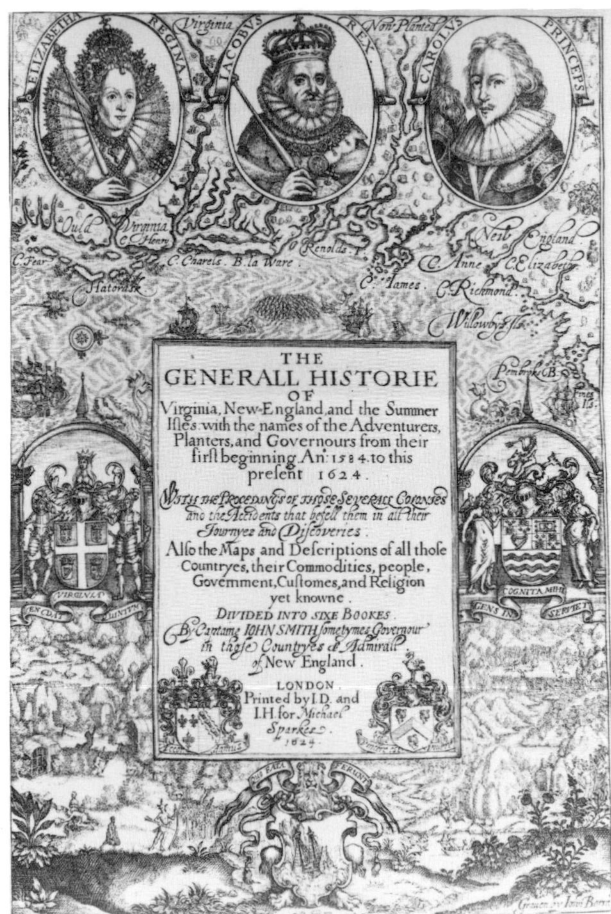
THE
GENERALL HISTORIE
OF
Virginia, New-England, and the Summer
Isles: with the names of the Adventurers,
Planters, and Governours from their
first beginning An: 1584. to this
present 1624.
With the Procedings of those Severall Colonies
and the Accidents that befell them in all their
Journyes and Discoveries.
Also the Maps and Descriptions of all those
Countryes, their Commodities, people,
Government, Customes, and Religion
yet knowne.
DIVIDED INTO SIXE BOOKES.
By Captaine IOHN SMITH sometymes Governour
in those Countryes & Admirall
of New England.
LONDON.
Printed by I.D. and
I.H. for Michael
Sparkes.
1624.

Engraved title page for the 1624 volume that collects Smith's writings about his experiences in the New World

Engravings from The true Travels, Adventures, and Observations of Captaine John Smith

his own time, it has made him a storybook hero for all time in an account so filled with braggadocio and derring-do that it has tempted many readers to agree with Thomas Fuller, who more than 300 years ago in his *The History of the Worthies of England* (1662) explained that "it soundeth much to the diminution of his [Smith's] deeds that he alone is the herald to proclaim them." But proclaim them he did, and with such vigor that his life has become legend. A year later, in 1631, John Smith was dead and buried in St. Sepulchre's Church in London. Earlier in 1631 he had published a rollickingly instructive book which he called *Advertisements for the unexperienced Planters of New-England, Or any where. Or, The Path-way to experience to erect a Plantation* . . . and in which he generously shared, sometimes with good-humored raillery, his own adventures and misadventures, expressing forthright notions of how others should have behaved or should behave in similar situations.

Colonist, explorer, professional soldier, and historian—John Smith was all of these. He seems also to have been an opportunist, writing to advance his own interests. He borrowed unashamedly from other writers about the New World, making their stories reflect on his own. But he was also a hardheaded and practical man who wrote clearly, presenting himself and his opinions with force and vigor, setting himself forth plainly, even vaingloriously, as capably at the center of all matters about which he wrote. He, John Smith, a person most anonymously named, was a person to be accounted for and to be held accountable as his story becomes history. What he had to say about his relationship with Pocahontas was expanded, and to his advantage, each time that he told it, so that it has grown, quite beyond the solid angularity of fact, to become America's first great legend. Historians may attack John Smith as a self-serving braggart, and braggart he was. He sang of himself but also of the bounty and beauty of the New World, its rugged shores, its fertile fields, sweet brooks and crystal springs, and of possibilities there for people bound in Europe by persecution or poverty. His may seem indeed to be a barbaric yawp, like the later yawp of Walt Whitman, celebrating himself in testimony to his right to celebrate an ideal of new opportunities for a new people. Self-proclaimed, he stands at the dawn of the literature of the New World, crowing like a chanticleer, and the echo of his voice in song and story has survived for more than 300 years. He has been called America's Odysseus and has been shown to have illustrated in his own life story many of the same traits and marvelous circumstances that have secured immortality for Odysseus, Jason, Robin Hood, and Siegfried, but with this difference—that he was his own Homer, the teller of his own tale. His autobiography as set forth in *The true Travels, Adventures, and Observations of Captaine John Smith* . . . may be thought to be finally as representative of the bold colonial adventurer of the seventeenth century as Benjamin Franklin's autobiography is representative of the self-reliant American of the eighteenth century or as Henry Adams's autobiography is representative of the self-suspecting retreat of the American in the nineteenth century. Like Franklin, John Smith was a man of letters but a man of much else besides.

Biographies:

Bradford Smith, *Captain John Smith, His Life and Legend* (Philadelphia: Lippincott, 1953);

Henry Wharton, *The Life of John Smith, English Soldier,* edited by Laura Polanyi Striker (Chapel Hill: University of North Carolina Press, 1957);

Philip L. Barbour, *The Three Worlds of Captain John Smith* (New York: Houghton Mifflin, 1964);

Everett Emerson, *Captain John Smith* (New York: Twayne, 1971);

Lewis Leary, "The Adventures of John Smith as Heroic Legend!," in *Essays on Early Virginia Literature Honoring Richard Beale Davis,* edited by J. A. Leo Lemay (New York: Burt Franklin, 1977), pp. 13-34.

Josiah Smith

(25 December 1704-19 October 1781)

M. Jimmie Killingsworth
New Mexico Institute of Mining and Technology

SELECTED BOOKS: *A Discourse Delivered at Boston, on July 11, 1726. Then Occasion'd by the Author's Ordination* . . . (Boston: Printed for S. Gerrish & T. Hancock, 1726);

A Sermon Preached in Boston, July 10th, 1726 . . . (Boston, 1727);

Humane Impositions Proved Unscriptural, or, The Divine Right of Private Judgment . . . (Boston: Printed for D. Henchman, 1729);

The Divine Right of Private Judgment Vindicated . . . (Boston, 1730);

The Duty of Parents to Instruct Their Children . . . (Boston: Printed for D. Henchman, 1730);

The Greatest Sufferers Not Always the Greatest Sinners. A Sermon Delivered in Charlestown, in the Province of South-Carolina, February 4th, 1727, 8. Then Occasioned by the Terrible Earthquake in New-England . . . (Boston, 1730);

No New Thing to be Slander'd . . . (Boston, 1730);

Solomon's Caution against the Cup . . . (Boston: Printed for D. Henchman, 1730);

The Young Man Warn'd: Or, Solomon's Counsel to His Son . . . (Boston: Printed for D. Henchman, 1730);

The Character and Duty of Minister and People . . . (Charlestown, S. C.: Printed by Lewis Timothy, 1736);

A Sermon Deliver'd at Charles-Town, in South Carolina, The Lord's-Day After the Funeral, and Sacred to the Memory of the Reverend Mr. Nathan Bassett . . . (Boston: Printed & sold by S. Kneeland & T. Green, 1739);

The Character, Preaching, &c. of the Reverend Mr. George Whitefield . . . (Boston: Printed by G. Rogers for J. Edward & H. Foster, 1740; Glasgow: Sold by Smith, 1741);

The Burning of Sodom, With It's Moral Causes, Improv'd in a Sermon Preach'd at Charlestown, South Carolina, after a Most Terrible Fire, which broke out on Nov. 18. 1740 . . . (Boston: Printed by D. Fowle, 1741);

Funeral Discourse in Charlestown, S. C. April 25, 1742, in Memory of Mrs. Hannah Dart . . . (Boston, 1742);

Jesus Persecuted in His Disciples . . . (Boston: Printed & sold by S. Kneeland & T. Green, 1745);

A Zeal of God Encourag'd and Guarded . . . (Boston: Printed & sold by S. Kneeland and T. Green, 1745);

Sermons on Several Important Subjects (Boston: Printed by Edes & Gill, 1757);

A Funeral Discourse, Sacred to the Memory of Mr. Joseph Moody . . . (Charlestown, S. C.: Printed by Peter Timothy, 1766);

The Church of Ephesus Arraign'd . . . (Charlestown, S. C.: Printed by Charles Crouch, 1768);

Success a Great Proof of St. Paul's Fidelity. Sacred to the Memory of the Reverend George Whitefield . . . (Charlestown, S. C.: Printed by Charles Crouch, 1770).

THE
Character, Preaching, &c.
OF THE REVEREND
Mr. GEORGE WHITEFIELD,
Impartially
Repreſented and Supported,
IN A
SERMON,
Preach'd in CHARLESTOWN, SOUTH-CAROLINA, *March* 26th *Anno Domini.* 1740.

By JOSIAH SMITH, V. D. M.

With a *PREFACE* by the REVEREND
Dr. *Colman* and Mr. *Cooper*
Of BOSTON, *New-England.*

2. Cor. iii. 6. *Who alſo hath made us able Miniſters of the New-Teſtament, not of the Letter, but of the Spirit.*
2 Cor. vi. 4. &c. *But in all Things approving ourſelves the Miniſters of* GOD, *in much Patience---in Labours, in Watchings, in Faſtings: By Pureneſs, by Knowlege, by Long-ſuffering, by Kindneſs, by the* HOLY GHOST, *by Love unfeign'd: By the Word of Truth--- by Honour and Diſhonour, by evil Report and good Report; as* Deceivers, *and yet* true.

BOSTON, Printed by G. ROGERS, for J. EDWARDS and H. FOSTER in Cornhill. 1740.

Title page for Smith's defense of evangelist George Whitefield. Like Whitefield, Smith supported the aims of the Great Awakening (John Carter Brown Library, Brown University)

Josiah Smith, the prolific and eloquent exponent of the Great Awakening in the South, was born in Charleston, South Carolina, the son of George and Dorothy Archar Smith. After spending most of his early life in Bermuda, he was educated at Harvard, from which he received an A.B. in 1725 and an A.M. *in absentia* in 1728. Ordained in Boston in 1726, he returned to Bermuda but was forced to abandon his settlement when it was devastated by hurricanes in 1728. He then moved to Cainhoy, South Carolina, to become pastor of the Independent Presbyterian church. In 1731 he married Elizabeth Darrell, with whom he raised seven children. He became the associate pastor of the influential Independent Church of Charleston in 1734 and its sole minister in 1742. Struck by palsy in 1749, Smith was left unable to articulate clearly. Though his congregation could no longer understand his speech, he was allowed to preach once a month—such was their fidelity to their minister and such was his love of the pulpit. An ardent Whig, he was forced to leave Charleston when it was captured during the Revolution. He moved with his family to Philadelphia, where he died in October 1781.

In more than twenty-five books of sermons and polemical writings of which no complete list currently exists, Smith demonstrates that he was a conscious and effective stylist. His sermons are written in the plain and simple manner characteristically found in the works of his New England brethren, with whom he constantly identified, both intellectually and spiritually. Though generally restrained in style and content, the sermons, especially those composed around the time of the great revivals of the late 1730s and early 1740s, occasionally exhibit a fiery eloquence. The explications of biblical texts and the style of Smith's earliest sermons betray his sensitivity to metaphor, which would also be the principal strength of the later sermons.

A blend of religious enthusiasm and practical rationality is everywhere evident in Smith's writings. In his pastoral sermons on the evils of the flesh he neither ignores nor dwells upon eternal punishment in hell but instead emphasizes practical consequences: for example, alcoholism destroys people's productivity in society as well as their souls. His belief that Christianity should produce an active moral life in this world is especially clear in his praise of Boston and its inhabitants and in his frequent condemnations of the more lax morality of his home city. When an earthquake struck Boston, he proclaimed that the greatest sufferers are not always the greatest sinners, but, when Charleston burned in 1740, he saw in the fire an act of God comparable to the burning of Sodom.

Smith attacked the conservative Presbyterians' insistence on the authority of the Westminster Confession, the Catechism, and other human "impositions" of scriptural lessons because of his commitment to the individual's right and ability to interpret scriptures according to reason and conscience. His defense of "the divine right of private judgment" in *Humane Impositions Proved Unscriptural* . . . (1729) incurred the disfavor of Hugh Fisher (who responded in a postscript to his *A Preservative from Damnable Errors* . . . , 1730) and of the presbytery in general. After defending his position in *The Divine Right of Private Judgment Vindicated* . . . (1730), Smith withdrew from the conflict, for he was not by nature combative or vindictive. His 1740 sermon in support of the character and preaching of George Whitefield, which was affixed to many of the posthumous collections of the controversial revivalist's writings, was less a polemic than a work of warm admiration designed to fan the fires of religious zeal. Largely because of Smith's efforts, the effects of the Great Awakening were felt more strongly in South Carolina than in any other Southern colony. Though he strongly encouraged an enthusiastic response to Christianity, he also recognized the danger of overzealousness and warned against it in *A Zeal of God Encourag'd and Guarded* . . . (1745). Smith has been remembered mainly for his connection with Whitefield, but he deserves his own place in religious and literary history as a dissenting minister whose sermons brought the power of New England preaching to the South.

References:

Richard Beale Davis, *Intellectual Life in the Colonial South, 1585-1763* (Knoxville: University of Tennessee Press, 1978), pp. 584, 608, 684-685, 697, 764-767, 1429;

Alan Heimert and Perry Miller, *The Great Awakening* (New York: Bobbs-Merrill, 1967), pp. 62-69;

Clifford K. Shipton, *Sibley Harvard Graduates*, volume 7 (Boston: Massachusetts Historical Society, 1945), pp. 569-585.

Richard Steere

(circa 1643-20 June 1721)

Peter L. Rumsey
Columbia University

BOOKS: *The History of the Babylonish Cabals; or, The Intrigues, Progression, Opposition, Defeat and Destruction of the Daniel-Catchers* . . . (London: Printed for R. Baldwin, 1682);

A Monumental Memorial of Marine Mercy Being An Acknowledgment of an High Hand of Divine Deliverance on the Deep in the Time of distress, in A Late Voyage from Boston in New-England, Anno 1683 (Boston: Printed by Richard Pierce for James Cowse, 1684);

The Daniel Catcher. The Life of the Prophet Daniel: In a Poem. To which is Added, Earth's Felicities, Heaven's Allowances, a Blank Poem. With several other Poems (Boston: Printed by John Allen for Nicholas Boon, 1713).

Richard Steere, an early American poet, was born at Chertsey, Surrey, England, where he seems to have spent his childhood and attended the local grammar school. On 6 January 1658, he was apprenticed to Master Henry Browne, cordwainer and citizen of London. Eight years later, Steere had completed his apprenticeship and was admitted to the Cordwainer Corporation. While in London, he was evidently attracted to the Whig cause and began to write in its behalf. His major work, *The History of the Babylonish Cabals* . . . (1682), a heroic, anti-Catholic poem, is an answer to *Absalom and Achitophel* (1681), John Dryden's satiric attack on the Earl of Shaftesbury (Achitophel) for his efforts to persuade Charles II's illegitimate son, the Duke of Monmouth (Absalom), to rebel against his father. In the same year, Steere also produced two satiric broadsides, *A Message from Tory-land to the Whig Makers* . . . (published on 11 July 1682) and *Rome's Thunderbolt, or Antichrist Displaid* (published circa August 1682). In *A Message from Tory-land*... the persona, an energetic Jesuit, freely confesses to all the evil deeds that the Whigs attributed to Papist conspirators, and in *Rome's Thunderbolt*... Steere attempted to convey the wickedness of the Roman See by employing figures from the book of Revelation—Rome is Babel; the Roman church is the Whore of Babylon; the pope is Antichrist.

Steere's propagandistic efforts apparently did not go unnoticed, for after Charles II's government began to silence the Whig presses in London, Steere fled to Boston, some time between fall 1682 and summer 1683. A nearly disastrous return voyage to London on the ship *Adventure* in December 1683 prompted Steere to write *A Monumental Memorial of Marine Mercy* (1684) upon his return to New England in May 1684. By 1685, he was acting as an agent for John Wheeler, merchant of New London. Upon Wheeler's death, Steere married Wheeler's widow, Elizabeth (circa 1692), and took over his business. While in New London, Steere again became involved in politics, advocating the Rogerene cause of John Rogers, a dissenting Seventh Day Baptist, and being fined by the Connecticut Court in 1695 for subscribing his name to an antiestablishment document which argued that "to compel people to pay for a Presbyterian ministry is against the Laws of England." In 1710, Steere left New London and resettled at Southold on Long Island. Elizabeth died in 1712, and Steere remarried twice thereafter. His second wife, Margaret Sylvester, whom he married in 1712, died in 1713, and a few months later, in March 1714, he married Bethiah Mapes. He died in Southold on 20 June 1721.

Steere's major American work, *The Daniel Catcher*..., is his finest. In addition to the title poem (a reworking of *The History of the Babylonish Cabal*...) and a modified version of *Rome's Thunderbolt*... (under the title "Antichrist Display'd"), Steere included a number of other poems which reveal a diversity of styles and attempts at experimentation.

The revision of Steere's earlier poems was minor and did not produce striking improvements in them. As an answer to Dryden's *Absalom and Achitophel, The Daniel Catcher* . . . remained inadequate. Its style imitates Dryden's rhythm, meter, and form, but falls short of the mark in its overall conception. The strictures which Steere imposed upon himself by choosing to imitate Dryden's form so closely proved too difficult to surmount. Like Dryden, Steere employed scriptural allegory, but his narrative structure, based upon the figure of the prophet Daniel, proved too weak to bear the burden of his attack. The result is a highly uneven work in which the allegorical parallels are often strained to the breaking point.

The Daniel Catcher.

THE LIFE Of the Prophet Daniel:

IN A POEM.

To which is Added,

Earth's Felicities, Heaven's Allowances,

A Blank POEM.

With ſeveral other Poems.

By *R. S.*

Printed in the Year 1713.

Title page for Steere's finest book. The title poem, a reworking of his earlier anti-Catholic poem, The History of the Babylonish Cabals, *is an answer to and imitation of John Dryden's* Absalom and Achitophel.

The other poems in *The Daniel Catcher*... are of considerable interest. "Upon the Caelestial Embassy" is of unusual subject matter for Puritan New England, because it is a poem on the Nativity (the Puritan establishment forbade the celebration of Christmas, viewing it as a pagan practice of the "Romish" church). In his poem Steere uses the paradox of Christ's humble beginnings and his glorious end as the focal point.

In "Sea-Storm nigh the Coast," which appears to be an outgrowth of parts of *A Monumental Memorial* . . . , Steere uses composite sea-land imagery—waves are "Liquid Mountains"—and a closely organized meter to convey a vivid impression of the overwhelming, chaotic force of the tempestuous sea.

"Earth's Felicities, Heaven's Allowances" would be noteworthy for no other reason than its being the first American attempt at blank verse. The reflective poem appears to be Steere's metaphysical assessment of the world around him. Beginning with the premise that the beauties of nature and man's happinesses are gifts freely bestowed by God, Steere moves on to enumerate these gifts and discourse upon them. He concludes on a traditional Puritan didactic note—earthly pleasures pose temptations for man, but they may and ought to be enjoyed in moderation. To do so is to put God's gifts to their proper use, for worldly joys and human happiness are but intimations of "Heav'ns Felicity," or "that Ocean of Delight" awaiting the godly in the next world.

In his range of subject matter, in his willingness to experiment with a variety of poetic forms, and in his ongoing attempt to find a poetic medium suited to his creative abilities, Richard Steere stands alone. Although the quality of his work is uneven at times, it displays a freshness and individuality absent in the largely imitative efforts of his New England contemporaries.

References:

Perry Miller and Thomas H. Johnson, eds., *The Puritans* (New York: Harper & Row, 1963), II: 667-669;

James Pierce Root, *A Record of the Descendants of John Steere* (Cambridge: Privately printed, 1890), pp. 14-15;

Donald P. Wharton, *Richard Steere: Colonial Merchant Poet,* Pennsylvania State University Studies, no. 44 (University Park: Pennsylvania State University Press, 1979).

James Sterling

(1701-10 November 1763)

O. Glade Hunsaker
Brigham Young University

SELECTED BOOKS: *The Rival Generals. A Tragedy as it was Acted at the Theatre-Royal in Dublin . . .* (Dublin: Printed by J. Carson for Pat. Dugan, 1722; London: Printed for A. Bettesworth, 1722);

The Loves of Hero and Leander from the Greek of Musaeus . . . , translation by Sterling (Dublin: Printed by Andrew Crooke, 1728; London: Printed for J. Walthoe, 1728);

The Poetical Works of the Rev. James Sterling . . . (Dublin: Printed by & for George Faulkner, 1734);

The Parricide. A Tragedy . . . (London: Printed for John Walthoe, 1736);

An Ode on the Times, address'd to the hope of Britain (London: Printed for R. Doddesley, 1738);

An Epistle to the Hon. Arthur Dobbs, Esq. in Europe, from a Clergyman in America (Dublin: Printed for J. Smith, 1752; revised edition, London: Sold by R. Dodsley & M. Cooper, 1752);

A Sermon, preached before his Excellency the Governor of Maryland, and both Houses of Assembly at Annapolis, December 13, 1754 (Annapolis: Printed by Jonas Green, 1755); republished as *Zeal against the Enemies of our Country Pathetically Recommended . . .* (London: Printed for J. Whiston, 1755).

James Sterling was born in Ireland at Dowrass, King's County, the son of Captain James Sterling and Patience Hansard Sterling. He received his early education at Mr. Lloyd's in Dublin and on 17 April 1716 entered Trinity College, Dublin, from which he graduated in 1720. A highly regarded young writer, Sterling completed his first play, a tragedy called *The Rival Generals* (1722), before he was twenty-one. It was successfully produced in Dublin, and in late 1722 or early 1723 Sterling married one of the play's cast, Nancy Lyddel, who by the late 1720s had become well known as an accomplished actress. Sterling's next tragedy, *The Parricide* (1736), was performed as early as 1726, and his translation, *The Loves of Hero and Leander from the Greek of Musaeus*... (1728), was reprinted at least three times.

His happiness over his early successes was marred, however, by the death of his wife in about 1732. Soon after Sterling took an M.A. degree and was ordained an Anglican clergyman, serving first as a military chaplain. In 1734 the poems he had written since the age of eighteen were published as *The Poetical Works of the Rev. James Sterling. . . .* J. A. Leo Lemay points out that none of these poems is as accomplished as those he later wrote in America; yet he was already experimenting with form and developing some of his dominant themes. He later expanded and revised some of these poems for publication in America. By 1736, when *The Parricide* was produced in London, he had asked to be assigned a church in America.

He first requested a church in Boston, but, according to Lemay, the people of Boston "wanted no part of a minister who was a playwright and had been married to an actress." On 16 September 1737 he was appointed a missionary to Maryland, where he was inducted as rector of All Hallows Parish, in Anne Arundel County, on 16 November 1737. In July 1739 he left this post to become rector of St. Anne's in Annapolis, and in spring 1740 he was chaplain to the General Assembly. That August he accepted the rectorship of a more wealthy parish, St. Paul's in Kent County, and he settled in Chestertown, where he lived until his death in 1763. On 19 September 1743 Sterling married Rebecca Holt, the widow of the Rev. Thomas Holt. Their only child, Rebecca, was born on 22 November 1744. Some time after this date Rebecca Holt Sterling died, and on 7 September 1749 Sterling married Mary Smith.

Sterling has come to be regarded as one of the finest writers of colonial Maryland. Many of the poems he wrote in America were published anonymously and have been attributed to him through the research of Lawrence C. Wroth and J. A. Leo Lemay, who calls Sterling the most "prolific of colonial Maryland poets." Most of his poems treat colonial ideals, usually public and occasional, in conventional verse. He is more credited with rhythmical skills than with the ability to evoke profound thought or powerful emotion. The first poem Sterling had published in America, "The Sixteenth Ode of Horace's Second Book . . . ," which appeared anonymously in the *Maryland Gazette* for 31 March 1747 and was subsequently reprinted in the *Pennsylvania Gazette*, is highly complimentary to his friend Gov. Samuel Ogle of Maryland and is described by Lemay as "competent" verse. An occasional poem of 1748, an epithalamium on the

AN
EPISTLE
TO THE
Hon. ARTHUR DOBBS, Esq;
In *EUROPE.*
FROM A
CLERGYMAN in AMERICA.
PART I.
India mittit opus; peregrè *sua Thura* Camœnæ.

LONDON:
Printed for the AUTHOR, and Sold by R. DODSLEY, in *Pall-mall*, and M. COOPER, in *Pater-noster-row.* 1752.

Title page for the London edition of Sterling's poem about the search for a Northwest Passage (John Carter Brown Library, Brown University)

marriage of two fellow Kent County residents, was also published anonymously in the *Maryland Gazette* (18 May 1748).

Sterling's next poetic effort was *An Epistle to the Hon. Arthur Dobbs, Esq. . . .* (1752), a 1,600-line poem in three parts, which Wroth describes as "high flown, windy, and very patriotic verse in praise of princes and potentates." Sterling had sent the poem, which praises Dobbs's search for the Northwest Passage, to London two years before its publication in what Lemay suggests may have been "the opening gambit in his play to gain a monopoly on northern trade." In about November 1751 Sterling sailed for Dublin, where he visited family and friends, and then went on to London, where he and others applied for a monopoly on trade along the Labrador coast in return for their promise to search for the Northwest Passage. This request for a monopoly enraged Benjamin Franklin and some fellow Philadelphians, with whom Sterling had earlier joined in financing Theodorus Swaine Drage's search for the passage. The application was denied, but Sterling's actions gained him enemies in the colonies.

Despite the controversy surrounding Sterling's poem, Lemay calls it "a major eighteenth century American poem," which was well received by contemporary reviewers. Yet, Lemay adds, today one might read it with interest of "the kind that the casual viewer gives to the fossil bones of a dinosaur."

On 12 May 1752, Sterling was appointed a customs collector in Maryland, a move that angered not only Franklin and his associates but also those Marylanders who opposed giving civil authority to the clergy. All opposition was overruled, however, and Sterling left for Maryland, where he arrived in August 1752 and took up his post.

On 12 December 1754 Sterling's occasional poem urging the colonies to unite in the effort to expel the French forces that had once again attacked British territory in North America was anonymously published in the *Maryland Gazette* and was reprinted in the *Pennsylvania Gazette* on 14 January 1755. His sermon to the Maryland Assembly on 13 December 1754 repeated the poem's theme, and Sterling continued to support patriotic efforts against the French in a 1756 essay urging his fellow colonists to outfit privateers to fight the enemy (*Maryland Gazette*, 12 August 1756).

In 1758 William Smith, the editor of the *American Magazine* in Philadelphia, accepted a number of Smith's most ambitious poems for publication in his magazine. Two of the more notable poems published there are "A Poem. On the Inventions of Letters and The Art of Printing . . ." and "The Royal Comet." The first is a revised and expanded version of a poem Sterling had had published as a broadside in Dublin in 1728, while "The Royal Comet" celebrates the King of Prussia's defense of the Protestant cause. Sterling's last published poem, which appeared in the *Pennsylvania Gazette* for 13 March 1760, is an occasional poem on the death of Gen. James Wolfe during the British defeat of the French on the Plains of Abraham, the decisive battle in the taking of New France by the British.

Much admired during his time, Sterling's poems are little read today. The most complete account of his life and works is to be found in J. A. Leo Lemay's *Men of Letters in Colonial Maryland* (1972), which provides detailed biography and bibliography, critical analyses of important poems, and discussions of his literary indebtedness and his philosophical position on political issues.

Periodical Publications:

"The Sixteenth Ode of Horace's Second Book, imitated and inscribed to His Excellency Samuel Ogle, Esq.," *Maryland Gazette*, 31 March 1747, p. 1;

"An Epithalamium . . . on the late Marriage of the Honourable Benedict Calvert, Esq.; with the agreeable young Lady, of your City, his Kinswoman," *Maryland Gazette*, 18 May 1748;

"A Poem, Occasioned by his Majesty's most gracious Benevolence to his British Colonies in America, lately invaded by the French," *Maryland Gazette*, 12 December 1754;

An essay urging Marylanders to fit out privateers, as Philopatris, *Maryland Gazette*, 12 August 1756;

"A Poem. On the Inventions of Letters and The Art of Printing . . . ," *American Magazine or Monthly Chronicle*, 1 (March 1758): 281-290;

"The Patriot, A Poem," *American Magazine or Monthly Chronicle*, 1 (April 1758): 332-335;

"The Dame of Cyprus," *American Magazine or Monthly Chronicle*, 1 (April 1758): 335;

"Leda's twin-sons . . . ," *American Magazine or Monthly Chronicle*, 1 (April 1758): 335-336;

"A Pastoral. To his Excellency George Thomas. . . ," *American Magazine or Monthly Chronicle*, 1 (May 1758): 390-397;

"The Royal Comet," *American Magazine or Monthly Chronicle*, 1 (August 1758): 550-552;

"Epitaph on the Late Lord Howe," *American Magazine or Monthly Chronicle*, 1 (September 1758): 604-605;

"Elogium," *American Magazine or Monthly Chronicle*, 1 (September 1758): 609;

"Apollinis Querla, Sive Epigramma," *American Magazine or Monthly Chronicle*, 1 (October 1758): 642;

"The 22d Ode of the first Book of Horace imitated; and inscribed to the Lady of his late Excellency Samuel Ogle, Esquire," *American Magazine or Monthly Chronicle*, 1 (October 1758): 642-643;

"Verses Occasioned by the Success of the British Arms in the Year 1759," *Maryland Gazette*, 3 January 1760;

"Prologue, spoken by Mr. Douglass," *Maryland Gazette*, 6 March 1760;

"Epilogue, spoken by Mrs. Douglass," *Maryland Gazette*, 6 March 1760;

"Panegyrical Verses on the Death of General Wolfe," *Pennsylvania Gazette*, 13 March 1760;

An essay on the relation between trade and agriculture, as Philo-patris, *Maryland Gazette*, 11 March 1762.

References:

J. A. Leo Lemay, "A Literary History of Colonial Maryland," Ph.D. dissertation, University of Pennsylvania, 1964;

Lemay, *Men of Letters in Colonial Maryland* (Knoxville: University of Tennessee Press, 1972), pp. 257-312, 372-382;

Lawrence C. Wroth, "James Sterling: Poet, Priest, and Prophet of Empire," American Antiquarian Society *Proceedings*, 41 (1931): 25.

Solomon Stoddard

(27 September 1643-11 February 1729)

Karl Keller
San Diego State University

SELECTED BOOKS: *The Safety of Appearing at the Day of Judgment, in the Righteousness of Christ* . . . (Boston: Printed by Samuel Green for Samuel Phillips, 1687; revised edition, Boston: Printed for D. Henchman, 1729; Edinburgh: Printed for M. Gray & for T. Vernor in London, 1742);

The Tryal of Assurance, Set Forth in a Sermon . . . (Boston: Printed by B. Green & J. Allen & sold by Michael Perry, 1696);

The Doctrine of Instituted Churches Explained and Proved from the Word of God (London: Printed for Ralph Smith, 1700);

The Necessity of Acknowledgment, of Offenses, in Order to Reconciliation . . . (Boston: Printed by T. Green, 1701);

God's Frown in the Death of Usefull Men. Shewed in a Sermon Preached at the Funeral of the Honourable Col. John Pynchon Esq. . . . (Boston: Printed by B. Green & J. Allen & sold by Benjamin Eliot, 1703);

The Sufficiency of One Good Sign to Prove a Man to Be in a State of Life . . . (Boston: Printed by B. Green & J. Allen, 1703);

The Way for a People to Live Long in the Land that God Hath Given Them . . . (Boston: Printed by Bartholomew Green & John Allen for Benj. Eliot, 1703);

The Danger of Speedy Degeneracy . . . (Boston: Printed by B. Green for Benj. Eliot, 1705);

The Falseness of Hopes of Many Professors . . . (Boston: Printed by B. Green?, 1708);

The Inexcusableness of Neglecting the Worship of God, Under a Pretence of Being in an Unconverted Condition . . . (Boston: Printed by B. Green & sold by Samuel Phillips, 1708);

An Appeal to the Learned. Being a Vindication of the Right of Visible Saints to the Lords Supper, though They be Destitute of a Saving Work of God's Spirit on Their Hearts: Against the Exceptions of Mr. Increase Mather (Boston: Printed by B. Green for Samuel Phillips, 1709);

Those Taught by God the Father to Know God the Son; Are Blessed . . . (Boston: Printed by B. Green for Benj. Eliot, 1712);

The Efficacy of the Fear of Hell to Restrain Men from Sin: and Other Sermons (Boston, 1713);

A Guide to Christ. Or the Way of Directing Souls That Are Under Conversion . . . (Boston: Printed by J. Allen for N. Boone, 1714);

Three Sermons Lately Preach'd at Boston Shewing I. The Vertue of Christ's Blood to Cleanse from Sin. II. That Natural Men Are Under the Government of Self-Love. III. That the Gospel is the Means of Conversion. To Which a Fourth is Added, To Stir up Young Men and Maidens to Praise the Name of the Lord (Boston: Printed by B. Green for Daniel Henchman, 1717);

The Duty of Gospel-Ministers to Preserve a People from Corruption . . . (Boston: Printed for Samuel Phillips, 1718);

The Presence of Christ with the Ministers of the Gospel . . . (Boston: Printed by B. Green, 1718);

A Treatise Concerning the Nature of Saving Conversion, and the Way Wherein It Is Wrought. Added, A Lecture-Sermon had at Boston, July 2, 1719. Wherein the Way to Know Sincerity and Hypocrisy is Cleared Up

(Boston: Printed by B. Green for Daniel Henchman, 1719);

An Answer to Some Cases of Conscience Respecting the Country . . . (Boston: Printed by B. Green & sold by Samuel Gerrish, 1722);

Question, Whether God Is Not Angry with the Country for Doing so Little to Convert the Indians? . . . (Boston: Printed by B. Green & sold by Samuel Gerrish, 1723);

The Defects of Preachers Reproved . . . (New London: Printed & sold by T. Green, 1724).

Solomon Stoddard was the first writer in the history of early American literature to have been born in America. Unlike other early American writers, he did not see himself as an exile or an outcast. The distinction suggests how he distinguished himself—in idea, style, image, purpose—in American literary history. With him we begin to understand the indigenous. Stoddard was one of the first writers on the American frontier, and he wrote out of a desire to satisfy the needs of colonial life in that wilderness. The way he framed dominant issues of his age—conversion, sacraments, community, the instituted church, the ministered nation—reshaped New England in his lifetime, most of the rest of the colonies by the Revolution, and also the American frontier then and afterward, well into the nineteenth century. In a number of ways, his words became the American Way.

Stoddard became a writer only reluctantly. He was born to Anthony and Mary Downing Stoddard, in Boston in 1643. Because the Stoddards, a family of wealthy merchants, had a reputation for articulate rebelliousness against colonial orthodoxy, it became easy for him to become a dissenter among Dissenters. He studied for the ministry at Harvard between 1658 and 1665, took his M.A. there in 1665, was appointed a fellow of the college in 1666, and was then appointed librarian in 1667. He made no attempt to publish his writings of the period, mainly poems and sermons, which still largely remain in manuscript.

Stoddard left Cambridge and Boston for the Barbados in 1667 to become the chaplain to Governor Daniel Searle, and he returned to the Bay Colony two years later, when he was invited to be the minister at Northampton, a frontier outpost and at the time the largest community outside Boston. He also made no effort to publish any of the writings, mainly sermons, of the first twenty years of his ministry. These exist today, as well, only as hundreds of manuscript pages of sermon notes.

Soon after his arrival in Northampton, Stoddard married Esther Warham Mather, widow of the previous minister, Eleazar Mather, and they had fourteen children. Those male children who survived into adulthood became ministers in the area (with the exception of one, John Stoddard, who became prominent in politics and finance in Connecticut), and all of the female children who survived married ministers in the area. His daughter Esther married Timothy Edwards, and their son was the well-known minister and philosopher Jonathan Edwards. A long list of prominent Americans descend from Stoddard, including poet Timothy Dwight, Aaron Burr, and novelist-essayist Gore Vidal.

When Stoddard went to Northampton he had serious doubts about the church practices instituted in the American congregations regarding conversion: the Full Covenant, which required a public profession of faith and acceptance into membership by the vote of a congregation; and the Half-Way Covenant, which was a compromise allowing membership to children and grandchildren of not-yet-professing and not-yet-admitted members. Because of those doubts he delayed his own membership and effectual calling until 1672, and between 1672 and 1677 he abandoned the practices of both the Full Covenant and the Half-Way Covenant regarding admission to the church and gradually thought out the more democratic practice of admitting all townspeople to the church and then allowing them to participate in the sacraments as a means of converting them. By late 1677 he was practicing his heresy, and by 1679 he was attempting to defend his revolutionary practice in a Reforming Synod in Boston. (There is some dispute among Stoddard scholars about the date of the beginning of Stoddard's change; some place it as early as 5 November 1677 and others as late as 1690.) At this synod, Stoddard delivered his first work written for a public, his "Nine Arguments Against Examinations Concerning a Work of Grace," which Increase Mather answered in 1680 with "Confutation of Solomon Stoddard's Observations Respecting the Lord's Supper." This debate was the beginning of Stoddard as a writer. He was thirty-six. The literary war continued for fifty years, and out of it came twenty-four published works by Stoddard. Necessity made him one of the most important writers/apologists of the period.

Stoddard's "Nine Arguments . . ." was a bold attack upon the artificial distinction the strict congregationalists made between the visible saints and the unregenerate, particularly the validity of public profession of faith as a test of church membership and town citizenship. It was also a justification of the open communion Stoddard had practiced in Northampton for several years, which was resulting in increased activity and several awakenings. Stoddard's contention that it was the individual's responsibility and not the minister's "to discern the Lord's body" was the beginning of a revolution. Earlier the settlers in the New England communities had believed that successes in their daily actions could be taken by them as evidence of their spiritual worth. This "visible sainthood" was leading to an aristocracy of the materially successful, and Stoddard believed that it was necessary for a person to look more deeply into oneself for evidence of one's spiritual worth. To him, individual conscience and individual introspection were greater tests of spiritual worth than any outward forms of success.

Because of the attraction to Stoddard's dissent, he was invited to appear and speak at Harvard commencements. His first published sermon (actually his first published work, delivered in 1685 and printed in 1687) was *The Safety of Appearing at the Day of Judgment, in the Righteousness of Christ....* Stoddard tried to get Increase Mather and Samuel Willard to write introductions to the publication, but they refused; the battlelines had been drawn. His sermon was a manifesto of dissent against the established theology of the colony, but more than that it was an affirmation of emotions over intellect, revelation over reason, in the conversion process. Perry Miller calls this work "one of the bridges by which New England passed from the seventeenth to the eighteenth century." What bridges the two eras is Stoddard's insistence that the whole person, with all his senses, intellect, and physical energy, be involved in the work of spiritual apprehension. Religion—whether at the point of conversion or at the point of taking the sacrament of the Lord's Supper—should involve one totally. This point of view, for the first time in American thought, made the spiritual aesthetic, for it demanded the involvement of the senses in all religious acts. To Stoddard it was "safe to appear" in church to take the sacrament if whole, if wholly stirred, if wholly involved.

Stoddard's first published work caused a large commotion. The hoped-for peace in the settlement of New England had been broken as never before. "Our neglect" of open conversion and communion, Stoddard wrote to fellow minister Edward Taylor in justification, "is the occasion of the great profaneness and corruption that hath overspread the land.... It [is] a frown on the land." Taylor replied: "We can date the beginnings of New England's apostacy in Mr. Stoddard's motions." According to an apocryphal story, several towns held meetings "to pray the devil out of Solomon Stoddard." And in 1670, so deep was the concern, the Mathers, who were his in-laws but also his antagonists in the developing drama, organized the Cambridge Association in an attempt to form a united front against "Stoddardeanism," by then spreading throughout the Connecticut Valley and indeed the entire colony. "Indeed," wrote Cotton Mather in alarm, "this dogma is a new thing; the assertions run counter to the common sense of the church in all ages and have an army to man against them."

Stoddard's *Sermon on Paul's Epistle to the Galatians*, delivered in 1690, was the third of his initial attempts to justify his revolutionary ideas and practices. Although not published at the time, it was a bold move that became widely known. At last Stoddard was completely open about his proposal that the Lord's Supper be instituted as a converting ordinance. Ecclesiastical purity held participation in the Lord's Supper as a seal on conversion, but with Stoddard all the respectable adults in a town would be given a common religious and social footing and not merely those approved by a minister and other elders of a congregation. The Mathers and their devotees in the east (the Boston area) and Edward Taylor and his like in the west (the Connecticut Valley) were furious at Stoddard's boldness on the issue. Taylor wrote hundreds of poems and sermons while the Mathers produced a good score monographs against him as a result.

In a work of 1696, *The Tryal of Assurance...*, Stoddard summarized his revolution of two decades: the inner spirit is not the object of rational inspection by others and therefore must be left to the feelings of the individual. "Don't let grace be in an arbitrary condition," he wrote; "let it flourish." Many who opposed the orthodoxy of the Mathers responded (perhaps politically, perhaps theologically) to Stoddard's position. Cotton Mather called it "an ill party thro' all the country" that would "throw all into confusion," but by the end of the century the momentum of Stoddard's position could not be stopped.

Although Stoddard was to write several other books in the next two decades spelling out his new sacramentalism further, most notably in *The Inexcusableness of Neglecting the Worship of God, Under a Pretence of Being in an Unconverted Condition...* (1708) and his *A Treatise Concerning the Nature of Saving Conversion...* (1719), after the turn of the century he by and large turned in his sermons and publications to other matters—

evangelicalism and a national church. Largely because he had succeeded so well in arguing against tests of conversion and in moving matters of grace over to matters of personal faith, he succeeded also in these new matters. His following had become so large that he was dubbed Pope of the Connecticut Valley. Cotton Mather said of him: "For one minister alone envisioning him[self] wielding a mitre in his western see . . . is to make himself a congregational pope."

Once while Stoddard was riding from Northampton to Hatfield, his party was ambushed by Indians. A Frenchman with the group took aim at Stoddard but was prevented from shooting him by an Indian who had lived among the English. He said: "That man [is] the Englishman's God."

Stoddard intensified the intracolonial war that he—and others, from the Brattle Street Church group of ministers in Boston and Cambridge to the Connecticut Valley group of rebel ministers—had brought about when he wrote and published *The Doctine of Instituted Churches* . . . (1700), which rejected strict congregationalism in favor of a new order of society, a national church. In both England and New England, the Puritans had encouraged each individual congregation of believers to elect its own minister, name its own officers, deliberate themselves upon sacraments and doctrines, and pass upon their membership themselves. But Stoddard, perhaps foreseeing the emergence of an American nation, argued for a greater unity of purpose and practice throughout all the Protestant colonies in America. It was a bold and heretical position. For Stoddard, Christian tradition provided no adequate congregational models, and he felt that change was necessary with the passage of time. In place of a congregational covenant, Stoddard argued for a national covenant, the binding of all believers together into an America of spirit. (His America of the time meant counties or associations of towns of like mind.) This move would free individuals of local conversion requirements (and therefore encourage more individuality of practice) and would create an itinerant ministry for the American frontier, but it implied and demanded as well severe prescription (for the sake of national unity) of such matters as prayer, music, preaching, baptism, communion, and ecclesiastical conduct. Personal experience, to Stoddard, was the only basis of doctrine, and yet strict doctrinal Calvinism was the way to bring individual believers into a national church. Stoddard never completely resolved this contradiction in his thinking.

The effectiveness of Stoddard's work moved the

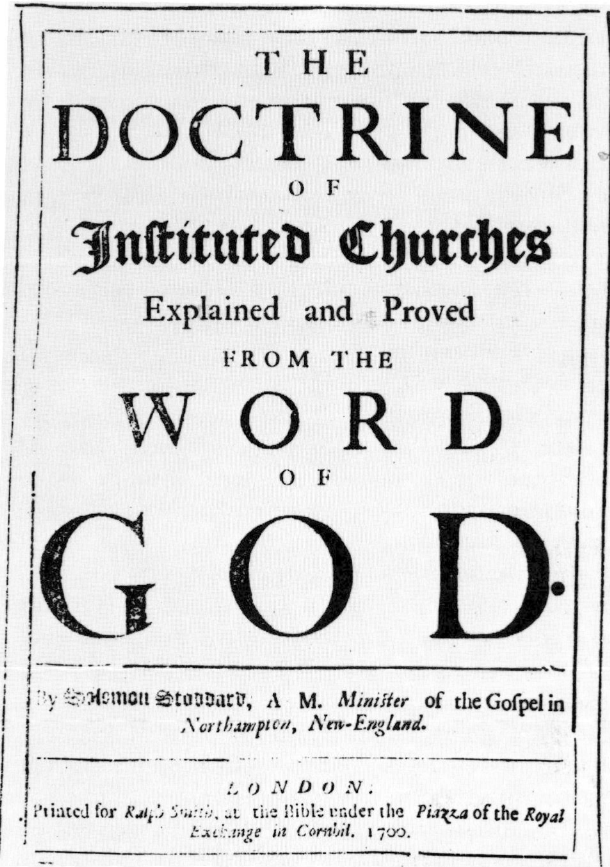
THE
DOCTRINE
OF
Instituted Churches
Explained and Proved
FROM THE
WORD
OF
GOD.

By Solomon Stoddard, A M. *Minister* of the Gofpel in *Northampton, New-England.*

LONDON:
Printed for *Ralph Smith*, at the Bible under the *Piazza* of the *Royal Exchange in Cornhil.* 1700.

Title page for Stoddard's call for the rejection of strict congregationalism in favor of a unified church. By centralizing the power then held by individual congregations, Stoddard hoped to bind all believers together into an America of spirit (John Carter Brown Library, Brown University).

Mathers and their cohorts in the pulpit in the east to even further anxiety, and in the next few years they wrote a number of books to try to stop the phenomenal Stoddard momentum, most notably Increase Mather's *The Order of the Gospel* (1700) and Cotton Mather's *Magnalia Christi Americana* (1702). When Stoddard preached his *The Necessity of Acknowledgment, of Offenses,* his annual sermon in Boston in 1701, he pointed to them and to other colonial leaders, ecclesiastical and civic, as the cause of disbelief in America. "The sins of the rulers make the land guilty." The work is remarkable for its audacious irreverence toward colonial authority but more so for holding America as a single covenanted nation of believers and for asserting that a ministry with effective evangelical language and emotion could bring that nation to a unity the other leaders could not create. Some historians feel that

Stoddard's sermon played a part in deposing Increase Mather from the presidency of Harvard, in promoting the founding of Yale University, and in shifting authority away from the theologians and colonial councils to the nationalist, evangelizing ministers like himself.

Stoddard had written these six works—each of them in the form of a manifesto—by the time he was sixty, but he was to write for another twenty-five years, refining the ideas of converting and conversion, communion and community, Millennium and nation that were being instituted gradually in New England. His works of these later years, mainly sermons by a notorious prophet written for special colonial occasions, became increasingly reactionary to the growing materialism and moralism of the period (*God's Frown in the Death of Usefull Men . . .*, 1703), increasingly reactionary to intellectuality (*The Way for a People to Live Long in the Land . . .*, 1703), and increasingly reactionary to the attitudes toward New England history and goals in the newer generation (*The Danger of Speedy Degeneracy . . .*, 1705).

What emerged mainly in Stoddard's sixties was an increased emphasis on evangelical preaching. He felt that the open communion and the secured community of believers that he had preached and written about for decades had not produced the regenerate New England he had hoped. His hope, as he expressed it in two important works, *The Inexcusableness of Neglecting the Worship of God...* (1708) and *The Falseness of Hopes of Many Professors . . .* (1708), now lay in ministerial appeal to the emotions in order to win the acceptance of the will and excite the religious affections of the new generations of Americans, especially in the frontier settlements: "As heaven needs an almighty power for the resurrection of bodies, so also for the resurrection of the churches." This statement was an admission of Stoddard's failure in the past but also proof of his inventiveness to meet frontier needs; he would do whatever necessary to make of America a lively believing people.

Again the Mathers objected, and Stoddard replied with one of the most important works of his later years, *An Appeal to the Learned . . .* (1709). It was at one and the same time a refutation of the Mathers' restrictiveness, a summary of Stoddard's preaching and writing up to that point, and a proposal of a solution in working regeneration through effectual language. The work was polemical in form and provincial in tone but nonetheless indicative of Stoddard's desperate need of the evangelized word, more than sacraments or church organization, to create and hold the believer. Only the word could make a Great Awakening.

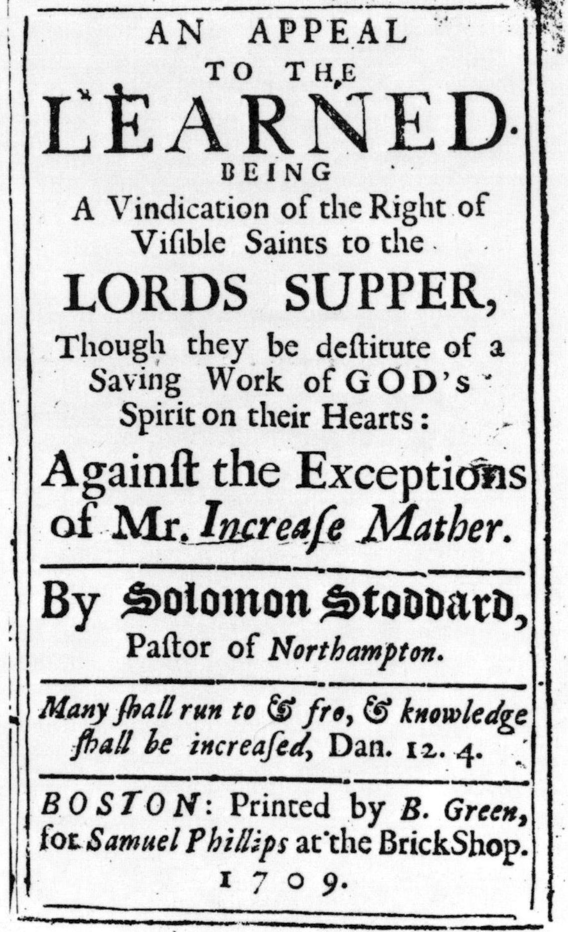
AN APPEAL
TO THE
LEARNED.
BEING
A Vindication of the Right of
Vifible Saints to the
LORDS SUPPER,
Though they be deftitute of a
Saving Work of GOD's
Spirit on their Hearts:
Againft the Exceptions
of Mr. *Increafe Mather.*

By Solomon Stoddard,
Paftor of *Northampton.*

Many fhall run to & fro, & knowledge fhall be increafed, Dan. 12. 4.

BOSTON: Printed by *B. Green,*
for *Samuel Phillips* at the BrickShop.
1709.

Title page for one of Stoddard's most important later works, which emphasizes the need for effective evangelical preaching to bring about regeneration (John Carter Brown Library, Brown University)

The Stoddard-Mather war of words of thirty years gave each side territory with the Mathers to the east but with their supremacy undercut severely by Stoddard's arguments; and with Stoddard and his supporters, an inbred network of close friends and relatives, to the west but with the emphasis shifting from sacraments and organization to organized evangelizing. By 1712 Stoddard was the first consistently evangelical American preacher, as indicated by a sermon of 1712, *Those Taught by God . . .*, and by a sequence of sermons in 1713, *The Efficacy of the Fear of Hell. . . .* In his later years the geopolitical battles of the past mattered less to him than the promotion of the means by which future generations might be effectually awakened. The light in hell fire, a "backward" looking at one's sins, a watch upon Christ in one's good feelings, one's whole being bestirred—these were Stoddard's subjects: "Zeal will inflame the heart. . . . When men are sensible to the breaking out of fire, . . . they will cry out earnestly. Men need to be frightened and not to be pleased." Awakenings followed, and Stoddard was again effective in Northampton and, through his large following among fellow ministers, on much of the rest of the colonial frontier.

Stoddard went even further in his sermon series *A Guide to Christ* . . . (1714) and proposed total submission of one's emotions to a mystical Christ. These sermons responded to the rationalist theologians of the time and promoted the evangelizers in the Stoddard mold. Perhaps these sermons and those continuing on up to 1720 are the work of an old man, for they are desperate in their promotion of direct enthusiasm, in their call for submissiveness, and in their finding a place for aesthetics in religious affections. God is less in power than in emotions, aesthetics, beauty.

All of Stoddard's final emphases were to find a place in the thinking of his grandson Jonathan Edwards, who replaced Stoddard at Northampton; in the thinking of several of the New Light ministers; and in some of the activities of the emerging Great Awakening. Yet most of Stoddard's writings in the last decade of his life were bound to a time and place. He was consistently a writer for occasions, as seen especially in his *An Answer to Some Cases of Conscience* . . . (1722), where he addressed economic and political problems of the Connecticut Valley and the colony. His approach was the same in all his later works: rulers need to be righteous, ministers need to be effective with the word, all Americans need to yield to Christ with their emotions, their whole beings—that is, a regenerate leadership making a regenerate nation.

When Stoddard died at eighty-six in 1729, all New England congregations had opened communion to regenerate and unregenerate alike—Stoddard's first mission. Most areas of New England were moving toward "national" organizations of congregations like the association Stoddard had formed in Hampshire County—his second mission. And the awakenings of three generations in a number of communities were converging gradually toward a Great Awakening—Stoddard's final mission. In 1740 when George Whitefield toured the colonies at the height of the Great Awakening, he said he felt he had just traveled through "the land of the great Stoddard."

Stoddard accomplished these things by becoming a writer—first as apologist for his revolutionary practices in his own congregation in Northampton; then in an increasingly aggressive literary war with ecclesiastical opponents, especially the intractable Mathers; and finally speaking out on colonial matters in sermons on key occasions in the interest of a regenerate America. He was a writer of necessity and as such indigenous to affairs American. He found, of necessity, effective language for his purposes—at first a language of equivocation as he sought to justify his changes in the New England Way; then a language of fresh usage and frontier invention as he championed the Connecticut Valley Way; and finally a language of the senses as he discovered the convergence of religion and aesthetics. "Stoddardeanism" has therefore become one of the great phases of early American thought and history.

Other:

Sermon on Paul's Epistle to the Galatians, in *Resources for American Literary Study*, 4 (1974): 205-224;

"Nine Arguments Against Examinations Concerning a Work of Grace," in *American Antiquarian Society Proceedings*, 86 (1976): 75-111.

References:

Ralph J. Coffman, *Solomon Stoddard* (Boston: Twayne, 1978);

James Goulding, "The Controversy between Solomon Stoddard and the Mathers: Western Versus Eastern Massachusetts Congregationalism," Ph.D. dissertation, Claremont Men's College, 1971;

David D. Hall, *The Faithful Shepherd: A History of the New England Ministry in the Seventeenth Century* (Chapel Hill: University of North Carolina Press, 1972);

E. Brooks Holifield, *The Covenant Sealed: The Development of Puritan Sacramental Theology in Old and New England, 1570-1720* (New Haven: Yale University Press, 1974);

James W. Jones, *The Shattered Synthesis: New England Puritanism before the Great Awakening* (New Haven: Yale University Press, 1973);

Karl Keller, "The Loose, Large Principles of Solomon Stoddard," *Early American Literature*, 16 (Spring 1981): 27-41;

Paul R. Lucas, "Valley of Discord: The Struggle for Power in the Puritan Churches of the Connecticut Valley, 1636-1720," Ph.D. dissertation, University of Minnesota, 1970;

Perry Miller, "Solomon Stoddard, 1643-1729,"

Harvard Theological Review, 34 (October 1941): 277-320;

Thomas A. Schafer, "Solomon Stoddard and the Theology of the Revival," in *A Miscellany of American Christianity: Essays in Honor of H. Shelton Smith*, edited by Stuart Clark Henry (Durham: Duke University Press, 1963), pp. 328-361;

Robert Lee Stuart, "The Table and the Desk: Conversion in the Writings Published by Solomon Stoddard and Jonathan Edwards during Their Northampton Ministries, 1682-1751," Ph.D. dissertation, Stanford University, 1970;

Harry G. Swanhart, "Solomon Stoddard: Puritan Patriarch. A Biography," Ph.D. dissertation, University of Michigan, 1961;

James Walsh, "Solomon Stoddard's Open Communion: A Reexamination," *New England Quarterly*, 43 (March 1970): 97-114;

Eugene E. White, "Solomon Stoddard's Theories of Persuasion," *Speech Monographs*, 29 (November 1952): 235-259;

William Williams, *The Death of a Prophet Lamented and Improved* (Boston: Printed by B. Green for D. Henchman, 1729).

Papers:

Stoddard's papers are scattered among the Boston Public Library; the Massachusetts Historical Society; the Forbes Library in Northampton, Massachusetts; the American Antiquarian Society; The New York Historical Society; the Baker Memorial Library at Dartmouth College; the Dawes Memorial Library at Marietta College; and the Historical Society of Pennsylvania.

Samuel Stone

(July 1602-20 July 1663)

Georgia Elliott
Princeton University

BOOK: *A Congregational Church is a Catholike Visible Church. Or An Examination of M. Hudson his Vindication Concerning the Integrality of the Catholike Visible Church . . .* (London: Printed by Peter Cole, 1652).

Samuel Stone traveled with John Cotton and Thomas Hooker to Boston in 1633 and became one of the leading clergymen in early New England. He was born at Hertford, England, the son of John Stone, and educated at Emmanuel College, Cambridge. On 13 June 1627 he was appointed curate at Stisted, Essex, where he remained until 13 September 1630, when he was suspended for nonconformity and sought refuge in New England. Hooker persuaded Stone to join him as an associate in a church at Newtown (now Cambridge) in New England, where they presided together nearly three years. In 1636 both Hooker and Stone moved to establish a new church in Hartford, Connecticut, a town named after Stone's birthplace in England. According to John Winthrop's *History of New England* (1853), Stone also served as chaplain under John Mason in the war against the Pequots in 1637. After Hooker's death in 1647, Stone continued as pastor of the Hartford church until his death in 1663.

Known for his ready wit and pleasant personality, Stone nevertheless became involved in a bitter dispute with a ruling elder over doctrinal differences, mainly the Half-Way Covenant, which caused a split in the church membership in 1659. He published one poem, an elegy for Thomas Hooker which was prefixed to Hooker's *A Survey of the Summe of Church-Discipline . . .* (1648) and one sermon, *A Congregational Church is a Catholike Visible Church. Or an Examination of M. Hudson . . .* (1652). In addition, he left two unpublished manuscripts, "Confutation of the Antinomians" and "A Body of Divinity," the latter called "a rich treasure" by Cotton Mather.

Other:

"In obitum viri Doctissimi Thomae Hookeri," in *A Survey of the Summe of Church-Discipline . . .*, by Thomas Hooker (London: Printed by A. M. for John Bellamy, 1648).

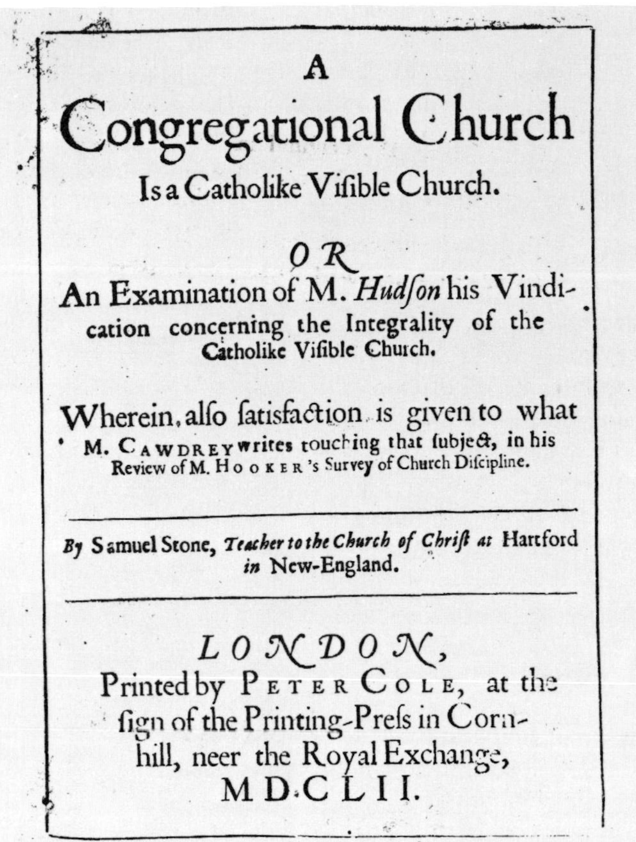
A

Congregational Church

Is a Catholike Visible Church.

OR

An Examination of M. *Hudson* his Vindication concerning the Integrality of the Catholike Visible Church.

Wherein, also satisfaction is given to what M. CAWDREY writes touching that subject, in his Review of M. HOOKER'S Survey of Church Discipline.

By Samuel Stone, *Teacher to the Church of Christ at* Hartford *in* New-England.

LONDON,

Printed by PETER COLE, at the sign of the Printing-Press in Cornhill, neer the Royal Exchange, MDCLII.

Title page for Stone's only published sermon (John Carter Brown Library, Brown University)

References:

Harold Jantz, *The First Century of New England Verse* (Worcester, Mass.: American Antiquarian Society, 1944);

William DeLoss Love, *The Colonial History of Hartford* (Hartford, Conn.: Published by the author, 1914);

Cotton Mather, *Magnalia Christi Americana* (London: Printed for Thomas Parkhurst, 1702), III: 62, 116-118;

George Leon Walker, *History of the First Church in Hartford* (Hartford, Conn.: Brown & Gross, 1884);

Alexander Young, *Chronicles of the First Planters of the Colony of Massachusetts Bay, from 1623 to 1636* (Boston: Little & Brown, 1846).

William Stoughton

(1631-7 July 1701)

Wesley T. Mott
University of Wisconsin

BOOKS: *New-Englands True Interest; Not to Lie: Or, A Treatise declaring from the Word of Truth the Terms on which we stand, and the Tenure by which we hold our hitherto-continued Precious and Pleasant Things . . .* (Cambridge: Printed by S. Green & M. Johnson, 1670);

A Narrative of the Proceedings of Sir Edmond Androsse and His Complices, Who Acted by an Illegal and Arbitrary Commission from the Late K. James, During his Government in New England. By Several Gentlemen who Were of his Council, attributed to Stoughton (Boston?, 1691);

The Address Of the Honorable the Lieutenant Governour Stoughton, In the Name of Himself and of His Majesties Council of the Province of the Massachusetts-Bay, unto His Excellency the Earl of Bellomont . . . (Boston: Printed by Bartholomew Green & John Allen, 1699).

(Boston Athenaeum)

William Stoughton.

William Stoughton, minister, political leader, and author of an important jeremiad, is best known as the remorseless judge of the Salem witch trials. Born probably in England, the son of Israel Stoughton, a founder of Dorchester, Massachusetts, Stoughton graduated from Harvard College (1650), where he studied divinity. He then went to England, where he received his M.A. at New College, Oxford (1653), and preached in Sussex. At the Restoration he was one of hundreds who refused to conform to standards imposed on the clergy as a prerequisite for their being sanctioned by the Church of England. Ejected from his fellowship as a result, he returned to New England in 1662 and preached at Dorchester.

Invited to give the election sermon on 29 April 1668 (*New-Englands True Interest; Not to Lie . . .*, 1670), Stoughton took the occasion to remind his audience of the "*Foundation-work*" needed to live up to God's "Expectations" for New England. Stressing God's "loving kindness and tender mercies" and "*our Advantages and Priviledges* in a Covenant-state," Stoughton chastised his contemporaries for falling short of the learning, virtue, and "Zeal" of the first generation. In one of the most famous sentences in any seventeenth-century jeremiad, he reminded New England that "God sifted a whole Nation that he might send choice Grain over into this Wilderness." Though the sermon has usually been cited for its gloomy depiction of the new generation's backsliding, scholars who have reassessed the nature of the "American jeremiad" now see in it an underlying optimism, a sense of the inevitable success of New England's "*solemn divine Probation.*"

Stoughton declined offers to become permanent

minister at Dorchester and Cambridge, turning his talents for the remainder of his life to politics. He served as selectman at Dorchester (1671-1674); as assistant or member of the upper house in the General Court, the chief governing, judicial, and legislative body of Massachusetts (1671-1677, 1680-1686); and as commissioner for the United Colonies of New England, a confederation of the Massachusetts Bay, Plymouth, Connecticut, and New Haven colonies formed for mutual cooperation and defense against the Indians and foreign threats (1674-1676, 1680-1686). He was sent to England in 1676 with Peter Bulkeley to defend the Bay Colony against charges that it had overstepped its charter. But when the agents returned in 1679, there was some sentiment that they had given up too much of the colony's autonomy, and Stoughton refused a subsequent appointment as agent to defend the charter before Charles II. The Massachusetts charter was voided by the Court of Chancery on 23 October 1684, and the General Court was dissolved. But Stoughton, who had carefully avoided offending the Crown during the charter crisis, was appointed deputy president of the new Council for New England under a commission received from King James II in May 1686; and on 26 July he was also named by Council President Joseph Dudley to head the courts. After Sir Edmund Andros arrived on 20 December with a royal commission as governor under yet another reorganization, Dudley was named chief justice, Stoughton judge assistant (3 March 1687). As a member of Andros's council until the hated governor was ousted in April 1689, Stoughton lost popularity. But he was an adaptable politician who quickly dissociated himself from the Andros regime; *A Narrative of the Proceedings of Sir Edmond Androsse . . .* (1691), a pamphlet critical of Andros, has been attributed to Stoughton. And when the charter was restored under William and Mary, the resilient Stoughton, through Increase Mather's intervention, received a royal commission as lieutenant-governor (14 May 1692), a post he held until his death.

By the time he was named lieutenant-governor the witchcraft hysteria was erupting in Massachusetts, and in the spring of 1692 Stoughton was named chief justice of the tribunal convened to deal with the matter. More responsible than any man for the atrocities committed by the court, Stoughton dispensed justice with incredible sternness. Indeed, when Governor Phips, increasingly alarmed at Stoughton's excessive zeal, reprieved eight of the condemned in January 1693, Stoughton angrily left the court. Unlike Samuel Sewall, Stoughton never publicly repented for his role in the witch trials. Remarkably, his contemporary reputation suffered little. Though lieutenant-governor, he served also as chief justice of Massachusetts from 22 December 1692 until shortly before his death, and when Phips went to England in 1694, Stoughton became acting governor, serving in that capacity for all but a year's interval until his death nearly seven years later.

A bachelor, Stoughton left much of his estate to the church, the poor, and the Dorchester schools. He was the greatest benefactor of Harvard College in the seventeenth century, having built Stoughton College in 1698-1699; though the structure was torn down in 1781, Stoughton Hall was erected on a different spot in 1805. Remembered today as a hanging judge, Stoughton died a widely respected, if opportunistic, colonial leader.

Other:

Cotton Mather, *The Wonders of the Invisible World . . .*, foreword by Stoughton (Boston: Printed by Benj. Harris for Sam. Phillips, 1693).

References:

Sacvan Bercovitch, *The American Jeremiad* (Madison: University of Wisconsin Press, 1978), pp. 59, 89, 173;

John W. Dean, "William Stoughton, Lieutenant-Governor of Massachusetts," *New-England Historical and Genealogical Register*, 50 (January 1896): 9-12;

Emory Elliott, *Power and the Pulpit in Puritan New England* (Princeton: Princeton University Press, 1975), pp. 91, 100-103;

David D. Hall, *The Faithful Shepherd: A History of the New England Ministry in the Seventeenth Century* (Chapel Hill: University of North Carolina Press, 1972), pp. 176, 182, 185;

Perry Miller, *The New England Mind: From Colony to Province* (Cambridge: Harvard University Press, 1953);

Samuel Eliot Morison, *Harvard College in the Seventeenth Century*, 2 volumes (Cambridge: Harvard University Press, 1936);

John Langdon Sibley, *Biographical Sketches of Graduates of Harvard University*, volume 1 (Cambridge: Charles William Sever, 1873), pp. 194-208.

Edward Taylor

Donald E. Stanford
Louisiana State University

BIRTH: Sketchley, Leicestershire, England, circa 1642, to William and Margaret Taylor.

EDUCATION: B.A., Harvard, 1671.

MARRIAGES: 5 November 1674 to Elizabeth Fitch; children: Samuel, Elizabeth, James, Abigail, Bathsheba, Elizabeth, Mary, Hezekiah. 6 June 1692 to Ruth Wyllys; children: Ruth, Naomi, Anna, Mehitabel, Keziah, Eldad.

DEATH: Westfield, Massachusetts, 24 June 1729.

SELECTED BOOKS: *The Poetical Works of Edward Taylor,* edited by Thomas H. Johnson (New York: Rockland Editions, 1939);

The Poems of Edward Taylor, edited by Donald E. Stanford (New Haven: Yale University Press, 1960; abridged, 1963);

Edward Taylor's Christographia, edited by Norman S. Grabo (New Haven & London: Yale University Press, 1962);

A Transcript of Edward Taylor's Metrical History of Christianity, edited by Stanford (Cleveland: Micro Photo, 1962; Ann Arbor: Books on Demand / University Microfilms International, 1977);

The Diary of Edward Taylor, edited by Francis Murphy (Springfield, Mass.: Connecticut Valley Historical Museum, 1964);

Edward Taylor's Treatise Concerning the Lord's Supper, edited by Grabo (East Lansing: Michigan State University Press, 1966);

The Unpublished Writings of Edward Taylor: volume 1, *Edward Taylor's "Church Records" and Related Sermons*; volume 2, *Edward Taylor vs. Solomon Stoddard: The Nature of the Lord's Supper*; volume 3, *Edward Taylor's Minor Poetry,* edited by Thomas M. and Virginia L. Davis (Boston: Twayne, 1981).

Edward Taylor, American Puritan poet and minister of the Congregational church at Westfield, Massachusetts, for over fifty years, is now considered the most important poet to appear in America in the seventeenth and eighteenth centuries. His fame is the result of two works, the *Preparatory Meditations . . .* (written 1682-1725) and *Gods Determinations touching his Elect . . .* (written 1682?), but he also wrote many other poems during his long life, and he was an indefatigable preacher. Over sixty of his sermons are extant as well as a long treatise, *The Harmony of the Gospels.* With the exception of two stanzas of verse, his works were unpublished in his lifetime. It remained for the twentieth century to discover his worth.

The year and place of Taylor's birth have not been established with certainty, but the most convincing evidence indicates that he was born in 1642 in the hamlet of Sketchley, Leicestershire, England. His mother, Margaret, died in 1657, his father, William, a yeoman farmer, in 1658. The civil war was raging in Leicestershire during his infancy, but by 1650 the future poet was enjoying the peace and stability of a prosperous midland farm. His poetry is replete with imagery drawn from the farm and from the countrysides of both Old and New England. The Leicestershire dialect occasionally appears in his colloquial verses, as do words drawn from the weaver's trade (in which he may have been employed at nearby Hinckley).

He was educated by a nonconformist schoolmaster, and he himself taught school for a short time at Bagworth. There is a tradition that he was a student at the University of Cambridge, but no evidence has been found to substantiate this claim. His firm religious convictions as a Protestant dissenter, formed in childhood and strengthened in the favorable atmosphere of Cromwell's regime, were severely tested during the first years of the Restoration. He refused to sign the Act of Uniformity of 1662 and was therefore prevented from teaching school and from worshiping in peace. On 26 April 1668, he sailed from Execution Dock, Wapping, bound for the Massachusetts Bay Colony.

His earliest verses, written in England, exhibit his lifelong love of the Protestant cause and his anti-Anglican and anti-Roman position. In "A Dialogue between the writer and a Maypole Dresser" the young poet berates the maypole dancers for worshiping the Roman harlot Flora when they "sacrificed a slaughtered tree to her." In "Another answer wherein is recited everie verse of the Pamphlet and answered particularly by E.T.," his answer to a papist pamphlet distributed in London in 1666 after the Great Fire, Taylor indulged in the coarse invective of Restoration satire to rebut the Catholic charge that Protestant heretics were responsible for the fire. He attacked the Church of Rome with the same kind of invective in the long poem written toward the end of his life, *The Metrical History of Christianity*. The most eloquent of his early poems, "The Lay-mans Lamentation," praises the zeal of the dissenting preachers silenced by the Act of Uniformity, which finally drove Taylor himself to the Bay Colony. In "A Letter sent to his Brother Joseph Taylor and his wife after a visit" Taylor exhibited his early interest in acrostic verse, a form in which he continued to write in Massachusetts. The names of himself, his brother, and his brother's wife appear in the initial and final letters of each line.

The hardships of Taylor's crossing of the Atlantic during the seventy days in which his ship was slowed by calms and buffeted by contrary winds are described in his diary, which also includes perceptive observations of natural phenomena, and of birds and fish, anticipating the imagery of his later poetry. On 5 July 1668, Taylor disembarked at Boston, and, after a visit with Charles Chauncy, president of Harvard, he entered Harvard College on 23 July as an upperclassman. He was the college butler in charge of kitchen utensils and responsible for collecting payment for food and drink consumed from the buttery—a position usually given a mature upperclassman. Taylor's life at Harvard for the next three years was busy and rigorous with recitations, disputations, and lectures carried on in Latin; with studies in Greek, Hebrew, logic, metaphysics, rhetoric, and astronomy; and with daily morning and evening prayers.

He provoked some gossip from his enemies because of his attentions to the wife of Goodman Steadman, so much so that if President Chauncy had not intervened on his behalf, he perhaps would not have received his degree from Harvard, and he had some trouble with his tutor, who had commanded Taylor to ascertain which students were imprisoning him in his room by fastening a nail above the door catch. Taylor failed to do so and was rebuked. These difficulties may have had some influence on his decision to leave Cambridge a few months after his graduation to take a church in Westfield, Massachusetts.

During his student years, Taylor continued to write poetry, including elegies on Zecharia Symmes, Francis Willoughby, and John Allen—all members of the Board of Overseers of Harvard College who died when Taylor was in residence at Harvard. Also extant is a fragment of an elegy which may be on the famous Richard Mather, founder of the Mather dynasty, who died in 1669. An elegy on Charles Chauncy, who died in 1672, was written during Taylor's first year at Westfield. All of these verses are similar in style, displaying more wordplay and wit than genuine feeling. The poem to Willoughby is acrostic, and the verses to Chauncy are an elaborate double acrostic. They are an interesting historical addition to the corpus of seventeenth-century funeral verse but are of little literary value. Taylor's later elegies to his wife and to Samuel Hooker are much more successful exercises in the genre.

It was customary for Harvard students to deliver declamations periodically. Taylor's "My last Declamation in the Colledge Hall," delivered 5 May 1671, defends in verse the value of the English language against the alleged superiority of the three ancient languages—Hebrew, Greek, and Latin—each of which (as Taylor explains in the complete title of his poem) was praised by other students in the language defended. We do not have the poems (or the prose) in Hebrew, Greek, and Latin to compare with Taylor's verses and to ascertain who won the argument, but the fact that such a debate was held at all gives an interesting sidelight on the state of learning among Harvard undergraduates of the seventeenth century. Taylor's effort cannot be called a literary success, but it is a stunning exercise in verbal wit in the course of which a dozen different figures of speech or other rhetorical devices are mentioned.

After graduating with his class from Harvard in 1671, Taylor was faced with the necessity of choosing a vocation. He decided to become a resident scholar at Harvard, and on 16 November he was, according to his diary, "instituted . . . scholar of the house." However, a few days later he was persuaded to undertake the hazardous journey of a hundred miles through deep snowdrifts in the dead of winter to Westfield to become minister to that small farming community in the Bay Colony. He remained in Westfield for the rest of his life, with only occasional visits to Boston and other New England towns.

By 1673 Taylor had a parsonage and a new, small meeting house, thirty-six feet square with a pyramidal roof and turret, built to serve also as a fort during the Indian troubles. The worshipers were summoned to meeting by the roll of a drum. By the summer of 1674 Taylor had fallen in love with Elizabeth Fitch of Norwich. On 8 September he sent her a love letter written in the florid rhetoric of the period, and the next month he composed for her an elaborate acrostic love poem. They were married 5 November 1674 and had eight children, five of whom died in infancy.

A war with the Indians, known as King Philip's War, began in June 1675 and was waged with savage ferocity on both sides. In the spring of 1676 the citizens of Westfield were asked to consider removal to the larger town of Springfield for their protection, but Taylor refused the invitation, a correct decision, for Westfield escaped serious damage. During these troubled times Taylor apparently composed little or no verse. The Indian chief King Philip was killed in August 1676, and with the coming of peace Taylor was finally able to organize his church. At his ceremony of ordination on 27 August 1679, Taylor preached his first extant sermon: *A Particular Church is Gods House,* in which he demonstrates with his customary Calvinistic rigidity that the members of this "Particular Church" at Westfield are among God's chosen people, the elect, as distinct from the damned; for all people, he said, are "either in a State of Wrath, or a State of Favourits."

Taylor now resumed his poetic activity. By about 1682 (the date is conjectural) he was composing his major poem *Gods Determinations touching his Elect: and The Elects Combat in their Conversion, and Coming up to God in Christ together with the Comfortable Effects thereof.* The long title (typical of the period) indicates the subject and movement of the poem—the various ways of God in converting the predestined elect to Christianity (specifically to orthodox Congregationalism) and the spiritual joys of saving grace once the Christian has ascertained the effects of grace in his soul. The poem is somewhat polemical in tone, suggesting that Taylor may have intended to publish it and distribute it to the citizens of Westfield for the purpose of convincing some of the more recalcitrant members of the community to accept saving grace and to enter into full communion with the church. There are a number of passages which are written to convince the reader that past sins are not certain signs of damnation and that excessive doubts as to a person's worthiness to accept full membership in the church are the devil's work. The poem was not published in Taylor's lifetime, but passages may have been read to his congregation during Sunday morning worship or at evening prayer meetings.

In justifying the ways of God to the elect and in exposing the machinations of the devil, Taylor had a number of previous works—such as John Milton's *Paradise Lost* (1667), John Bunyan's *The Holy War* (1682), Michael Wigglesworth's *The Day of Doom* (1662), and Lorenzo Scupoli's *The Spiritual Conflict* (translated from the Italian in 1613)—which could have served as models for his own poem of spiritual combat. As in Milton's poem, Taylor depicts spiritual combat, and he attempts to explain God's ways of bringing sinners to heaven, but his religious thinking differs from Milton's (Milton was not a Calvinist), and Taylor's homely, colloquial style is quite different from the sonorous and sophisticated blank verse of *Paradise Lost.* Taylor's poem is closer to Bunyan's prose work *The Holy War.* Both works are Calvinistic, and both describe in allegorical terms the combat between the soul and Satan. In *The Day of Doom* Wigglesworth expresses Calvinistic ideas identical to those of Taylor, but his verse, written in awkward fourteeners, is far inferior to Taylor's, and he displays considerably more zest in dwelling on divine wrath and the tortures of the damned in hell than does Taylor, who prefers to emphasize the "comfortable effects" of God's grace to the saved in heaven. Scupoli's *Spiritual Conflict* emphasizes the necessity of overcoming the passions in cleansing the soul from sin, and the same notion is to be found in *Gods Determinations touching his Elect . . . ,* but it is not the central theme of the poem. A possible source for the psychological aspects of Taylor's poem, and one much closer to home, is William Ames's *Conscience with the Power and Cases thereof* (1639), a copy of which (in Latin) was in Taylor's library. Ames's psychological profile of the devil as one who tempts men to damnation by convincing them they are not of the elect is similar to Taylor's concept of Satan. Sermons and tracts depicting what John Downame called *Christian Warfare* (1633), that is the clash between personified virtues and vices, were numerous in Taylor's day, and, despite what some scholars have suggested, they probably had more influence on the poem than did the morality plays or the Elizabethan drama.

Gods Determinations touching his Elect . . . is a dramatization of Taylor's Calvinistic religious beliefs concerning predestination, creation, the nature of God, original sin, saving grace, redemption through faith in Christ, the division of mankind into the damned and the elect, and the joys of eternal salvation. There is some allegory, and the devil reminds us of the personified vices of the morality plays, but the poem is not an exercise in symbolism nor in Neoplatonism. Heaven and hell are depicted as real places. Christ, Satan, and the angels may sometimes take on the physical

Taylor's gravestone in Westfield, Massachusetts

attributes of real persons.

The poem opens with the creation of the physical universe. For Taylor God made the world out of nothing, and he can return it to nothing if he chooses. His cosmology was Ptolemaic and pre-Newtonic. That is, the earth is stationary, and the sun moves around it. "Who in this Bowling Alley bowld the Sun?," he asks in his preface. The answer, of course, is God. The poem proceeds with a depiction of original sin and its effect on man, who is now God's enemy. The two major attributes of God, Justice and Mercy, are personified, and they engage in a debate on the destiny of sinful man, Justice arguing for eternal punishment, Mercy for compassion. Mercy wins the debate for the elect. By becoming incarnate in Christ, he purchases redemption for the elect, who are seen at the end of the poem riding in God's coach up to heaven. The rest of mankind slip down into hell.

The major part of the poem depicts the various methods by which God, through Christ, brings salvation to the elect. Some, the saints, receive grace quickly and easily, but most of the elect, the Converts, come to Christ after varying degrees of difficulty. The struggle for their salvation is dramatically presented as a combat for the souls of the elect between Mercy and Justice on the one hand and the devil on the other. The converts are divided into three ranks—those who are captured by Mercy after a short struggle, those who are captured by Justice after a longer struggle, and those who are finally captured by Justice after a fierce and prolonged battle. The effect of sin on natural man and the combats for his redemption are graphically presented, often in a colloquial, down-to-earth style. Of disobedient man's terror of God's wrath Taylor writes:

> Then like a Child that fears the Poker Clapp
> Him on his face doth on his Mothers lap
> Doth hold his breath, lies still for fear least hee
> Should by his breathing lowd discover'd bee.

Satan, raging at those of the elect who deserted him for Christ, says that now they have two enemies—God and Satan—both of whom will never trust them: "You'l then have sharper service than the Whale, / Between the Sword fish, and the Threshers taile."

For the modern reader the most interesting part of the poem, perhaps, is to be found in what Taylor calls "Satans Sophestry," in the devil's psychological warfare against those who may wish to think of themselves as the elect. His temptations range from appeals to the baser passions to the attempt by subtle arguments to insinuate doubts in the soul's assurance of saving faith. One of his most insidious arguments is that, if a person has any doubts at all about the possibilities of his spiritual regeneration, then he is not one of the elect because God is supposed to give the elect assurance of saving faith. On the other hand, if a person believes he is assured of saving faith, then he (poor sinner that he is) is guilty of pride, the cardinal sin, and so damned. Another line of attack is to convince the sinner that his so-called love of God is really love of self (a sin) and that his real motivation is fear of hell and desire for the joys of heaven. A third method of attack is what Taylor calls the "ath'istick Hoodwinke"—that the attributes of the Christian God—his ubiquitousness and his incarnation in "a mortal clod"—are contrary to reason and to common sense and that in fact God does not exist. These arguments and many more were probably suggested to Taylor by such books as William Ames's *Conscience with the Power and Cases thereof*.

Some of the best poetry in *Gods Determinations*

touching his Elect . . . is in "Christ's Reply," in which he fortifies the elect against Satan's arguments and arouses their martial ardor to lead the good life. Christ begins:

I am a Captain to your Will,
You found me Gracious, so shall still,
Whilst that my Will is your Design.

and he concludes:

To him that smiteth, hip and thigh,
My foes as his: Walks warily,
I'le give him Grace: he'st give me praise.
Let him whose foot doth hit a Stone
Through weakeness, not rebellion
Not faint, but think on former dayes.

The final lines, in which the saints express their joy in the experience of salvation, are also moving:

In Heaven soaring up, I dropt an Eare
On Earth: and oh! sweet Melody:
And listening, found it was the Saints who were
Encoacht for Heaven that sang for Joy.
For in Christs Coach they sweetly sing;
As they to Glory ride therein.

Unlike Wigglesworth, Taylor, here and in the *Preparatory Meditations . . .*, is more effective when he is depicting the sweetness of God's grace than when he is describing the pains of hell.

Gods Determinations touching his Elect . . ., unlike Milton's *Paradise Lost*, is a "dated" poem, quite obviously of its period. It does not have the universal and permanent appeal of Milton's epic, nor can Taylor at any time equal the skill of Milton's blank verse. The poem is like an anthology of poems written in various meters and in various styles, sometimes colloquial, sometimes ornate, sometimes plain and direct, but it is given coherence and dramatic effectiveness by a single theme (the redemption of the elect) and a single narrative line (the rise of the elect from anguish and despair to the glories of heaven). It is the best long poem written in seventeenth-century America.

At about the same time he was writing *Gods Determinations touching his Elect . . .*, Taylor was also composing a series of occasional poems. Only one can be dated precisely—"Upon the Sweeping Flood Aug: 13. 14, 1683." This, the most powerful of the series, has been widely admired. (Joyce Carol Oates used its title as the title for a collection of her short stories.) The flood, which Taylor refers to in his church record, is given allegorical and religious significance: the storm and flood were sent by God to drown man's carnal love, for the sins of man have acted as a purge on the heavens. Allegorizing natural events, "occurants" as Taylor called them, was habitual among Puritan writers. Several other occasional poems are also allegorical. In the charming "Upon a Wasp Child with Cold," the frozen insect, as he is warmed by the sun, illustrates the action of God's grace on the human soul. In "Huswifery" the central image, the spinning wheel, represents one of God's elect (the poet), and the thread woven by the wheel will be woven by God into a web of glory for the saint in heaven. The spider in "Upon a Spider Catching a Fly" is the devil destroying sinful, natural man, and in "The Ebb and Flow" the tide suggests Taylor's rising and falling expectations of election. Allegory occurs also in Taylor's most moving occasional poem, two stanzas of which, published in Cotton Mather's *Right Thoughts in Sad Hours . . .* (1689), were the only lines by Taylor to appear in print during his lifetime. "Upon Wedlock and Death of Children," written in 1682 or 1683, refers to the deaths of two of his children and to his marriage to Elizabeth Fitch, which he calls a "True-Love Knot." The word *knot* has the seventeenth-century meaning of "garden" as well as the modern meaning. Because theirs is true love, the knot can never be untied; it is a Gordian knot. From this garden sprang four flowers, two of which grew to maturity, two of which died: "But oh! the tortures, Vomit, screechings, groans, / And six weeks Fever would pierce hearts like stones." But Taylor's grief is assuaged with the acceptance of God's will:

Lord, theyre thine.
I piecemeal pass to Glory bright in them.
I joy, may I sweet Flowers for Glory breed,
Whether thou getst them green, or lets them seed.

In 1682 Taylor embarked upon his greatest work, the major poetic achievement of Colonial America. *Preparatory Meditations before my approach to the Lords Supper* is a series of more than two-hundred poems grouped in two series written "Chiefly upon the Doctrin preached upon the Day of administration" from 1682 to 1725. Unpublished until the twentieth century, they are a private spiritual diary of great significance to our understanding of the religious and psychological history of the period. The poems are uneven in poetic merit and frequently repetitious in theme and diction, but a few of them deserve a place in any anthology of seventeenth- and early-eighteenth-century poetry, together with the poems of John Donne, George Herbert, and Richard Crashaw to which they bear resemblance. For they are written in the metaphysical and baroque style and may properly be considered the last exemplars of the metaphysical school.

In his imagery Taylor frequently made use of the metaphysical conceit of what Samuel Johnson called, in commenting on Donne, *discordia concors* "a combination of dissimilar images. . . . the most heterogenous ideas are yoked by violence together." But Taylor is sometimes even more fantastic than Donne. His imagery may be as extravagant as that of Crashaw or the now-forgotten poet John Cleveland, whom Taylor mentions in his poem on Pope Joan. Today we would call such yoking of images surrealistic, as in his famous line "Should Stars Wooe Lobster Claws." The strongest influence from the metaphysical school is George Herbert, an Anglican poet and preacher, widely respected by the American Puritans in spite of doctrinal differences and especially admired by Taylor, who was perhaps at his best when writing under Herbert's influence, as in meditation six of the first series, "Am I thy Gold?"

In his diction Taylor combined the colloquial with the cosmic (again like Donne), employing abstruse theological or philosophical terms with the homely idiom of the farm or the weaver's trade. The line "My tazzled Thoughts twirld into Snick-snarls run" illustrates his fondness for "domestic diction" and also the influence of the sixteenth-century rhetorician Petrus Ramus, the followers of whom eschewed the ornate style and, like Emerson later, preached that the poet should "fasten words to things." Taylor's frequent use of the plain style is Ramist. His occasional employment of the ornate style is derived from the King James version of the Bible, and especially from the Song of Solomon, which Taylor loved and which had a pervasive influence on his last meditations. Taylor also employed, sometimes to excess, the various rhetorical devices of the sixteenth- and seventeenth-century handbooks such as irony, synecdoche, metonymy, *meiosis* (diminishing), and amplification. He was especially fond of amplification, which combined with *ploce* (repetition of a word) and *polyptoton* (repetition of a word root) results in what Yvor Winters has called "a punning piety." In meditation 2.48 he writes with reference to the devil and the powers of darkness:

> Their Might's a little mite, Powers powerless fall.
> My Mite Almighty may not let down slide.
> I will not trust unto this Might of mine:
> Nor in my Mite distrust, while I am thine.

In the emblem tradition as it appears in the poetry of Francis Quarles (1592-1644), a poet the Puritans admired, a poem makes a moral, epigrammatic comment on a picture that illustrates a theological or philosophical idea. The tradition is also evident in Taylor's verse, most obviously "Upon a Spider Catching a Fly," where the spider in his web symbolizes the devil. Typology as used in biblical exegesis—an object, event, or person in the Old Testament (the type) foreshadows an object, event, or person in the New Testament (the Antitype)—is also pervasive, especially in the meditations of the second series. The Jewish Passover considered as a type of Christian Communion, or Lord's Supper as Taylor called it, is one of Taylor's favorite constructs.

Taylor's meditations are an important part of a long tradition of meditation writing in verse and prose, beginning, as far as verse is concerned, with Robert Southwell and continuing through John Donne, George Herbert, Richard Crashaw, Henry Vaughan, Andrew Marvell, Thomas Traherne, and, finally, Taylor. Richard Baxter's treatise, *The Saints Everlasting Rest* (1650), which had considerable influence on meditation writing in verse, advocated an orderly method of meditation involving the three faculties of the soul—memory, understanding, and will (the emotions) in that order. Louis Martz has shown in his introduction to Donald E. Stanford's edition of Taylor's poems that some of Taylor's *Preparatory Meditations* . . . are organized according to this tripartite division. Frequently the Puritan poet appears to be following another threefold pattern—despair as he contemplates the sins of mankind and his own personal sin, joy when he thinks of Christ's promise of redemption to the elect, and hope and resolution when he considers the possibility that he too may be one of the elect. There are also many meditations which appear to have no preset pattern. Taylor was writing at the end of, that is during the decadence of, the meditative tradition, and his poems usually do not have the closely knit logical organization of the best poems of Donne and Herbert.

Taylor wrote these poems, as the title indicates, in preparation for his administration of Communion, which he and his fellow Congregationalists called the Lord's Supper, one of the two Puritan sacraments, the other being Baptism. The Lord's Supper was considered the more important of the two. It was taken with the utmost seriousness by

Taylor, who believed that Christ's spirit was really present in the elements. He was a conservative in his attitude toward its administration. He believed that only those members of his congregation who considered themselves regenerate and in full communion with the church should participate in the Lord's Supper, and he was scandalized when Solomon Stoddard (1643-1729), minister of the Congregational church in the nearby town of Northampton, liberalized the communion service and admitted unregenerate persons to it. Participation required preparation on the part of congregation and minister, for he who took Communion while in a state of sin ate and drank his own damnation. Taylor's preparation consisted of prayer and the writing of a preparatory meditation. There was a long tradition as to the necessity of and the method of preparation, and a number of treatises were published on the subject. For example, Thomas Doolittle's *A Treatise Concerning the Lord's Supper* (ninth edition, 1675) was in the library of Richard Taylor (the poet's brother), and Taylor was probably familiar with it. Doolittle in his directions for preparatory meditation urges the believer to reflect on the love of God demonstrated in man's redemption, on the sufferings of Christ, on the benefits purchased by the death of Christ, and on the believer's sins. He suggests that the believer make a catalogue of his sins, which Taylor often did.

Of the more than 200 meditations, a number appear to be independent or occasional poems, but some form well-defined, coherent groups. The central theme of the forty-nine poems of the first series is *love*—the divine love of God and Christ for man as proven by Christ's saving grace to the elect and, conversely, the human love that the elect should have for Christ and God. Three unnumbered poems, entitled "The Experience," "The Return," and "The Reflexion," which Taylor placed among his first meditations, graphically depict the minister-poet's love of Christ, and one of them, "The Reflexion," presents what appears to be a mystic moment in which Taylor actually saw a vision of Christ at the Communion table:

> Once at thy Feast, I saw thee Pearle-like stand
> 'Tween Heaven, and Earth where Heavens
> Bright glory all
> In streams fell on thee, as a floodgate and,
> Like Sun Beams through thee on the
> World to Fall.

The experience may have been the inspiration for the first series of preparatory meditations.

Meditations 1-30 of the second series are a contemplation of the truths of scripture as seen typologically. Each poem presents a series of parallels, of types and antitypes, to show that persons and events in the life of Christ were foreshadowed in the Old Testament. The theme of what Taylor called "blessed theanthropy," the perfect union of the human and the divine in Christ, unifies the group. Christ is seen as the supreme figure in all human history, and the various personages of the Old Testament—such as Noah, Joseph, Moses, Samson—all foreshadowed Christ.

Taylor's Christological theme is continued in another group of poems in the second series, meditations 31-56, fourteen of which are directly related to his fourteen sermons which have been published in *Christographia*. In these poems Taylor attacks the various "heresies" which are not in agreement with his view of Christ's perfect humanity and divinity, specifically that of William Sherlock (1641-1707), who argued that the trinity consisted of three "minds" rather than three persons and who denounced what he considered to be excessive worship of Christ as a person, and that of Faustus Socinus (1539-1606), who believed in the unipersonality of God and denied the divinity of Christ. These meditations are more than mere attacks on heresies, however. They are moving and sometimes eloquent statements of Taylor's belief in the perfect humanity and perfect divinity of Christ. Meditations 102-111 are an attack on Stoddardeanism, which Taylor considered almost as dangerous as heresy. In them he vitriolically attacks his fellow pastor, Solomon Stoddard, for allowing all members of the congregation at his Northampton church to partake of the Lord's Supper whether or not they considered themselves regenerate. Stoddard considered the Lord's Supper to be a converting and regenerating ordinance and not a sacrament for the regenerate only as did Taylor. Taylor also preached a series of sermons against Stoddard.

Toward the end of his life Taylor wrote a series of meditations (series two, 115-133) on sequential texts from the Song of Solomon, or Canticles, which many Christians of the seventeenth century considered to be an allegorical poem celebrating the "wedding" of Christ with the members of his church. Taylor adopts the view of Origen, a church father whom he greatly admired, that Canticles may be interpreted as a celebration of the wedding of Christ with the individual soul. In these moving poems, heavily influenced by the diction and imagery of the Bible, Taylor meditates on his union with Christ with almost mystical intensity.

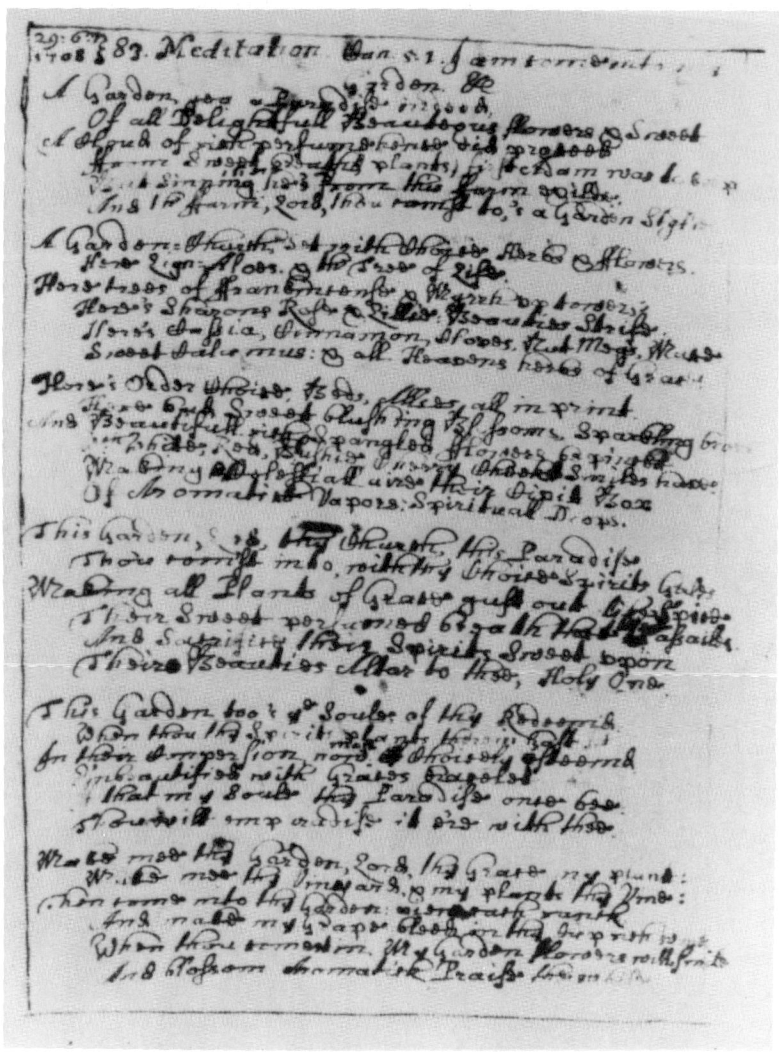

Manuscript for meditation 83 from Preparatory Meditations, *second series (Beinecke Rare Book and Manuscript Library, Yale University)*

There appears to be little agreement on which of Taylor's many meditations are the best poems. The religious ecstasy of meditation 1.20 on the ascension of Christ has been frequently praised:

God is Gone up with a triumphant Shout
    The Lord with sounding Trumpets melodies.
Sing Praise, sing Praise, sing Praise, sing Praises out,
    Unto our King sing praise seraphickwise.
    Lift up your Heads ye lasting Doore they sing
    And let the King of Glory Enter in.

The quiet Herbertian piety of meditation 1.6 has its adherents. But perhaps the most impressive of all his poems is meditation 2.112, which so powerfully and so precisely summarizes the doctrine of Christ's redemptive mission and the elect's victory over death:

Infinities fierce firy arrow red
    Shot from the splendid Bow of Justice bright
Did smite thee down, for thine. Thou art their head.
    They di'de in thee. Their death did on thee light.
    They di'de their Death in thee, thy Death is theirs.
    Hence thine is mine, thy death my trespass clears.

How sweet is this: my Death lies buried
    Within thy Grave my Lord, deep under ground,
It is unskin'd, as Carrion rotten Dead.
    For Grace's hand gave Death its deadly wound.
    Deaths no such terrour on th'Saints blesst Coast.
    Its but a harmless Shade: No walking Ghost.

In 1688, when he heard that Stoddard was about to allow unregenerate sinners to partake of the Lord's Supper, Taylor sent him a letter opposing the move. Stoddard laconically replied that he was not at leisure to go into the reasons for his innovation and then proceeded to liberalize the communion service in the manner Taylor feared. The church at Northampton appears to have followed Stoddard's practice until his grandson, the great Calvinist preacher Jonathan Edwards, returned to the conservative restrictions of former days, a decision which was eventually instrumental in his being discharged of his duties as pastor of that church and sent out to preach to the Indians. The controversy over Stoddard's practice was widespread and bitter; yet it was engaged in by some of the chief pastors of the period, including Increase and Cotton Mather.

In 1690 Taylor entered in his commonplace book six syllogisms arguing that the Lord's Supper is not a converting ordinance, and in this same year, after reading a sermon by Stoddard defending his practice, he wrote in his book thirty-four pages of animadversions against Stoddard. He made use of this material in 1694 in his series of sermons preached on his own doctrine of the Lord's Supper. In the course of these sermons he continually attacks Stoddard for destroying a precious sacrament.

The first Mrs. Taylor died 7 July 1689. Taylor's moving elegy on her describes the joys and griefs of their married life, especially those caused by the deaths of their children, and his own grief at the death of the children's mother:

> Five Babes thou tookst from me before this Stroake.
> Thine arrows then into my bowells broake,
> But now they pierce into my bosom smart,
> Do strike and stob me in the very heart.

On 6 June 1692, Taylor married Ruth Wyllys of Hartford, who survived him.

Late in 1697 Taylor engaged in controversy with Benjamin Ruggles, pastor of the church at Suffield in the Bay Colony, who began to express what Taylor considered to be dangerous Presbyterian views, dangerous not for doctrinal reasons—for the doctrines of the two churches were almost identical—but because Presbyterianism would deprive the independent Congregational minister of power over his church and place it in the hands of a church synod. Taylor's struggle against the establishment of Presbyterianism in New England is described in the Westfield church record and is referred to in his poem on the death of Samuel Hooker (circa 1635-1697), minister of the Congregational church in Farmington, Connecticut. In this most powerful of all of Taylor's elegies Ruggles is referred to as one of several "Young Cockerills" and Presbyterianism is called "refined Prelacy at best." The next year Taylor wrote an elegy on his sister-in-law Mehetabel Woodbridge. On 18 January 1701 James Taylor, Taylor's son by his first wife, died in Barbados. The poet refers to his death in meditation 2.40: "Under thy Rod, my God, thy smarting Rod, / That hath off broke my James, that Primrose, Why?" In the same year Taylor began, on 31 August, a series of fourteen sermons, entitled *Christographia*, on the nature of Christ's person and the unity of the divine and human natures in Christ. The series was finished on 10 October 1703. In his day, Taylor had a reputation for pulpit eloquence. His Harvard classmate Samuel Sewall wrote in his *Letter-Book*, "I have heard him preach a sermon at the Old South upon short warning which as the phrase in England is, might have been preached at Paul's Cross." Sewall, who lived in Boston, had access to the best preaching of the day. Taylor's poetry was almost completely unknown in his lifetime, but now that almost all of Taylor's extant poetry and prose have been published, it seems unlikely that his reputation as a preacher will ever equal his reputation as a poet. In his sermons he never exhibits the power and the beauty of the great Calvinist preacher Jonathan Edwards.

In structure and style his sermons are in the tradition of the Puritan preaching of his time. There is usually a three-fold structure—doctrine, reason, and use—or as Taylor put it on the title page of *Christographia*, each sermon is "Opened, Confirmed, and Practically improved." The purpose of the Puritan sermon was to explain the scripture and to instruct the congregation in the practical application of scriptural doctrine. Taylor came naturally to the plain style he employed, for most Puritan divines preferred it to the learned and ornate style of the Anglican preachers. Yet he was also preaching to a congregation of poorly educated farmers for whom a plain style and at times colloquial diction were necessary. He refers to the Quakers as "the old Clucking hen of antichrist" and to natural man as "a mushroom." In his attacks on Stoddard he refers to the Communion bread: "Hands off: its Childrens bread; a Crumb of it may not fall to dogs. But all of it belongs to every Child in the Family." However, Taylor's talent as a poet sometimes appears in his sermons, especially in passages depicting the sweetness of saving grace and the mystical union of Christ and the believer.

In June 1705 the bones of a "monster" were

discovered at Claverack on the bank of the Hudson River near Albany, New York. The discovery caused considerable excitement, and accounts of the remains appeared in the *Boston News-Letter* and several years later in the *Philosophical Transactions of the Royal Society*. At the time their discovery was considered proof of the existence of giants in the earth before the flood. Today the bones are thought to be mastodon remains, the first to be discovered in America.

At least two of the teeth were brought to Taylor in Westfield for examination. He claimed that one weighed five pounds, the other two. Combining this evidence with the report that a thigh bone seventeen-feet long had also been discovered and that the ground was discolored for seventy feet, Taylor constructed in his imagination a marvelous giant seventy-feet tall and described him in a remarkable poem of one hundred and ninety verses, entitled "The Description of the great Bones dug up at Claverack. . . ." Taylor, like his contemporaries Increase and Cotton Mather, had a fondness for prodigies and remarkable providences.

Early in the eighteenth century (the exact date has never been determined) Taylor began a long poem which eventually ran to well over 20,000 lines. The first part of the poem presents the sufferings and persecutions of the Christians from the beginning until the twelfth century, and, after a lacuna in the manuscript, there is an account of the martyrdoms of Queen Mary's reign in England. The poem is untitled. Donald E. Stanford, who in 1960 made and later published a transcript of the poem, called it *A Metrical History of Christianity*. The primary sources are the *Magdeburg Centuries* (1567-1574) of Matthias Flaccus and the well-known book *Actes and Monuments of these Latter Perilous Days*, first published in English in 1563 and usually known as *The Book of Martyrs* by John Foxe. Written in decasyllabic couplets and in eight other verse forms, Taylor's long and frequently tedious poem is uneven in literary merit, varying from the crudest doggerel to exalted hymns to God's grace. There are a few powerful lines on the operation of God's justice, but there are also unnecessarily detailed descriptions of the physical agonies of the martyrs and some extremely vitriolic language in several attacks on the Papacy reminiscent of the pamphlet war of the previous century.

Taylor as pastor was a stern disciplinarian, and he occasionally had to put down uprisings in his congregation. In 1712 a faction was formed against him by Benjamin Smith, who refused to accept admonishment for disobedience in a dispute with Taylor regarding the guardianship of one Henry Lee, the faction claiming that such disciplinary action as well as loosing and binding the members of the church lay with the church as a whole and not with the minister. Taylor, who he said "Knew my office," threatened the whole congregation with deprivation of the sacrament of the Lord's Supper if they did not support him against the faction. The majority of them, apparently, desired to remain neutral but submitted eventually. Taylor was much perturbed by the affair and left an account of it on several pages of folio size in the church record, and on 2 December 1713 and 31 January 1714, he preached to his congregation on pastoral authority.

Taylor was ill and enfeebled in the final years of his life, but he persisted in writing poems until almost the end. "Upon my recovery out of a threatening Sickness," which begins, "What, is the golden Gate of Paradise / Lockt up 'gain that yet I may not enter?," was written in December 1720. In January 1721 he composed "A Valediction to all the World preparatory for Death," a flawed, eccentric, but moving, poem (which exists in several heavily corrected versions). In it Taylor bids farewell to the physical world including the stars, sun, moon, and air, while he eagerly anticipates the joys of singing, above the angels, God's praises in heaven. Throughout the eight cantos he enumerates in vivid detail the pleasures and sorrows of earthly life, including his "study, Books, Pen, Inke, and Paper," all of which he is about to relinquish for his life in a heaven which he believes in and depicts with absolute conviction:

> When I've skipt ore the purling Stile with joy
> Twixt Swift wing'd Time and Fixt Eternity
> And am got in the heavenly strand on High
> My Harp shall sing thy praise melodiously.

In order to make his music acceptable to God, he will seek aid from the birds, flowers, and angels:

> And first I'de borrow of all birds within
> The Woods where they their bagpipes blow make sing
> And thence I run to sweet fine flowers whose tune
> Is silent given in beauty and perfume
> Then at the Angells doore, those happy Friends
> And 'treat them me their melodie to lend,
> And mix their tunes with mine. . . .

In 1723 Taylor wrote his elegy on Increase Mather (1639-1723), who had died on 23 August. The long title begins "A funerall Teare dropt upon the Coffin of that holy [man of] God, Dr. Increase Mather. . . ."

Mather is praised as a champion of Congregational orthodoxy, and his opponents, especially the Roman Catholics who made Mather "their Maypole Music," are denounced at some length. Timothy Cutler, a rector of Yale University who defected to Anglicanism, is more briefly dismissed: "Cutler's Cutlery gave th' killing Stob." In October 1725 Taylor wrote his last preparatory meditation, which begins: "Heart sick my Lord heart sick of Love to thee!" During his final years Taylor composed a scurrilous attack upon the so-called Pope Joan, the legendary Pope John VIII of the ninth century, who according to some Protestant apologists was a woman disguised as a man. The myth had wide circulation from medieval times through the seventeenth century. The poem is in six versions or drafts and several fragments, indicating that Taylor spent more time on the poem than it was worth.

The exact composition date of "A Fig for thee Oh! Death" is not known, but the handwriting suggests it was a very late poem, and it makes a suitable conclusion to any collection of Taylor's poetry. He begins his poem with an address to Death as

> Thou King of Terrours with thy Gastly Eyes
> With Butter teeth, bare bones Grim looks likewise.
> And Grizzly Hide, and clawing Tallons, fell,
> Opning to Sinners Vile, Trap Door of Hell.

But Death, through Christ's grace, has lost its terror for him. Death can seize only the body,

> Till she hath slept out quite her fatall Sleep.
> When the last Cock shall Crow the last day in
> And the Arch Angells Trumpets sound shall ring
> Then th' Eye Omniscient seek shall all their round
> Each dust death's mill had very finely ground.

The poem concludes with a vision of the soul and body as two lovers in heaven:

> The Soule and Body now, as two true Lovers
> Ery night how they do hug and kiss each other.
> And join hand in hand thus through the skies
> Up to Eternall glory glorious rise.

Taylor died on 24 June 1729 and was interred in the old burying ground at Westfield, Massachusetts. His interesting tombstone, engraved with the face of a primitive angel, fell into disrepair but has now been reconstructed.

There are few contemporary descriptions of Taylor. The most detailed account is by his grandson Ezra Stiles, president of Yale College, who said that he was "a vigorous advocate for Oliver Cromwell, civil and religious liberty. . . . greatly detested King James . . . gloried in King William and the Revolution of 1688. . . . A man of small stature, but firm; of quick passions, yet serious and grave. Exemplary in piety, and for a very sacred observance of the Lord's Day."

Other:

Cotton Mather, *Right Thoughts in Sad Hours. . .*, includes two stanzas of "Upon Wedlock and Death of Children," by Taylor (London: Printed by James Astwood, 1689).

Bibliography:

Constance J. Gefvert, *Edward Taylor: An Annotated Bibliography, 1668-1970* (Kent, Ohio: Kent State University Press, 1971).

Biography:

Norman S. Grabo, *Edward Taylor* (New York: Twayne, 1961).

References:

Ursula Brumm, "Edward Taylor and the Poetic Use of Religious Imagery," in *Typology and Early American Literature*, edited by Sacvan Bercovitch (Amherst: University of Massachusetts Press, 1972), pp. 191-206;

Brumm, "Edward Taylor's Meditations on the Lord's Supper," in *American Thought and Religious Typology*, translated by John Hoaglund (New Brunswick: Rutgers University Press, 1979), pp. 56-85;

E. F. Carlisle, "The Puritan Structure of Edward Taylor's Poetry," *American Quarterly*, 20 (1968): 147-163;

Michael J. Colacurcio, "Gods Determinations Touching Half-Way Membership: Occasion and Audience in Edward Taylor," *American Literature*, 39 (November 1967): 298-314;

Early American Literature, special Taylor issue, 4, no. 3 (Winter 1969-1970);

Albert Gelpi, *The Tenth Muse: The Psyche of the American Poet* (Cambridge: Harvard University Press), pp. 13-54;

Norman S. Grabo, "Edward Taylor's Spiritual Huswifery," *PMLA*, 74 (December 1964): 554-560;

Clark Griffith, "Edward Taylor and the Momentum of Metaphor," *ELH*, 33 (1966): 448-460;

Alan B. Howard, "The World as Emblem: Language and Vision in the Poetry of Edward Taylor," *American Literature*, 44 (November 1972): 359-384;

Donald Junkins, "Edward Taylor's Revisions," *American Literature*, 37 (May 1965): 135-152;

Karl Keller, *The Example of Edward Taylor* (Amherst: University of Massachusetts Press, 1975);

Keller, " 'The World Slickt up in Types': Edward Taylor as a Version of Emerson," *Early American Literature*, 5 (Spring 1970): 124-140;

John Hoyt Lockwood, *Westfield and Its Historic Influences 1669-1919: The Life of an Early Town* (Springfield, Mass.: Privately printed, 1922), I: 102-321;

Charles W. Mignon, "Christ the Glory of All Types: The Initial Sermon from Edward Taylor's 'Upon the Types of the Old Testament,' " *William and Mary Quarterly*, 37 (April 1980): 286-301;

Mignon, "The Nebraska Edward Taylor Manuscript," *Early American Literature*, 12 (Winter 1977/1978): 296-301;

Robert Reiter, "Poetry and Typology: Edward Taylor's *Preparatory Meditations*, Second Series, Numbers 1-30," *Early American Literature*, 5 (Spring 1970): 111-123;

Gene Russell, *A Concordance to the Poems of Edward Taylor* (Washington, D.C.: Microcard Editions, 1973);

William J. Scheick, *The Will and the Word: The Poetry of Edward Taylor* (Athens: University of Georgia Press, 1974);

Donald E. Stanford, "The Earliest Poems of Edward Taylor," *American Literature*, 32 (May 1960): 136-151;

Stanford, "Edward Taylor," in *Major Writers of Early American Literature*, edited by Everett Emerson (Madison: University of Wisconsin Press, 1972), pp. 59-91;

Stanford, *Edward Taylor*, University of Minnesota Pamphlets on American Writers, no. 52 (Minneapolis: University of Minnesota Press, 1965);

Stanford, "Edward Taylor and the Lord's Supper," *American Literature*, 27 (May 1955): 172-178;

Stanford, "Edward Taylor's Metrical History of Christianity," *American Literature*, 33 (November 1961): 279-295;

Stanford, "Edward Taylor's 'Spiritual Relation,' " *American Literature*, 35 (January 1964): 467-475;

Stanford, "The Giant Bones of Claverack, 1705," *New York History*, 45 (January 1959): 47-61;

Stanford, "The Parentage of Edward Taylor," *American Literature*, 33 (May 1961): 215-221;

Jean L. Thomas, "Drama and Doctrine in *Gods Determinations*," *American Literature*, 36 (January 1965): 452-462;

Peter Thorpe, "Edward Taylor as Poet," *New England Quarterly*, 39 (1966): 356-372;

Austin Warren, "Edward Taylor," in his *Rage for Order* (Ann Arbor: University of Michigan Press, 1948), pp. 1-18;

Warren, "Edward Taylor," in *Major Writers of America*, edited by Perry Miller (New York: Harcourt, Brace & World, 1962), I: 51-62.

Papers:

Most of Taylor's papers are in the Beinecke Rare Book and Manuscript Library of Yale University; the Redwood Library and Athenaeum in Newport, Rhode Island; the Boston Public Library, the Westfield Athenaeum in Westfield, Massachusetts; and the Massachusetts Historical Society in Boston.

Benjamin Tompson

(14 July 1642-13 April 1714)

Peter White
University of New Mexico

BOOKS: *New Englands Crisis. Or a Brief Narrative of New Englands Lamentable Estate at present, compar'd with the former (but few) years of Prosperity* . . . (Boston: Printed & sold by John Foster, 1676); first two parts republished as *Sad and Deplorable News from New England* (London: Printed for H. J., 1676); revised and enlarged as *New-Englands Tears For Her Present Miseries: Or, A Late and True Relation of the Calamities of New-England Since April last past* . . . (London: Printed for N. S., 1676);

Benjamin Tompson, 1642-1714, First Native-Born American Poet: His Poems, edited by Howard Judson Hall (Boston & New York: Houghton Mifflin, 1924);

Benjamin Tompson, Colonial Bard: A Critical Edition, edited by Peter White (University Park: Pennsylvania State University Press, 1980).

Benjamin Tompson was the first native-born American poet of note. He wrote the first volume of American poetry to be republished in England (there is some evidence that his *New Englands Crisis* . . . (1676) was the first American book of any kind to be republished in England); he was called upon by Cotton Mather and William Hubbard to write prefatory poems for their colonial histories; he greeted Lord Bellamont in Boston in 1699 with a pastoral skit and poetic recitation that parodied Nathaniel Ward's *The Simple Cobbler of Aggawam* . . . (1647); and he was lauded by his contemporaries as "the Renouned Poet of New England." About thirty of his poems exist today, roughly half in manuscript form. He is particularly noted for his ability to describe the spiritual emptiness of the second generation of American Puritans in the Massachusetts Bay Colony and for his talent in legendizing the famous patriarchs of the first generation. Tompson was a well-educated, worldly, and witty poet who frequently took it upon himself to be the colony's spokesman.

Very little is known about the life of this Puritan poet. He was born in Braintree, Massachusetts, on 14 July 1642 to Abigail and the Reverend William Tompson, one of the colony's more influential and respected ministers. In 1654 Benjamin Tompson was adopted by the Blanchard family of Charlestown because his mother died "of a cold taken while walking to church" and because his father had been sent to Virginia on a missionary pilgrimage to the Indians and Anglicans of the Southern colonies, and later appears to have fallen into a "deep melancholy," most probably due to the pressures of frontier existence. Benjamin was well-cared for by the Blanchards, who provided for his education at Harvard, where he took his degree in 1662. Rejecting the normal expectation that he would enter the ministry, Tompson embarked on a varied and worldly career in mathematics, teaching, practicing medicine, and writing poetry. He taught classical languages in the grammar schools of Boston, Roxbury, Charlestown, and Braintree, but he seems to have spent a good deal of his intellectual and emotional energy in suing municipalities for fair compensation for teaching or in petitioning families like the Mathers for land and other privileges. Some scholars have seen his contentious behavior as erratic and eccentric, and he did at least live a varied and sometimes unusual life: he probably practiced some form of alchemy; he wrote at least one witty funeral elegy and a host of other satirical poems; he practiced medicine during King Philip's War in 1676; he was twice married (first in 1667 to Susanna Kirkland and a second time, in 1698, to Prudence Payson, a wealthy woman); and he appears to have spent untold years in trying to achieve fame and patronage both here in America and in England. Although it is difficult to draw any firm conclusions from the sketchy details of his long life, his extant poetry reveals a man of imagination, wit, temper, sensitivity, and learning.

As a poet, Benjamin Tompson generally adopted one of two roles: he was either the spokesman for the Holy Commonwealth, who chastized backsliders or elegized the patriarchs, or he was the father and friend, who lamented the loss of loved ones with notable simplicity and sincerity. In his public verse, either elegiac, occasional, or mock-epic, he used his knowledge of classical languages, medieval theology, and world history, and he

New-Englands Tears

FOR HER

Preſent Miſeries:

OR,

A Late and True RELATION of the CALAMITIES of

NEW-ENGLAND

Since *APRIL* laſt paſt.

With an Account of the Battel between the *Engliſh* and *Indians* upon *Seaconk Plain*:

And of the *Indians* Burning and Deſtroying of *Marlbury*, *Rehoboth*, *Chelmsford*, *Sudbury*, and *Providence*.

With the Death of *Antononies* the Grand *Indian* Sachem; And a RELATION of a Fortification begun by Women upon *Boſton Neck*. Together with an Elegy on the Death of *John Winthrop* Eſq; late Governour of *Connecticott*, and Fellow of the *Royal Society*.

Written by an Inhabitant of Boſton *in* New England *to his Friend in* London. With Allowance.

LONDON Printed for *N. S.* 1676.

Title page for the revised and enlarged edition of Tompson's poem about King Philip's War (John Carter Brown Library, Brown University)

frequently employed alchemical, astrological, or medical terminology to satirize the loss of leadership and direction in the New Israel. He was quite capable of exploiting the linguistic aspects of language in the popular poetic forms of the day, especially in the anagram, and he seems to have been particularly adept at describing colonial warfare with a kind of "journalistic" flair. In many of his poems he practiced baroque techniques: the conceit, the paradox, startling imagery, or elaborate arguments. He frequently achieved remarkable effects by juxtaposing dream visions of the celestial realms with shockingly vivid depictions of human mortality, bodily corruption, or unchecked appetite. Modern readers can see in Tompson's poetry the fearfulness with which the Indians were viewed, the hostility extended toward "heretical" elements, and the specter of death and violence on the frontier. But we may also read in his works the Puritans' respect for the significance of language, learning, piety, humor, and sentiment. Tompson's work, thus, presents a microcosmic picture of early American taste.

Tompson's first surviving poetic effort, "Remarks on the Bright, and dark side of Mr. William Tompson," was written in 1666, four years after he had graduated from Harvard College. It is an important poem because it presents the poet's public attitude toward his father's career and the Puritans' "errand into the wilderness." Using the standard typological reading of history, Tompson sees his father as a type of Melchizedek, Lazarus, Daniel, and Nehemiah, all characters who were in one way or another threatened by persecutors or who were responsible for the rebuilding of Zion. Like Tompson's father, who vacillated between lucidity and insanity for eight years, these biblical heroes are remembered for their ultimate victories over demonic adversity and doom. Cotton Mather, in the *Magnalia Christi Americana* (1702), reports that William Tompson overcame the devil in a deathbed struggle to rest in the peace and security of Christ. Tompson's "Remarks on the Bright, and dark side of Mr. William Tompson" serves in the *Magnalia Christi Americana* as the poetic counterpart of Mather's hagiography. But another, unpublished poem, "Gulielmi Tompsoni Braintreensis," presents a somewhat different impression of Benjamin Tompson's concern for his father's sacrifices. This six-line elegy calls his father New England's Boanerges, "a thundering textman," who, much to the shame of the congregation of Braintree, lies "tombless," that is in a plain grave, while the surviving "Virgins slumber" and "Others wantonize." Here, Tompson is not so charitable toward his neighbors, who failed to provide their minister with an appropriate mark of his status and who appear to be failing to carry on the great work in the wilderness.

The following year Tompson further indulged his tendency toward individuality in a slightly different way. At the death of Robert Woodmancy, headmaster of the Boston Latin School, in 1667, Tompson composed one of the most unusual elegies of the colonial period, *The Grammarians Funeral . . .*, not published until 1708 upon the death of the well-known schoolmaster and Latin scholar Ezekiel Cheever. In this seventy-six-line broadside tribute Tompson personifies various rules of Latin and puns upon the meaning of Latin verbs to create a scene of hilarity and frivolity not often associated with Puritanical behavior. Not surprisingly, scholars have practically ignored analysis of this poem; it so drastically contradicts the image of the dour and repressed Puritan. In Tompson's elegy the personified figures act a little like bumpkins at a county fair jostling one another, declining responsibility, serving refreshments, and welcoming pagan deities. The final six lines of the poem, however, restore some decorum to the event and may well have rescued Tompson from charges of blasphemy. Because Tompson replaced Robert Woodmancy as the master of the Boston Latin School in 1667, one wonders if Tompson may have refrained from publishing this comic piece from the fear of losing that important appointment. Two years later Ezekiel Cheever replaced Tompson as the headmaster of Boston's best-known school, leading one to wonder if Tompson released the poem in 1708 to achieve a kind of gentle vengeance upon his competitor Cheever.

Tompson did not teach between 1674 and 1679, perhaps because of continuing disagreements with the local school authorities, and during this five-year period he produced most of his better-known poetry, principally *New Englands Crisis . . .* and its revised and enlarged version, *New-Englands Tears . . . .* Although the colonial records are not clear, there is enough evidence to suggest that Tompson declared himself a physician during King Philip's War in 1676. His experiences may have provided him with the material for *New Englands Crisis . . .*, his "jeremiad" account of the bloody confrontation between the colonists and several tribes of the Algonquian Confederation under Metacomet (King Philip), the Wampanoag chieftain. Given the temper of the times, Tompson has a relatively balanced approach toward this conflict. Naturally he sees the war from the English-American point of view; the Indians are heathen savages bent upon the destruction of the chosen people. But, significantly, in the general prologue to the poem, he castigates the Puritans for greed, illegal acquisitions of lands, hypocrisy, sensuality, and loss of political and spiritual vision. The poem had a tremendous appeal to English readers, so powerful in fact that a pirated version of the first two parts appeared in London in 1676 under the title *Sad and Deplorable News from New England . . . .* The second and official version, *New-Englands Tears . . .*, appeared in London later that year with revisions and additions by Tompson. In both *New Englands Crisis . . .* and *New-Englands Tears . . .* Tompson covers events in media res, employing a kind of eyewitness perspective interwoven with elegies, typological analyses, classical allusions, satirical attacks, and witty compositions on, for example, the "Amazonian Dames" who sandbagged Boston Neck much to the disgrace of the momentarily cowardly males. Tompson drew upon many traditions of Puritan literature for his portrait of the conflict, but perhaps he was most indebted to the highly popular Indian captivity narrative, which encouraged a bit of sensationalism in the form of portraits of violence, confusion, chaos, and suffering. In the set speech of King Philip, though, Tompson innovatively used Pidgin-English to sharpen the satirical barbs cast at the enemy. Overall, *New Englands Crisis . . .* is one of the most interesting seventeenth-century poems of America; it is lively, vivid, and frequently original.

The year 1676 may have been Tompson's most productive year, but it was also marked by tragedies throughout the colonies. Tompson announced the death of John Winthrop, Jr., governor of Connecticut and member of the Royal Society, in *A FUNERAL TRIBUTE to John Winthrope* (1676), a broadside elegy which begins: "Another Black Parenthesis of woe / The *Printer* wills that all the World should know." Typically the persona in this elegy sees himself as reluctantly accepting the role of reporter to the world for New England's affairs. He must, however painful the task, inform his tearful readers throughout civilized society of the extent of God's case against sinful New England. According to the poet, John Winthrop, from whose family Tompson almost certainly sought patronage, was a peerless pillar in the community of saints, a physician to the colony, a type of Roman statesman, and an alchemist in the mold of Paracelsus. While this elegy is conventional in many ways, it demonstrates Tompson's ability to create fantastic scenes employing exotic imagery, rich allusion, and coherent typological patterns.

By the following year, Tompson's fame had apparently warranted recognition from the Bay Colony's elite: William Hubbard, who later became President of Harvard College, asked Tompson to write a prefatory poem to his *A Narrative of the Troubles with the Indians in New-England . . .* (1677). Naturally flattered by the request, the colonial bard responded by returning the compliment, congratulating Hubbard as the only writer since the Old Testament Nathan, or Samuel Purchase, or Richard Hakluyt to portray historical exploration and military strategies accurately. Roger Williams, the Indians' "*grand* Apostle," as Tompson calls him, wrote on the natives' language, but Hubbard wrote "*how they burn, / Rob, kill and Roast, lead Captives, flay, blaspheme.*" Sensing that Tompson could be relied upon to compose sympathetic introductory poems, Cotton Mather called upon his former schoolmaster in 1702 to recommend the *Magnalia Christi Americana* to the public. This time, however, the older and more confident poet took the opportunity to poke some fun at the self-important Mather, his most famous pupil. By ingeniously punning upon the terminology of the classical-school curriculum and by skillful allusion to the Bible, Tompson delicately satirizes Mather's achievement as a kind of wizardry, or necromancy, and this only a few years after the legal proceedings against the so-called witches of Salem. No contemporary reader could fail to catch the rather bold import of this poem.

In the last two decades of the seventeenth century, Tompson seems to have been relatively content to serve as headmaster of the Braintree grammar school. Although the court records show that he occasionally petitioned for more land or higher wages, he remained the better part of the time in Braintree and produced elegies for family members or friends, raised his eight children and twenty-eight grandchildren, practiced medicine, and served as town clerk. Two anagrams on Edmund and Humphrey Davie, written in 1682, seem to reflect a more mature or, perhaps, a more resigned attitude toward life in the wilderness. Gone is that sense of urgency and ambition, sometimes bitterness, that characterizes his early work. The Davies were intellectual and influential members of the Puritan community, and most probably Tompson received some patronage from them. In return, Tompson composed anagrammatic elegies for Humphrey Davie's son, Edmund, and wife, Mary, who died within a year of each other. Tompson focused the elegies upon the splendors of the New Jerusalem of heaven, the celestial city where transcendent souls are crowned with glory and light. In much the same vein, Tompson returned to these themes and image patterns in 1710, when he composed *A Neighbour's Tears Sprinkled on the Dust of the Amiable Virgin, Mrs. Rebeckah Sewall . . .*, a broadside elegy on Judge Samuel Sewall's granddaughter, Rebeckah, who died at the age of six. Drawing upon the language of the Bible and the funerary imagery of the Puritan gravestone, Tompson portrays young Rebeckah as a "pretty Lamb" amidst a "flock of Doves," a "New made Creature . . . so bright," but a "rare plant . . . cropt before mine Eyes." This language is remarkably similar to that of Anne Bradstreet's elegies for her grandchildren. One of the very few surviving poems in which Tompson alludes to his own misfortunes, this elegy ends with a direct statement: "Pleasant Rebeckah, heres to thee a Tear / Hugg my sweet Mary if you chance to see her." Tompson's daughter Mary had died on 28 March 1700, at the age of seven.

Near the end of May in the last year of the seventeenth century, Benjamin Tompson reached the zenith of his career as New England's "Renouned Poet." Finally, after two years' anticipation, New England was about to greet their new Royal Governor, Richard Coote, the first Earl of Bellamont, who had tarried in New York, enjoying the hospitality of his subjects there. To welcome such an eminent guest, Benjamin Tompson composed a kind of pastoral skit in which various classical deities, legendary Indian chiefs, aged patriachs, shepherds, and nymphs pay respects to Bellamont on his progress from Dedham, Massachusetts, to Boston. It is uncertain whether Tompson devised this "Rural bitt," as he called it, through his own inspiration or through a commission from higher authorities. One hundred years later, Ebenezer Parkman wrote to Mather Byles of Tompson's celebrated portrayal of Nathaniel Ward, author of *The Simple Cobbler of Agawaam . . .*, and how, as legend has it, Tompson, dressed as a shoemaker, "ran out from his stall to pay his homely Complements to his Lordship." But Tompson's address to the governor is more than just a "homely" or "Rural bitt." In many ways emblematic of his career, it is public, patriotic, bold, witty, and sincere. It displays learning in an unostentatious way, makes reference to historical, contemporary, and worldly events, and traces the progress of American settlement with high hopes for future greatness.

But Benjamin Tompson was not able to sustain such optimism. On 20 June 1713, in the only extant poem which might be read as a purely personal statement, the colonial comic delivers a rather sweeping indictment against a life of aspiration in the New World and meditates upon his approaching death:

> I feel this World too mean, and low.
> Patron's a lie: Friendship a Show
> Preferment trouble: Grandure Vaine
> Law a pretence: a Bubble Gaine
> Merit a flash: a Blaze Esteem
> Promise a Rush: and Hope a Dream
> Faith a Disguise; a Truth Deceit
> Wealth but a Trap: and Health a Cheat
> These dangerous Rocks, Lord help me Shun
> Age tells me my Days work is done.

This "Aged Sylvan," as Tompson called himself, died ten months later and was buried in Roxbury, now a part of Boston. His "last lines" express some conventionally Puritanical ideas but in a remarkably striking, original way. To be sure, the final couplet clears Tompson of an unorthodox pessimism, but still there is the lingering impression that, tired of his search for social utopianism and personal recognition, he has given up the struggle. It is all the more frustrating, then, that so little biographical and literary information is available. Manuscript poems are limited to two autograph poems, three letters, and a few legal documents in addition to poems copied by others. Perhaps continuing research may eventually unearth a store of biographical and literary information.

Other:

"UPON the NATIVES," in *A Narrative of the Troubles with the Indians in New-England . . .*, by William Hubbard (Boston: Printed by John Foster, 1677);

"Remarks on the Bright, and dark side of Mr. William Tompson" and "Celeberrimi COTTONI MATHERI, Celebratio," in *Magnalia Christi Americana*, by Cotton Mather (London: Printed for Tho. Parkhurst, 1702);

Kenneth B. Murdock, ed., *Handkerchiefs from Paul, Being Pious and Consolatory Verses of Puritan Massachusetts*, includes poems by Tompson (Cambridge: Harvard University Press, 1927).

References:

Neil T. Eckstein, "The Pastoral and the Primitive in Benjamin Tompson's 'Address to Lord Bellamont,'" *Early American Literature*, 8 (February 1973): 111-116;

Edwin S. Fussell, "Benjamin Tompson, Public Poet," *New England Quarterly*, 26 (December 1953): 494-511;

Howard Judson Hall, Introduction to *Benjamin Tompson, 1642-1714, first Native-Born Poet of America: His Poems*, edited by Hall (Boston & New York: Houghton Mifflin, 1924);

Kenneth B. Murdock, Introduction to *Handkerchiefs from Paul, Being Pious and Consolatory Verses of Puritan Massachusetts*, edited by Murdock (Cambridge: Harvard University Press, 1927);

Peter White, Introduction to *Benjamin Tompson, Colonial Bard: A Critical Edition*, edited by White (University Park: Pennsylvania State University Press, 1980).

Papers:

The following institutions have books or documents relating to Tompson: The Massachusetts Historical Society; The Essex Institute, Salem, Massachusetts; The Henry E. Huntington Library; The John Carter Brown Library, Brown University; The Boston Athenaeum; Yale University Library; Houghton Library, Harvard University; The Connecticut Historical Society; New York Public Library; and Boston Public Library.

Nathaniel Ward

(circa 1578-1652)

Rosamond Rosenmeier
University of Massachusetts, Boston

SELECTED BOOKS: *The Simple Cobbler of Aggawam in America. Willing to Help 'Mend his Native Country, Lamentably Tattered, Both in the Upper-Leather and Sole, With All the Honest Stitches He Can Take. And as Willing Never to Bee Paid for His Work, by Old England Wonted Pay . . .* as Theodore de la Guard (London: Printed by J. D. & R. I. for S. Bowtell, 1647; Boston: Printed for Daniel Henchman, 1713);

A Religious Retreat Sounded to a Religious Army, by One that Desires to Be Faithful to his Country . . . (London: Printed for S. Bowtell, 1647);

A Word to Mr. Peters, and Two Words for the Parliament and Kingdom. Or, An Answer to a Scandalous Pamphlet, Entituled, A Word for the Armie, and Two Words to the Kingdom: Subscribed by Hugh Peters. Wherein the Authority of Parliament is Infringed, the Fundamentall Laws of the Land Subverted; the Famous City of London Blemished; and All the Godly Ministers of the City Scandalized . . ., attributed to Ward (London: Printed by Fr.

Neile for Tho. Underhill, 1647);

To the High and Honorable Parliament of England Now Assembled at Westminster. The Humble Petitions, Serious Suggestions, and Dutifull Expostulations of Some Moderate and Loyall Gentlemen, Yeomen, and Freeholders of the Easterne Association (London: Printed for R. Smith, 1648);

A Sermon preached before the Honourable House of Commons at their Late Monethly Fast, Being on Wednesday, June 30. 1647 . . . (London: Printed by R. I. for Stephen Bowtell & William Bishop, 1649).

Lawyer, minister, satirist, Nathaniel Ward was born in Haverhill, Suffolk, England, circa 1578. The son of John Ward, a Puritan minister at Bury St. Edmunds, Nathaniel studied law at Emmanuel College, Cambridge, and took his M.A. in 1603. After practicing law in England, he traveled in 1616 to the Continent, where he visited the court of the Elector Palatine at Heidelberg. Influenced by the Calvinist preacher David Pareus, he decided to become a minister, was ordained in Germany in 1618, and served as chaplain to an English factory at Ebling until 1624. Returning to England, he served as curate of St. James's, Picadilly (1626-1628), and then as rector of Stondon-Massey in Essex (1628-1633). Advanced study, European travel, and training in law combined to enrich Ward's ministry and career as a writer.

Since his days at Ebling and at Emmanuel College, Ward had been acquainted with the founders of the Massachusetts Bay Colony. Ward's wife, of whom little is known, died in 1631, and in 1633, Ward was silenced by Archbishop Laud for Nonconformity. All of these factors led to his decision to emigrate; he sailed for Massachusetts in 1634. There he served as copastor at Agawam (renamed Ipswich shortly after his arrival) but resigned in 1636, perhaps because of ill health. Because of his background in law, Ward was asked in 1641 to help compile *The Body of Liberties,* the first code of laws in the colony and later used as the basis for the 1648 code. Ward's compilation essentially insured for Massachusetts a government of laws rather than of men and guaranteed certain rights of person and property to its citizens. After another attempt at frontier life, in Haverhill, Massachusetts, Ward moved back to Boston, where in 1645 he wrote *The Simple Cobbler of Aggawam in America . . .*, published in England in 1647 under the pseudonym Theodore de la Guard.

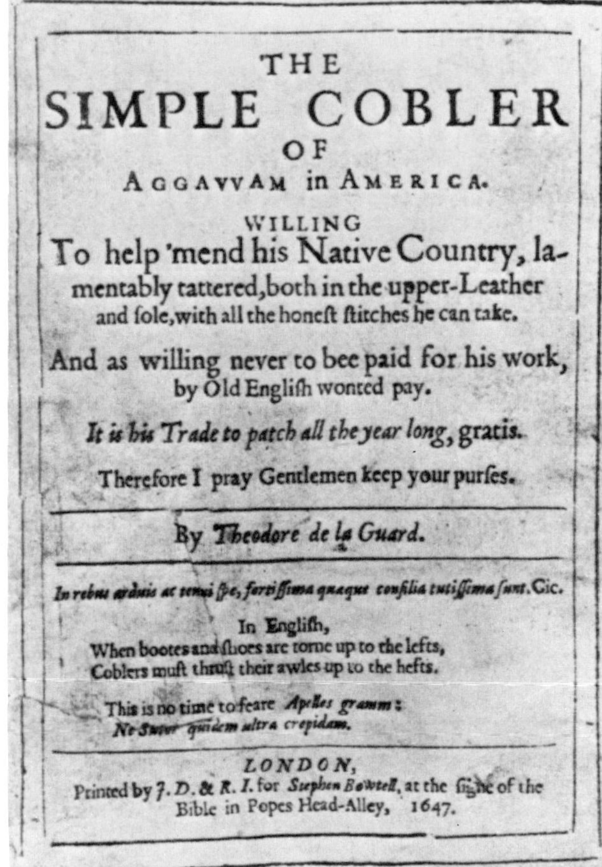
THE
SIMPLE COBLER
OF
AGGAVVAM in AMERICA.
WILLING
To help 'mend his Native Country, lamentably tattered, both in the upper-Leather and sole, with all the honeſt ſtitches he can take.
And as willing never to bee paid for his work, by Old Engliſh wonted pay.
It is his Trade to patch all the year long, gratis.
Therefore I pray Gentlemen keep your purſes.
By *Theodore de la Guard.*
In rebus arduis ac tenui ſpe, fortiſſima quæque conſilia tutiſſima ſunt. Cic.
In Engliſh,
When bootes and ſhoes are torne up to the lefts,
Coblers muſt thruſt their awles up to the hefts.
This is no time to feare *Apelles gramm:*
Ne Sutor quidem ultra crepidam.
LONDON,
Printed by *J. D. & R. I.* for *Stephen Bowtell,* at the ſigne of the Bible in Popes Head-Alley, 1647.

Title page for Ward's immediately popular first book: a witty attack on the breakdown of the social fabric of New and Old England, followed by a program for restoration of social harmony

Ward returned to England that year, preached before Parliament, and published pamphlets opposing religious toleration and attacking the power of the army. In 1648 Ward was made minister at Shenfield, where, comfortably settled, he remained until his death in 1652. He contributed a dedicatory poem to Anne Bradstreet's volume of poetry *The Tenth Muse Lately Sprung Up in America,* published in 1650, and he may have been influential in securing the book's publication.

The immediate popularity of *The Simple Cobbler of Aggawam in America . . .* (it went through four editions in 1647) suggests that its style and message had enormous appeal for English audiences. Essentially a plea for stability in social and political life, the work reveals Ward's allegiance to the ideals of harmony and mutual accommodation rather than to the correctness of the fine points of theological interpretation. He was suspicious of theological debate; he felt that the devil, who "cannot sting the vitals of the Elect mortally," can nevertheless "fly-blow their Intellectuals miserably." Using characteristic neologisms he wrote, "I am neither Presbyterian, nor Plebsbyterian, but an Interpendent"; he felt he was called "to sit and study . . . how Parliament will commoderate a way out of both. . . ."

As the implicit reference to Acts 2: 17-21 in the first sentence of *The Simple Cobbler of Aggawam in America* . . . makes clear, Ward considered the world to be in its latter days and Christ's Second Coming to be imminent. Thus the appeal to his readers to conserve the ancient truths and beware the "contagion" of "unsound mindes" takes on a special urgency. Attacking the breakdown in the social fabric, Ward prefaces his work with the statement that his native country is "lamentably tattered," both in the "upper-leather and sole," and that he is willing to help to mend it "with all the honest stitches he can take." He then lists and disposes of ten objections to his basic contention that diverse "Opinionists" should not be tolerated, and finally turns to a series of recommendations for reforming and restoring English society to harmony and wholeness.

The major metaphors of clothing, stitching, and building are used with particular virulence in a brief but well-known dissertation on "women's fashions," inserted at the conclusion of the initial ten-point argument. Ward's most contorted language is reserved for this invective. The discussion of dress is, of course, symbolic, and suggests several points about Ward's view of women, of men, and of "royled waters" in which Satan "loves to fish." Ward clearly considers male and female roles to be among those "Truths of God [which are] the pillars of the world." He fears not just the faddishness of women, but as he says later, the "dehomination" of men by the devil. In a time characterized by excesses, Ward finds both an "over-franchized people" and an "over-risen king." The result is men deprived of their civil rights, or in danger of being so; such men, Ward says, "are but women." This sense of the undoing of sexual identity is revealed in Ward's mention of "fashions" peculiar to certain women in New England. Ward implicitly decries the example Anne Hutchinson presents to women. Elsewhere, however, Ward deifies women, when he, following Paul, speaks of the New Jerusalem as a "mother" and of commonwealths as mothers. He furthermore pictures England's distress in female terms; he writes that "all her beauty departed, the Lord has covered *Sion* with a cloude. . . ." These and other passages reveal a complex misogyny; this section of *The Simple Cobbler* . . . includes, as well, a touching confession of Ward's loneliness, as a widower of twelve years.

In his dedicatory poem for Anne Bradstreet's book, Ward echoes this concern for the stability of men's and women's sexual roles. In a mock-jovial voice he comments that Bradstreet's work is hard to distinguish from that of Guillaume du Bartas, one of Bradstreet's models. Ward's comments indicate that he finds Bradstreet unique among her sex, and his praise is tempered with caution: "Let men look to't, least women weare the Spurs."

Ward contrived an original stylistic technique: punning, coining new words, and sprinkling the text with irreverent references to Latin and Greek. Beneath this crotchety, irregular surface lies a deep concern for the restoration of a balance between what he calls the "parapoints" of society: a "royal" king, and "loyal" subjects, each in its place. After his return to England Ward continued to put forth these ideas in his sermons and public addresses. If his admonitions did not take effect, his originalities of style certainly did. He had several imitators who came so close to Ward's style that attribution of a number of pamphlets similar to *The Simple Cobbler of Aggawam* . . . is still being debated.

Other:

The Body of Liberties. The Liberties of the Massachusetts Colonie in New England, 1641, compiled by Ward and others, Massachusetts Historical Society *Collections,* third series 8 (1641); Old South Leaflet, volume 7, number 164 (Boston: Directors of the Old South Work, 1905).

References:

John Ward Dean, *Memoir of the Rev. Nathaniel Ward* (Albany: J. Munsell, 1868);

Shirley Wilcox Harvey, "Nathaniel Ward: His Life and Works, Together with an Edited Text of his Simple Cobbler," Ph.D. dissertation, Boston University, 1936;

Samuel Eliot Morison, "Nathaniel Ward: Lawmaker and Wit," in his *Builders of the Bay Colony* (Boston & New York: Houghton Mifflin, 1930), pp. 217-243;

Vernon L. Parrington, *The Colonial Mind, 1620-*

1800, volume 1 of *Main Currents in American Thought* (New York: Harcourt, Brace, 1927), pp. 76-81;

P. M. Zall, Introduction to *The Simple Cobbler of Aggawam in America* (Lincoln: University of Nebraska Press, 1969), pp. ix-xviii.

John Wheelwright

(circa 1592-15 November 1679)

Mark R. Patterson
University of Washington

John Wheelwright (The State House, Boston)

BOOKS: *Mercurius Americanus, Mr. Welds his Antitype, or Massachusetts Great Apologie Examined, Being Observations upon a Paper Styled, A Short Story of the Rise, Reign, and Ruine of the Familists, Libertines, &c. Which Infected the Churches of New-England, &c. . . .* (London, 1645);

A Sermon Preached at Boston in New England upon a Fast Day, the 19th of January, 1636-37 (Cambridge: J. Wilson, 1867);

John Wheelwright. His Writings . . . (Boston: Printed for the Prince Society, 1876).

John Wheelwright, colonial minister and nonconformist, is best remembered for his association with Anne Hutchinson and his long conflict with John Winthrop and the Massachusetts Bay Colony during the Antinomian controversy. Wheelwright was probably born in Saleby, Lincolnshire, England, to Robert Wheelwright, a moderately wealthy landholder. Matriculating at Sydney-Sussex College, Cambridge, when he was eighteen, Wheelwright became friends with Oliver Cromwell before receiving his A.B. in 1614. He received his A.M. in 1618, and took orders the following year. In 1621 he married Marie Storre, daughter of Thomas Storre, vicar of Bilsby, and on 9 April 1623 he succeeded to the vicarage upon the death of his father-in-law. Sometime between 1628 and 1630, after bearing three children, his wife died; thereupon, in 1630, he married Mary Hutchinson, whose brother, William, was married to Anne Hutchinson.

Wheelwright's nonconformist beliefs emerged during the early 1630s, and in 1633 a successor to Wheelwright's vicarage was inducted. Wheelwright was soon completely silenced by his superiors. Perhaps already thinking of emigrating, Wheelwright had purchased land in New Hampshire in 1629, but he remained in Lincolnshire, although unable to preach, until 1636, when he left for America. He arrived in Boston with his wife and five children on 26 May 1636 and was admitted to the church on 12 June. After John Winthrop, fearing Wheelwright's beliefs were Antinomian, rejected his selection as second teacher of the church in Boston (behind John Cotton), Wheelwright became pastor of the new church in Mount Woolaston (now Quincy).

Shortly after assuming his duties, Wheelwright became embroiled in the Antinomian controversy, which centered on his sister-in-law, Anne Hutchinson. The Antinomians stressed the absolute superiority of faith and personal revelation over outward signs of sanctification, thus threatening the power of the community to control belief. In January 1637, Wheelwright belligerently preached a fast-day sermon, the contents of which seemed to oppose the legal authority of John Winthrop and other powerful Boston leaders. Because of his emphasis on justification by faith alone, he was brought before the General Court and was closely questioned for several days, until his conviction for "sedition and contempt of civil authority." Strong opposition to this decision from Governor Henry Vane and several magistrates caused the court to postpone final judgment; it was not until the first synod in August and September 1637 that a final decision was reached. Having lost his main support when now ex-governor Vane returned to England and John Cotton implicitly revised his extreme statements on faith, Wheelwright was finally "disfranchised and banished" by the court on 2 November 1637. Unwilling to continue his opposition, he hurriedly prepared for his exile.

Declining to live in Rhode Island with other settlers and exiles from the Massachusetts Bay Colony, Wheelwright spent the unusually severe winter at Squamscot, New Hampshire. In April 1638 he purchased land from the Indians and, with family and friends, founded Exeter, New Hampshire. Despite the settlement's prosperity, Wheelwright remained uneasily just out of Boston's jurisdiction until the Massachusetts Bay Colony annexed Wheelwright's community in 1643. In the spring of that year, Wheelwright moved to Wells, Maine, along with a number of Exeter parishioners. Here he attempted to reconcile himself with the authorities in Boston by sending letters of repentance to the General Court and Governor Winthrop. Perhaps convinced by the submissive tone of the letters, the legislature lifted his banishment on 9 May 1644. Nevertheless, when John Winthrop and Thomas Weld published their attack on the Antinomians, Wheelwright rebutted it with his own pamphlet, *Mercurius Americanus . . .* (1645). He remained at Wells until 1647, when he was asked to be minister at Hampton, New Hampshire. In 1654, during his ministry at Hampton (1647-1656), he was finally vindicated by the Massachusetts legislature.

In late 1655 or early 1656, Wheelwright returned to England to see and perhaps advise his old friends, particularly Cromwell, who were now in power. Wheelwright remained in England after the Restoration until 1662, when the increasingly uncertain political situation of the Puritans made his return to America advisable. At age seventy he became the pastor at Salisbury, New Hampshire, where he served until his death on 15 November 1679.

References:

Charles H. Bell, Memoir of Wheelwright, in *John Wheelwright. His Writings* (Boston: Printed for the Prince Society, 1876);

John Heard, Jr., *John Wheelwright 1592-1679* (Boston: Houghton Mifflin, 1939).

Alexander Whitaker

(1585-1617)

Michael A. Lofaro
University of Tennessee

BOOK: *Good Newes from Virginia . . .* (London: Printed by Felix Kyngston for William Welby, 1613).

Alexander Whitaker's importance rests upon his sermon *Good Newes from Virginia,* the only substantial piece of his writings that survives. Whitaker sent this work from Henrico, Virginia, to his friend William Crashaw in England after 28 July 1612, and when it was published in 1613, it became the first American sermon to appear in print.

Born the first child of William Whitaker and Susan Culverwell in 1585, Alexander Whitaker went to Eton in 1598, and in 1602 to Trinity College, Cambridge, his father's alma mater. Here he completed his B.A. in two or three years and his M.A. in 1608 before receiving holy orders in 1609. Evidently moved deeply by his friend Crashaw's sermon before the Virginia Council on 21 February 1609, Whitaker left England on 27 May 1611 to bring the gospel to America. In Virginia he served as the minister for Henrico, for the town of New Bermuda, and for those communities further upriver. As the minister to Sir Thomas Dale at Jamestown he very likely instructed and baptized that nobleman's ward, Pocahontas, to gain a first and highly influential convert for the English church in America.

According to Crashaw's introduction to *Good Newes from Virginia . . . ,* Whitaker seeks to answer "the calumnies and slanders, raised vpon our Colonies, and the Countrey it selfe" in his sermon. The minister attempts to demonstrate that the Virginia Plantation is now on sound footing, having withstood the verbal and physical attacks of its adversaries, both from within and without, verbal and physical, white and Indian, and that it is worthy of additional support from the Virginia Company and all Englishmen. It is highly probable that Whitaker expanded his original sermon as delivered in Virginia before he sent it to the Virginia Company in London. His fairly detailed comments on the habits of the Indians and on natural resources and topography would be redundant for those who viewed them on a regular basis, but these descriptions were eagerly received in England and are now of unquestioned historical significance. These relatively unintegrated passages place *Good Newes from Virginia* well within the realm of the earliest English travel, promotion, and propaganda narratives dealing with America.

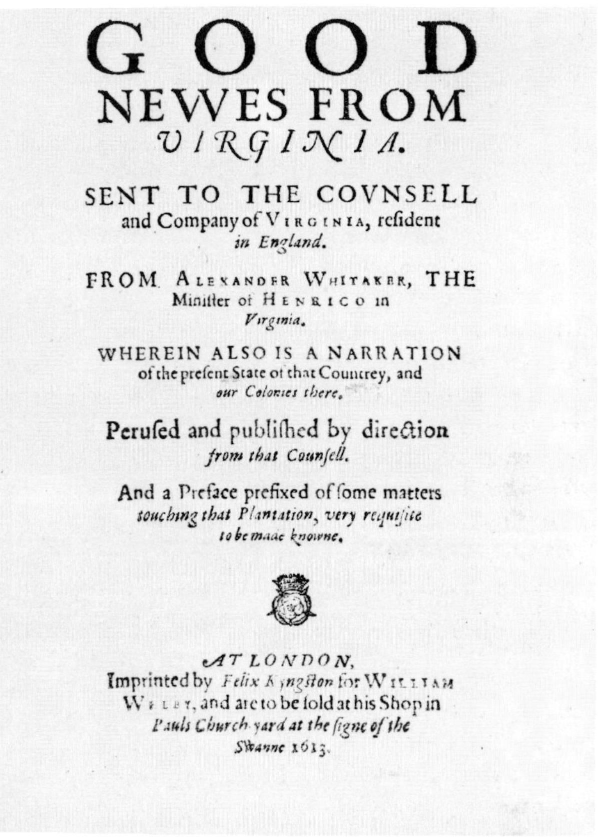

GOOD
NEWES FROM
VIRGINIA.
SENT TO THE COVNSELL
and Company of VIRGINIA, reſident
in England.
FROM ALEXANDER WHITAKER, THE
Miniſter of HENRICO in
Virginia.
WHEREIN ALSO IS A NARRATION
of the preſent State of that Countrey, and
our Colonies there.
Peruſed and publiſhed by direction
from that Counſell.
And a Preface prefixed of ſome matters
touching that Plantation, very requiſite
to be made knowne.

AT LONDON,
Imprinted by *Felix Kyngſton* for WILLIAM
WELBY, and are to be ſold at his Shop in
Pauls Church-yard at the ſigne of the
Swanne 1613.

Title page for Whitaker's sermonic defense of Virginia, the first American sermon to appear in print (John Carter Brown Library, Brown University)

Alexander Whitaker died at the age of thirty-two in the spring of 1617. His ministry of six years in Virginia ended abruptly when he drowned crossing the James River.

Letters:

["To William Crashaw," 9 August, 1611], in *The Genesis of the United States,* by Alexander

Brown (Boston: Houghton Mifflin, 1897), I: 497-500;

"To the Right Worshipful Sir Thomas Smith [Smythe], Knight, Treasurer of the English Colonie in Virginia" [28 July, 1612],in Brown, II: 578-579;

"To my verie deere and louing Cosen M.[aster] G.[ouge] Minister of the B.[lack] F.[riars] in London" [18 June, 1614], in *A True Discourse of the Present Estate of Virginia,* by Ralph Hamor (London: Printed by John Beale for W. Welby, 1615).

References:

Richard Beale Davis, *Intellectual Life in the Colonial South, 1585-1763,* three volumes (Knoxville: University of Tennessee Press, 1978);

William H. Littleton, "Alexander Whitaker (1585-1617), 'The Apostle of Virginia,' " *Historical Magazine of the Protestant Episcopal Church,* 29 (1960): 325-348;

Harry C. Porter, "Alexander Whitaker: Cambridge Apostle to Virginia," *William and Mary Quarterly,* third series 14 (July 1957), 317-343.

Andrew White

(1579-27 December 1656)

Daniel E. Williams
Universität Tübingen

BOOKS: *A Declaration of Lord Baltemore's Plantation in Mary-land* (London, 1633); republished, edited by Lawrence C. Wroth (Baltimore: Lord Baltimore Press, 1929); Latin version: "Declaratio Coloniae Domini Baronis de Baltamoro in Terra Marie prope Virginiam. . . ," translated into English by Nathan C. Brooks, in *Tracts,* edited by Peter Force, volume 4, no. 12 (Washington, D.C.: Peter Force, 1846); original Latin and revised English translation in *Woodstock Letters,* 1 (1872): 12-24; further revised translation, "An Account of the Colony of the Lord Baron of Baltamore," in *Narratives of Early Maryland,* edited by Clayton C. Hall (New York: Scribners, 1910), pp. 1-10;

A Relation of the successful beginnings of the Lord Baltimore's Plantation in Maryland (London, 1634); republished in Shea's *Early Southern Tracts,* no. 1 (Albany, N.Y.: Printed by J. Maunsell, 1865); Latin version: "Relatio itineris in Marylandiam," translated into English by Brooks, in *Tracts,* edited by Peter Force, volume 4, no. 12 (Washington, D.C.: Peter Force, 1846); original Latin and revised English translation in *Woodstock Letters,* 1 (1872): 71-80, 145-155; second English version ("Lechford version"): "A Briefe Relation of the Voyage Unto Maryland," in *Narratives of Early Maryland,* pp. 25-45;

A Relation of Maryland (London: Sold by William Peasley & John Morgan, 1635); republished in *Narratives of Early Maryland,* pp. 63-112.

The history of early Maryland is incomplete without the story of Father Andrew White. An English Jesuit priest, White was actively involved in the Maryland colony throughout its planning stages and its first decade of existence. During these early years he filled several significant roles: sacred and secular adviser, first superior of the Maryland Mission, priest, missionary, New World enthusiast, colonist, propagandist, and historian. Directly and indirectly, White's influence was felt by many—by the Indians and the colonists he administered to both physically and spiritually and by those in Europe who relied on his writings for their image of the new colony. Today his influence continues; his descriptions of Maryland provide some of the most valuable information concerning the people, places, and events of the early colony.

Little is known concerning White's early years. He was born in 1579, probably into a London Catholic family of some means. Like many English recusants of this period, he was educated on the Continent at various seminaries specifically established for English Catholics. After first matriculating at Douai College in 1593, he entered St. Alban's College in Valladolid that same year and the following year studied at St. Hermenegild's College in Seville. After returning to Douai in 1605 he was ordained a secular priest and immediately volunteered for missionary work in England. But White returned to his native country at a time when anti-Catholic sentiment was about to burst into intense rage and open persecution. Angered by a lack of religious freedom, a small band of English Catholics had conspired to blow up both King James I and Parliament on 5 November 1605. The conspiracy was betrayed, however, and on the night of 4-5 November at least twenty barrels of gunpowder were discovered in a cellar underneath the palace at Westminster. Although the leaders of the Gunpowder Plot were either killed trying to escape or executed, many other Catholics were persecuted as well during the anti-Catholic fury which followed. White was arrested and imprisoned for several months before being banished on pain of death. Fleeing to the Continent, he was accepted into the Society of Jesus in 1607 and entered the new novitiate, St. John's College, at Louvain, where he remained until 1609 when he took his first set of vows. He was then sent back to England, despite the possibility of imprisonment and execution, and in 1612 he was known to have been in London and in several southern counties.

For the next decade and a half White divided his time between missionary work in England and professorial duties on the Continent. During the first few years which followed his return to the Continent, he served as professor of sacred studies, dogmatic theology, Hebrew, and Greek, first at Louvain, then later at Liège. When he was not teaching, he returned to England to continue his missionary work. In 1619 he took his final four vows and was sent once more back to England, where he remained for about three years. In 1623 White returned to teaching and was appointed prefect for studies at Louvain. Two years later, after moving to Liège, he was again appointed prefect of studies. During this period of his life White had achieved some prominence in English Catholic circles and was well known as a strict follower of St. Thomas Aquinas. As prefect of studies in charge of the higher courses, he started a controversy over the methods and principles of theological training, writing a number of propositions supporting his conservative Thomist views. This controversy was finally resolved in 1629 when Father Vitelleschi, general of the Society of Jesus in Rome, decided in favor of more liberal methods. It was at this time that White, fifty years old, concluded his career as a professor and requested permission to begin another—

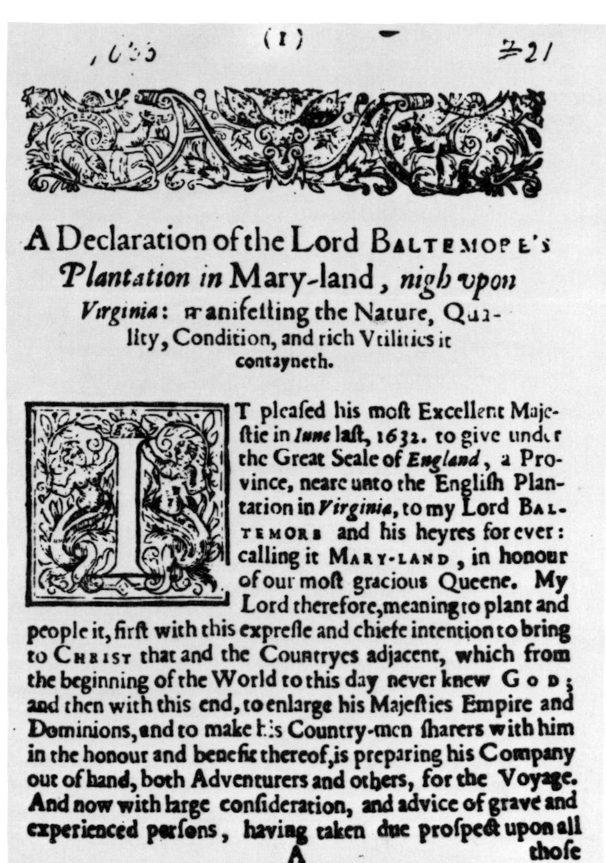

(1)

A Declaration of the Lord BALTEMORE'S *Plantation in* Mary-land, *nigh upon Virginia*: manifesting the Nature, Quality, Condition, and rich Vtilities it contayneth.

IT pleased his most Excellent Majestie in *Iune* last, 1632. to give under the Great Seale of *England*, a Province, neare unto the English Plantation in *Virginia*, to my Lord BALTEMORE and his heyres for ever: calling it MARY-LAND, in honour of our most gracious Queene. My Lord therefore, meaning to plant and people it, first with this expresse and chiefe intention to bring to CHRIST that and the Countryes adjacent, which from the beginning of the World to this day never knew GOD; and then with this end, to enlarge his Majesties Empire and Dominions, and to make his Country-men sharers with him in the honour and benefit thereof, is preparing his Company out of hand, both Adventurers and others, for the Voyage. And now with large consideration, and advice of grave and experienced persons, having taken due prospect upon all

A those

First page for White's pamphlet promoting the recently chartered colony of Maryland, written a few months before he left England with the first group of settlers (from a facsimile at John Carter Brown Library, Brown University; the only extant copy belongs to the Archdiocese of Westminster)

missionary in the New World.

During the 1620s, when White had periodically traveled to England, he had met George Calvert, first Lord of Baltimore, and had become interested in Baltimore's plans for colonization. The two men maintained a correspondence discussing the possibility of an English Catholic settlement in the New World, a correspondence which continued during the time Baltimore spent in Newfoundland attempting to establish Avalon, his first colonization project. After the Avalon project was abandoned in favor of a warmer climate and after the death of Baltimore in 1632, White continued both his interest in an English Catholic settlement and his relationship with the Calvert family. Once the Maryland charter was granted to Cecilius, second Lord Baltimore, White was chosen to be founder and first superior of the Maryland Mission.

In order to attract further support, White wrote *A Declaration of Lord Baltemore's Plantation in Mary-land* (he also wrote a Latin version, "Declaratio Coloniae Domini Baronis de Baltamoro . . .") a few months before his departure for the colony in 1633. This brief promotional pamphlet, which Baltimore corrected before publication, favorably described the possibilities and conditions of settlement. Relying on the accounts of Capt. John Smith and the observations of the first Lord Baltimore, White characterized Maryland as a land of incredible fertility, where both the "seeds of religion" and a variety of worldly enterprises would result in great harvests. Although clearly more interested in the prospects of a spiritual harvest, he did not neglect to mention Maryland's fertility, stating that "three harvests a year" are possible. White further related the story of one New World farmer who grew so many peaches "that he gave a hundred bushels to his pigs last year."

Final preparations for the expedition were made during the summer and early fall of 1633, but departure from Gravesend was delayed until every colonist took an elaborate oath of allegiance to the English crown, the result of continued anti-Catholic sentiment and opposition from those backing the Virginia colony. White and the rest of his Jesuit party waited until the two ships, the *Ark* and the *Dove*, reached the Isle of Wight before boarding in order to escape the oath and unwanted notice. Finally, on Friday, 22 November, the ships set sail for America.

The history of the voyage and the first few weeks in Maryland has been preserved in White's *A Relation of the successful beginnings of the Lord Baltimore's Plantation in Maryland* (1634). This narrative, a combination travel journal and promotional tract, was actually written in three versions, one in Latin and two in English, and the three original manuscripts accompanied the *Ark* on its return voyage back to England two months after landing. The three versions are similar. The Latin version, "Relatio itineris in Marylandiam," was intended for White's superiors in Rôme and expresses a greater acknowledgment of providence. Of the two English versions, one was published in London in order to encourage settlement and investment and, consequently, revealed little of the hardships encountered by the first settlers. The second English version, "A Briefe Relation of the Voyage Unto Maryland," was included in a letter Governor Leonard Calvert sent to his business partner, Sir Richard Lechford. In the two English versions White concentrated more on Maryland's worldly advantages than on its spiritual opportunities. Nevertheless, in all three the hand of God guiding and protecting the colonists was apparent as White related how the expedition was threatened with conspiracy, pirates, storms at sea, shortages of supplies, rebellion, Virginian opposition, and Indian attack. During one particularly terrible storm at sea White exclaimed that "it seemed all the sprights and witches of Maryland were now set in Battaile array against us." When the expedition finally managed to escape each danger, White not only believed that God had delivered them but that God had taken a special interest in their enterprise. After barely escaping a sea battle in the Caribbean with five Spanish men-of-war, he remarked: "But god who endeavoreth the spirituall good of Maryland preserved us from danger." He was convinced that God protected them so that they might "Bring the light of his holy law to those distressed, poore infidels."

Yet despite his missionary zeal, White again did not fail to describe the worldly beauty and advantages around him, and he included some of the most favorable New World descriptions published in England. His appreciative lists of all the fruits, vegetables, trees, and animals he observed are long and sometimes poetic. The Chesapeake Bay is described as "the most delightfull water I ever saw" and the Potomac River is "the sweetest and greatest river I have ever seene, so that the Thames is but a little finger to it." He characterizes St. Mary's, the site of the first settlement, as "noble a seat as could be wished, and as good ground as I suppose is in all Europe." He concludes his narrative by again returning to the theme of fertility: "the soyle, which is excellent so that we cannot sett downe a foot, but tread on Strawberries, raspires [raspberries], fallen mulberrie vines, acchorns, walnuts, saxafras [sassafras] etc."

Historically White's narrative is of great value and is considered to be the authority on the founding of Maryland. His descriptions of the rivalries between different colonies accurately reveal how tense relations sometimes were. Before leaving England, Baltimore ordered his two ships not to approach the Virginia forts too closely, lest they be fired upon. After arriving in Barbados in January 1634 White remarked how the officials there exploited the ocean-weary colonists by raising prices so high "that nothing could be had, but it Cost us our eies [eyes]." Reaching the Chesapeake, he described how William Claiborne, one of Baltimore's "chiefe enemies," had incited the Indians against the Maryland expedition so that "500 bowmen came to meet them at the water side."

In addition to the promotional descriptions and historical information, White's narrative reveals something of the man himself. One of the most charming images is the fifty-four-year-old's excitement over a race between his ship, the *Ark*, and another London merchant ship. "Here we had a greate recreation to see that ship and ours runne for the fame with all the cloath they could make, an howers space with faire winde and weather, and pleasant sound of trumpetts." Equally engaging is the Jesuit professor's description of his first chapel in Maryland. Although accustomed to the finest cathedrals in Spain and France, the devout and determined priest immediately moved into a small Indian hut, made from bark, and there celebrated mass, "haveing it dressed a little better than by the Indians." Ultimately, one cannot help but admire the power of White's faith, a power strong enough to cure the sick, convert the wicked, and establish a colony.

White spent eleven years in Maryland, from 1634 to 1645. During this period he actively pursued his missionary work among both colonists and Indians, becoming something of a Maryland folk hero for his successful conversions and miraculous cures. Two of his best-known stories concern his successful efforts to convert an influential Piscataway "tayac" (or emperor) and his curing a dying Indian with a relic of the Holy Cross. White traveled widely in the region, visiting Indian villages, and from 1639 onward he lived exclusively with the Indians, learning their different dialects well enough to compile an Indian dictionary, a grammar, and a catechism. (Only the catechism is known to exist today.)

Not all of White's experiences were fortunate. During the late 1630s his health began to decline, the result of both age and hardship. Twice he was seriously ill and was expected to die, as several other Jesuit missionaries in Maryland already had. Also his hearing began to fade, but, true to character, White only complained that deafness interfered with his hearing confessions and learning the Indian dialects. Of a more serious nature, his relationship with Baltimore began to fail as well. After the Jesuits had been given land by the Indians, a conflict erupted with Baltimore over ultimate jurisdiction. In 1639 White wrote a long letter to Baltimore, attempting to restore good relations between the Lord Proprietor and the Jesuits. But White's vision of a Catholic kingdom differed with Baltimore's more pecuniary interests, and relations never returned to their former harmony.

White's final experiences in Maryland ended in indignity when the English civil war spilled over to America. In late 1644 White and another Jesuit priest were taken prisoner by Virginia Puritans and carried in chains back to England, where the sixty-six-year-old missionary was then imprisoned in Newgate. He was tried on a charge of treason for being a priest in England, but, after pleading that he had entered the country against his will, he was merely banished. In exile on the Continent for a second time, he vainly petitioned his superiors for permission to return to Maryland, but permission was denied due to his advanced age and ill health. His last years were spent in relative obscurity. Under an assumed name he returned to England and became a private chaplain to a noble family in Hampshire. He died in 1656.

In his efforts to achieve good relations between colonists and Indians White's influence was felt for generations. As a writer he influenced many who had never heard of his name, both those considering emigration and those simply curious about the New World. In 1635 Baltimore supervised the publication of *A Relation of Maryland*, a highly favorable prospectus for emigration largely based on White's previous narratives and possibly incorporating new material by White, but including much material by others as well. This pamphlet did much to encourage settlement and to create a positive image of the new colony. Ultimately Maryland was one of the most successful of the early colonization efforts, and Father Andrew White—Old World professor and New World missionary—contributed much to this success.

References:

Elizabeth Baer, *Seventeenth Century Maryland; A Bibliography* (Baltimore: John Work Garrett Library, 1949);

Edwin Warfield Beitzell, *The Jesuit Missions of St. Mary's County, Maryland* (Abell, Md., 1960);

Bernard Ulysses Campbell, "Sketch of the Early Missions in Maryland," *U.S. Catholic Magazine, 2* (1848): 529-535, 580-585;

"Extracts from the Annual Letters of the English Province of the Society of Jesus," in *Narratives of Early Maryland*, edited by Clayton C. Hall (New York: Scribners, 1910), pp. 113-144;

Henry J. Foley, *Records of the English Province of the Society of Jesus*, 7 volumes (London: Burns & Oates, 1875-1883);

Thomas Hughes, *History of the Society of Jesus in North America* (Cleveland: Burrows Brothers, 1907);

J. A. Leo Lemay, *Men of Letters in Colonial Maryland* (Knoxville: University of Tennessee Press, 1972), pp. 8-27;

John Gilmary Shea, *History of the Catholic Missions Among the Indian Tribes of the United States 1529-1854* (New York: Dunigan, 1855; republished, New York: AMS Press, 1973);

Bernard C. Steiner, "Beginnings of Maryland 1631-1639," *Johns Hopkins University Studies in Historical and Political Sciences*, 21, nos. 8-10 (1903): 7-112.

Samuel Whiting

(20 November 1597-11 December 1679)

Wesley T. Mott
University of Wisconsin

BOOKS: *Oratio, Quam Comitijs Cantabrigiensibus Americanis Peroravit . . . Anno M.DC.XL.IX.* (Cambridge?, 1649; Boston: Printed by B. Green, 1709);

A Discourse of the Last Judgement . . . (Cambridge: Printed by S. Green & M. Johnson, 1664);

Abraham's Humble Intercession for Sodom . . . (Cambridge: Printed by Samuel Green, 1666).

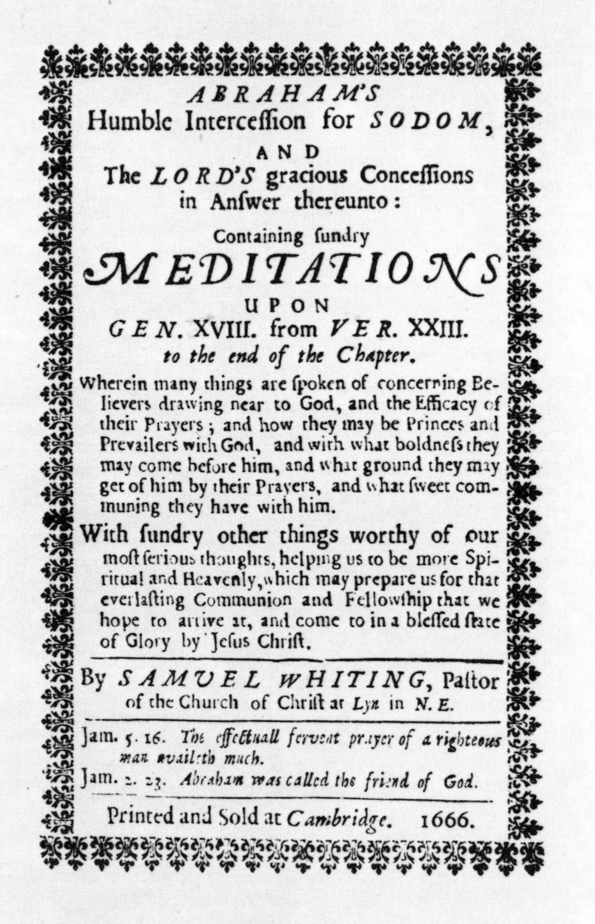

ABRAHAM'S
Humble Interceffion for *SODOM*,
AND
The *LORD'S* gracious Conceffions in Anfwer thereunto:
Containing fundry
MEDITATIONS
UPON
GEN. XVIII. from *VER.* XXIII.
to the end of the Chapter.

Wherein many things are fpoken of concerning Believers drawing near to God, and the Efficacy of their Prayers; and how they may be Princes and Prevailers with God, and with what boldnefs they may come before him, and what ground they may get of him by their Prayers, and what fweet communing they have with him.

With fundry other things worthy of our moft ferious thoughts, helping us to be more Spiritual and Heavenly, which may prepare us for that everlafting Communion and Fellowfhip that we hope to arrive at, and come to in a bleffed ftate of Glory by Jefus Chrift.

By *SAMUEL WHITING*, Paftor of the Church of Chrift at *Lyn* in *N. E.*

Jam. 5. 16. *The effectuall fervent prayer of a righteous man availeth much.*
Jam. 2. 23. *Abraham was called the friend of God.*

Printed and Sold at *Cambridge.* 1666.

Title page for Whiting's 1666 book, which, despite its warnings to the wicked, reflects its author's well-known toleration and quiet temper (John Carter Brown Library, Brown University)

Samuel Whiting, a leading New England minister and author of one of the earliest spiritual biographies in America, was born at Boston, Lincolnshire, son of John Whiting, mayor of Boston in 1600 and 1608. Related to the Reverend John Cotton, he received his A.B. (1616) and A.M. (1620) at the great Puritan college, Emmanuel, at Cambridge. On 6 August 1629 he married his second wife, Elizabeth St. John, daughter of a member of parliament and sister of Oliver St. John, future chief justice of England under Cromwell. Earlier prosecuted for nonconformist preaching and practices at Lynn Regis, Whiting was harassed again after his second marriage in his ministry at Skirbeck. Having seen Cotton flee England in disguise, he brought his wife, his daughter from his first marriage, Dorothy, and his son Samuel to New England in 1636. They settled at Saugus (renamed Lynn in honor of Whiting's English pastorate), where, until his death more than four decades later, Whiting served as minister.

Whiting's career was remarkably varied. A proficient scholar in Hebrew, he also delivered a Latin oration in 1649 at Harvard College, of which he was named overseer in 1654. He was invited to give the artillery sermon for 1660 and is believed to have presided over the synod of 1662. Though called upon by the Bay Colony for leadership in many capacities, Whiting was known for his toleration and beloved for his "quiet temper." In his *Magnalia Christi Americana* (1702) Cotton Mather noted that Whiting's "very Countenance had an amiable Smile continually sweetening of it." At the height of the Antinomian crisis in 1637, Whiting apparently did not take part in the synod or legal proceedings that led to the banishment of John Wheelwright, who had been his neighbor in England and with whom he had sailed to New England; yet after 1650 Whiting shared the concern of many that as the great New England founders died off, the authority of the clergy was diminishing. His spiritual biography, "Concerning the Life of the Famous Mr. Cotton, Teacher to the Church of Christ at Boston, in New-England," was written in 1653 both as a consoling reminder of John Cotton's contribution to the Puritan cause and as an example to others. (Though not published until 1769, Whiting's sketch was used by John Norton and Cotton Mather in their more elaborate biographies of Cotton.) Later, in the face of mounting interference by civil courts, Whiting fought to maintain the preeminence of churches in matters of discipline.

Whiting's *A Discourse of the Last Judgement*... (1664), an extended outline of sermon notes, was so popular that he soon published a more substantial volume, *Abraham's Humble Intercession for Sodom*... (1666). This work, orthodox as it is, also reflects Whiting's mild, introspective nature. He urges his reader "To be familiar with God, and to commune sweetly with him in Prayer, as he does with us in his gracious Answers." He threatens that God will destroy the wicked, but terror here is primarily an incentive for the reader to long for the great "comforts" of salvation. In great pain from bladder stones for many years, Whiting "bore his Affliction with incomparable Patience" and to the end was a respected voice among the New England clergy.

Other:

"Concerning the Life of the Famous Mr. Cotton, Teacher to the Church of Christ at Boston, in New-England," in *A Collection of Original Papers Relative to the History of the Colony of Massachusetts-Bay*, edited by Thomas Hutchinson (Boston: Printed by Thomas & John Fleet, 1769).

References:

Cotton Mather, *Magnalia Christi Americana* (London: Printed for Thomas Parkhurst, 1702), III: 156-161;

William Whiting, *Memoir of Rev. Samuel Whiting, D.D.* (Boston: Rand, Avery, 1872);

Alexander Young, Notes to "Concerning the Life of the Famous Mr. Cotton. . . ," in *Chronicles of the First Planters of the Colony of Massachusetts Bay, from 1623 to 1636*, edited by Young (Boston: Little & Brown, 1846), pp. 419-431.

Michael Wigglesworth

Ronald A. Bosco
State University of New York at Albany

BIRTH: Probably Yorkshire, England, 18 October 1631, to Edward and Esther Wigglesworth.

EDUCATION: A.B., 1651; A.M., 1653; Harvard College.

MARRIAGES: 1655 to Mary Reyner; daughter: Mercy. 1679 to Martha Mudge; children: Abigail, Mary, Martha, Esther, Dorothy, Samuel. 1691 to Sybil Sparhawk Avery; son: Edward.

DEATH: Malden, Massachusetts, 10 June 1705.

BOOKS: *The Day of Doom: or, a Description of the Great and Last Judgment. With a Short Discourse about Eternity* (Boston: Printed by Samuel Green, 1662; London: Printed by W.G. for John Sims, 1673);

Meat Out of the Eater: or Meditations concerning the necessity, end, and usefulness of Afflictions unto God's children . . . (Boston: Printed by

Samuel Green & M. Johnson, 1670);

The Diary of Michael Wigglesworth, 1653-1657, edited by Edmund S. Morgan (New York: Harper & Row, 1965; London: Harper & Row, 1966).

As is true of many colonial figures, Wigglesworth's fame during his life and in the minds of succeeding generations of New Englanders lies in a few, though momentous, public contributions to the spiritual life of his culture. Although the subject of several short studies in the nineteenth century and of a sympathetic full-length biography in this century, Wigglesworth's private, personal life is surrounded by much ambiguity and conjecture. Even his brief "Autobiography" and his more detailed diary for the years 1653-1657, both of which have been published, are of little help, for consistent with the established Puritan tradition of personal letters, they emphasize Wigglesworth's spiritual growth: a conventional, repetitive process of spiritual doubt, followed by humiliation, followed by assurance.

What is known, then, of Malden's famous pastor, physician, and poet is at best sketchy and derivative. The son of Edward and Esther Wigglesworth, he and his parents left the Yorkshire district in England and arrived at Charlestown in New England in 1638. After a brief stay, they traveled to New Haven, Connecticut, where they settled in October of that year. Prepared for college by Ezekiel Cheever, under whom he was writing Latin compositions by the age of nine, young Wigglesworth had to interrupt his education and return home to help support the family when his father became ill. In frail health himself, Wigglesworth remained at home for five years, until, at the age of fourteen, he resumed his studies. When he was seventeen, he entered Harvard College with the class of 1651, obtaining both his A.B. and A.M. degrees there. From 1652 to 1654 he remained at Harvard as a fellow and a tutor of the college; Shubael Dummer, John Eliot, Eleazer Mather, and Increase Mather were among his pupils at this time. Wigglesworth began to preach occasionally around Boston in 1653, and sometime during 1654 or 1655 he was invited to settle as minister at Malden, where he was formally ordained on 7 September 1656.

Wigglesworth was able to discharge his duties at the Malden church for only a year or so. In 1657 he became the victim of a painful, lingering disease that lasted almost without interruption until 1686. During that thirty-year period he shared (with limited success) authority over the Malden congregation with colleagues Benjamin Bunker (from 1663 to 1670), Benjamin Blackman (from 1674 to 1678), and Thomas Cheever, Ezekiel Cheever's son (from 1681 to 1686). On 23 September 1663, when his health had become so impaired that he had to suspend completely his pastoral labors, Wigglesworth sailed to Bermuda in the hope of a cure. That plan failing, he returned to Malden at the end of nine months and resumed his ministry as best he could.

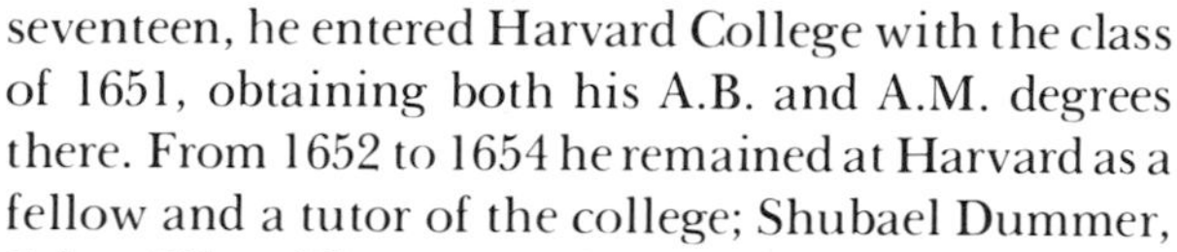

Though his ministry was drastically reduced during the period from 1663 to 1686, this time was nevertheless productive for Wigglesworth. He maintained a medical practice in Malden, and in addition to overseeing the reprinting of *The Day of Doom* (1662) in 1666 and 1670, he had *Meat Out of the Eater* published in 1670. Although the matter has never been settled fully, it appears, according to a letter Wigglesworth wrote to Increase Mather in 1684, that the trustees of the Harvard Corporation invited Wigglesworth to become president of the college after the death of John Rogers in July 1684. Wigglesworth declined, saying, "I cannot think my bodily health and strength competent to undertake . . . such a weighty work as you mention. . . . Wherefore I hope the Colledge & Overseers will think of and apply themselves to a fitter person." However, in 1685, when the Malden church had become financially and administratively reduced to the point of public scandal, Wigglesworth made a startling recovery. At that time, as Cotton Mather observed in *A Faithful Man, Described and Rewarded* . . . (1705), "It pleased God . . . wondrously to restore His *Faithful Servant*. He that had been for nearly Twenty years almost *Buried Alive*, comes abroad again." Thomas Cheever was dismissed from his position as Wigglesworth's colleague early in 1686, and by May, Wigglesworth had so regained his health that he was able to preach the annual Massachusetts election sermon. A second testimony to his pulpit talent and renewed vigor came in 1696, when he was invited to preach the annual artillery election sermon. Neither sermon was ever published. Routinely preaching two or three times a week and, without concern for his personal comfort, working daily to preserve the spiritual as well as physical well-being of his flock, Wigglesworth fulfilled his charge with uncommon energy for the last twenty years of his life.

Wigglesworth's three marriages have been the

subject of considerable controversy and genealogical discussion. Some scholars have argued that the death of his first wife, his cousin Mary Reyner, in 1659, exacerbated his declining physical condition and encouraged a state of depression which lasted until his second marriage in 1679. That marriage, to Martha Mudge, his housekeeper, who was about twenty-five years his junior and was once unkindly characterized by Increase Mather as "your servant mayd . . . of obscure parentage . . . & of no church, nor so much as Baptised," is the most controversial. The senior clergymen of Boston, under the leadership of Increase Mather, were scandalized by the match, while an outraged Malden congregation voted to reduce Wigglesworth's salary. Nevertheless, as his biographers surmise, the marriage seems to have been a happy one and not without significant therapeutic benefits for the aging, ailing minister. For instance, during the first year of marriage, Wigglesworth, representing Malden, was elected a freeman of the colony, and with Martha he began a family that would eventually include six children—all after twenty years of apparent physical and sexual debilitation. Additionally, he returned to his poetry, revising both *The Day of Doom* and *Meat Out of the Eater* for new editions. Finally, to paraphase Cotton Mather's statement, Wigglesworth returned from the grave during the 1680s to resume a productive ministerial career that, as all agree, merited in the end Malden's esteem and love. To the extent that one may be redeemed of twenty years worth of troubles by his children and grandchildren, Wigglesworth was many times blessed, for his son Samuel, whose mother was Martha, was widely known in the eighteenth century as physician and pastor of what is now Hamilton, Massachusetts; his son Edward, whose mother was Sybil Avery, Wigglesworth's third wife, was the first Hollis Professor of Divinity at Harvard College; his grandson Edward was the second Hollis Professor; and his great-grandson David Tappan was the third.

As a poet, Wigglesworth enjoyed a singularly high reputation during the colonial period; however, that reputation has diminished appreciably over the past century, in part because Wigglesworth has not been the subject of serious critical scholarship, in part because in what scholarship there is Wigglesworth's poetry invariably suffers in comparisons between it and the poetry of contemporaries Anne Bradstreet and Edward Taylor, and in part because Wigglesworth's aesthetic bias, which was fashioned out of an appreciation of the Puritan plain style and a conviction of the rightness of New England's brand of Calvinism, strikes contemporary readers as more appropriate to the pulpit than to poetic stanzas. However, if we accept Cotton Mather's account of the reason that Wigglesworth took to poetry in the first place, we discover that Wigglesworth was aware of what today we consider the limitations of his poetry, and that from his point of view (and from the point of view of the several generations of colonials raised on the poetry) the intentionally didactic or sermonic aspect, orthodox content, and plain style of his poetry were its very strengths. Referring to the period from 1657 to 1662, when Wigglesworth was first struck with his affliction and turned to poetry, Mather wrote: "And that he might yet more *Faithfully* set himself to Do Good, when he could not *Preach*, he *Wrote* several Composures, as are for Truth's dressed up in a *Plain Meeter*."

Without doubt, *The Day of Doom* (1662) is Wigglesworth's best-known work. An immediate success, the volume contains, in addition to the title poem, verses addressed "To the Christian Reader," "A Prayer unto Christ the Judge of the World," "A Short Discourse on Eternity," "A Postscript unto the Reader," and "Vanity of Vanities; A Song of Emptiness. . . ." In the 1673 London edition, a poem of 104 lines entitled "I walk'd and did a little Molehill view" appeared, but that poem, which uncharacteristically for Wigglesworth develops natural subjects, has been all but discredited by modern scholarship as coming from Wigglesworth's hand. In "A Prayer unto Christ the Judge of the World," the prefatory lines to *The Day of Doom*, the poet acknowledges the Puritan bent of both his verses and his imagination:

O Dearest Dread, most glorious King,
I'le of thy justest Judgments sing:
Do thou my head and heart inspire,
To Sing aright, as I desire.
Thee, thee alone I'le invocate,
For I do much abominate
To call the *Muses* to mine aid:
Which is th' Unchristian use, and trade
Of some that Christians would be thought,
And yet they worship worse then nought.
Oh! what a deal of Blasphemy,
And Heathenish Impiety,
In Christian Poets may be found.

. . . .

Oh! guide me by thy sacred Sprite
So to indite, and so to write,
That I thine holy Name may praise,
And teach the Sons of men thy wayes.

The first native American "best-seller," the volume was reprinted regularly until the end of the eighteenth century, and the title poem was memorized by successive generations of New England schoolchildren, for whom it was an entertaining and instructive supplement to catechism and Bible. Filled with biblical allusion and direct reference and written in the ballad meter, "The Day of Doom" presents a vision of the judgment day wherein the reader, much like the reader of a Puritan sermon might be, is charged to look after his spiritual condition at the same time as he is urged to see the wisdom and justice of doctrines such as predestination and the final mercifulness of Calvin's God toward the saints. Characters in the poem include a wide range of sinners ("whining hypocrites," "Idolaters, false worshippers, / Prophaners of Gods Name," "Blasphemers lewd, and Swearers shrewd, / Scoffers at Purity," and "Sabbath-polluters, Saints persecuters, / Presumptuous men and proud"—to name a few) who are contrasted to Christ's notable saints (his "holy Martyrs," his faithful "Sheep," his "Flock of Lambs"—"all sound Believers [Gospel receivers]"). Of course, the saints represent the ideal, and their faithful service to Christ only heightens the "endless pains, and scalding flames, / [of those] . . . waiting for Damnation." Once all the sinners are condemned to hell (unborn babes are sent to the easiest room in hell), the reward waiting for the saints is elaborated upon with an intensity that should have moved all Puritans, including marginal ones, to repent and be saved. The concluding stanzas of the poem celebrate the saints' union with God with as much sentiment and self-righteousness as the plain style allowed:

O blessed state of the Renate!
    O wondrous Happiness,
To which they're brought, beyond what thought
    can reach, or words express!
Griefs water-course, and sorrows source,
    are turn'd to joyful streams,
Their old distress and heaviness
    are vanished like dreams.

For God above in arms of love
    doth clearly them embrace,
And fills their sprights with such delights,
    and pleasures in his grace;
As shall not fail, nor yet grow stale
    through frequency of use:
Nor do they fear Gods favour there,
    to forfeit by abuse.

For there the Saints are perfect Saints,
    and holy ones indeed,
From all the sin that dwelt within
    their mortal bodies freed:
Made Kings and Priests to God through Christs
    dear loves transcendency,
There to remain, and there to reign
    with him Eternally.

For both its occasion and its style, "God's Controversy with New-England," written in the same year that *The Day of Doom* was published, is probably the more genuinely "native" of the two. Whereas *The Day of Doom* develops content that is universal and universally applicable, "God's Controversy with New-England" is directed at the specific condition of a fallen New England. Composed at the time that New England clergymen were first preaching against declension, the poem enlarges on the subject of "New-England Planted, Prospered, Declining, Threatned, Punished" for the edification of God's latest chosen people. "God's Controversy with New-England" is, then, a poetic jeremiad, cautioning New Englanders that the plight of a fallen Israel is theirs unless they return to the ideals of the founders and give up the path of worldliness and carnal security which they now follow. The occasion for the poem was a drought that affected New England in 1661-1662, a calamity that Wigglesworth interpreted as a punishment from God for New England's backsliding and a warning from God in which the final dissolution of New England into a place of "barrenness," of "great & parching drought" is foreshadowed. Although the emotive impact of "The Day of Doom" is clearly more sustained than that of "God's Controversy with New-England," it is suggestive that, as Wigglesworth reveals a deep love for New England and a desire to see New England's potential fulfilled in the second poem, the assumption that such feelings were shared among his contemporaries leads one to wonder about the popularity this poem might have achieved, had it been published in the seventeenth century. As much as "The Day of Doom" moved saints and sinners to consider their ways, affirmative sentiments such as these from the conclusion of "God's Controversy with New-England" might have moved many to repent and reform:

Ah dear New England! dearest land to me;
    Which unto God hast hitherto been dear,
And mayst be more dear than formerlie,
    If to his voice thou wilt incline thine ear.
. . . .
Thou still hast in thee many praying saints,

Of great account, and precious with the Lord,
Who dayly powre out unto him their plaints,
And strive to please him both in deed & word.

Cheer on, sweet souls, my heart is with you all,
And shall be with you, maugre Sathan's might:
And whereso'ere this body be a Thrall,
Still in New-England shall be my delight.

Meat Out of the Eater, Wigglesworth's final major poetic effort, was completed in 1669 and published in 1670. The most introspective and, in that, personal of Wigglesworth's poetry, *Meat Out of the Eater* consists of a series of meditations and songs "about ye cross" written as much to console as to edify "enduring" Christians. In many respects, Wigglesworth was his own model for the enduring Christian, though the sense of Puritan modesty so apparent in his diary would never have allowed him to admit that he was his own source. But after years of infirmity, depression, and frustration, which affected his private life and his ability to discharge his ministerial duties, compensations for which the poet argues in *"Tolle Crucem,"* the volume's opening poem, or that are developed in the many songs and meditations that constitute the volume's long section of "Riddles Unriddled, or Christian Paradoxes" must have been derived from personal experience. Songs that elaborate riddles such as "Sick Men's Health," "Strength in Weakness," and "Joy in Sorrow" exhibit a poignancy and represent an expression of inner conviction that during the late-seventeenth or early-eighteenth centuries are otherwise found only in Edward Taylor's meditations.

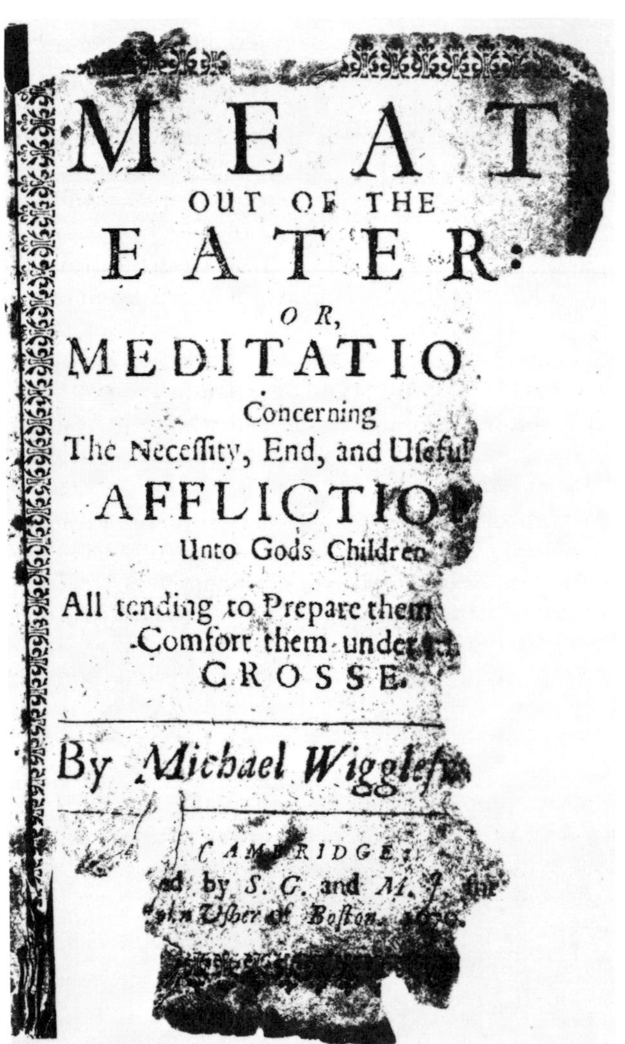
MEAT
OUT OF THE
EATER:
OR,
MEDITATIO
Concerning
The Neceffity, End, and Ufeful
AFFLICTIO
Unto Gods Children
All tending to Prepare them
Comfort them under
CROSSE.
By Michael Wiggle
CAMBRIDGE:
by S. G. and M.
Ufher of Bofton.

Title page for Wigglesworth's introspective, poetic meditations born of his years of mental and physical suffering (John Carter Brown Library, Brown University)

By 1689, when *Meat Out of the Eater* appeared in a fourth edition, Wigglesworth had a secure and appreciative following for his poetry, and he had resumed the challenges of his ministry. "God's Controversy with New-England" and his two major volumes of verse were, then, accomplishments of what Wigglesworth had likely assumed were unproductive "career" years. Yet the popular response to *The Day of Doom* and *Meat Out of the Eater* by his contemporaries should have shown him that as a poet he was effectively about the Lord's work. Contemporary readers should also be impressed, for no American poet enjoyed such wide appeal and literary success at home or abroad until the Fireside poets emerged in the nineteenth century. In addition to his major poetry, seven other pieces survive from the period 1660-1705. All remained in manuscript until after Wigglesworth's death, though four were published soon afterward by Cotton Mather in an appendix to *A Faithful Man, Described and Rewarded . . .* (1705), the funeral sermon he preached to Wigglesworth's Malden congregation. Three of these seven poems are highly occasional or topical (one, written in 1670, is on the death of Benjamin Bunker, Wigglesworth's colleague at the Malden church; another, written in 1673, is on the return of his friend John Foster, who was imprisoned by the Moors). The remaining four poems are personal expressions of disappointment and anxiety compensated for by Christ's love and the promise of eternal life. Of these, "Death Expected and Welcomed," a brief poem of twelve lines probably written in 1705, offers an apt summary of Wigglesworth's career and poetic concerns:

> Welcome, sweet rest, by me so long desired,
> Who have with sins and griefs so long been tired.
> And welcome, Death, my Father's messinger,
> Of my felicity the hastener.
> Welcome, good Angels, who, for me distrest,
> Are come to guard me to eternal rest.
> Welcome, O Christ! who hast my soul redeemed:
> Whose favor I have more than life esteemed.
> O! do not now my sinful soul forsake,
> But to thyself, thy servant gathering, take.
> Into thine hands I recommend my spirit,
> Trusting, through thee, eternal life to inherit.

Other:

"*Christe, parum doleo quia te non diligio multum*," in *A Faithful Man, Described and Rewarded. Some Observable & Serviceable Passages in the Life and Death of Mr. Michael Wigglesworth*, by Cotton Mather (Boston: Printed by B. Green for Benj. Eliot, 1705), p. 42;

"*Ira premit, peccata gravant, afflictio frangit*," in *A Faithful Man, Described and Rewarded . . .* , p. 43;

"Death Expected and Welcomed," in *A Faithful Man, Described and Rewarded . . .* , p. 45;

"A Farewell to the World," in *A Faithful Man, Described and Rewarded . . .* , pp. 46-48;

"Autobiography," *New England Historical and Genealogical Register*, 17 (1863): 137-139;

"Upon the Return of My Dear Friend Mr. Foster with His Son Out of Captivity under the Moors," *American Historical Record*, 1 (1871): 393;

"Upon the Much Lamented Death of That Precious Servant of Christ, Mr. Benjamin Buncker," *New England Historical and Genealogical Register*, 26 (1872): 11-12;

"When as the wayes of Jesus Christ," *New England Historical and Genealogical Register*, 26 (1872): 12;

"God's Controversy with New-England," *Proceedings of the Massachusetts Historical Society*, 12 (1873): 83-93.

Biographies:

John Ward Dean, *Memoir of Rev. Michael Wigglesworth, Author of The Day of Doom* (Albany, N.Y.: Munsell, 1871);

Richard Crowder, *No Featherbed to Heaven: A Biography of Michael Wigglesworth* (Ann Arbor: Michigan State University Press, 1962).

References:

O. M. Brack, Jr., "Michael Wigglesworth and the Attribution of 'I Walk'd and Did a Little Mole-Hill View,' " *Seventeenth-Century News*, 28 (Fall 1970): 41-44;

Deloraine P. Corey, *The History of Malden, Massachusetts, 1633-1785* (Malden, 1899), pp. 186-295;

Robert Daly, *God's Altar: The World and the Flesh in Puritan Poetry* (Berkeley, Los Angeles & London: University of California Press, 1978);

Richard M. Gummere, *Seven Wise Men of Colonial America* (Cambridge: Harvard University Press, 1967), pp. 25-40;

Cotton Mather, *A Faithful Man, Described and Rewarded. Some Observable & Serviceable Passages in the Life and Death of Mr. Michael Wigglesworth . . .* (Boston: Printed by B. Green for Benj. Eliot, 1705);

F. O. Matthiessen, "Michael Wigglesworth, A Puritan Artist," *New England Quarterly*, 1 (October 1928): 491-504;

John Langdon Sibley, "Michael Wigglesworth," in *Biographical Sketches of Graduates of Harvard University*, volume 1 (Cambridge, Mass.: Charles William Sever, 1873), pp. 259-286;

William B. Sprague, *Annals of the American Pulpit; or Commemorative Notices of Distinguished American Clergymen of Various Denominations* (New York: Carter, 1866), I: 143-146.

Papers:

Wigglesworth's fragmentary manuscripts are housed at the New England Historic Genealogical Society and the Massachusetts Historical Society, both in Boston.

Samuel Willard

(31 January 1640-12 September 1707)

Peter L. Rumsey
Columbia University

BOOKS: *Useful Instructions for a professing People in Times of great Security and Degeneracy . . .* (Cambridge: Printed by Samuel Green, 1673);

The Heart Garrisoned. Or, The Wisdome, and Care of the Spiritual Souldier above all things to safeguard his Heart . . . (Cambridge: Printed by Samuel Green, 1676);

A Sermon Preached upon Ezekiel 22.30, 31. Occasioned by the Death of the much honoured John Leveret, Esq; Governour of the Colony of Massachusetts. N-E . . . (Boston: Printed by John Foster, 1679);

The Duty of a People that have Renewed their Covenant with God . . . (Boston: Printed by John Foster, 1680);

Ne Sutor Ultra Crepidam. Or Brief Animadversions Upon the New-England Anabaptists late Fallacious Narrative . . . (Boston: Printed by S. Green upon assignment of S. Sewall & sold by Sam. Phillips, 1681);

Covenant-Keeping The Way to Blessedness . . . (Boston: Printed by James Glen for Samuel Sewall, 1682);

The Fiery Tryal no strange thing . . . (Boston: Printed for Samuel Sewall, 1682);

The High Esteem Which God hath of the Death of his Saints. As it was Delivered in a Sermon Preached October 7, 1683. Occasioned by the Death of the Worshipful John Hull Esq. . . . (Boston: Printed by Samuel Green for Samuel Sewall, 1683);

Mercy Magnified on a Penitent Prodigal, Or a Brief Discourse, wherein Christs Parable of the Lost Son found, is Opened and Applied . . . (Boston: Printed by Samuel Green for Samuel Phillips, 1684);

The Child's Portion: Or the unseen Glory of the Children of God, Asserted, and proved: Together with several other Sermons . . . (Boston: Printed by Samuel Green & sold by Samuel Phillips, 1684);

A Brief Discourse of Justification . . . (Boston: Printed by S. Green for Samuel Phillips, 1686);

Heavenly Merchandize: Or the Purchase of Truth Recommended, and the Selling of it Disswaded . . . (Boston: Printed by Samuel Green & sold by Joseph Brunning, 1686);

A Brief Discourse Concerning that Ceremony of Laying the Hand on the Bible in Swearing (London: Printed by J. A., 1689);

The Principles of the Protestant Religion Maintained, And Churches of New-England, in the Profession and Exercise thereof Defended, Against all the Calumnies of one George Keith, A Quaker . . ., by Willard, James Allin, Joshua Moody, and Cotton Mather (Boston: Printed by Richard Pierce, 1690);

The Barren Fig Trees Doom . . . (Boston: Printed by Benjamin Harris & John Allen, 1691);

The Danger of Taking God's Name in Vain . . . (Boston: Printed by Benjamin Harris & John Allen, 1691);

The Mourners Cordial Against Excessive Sorrow . . . (Boston: Printed by Benjamin Harris & John Allen, 1691);

Promise-Keeping. A Great Duty . . . (Boston: Printed by Benjamin Harris & John Allen, 1691);

The Sinfulness of Worshipping God With Men's Institutions . . . (Boston: Printed by Benjamin Harris & John Allen, 1691);

Some Miscellany Observations On our present Debates respecting Witchcrafts . . . (Philadelphia: Printed by William Bradford for Hezekiah Usher, 1692);

The Doctrine of the Covenant of Redemption . . . (Boston: Printed by Benj. Harris, 1693);

Rules for the Discerning of the Present Times . . . (Boston: Printed by Benjamin Harris, 1693);

The Character of a Good Ruler . . . (Boston: Printed by Benjamin Harris for Michael Perry, 1694);

The Law Established by the Gospel . . . (Boston: Printed by Bartholomew Green, 1694);

Reformation The Great Duty of an Afflicted People . . . (Boston: Printed & sold by Bartholomew Green, 1694);

Impenitent Sinners Warned of their Misery and Summoned to Judgement . . . (Boston: Printed by B. Green & J. Allen, 1698);

The Man of War. A Sermon Preached to the Artillery Company . . . (Boston: Printed by B. Green & J. Allen, 1699);

Spiritual Desertions Discovered and Remedied . . . (Boston: Printed by B. Green & J. Allen for Michael Perry & Benjamin Eliot, 1699);

The Fountain Opened: Or, The Great Gospel Priviledge of having Christ exhibited to Sinfull Men . . . (Boston: Printed by B. Green & J. Allen for Samuel Sewall, Jr., 1700);

Love's Pedigree. Or A Discourse shewing the Grace of Love in a Believer to be of a Divine Original . . . (Boston: Printed by B. Green & J. Allen & sold by Benjamin Eliot, 1700);

Morality Not to be Relied on for Life . . . (Boston: Printed by B. Green & J. Allen for Benjamin Eliot, 1700);

The Peril of the Times Displayed . . . (Boston: Printed by B. Green & J. Allen for Benjamin Eliot, 1700);

A Remedy Against Despair . . . (Boston: Printed by B. Green & J. Allen & sold by S. Phillips, 1700);

The Truly Blessed Man . . . (Boston: Printed by B. Green & J. Allen for Michael Perry, 1700; London, 1722);

The Best Priviledge . . . (Boston: Printed by B. Green & J. Allen for Benjamin Eliot, 1701);

The Checkered State of the Gospel Church . . . (Boston: Printed by B. Green & J. Allen for Samuel Sewall, Jr., 1701);

The Christians Exercise by Satans Temptation . . . (Boston: Printed by B. Green & J. Allen for Benjamin Eliot, 1701);

The Fear of an Oath. Or, Some Cautions to be used about Swearing . . . (Boston: Printed for Nicholas Boone, 1701);

Prognostics of Impending Calamities . . . (Boston: Printed by B. Green & J. Allen for Nicholas Boone, 1701);

Walking With God, The Great Duty and Priviledge of true Christians . . . (Boston: Printed by B. Green & J. Allen & sold by Benjamin Eliot, 1701);

A Brief Reply to Mr. George Keith, in Answer To a Script of his, Entituled, A Refutation of a Dangerous and Hurtful Opinion, Maintained by Mr. Samuel Willard (Boston: Printed for & sold by Samuel Phillips, 1703);

Israel's True Safety . . . (Boston: Printed by B. Green for Samuel Phillips, 1704);

The Just Man's Prerogative . . . (Boston: Printed by B. Green & sold by Nicholas Boone, 1706);

A Thanksgiving Sermon Preach'd at Boston in New England, December, 1705. On the Return of a Gentleman from his Travels (London: Printed for R. Smith, 1709);

Some Brief Sacramental Meditations, Preparatory for Communion at the Great Ordinance of the Supper (Boston: Printed by B. Green for Benjamin Eliot, 1711);

A Compleat Body of Divinity in Two Hundred and Fifty Expository Lectures on the Assembly's Shorter Catechism . . . (Boston: Printed by B. Green & S. Kneeland for B. Eliot & D. Henchman, 1726);

Brief Directions to a Young Scholar Designing the Ministry, for the Study of Divinity (Boston: Printed by J. Draper for T. Hancock, 1735).

Samuel Willard, the son of Simon and Mary Sharpe Willard, was born and raised in Concord, Massachusetts. Upon his graduation from Harvard in 1659, he became minister at Groton, Massachusetts, serving until the destruction of Groton by Indian attacks in 1676. Willard was then called to preach at Third Church (commonly called Old South) in Boston, where he remained for the rest of his life.

Willard was an influential figure and a prolific writer, second only to the Mathers and Benjamin Colman in the number of works he had published. His writings display an orthodox view of the issues of his day, tempered by common sense. When, in 1671, Elizabeth Knap (or Knapp) put on an exhibition of apparent demonic possession attended by fits and convulsions which had many of the people of Groton suspecting that witchcraft had broken out in their midst, Willard was able to quell the furor and wrote a remarkably objective series of observations on the incident, "A briefe account of a strange and unusuall Providence of God, befallen to Elizabeth Knap of Groton in 1671-1672."

For the most part, Willard tended to be conservative and to side with the establishment in its consistent persecution of members of various religious sects, as his strong statement against toleration for the Anabaptists in *Ne Sutor Ultra Crepidam* . . . (1681) clearly demonstrates. Yet, unlike some other Puritan ministers, Willard was flexible and able to bow to reason. In 1692, during the early stages of the witchcraft proceedings at Salem, he consistently aligned himself with the government position of advocating the vigorous prosecution and condemnation of people suspected of being witches, but he moved away from that stand when it became obvious to him that the judgments

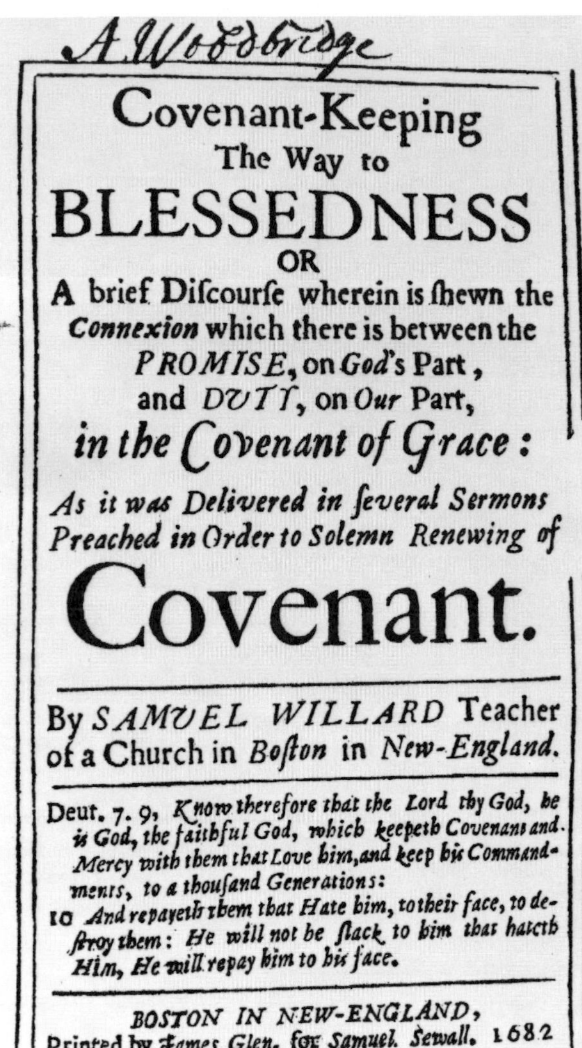

A Woodbridge

Covenant-Keeping
The Way to
BLESSEDNESS
OR
A brief Diſcourſe wherein is ſhewn the
Connexion which there is between the
PROMISE, on *God's* Part,
and *DUTY*, on *Our* Part,
in the Covenant of Grace:
As it was Delivered in ſeveral Sermons
Preached in Order to Solemn Renewing of
Covenant.

By *SAMUEL WILLARD* Teacher
of a Church in *Boſton* in *New-England.*

Deut. 7. 9, *Know therefore that the Lord thy God, he is God, the faithful God, which keepeth Covenant and Mercy with them that Love him, and keep his Commandments, to a thouſand Generations:*
10 *And repayeth them that Hate him, to their face, to deſtroy them: He will not be ſlack to him that hateth Him, He will repay him to his face.*

BOSTON IN NEW-ENGLAND,
Printed by *James Glen,* for *Samuel Sewall.* 1682

Title page for one of the forty-three books Willard had published during his lifetime

were in error. In a bold move, considering the theological climate at the time, Willard published anonymously in 1692 *Some Miscellany Observations* . . . (popularly known as "The Dialogue between S. & B."), in which he sought a middle path of reconciliation between those citizens who favored trying and executing so-called witches and those who felt that the notion of accusing their neighbors of witchcraft bordered upon the ridiculous. A few years later, Willard acknowledged the error of his initial participation in the witchcraft delusion by publicly reading his confession before the congregation of Old South Church on 14 January 1697. Willard became vice-president of Harvard on 6 September 1701 and served until his death, retaining at the same time his association with the Old South congregation. In April 1707, Willard began to suffer from convulsion fits, and he died seven months later.

More than forty-five of Willard's works are extant in published form, the majority being typical Puritan sermons. In one of his most notable collections, *The Barren Fig Trees Doom* (1691), Willard maintained that church membership was "not only a title of dignity, but also an obligation to Service." His major work is *A Compleat Body of Divinity* . . . (1726), a systematic compilation of years of monthly lectures delivered on *The Shorter Catechism*, compiled by the Westminster Assembly in 1644. Willard's massive work, the first printed in folio in America, was received with considerable interest and stands as a monument of orthodox Puritan theology.

Willard's works, ranging from sermons and theological treatises to observations of witchcraft and polemical responses to outspoken Quaker critics, show him to have been active in many different phases of colonial community life. He wrote in a traditional straightforward style and, while he was uniformly orthodox in his outlook upon life and religion, he was not dogmatic and showed a willingness to alter his views when reason dictated that it would be common sense to do so.

Other:

"A briefe account of a strange and unusuall Providence of God, befallen to Elizabeth Knap of Groton in 1671-1672," *Collections of the Massachusetts Historical Society*, 38: 555-570.

References:

An Historical Catalogue of the Old South Church (Boston: Privately printed, 1883);

Ernest Benson Lowrie, *The Shape of the Puritan Mind* (New Haven: Yale University Press, 1974);

William G. McLoughlin, *New England Dissent, 1630-1833* (Cambridge: Harvard University Press, 1971), pp. 105-107;

Perry Miller, *The New England Mind: From Colony to Province* (Cambridge: Harvard University Press, 1953);

Miller and Thomas H. Johnson, eds., *The Puritans*, 2 volumes (New York: Harper & Row, 1963);

John Langdon Sibley, *Biographical Sketches of Harvard Graduates*, volume 2 (Cambridge: Charles William Sever, 1881), pp. 13-36;

Seymour Van Dyken, *Samuel Willard, Preacher of Orthodoxy in Era of Change* (Grand Rapids, Mich.: Eerdmans, 1972).

Papers:

The Massachusetts Historical Society has John Hull's copies of sermons delivered between 1671 and 1679. Willard's commonplace book is at Harvard University.

Roger Williams

Richard VanDerBeets
San Jose State University

BIRTH: Smithfield, London, circa 1603, to James and Alice Pemberton Williams.

EDUCATION: B.A., Pembroke College, Cambridge, 1627.

MARRIAGE: 15 December 1629 to Mary Barnard; children: Mary, Joseph, Freeborn, Providence, Mercy, Daniel.

DEATH: Providence, Rhode Island, between 16 January and 15 March 1683.

SELECTED BOOKS: *A Key into the Language of America* . . . (London: Printed by Gregory Dexter, 1643);

Mr. Cotton's Letter Lately Printed, Examined, and Answered (London, 1644);

Queries of the Highest Consideration . . . (London, 1644);

The Bloudy Tenent of Persecution, for cause of Conscience, discussed, in a Conference between truth and peace . . . (London, 1644);

Christenings Make Not Christians (London, 1645);

Experiments of Spiritual Life & Health . . . (London, 1652);

The Fourth Paper Presented by Major Butler . . . (London: Printed for G. Calvert, 1652);

The Bloody Tenent Yet More Bloody . . . (London: Printed for G. Calvert, 1652);

The Hireling Ministry None of Christs . . . (London, 1652);

The Examiner Defended, attributed to Williams (London: Printed by James Cottrel, 1652);

George Fox Digg'd Out of His Burrowes . . . (Boston: Printed by John Foster, 1676).

COLLECTION: *The Writings of Roger Williams,* 6 volumes (Providence: Narragansett Club Publications, 1866-1874); enlarged as *The Complete Writings of Roger Williams,* 7 volumes (New York: Russell & Russell, 1963).

Although Roger Williams by no means originated the concept of separation of church and state or the notion that one's religious beliefs are inviolably private matters, it is for these two principles that he is best known. Williams was indeed an early apostle of and forceful spokesman for those ideas which are now central to American thought. Yet it must be remembered that he was a profoundly devout Separatist Puritan whose political and social ideas were always subordinate in importance to his religious thought. The basis for his abiding interest in political democracy, for example, was principally that it afforded the elect the necessary freedom to work out the problems of existence in a climate conducive to religious expression. *A Key into the Language of America* . . . (1643), unlike the usual handbook for traders or missionaries, is largely concerned with the spiritual benefits that observation of the Indian may provide the white man; and in Williams's later life his scathing attack on the already much-harassed Quakers derived from his staunch and rationalist Calvinism at the expense of his political and social liberalism. From the beginning, religion was the principal influence in Williams's life. "From my Childhood," he later wrote of his early conversion to Puritanism, "the Father of Lights and Mercies toucht my Soul with a Love to himself, to his only begotten, the true Lord Jesus, to his Holy Scriptures."

Roger Williams, the third of four children, was born in the Smithfield district of London, very likely in 1603 (the register of the parish church in which he was born was destroyed in the London fire of 1666). His father, James, was a tailor and textile retailer; his mother, Alice Pemberton, came from a family of tradesmen of somewhat higher social standing than her husband's. There are no records of Roger Williams's early education, yet his training cannot have been simply that of a merchant apprentice. While still a boy, his accomplishments earned him the patronage of Sir Edward Coke, who aided his subsequent enrollment and education at Charterhouse and later at Cambridge. After receiving his bachelor's degree and working briefly on an M.A., he left Cambridge in 1629 to take a position as household chaplain to Sir William Masham. During this period he met the man who would later become one of his chief adversaries in New England, John Cotton, and the woman who would become his wife, Mary Barnard. In December of 1630, Williams and his wife left England for America, going first to Boston, where he declined a position with the Nonseparatist church, then to Salem, and finally to Plymouth, where his career as a trader, friend to the Indians, writer, and controversialist began. Here he questioned the existing edict that Christian rulers had divine right to the lands of the heathen, thereby questioning the very King's Charter of the Massachusetts colonists; this challenge he based on his belief in the separation of spiritual and material prerogatives. Returning to Salem in 1633, Williams became embroiled in the debate over the General Court's oath of allegiance, again arguing from his position of the distinction between civil and religious policy. In 1634 he was invited by the Salem congregation to become their pastor, and in 1635 an outraged General Court ordered that he be sent back to England in order to keep him from further disrupting the body politic of the colonies. To avoid deportation, Williams fled south from Salem to an Indian settlement and thence, with a group of some dozen other Englishmen, to the mouth of the Moshassuck River, among the Narragansett Indians, to found the settlement he called Providence. In early 1643, to ensure the independence and survival of the now considerably expanded Providence Plantations, Williams sailed for England to obtain a charter. It was during this two months' voyage that he drafted his first published work, *A Key into the Language of America . . .* , printed in London soon after his arrival in the summer of 1643.

One of the motives behind the Puritan emigration, other than to escape persecution, was to convert the Indians and propagate the gospel; Roger

H. Bouchard statue of Williams at the International Monument of the Reformation in Geneva, Switzerland

Williams never lost sight of this objective. "One of the English preachers," wrote a contemporary of Williams's about his relations with the Indians, "in a special good intent of doing good to their soules, hath spent much time in attaining to their Language. . . . It is hoped that he may be an instrument of good amongst them." Divided into thirty-two chapters, *A Key into the Language of America . . .* is not a dictionary; rather it is structured as a history of the Indians "from their Birth to their Burialls." The reader is introduced to a variety of Narragansett customs and habits relating to foodstuffs, houses, family relationships, hunting and fishing, trading and money, and marriage; native beliefs about nature, the stars, and animal life are also presented. The religion of the Indians, not surprisingly, is treated in the longest chapter of the book; in general, Williams found the Indians to be genuinely concerned about their spiritual state. Publication of *A Key into the Language of America . . .* had two interesting and immediate consequences: the Massachusetts Bay Puritans were

THE
BLOVDY TENENT,
of PERSECUTION, for cause of
CONSCIENCE, discussed, in
A Conference betweene
TRVTH and PEACE.
VVHO,
In all tender Affection, present to the High
Court of Parliament, (as the Result of
their Discourse) these, (amongst other
Passages) of highest consideration.

Printed in the Year. 1644.

Title page for Williams's influential arguments for liberty of conscience and the separation of church and state

shamed into more active missionary work, and Williams obtained his charter.

While in England in 1644 he wrote four other works. *Mr. Cotton's Letter Lately Printed, Examined, and Answered* is a sharp reply to *A Letter of Mr. John Cottons Teacher of the Church in Boston, in New-England, To Mr. Williams . . .* (1643), which Cotton had written soon after Williams's banishment to justify that action. Williams's answer contains his version of the events, a defense of his Separatist position and an attack on the casuistry of the idea of Nonseparation, and a series of examples of Massachusetts Bay intolerance. He characterizes Cotton as one "swimming with the stream of outward credit and profit, and smiting with the fist and sword of persecution such as dare not joyn in worship with him" and charges that Cotton's professed moderation is in reality masked intolerance. Following the publication of Williams's work, Cotton's prestige as the spokesman for the New England Way was considerably damaged. In *Queries of the Highest Consideration . . .* Williams addresses the Westminster Assembly and attacks the ideas set forth in its *An Apologetical Narration* (1644), which attempted to advance Congregationalism as the via media between Separatism and Presbyterianism. Williams sees again the dangers of a close relationship between church and state and the resultant orthodoxy from which dissenters are banished.

The Bloudy Tenent of Persecution . . ., the most notable of Williams's four works written in 1644, is his return to the battle with Cotton. A letter had been sent to Cotton, presumably from an Anabaptist prisoner in Newgate complaining of persecution because of his beliefs. Cotton's answer justifies persecution for the sake of conscience; *The Bloudy Tenent . . .* is an assault upon this theory and a statement of Williams's convictions about the separation of civil and religious commitments and of freedom of conscience. The work is divided into two halves: the first part is a point-by-point rebuttal of Cotton's defense of persecution cast in a colloquy between Truth and Peace, with Williams's own plea for liberty of conscience as a fundamental human right; the second half comprises his attack on *A Model of Church and Civil Power* (1635), a statement of the New England theory of the relationship between church and state which Williams attributes to Cotton, though in fact it is by a group of clergymen. Williams stresses the absolute necessity of separation of church and state, which, based on the concept of the civil state as solely a secular institution, he had already effected at Providence. In his denunciation of magisterial intervention in religious affairs, Williams draws numerous examples from scripture and from English history to undercut the reasoning of *A Model of Church and Civil Power*. His central position is that the civil government, although an ordinance of God, has only the power given it by the people. Consequently, the magistrate's authority is but a delegated one. Election of magistrates by the people, then, renders incongruous the interference of these officials in church affairs, for that would imply that the people originally had the power to govern the church—a notion Williams thought so bizarre as to pull Christ and God out of heaven and "subject them unto naturall, sinful, inconstant man, and so consequently to Satan Himselfe." It is no surprise that Parliament placed *The Bloudy Tenent . . .* on its list of books to be burned. Believing as he did that no true church had existed since the Apostasy, Williams could not abide people being forced into worshiping in a national church. Better, he felt, if men were left free to seek truth by whatever illuminations they had, as in fact they were doing in Providence, with no coercion from civil magistrates. *The Bloudy Tenent*... has been influential from the time it was written in determining views on religious liberty and the dissociation of church and state. During the period 1643-1649 more than 120 pamphlets appeared either attacking or defending Williams. And its influence, only four years after it was written, on the English Revolution of 1648 is clear from the Levellers' advocacy of a democratic government in which the common people of England could participate. In time, of course, the idea that all political power resided with the people did take hold, as did the idea of religious liberty: the Constitution of the United States proclaims the power of the people in its preamble; religious freedom is guaranteed in the First Amendment.

Christenings Make Not Christians is the last work of Williams's first mission to England, although it was not published until 1645 after he had already returned to America. It treats the matter of conversion, the application of the term *Christian* to an entire nation, and the necessity for the civilized to become fully Christianized before converting the Indian.

Williams returned to America in 1644, having obtained his charter, and upon his return he was elected Chief Officer of the Providence Plantations. This office he held for three years, during which time his principal task was to get the charter ratified. Dissension continued to infect the colony, largely through the covert actions of the Massachusetts Magistrates, despite the institution of a central government in Rhode Island in 1647. Then, with the execution of King Charles in 1649, the validity of the charter itself came into question. As a result of these complications, Williams undertook a second trip to England in 1651. This stay resulted in another series of publications, notably *The Bloody Tenent Yet More Bloody* . . . (1652), which continues the controversy with John Cotton. A reply to Cotton's *Bloudy Tenent, Washed, and Made White in the Bloud of the Lambe* (1647), it reiterates Williams's arguments for the separation of civil and religious administrations and for complete soul liberty, yet with the increased vigor and conviction that eight years additional thought had provided him. The doctrine of persecution is, he writes, "one of the most Seditious, Destructive, Blasphemous, and Bloudiest in any or in all Nations of the World." *Experiments of Spiritual Life & Health* . . . (1652), written two years earlier than its date of publication, is in fact a long devotional letter from Williams to his wife, Mary, who had been recovering from serious illness and was troubled over her spiritual state. *The Hireling Ministry None of Christs* . . . (1652) addresses the matter of legal establishment of religion and compulsory support of the clergy. Williams attacks the motives of a mercenary and "Hireling Ministry" interested primarily in "fatter and rancker pastures." His stand for a devout ministry based solely on spiritual worth was unsuccessful insofar as Parliament, not yet ready to forgo the collection of tithes, was not influenced to change its position. *The Fourth Paper Presented by Major Butler*... (1652) is also a topical publication, in support of the views of Major Charles Butler, an officer in Cromwell's army and a fervent tolerationist opposed to any kind of an established church. Butler had written a series of four pamphlets, the last of which advocated the toleration of the Jews. Williams agreed and further argued that Jews, long denied admission into England, be extended their civil rights. He was successful enough to at least induce Cromwell to remove some exclusionary immigration ordinances. *The Examiner Defended* (1652), one final pamphlet on the relationship of church and state, was published anonymously but is almost certainly by Williams. It is a defense of the views in another anonymous pamphlet, *Zeal Examined* (1652), which had been in turn attacked by the pamphlet *The Examiner Examined* (1652), also anonymous. Although it adds nothing new to his canon, this little tract to an unknown adversary does compactly summarize Williams's major ideas.

In 1654 Roger Williams returned to America to play a leading role in determining the policies of his Plantations. Consequently, when Massachusetts closed her doors to the Quakers in 1656, Providence threw open hers. Yet it was this act, followed by a significant influx of Quakers, that ultimately provoked Williams's intemperate and seemingly uncharacteristic denunciation of what he termed "the cursed sect" in *George Fox Digg'd Out of His Burrowes* . . . (1676). The Society of Friends under the leadership of George Fox was in fact a noisy, fanatical, and unruly group who, Williams felt, downgraded the scriptures with the belief that their "inner light"—which Calvinists interpreted as the heresy of enthusiasm—would win them eternal salvation without study of the Bible or an educated ministry. Fox's arguments for the doctrines, published in his *The Great Mystery of the Great Whore* (1659), Williams found to be "weak and silly... Anti-Christian and Blasphemous." The Quakers' repudiation of the significance of the Bible and their claim to the immediacy and infallibility of

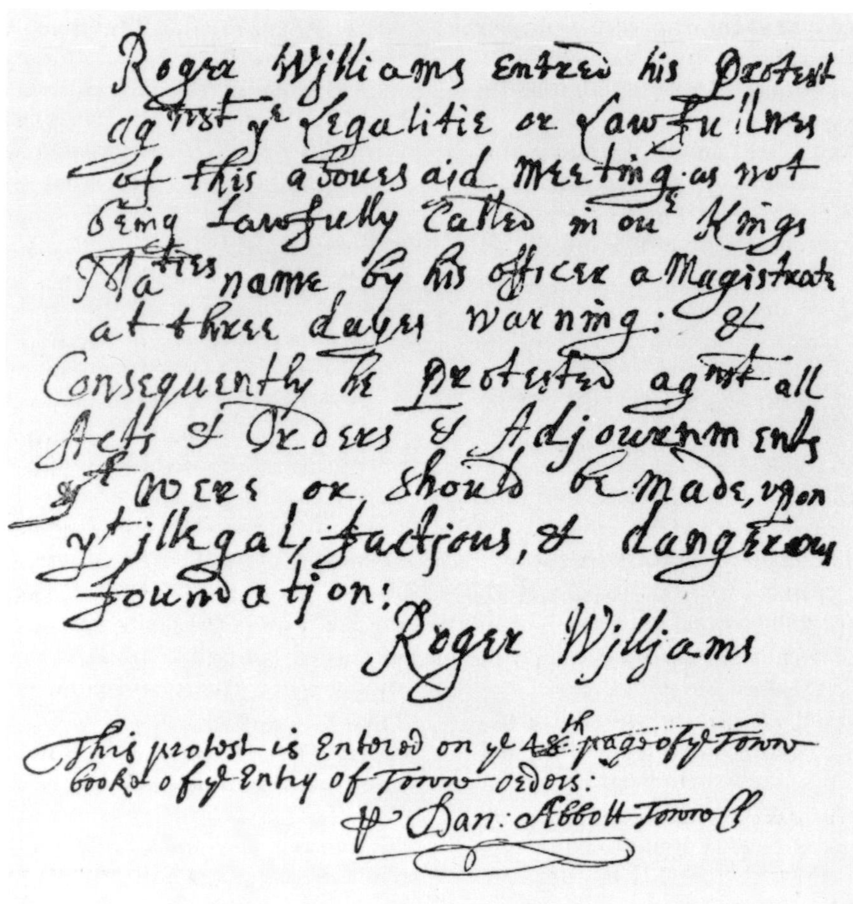

Roger Williams entred his protest
agnst ye Legalitie or Lawfullness
of this aboves aid meeting as not
being Lawfully Called in our Kings
Maties name by his officer a Magistrate
at three dayes warning: &
Consequently he protested agnst all
Acts & Orders & Adjournments
yt were or should be made, upon
yt illegal, factious, & dangerous
foundation:
Roger Williams

This protest is Entered on ye 48th page of ye Towne
booke of ye Entry of Towne Orders:
p Dan: Abbott Towne Clk

Williams's 8 December 1680 protest over a meeting of the Providence town council that was held without the legally specified three-days' notice (Rhode Island Historical Society)

the inner light earned them Williams's disgust and everlasting scorn.

Williams's final public role was, ironically, as unsuccessful negotiator for the Narragansetts with New England during King Philip's War (1675-1676), in which that tribe was annihilated at the Great Swamp Fight and the political power of the Indian in New England destroyed. Owing to progressively bad health and lameness during the last seven years of his life, Williams in effect withdrew from public affairs. The precise date of his death, like that of his birth, is not known; he died at the age of eighty sometime between January 16 and March 15 in the year 1683. Any assessment of Roger Williams's importance must necessarily begin with his insistence on the absolute religious freedom that has now become one of the distinctive features of the American way of life. In addition, his career and engagement in a variety of activities included such accomplishments as the founding of a colony on principles of political democracy and religious equality and the writing and publication of widely influential tracts espousing the idea of soul liberty, a principle of unquestioned validity for enlightened Americans today. These and all his earthly works were drawn from and nourished by the wellspring of Williams's highest and most abiding principle: love of God, man, and truth.

Letters:

Letters of Roger Williams, 1632-82, volume 6 of *The Complete Writings of Roger Williams* (New York: Russell & Russell, 1963).

Biographies:

James D. Knowles, *Memoirs of Roger Williams* (Boston: Edmons, 1834);

Romeo Elton, *Life of Roger Williams* (Providence: A. Cockshaw, 1853);

Oscar S. Straus, *The Pioneer of Religious Liberty* (New York: Century, 1894);

Edmund J. Carpenter, *Roger Williams: A Study of*

the Life, Times and Character of a Political Pioneer (New York: Grafton Press, 1909);

Emily Easton, *Roger Williams: Prophet and Pioneer* (Boston: Houghton Mifflin, 1930);

James E. Ernst, *Roger Williams: New England Firebrand* (New York: Macmillan, 1932);

Samuel H. Brockunier, *The Irrepressible Democrat: Roger Williams* (New York: Ronald Press, 1940);

Perry Miller, *Roger Williams* (Indianapolis: Bobbs-Merrill, 1953);

Ola Elizabeth Winslow, *Master Roger Williams: A Biography* (New York: Macmillan, 1957);

Cyclone Covey, *The Gentle Radical: Roger Williams* (New York: Macmillan, 1966).

References:

Mauro Calamandrei, "Neglected Aspects of Roger Williams' Thought," *Church History*, 21 (September 1952): 239-258;

Henry Chupack, *Roger Williams* (New York: Twayne, 1969);

Theodore P. Greene, ed., *Roger Williams and the Massachusetts Magistrates* (Boston: D. C. Heath, 1964);

Hans R. Guggisberg, "Religious Freedom and the History of the Christian World in Roger Williams' Thought," *Early American Literature*, 12 (Spring 1977): 36-48;

Elizabeth Hirsch, "John Cotton and Roger Williams: Their Controversy Concerning Religious Liberty," *Church History*, 10 (March 1941): 38-51;

Irwin H. Polishook, *Roger Williams, John Cotton, and Religious Freedom* (Englewood Cliffs, N.J.: Prentice-Hall, 1967);

Richard Reinitz, "The Separatist Background of Roger Williams' Argument for Religious Toleration," in *Typology and Early American Literature*, edited by Sacvan Bercovitch (Amherst: University of Massachusetts Press, 1972);

John J. Teunissen and Evelyn J. Hinz, Introduction to *A Key into the Language of America*, edited by Teunissen and Hinz (Detroit: Wayne State University Press, 1973).

Papers:

There are collections of Williams's papers at the Rhode Island Historical Society Library, the Massachusetts Historical Society, and Providence City Hall.

John Wilson

(1588-7 August 1667)

John Harmon McElroy
University of Arizona

BOOKS: *A Song, Or, Story, For the Lasting Remembrance of divers famous works, which God hath done in our time . . .* (London: Printed by R. Young for I. Bartlet, 1626); republished as *A Song of Deliverance for the Lasting Remembrance of Gods Wonderful Works, Never to Be Forgotten . . .* (Boston: Printed by John Foster, 1680);

The Day Breaking, if not the Sun-Rising of the Gospell with the Indians in New-England . . ., attributed to Wilson (London: Printed by R. Cotes for F. Clifton, 1647);

A Seasonable Watch-Word Unto Christians Against the Dreams & Dreamers of This Generation . . . (Cambridge: Printed by S. Green & S. Green, 1677).

John Wilson, for thirty-five years pastor of the first church organized in Boston, considered poetry a part of his ministry and had so ready a faculty for putting his devout thoughts into verse that he sent poems to "All Persons, in All Places, on All Occasions." According to his son, his occasional religious verse would have made "a large Folio," had it been collected. The few of his Latin and English poems that he had published during his life or that have otherwise survived can be found in Kenneth B. Murdock's collection *Handkerchiefs from Paul, Being Pious and Consolatory Verse of Puritan Massachusetts* (1927). This couplet about Job, from the poem Wilson wrote to one of his daughters on the death of her firstborn, exemplifies the nature of his poetical talent: "[Job's] *Life* was only given him for a Prey / Yet all his Troubles were to *Heaven* the way." In seventeenth-century Boston Wilson was particularly well known for making anagrams and poems based on them and for extemporaneous preaching in a "Seraphical Voice." Only one of his sermons, derived from auditors' notes after his death, was ever published. *A Seasonable Watch-Word Unto Christians Against the Dreams & Dreamers of This Generation* (1677), his valedictory sermon to the First Church, reminded his parishioners that their kind had not come into the American wilderness to "follow their own humours" or to tolerate the ranting of Quaker "dreamers" but rather to live by the ordinances of God preached by faithful ministers of his word. Wilson's admirers also published after his death *A Song of Deliverance for the Lasting Remembrance of Gods Wonderful Works* (1680), his long poem (originally printed in London in 1626) commemorating England's defeat of the Spanish Armada and the "Papist" Gunpowder Plot as providences of God against "His enemies" and describing the plagues that followed those events as God's chastisements of England for its ingratitude.

A native of Windsor, where his father, William, was canon, Wilson was born into the English hierarchy. His mother, Elizabeth Woodhall, was a niece of Archbishop Grindal. After studying at Eton, he took B.A. (1610) and M.A. (1613) degrees at King's College, Cambridge, to follow his parent into the established church. But his conversion to Puritanism some time before 1610 cost him his natural preferment, including a comfortable lifetime fellowship at King's. High-placed family friends lessened the persecution he suffered for his nonconformity. By the time of his emigration in 1630 with the Winthrop company, he had been married for at least fifteen years to Elizabeth Mansfield (with whom he fathered three surviving children: Elizabeth, Mary, and John) and had been for a dozen years lecturer at Sudbury in Suffolk, a stronghold of Puritanism that sent more immigrants to New England than any other town or village in East Anglia.

His commitment to the church-state of Massachusetts Bay was complete. As the chief object of Anne Hutchinson's attack on the clergy during the Antinomian Controversy of 1636-1638, he aligned himself with his friend John Winthrop to suppress her numerous adherents and in the end spoke the words of her excommunication: "in the name of our Lord Jesus Christ and in the name of the Church I doe not only pronounce you worthy to be cast out, but *I doe cast you out* and in the name of Christ *I doe deliver you up to Sathan* that you may learne no more to blaspheme to seduce and to lye." In the midst of this crisis, having been selected by lot, he went as chaplain in the expedition against the Pequot Indians in Connecticut, a service for which he was awarded a grant of land. In mid-century he was active in the punishing and hanging of defiant Quakers. A minister whose purse was "continually emptying it self into the hands of the *Needy*," including poor Indians, he was associated with the Reverend John Eliot in the earliest work of converting the tribes of New England to Christianity. (*The Day Breaking, if not the Sun-Rising of the Gospell with the Indians in New-England . . .* , a tract published in London in 1647, has been partly and wholly attributed to him.) Wrongdoers scourged in public he customarily summoned to his house soon afterward, and "having first expressed his Bounty to them, he would then bestow upon them such gracious Admonitions and Exhortations, as made them to become, instead of *Desperate*, remarkably *Penitent*." He was, "like *John, a Son of Thunder*, against *Seducers*, yet he was like that Blessed, and Beloved Apostle also, all made up of *Love*." Cotton Mather's characterization resembles Hawthorne's portrait of Wilson, in *The Scarlet Letter* (1850), as a clergyman of stern orthodoxy whose "genial benevolence" in his private life won for him "warmer affection than was accorded to any of his professional contemporaries."

Other:

Kenneth B. Murdock, ed., *Handkerchiefs from Paul, Being Pious and Consolatory Verse of Puritan Massachusetts*, includes poems by Wilson (Cambridge: Harvard University Press, 1927).

References:

Cotton Mather, *Johannes in Eremo. Memoirs, Relating to the Lives of the Ever Memorable, Mr. John Cotton, who Dyed, 23.D. 10.M. 1652. Mr. John Norton, who Dyed 5.D. 2.M. 1663. Mr. John Wilson, who Dyed 7.D. 6.M. 1667. Mr. John Davenport, who Dyed, 15.D. 1.M. 1670 . . .* (Boston: Printed for & sold by Michael Perry, 1696);

Kenneth B. Murdock, Preface to *Handkerchiefs from Paul, Being Pious and Consolatory Verse of Puritan Massachusetts*, edited by Murdock (Cambridge: Harvard University Press, 1927);

John Wilson (son), Preface to *A Song of Deliverance for the Lasting Remembrance of Gods Wonderful Works* (Boston: Printed by John Foster, 1680).

Papers:
The Beinecke Rare Book and Manuscript Library at Yale University has a collection of Wilson's letters.

John Winthrop

Everett Emerson
University of North Carolina at Chapel Hill

BIRTH: Near Groton, Suffolk, England, 22 January 1588, to Adam and Anne Browne Winthrop.

EDUCATION: Trinity College, Cambridge University, 1603-1605; Gray's Inn, London, 1613.

MARRIAGES: April 1605 to Mary Forth; children: John, Henry, Forth, Mary, Anne, Anne. 1616 to Thomasine Clopton; unnamed daughter. April 1618 to Margaret Tyndal; children: Stephen, Adam, Deane, Nathaniel, Samuel, Anne, William, Sarah. 1647 to Martha Rainsboro Coytmore; child: Joshua.

DEATH: Boston, Massachusetts, 26 March 1649.

SELECTED BOOKS: *Antinomians and Familists condemned by the synod of elders in New-England: with the proceedings of the magistrates against them, and their apology for the same* . . . (London: Printed for R. Smith, 1644); republished as *A Short Story of the rise, reign, and ruin of the Antinomians, Familists & libertines* . . . (London: Printed for Ralph Smith, 1644);

A Declaration of Former Passages and Proceedings Betwixt the English and the Narrowgansets, with Their Confederates, Wherein the Grounds and Justice of the Ensuing Warre are Opened and Cleared... (Cambridge: Printed by Stephen Daye, 1645);

A Journal of the Transactions and Occurrences in the Settlement of Massachusetts and the Other New-England Colonies, from the Year 1630 to 1644 (Hartford: Printed by Elisha Babcock, 1790); reedited as *The History of New England from 1630 to 1649,* two volumes, edited by James Savage (volume 1, Boston: Printed by Phelps & Farnham, 1825; volume 2, Boston: Printed by T. B. Wait & son, 1826; revised and enlarged again, Boston: Little, Brown, 1853);

Winthrop Papers, 5 volumes (Boston: Massachusetts Historical Society, 1929-1947).

Portrait painted in England before 1630 (The State House, Boston)

The first and the most important governor of the Massachusetts Bay colony, John Winthrop had a powerful voice in determining the character of that colony and thus was influential in shaping the nature of American Puritanism. His sermon "Christian Charitie. A Modell Hereof," delivered in 1630 on the way to America, is the most exalted statement of Puritan aspirations. The journal that he kept from 1630 to 1648 serves as a vital record of the activities of the colony, and it, along with his other writings—on such topics as his religious experience, the nature of nonseparatist Congregationalism, Antinomianism, the authority of the magistrate and the liberty of the people—makes him one of the two most important nonclerical prose writers of early New England, the other being the governor of the Plymouth colony, William Bradford. It was characteristic that he should deliver his most important speech in 1645 after he had been acquitted of the charge of exceeding his authority and that his speech should be both modest, as he referred to his own qualifications for leadership, and supremely confident, as he discussed his notion of the authority of his office. This "little speech" was apparently unexpected by those present, but now it seems altogether in character to those who have examined the life and writings of John Winthrop.

Born the son of the lord of the manor at Groton in Suffolk, John Winthrop was brought up on the estate that had been granted to his grandfather at the time of the dissolution of the English monasteries under Henry VIII. John's father served for many years as auditor of Trinity College, Cambridge, and there the future American governor was enrolled at the age of fourteen. While at Cambridge, he became desperately ill and, as a result, experienced a religious conversion that identified him thereafter with the Puritan group within the Church of England. Gentlemen such as Winthrop seldom remained for long at the university, and he was soon back at home and almost immediately married. His wife, Mary Forth, bore him six children in the next ten years, the oldest—John, Junior—becoming an important New Englander in his own right. As a dowry the young husband was given lands at Great Stambridge, but before long the elder Winthrop made John lord of the Groton manor. In 1613 the future Massachusetts governor studied law at Gray's Inn in London, and at Groton he had the opportunity to practice the law as justice of the peace.

The only surviving record of this time, the section of Winthrop's "Experiencia" written in 1607-1613, deals with his religious travail. For instance, he recorded that he had made "a new Covenant with the Lorde" in April 1606 that he would, with grace, reform his "pride, covetousnesse, love of this worlde, vanitie of minde, unthankfulnesse, slouth. . . ." One should not suppose that Winthrop was in fact an especially covetous or worldly person; his list of sins is a typical Puritan one. Winthrop also recorded "a speciall providence of God that my wife taking upp a measse of porridge, before the children or anybodye had eaten of it, she espied therein a great spider." The recognition of such providences was, like the cataloging of sins, the duty of a devout Puritan; Winthrop would record many of God's intervening acts.

After ten years of marriage, Mary Winthrop died. Soon, in 1616, Winthrop married again, to Thomasine Clopton, but within a year his second wife was dead. His third wife, Margaret Tyndal, whom he married in 1618, was to be his marriage partner for almost thirty years. As head of a large household that could be expected to become larger, Winthrop now needed to increase his income. The practice of law being lucrative, he turned to it more and more, and soon he found that he was obliged to spend long periods in London, where in 1627 he was appointed attorney to His Majesty's Court of Wards and Liveries. Because John and Margaret were frequently separated, first by his work in London, later for a time by the Atlantic Ocean, they created a correspondence, a celebrated one, that gives a most engaging insight into their love and devotion to each other.

Winthrop's office in London brought him close to the growing tension between Charles I and Parliament. Winthrop and other Puritans put their trust in Parliament, but in March 1629 Charles dissolved it and indicated that he did not intend to trouble himself further with that institution. Moreover, on the Continent, in both France and Germany, Roman Catholic forces were triumphing over Protestant ones. In May 1629 Winthrop wrote to his wife: "the Lorde hath admonished, threatened, corrected, and astonished vs, yet we growe worse and worse, so as his spirit will not allwayes striue with us, he must needs giue waye to furye at last: he hath smitten all the other Churches before eyes, and hath made them to drinke of the bitter cuppe of tribulation, euen vnto death; we sawe this, and humbled not ourselues, to turne from our euill wayes, but haue provoked him more then all the nations rounde about vs: therefore he is turninge the cuppe towards vs also, and because we are the last, our portion must be, to drinke the verye dreggs which remaine: my deare wife, I am veryly perswaded, God will bringe some heauye Affliction vpon this lande, and that speedylye: but be of good

Comfort, the hardest that can come will be a meanes to mortifie this bodye of Corruption, which is a thousand tymes more dangerous to vs then any outward tribulation, and to bringe vs into neerer communion with our Lo: Jes: Christ, and more Assurance of his kingdome. If the Lord seeth it wilbe good for vs, he will prouide a shelter and a hidinge place for vs and ours. . . ."

Even before this letter was written, the place where Winthrop would go with his family was being prepared. In late April of this same year some two hundred colonists left for New England, the vanguard of a much larger group whose enterprise was to be authorized by a royal charter as the Massachusetts Bay Company. Winthrop soon met with those planning to be part of the colony, all Puritans and most attracted to the Congregational variety of Puritanism, and in August he brought together a group to discuss the notion. For this meeting, apparently, he drafted a document, "General Observations For the Plantation of New England," to which he added, perhaps before the meeting, perhaps as a result, "Obiections against this intended Plantation for New E: Answered and resolued" and "Reasons to be considered for iustifieinge the vdertakeres of the intended Plantation in New England, and for incouraginge such whose hartes God shall moue to ioyne with them in it." In these carefully drafted analyses, Winthrop tried to persuade himself as well as others that their plan was wise. The lengthy documents set forth a multitude of reasons for the undertaking: the opportunity for missionary activity, the need to escape the anticipated destruction of European churches, overcrowded conditions, the corruption of education and religion in England, and the virtue of setting an example in the founding in the New World of "a particular church" (by which the would-be colonists meant a church of the congregational type). Also noted was the fact that "God hath consumed the Natiues [of New England] with a great Plauge in those partes, soe as there be few Inhabitantes lefte." As a result of this conference, John Winthrop was among those who signed an agreement at Cambridge in late August "to embarke for the said plantacion by the first of march next . . . to the ende to passe the Seas (vnder Gods protection) to inhabite and continue in new England." In October Winthrop was elected governor of the company. Scrupulous always, Winthrop drafted for himself "Perticular Considerations in the case of J: W:," in which he noted that he judged himself called to the work as governor by both men and God and that his financial condition demands such a change.

By design or fortune, the charter of the Massachusetts Bay Company did not prescribe, as such documents normally did, that meetings of the company would be held in London or some other specified place in New England. The result was that the would-be colonists were able to take a step that would have highly significant consequences: they arranged for the transfer of the charter and the governance of the company to New England. By this agreement, the founders prevented the royal government or others who might be unsympathetic with their plans to create a Puritan colony from seizing control of the company. Very possibly this arrangement was John Winthrop's idea; at any rate its adoption meant that his position as governor gave him considerable power to shape the new colony—to make it a Puritan commonwealth.

On 8 April 1630 Winthrop and three of his sons were together on the *Arbella*, bound for America. With his arrival aboard ship, Winthrop began his extremely valuable journal, part of which was first published as *A Journal of the Transactions and Occurrences in the Settlement of Massachusetts and the Other New-England Colonies, from the Year 1630 to 1644* (1790). A more complete version was later published as *The History of New England from 1630 to 1649* (1825-1826). Many of the journal entries are brief and strictly factual; others are fuller and give a strong sense of the governor's personality, motives, and values. On board ship also Winthrop delivered the address that is his best-known work, a sermon entitled "Christian Charitie. A Modell Hereof." With frequent citation of the Bible as his authority, Winthrop declares that people need one another and that personal relations should be governed by the rules of justice and mercy. His fundamental notion is the covenant. Specifically he reminds the colonists that he and they are a body of professing Christians that "ought to account our selues knitt together" since "through a special overruleing providence, and a more than an ordinary approbation of the Churches of Christ" they have been commissioned by God to create a Christian community. If they keep, in St. Paul's words, "the vnitie of spirit in the bond of peace," then "the Lord will be our God and delight to dwell among vs." But, he warns, the new community will be exposing itself by its ambition. Using St. Matthew's term, Winthrop describes the new settlement as "a Citty vpon a Hill" that "the eies of all people" will be watching. Therefore "wee are Commaunded this day to loue the Lord our God, and to loue one another [,] to walke in his wayes and

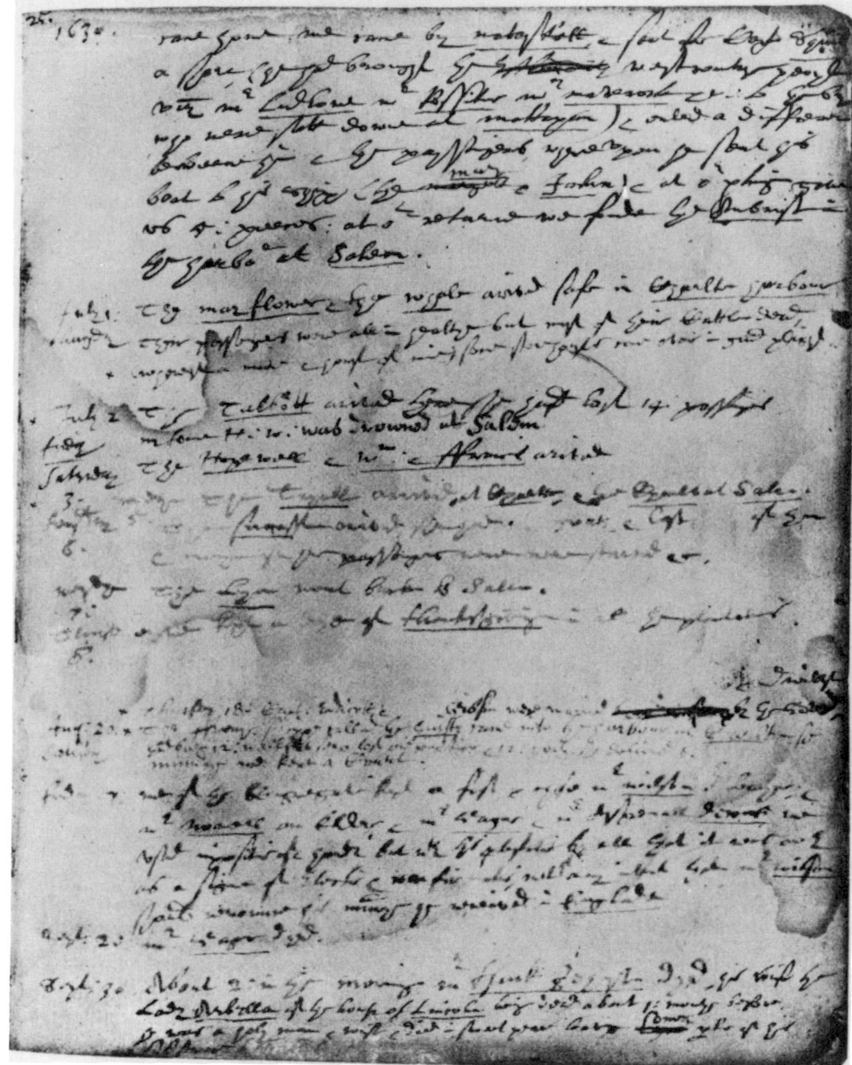

Entries for 17 June-30 September 1630 in the first volume of Winthrop's journal (Massachusetts Historical Society)

to keepe his Commaundements and Ordinance, and his lawes, and the Articles of our Covenant with him. . . ." The much-discussed sermon is often judged to set forth the position of the whole body of the Massachusetts settlers, but soon in the new commonwealth there was to be conflict over many issues. Conflict, as well as Winthrop's principle of community, was to shape the new society.

Winthrop's journal reports the arrival of the *Arbella* in mid-June, and then, with less detail, it describes the creation of a congregational church, the arrival of other ships with colonists, and the movement of people and supplies. Winthrop's surviving letters from this period, including several affectionate ones to his wife (who was not to arrive till the fall of 1631), provide little information about the new land; instead they catalogue the supplies that the colony required. The first extended journal entry tells of the wintry deaths from exposure of a group that attempted to travel from Boston, where Winthrop had settled, to Plymouth, where a more radical religious group, the Separatists, had been established for a decade.

As governor of the colony, Winthrop has been judged responsible for the fact that the Massachusetts Bay Company's council shared some of the governing power with all the able-bodied men of the colony, except servants. The records of the company show that as a result of this sharing of political power, 225 men had taken an oath admitting them as "freemen" by May 1631. Later the right to hold the status of freeman was limited to those who had been admitted to membership in a church. Political power, Puritan leaders argued, belonged only in the hands of godly men. Thus, the franchise was reserved to those sympathetic with Puritan religious ideals.

Some of the Puritans of Massachusetts Bay were Separatists who wanted the churches they were founding to make a radical break with the Church of England, while others were traditionalists who were not ready to abandon the ways that they had known in the Church of England. Winthrop advocated a middle course, as when he had to contend with Roger Williams, who in 1631 refused to become a member of the Boston church because its members would not make a public declaration announcing themselves as Separatists, and to contend also in 1631 with a faction within the Watertown church that was unwilling to denounce the Roman Catholic church. It was in the context of these disputes that Winthrop prepared, probably in March 1631, a brief document, "Reasons to proue a necessitye of reformation from the Corruptions of Antechrist which hath defiled the Christian Churches, and yet without an absolute separation from them . . . ," which advocates the middle way. The Massachusetts Bay Puritans believed it important to deny that they had separated from the Church of England—as the Plymouth Separatists boasted that they had done because Winthrop and his fellows intended to maintain in America the principle of compulsory uniformity. They intended to create separate churches that were governed by their individual congregations, but everyone was expected to attend the church of his town. Had Winthrop recognized the right to separate from a corrupt church, immigrants to Massachusetts Bay could apply his logic to declare themselves dissatisfied with the churches they found in order to create new, competing ones. Therefore Winthrop maintained in his "Reasons to proue a necessitye of reformation. . . ," that particular churches existing both in the days of Catholic Mary and in the days of Protestant Elizabeth might well have been "true Churches" though corrupt, since "the Corruption of a thinge dothe not nullifie a thinge so longe as the thinge hath a beinge in the same nature, that it had, when it was in the best beinge: so it is with the particular Congregations."

Frequently summoned to intervene and make peace between conflicting parties, Winthrop had to contend with conflicts relating to jurisdiction, conflicts with the Indians, questions as to what was a just price for services and commodities, and even arguments over Deputy-Governor Thomas Dudley's adornment of his house. All these matters are reported impersonally in Winthrop's journal, with Winthrop identifying himself merely as "the governour." Occasionally his record sets forth his own position, as when Dudley questioned Winthrop's authority and its source.

Because, in a move unanticipated by the royal government that granted its charter, the company's charter and governance had been transferred to New England, the colony could practice self-government and was left free to become highly distinctive. With their religious orientation, leaders of both church and state modeled the new commonwealth after ancient Israel, and, while in principle they separated secular from spiritual authority, they saw the two working together cooperatively. Despite this division, Winthrop was a strong governor—though he took moderate positions on most issues. Nonetheless he was challenged again and again. His most difficult cases came in the early years of the colony. The first concerned the attractive but iconoclastic religious radical Roger Williams, who was critical of the state that Winthrop headed. In Massachusetts the cooperation of the church and state meant that all residents of a town, whether or not they were church members, were expected to attend religious services together, but Williams argued that those who had not been converted and thus were not members should not be permitted to attend services. Moreover, Winthrop believed that the magistrate, or secular political official, derived his authority from God, while Williams insisted that the magistrate's power was from the people and that he was utterly lacking in authority over spiritual matters. This disagreement was based on conflicting ideas about the relationship between church and state: Williams argued for an absolute separation of the two, but for Winthrop and the other leaders of the colony the fundamental characteristic of their new commonwealth was its basis in a covenant with God, a covenant that made it a Holy Commonwealth. When Williams refused to keep his beliefs to himself but instead sought to teach them, Winthrop and the other magistrates decided to send him back to England. Williams then fled to Rhode Island, where he was free to do as he would. Despite his disagreement with Winthrop, Williams wrote admiringly to the Massachusetts governor that Winthrop had "bene alwayes pleased lovingly to answer my boldnes in civil things."

Winthrop was less kindly disposed toward a second dissenter within the commonwealth. In 1634 Anne Hutchinson followed John Cotton, her favorite clergyman, from England to Boston, where she attracted a large following to her house, which was just across the street from Winthrop's. At first, she met with a group of women only to discuss the sermons that had been delivered the previous week. Then a second group, this time of men, began to listen to her. As her authority grew, she became more critical of what she was discussing. She argued that most of the ministers (but not John Cotton) were preaching not the New Covenant of faith but the Old Covenant of works when they taught that "sanctification"—leading a righteous life—was evidence of salvation. Instead she taught that those who are converted find the person of the Holy Ghost dwelling within them and that this indwelling, not the ability to perform good works, is what one who cares about the state of his soul should look for. Hutchinson derived her theological views from John Cotton, and, though for a while he encouraged her, she was becoming a divisive force within Boston. Soon her influence spread even beyond her town, as she and her followers crusaded against the many ministers they called "legalists," those who emphasized good works. This crusade more clearly threatened Winthrop and what he believed in when in 1636 one of her admirers, Henry Vane, was elected governor, though he was only twenty-three and a recent arrival from England.

Besides the factionalism that the Hutchinsonians created, their teachings were in conflict with one of the central principles upon which the colony had been founded, the doctrine that the health and welfare of the new society depended upon the "Christian Charitie" of its members. Such a principle could be questioned on theological grounds because it failed to take into account man's depravity, his sinfulness, and his helplessness without God's grace. The magistrates of Massachusetts Bay, however, were hardly in a position to listen to those who argued such notions. Among the Hutchinsonian positions, as Winthrop outlined them, were:

> No Christian must be prest to duties of holinesse.
> No Christian must be exhorted to faith, love, and prayer, &c. except we know he hath the Spirit.
> God loves a man never the better for any holinesse in him, and never the lesse, be he never so unholy.

In fact, said Winthrop, Hutchinson's followers attacked the magistrates and identified them as "Ahabs, Amaziahs, Scribes and Pharisees, enemies to Christ, led by Satan, that old enemy of Free Grace. . . ."

In May 1637 Winthrop was once again elected governor, and in November Hutchinson was tried, with Winthrop the leading questioner. The whole complicated issue was slow to be resolved, as Hutchinson was a highly intelligent woman. Only when she claimed that her knowledge came by an immediate revelation, by God's own voice, could the General Court find grounds by which to banish her.

Some time later Winthrop prepared the relevant documents for publication as *Antinomians and Familists condemned by the synod of elders in New-England. . . .* His work is best known by the title it was given in its second and third editions, *A Short Story of the rise, reign, and ruin of the Antinomians, Familists & libertines . . .*, which along with the first appeared in 1644. In this work Winthrop passed this well-known judgment on his troublesome opponent: "This *American Jesabel* kept her strength and reputation, even among the people of God, till the hand of Civill Justice laid hold of her, and then she began evidently to decline and the faithfull to bee freed from her forgeries. . . ."

One of the consequences of the "Antinomian controversy" was that the General Court passed an order "that no town or person shall receive any stranger, resorting hither with intent to reside in this jurisdiction, nor allow any lot or habitation to any, or entertain any above three weeks, except such person shall have allowance under the hands of some one on the council, or two of the magistrates." The effect of this order was to permit the magistrates to determine what opinions were to be heard in the colony, an important power. Winthrop took it upon himself to speak in "Defense of an Order of Court," arguing that the welfare of the commonwealth is sufficient warrant for the denial of admission to those likely to disturb the public weal. He also noted that the principle had been invoked before the General Court's order was adopted in the banishment of Roger Williams.

When his defense was criticized in writing by Henry Vane, Winthrop prepared in 1637 "A Reply in Further Defense," in which he defended the authority that the order gave to the magistrates on three grounds: that the magistrates are all church members and as such subject to correction by their churches, that they are freemen "regulated by oath, to direct their aymes to the wellfare of this civill body," and that they are magistrates "regulated by their relation to the people" and thus subject to impeachment. This document, which has received too little attention, shows Winthrop to be an acute student of the law as well as a careful reader of the Bible. He tried not to claim too much wisdom for the magistrates whose authority he seeks to justify, admitting that "in some cases a man that is a true christian may be rejected or denyed residence . . . ," but he noted that the situation which provoked the court's order demanded action, for "the hearts of the faithfull were sadded by the spreading of diverse new and unsound opinions, and the uncharitable censures which they laye under by occasion of them, how brotherly love and communion decayed, how the ordinances of religion were neglected. . . ." This statement provides a clear indication of Winthrop's priorities.

As might be expected, the controversy had considerable influence on early Massachusetts history. It increased not only the power of the state to control opinion but also, by discouraging those who would question them, the power of the clergy. It also changed the religious spirit of the commonwealth, making it less pietistic, less enthusiastic, more given to a rigid morality. Fewer people believed themselves to have been converted, and ministers began to denounce the unconverted. The line between church members and nonmembers was more sharply drawn, and the sense of community that Winthrop had advocated in his "Christian Charitie" sermon was becoming forgotten.

The Antinomian controversy led to Winthrop's writing in 1636, at age forty-eight, his essay "Christian Experience," which describes, as do many such Puritan spiritual autobiographies, the writer's sinful youth, when his "lusts were so masterly as no good could fasten upon mee." He goes on to relate how he benefited from the effective preaching of the Puritan Ezekiel Culverwell and later from the writings of the well-known Puritan teacher William Perkins. Nonetheless he continued to experience both periods of peace and comfort and periods when "worldly imployments, and the love of temporall things did steal away my heart" from Christ. The "voice of peace" had come to Winthrop by the time of his writings, but he seems to have assumed that his life would continue on its zig-zag course.

Winthrop was not the only governor of the Massachusetts Bay Colony during his lifetime, but because he served as governor for ten years and deputy governor for nine, he was always close to the center of power. The task of government continued to grow, as the colony increased in size, with 3,000 new settlers in 1638 alone. Within its first decade eighteen towns were created, a college was founded, and colonists went out to create a second Puritan commonwealth in Connecticut. Growth and prosperity brought new problems to Winthrop, such as the need to create a more complex government, and conflicts had to be resolved over the division of political power. Massachusetts government was more democratic in principle than in practice, and Winthrop wanted to keep it that way. Israel Stoughton, who came in conflict with him, judged Winthrop to be "a man of men," "a godly man and a worthy magistrate" but also noted that "he is but a man, and some say they have idolized him and do now confess their error."

By 1640 English Puritans could see that they needed no longer to leave their country, for the King was being openly defied and ministers could no longer be silenced nor hated rituals be required. A few leaders left New England for their mother country to play roles in the struggle that was to ensue; Winthrop remained in the New World, where there were new challenges to meet, such as Dr. Robert Child's remonstrance against the restriction of political rights to those who were church members. Winthrop replied that since colonies "have been the foundations of great commonwealths," Massachusetts had acted within its rights. Eventually Child made his peace with Massachusetts. As a result of continuing clashes with the Indians, Winthrop wrote a warning that the time would come when the colonists would have to punish the Rhode Island Indians, who had been fighting with the Mohegans. His account of the battle and his fears for the future were published in a seven-page pamphlet entitled *A Declaration of Former Passages and Proceedings Betwixt the English and the Narrowgansets* . . . (1645). Moreover, he had to face the consequences of giving the administration of his American estate to a man convicted of bigamy, lying, and forgery; James Luxford had acquired £2600 of debts, mostly without his master's knowledge, and Winthrop was obliged to sell many of his lands. He had to face, too, the death of his beloved wife Margaret in 1647. But like other Puritans who believed that man was not meant to live alone, he remarried the same year, this time his wife being a widow, Martha Rainsboro Coytmore, and soon found himself a father again—for the sixteenth time. The Massachusetts governor kept busy, as his journal records, but death caught up with him in his sixty-second year, on 26 March 1649.

John Winthrop was the great political leader of early New England. He has never been treated as a literary figure, though Moses Coit Tyler provided his readers with selections from "Christian

Charitie" and from his journal, along with admiring comments. More recently his sermon on the *Arbella* has become the most quoted document for describing Puritan aspirations. What Winthrop's record of his New World experiences is to be called has yet to be decided; the journal is clearly one of the two most important sources of information about early New England. Winthrop himself called his work a history; that is, while he gave no name to the first volume of his manuscript, he called each of the other two "A Continuation of the History of New England." Like William Bradford's history in that it remained unpublished for many years (till 1790), Winthrop's great work differs from Bradford's in that it was not composed, with an introductory description of the background of his undertaking; and it is far less philosophical than Bradford's history. Since it is mostly a day-by-day record, it seems more accurate to call the work a journal rather than a history. A substantial work of nearly 200,000 words, it is still best read in the edition prepared by James Savage and published in 1853.

Despite its lack of structure, Winthrop's journal is unified both by the author's personality and his preoccupations. Winthrop constantly reminds his reader that the Massachusetts colonists were living on the edge of wilderness. He tells, for instance, how he survived a night in the woods, after darkness suddenly fell upon him and prevented him from finding his way as he was walking a short distance from his farmhouse. Other stories of survival in his journal include that of a maidservant who was lost for seven days in February, without food, before she found her way to the Salem settlement. There are also accounts of those who failed to survive. Quite as present as the wilderness in Winthrop's pages is his religious perspective. He notes that "it is useful to observe, as we go along, such especial providences of God as were manifested for the good of these plantations." When a neighbor saw a Cambridge house on fire and aroused its sleeping occupants and "saved all," Winthrop credited God's special providence. When the books of his son John were attacked by mice, he saw God's hand. One volume contained "the Greek testament, the psalms, and the common prayer . . . bound together. He found the common prayer eaten with mice, every leaf of it, and not any of the two others touched, nor any other of his books, though there were above a thousand." Thus God revealed his judgment on set forms of prayer.

The punishment of sin is another of Winthrop's favorite topics. "As people increased, so sin abounded," he noted, "and especially the sin of uncleanness, and still the providence of God found them out." Thus Winthrop introduces a long account of a boy "found in buggery with a cow" and celebrates the boy's conversion while he was on the ladder, awaiting hanging. This toughmindedness is occasionally qualified by a recognition of the value of restraint, as when Winthrop sets forth the importance of leaving the punishment of certain offenses "to the wisdom of the judges," a position he set forth in a 1645 speech.

Though its lack of continuity and connections discourages the reading of Winthrop's journal straight through, the work is consistently valuable to anyone interested in early America, though sometimes the writer's sense of proportion may seem peculiar, as when he provides a detailed account of the deliberations concerning a legal question that today seems trivial. Usually Winthrop's attention to the specific, his terseness, and his clarity make his writing vivid and engaging, as in this entry for the year 1642:

> Nine bachelors commenced at Cambridge; they were young men of good hope, and performed their acts, so as gave good proof of their proficiency in the tongues and arts. The general court has settled a government or superintendency over the college, viz., all the magistrates and elders over the six nearest churches and the president, or the greatest part of these. Most of them were now present at this first commencement, and dined at the college with the scholars' ordinary commons, which was done for the students' encouragement, etc., and it gave good content to all.

Besides his "Christian Charitie" sermon, his statement on nonseparation, and his two defenses of 1637, Winthrop left three important documents setting forth his position on major issues. The first from 1643 sets forth Winthrop's stand on the much-debated issue of the negative vote. The General Court had been divided into two bodies, the deputies and the magistrates. Though both were elected by the freemen, the deputies were considered to represent the people and were to keep the government informed of public opinion; the magistrates, on the other hand, were expected to consult only their own wisdom and judgment. In decision making, the magistrates had a veto power, which the deputies sought to eliminate; whereupon as Winthrop records in his journal, "one of the magistrates wrote a small treatise, wherein he laid down the original of it from the patent [the charter of the company], and the establishing of it by order of the general court in 1634, showing thereby how it was fundamental to our government, which, if it were taken away, would be a mere democracy." This view of democracy stands out in Winthrop's "Defense of the Negative Vote," in which he labels the Massachusetts government "a mixt Aristocratie" and argues that since the deputies are "the Democraticall parte of our Gouerment," without the magistrates' veto power, Massachusetts would be "a meere Democratie" which civilized countries consider "the meanest and worst of all formes of Goverment. . . ." To reduce the power of the magistrates would be "to incurre Scandall," for it would mean "undervaluing the gifts of God, as wisdome, learning etc., and the Ordinance of magistracye."

Puritans such as Winthrop did not believe that all men were created equal. Theirs was a hierarchical society, and those who questioned the acts of the magistrates were judged to be demonstrating that they were fallen sons of Adam. If the people had no rulers but themselves, it was believed, sinfulness would prevail.

The great powers of the Massachusetts magistrates included the authority to prescribe the penalty to be administered to those found guilty of crimes. This practice led to the charge that the magistrates were guilty of arbitrary government. In response, as Winthrop notes in his journal, he "now wrote a small treatise about these points, showing what arbitrary government was, and that our government (in the state it now stood) was not arbitrary, neither in the ground and foundation of it, nor in the exercise and administration thereof." In his "Discourse on Arbitrary Government," written in 1644, Winthrop expanded his notion of the nature of magistracy. God himself created the concept of the government, he taught, with the people's governors serving as God's "vicegerents." To his agents, God provides a few precedents: the laws he gave to the ancient Commonwealth of Israel. For God to prescribe each action to be undertaken by his magistrates would destroy the ordinance of magistracy. Then Winthrop stated his position boldly: "Judges are Gods vpon earthe: therefore, in their Administrations, they are to holde forthe the wisdome and mercye of God, (which are his Attributes) as well as his Justice: as occasion shall require, either in respecte of the qualitye of the person, or for a more generall good: or evident repentance, in some cases of less public consequence, or avoyding imminent danger to the state, and such like prevalent Considerations." For Winthrop the great discretionary powers of the magistrates are in the nature of the office. He further clarifies his position when he writes that God has given "power and gifts to men to interprett his Lawes: and this belongs principally to the highest Authoritye in a Common Wealth and subordinately to other magistrates and Judges accordinge to their severall places."

Perhaps most important is the speech Winthrop delivered to the General Court after he had been acquitted in 1645 of the charge of exceeding his authority as a magistrate. Winthrop "desired leave for a little speech, which was," he recorded, "to this effect." Then, with a very modest introduction, he lectured the court and especially those who had complained of his behavior, with an unusual blend of humility and absolute self-assurance:

> The great questions that have troubled the country, are about the authority of the magistrates and the liberty of the people. It is yourselves who have called us to this office, and being called by you, we have our authority from God, in way of an ordinance, such as hath the image of God eminently stamped upon it, the contempt and violation whereof hath been vindicated with examples of divine vengeance. I entreat you to consider, that when you choose magistrates, you take them from among yourselves, men subject to like passions as you are. Therefore when you see infirmities in us, you should reflect upon your own, and that would make you bear the more with us, and not be severe censurers of the failings of your magistrates, when you have continual experience of the like infirmities in yourselves and others. We account him a good servant, who breaks not his covenant. The covenant between you and us is the oath you have taken of us, which is to this purpose, that we shall govern you and judge your causes by the rules of God's laws and our own, according to our best skill.

Having explained the principle of the authority of the magistrates, Winthrop defined the liberty of the people, distinguishing between natural liberty, the power to do as one wishes, and moral liberty, the "liberty to that only which is good, just, and honest." He warned his listeners to seek only moral liberty, cheerfully submitting themselves to due authority. There was nothing novel or original in Winthrop's "little speech"; rather it set forth exactly and at a singularly opportune moment the accepted doctrines that the Massachusetts clergy had been

A

DECLARATION OF FORMER PASSAGES AND PROCEEDINGS BETWIXT THE ENGLISH and the Narrowganſets, with their confederates, Wherin the grounds and iuſtice of the enſuing warre are opened and cleared.

Publiſhed, by order of the Commiſſioners for the united Colonies: At Boſton the 11 of the ſixth month

1645.

THE moſt conſiderable part of the Engliſh Colonies profeſſe they came into theſe parts of the world with deſire to advance the kingdome of the Lord Jeſus Chriſt, and to injoye his precious Ordinances with peace, and (to his praiſe they confeſſe) he hath not failed their expectation hitherto, they have found ſafety, warmth and refreſhing under his wing to the ſatisfaction of their ſoules. But they know, and have conſidered that their Lord & maſter is King of righteouſnes and peace, that he gives anſwerable lawes, and caſts his ſubjects into ſuch a mould and frame; that (in their weak meaſure) they may hold forth his virtues in their courſe and carriage, not only with the nations of Europe, but with the barbarous natives of this wildernes. And accordingly both in their treaties & converſe they have had an awfull reſpect to divine rules, endeavouring to walk uprightly and inoffenſively, & in the midſt of many injuries and inſolencies to exerciſe much patience and long ſuffering towards them.

The Pequots grew to an exceſſe of violence and outrage, and proudly turned aſide from all wayes of juſtice & peace, before the ſword was drawn or any hoſtile attempts made againſt them. During thoſe warrs, & after the Pequots were ſubdued, the Engliſh Colonies were carefull to continue and eſtabliſh peace with the reſt of the Indians, both for the preſent & for poſterity, as by ſeveral treaties with the Narrowganſet & Mohiggin Sagamores may appeare: which treaties for a while were in ſome good meaſure duly obſerved by all the Indians, but of late the Narrowganſets & eſpecialy the Niantecks their confederates have many wayes injuriouſly brokē & violated the ſame by entertaining and keeping amongſt them, not only many of the Pequot nation, but ſuch of them as have had their hands in the blood & murder of the Engliſh, ſeizing and poſſeſſing at leaſt a part of the Pequots

country

First page for Winthrop's account of the colonists' clashes with the Indians and the threat of future warfare

preaching for a decade and a half. The speech is masterful; it is frequently cited as the definitive statement of the Puritan concepts of the authority of the magistrates and the liberty of the people. Cotton Mather commented in his "Nehemias Americanus. The Life of John Winthrop" (in *Magnalia Christi Americana*, 1702) that with this speech Winthrop so won the admiration of his people that they would have no one else as governor as long as Winthrop lived.

These political statements, the sermon delivered on the *Arbella*, and his journal are of continuing importance to those interested in the Massachusetts Bay Colony, the most closely examined chapter of American history. Winthrop was a leader who devoted himself to principle without compromising his practical ability to govern and a leader who never put his own worldly interests ahead of his social responsibilities. While one could wish that the record he left was less impersonal, from all accounts it was an important aspect of his personality that he sought to be objective in all his dealings with people, with the notable exception, as far as the printed record shows, of his dealings with his beloved wife Margaret. John Winthrop was not an authoritarian personality; he derived his belief in the authority of his office from the Bible as he had been taught to read it. His limitations were those of his age.

Other:

David D. Hall, ed., *The Antinomian Controversy, 1636-1638. A Documentary History*, includes Winthrop's *A Short Story of the rise, reign, and ruin of the Antinomians, Familists & libertines* (Middletown, Conn.: Wesleyan University Press, 1968).

Letters:

Everett Emerson, ed., *Letters from New England: The Massachusetts Bay Colony, 1629-1639*, includes twenty-one letters from Winthrop (Amherst: University of Massachusetts Press, 1976).

Biographies:

Robert C. Winthrop, *Life and Letters of John Winthrop*, 2 volumes, second edition (Boston: Little, Brown, 1869);

Lawrence Shaw Mayo, *The Winthrop Family in America* (Boston: Massachusetts Historical Society, 1948);

Edmund S. Morgan, *The Puritan Dilemma: The Story of John Winthrop* (Boston: Little, Brown, 1958);

Richard S. Dunn, *Puritans and Yankees: The Winthrop Dynasty of New England, 1630-1717* (Princeton: Princeton University Press, 1962).

References:

Everett Emerson, *Puritanism in America, 1620-1750* (Boston: G. K. Hall, 1977);

Cotton Mather, *Magnalia Christi Americana* (London: Printed for Thomas Parkhurst, 1702);

Perry Miller, *The New England Mind: The Seventeenth Century* (Cambridge: Harvard University Press, 1939);

Miller, *Orthodoxy in Massachusetts, 1630-1650* (Cambridge: Harvard University Press, 1933);

Samuel Eliot Morison, *Builders of the Bay Colony* (Boston: Houghton Mifflin, 1958);

Darrett B. Rutman, *Winthrop's Boston: A Portrait of a Puritan Town, 1630-1649* (Chapel Hill: University of North Carolina Press, 1965);

Daniel B. Shea, *Spiritual Autobiography in Early America* (Princeton: Princeton University Press, 1968);

Nathaniel B. Shurtleff, ed., *Records of the Governor and Company of the Massachusetts Bay*, 6 volumes (Boston: Printed by order of the legislature, 1853-1854);

Larzer Ziff, *The Career of John Cotton: Puritanism and the American Experience* (Princeton: Princeton University Press, 1962).

Papers:

The Winthrop papers are housed at the Massachusetts Historical Society in Boston.

John Winthrop, Jr.

(12 February 1606-5 April 1676)

Alasdair Macphail
Connecticut College

BOOKS: *An Exposition upon Sir George Ripley's Epistle to King Edward IV, anonymous, in Chymical, Medicinal, and Chyrurgical Addresses Made to Samuel Hartlib, Esquire* (London: Printed by G. Dawson for Giles Calvert, 1655); revised, enlarged, and republished under the pseudonym Eirenaeus Philalethes* (London: Printed for William Cooper, 1677); republished in *Ripley reviv'd: or An Exposition upon Sir George Ripley's Hermetico-Poetical Works* (London: Printed by T. Ratcliff & N. Thompson for W. Cooper, 1678);

Introitus Apertus ad Occlusum Regis Palatium, as Eirenaeus Philalethes (Amsterdam: Apud Joannem Janssonium à Waesberge & viduam ac haeredes Elizei Weyerstraet, 1667); republished as *Secrets Reveal'd; Or, an Open Entrance to the Shut-Palace of the King: Containing the Greatest Treasure in Chymistry, Never Yet so Plainly Discovered* (London: Printed by W. Godbid for W. Cooper, 1669);

Tres tractatus de metallorum transmutatione, as Eirenaeus Philalethes (Amsterdam: Apud Johannem Janssonium à Waesberge & viduam Elizei

*Although there is no conclusive evidence, some scholars believe that John Winthrop, Jr., is the alchemist whose works were published under the pseudonym Eirenaeus Philalethes between 1655 and 1683.

John Winthrop, Jr., circa 1635

Weyerstraet, 1668); republished as *Three Tracts of the Great Medicine of Philosophers for Humane and Metalline Bodies* (London: Printed & sold by T. Sowle, 1694);

An Exposition upon Sir George Ripley's Preface, as Eirenaeus Philalethes (London: Printed for William Cooper, 1677); republished in *Ripley reviv'd . . .*;

An Exposition upon the First Six Gates of Sir George Ripley's Compound of Alchymie [and] *Experiments for the Preparation of the Sophick Mercury,* as Eirenaeus Philalethes (London: Printed for William Cooper, 1677); republished in *Ripley reviv'd . . .*;

A Breviary of Alchemy; Or A Commentary upon Sir George Ripley's Recapitulation, as Eirenaeus Philalethes (London: Printed for William Cooper, 1677); republished in *Ripley reviv'd . . .*;

An Exposition upon Sir George Ripley's Vision, as Eirenaeus Philalethes (London: Printed for William Cooper, 1678); republished in *Ripley reviv'd . . .*;

Opus tripartitum de philosophorum arcanis, as Eirenaeus Philalethes (London: Printed for William Cooper, 1678); English translation (London: Printed for William Cooper, 1678);

The Secret of the Immortal Liquor called Alkahest or Ignis-Aqua, as Eirenaeus Philalethes (London: Printed for William Cooper, 1683);

Winthrop Papers, 5 volumes (Boston: Massachusetts Historical Society, 1929-1947).

John Winthrop, Jr., was the eldest and most noteworthy child of Massachusetts's first governor, after whom he was named. He was born on 12 February 1606 at Groton Manor, the Winthrops' modest ancestral estate in Suffolk, England. His father was only eighteen at the time and was married to Mary Forth, the first of his four wives, who bore him five more children before dying in childbirth in June 1615. The last two of these children, both named Anne, died in infancy, and two others died in early manhood, both in 1630: Henry (born 1608) drowned in a tidal creek on 2 July, only days after the Winthrop Fleet had landed some 1,000 immigrant Puritans in Massachusetts; while back in England Forth (born in late 1609 or early 1610) took ill and died suddenly in November. John Winthrop, Jr., however, lived to be seventy. He succumbed on 5 April 1676 to a respiratory ailment while on an official visit to Massachusetts from Connecticut (where he had been the colony's leading citizen since 1646 and its governor since 1657), whence he and James Richards had come as commissioners to the United Colonies of New England then assembled in Boston to deal with the bloody crisis of King Philip's War.

The Connecticut John Winthrop ranks high among the founders of New England not only for his political acumen and diplomatic skill but also, and more particularly, for his interest in science, for his entrepreneurial bent, and for his tolerant, low-key adherence to Puritan orthodoxy. "Among second-generation New Englanders," writes Richard S. Dunn in an insightful 1962 study of the Winthrop dynasty, "there was no more attractive figure than John Winthrop, Jr. Founder of three towns, industrialist, scientist, doctor, governor, diplomat, farmer, land speculator, he reflected almost every aspect of his burgeoning society. Religion framed his life, but he did not experience his father's crusading zeal. He was energetic and public spirited, but preferred science to politics. Whereas the elder Winthrop wrote didactic tracts and diaries of religious meditations, the son kept medical and alchemical notebooks." Even his portrait, adds Dunn, "has a half-humorous friendly look." Dunn's congenial assessment of the younger Winthrop is generally accepted by historians today.

So too is the lasting impression (which was most forcefully expressed by William B. Weeden in 1890), that John Winthrop, Jr., was "one of the best-instructed men in the science and exact knowledge of his day." That claim, however, is something of an exaggeration. It is not supported by the level of intellectual accomplishment which is found in Winthrop's extant papers. This admirable colonist was a self-instructed dilettante, and as far as we know he contributed nothing of consequence to the fields of inquiry which so occupied his mind when it was not otherwise engaged in the demands of public office or private affairs. From early manhood to old age, John Winthrop, Jr., displayed a restless, inquiring temperament but very little inclination to apply himself steadily to tasks which did not yield quick returns. Great at beginning projects, he tended to leave it up to someone else to see them to fruition or to cope with their frustrations.

Brought up on the family manor with his brothers Henry and Forth, his sister Mary (born 1612), and in time with more siblings from his father's third marriage to Margaret Tyndal in 1618, John Winthrop, Jr., attended the King Edward VI Grammar School at nearby Bury St. Edmunds. At the age of sixteen he was sent to Trinity College, Dublin, where there was little in the way of religious oaths and other trappings of Anglicanism to offend the Puritan sensitivities of the senior John Winthrop. The youth quickly became homesick despite the temporary presence in Dublin of his aunt Lucy and her husband, Emmanuel Downing, lawyer, businessman, and a person of growing influence in Puritan circles in England. Winthrop had no interest in his studies and was either unwilling or unable to apply himself to the task at hand. This lack of perseverance has led his most recent biographer, Robert C. Black III, to declare that "so pronounced was this form of immaturity that it was already in the way of becoming a character defect." Indeed, writes Black, "this defect would linger for years, until the generally remarkable career of John Winthrop, Jr., became uncomfortably littered with unfinished tasks and abandoned designs."

Home again at the age of seventeen, Winthrop next tried studying for his father's profession at the Inner Temple in London, but within two years he abandoned his law books in order to indulge his wanderlust, which soon took him to La Rochelle as a clerk of sorts with the Duke of Buckingham's inept expeditionary force of 1627 and, after that brief assignment, to Leghorn and later to Constantinople as tourist in 1628-1629. It was at this point that events at home converged with his own quest for adventure, for the next year his father set off for Massachusetts and charged him to oversee a multitude of loose ends before following in the wake of the Winthrop Fleet. The restlessness of youth was now eagerly put to the service of the governor of the Massachusetts Bay Company, and John Winthrop, Jr., stayed behind tidying up the family's extremely complex financial affairs and looking after his pregnant stepmother. It would appear that he discharged these responsibilities cheerfully and competently, and that he matured in the process. The tragic loss of his two brothers at this time must have contributed to this maturation—especially since Henry left a widow and infant daughter unprovided for in America, and Forth had a fiancée who had anticipated leaving England as his wife. The care of others increasingly became Winthrop's concern. As heir of entail to his father's landed estate, he went so far as to break the entail of his own accord in order to provide funds for the emigration and to help make adequate settlements on his stepmother and her children. Also before leaving England he married Martha Fones in February 1631.

Sometime in August 1631, Winthrop set sail for the New World on the *Lion* with his bride, his stepmother (now safely delivered of her child), and those of his half-brothers and sisters who had not previously accompanied the governor (with the exception of Deane, left behind to complete his schooling). His party arrived in Boston on 2 November. As befitted the eldest son of the colony's leading magistrate and a man of obvious potential in his own right, the younger Winthrop gained almost immediate visibility and influence in Massachusetts. He joined the Boston church early in 1632, was admitted to freemanship that April, and was elevated on 9 May to the office of assistant by vote of the colony's General Court (or legislature). This appointment was the beginning of Winthrop's lifelong service to the commonweal—first to Massachusetts, where for eighteen years he was continuously reelected to be an assistant (1632-1649), and subsequently of Connecticut, where he had finally migrated when founding New London in 1646, where he was repeatedly elected governor from 1657 until his death in 1676, and from whence he brought off his finest diplomatic triumph by securing, as the colony's agent in London, a most favorable royal charter in 1662.

Much in motion during his early years in

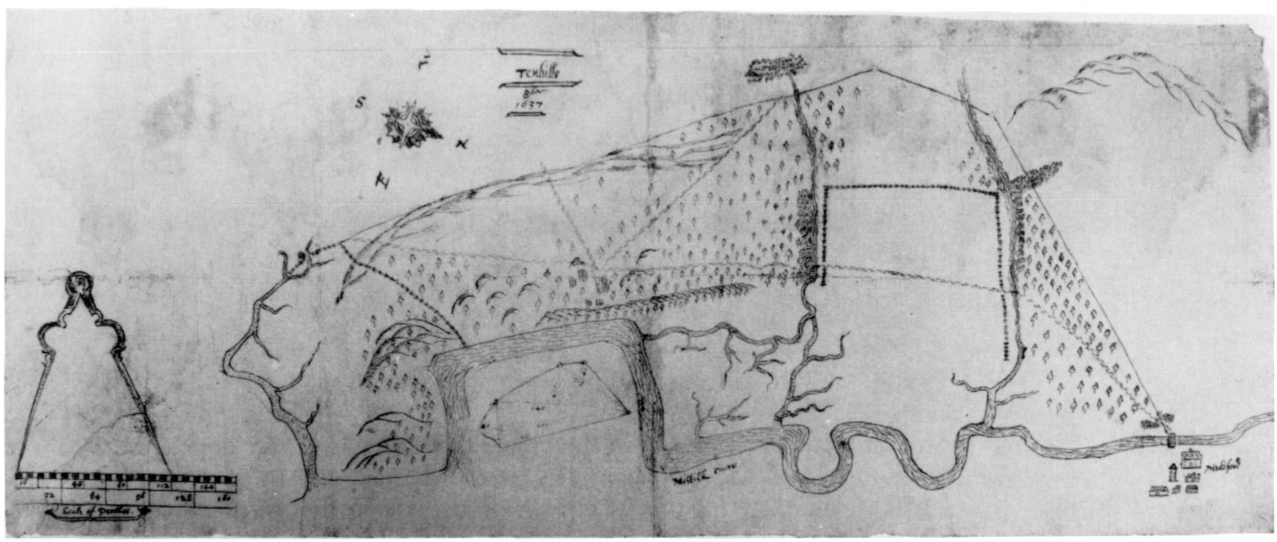

John Winthrop, Jr.'s map of his father's farm, Tenhills (Massachusetts Historical Society)

America, Winthrop originally settled in Agawam (later Ipswich) in 1633 and was instrumental in founding what soon became a major Bay Colony community. It was there that he lost his wife and infant daughter late in the summer of 1634. The following spring he returned to England on private and public business, proving himself energetic on both counts. He married Elizabeth Reade, who was the stepdaughter of the Reverend Hugh Peter and with whom he appears to have had a happy marriage until her death, thirty-seven years later, on 1 December 1672. On behalf of the colony he helped his uncle Emmanuel Downing, before the Court of King's Bench, to fend off a writ of quo warranto that threatened the Massachusetts charter of 1629 in favor of the rival territorial claim of the so-called "Warwick patent." At the same time that he was working in the interest of Massachusetts, Winthrop made an arrangement with Lord Say and Seale and Lord Brook to settle a plantation at the mouth of the Connecticut River and in return was made governor of that territory for one year. Thus began his connection with what later became part of Connecticut.

Back in New England by the fall of 1635, Winthrop soon tired of his municipal obligations in Ipswich and began spending much of his time in Boston involved with a variety of schemes: with the irregular expansion of settlement westward into the Connecticut Valley and along the coast to Saybrook, which he helped found in 1636 as he had promised their lordships; with the declining fortunes of the beaver trade in which he briefly invested; and with the problem-beset Saugus ironworks, which he began in 1643 with capital he had raised mainly in England during a second return visit in 1641-1642. His wife, meanwhile, stayed mostly in Ipswich. She was none too happy with the place but was kept extremely busy giving birth at regular intervals to their seven children—five daughters, one of whom died young, and two sons: Fitz-John, born 14 March 1638, and Wait-Still, born 17 February 1642, while her husband was in England raising funds for his projects and cultivating the friendship of London's men of learning.

Winthrop had brought with him to America the nucleus of a library that, by the time he came back from this second trip to England, numbered more than one thousand books. Eventually his library became the finest private collection in all of early New England. Without a doubt it was the mainstay of the considerable erudition which Winthrop acquired during the course of his life. For, unlike the New England clergy who made up most of the local intelligentsia and were all university men, Winthrop was primarily self-educated and secular in his intellectual pursuits. Consequently, it is largely through the contents of this remarkable library that we can appreciate the cast of a mind that was only nominally Puritan. Some 250 of Winthrop's books were presented to the New York Society Library by his descendants, and these volumes have been much noted by historians. "In the strictly scientific books," C. A. Brown observed in 1928, "52 relate to chemistry or alchemy, 33 to medicine, 10 to physics, 9 to astronomy, 8 to mathematics and geometry, 8 to natural history, 3 to navigation, and a dozen or more scattered volumes to geography, metallurgy, military science, agriculture, and political economy." Samuel Eliot Morison added to this list his own breakdown of the collection in 1936: "Besides scientific works, the Winthrop library contains books of religion, travel, philosophy, law, and sundry grammars and dictionaries. Half of the books are in Latin, 71 in English, 23 in German, 17 in French, 12 in Dutch, 7 in Italian, 4 in Greek, and 1 in Spanish." Furthermore, the Winthrop library does not appear to have been the haphazard accumulation of a gentleman's fancy but a carefully selected working library, access to which was much appreciated by Winthrop's closer friends. And through the good offices of his more distant friends the younger Winthrop was able to obtain new publications from overseas before the edition was "quite worn out," as he put it in one of many letters requesting a particular and timely volume not otherwise available in the New World.

Despite all his commitments and accomplishments in middle age, Winthrop increasingly became aware of the distance separating him from a part of English life which he had only begun to discover before becoming a colonist but which he now enjoyed more and more every time he returned to the mother country. In a letter to Sir Robert Moray, the first president of the Royal Society, whom he had come to know in 1661-1662, he admitted to "sad & serious thoughts about the unhappinesse of the condition of a wilderness life so remote from the fountains of learning & and noble sciences." Winthrop's reference is not to the English universities, which were the fonts of received academic wisdom and theological expertise, but to the City of London with its new and secular learning, its cosmopolitan scholarship, and, most important, its empirical scientists. Whereas his own father had valued the degree of isolation afforded by the Atlantic Ocean as a protective moat around the Puritan commonwealth, John Winthrop, Jr., viewed it differently. To him, the sea was both an obstacle that must repeatedly be surmounted in the quest for knowledge and contacts, and a void into which some of his papers vanished forever—as when Ben Gilliam's ship was taken by the Dutch in 1665 or when Captain Scarlett's went down in 1666. Elected to the Royal Society in 1661 as one of its earliest, if not exactly founding, members, Winthrop thereafter expressed "constant sorrow that . . . my remoteness makes [me] so little capable of doing that service to which my desire & indeavours have beene and are greatly fixed & devoted."

Ironically, it probably was the "remoteness" of Winthrop's chosen home that most qualified him in London's eye for membership in a society devoted to explaining the physical world. As its first colonial member he was ideally located to supply the society with a steady flow of information about, and curiosities from, the New World. Thus the distance which he lamented had potential advantages to science. But the loss of correspondence, the weight of civic responsibilities, and an unsystematic—even dilettantish—approach to investigation all conspired against Winthrop's fulfilling this expectation to his own satisfaction. Thus the acclaim traditionally accorded him for his scientific pursuits is more rightly derived from his association with some of Europe's leading empiricists than from his personal contribution to their collective endeavor.

Winthrop's most sustained communication is a short essay on the planting, care, and usefulness of Indian corn, over the nutritional benefits of which some English minds had been divided ever since John Gerard's 1636 dismissal of this foreign plant as "a more convenient food for swine than man." Winthrop's opinion on this mildly controversial issue had been requested by Robert Boyle, but his paper, which praised the plant exceedingly, was not given full display in the Society's *Philosophical Transactions*. The paper was merely summarized in 1678, about a decade after Winthrop had written it and two years after he had died. (Indeed, the piece was not printed in full until 1937, when it appeared in a New England journal.) Viewed in the transatlantic context where it properly belongs, the substance of Winthrop's correspondence with the members of the Royal Society is not as impressive as the fact that he corresponded with such luminaries at all.

His letters to England described such New World "wonders" as certain miniature oak trees; a knobby bark "of a very healing nature"; wheat that had been "blasted" in a startling way; black caterpillars that destroyed whole apple orchards in no time at all; a "great pillar" of water rising up, he is informed, from the Caribbean sea rather than falling down "from the cloudes above"; and even "a strange kind of fish" which Winthrop carefully diagrams but which the society concludes (in a rather dismissive footnote) "is improperly termed a fish; it belongs to the tribe of *vermes* in modern natural history, and is *asterias caput medusae* of Linnaeus." He sent a box of milkweed pods with the speculation that the "silke downe" within might have commercial possibilities, a potential Winthrop allowed he had not yet had time to explore. (Nothing further came of this idea.) Another packet enclosed as a "novelty" two short essays "of Latin composed by two Indians now scholars in the college of this country and," Winthrop assured the society, "the writing is with their owne hands." More miraculous yet was his secondhand account of a hill about a quarter of a mile from the Kennebec River that, "leaping over" the intervening trees, ended upside-down in the river itself. There evidently had been no earthquake or other freak of nature known to his informant, so Winthrop was perfectly at a loss for an explanation and pronounces the whole thing "a matter too hard for man to comprehend."

Clearly remoteness was not the only factor making Winthrop a peripheral member of the Royal Society. He scrupled to publish his plan for "a way of trade and banke without money" or to push for its adoption even though the acute shortage of specie hampered the flow of trade within the colonies. He personally abandoned further "triall of the instrument for depth at sea [because] the motion of the waves unhookes the lead," and he did not engage a sailor to test his gadget out in a calmer weather. Similarly, he had some "new notions about findinge the longitude at sea" which he believed would be of great service since he had heard of too many captains sailing for Barbados "who, after long tyme beatinge every way for it, could not find it," but he did not seek the help of any seafaring man to conduct the experiment for him. Instead, having already committed these "notions" to paper only to see them "perish" en route to London, he elected not to write them down again "thinking it best to be silent. . . , it being yet but in the theory, especially as to an experiment by practicall observation in a long sea voyage." During the last two decades of his life, however, he never again had the opportunity to conduct such an experiment in the course of a transatlantic crossing. Not only did Winthrop remain in America, but he lived in Hartford and was thus removed from ready access to the sea.

Even in old age, John Winthrop, Jr., appears to have had intriguing ideas, but he rarely developed them himself or entrusted them to the care of others, as had so often been his wont when he was a younger man. Yet he was deemed genuinely successful in his day as an alchemist and as a physician, and he had a small medical practice during much of his adult life. Winthrop may be the author of a number of alchemy tracts by one Eirenaeus Philalethes, whom George Starkey (1627-1665) asserted was a New Englander jealous of his anonymity. If Eirenaeus Philalethes was indeed a New Englander (and the evidence is only circumstantial), R. S. Wilkinson and others believe that he is more likely to have been John Winthrop, Jr., than any other contemporary colonist known to have had a lasting interest in alchemy. Winthrop deserves the recognition he was accorded as a metallurgist (though his prospecting was stymied much of the time by Indian troubles) and as an entrepreneur (though he was soon disappointed as promoter of the Beverly saltworks and the Saugus ironworks).

Winthrop put his telescope, an advanced one for his day, to excellent use on 6 August 1644, when he spotted a star that seemed to accompany Jupiter's four known moons. The following January he was at his scientific best when reporting this exciting and potentially important find. He wrote with modesty and a due sense of reservation on account of the fact that, first, his was but "a single affirmation" of this new "moon," and second, he was "not without some consideration whether that fifthe moon might not be some fixed star with which Jupiter might at that time be in near conjunction." This second consideration seems to modern astronomers to explain the sighting. Early in the twentieth century he was briefly credited with discovering the fifth satellite of Jupiter, but by 1948 it was acknowledged that this honor rightly belongs to Edward Emerson Barnard in 1892. With only a three-and-a-half foot telescope at his disposal—the same instrument that he bequeathed to Harvard College, where it has been preserved and examined—Winthrop could not possibly have spotted Jupiter's elusive fifth satellite. He most probably glimpsed the star now known as CPO-23, 14844, which indeed, as John W. Streeter explained in 1948, would then have been "in near conjunction" to Jupiter from the vantage of one standing in New England.

Winthrop's claim to scientific fame was exaggerated by his admirers in the late nineteenth and early twentieth centuries and does not conform at all to his own humble protestation that, as a member of the Royal Society, he was "unworthy I acknowledge of that honour." He may have preferred science to politics, as several historians have claimed on his behalf, but his lasting accomplishments were political rather than scientific or entrepreneurial, and they owed much to his generous, open-minded disposition. It was this that earned him the friendship of dissidents such as Dr. Robert Child and the Reverend Roger Williams, whom his father had helped hound out of Massachusetts, and it was this same charitable and inquiring temperament that won him the loyalty of ordinary people, like those of Ipswich who tried in vain to keep him from moving to New London in the 1640s, or those of New London who were loathe to see him move to Hartford in the 1650s. On both sides of the Atlantic, it seems, these sterling qualities were appreciated by all who knew him, and his English friend Henry Oldenburg of the Royal Society declared in 1672, "You are a person most curious and able, and of a nature prone to pardon." And as the recent biographer of John Winthrop, Jr., has so rightly observed: "A finer compliment could hardly be bestowed upon any man."

Letters:

"Extract of a Letter from John Winthrop, Esq., Governor of Connecticut in New England, to the Editor, concerning some Natural Curiosities of those Parts, especially a strange and curious Fish, sent for the Repository of the R[oyal] S[ociety]," *Philosophical Transactions . . . Abridged . . .*, volume 2, edited by John Lowthrop (London: Printed by the Society, 1731), pp. 421-423;

In Connecticut Historical Society *Collections*, 1 (1860);

Correspondence of Hartlib, Oldenburg, and others of the Founders of the Royal Society, with Governor John Winthrop of Connecticut, 1661-1672, edited by Robert C. Winthrop (Boston: J. Wilson, 1878);

In Massachusetts Historical Society *Collections*, fifth series 8 (1882): 3-177;

"Winthrop-Davenport Papers," *New York Public Library Bulletin*, 3 (1899): 393-408.

References:

Robert C. Black III, *The Younger John Winthrop*, (New York: Columbia University Press, 1966);

C. A. Brown, "Scientific Notes from the Books and Letters of John Winthrop, Jr. (1606-1676)," *Isis: Quarterly Organ of the History of Science Society*, 36 (1928): 325-342;

Richard S. Dunn, "John Winthrop, Jr. and the Narragansett Country," *William and Mary Quarterly*, third series 13 (1956): 68-86;

Dunn, "John Winthrop, Jr., Connecticut Expansionist: The Failure of His Designs on Long Island, 1663-1675," *New England Quarterly*, 29 (1956), pp. 3-26;

Dunn, *Puritans and Yankees: The Winthrop Dynasty of New England, 1630-1717* (Princeton: Princeton University Press, 1962);

Frederick J. Kingsbury, "John Winthrop, Jr.," American Antiquarian Society *Proceedings* (1899): 295-306;

Filmer Mood, "John Winthrop, Jr. On Indian Corn," *New England Quarterly*, 20 (1937), pp. 121-133;

Samuel Eliot Morison, *Builders of the Bay Colony: A Gallery of our Intellectual Ancestors* (Boston & New York: Houghton Mifflin, 1930);

Morison, *Puritan Pranaos: Studies in the Intellectual Life of New England in the Seventeenth-Century* (New York: New York University Press, 1936);

John W. Streeter, "John Winthrop, Jr., and the Fifth Satellite of Jupiter," *Isis*, 39 (1948), pp. 159-162;

William B. Weeden, *Economic and Social History of New England, 1620-1789*, 2 volumes (Boston: Houghton, Mifflin, 1890);

R. S. Wilkinson, "The Alchemical Library of John Winthrop, Jr.," *Ambix*, 11 (February 1966): 33-51; 13 (October 1966): 139-186;

Wilkinson, "The Problem of the Identity of Eirenaeus Philalethes," *Ambix*, 12 (February 1964): 24-43;

Wilkinson and J. W. Hamilton-Jones, "The Identity of Eirenaeus Philalethes," letters to the editor, *Ambix*, 13 (February 1965): 52-54.

Papers:

The Winthrop papers are housed at the Massachusetts Historical Society, Boston.

John Wise
(August 1652-8 April 1725)

Richard Silver
Stanford University

SELECTED BOOKS: *The Churches Quarrel Espoused* . . . (New York: Printed & sold by William Bradford, 1713);

A Vindication of the Government of New England Churches (Boston: Printed by J. Allen for N. Boone, 1717);

A Word of Comfort to a Melancholy Country; Or, the Bank of Credit Erected in Massachusetts Fairly Defended . . . (Boston: Printed by J. Franklin, 1721).

John Wise was probably the most original prose writer in colonial America. His works were filled with rough country humor, homely metaphors, and practical examples that appealed directly to the common townsfolk of New England rather than to the learned ministerial elite.

Wise was born in Roxbury, Massachusetts, in August 1652, the son of Joseph Wise, a former indentured servant. From shortly after his 1673 graduation from Harvard College until November 1677, Wise served as minister in Branford, Connecticut. During that time he also briefly acted as chaplain to the colonial troops in King Philip's War (1675-1676). Wise accepted a call from the Hatfield, Massachusetts, congregation in 1677 and served as minister there until 1682. While in Hatfield, he married Abigail Gardner of Muddy River, Massachusetts, in December 1678, and in November 1679 Jeremiah Wise, the first of John Wise's seven children, was born. In 1682 Wise accepted an offer to become the first minister of the newly created Chebacco parish in the township of Ipswich.

It was as minister in Ipswich that Wise achieved fame as a defender of the rights of the colonists and as a staunch supporter of the Congregationalist form of church government. His first notable test came in 1687 when he advised his parishioners to resist Edmund Andros's efforts to impose a poll and property tax on Massachusetts residents. Andros directed town residents to appoint tax commissioners to collect the new levies, but a number of Massachusetts towns, led by Ipswich, refused to appoint these officials without a directive from the Massachusetts General Assembly. Andros was infuriated by this resistance, and for his part in the protest Wise was imprisoned for twenty-one days, fined £50, and suspended from the ministry. When he appealed his sentence and claimed the rights of a free-born Englishman, he was told by the judge, "Mr. Wise, you have no more privileges Left you, than not to be Sould for Slaves."

When Andros was deposed in 1689 and the Dominion of New England was abolished, Wise was fully exonerated. His courageous stand against Andros was rewarded by an appointment as chaplain to the colonial military expedition against Quebec in 1690. Though the military misson was a failure, Wise distinguished himself by his efficient actions and intelligent advice. Two years later Wise again displayed his courage and good sense when he vigorously defended his former parishioners John and Elizabeth Procter in the Salem witch trials. But despite Wise's warning against reliance on spectral evidence, John Procter was hanged, and his wife escaped execution only upon a plea of pregnancy.

After 1692 Wise disappeared from the public scene until 1713, when he appeared as the author of the remarkable work *The Churches Quarrel Espoused*. . . . Reprinted in 1715, the piece was a satirical reply to the Proposals of 1705 sponsored by Cotton Mather. The proposals, signed by such New England luminaries as Mather, Samuel Willard, and Ebenezer Pemberton, advocated the establishment of ministerial associations that would broaden the power of the clergy at the expense of the individual congregations and called for the establishment of standing councils with final authority in ecclesiastical matters. Though the proposals were never enacted in Massachusetts, the acceptance of the Saybrook Platform in Connecticut in 1708 had kept the issue of ecclesiastical authority alive, and, when Wise turned to the question in 1713, it was still an important point of contention.

In *The Churches Quarrel Espoused* . . . Wise defended each congregation's right to determine questions of church discipline and the selection of new ministers. He cited as his authority the Cambridge Platform of 1648. The novelty of *The Churches Quarrel Espoused* . . . lay in the quality of Wise's rhetoric and in the audience that Wise addressed. Wise directed his appeal to the common town dweller, deliberately using homely metaphors, rough humor, and common images to illustrate the dangers the proposals posed to the rights of the congregations. Warning his readers that though the proposals "be but a Calf now, yet in time it may grow to become a sturdy Ox that will know no Whoa," he replied to each of the sixteen points in the proposals and exposed them as threats to the liberty and free choice of the common New Englander. Because the proposals placed overseers on the individual ministers, Wise felt that they "Out Pope't the Pope Himself" and threatened New England with a form of Catholic hierarchy. For Wise, the proposals represented the danger of an arbitrary ecclesiastical rule that violated the principles of New England Congregationalism.

Wise's satirical attack on the proposals was followed in 1717 by *A Vindication of the Government of New England Churches.* In this short treatise the Ipswich minister defended Congregationalism through five demonstrations: defenses based on authorities from antiquity, natural law, holy scripture, the constitution of the colony, and the providence of God. The most original defense was the demonstration from natural law. Borrowing from Samuel Pufendorf's *De jure naturae et gentium,* first published in 1671, Wise examined the merits of the monarchical, aristocratic, and democratic forms of civil government and concluded that since the "End of all good Government is to Cultivate Humanity and Promote the happiness of all," democracy was "the form of Government, which the Light of Nature does most highly value." Because Congregationalism was the most democratic form of ecclesiastical government, Wise concluded that it was preferable to any other form of church organization.

Wise's appeal to natural law marked a revolutionary departure from the usual clerical defense of Congregationalism. While ministers such as Increase Mather, in his work *A Disquisition Concerning Ecclesiastical Councils* (1716), supported Congregationalism by an appeal to holy scripture and early Puritan practice, Wise based his defense on the common man's desire to preserve as much of his natural liberty as possible within an ordered society. In presenting this rationalistic defense Wise spoke directly to the fears and concerns of his parishioners.

A similar practical tone and appeal marked Wise's last public writing, his 1721 pamphlet entitled *A Word of Comfort to a Melancholy Country.* . . . In this work Wise defended the

A

Word of Comfort

TO A

Melancholy Country.

OR THE

Bank of Credit

Erected in the

Maſſachuſetts-Bay,

Fairly Defended by a Diſcovery of the Great Benefit, accruing by it to the the Whole PROVINCE; With a Remedy for Recovering a Civil State when Sinking under Deſperation by a Defeat on their *Bank of Credit.*

By AMICUS PATRIÆ.

Maximus in Republica nodus eſt, et ad Res Præclare, Gerendas Impedimentum, Inopia Rei Pecuniariæ. Cicer.

The Want of Money (or a Sufficient Medium of Trade) is the greateſt of all Interruptions in a Common Wealth; and puts by, or Obſtructs the carrying on of Buſineſs in a Flouriſhing Manner.

BOSTON: Printed in the Year, 1721.

Title page for Wise's pamphlet defending the establishment of a private land bank that would issue paper currency (John Carter Brown Library, Brown University)

establishment in Massachusetts of a private land bank that would issue paper currency. Wise supported an inflationary policy because he feared that a reliance on metallic currency would retard Massachusetts's economic development, and he saw the issuance of paper currency as a means to encourage manufacturing, to increase the prices paid for agricultural goods, and to join all of the colony's residents in a web of commerce that depended on mutual good faith and active trade.

Wise died on 8 April 1725. His two works on church government were reprinted in 1772 after the Bolton, Massachusetts, controversy over the question of local autonomy once again disrupted the Massachusetts churches.

Biography:

George Allan Cook, *John Wise: American Democrat* (New York: King's Crown Press, 1952).

References:

Timothy Breen, *The Character of a Good Ruler: Puritan Political Ideas in New England 1630-1730* (New York: Norton, 1970);

John Ericson, "John Wise: Colonial Conservative," Ph.D. dissertation, Stanford University, 1961;

Richard Gummere, "John Wise: A Classical Controversialist," *Essex Institute Historical Collections,* 92 (1956): 265-273;

Carolyn Hopping, "New England Puritanism and American Democracy," *Melbourne Historical Journal,* 7 (1968): 24-48;

Perry Miller, *The New England Mind: From Colony to Province* (Cambridge: Harvard University Press, 1953), pp. 288-302;

Vernon Lewis Parrington, *The Colonial Mind, 1620-1800,* volume 1 of *Main Currents in American Thought* (New York: Harcourt, Brace, 1927), pp. 118-125;

Clinton Rossiter, "John Wise: Colonial Democrat," *New England Quarterly,* 22 (1949): 3-32;

Moses Coit Tyler, *A History of American Literature: 1607-1765* (New York: Putnam's, 1878), pp. 350-360.

Papers:

The Archives Division in the Massachusetts State House, Boston, has six documents relating to Wise.

Roger Wolcott

(4 January 1679-17 May 1767)

William J. Scheick
University of Texas at Austin

BOOKS: *Poetical Meditations, Being the Improvement of Some Vacant Hours . . .* (New London: Printed & sold by T. Green, 1725);

A Letter to the Reverend Mr. Noah Hobart (Boston: Printed by Green & Russell, 1761);

The Wolcott Papers, 1750-1754, Collections of the Connecticut Historical Society, 16 (1916).

Roger Wolcott may have been the first poet of Connecticut, and his *Poetical Meditations . . .* (1725) was indeed the first book of verse published in that colony. Within this historical context Wolcott's meditations and the epic published with them exemplify how the traditions and typological vocabulary of seventeenth-century Puritanism metamorphosed into the more worldly concerns and poetic conventions (especially the use of classical allusion) characteristic of eighteenth-century American writing. Similarly instructive is the important influence of family heritage on *Poetical Meditations . . . ,* specifically the Wolcott family's attainment (over three generations) of local and colony-wide power and its acquisition of landholdings in Windsor and elsewhere in central Connecticut, where Roger's paternal grandfather settled several years after his arrival in the New World in 1630.

Born on 4 January 1679 at Windsor, Roger was the youngest child of Martha Pitkin Wolcott and Simon Wolcott. Living in his father's inherited rustic residence in Windsor, along the Connecticut River, Roger received no formal education and, in fact, did not begin to read and write until after eleven years of age. But like Benjamin Franklin, his younger contemporary, Roger rose from relative poverty—what he referred to as "a time when my father's outward estate was at the lowest ebb"—to fame and financial security by enterprisingly cultivating opportunities for a yield of personal and public fruit. Typically, five years after his apprenticeship to a clothier in 1694, Wolcott started his own clothing business, which proved to be a successful undertaking. Nearly three years later, in 1701, he married Sarah Drake, a second cousin, and they raised a family of fifteen children on Wolcott lands in Windsor.

The Wolcott heritage included more than land; Roger's grandfather had for many years served as a Windsor representative in the House of Magistrates; Roger's father had performed various services for the General Court and had been appointed captain of the Simsbury militia. This family tradition of public service informed Roger Wolcott's admission to the bar in May 1709 and his election in October to the post of deputy from Windsor to the General Assembly, a position he would hold for seven terms. During subsequent years Wolcott's political career expanded steadily. The public offices he held included: Justice of the Peace of the County of Hartford (1710), commissary of the Connecticut stores in the expedition against Canada (1711), assistant to the General Assembly (1714-1717, 1720-1741), Judge of the County Court (1721), a judge of the Superior Court (1732), Deputy Governor (1741-1750), and Governor of Connecticut (1750-1753, 1755). After his last term as governor, Wolcott, at seventy-seven years of age, retired from an active political life.

In spite of the number of official documents he had to compose in the course of his public duties and in spite of his lack of formal education, Wolcott seems occasionally to have enjoyed writing during his few leisure hours. These somewhat more personal works, however, are not essentially private, even when they appear to be. The title of Wolcott's earliest publication, *Poetical Meditations, Being the Improvement of Some Vacant Hours,* suggests the personal use of leisure time for religious meditation; but in fact this implication disguises a covert public and political design, the attempt of Wolcott and his allies to present their side in a land dispute.

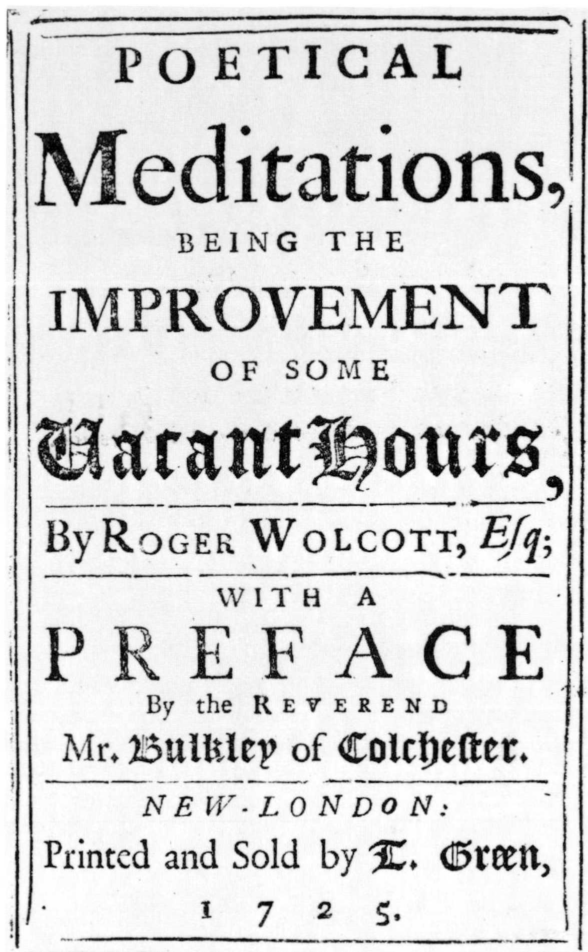
POETICAL
Meditations,
BEING THE
IMPROVEMENT
OF SOME
Vacant Hours,
By ROGER WOLCOTT, *Esq*;
WITH A
PREFACE
By the REVEREND
Mr. Bulkley of Colchester.
NEW-LONDON:
Printed and Sold by T. Green,
1725.

Title page for the first volume of verse published in Connecticut. Despite the implications of its title, the book is largely the attempt of Wolcott and his allies to present their side in a land dispute (John Carter Brown Library, Brown University).

Twenty years later in 1745 Wolcott produced a journal while or shortly after serving as a major general in the Connecticut forces which conducted a successful forty-nine-day siege against the French at Louisburg and on the islands of Cape Breton and St. Johns. In this personal account written with a public audience in mind but not published until 1860, Wolcott, who at the age of sixty-six was the oldest member of the Connecticut troops, gives six reasons for the defeat of the French; the principal factor, Wolcott notes, was that the Connecticut forces were composed of freemen rather than of mercenaries, who constituted the military defense of Louisburg.

Less public, though by no means genuinely confessional or private, is a brief autobiography which Wolcott completed on 10 June 1755, perhaps for his posterity (an intention characteristic of the authors of such works during the eighteenth century). Occasionally inaccurate, often elliptical and unquestionably selective, this document still provides a basically trustworthy outline of Wolcott's public life and emphasizes a theme prevalent in other eighteenth-century American works in its genre as well as in many seventeenth-century New England Puritan histories and biographies: how a decline in one's life is followed by a rise in fortune. Yet this theme pertains to Wolcott's material welfare—physical health, business ventures, land acquisition, the public esteem accorded him—not to his spiritual state, the province of the histories, biographies, and autobiographies of his Puritan predecessors. Wolcott's autobiography, which remained unpublished until 1881, also preserves his elegiac verses on the deaths of his son in 1711, of his daughter in 1735, and of his wife in 1747. Extremely conventional, these works reveal little of Wolcott's private self.

On 12 July 1759, several years into his retirement from an active public life, Wolcott completed a short history of Connecticut that he intended to send to the president of Yale College, Thomas Clap, who was writing an account of the colony. Like William Bradford, whose manuscript history of the Plymouth colony he had not read, Wolcott speaks of himself in the third person in his history and stresses the theme, at once both public and personal for him, that periods of strife or decline finally end in improvements: "What one Governor suffers and another gains by an intrigue is of no great importance to the public, yet in my opinion it is best to let things proceed in their natural course." Still later during his retirement, Wolcott published *A Letter to the Reverend Mr. Noah Hobart* (1761), a twenty-four-page prose work replying to a book by Hobart that defended a clerical position on church authority associated with the Old Lights of the Massachusetts ministerial establishment and specifically at issue in the installment of Reverend James Dana at Wallingford, Connecticut, in 1758. Dana was ordained as Wallingford's minister in spite of the county consociation's ruling against his installment; and when the Wallingford congregation further ignored the consociation's dissolution of their pastoral relation with Dana, it and the ordaining council were sentenced by the consociation to the status of noncommunicants. In his letter dated 25 April 1760, Wolcott replied to Hobart (who defended Dana) by positing a correspondence between political and religious government and by concluding that in the settlement of ecclesiastical disputes the rights of church members supersede the assertion of "papal" ministerial power. A hortatory note is sounded as well in "A Letter to the Freemen of Connecticut" (*Connecticut Gazette*, 28 March 1761), Wolcott's final attack on ambition and strife.

As overtly public documents Wolcott's last two publications might appear a polar extreme to his first book, the seemingly more private *Poetical Meditations*. *Poetical Meditations*, however, evokes this impression of privacy to conceal the author's public interests. Wolcott's poems—a dedicatory poem (dated 4 January 1722/23) to Reverend Timothy Edwards (Jonathan Edwards's father, minister at Windsor), six meditations, and an epic account in heroic couplets celebrating John Winthrop, Jr.'s role in securing a charter for colonial Connecticut from King Charles II—are preceded by a fifty-six-page preface (dated 21 December 1724) by John Bulkley and followed by an advertisement for wool by Joseph Dewey, who financed the publication of the book. As JoElla Doggett has disclosed, Bulkley, Wolcott, and Dewey were about the same age, were related through extended family and community bonds, and were all involved on one side of the then-current arguments concerning ownership of land in central Connecticut.

This land issue is central to Bulkley's preface, which draws primarily upon the philosophy of John Locke and secondarily upon scripture to argue the inferiority of humans in the state of nature to those joined in a civil condition; hence, Bulkley concludes, because Native Americans did not transform the wilderness out of its common state through cultivation and regulation, they possessed no natural right to their land and so properly could not sell any of it. This argument, as Doggett has observed, was intended to undermine claims by the Dutch and by several Pilgrims of Plymouth, who purchased territories from Native Americans in Connecticut in 1633. Moreover, in the minds of the English colonists the conflict between Dutch claims (originating from the Pequot victors in the disputed area) and Pilgrim claims (originating from the defeated Wangunks in the disputed area) was definitively resolved by the successful defeat of the Pequots in the Pequot War of 1637 by the English settlers, who subsequently cultivated the contested territory. This resolution, however, was subverted by the fact that Major John Mason, the military hero of the Pequot War, received all of the Mohegan land, for some of which he paid. Debate ensued concerning whether Mason had purchased or been given this land, whether in either case he had received this territory in trusteeship for Native Americans, or whether (as Wolcott's allies argued) he had contracted for the lands as an agent of the Connecticut colony. Mason's death in 1672 left these questions unanswered, and exactly fifty years later one of Mason's descendents, approaching the General Court on the subject, insisted on reimbursement from certain present landowners in the disputed area and reinstatement of the Mason family trusteeship over the former Mohegan territory. The land involved in this suit included holdings by Bulkley, Dewey, and Wolcott; and the threat to these holdings provided the impetus for the publication of *Poetical Meditations*, ostensibly a private work written for "the improvement of some vacant hours," but in fact a covert defense of

Wolcott's, Bulkley's, and Dewey's investments in land.

While the title of Wolcott's book invites the reader to anticipate verse written for spiritual self-improvement reflecting the poet's private and inward orientation exempt from material concerns, only six meditations appear in the volume. Of these poems (with distinct elegiac undertones), which comprise a total of eighteen pages, only one could be classified as personal (announcing, finally, that one must use one's talents even if pride is a potential consequence). Similarly deceptive are Bulkley's prefatory references to Wolcott's epic on John Winthrop, Jr.'s attainment of the Connecticut charter. Although avoiding any mention of the meditations, Bulkley echoes the title of the book when he associates Wolcott's use of his leisure time in writing verse with the example of "the Eminent *Sages* and earliest *Writers* History gives us any Knowledge of, who have taken the same way to raise up Monuments to, and eternize the Names and Actions of their Admired *Heroes*." This mode of celebrating Winthrop, Bulkley insists, constitutes "the design of" Wolcott's epic, there "being no other" intent "as to the main of it at least." Bulkley's feeble qualification—"as to the main of it at least"—intimates the presence of some hidden intention in the poem.

Wolcott too asserts from the first that his poem will "Endear a WINTHROP's Memory / To Us, and to our Last Posterity," a claim reiterated in the closing lines of the epic. Indeed Winthrop figures prominently in the poem, but he functions less as a celebrated personage than as a narrative voice which presents a case for Wolcott's position in the land controversy involving the family of John Mason. Within the opening and closing frame narrated in Wolcott's authorial voice, Winthrop gives a long account of Charles II, an account which in turn frames a narrative in which Winthrop speaks the words of John Mason, whose "Prudent and Invulnerable mind" during the Pequot War is praised by Winthrop. This frame-within-a-frame pattern is carried out so carefully that at one point in Mason's narrative Charles II parenthetically interrupts Winthrop with a request for clarification of a Native American expression. A clue to the significance of this frame-within-a-frame narrative emerges at the close of the epic, when King Charles grants Connecticut a charter: "*Chief in the Patent* WINTHROP *Thou shalt stand, / And Valiant* MASON *next at thy Right Hand*." Just as Mason's words are framed by Winthrop's voice in the epic, Mason's heroism and victory in the Pequot War as well as, the authorial voice implies, his subsequent land agreements with Native Americans are, as it were, framed by the agency of the civil authority of Connecticut, represented by Winthrop: "*Let all Officers in Civil Trust, / Always Espouse their Country's Interest*." In other words, the descendents of Mason should desist in their claims to the Native American lands "acquired" by their ancestor, for he was only a loyal agent of the colony; the authority of this colony was represented by Winthrop, at whose right hand (the hand of friendship) Mason is said, by Charles II, to stand and in whose words the reader is told that the Native Americans, recognizing that their failure to cultivate the land constituted nonownership, willingly, with a handshake, ceded their territories to the settlers, whose lands are "now by Deeds and Leagues Secure." The Connecticut courts eventually agreed, deciding in favor of Wolcott and his allies.

In Wolcott's poetry Native Americans not only fare badly as a race but are also presented unrealistically, even at one point improbably complaining about "humbly wait[ing] . . . Cap in hand." Such artificiality characterizes as well Wolcott's depiction of nature, descriptions verging on genuine observation but always blighted by intrusive classical allusions. Wolcott's verse in fact never evinces natural moments of any sort. This deficiency emanates less from extrinsic influences—such as previous accounts of the Pequot War, descriptive catalogues in the travel literature of the preceding century, and the Neoclassical tradition of English verse—than from the intrinsic suppression of poetic impulse by political purpose.

While *Poetical Meditations* is no aesthetic landmark in American letters, it does demarcate the transformation of New England Puritan imagery and poetic forms from modes of religious expression (whether meditative or epic) to modes of purely political expression. Specifically, its six quasi-meditations are intended to predispose the reader favorably toward an epic poem that covertly argues for a particular position in a controversy over land while overtly proclaiming its purpose to be the leisurely celebration of a well-recognized hero of the Connecticut colony. In *Poetical Meditations* the Puritan religioliterary heritage merely serves as a vehicle for Wolcott's defense of his political self-interest.

Other:

"A Letter to the Freemen of Connecticut," *Connecticut Gazette* (28 March 1761), n.p.;

"Journal of Roger Wolcott at the Siege of

Louisbourg, 1745," *Collections of the Connecticut Historical Society,* 1 (1860): 131-161;

"Autobiography" [10 June 1755], in Samuel Wolcott, *Memorial of Henry Wolcott* (New York: Anson Randolph, 1881), pp. 83-90;

"Roger Wolcott's Memoir Relating to Connecticut" [12 June 1759], *Collections of the Connecticut Historical Society,* 3 (1895): 323-336;

Perry Miller and Thomas H. Johnson, eds., *The Puritans: A Source Book of Their Writings,* volume 2, includes poems by Wolcott (New York: Harper & Row, 1963);

Kenneth Silverman, ed., *Colonial American Poetry,* includes poems by Wolcott (New York: Hafner, 1968);

Harrison T. Messerole, ed., *Seventeenth-Century American Poetry,* includes poems by Wolcott (New York: New York University Press, 1968).

Bibliography:

William J. Scheick and JoElla Doggett, *Seventeenth-Century American Poetry: A Reference Guide* (Boston: G. K. Hall, 1977), pp. 171-172.

Reference:

JoElla Doggett, "Roger Wolcott's *Poetical Meditations*: A Critical Edition and Appraisal," Ph.D. dissertation, University of Texas at Austin, 1974.

Papers:

The bulk of the Wolcott papers are held by the Connecticut Historical Society.

William Wood

(birth date and death date unknown)

Jane Gold
George Washington University

BOOK: *New Englands Prospect; A True, Lively and Experimentall Description of that Part of America Commonly Called New England . . .* (London: Printed by T. Cotes for John Bellamie, 1634; Boston: Printed by T. & J. Fleet and Green & Russell, 1764).

William Wood, author of *New Englands Prospect* . . . (1634), the earliest comprehensive record of New England's natural resources and inhabitants prior to European colonization, arrived in Massachusetts in 1629. Alden T. Vaughan, editor of the latest edition of Wood's book, speculates that Wood was probably one of John Endecott's scouting party that settled in Salem a year before the royal charter established the Massachusetts Bay Colony; this theory would account for Wood's scanty references to English colonists and for the uncharacteristically secular tone of this early work. Records of the Massachusetts Bay Colony report that he was admitted a freeman in May 1631. In August 1633 he went back to England, intending to return to America, and in September 1634 the General Court sent "lettres of thankfullnes" to Wood among others "that have been benefactors to this plantation." Although several biographers identify him as a William Wood who is mentioned in several sources as living in New England in the late 1630s, there is no supporting evidence for this supposition. Nothing is known definitively about his life, including the dates and places of his birth and death.

To refute "many scandalous and false reports past upon the Country," Wood undertook in *New Englands Prospect* . . . to provide his readers "the true, and faithfull relation of some few yeares travels and experience. . . ." But despite his efforts at objectivity, he clearly delights in New England, and from a firsthand vantage point he favorably compares its geography, climate, soil, and crop production with England's. Similarly, he attributes reports of death among colonists to unhealthful conditions on the voyage over and reports of suffering to the improvidence of those who came without adequate provisions. In the one chapter that specifically discusses evils afflicting the plantations, he speaks only of wolves ("ravening runnagadoes" which devour cattle), frogs, insects, and the rattlesnake, "a most poysonous and dangerous

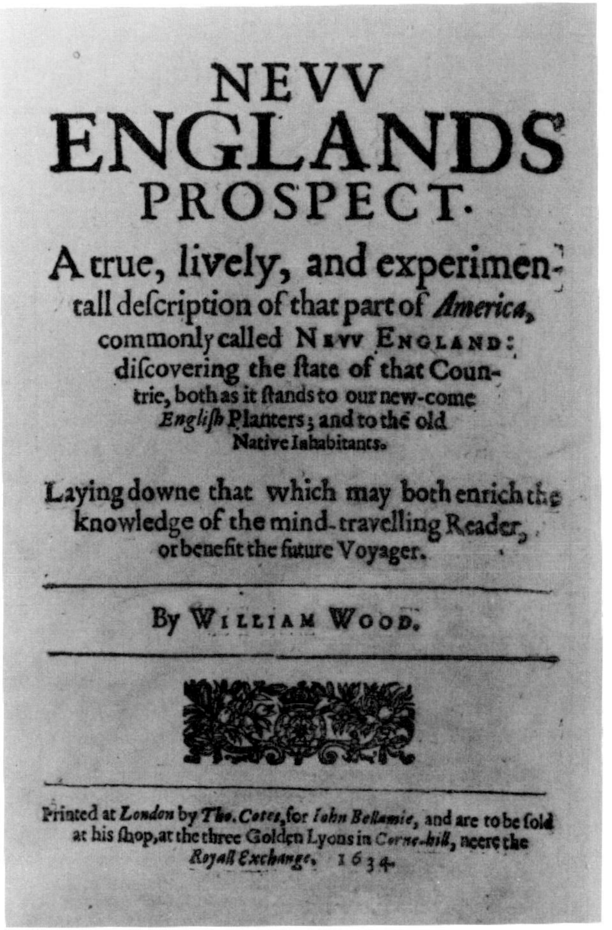

NEVV
ENGLANDS
PROSPECT.

A true, lively, and experimentall deſcription of that part of *America*, commonly called Nevv England: diſcovering the ſtate of that Countrie, both as it ſtands to our new-come *Engliſh* Planters; and to the old Native Inhabitants.

Laying downe that which may both enrich the knowledge of the mind-travelling Reader, or benefit the future Voyager.

By William Wood.

Printed at *London* by *Tho. Cotes*, for *Iohn Bellamie*, and are to be ſold at his ſhop, at the three Golden Lyons in *Corne-hill*, neere the *Royall Exchange*. 1634.

Title page for Wood's enthusiastic description of New England, written in response to "many scandalous and false reports past upon the Country"

creature, yet nothing so bad as the report goes of him in *England*. . . ." Thus he downplays the hazards while stressing the unique opportunities and economic advantages awaiting the adventurous, industrious, and provident settler.

Part 1 describes New England's geography, climate, soil, plants, and animal life as well as the conditions affecting the few English settlements. Part 2 describes the coastal Indians, assessing each tribe individually and offering observations on such aspects as their appearance, diet, government, marriage customs, religion, warfare, sports, and mourning for the dead. Following part 2 is "a small nomenclator" of the Indian Language. Part 2 is most notable for Wood's generally sympathetic although not uncritical portrayal of these Indians. Despite his lighthearted treatment, he acknowledges them to be "wise, lofty-spirited, constant in friendship to one another; true in their promise, and more industrious than many others."

Written in a lively and descriptive style, *New Englands Prospect* . . . combines graceful prose with creditable verse, as Wood embellishes his richly informative material with vivid anecdotes and witty observations.

New Englands Prospect . . . aroused great public interest and was widely recommended to those seeking further knowledge about New England. Thomas Morton referred to it frequently in his *New English Canaan* . . . (1637); two hundred years later, Alonzo Lewis borrowed much of his description directly from Wood for his *History of Lynn* (1844); and, in 1878, Moses Coit Tyler praised it as "a very sprightly and masterful specimen of descriptive literature." But the book's lasting significance goes beyond its descriptive merits. Because Wood "wrote on American topics from an English background and in an English idiom," Vaughan credits him with having "foreshadowed an emergent literary tradition." Moreover, *New Englands Prospect* . . . provides remarkable insight into the natural factors influencing the white settlers in their new environment: the flora and fauna, the customs of the Indian inhabitants, and the dramatic interaction of the two races on the new continent.

References:

Frederick Freeman, *The History of Cape Cod*, volume 1 (Boston: Rand & Avery, 1858), pp. 127-128;

Alonzo Lewis, *The History of Lynn, including Nahant* (Boston: Samuel N. Dickinson, 1844);

James Savage, *A Genealogical Dictionary of the First Settlers of New England*, volume 4 (Boston: Little, Brown, 1862), p. 630;

Moses Coit Tyler, *A History of American Literature, 1607-1783*, volume 1 (New York: Putnam's, 1878), pp. 170-179;

Alden T. Vaughan, Introduction to *New England's Prospect*, edited by Vaughan (Amherst: University of Massachusetts Press, 1977).

Benjamin Woodbridge

(1622-1 November 1684)

Rosamond Rosenmeier
University of Massachusetts, Boston

BOOKS: *Church Members set in Joynt; or, A Discovery of the Unwarrantable and Disorderly Practice of Private Christians in Usurping the Peculiar Office and Work of Christs Own Pastours, Namely Publike Preaching* . . . (London: Printed by E. Paxton, 1648);

Justification by Faith: or, A Confutation of that Antinomian Error, That Justification is Before Faith . . . (London: Printed by John Field for Edmund Paxton, 1652);

The Method of Grace in the Justification of Sinners . . . (London: Printed by T. R. & E. M. for E. Paxton, 1656).

Poet, minister, and well-known writer on theology, Benjamin Woodbridge was born in Stanton, Wiltshire, England, in 1622, the son of John and Sarah Parker Woodbridge. He began his university studies at Magdalen College, Oxford, in 1638, but sailed to Massachusetts in 1640 to join his older brother John and his uncle, Thomas Parker. In Massachusetts he entered the newly established Harvard College in 1642 and in that year became its first graduate, graduating at the head of his class.

Woodbridge returned to England in 1647, accompanied by his brother John, who is credited with carrying with him a manuscript of fifteen poems by their sister-in-law, Anne Bradstreet. In 1650 the publisher Stephen Bowtell published Bradstreet's *The Tenth Muse Lately Sprung Up in America* . . . , with a prefatory poem by Benjamin Woodbridge. Unlike his brother, Benjamin Woodbridge did not return to New England. While serving as minister at Salisbury, he once again studied at Magdalen College, where he completed his M.A. in 1648, and then succeeded Dr. William Twisse at Newbury, in Berkshire. He seems to have kept in touch with his New English friends, for Samuel Sewall, in his *Phaenomena Quaedam Apocalyptica* . . . (1697), notes with pride Woodbridge's call to the ministry at Newbury, Berkshire, as if the "learned and ingenious" young man were a native of the Newbury, Massachusetts, region.

Woodbridge is best known for his elegy for John Cotton, "Upon the TOMB of the Most Reverend Mr. John Cotton . . . ," written shortly after Cotton's death in 1652. First published as a broadside, printed circa 1667, it was later republished in Cotton Mather's *Magnalia Christi Americana* (1702), where it concludes Mather's spiritual biography of Cotton. After beginning with rather wooden praise for Cotton's moral qualities, the poem, with increasing vigor, celebrates Cotton as peacemaker, seer, and minister whose spirit lives on in every heart, and whose work will be carried forward by Cotton's younger colleague and biographer, John Norton. The poetic tension builds, as if the act of eulogizing Cotton's "Might and Heavenly Eloquence" is leading the poet to discover and express his own powers.

An emphasis on contradictions in Cotton's personality, even to the point of paradox, characterizes Woodbridge's handling of the poetic statement. Cotton is a "Noble Spirit, Servant unto all," embracing high and low, old and young, joy and sorrow, fear and confidence. The fact that his spirit is an embodiment of such contradictions seems to account for the "daz'ling fervent Influences" of Cotton's ministry. Like a heavenly body, Cotton moved "on Earth from East to West," in a path that is also contradictory; although Cotton went down like the sun he also went "up to Heaven for Rest." Cotton, like Christ, the poem concludes, lives in death. Woodbridge also calls Cotton "a living breathing Bible" and predicts that Cotton, at the Resurrection, will come forth "in a *New Edition* / . . . without *Errata's*." This figure of speech may have provided Benjamin Franklin with the idea for the conclusion of his own epitaph, in which he likens his body to a book that will "appear once more, / In a new and more elegant edition, / Revised and corrected / By / THE AUTHOR."

A more sustained mastery of poetic elements marks Woodbridge's fine commendatory poem "Upon the Author, by a known Friend," included in Anne Bradstreet's *The Tenth Muse* . . . (1650) and reprinted in her *Several Poems* (1678). There Woodbridge focuses on the issue of gender. He begins with the assertion that Bradstreet "proves" that all of the traditionally female muses, virtues, and graces are "not nine, eleven nor three / . . . but one unity." Furthermore, while the arts have been monopolized by men, Woodbridge now tells them, "In your own Arts, confess your selves out-done, / The Moon hath totally eclips'd the sun." The "bright silver" of Bradstreet's moon makes the gold of the masculine sun (the great poetry of the past) "look dim," and in turn the sun outshines "our pale lamps" (lesser talents, Woodbridge's own perhaps included), and other mortal "Fires." As an outspoken champion of a woman poet, Woodbridge may be endeared to modern readers; few, however, would agree that Bradstreet's art ranks above the entire English tradition.

Although these two minor works demonstrate poetic talent, Woodbridge's life was devoted to preaching rather than to poetry, and only these two poems are extant. Both poems (written after his return to England) demonstrate a transatlantic perspective, as do the subjects of Woodbridge's extant sermons from this period. The errors of Antinomianism and the evidence of works are concerns he shared with his New English colleagues. Although they differ in their assessments of his personality and temperament, historians agree that Woodbridge was deeply learned and a brilliant logician and that his judgments were characterized by independence. He seems to have found truth not fully represented in any one ecclesiastical polity, seeing elements of his faith present in the Anglican, Presbyterian, and Congregational versions of Protestantism.

Following a highly successful ministry at Newbury, in the years prior to the Restoration, Woodbridge, with other Presbyterians, was silenced by the Act of Uniformity in 1662, despite the fact that he had sought accommodation as a member of the Savoy Conference in 1661. Having been removed from the Newbury pulpit, he preached privately there but was harassed and imprisoned several times. In 1665 he consented to ordination in the Church of England. Favored by Charles II, he was offered a canonry at Windsor, which, after long deliberation, he refused; for a time he served as chaplain to Charles. But some time after 1665, Woodbridge again found he could not conform, and he returned to private preaching until an indulgence from Charles in 1672 allowed him to preach in public once more. In 1683 he retired to Englefield in Berkshire and died there 1 November 1684.

While Woodbridge was not a religious tolerationist, there was an ecumenical quality to his religious quest. His reference in the Cotton elegy to "the happy Israel in AMERICA" is to a spiritual congregation, a priesthood of all believers in a universal "church" that includes the Israel in England and in the world.

Other:

"Upon the Author, by a known Friend," in *The Tenth Muse Lately Sprung Up in America . . .*, by Anne Bradstreet (London: Printed for Stephen Bowtell, 1650); republished in *Seventeenth-Century American Poetry*, edited by Harrison T. Messerole (New York: New York University Press, 1968), p. 409;

"Upon the TOMB of the Most Reverend Mr. John Cotton, late Teacher of the Church of Boston in New-England," in *Magnalia Christi Americana*, by Cotton Mather (London: Printed for Thomas Parkhurst, 1702); republished in *Seventeenth-Century American Poetry*, pp. 410-411.

Reference:

John Langdon Sibley, *Biographical Sketches of Graduates of Harvard University, in Cambridge, Massachusetts*, volume 1 (Cambridge, Mass.: Charles William Sever, 1873), pp. 20-27.

John Peter Zenger
(1697-28 July 1746)

Thomas P. Slaughter
Rutgers University

John Peter Zenger, printer, was born in Germany and immigrated to New York at the age of thirteen with his parents, his younger brother and sister, and a large group of Palatine Germans. His father died en route. In 1711 his widowed mother, Johanna, indentured him to printer William Bradford for a term of eight years. After the expiration of his indenture, Zenger lived first in Philadelphia, where he married Mary White on 28 July 1719, and then in Chestertown, Kent County, Maryland. In 1720 he successfully petitioned the Maryland assembly to be allowed to print the session laws. Soon thereafter he returned to New York. By then a widower, he married Anna Catherina Maulin on 11 September 1722.

After a short-lived partnership with his former master (Bradford), Zenger entered into his own printing business in 1726. In the course of his career he printed polemical tracts, some theological works, and books in the Dutch language. In 1730 he published the first arithmetic text printed in America, Peter Venema's *Arithmetica of Cyffer-Konst. . . .*

Zenger is chiefly known as editor of the *New York Weekly Journal,* which he began publishing on 5 November 1733, and for his trial on charges of seditious libel resulting from articles printed in the *Journal* in 1733-1734. Until recently, the Zenger trial was described by historians as a landmark case in the cause of freedom of the press and as a crucial victory of popular will over aristocratic government. It is now clear that Zenger and his associates were neither the political democrats nor the radical legal reformers that earlier historians considered them. Historians such as Stanley N. Katz now believe that they were, in fact, "a somewhat narrow-minded political faction seeking immediate political gain rather than long-term governmental or legal reform," and, Katz asserts, "The reformation of the law of libel and the associated unshackling of the press came about, when they did, as if Peter Zenger had never existed." Yet, as a popular symbol of the struggle between the forces of liberty and oppression, Zenger and his case left a heritage of great historical importance. For more than a century after his trial his name and cause would be resurrected time and again to arouse emotions on behalf of free speech and other "liberty" causes. The standard of Zenger and freedom of the press would be raised in political battle not only against George III but by political foes of George Washington, John Adams, and other political figures of lesser renown.

The chain of events which ended in Zenger's trial began with the arrival of William Cosby as governor of New York in August 1732. Political opposition to the governor immediately arose over the issue of salary paid to Rip Van Dam, who, as senior member of the provincial council, had assumed executive powers and been paid the governor's salary between the death of the previous governor and Cosby's arrival. Cosby sued for a portion of the governor's salary which Van Dam refused to relinquish.

Chief Justice Lewis Morris agreed with Van Dam's lawyers, James Alexander and William Smith, that the New York Supreme Court had no right to exercise equity jurisdiction over the case. Cosby thus lost his suit by default and, provoked by Morris's published decision, dismissed him from the court. Morris then began a political campaign to destroy the governor. Morris was joined in this dispute by Alexander and Smith and the influential scientist and politician Cadwallader Colden, all of whom were piqued at having been excluded from the governor's council.

This opposition group organized their political campaign in the by-elections and municipal elections of 1733 on a "popular" program endorsing the impartial administration of justice, the independence of the three branches of government, the appointment of qualified and genuinely local officials, and the protection of private-property rights. They adopted the slogan of "King George, Liberty, and Law." After the elections of 1733, they established the *New York Weekly Journal* on 5 November 1733. The guiding intellect and actual editor of the *Journal* was James Alexander, not Zenger, who printed the paper in his little printing

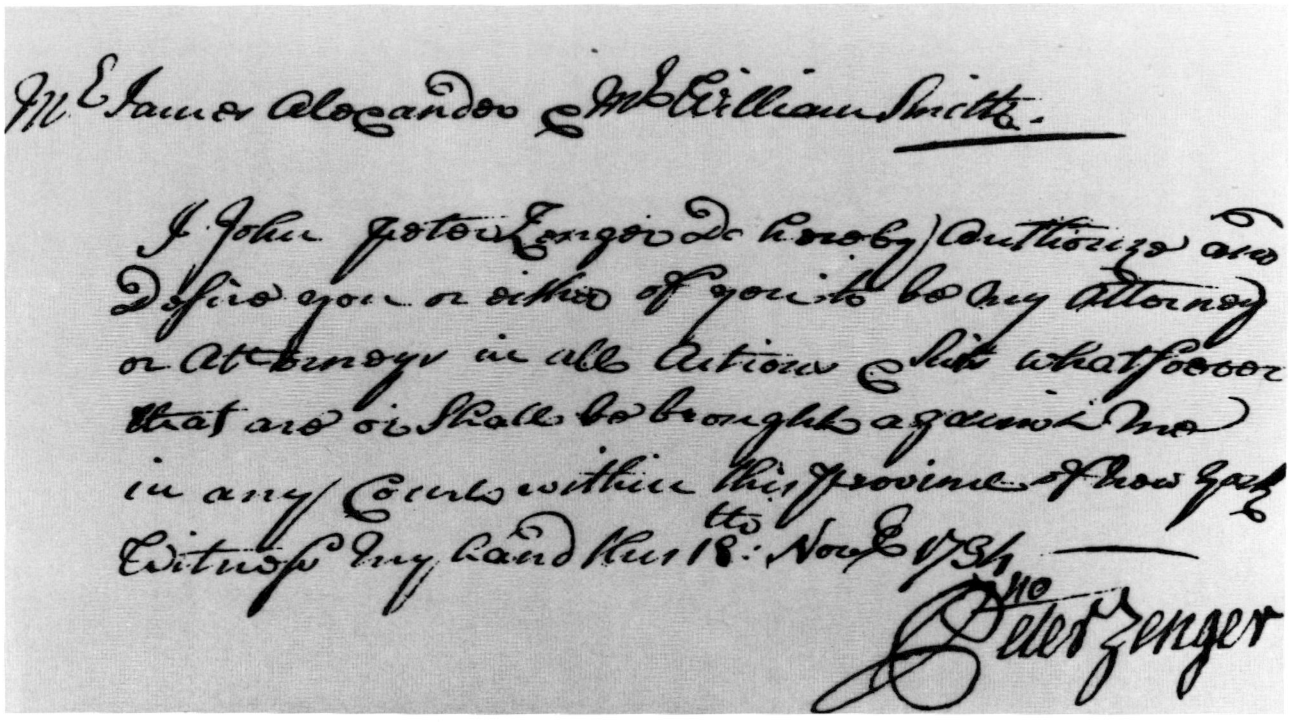

Mr. James Alexander & Mr. William Smith.

I John Peter Zenger do hereby Authorize and Desire you or either of you to be my Attorney or Attorneys in all Actions & Suits whatsoever that are or shall be brought against me in any Courts within this Province of New York Witness my hand this 18th Nov. 1734

Jno Peter Zenger

Document signed by Zenger giving power of attorney to James Alexander and William Smith

shop. Alexander used the paper purely as a vehicle for attacking the governor.

The only major restraint on freedom to print in England was the law of libel. The law of seditious libel was intended to protect the government from defamatory threats to public order. In eighteenth-century England the courts of King's Bench assumed jurisdiction over such cases. Both judges and juries were involved, but the jury's role was highly circumscribed. Only judges could decide the law—whether words were libelous under the law. The jury's decision was only of fact—whether the words had been communicated and whether the accused individuals had committed the act. The common-law crime of seditious libel was generally acknowledged to hold in New York, although no statute defining it had ever been adopted in the colony. American law was not consistent on the point, and there existed traditions which claimed the right of jury trial with jury power to decide both law and fact in such cases. Newspaperman William Bradford had raised the claim of right to jury trial with unlimited power to judge law and fact in 1692. The issue surfaced again successfully fifteen years later in the seditious libel trial of preacher Francis Makemie in New York.

The issue of freedom of the press thus became the volatile issue of debate in the *Journal* and its political rival, William Bradford's *Gazette*. In the course of the debates the *Journal* broke little new ground and offered little precision in its defense of freedom of the press. It did consistently favor an expanded role for juries in libel prosecutions. The *Journal* implicitly supported the view that juries should decide law and fact in cases of libel and endorsed the notion of freedom from prior restraint, subject to future punishment by law, as judged by a local jury. These views hardly made the Morris faction radical exponents of free speech as historians later portrayed them. Their goals were extremely limited, designed only to achieve political advantage.

By the ruling standard of English law, the *Journal* clearly libeled the government. Words which posed a threat to the security of government were criminal, and Cosby's administration felt itself menaced by the *Journal*'s satires, reportage, and political essays. In January 1734, however, a New York grand jury refused to return indictments against Zenger for seditious libel. The assembly also refused to cooperate in Governor Cosby's prosecution of his political enemies. Finally, the Governor's

A modern painting of Andrew Hamilton conducting the defense at Zenger's trial

Council decided that four numbers of the *Journal* (numbers 7, 47, 48, and 49) were seditious and ordered them burned. The government was unable to discover the authors of the offending articles, so Zenger, the printer, was alone ordered imprisoned and tried for the crime.

Zenger's employers left him in prison as a symbol for their cause, refusing to post minimal bond, and Alexander continued to publish the *Journal*. Zenger thus remained in jail for more than eight months before his trial was brought to a close in August 1735. After Zenger's lawyers, Smith and Alexander, attacked the validity of the judges appointed to hear the case, they were disbarred, and Alexander engaged Andrew Hamilton of Philadelphia to defend Zenger. Hamilton brilliantly chose to address the jury rather than the law (on which he certainly must have lost the case). He argued that the court's law was outmoded and that it usurped the rights of the jury. He maintained that truth *was* a defense against the accusation of libel and that the jury had a perfect right to return a general verdict where law and fact were intertwined, despite instructions of the judge. The jury accepted Hamilton's contention that falsehood was a necessary ingredient of libel and acquitted Zenger. In 1737, after New York's tumultuous party politics turned in his favor, Zenger became New York's public printer, and the following year he was made public printer for New Jersey as well.

Public opinion, not the law, was with Hamilton and Zenger in their victory in the libel case. The case established no legal precedent in the colony or elsewhere in America. It was not until 1843 that the substantive law of libel was amended in England. In America it took the furor over the Sedition Act of 1798 to bring about the changes often credited to the Zenger case. In New York it was 1805 before the principles espoused by Hamilton became the law of the state.

A Brief Narrative of the Case and Tryal of John Peter Zenger (1736) was the major literary document to come out of this affair. Although it is often wrongly attributed to Zenger, the idea for publishing the account was James Alexander's, and he probably wrote most of it. It was first published in New York in June 1736 and was reprinted fifteen times in England and America before the end of the eighteenth century. In 1738 alone four or five London editions appeared. It was republished in defense of Alexander McDougall in 1770 against a similar charge of seditious libel by the New York Assembly. In 1752 London supporters of William Owen and during the years 1763-1774 those of John Wilkes used the narrative as part of their campaigns to defend these men against charges of seditious libel. In 1799 the narrative was published in Boston by foes of the Federalist Sedition Act of 1798.

Both the case and the narrative had, then, immense symbolic significance in the cause of freedom of the press. Even though historians have been wrong to emphasize the legal significance of the case and John Peter Zenger's actual involvement for the cause, it would be difficult to overestimate the political role played by Alexander, the true author of the narrative, and by Zenger's lawyer, Andrew Hamilton.

References:

Stanley Nider Katz, ed., *A Brief Narrative of the Case and Trial of John Peter Zenger, Printer of the New York Weekly Journal by James Alexander* (Cambridge, Mass.: Harvard University Press, 1963; revised, 1972);

Livingston Rutherford, *John Peter Zenger, His Press, His Trial and a Bibliography of Zenger Imprints* (Gloucester, Mass.: Peter Smith, 1963).

Supplementary Reading List

Ahlstrom, Sydney E. *A Religious History of the American People.* New Haven & London: Yale University Press, 1972.

Ahlstrom, ed. *Theology in America. The Major Protestant Voices from Puritanism to Neo-Orthodoxy.* Indianapolis & New York: Bobbs-Merrill, 1967.

Bailyn, Bernard. *Education in the Forming of American Society.* Chapel Hill: University of North Carolina Press, 1960.

Bailyn. *The New England Merchants in the Seventeenth Century.* Cambridge: Harvard University Press, 1955.

Bailyn and John Clive. "England's Cultural Provinces: Scotland and America," third series 11 (April 1954): 200-213.

Baritz, Loren. *City on a Hill, A History of Ideas and Myths in America.* New York: Wiley, 1964.

Bercovitch, Sacvan. *The American Jeremiad.* Madison: University of Wisconsin Press, 1978.

Bercovitch. *The Puritan Origins of the American Self.* New Haven: Yale University Press, 1975.

Bercovitch, ed. *The American Puritan Imagination: Essays in Revaluation.* New York & London: Cambridge University Press, 1974.

Bercovitch, ed. *Typology and Early American Literature.* Amherst: University of Massachusetts Press, 1972.

Blench, J. W. *Preaching in England in the Late Fifteenth and Sixteenth Centuries; A Study of English Sermons, 1450-c. 1600.* New York: Barnes & Noble, 1964.

Breen, T. H. *The Character of the Good Ruler; A Study of Puritan Political Ideas in New England, 1630-1730.* New Haven: Yale University Press, 1970.

Brumm, Ursula. *American Thought and Religious Typology,* translated by John Hooglund. New Brunswick: Rutgers University Press, 1970.

Carroll, Peter N. *Puritanism and the Wilderness: The Intellectual Significance of the New England Frontier, 1629-1700.* New York: Columbia University Press, 1969.

Coolidge, John S. *The Pauline Renaissance in England: Puritanism and the Bible.* Oxford: Clarendon Press, 1970.

Crowder, Richard. *No Featherbed to Heaven: A Biography of Michael Wigglesworth, 1631-1705.* East Lansing: Michigan State University Press, 1962.

Daly, Robert. *God's Altar: The World and the Flesh in Puritan Poetry.* Berkeley: University of California Press, 1978.

Daniélou, Jean. *From Shadows to Reality: Studies in the Biblical Typology of the Fathers,* translated by Wulstan Hibberd. London: Burns & Oates, 1960.

Davies, Horton. *Worship and Theology in England,* volume 1: *From Cranmer to Hooker, 1534-1603.* Princeton: Princeton University Press, 1970.

Davies. *Worship and Theology in England,* volume 3: *From Watts and Wesley to Maurice, 1690-1850.* Princeton: Princeton University Press, 1961.

Davis, Richard Beale. *Intellectual Life in the Colonial South, 1585-1763,* 3 volumes. Knoxville: University of Tennessee Press, 1978.

Dunn, Richard S. *Puritans and Yankees; The Winthrop Dynasty of New England, 1630-1717.* Princeton: Princeton University Press, 1962.

Elliott, Emory. "The Development of the Puritan Sermon and Elegy: 1660-1750," *Early American Literature,* 15 (Fall 1980): 151-164.

Elliott. *Power and the Pulpit in Puritan New England.* Princeton: Princeton University Press, 1975.

Elliott, ed. *Puritan Influences in American Literature.* Urbana: University of Illinois, 1979.

Emerson, Everett H. "Calvin and Covenant Theology," *Church History,* 25 (June 1956): 136-144.

Emerson. *English Puritanism from John Hooper to John Milton.* Durham: Duke University Press, 1968.

Emerson. *John Cotton.* New York: Twayne, 1965.

Emerson. *Puritanism in America, 1620-1750.* Boston: Twayne, 1977.

Emerson, ed. *Major Writers of Early American Literature.* Madison: University of Wisconsin Press, 1972.

Franklin, Phyllis. *Show Thyself a Man. A Comparison of Benjamin Franklin and Cotton Mather.* The Hague & Paris: Mouton, 1969.

Frederick, John T. "Literary Art in Thomas Hooker's *The Poor Doubting Christian,*" *American Literature,* 40 (March 1968): 1-8.

Frederick. "Literary Art in Thomas Shepard's *Parable of the Ten Virgins,*" *Seventeenth Century News,* 26 (Spring 1968): 4-6.

Gilmore, Michael T., ed. *Early American Literature: A Collection of Critical Essays.* Englewood Cliffs, N. J.: Prentice-Hall, 1980.

Grabo, Norman. *Edward Taylor.* New York: Twayne, 1961.

Grabo, "John Cotton's Aesthetic: A Sketch," *Early American Literature,* 3 (Spring 1968): 4-10.

Grabo, "Puritan Devotion and American Literary Theory," in *Themes and Directions in American Literature,* edited by Ray B. Browne and Donald Pizer. Lafayette: Purdue University Press, 1969, pp. 6-23.

Grabo, "The Veiled Vision: The Role of Aesthetics in Early American Intellectual History," *William and Mary Quarterly,* third series 19 (October 1962): 493-510.

Hall, David D. *The Faithful Shepherd: A History of the New England Ministry in the Seventeenth Century.* Chapel Hill: University of North Carolina Press, 1972.

Hall, comp. *Puritanism in Seventeenth-Century Massachusetts.* New York: Holt, Rinehart & Winston, 1968.

Haller, William. *The Puritan Frontier: Town Planting in New England Colonial Development, 1630-1660.* New York: Columbia University Press, 1951.

Haller, *The Rise of Puritanism.* New York: Columbia University Press, 1938.

Haroutunian, Joseph. *Piety Versus Moralism: The Passing of the New England Theology.* New York: Holt, 1932.

Heimert, Alan E. "Puritanism, the Wilderness, and the Frontier," *New England Quarterly,* 26 (September 1953): 361-382.

Holmes, Thomas James. *Cotton Mather: A Bibliography of His Works,* 3 volumes. Cambridge: Harvard University Press, 1940.

Holmes, "Cotton Mather and His Writings on Witchcraft," *Papers of the Bibliographical Society of America,* 18, parts 1 and 2 (1924): 31-59.

Holmes. *Increase Mather: A Bibliography of His Works,* 2 volumes. Cleveland: Privately printed, 1931.

Israel, Calvin, ed. *Discoveries & Considerations: Essays on Early American Literature & Aesthetics: Presented to Harold Jantz.* Albany: State University of New York Press, 1976.

Jantz, Harold S. *The First Century of New England Verse.* Worcester, Mass.: American Antiquarian Society, 1944.

Kagle, Steven E. *American Diary Literature: 1620-1799.* Boston: Twayne, 1979.

Keller, Karl. *The Example of Edward Taylor.* Amherst: University of Massachusetts Press, 1975.

Lemay, J. A. Leo. *Man of Letters in Colonial Maryland.* Knoxville: University of Tennessee Press, 1972.

Levin, David. *Cotton Mather: The Young Life of the Lord's Remembrancer, 1663-1703.* Cambridge & London: Harvard University Press, 1978.

Levin. *In Defense of Historical Literature.* New York: Hill & Wang, 1967.

Lowance, Mason I., Jr. *The Language of Canaan: Metaphor and Symbol in New England from the Puritans to the Transcendentalists.* Cambridge & London: Harvard University Press, 1980.

McGiffert, Michael, ed. *Puritanism and the American Experience.* Reading, Mass.: Addison-Wesley, 1969.

McGiffert and Winfred E. Bernhard, eds. *God's Plot: The Paradoxes of Puritan Piety. Being an Autobiography & Journal of Thomas Shepard.* Amherst: University of Massachusetts Press, 1972.

Meserole, Harrison T., ed. *Seventeenth-Century American Poetry.* New York: New York University Press, 1968.

Middlekauff, Robert. *The Mathers: Three Generations of Puritan Intellectuals, 1596-1728.* New York: Oxford University Press, 1971.

Miller, Perry. *Errand into the Wilderness.* Cambridge: Harvard University Press, 1956.

Miller. *The New England Mind: From Colony to Province.* Cambridge: Harvard University Press, 1953.

Miller. *The New England Mind: The Seventeenth Century.* New York: Macmillan, 1939.

Miller. *Orthodoxy in Massachusetts, 1630-1650.* Cambridge: Harvard University Press, 1933.

Miller and Thomas Johnson, eds. *The Puritans,* 2 volumes. New York: American Book Company, 1938; revised edition, New York: Harper & Row, 1963.

Morgan, Edmund S. *The Puritan Dilemma: The Story of John Winthrop.* Boston: Little, Brown, 1958.

Morgan. *The Puritan Family: Religion & Domestic Relations in Seventeenth-Century New England.* Boston: Boston Public Library, 1944; revised and enlarged edition, New York & London: Harper & Row, 1966.

Morgan. *Visible Saints: The History of a Puritan Idea.* New York: New York University Press, 1963.

Morgan, ed. *Puritan Political Ideas, 1558-1794.* Indianapolis: Bobbs-Merrill, 1965.

Morison, Samuel Eliot. *Builders of the Bay Colony.* Boston & New York: Houghton Mifflin, 1930.

Morison. *The Founding of Harvard College.* Cambridge: Harvard University Press, 1935.

Morison. *Harvard College in the Seventeenth Century,* 2 volumes. Cambridge: Harvard University Press, 1936.

Morison, *The Puritan Pronaos: Studies in the Intellectual Life of New England in the Seventeenth Century.* New York: New York University Press, 1936. Revised as *The Intellectual Life of Colonial New England.* New York: New York University Press, 1956.

Murdock, Kenneth B. "Clio in the Wilderness: History and Biography in Puritan New England," *Church History,* 24 (September 1955): 221-238; revised and republished in *Early American Literature,* 6 (Winter 1971-1972): 201-219.

Murdock. *Increase Mather: The Foremost American Puritan.* Cambridge: Harvard University Press, 1925.

Murdock. *Literature and Theology in Colonial New England.* Cambridge: Harvard University Press, 1949.

Nye, Russel B. *American Literary History: 1607-1830.* New York: Knopf, 1970.

Pettit, Norman. *The Heart Prepared: Grace and Conversion in Puritan Spiritual Life.* New Haven: Yale University Press, 1966.

Piercy, Josephine K. *Studies in Literary Types in Seventeenth Century America (1607-1710).* New Haven: Yale University Press, 1939.

Plumstead, A. W., ed. *The Wall and the Garden: The Massachusetts Election Sermons, 1670-1775.* Minneapolis: University of Minnesota Press, 1968.

Powell, Sumner Chilton. *Puritan Village, The Formation of a New England Town.* Middletown, Conn.: Wesleyan University Press, 1963.

Rutman, Darrett B. *American Puritanism; Faith and Practice.* Philadelphia: Lippincott, 1970.

Sasek, Lawrence A. *The Literary Temper of the English Puritans.* Baton Rouge: Louisiana State University Press, 1961.

Schneider, Herbert W. *The Puritan Mind.* New York: Holt, 1930.

Seelye, John. *Prophetic Waters: The River in Early American Life and Literature.* New York: Oxford University Press, 1977.

Shea, Daniel B., Jr. *Spiritual Autobiography in Early America.* Princeton: Princeton University Press, 1968.

Silverman, Kenneth. *The Life and Times of Cotton Mather.* New York: Harper & Row, 1983.

Silverman, ed. *Colonial American Poetry.* New York: Hafner, 1968.

Tichi, Cecilia. *New World, New Earth: Environmental Reform in American Literature from the Puritans through Whitman.* New Haven: Yale University Press, 1979.

Tyler, Moses Coit. *A History of American Literature: 1607-1765.* New York: Putnam's, 1878.

Walzer, Michael L. *The Revolution of the Saints; A Study in the Origins of Radical Politics.* Cambridge: Harvard University Press, 1965.

Watts, Emily Stipes. *The Poetry of American Women from 1632 to 1945.* Austin: University of Texas Press, 1977.

Wright, Louis B. *The Cultural Life of the American Colonies: 1607-1763.* New York: Harper, 1957.

Wright. *Culture on the Moving Frontier.* Bloomington: University of Indiana Press, 1955.

Wright, Thomas G. *Literary Culture in Early New England, 1620-1730.* New Haven: Yale University Press, 1920.

Ziff, Larzer. *The Career of John Cotton: Puritanism and the American Experience.* Princeton: Princeton University Press, 1962.

Ziff. *Puritanism in America; New Culture in a New World.* New York: Viking, 1973.

Contributors

Richard E. Amacher .... *Auburn University*
Robert D. Arner .... *University of Cincinnati*
Alan Axelrod .... *Henry Francis du Pont Winterthur Museum*
Ronald A. Bosco .... *State University of New York at Albany*
Carl Bredahl .... *University of Florida*
Ursula Brumm .... *Freie Universität Berlin*
Sargent Bush, Jr. .... *University of Wisconsin, Madison*
Richard Cogley .... *Arendtsville, Pennsylvania*
Robert Daly .... *State University of New York at Buffalo*
Jane Donahue Eberwein .... *Oakland University*
Georgia Elliott .... *Princeton University*
Everett Emerson .... *University of North Carolina at Chapel Hill*
Jane Gold .... *George Washington University*
Paul W. Harris .... *University of Michigan*
Robert W. Hill .... *Clemson University*
John R. Holmes .... *Kent State University*
O. Glade Hunsaker .... *Brigham Young University*
Jeffrey M. Jeske .... *University of California, Los Angeles*
Davis D. Joyce .... *University of Tulsa*
Karl Keller .... *San Diego State University*
Wyn Kelley .... *Stanford University*
Homer D. Kemp .... *Tennessee Technological University*
M. Jimmie Killingsworth .... *New Mexico Institute of Mining and Technology*
Harald Alfred Kittel .... *Freie Universität Berlin*
Michael P. Kramer .... *University of California, Davis*
James Lawton .... *Brookline, Massachusetts*
Lewis Leary .... *University of North Carolina at Chapel Hill*
Michael A. Lofaro .... *University of Tennessee*
Mason I. Lowance, Jr. .... *University of Massachusetts, Amherst*
R. C. Gordon-McCutchan .... *University of California, Santa Barbara*
John Harmon McElroy .... *University of Arizona*
Alasdair Macphail .... *Connecticut College*
Wendy Martin .... *Queens College*
Robert Micklus .... *State University of New York at Binghamton*
Randall M. Miller .... *St. Joseph's University*
Susan Mizruchi .... *Princeton University*
Wesley T. Mott .... *University of Wisconsin*
Mark R. Patterson .... *University of Washington*
Richard M. Preston .... *Princeton University*
Catherine Rainwater .... *University of Texas at Austin*
Kenneth A. Requa .... *Seattle, Washington*
Rosamond Rosenmeier .... *University of Massachusetts, Boston*
Paul Royster .... *New York, New York*
Max Rudin .... *Columbia University*
Peter L. Rumsey .... *Columbia University*
William J. Scheick .... *University of Texas at Austin*
Frank Shuffelton .... *University of Rochester*
Richard Silver .... *Stanford University*

Nancy Craig Simmons .... *Virginia Polytechnic Institute*
Thomas P. Slaughter .... *Rutgers University*
Ann Stanford .... *California State University, Northridge*
Donald E. Stanford .... *Louisiana State University*
Richard VanDerBeets .... *San Jose State University*
Peter White .... *University of New Mexico*
Daniel E. Williams .... *Universität Tübingen*
Robert P. Winston .... *Dickinson College*

Cumulative Index

Dictionary of Literary Biography, Volumes 1-24
Dictionary of Literary Biography Yearbook, 1980, 1981, 1982
Dictionary of Literary Biography Documentary Series, Volumes 1-4

Cumulative Index

DLB before number: *Dictionary of Literary Biography*, Volumes 1-24
Y before number: *Dictionary of Literary Biography Yearbook*, 1980, 1981, 1982
DS before number: *Dictionary of Literary Biography Documentary Series*, Volumes 1-4

A

B

C

D

E

F

G

H

I

J

K

L

M

N

O

P

Q

R

S

T

U

V

W

Y

Z